Teaching Students with Language and Communication Disabilities

FIFTH EDITION

S. Jay Kuder

Rowan University

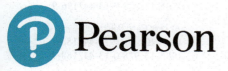

330 Hudson Street, NY NY 10013

Editorial Director: *Kevin Davis*
Executive Portfolio Manager: *Julie Peters*
Managing Content Producer: *Megan Moffo*
Portfolio Management Assistant: *Maria Feliberty*
Development Editor: *Jill Ross*
Executive Product Marketing Manager:
   Christopher Barry
Executive Field Marketing Manager: *Krista Clark*
Manufacturing Buyer: *Carol Melville*

Cover Design: *Carie Keller, Cenveo® Publisher Services*
Cover Art: *WavebreakmediaMicro/Fotolia*
Editorial Production and Composition Services: *Cenveo Publisher Services*
Full-Service Project Manager: *Bonnie Boehme and Revathi Viswanathan, Cenveo Publisher Services*
Text Font: *Albertina MT Pro*

Credits and acknowledgments for materials borrowed from other sources and reproduced, with permission, in this textbook appear on appropriate page within text, or below.

Every effort has been made to provide accurate and current Internet information in this book. However, the Internet and information posted on it are constantly changing, so it is inevitable that some of the Internet addresses listed in this textbook will change.

Library of Congress Cataloging-in-Publication Data
Names: Kuder, S. Jay, author.
Title: Teaching students with language and communication disabilities / S. Jay Kuder, Rowan University.
Description: Fifth edition. | Boston, MA : Pearson Education, Inc., [2018] | Includes bibliographical references and index.
Identifiers: LCCN 2017004092| ISBN 9780134618883 | ISBN 0134618882
Subjects: LCSH: Children with disabilities—Education—United States. | Language arts--United States. | Language disorders in children—United States. | Communicative disorders in children—United States.
Classification: LCC LC4028 .K83 2018 | DDC 371.91/4—dc23 LC record available at https://lccn.loc.gov/2017004092

23 2022

Print Edition
ISBN 10:   0-13-461888-2
ISBN 13: 978-0-13-461888-3

eText Instant Access
ISBN 10:   0-13-447196-2
ISBN 13: 978-0-13-447196-9

Access Card Package
ISBN 10:   0-13-447188-1
ISBN 13: 978-0-13-447188-4

Contents

Preface

In response to legislation such as the Individuals with Disabilities Education Act and the No Child Left Behind Act, most students with disabilities are now expected to be taught the same curriculum as their peers without disabilities. To be successful in a more challenging curriculum, these students must have the language skills, both spoken and written, that are required.

The purpose of this book is to help teachers and other professionals who work with children identify, understand, and help those with language difficulties so that they can achieve success in school and in life after formal schooling is completed. To achieve these goals, it is essential that all educators, special and regular, understand language—what it is and how to help children experiencing difficulty with it. This book is designed to assist teachers and other education professionals to acquire knowledge about language, language development, language disorders, and evidence-based practices for enhancing language skills that will enable them to become more effective teachers and/or clinicians.

New to This Edition

The fifth edition of *Teaching Students with Language and Communication Disabilities* includes a number of significant changes. In addition to an update of the research literature, the following are new to this edition:

- The Enhanced Pearson eText is the digital version of the text and includes a number of new resources:
  - Videos that illustrate and extend the text
  - "Apply Your Knowledge" video-based activities that enable students to immediately apply their knowledge
  - Quizzes embedded throughout each chapter
- The content on language assessment and intervention has been reconceptualized and reframed to better match the Response to Intervention (RTI) model that is becoming more prevalent in the United States.
- Chapter 13 (Language Assessment and Instruction in the Classroom) is now focused on classroom-based language assessment and instruction that are consistent with the first two tiers common to most RTI models.
- Chapter 14 (Intensive Language and Communication Assessment and Instruction) focuses on the more extensive and intensive assessment and instructional methods usually associated with tier 3. Such instruction is usually provided by a special educator and/or a speech-language specialist.
- Throughout the book, there are expanded discussions of emerging technologies, such as the use of mobile apps, that are enabling teachers to provide more individualized instruction to students at a lower cost.

This edition includes a co-author with expertise in second language acquisition—my daughter, Emily Kuder. Emily is a certified teacher of Spanish who has expertise in the

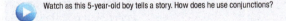
Watch as this 5-year-old boy tells a story. How does he use conjunctions?

Stage V (MLU = 3.75–4.5; Age = 41–46 Months)

There are no major new structures that emerge in Stage V. Instead, this stage is marked by elaboration and refinement of structures that emerged in earlier stages. The child continues adding grammatical morphemes; more frequently uses adjectives, adverbs, and embedded sentences; and more consistently uses inversion in questions (*Are you going to the store?*). In short, the child is learning to become a more effective (and more social) communicator.

This description of the syntactic development of children between 1 and 4 years of age is complete for the purpose intended here, although there has been no attempt to describe every feature that develops during this period. Instead, the goal has been to describe major accomplishments that illustrate the general course of development and provide background for an understanding of what happens when children fail to develop in the expected ways.

By the time most children enter kindergarten, they are able to understand and use quite complex and sophisticated language. They have mastered the use of pronouns and grammatical morphemes and can use all adult sentence forms, including compound and complex sentences. But they have not learned everything there is to know about language. There is still much to be learned after children enter formal schooling. Before examining syntactic development during the school years, however, we need to look at the development of two other aspects of language in the preschool years: semantics and pragmatics.

Apply Your Knowledge 5.2: Stage V+

Watch the video of a 6-year-old boy having a conversation with an adult, and then answer the question.

linguistic structures of Spanish, language education, and second language acquisition. She brings a new and welcome perspective to this text.

I hope that faculty and students will find this edition more up-to-date and more grounded in effective practice research while continuing to be readable and practical. My goal, as always, is to present information about language in a form that teachers and other education professionals can use to help children enhance language and literacy skills.

About the Authors

Dr. S. Jay Kuder is a professor in the Department of Interdisciplinary and Inclusive Education at Rowan University in Glassboro, New Jersey. Dr. Kuder's research interests are in the development of effective practices for enhancing the language and literacy skills of children with disabilities. His recent research has focused on the use of technology to enhance communication and social skills in students with autism spectrum disorders. Dr. Kuder holds a master's degree in special education from Temple University and a doctoral degree in applied psycholinguistics from Boston University. He is a member of the American Speech-Language-Hearing Association and the Council for Exceptional Children and is a fellow of the American Association on Intellectual Disabilities.

Emily E. Kuder is a doctoral student in the Department of Spanish and Portuguese at the University of Wisconsin–Madison. Her research interests include second and subsequent language learning and maintenance as well as second language teaching. Emily holds a master's degree in Spanish literature and pedagogy from the University of Delaware and is a certified teacher of Spanish. Emily is currently completing research on the prosodic behaviors of teachers in the second language classroom setting. She teaches courses in instrumental Spanish in addition to Spanish courses intended for heritage speakers and advanced courses in language practice, conversation, and phonetics.

Acknowledgments

I thank my colleagues and students at Rowan University who have continued to challenge me with their questions and discussions. In addition, I thank those individuals who reviewed earlier versions of this book. Their suggestions have been helpful in developing the fifth edition. I would also like to acknowledge the following individuals who reviewed this edition for Pearson: Dr. Steven A. Crites, Northern Kentucky University; Karen H. Douglas, Illinois State University; Rhonda V. Kraai, Eastern Michigan University; Rachel Mathews, Longwood University; and Christine R. Ogilvie, Florida State University. Finally, I thank my wife, Lucy, and my children, Julia, Emily, and Suzanne, for continuing to inspire me with their love and their amazing achievements.

Language and Language Disorders

In this chapter we will explore the meaning of the terms speech, language, *and* communication. *It is important to understand the meaning of each of these terms since they will be used throughout the text. In addition, they are frequently used—and sometimes misused—to describe the difficulties experienced by some students.*

Once we are reasonably sure what we are talking about, it is possible to begin to identify children with language disorders. In this chapter we will also discuss the concept of language disorder *and consider some criteria for identifying students with language difficulties.*

Learning Outcomes

After reading this chapter, you should be able to:

1. Differentiate among *speech,* *language,* and *communication* and explain the characteristics of each.
2. Describe the characteristics of language disorders.

Kevin: A Case Study

Kevin is a 9-year-old student in a regular fourth-grade classroom. Kevin seems bright and usually works hard, but he is a puzzle to his teacher. Sometimes it seems as though he's just not all there. He misunderstands directions—failing to complete all of the assignment or even working on the wrong pages. He is reluctant to answer questions in class. When he does answer, he stops and starts and seems confused. Kevin is a slow, hesitant reader. His teacher, Mrs. Ross, has noticed that his comprehension of text often seems to be ahead of his ability to read the words themselves. He is a poor speller. In his writing he tends to use short, choppy sentences, and his output is often poorly organized. Although Kevin is good in math, he has difficulty with word problems. In addition to these problems with his schoolwork, Kevin often appears to be lost among his fellow students. He hangs behind the others when they go out to play and often eats by himself at lunch.

Mrs. Ross would like to help Kevin, but she is not sure what is wrong. Is he immature? Should he be referred for special education? Could there be some medical reason for Kevin's problems?

Kevin is typical of students who have problems with language and communication. He may be experiencing difficulty understanding incoming language and producing appropriate spoken responses of his own. He appears to lack some of the subtle communication skills that are critical to social acceptance by his peers. He is at risk for academic as well as social difficulties. If nothing is done, it is likely that Kevin's problems will get worse. As the pace of learning increases in middle and high school, he is likely to fall further behind. But what *should* be done? And just what is Kevin's problem?

In order to understand Kevin and children like him, it is first necessary to understand the nature of language and the related concepts of speech and communication. This may help in determining what kind of difficulty Kevin is experiencing. It may even help in the development of procedures to help Kevin and children like him to enhance their skills in language and communication.

Speech, Language, and Communication

Speech

Speech, language, and communication are all words that are sometimes used in describing the language production and language difficulties of children. It may be that Kevin has a speech problem. He may also have a language problem. Is this just another way of saying the same thing? He may well have some problems communicating with others. How can we describe the problem that Kevin, and other students like him, are having? Does it make any difference what we call his problem, or is this just a tiresome academic debate?

In order to answer these questions, it is necessary to know just what we mean by the terms *speech*, *language*, and *communication*. They are often used loosely, even by some professionals, in describing the difficulties many children face in learning and interacting. But each of these terms has a particular meaning that has implications for understanding and helping students. To understand what *speech*, *language*, and *communication* mean, we have to ask some other questions. Is it possible to have speech without language? Consider the 3-month-old baby as she begins to babble. Listen to the sounds she makes: "bah," "gah," "buh." Are these speech sounds? Linguists (people who study language) say that these *are* speech sounds because they have characteristics that are identical to the same sounds produced by adults. What about people with echolalia? This is a condition prevalent in some children with autism spectrum disorders in which they repeat what they hear. For example, I might say, "What did you have for dinner?" and a person with echolalia might respond, "What did you have for dinner?" Did this person use speech? Of course, the answer is yes.

In each of these examples, it is clear that speech is being used, but most linguists would say that in neither case is true *language* being used. Although Mommy or Daddy may claim to understand what baby is saying, most outsiders would have a hard time interpreting the sounds being uttered. The baby's speech could hardly be said to be conforming to the rules of adult language. In the case of an individual with echolalia, although the speech output is certainly in the form of language, it is not being used in a meaningful way. It is not an appropriate response within the context of the conversation.

These observations can help us differentiate between speech and language. **Speech** can be defined as the neuromuscular act of producing sounds that are used in language. Not all sounds are speech sounds in a particular language. For example, a person can make clicking sounds with his or her tongue. Although these may actually be speech sounds in some African languages, they are not speech sounds in English. Speech, then, is a physiological act in which the muscles involved in speech production are coordinated by the brain to produce the sounds of language.

Language

Language is unique to humans. It is, in fact, what makes us human. Do you agree?

 Watch the video of Kanzi, a bonobo with remarkable language abilities. How do animals like Kanzi help us understand what makes human language unique?
https://www.youtube.com/watch?v=2Dhc2zePJFE

While many linguists claim that language is only found in humans, research with many types of animals over the past 50 years has challenged this claim while helping us to clarify our understanding of language itself. This research has found that some animals

---

Box 1.1   Do Animals Have Language?

In their book titled *Apes, Language, and the Human Mind*, Savage-Rumbaugh, Shanker, and Taylor (1998) describe the remarkable language (and other accomplishments) of Kanzi, a bonobo (a species of ape from Africa). The authors recount this event:

> One day when Kanzi was visiting Austin (a chimpanzee), he wanted some cereal that had been prepared specifically for Austin. He was told, "You can have some cereal if you give Austin your monster mask to play with." Kanzi immediately found his monster mask and handed it to Austin, then pointed to Austin's cereal. When told, "Let's go to the trailer and make a water balloon," Kanzi went to the trailer, got a balloon out of the backpack, and held it under the water faucet. (p. 139)

What does an interaction such as this mean? Did Kanzi really understand what was being said to him? He certainly responded as if he did. But what did he understand? Did he understand the grammar of the complex sentence that he heard? Did he understand the words? Or did he just understand the situation and "figure out" what was expected of him?

These are questions that have long fascinated psychologists and linguists alike. Although early attempts by Winthrop and Luella Kellogg in the 1930s and Keith and Kathy Hayes in the 1940s to induce language in chimps by raising them just as they would a human infant were largely a failure, the interest in nonhuman primate language did not disappear. Beginning in the 1960s, with research by Beatrice and Allan Gardner of the University of Nevada, interest in the potential language abilities of chimps and other nonhuman primates was revived. Using American Sign Language as the means of communication, the Gardners successfully trained a chimp named Washoe to use over 100 signs. Even more exciting, they claimed that Washoe created new signs by combining signs she had already learned (Gardner & Gardner, 1969).

Many of the claims put forward by the researchers on the language abilities of chimpanzees and apes have been challenged by other scientists. For example, after examining some of the Gardners' earlier research, Dr. Herbert Terrace of Columbia University (Terrace, 1980) concluded that many of the claims for evidence of chimps' language abilities were overblown and that the supposed uses of language were, in fact, merely instances of sophisticated imitation.

The debate on whether language is unique to humans will continue. It is a fascinating debate because it raises questions about what defines language as well as what it means to be human.

---

appear to have language skills that approach those of humans. Certainly, many species have highly effective communication systems. See Box 1.1 for details on some of the research on language in animals.

Although some animals have demonstrated remarkable abilities to communicate, linguists such as Noam Chomsky and psychologists like Steven Pinker (1994) claim that language is, indeed, unique to humans. Chomsky and his colleagues (Hauser, Chomsky, & Fitch, 2002) claim that the systems of communication of bees and chimps differ qualitatively from human language because they lack the rich expressive and open-ended power of human language. While they acknowledge that humans have much in common with other animals that helps them to develop language in the "broad sense," they also believe that there are aspects of language that are unique to humans. Pinker (1994) argues for the existence of what he calls a language "instinct," a unique feature of humans that is based on the biological development of our brains. Pinker and his colleague Ray Jackendoff (2005) claim that language is a unique adaptation of the human species for the purpose of communication.

 Watch this video of Professor Noam Chomsky as he discusses language learning. How do what he calls the "big questions" about language help us understand the universality of language?
https://www.youtube.com/watch?v=Zg1bHzBoggk

While some linguists (for example, Brian MacWhinney, 1999) reject the idea that language is innate and solely the result of biological determinism, there can be little doubt that language is universal in humans. It has been estimated that there are nearly 7,000 languages being spoken today somewhere in the world (Lewis, 2009). Languages are found in all types of societies—urban and rural, industrialized and agricultural—in all regions of the world (search for the Ethnologue website to view a map showing languages of the world).

So, what is language? Before we can arrive at a definition, it is necessary to ask another question. Is it possible to have language without speech? The answer is yes. One example is American Sign Language (ASL). Most linguists agree that American Sign Language is a language (Battison, 2000). It is the primary mode of communication of many people who are deaf. It is a gestural language that has its own unique grammatical structure. But why is it considered a language? What makes it so?

One feature may be obvious: A true language *communicates*. It communicates thoughts, ideas, and meaning. Although communication is a necessary feature of language, it is not sufficient to describe language. Linguists say that in order for a system of communication to be a language, it must be shared by a group of people. They call this feature a *shared code*. That is, although not everyone may know ASL (just as not everyone knows Hungarian), those who know the language being used can communicate with each other. You might ask, "How large does the group need to be?" Now that is another interesting question. There have been occasional reports in the press of twins who share a "secret language." Researchers who have studied this phenomenon have concluded that, although some twins do indeed develop unique words and sentence structures, most grow out of this stage quickly (Bishop & Bishop, 1998). Even if it lasts just a short time, is this really a language? After all, it is a system of communication that is shared by more than one person. In order to answer this question, we need to know more about what makes a system of communication a language.

A third feature of language is that it consists of *arbitrary symbols*. That is, the symbols have meaning simply because we say they do. There is no reason that a tree might not be called a "smook." There is nothing green and leafy about the word *tree*. Although a few ASL signs are iconic (they look like the things they represent), most are arbitrary symbols. Therefore, ASL has this feature of language. Another feature of language is that it is *generative*. Given a finite set of words and a finite number of rules, speakers can generate an infinite number of sentences. Although you are an educated person who has read widely, there are certainly sentences in this book that you have never encountered before. This is due to the generative property of language. Finally, language is *creative*. New words are constantly entering the language while existing words drop out of usage or change their meaning. Consider some of the new words that have entered the English language—*byte, Teflon, laser*. How about words that have acquired additional meanings—*gay, cool, neat*?

You can see that language is a complex phenomenon and, as such, is difficult to define. Even linguists sometimes have difficulty defining whether a communication system is a language. **Dialects** are variants of a language. They may differ in just one component (think of regional differences for words such as "bag" and "sack" in the United States) or in many components (for example, regional dialects in Italy that can vary so much that speakers from different areas cannot understand each other). At what point does a dialect actually become a separate language? This is a really difficult question and one that linguists continue to struggle with (e.g., Backus, 1999). Although there is no definitive answer to the question of the point at which a dialect can be considered a separate language, asking questions such as this helps us better understand what defines a language.

 Watch this video about "accent" and "dialect." How do the words differ in meaning?

Watch this video of a 6-year-old child "translating" Australian dialect into standard English dialect. Note how words and their meanings can differ from one community to another even when the same language is used.
https://www.youtube.com/watch?v=4d1gXvuJ-ZY

Because language is such a complex phenomenon and still not completely understood, there is not a single, widely accepted definition. Let's see if we can build our own definition of language. It seems that most of the experts agree that language is **symbolic** and **rule-based**. Our discussion of the use of language suggests that communication through a **shared code** (or, as Hulit, Fahey, & Howard [2014] put it, "conventions") is essential. So, putting it all together, we arrive at the following definition that we will use in this book:

> **Language** is a rule-governed symbol system for communicating meaning through a shared code of arbitrary symbols.

This definition conveys the idea that language involves communication that is shared by a community. Another important feature of language is that it is both receptive and expressive. That is, it involves both the understanding of language (receptive) and the production of language (expressive). Young children and some children with disabilities may not be able to produce the adult form of words, but if they consistently respond to language input, they can be said to have developed language.

Apply Your Knowledge 1.1: Receptive/Expressive Language

To better understand the difference between expressive and receptive language, watch the video of a mother and her young child playing with blocks and then respond to the questions.

Communication

Is it possible to communicate without language? If you have ever been in a noisy room, the answer should be obvious. A lot of communication can occur nonlinguistically. A smile, a shift in body position, a gesture, or even the raise of an eyebrow can communicate a great deal. Sometimes these communicative attempts may be misinterpreted, causing problems. But, clearly, it is possible to communicate without spoken language.

Communication is the broadest of the terms that we have attempted to define. **Communication** has been defined by one author as "the process participants use to exchange information and ideas, needs and desires" (Owens, 2015, p. 9). In order for communication to take place, there must be four elements:

1. A sender of the message
2. A receiver of the message
3. A shared intent to communicate
4. A shared means of communication

When all of these elements are present, communication may occur (see Figure 1.1(a)). But when one or more of these elements is missing, there may be a breakdown in communication. Figure 1.1(b) shows what may happen if you meet someone in a foreign country. You may both want to communicate, but unless you share a common language, you may be unable to do so. Although you share the intent to communicate, you lack a shared means of communication. However, if you can get your messages across with gestures and facial expressions, you may be able to communicate with each other after all. Conversely,

Components of Communication

(a) Successful Communication

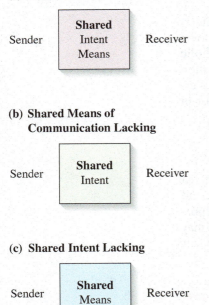

Sender — [Shared / Intent / Means] — Receiver

(b) Shared Means of Communication Lacking

Sender — [Shared / Intent] — Receiver

(c) Shared Intent Lacking

Sender — [Shared / Means] — Receiver

two speakers may share the means to communicate (i.e., a common language) but not share the same communicative intent (see Figure 1.1(c)). For example, if I am teaching a class and suddenly feel hot, I may look at a student in the class who is seated near the window and say, "Gee, it's hot in here." If the student's response is to say, "Yes, it is," we have failed to communicate. My intent was for the student to open the window. The student's understanding of my message was that I was simply commenting on the room temperature. For communication to be successful, all of its elements must be in place: a speaker, a listener, a shared intent to communicate, and a shared means of communication.

We have seen that speech and language can be used for communication but are not essential for communication. Communication can take place without either speech or language being used. Similarly, language can be either spoken or nonspoken (e.g., ASL). Speech can be used to express language or for nonlanguage utterances (e.g., babble or echolalia) (see Figure 1.2).

For our purposes it is important to understand the distinctions among speech, language, and communication because these distinctions can help us be more specific about the nature of the problems of a student such as Kevin. It could be that his difficulties are primarily the result of speech problems, such as misarticulation. This could account for some of his reluctance to talk in class and for some of his difficulties in socializing with his peers. But a speech problem alone would not explain Kevin's difficulties in understanding language or his problems with reading and writing. Kevin clearly has some difficulty communicating with others. This could be caused by misunderstanding the communicative intentions of others or by deficiencies in the language skills that are necessary for communication. It is most likely that Kevin has a language disorder. His difficulty in using and interpreting language for learning and socialization support this conclusion.

 Check Your Understanding 1.1
Click here to gauge your understanding of the concepts in this section.

FIGURE 1.2

Speech, Language, and Communication

Speech: The neuromuscular act of producing sounds that are used in language.

Language: A rule-governed symbol system for communicating meaning through a shared code of arbitrary symbols. Language:

- Communicates.
- Is a shared code.
- Consists of arbitrary symbols.
- Is generative.
- Is creative.

Communication: "The process participants use to exchange information and ideas, needs and desires" (Owens, 2015). In order for communication to take place, there must be a:

- Sender of the message.
- Receiver of the message.
- Shared intent to communicate.
- Shared means of communication.

Language Disorder

Children with speech and language disorders constitute the second largest category of students with disabilities identified under the Individuals with Disabilities Education Act (IDEA). In the 2011 to 2012 school year, nearly 1.4 million children (about 2.8% of the total school population) in the United States received services for a speech or language disability (U.S. Department of Education, 2015). As large as this number is, it likely underestimates the incidence of speech and language disorders in the school-age population. The IDEA number is based solely on those children who have a primary classification as being speech and language impaired. However, many children with other disabilities (e.g., autism, intellectual disabilities, learning disabilities) have significant speech and/or language disorders. The National Institute on Deafness and Other Communication Disorders (2015) estimates that the prevalence of speech and language disorders is closer to 6 percent of the school-age population. That would mean approximately 3,000,000 children in the United States have a speech or language disorder.

However, there may be far more children with speech and language difficulties who are not receiving services. Current estimates are that about 17 percent of the total U.S. population has some type of communication disorder (Owens, Farinella, & Metz, 2015). Children with language "difficulties" may lag behind their peers in one or more areas of language, but their problems may be less pervasive and less severe than those of children identified as language "disordered." Even though they may have less serious language challenges, students with language difficulties may be at risk for reading and writing difficulties.

The American Speech-Language-Hearing Association (ASHA) has defined **language disorder** as follows:

> A language disorder is impaired comprehension and/or use of spoken, written, and/or other symbol systems. This disorder may involve (1) the form of language (phonology, morphology, syntax), (2) the content of language (semantics), and/or (3) the function of language in communication (pragmatics) in any combination. (ASHA, 1993, p. 40)

Let's take a look at this definition in more detail. The first major point highlighted by the ASHA definition is that language disorder includes both *comprehension* of language and language *production*. Children who have comprehension (receptive language) difficulties may have a hard time following directions and may appear to be inattentive. Students who have problems with language production (expressive language) may be reluctant to participate in activities that require the use of language. They may use more immature language than do their peers. They might also have difficulty relating personal experiences or retelling stories. Sometimes the productive language problems are more obvious, but difficulties in comprehension can be as much as or more of a problem in the classroom.

The second major point made by the definition is that the disorder can be identified in *either spoken or written* language. Usually we think of a language disorder as referring just to *spoken* language problems. But the definition points out that language is an essential part of writing as well. Sometimes problems in writing are caused by an underlying difficulty in using language.

The third major point is that language disorders can occur in *one or more* aspects of language. We will examine these elements of language in more detail in the next chapter, but the important point is that a language disorder can be pervasive or limited in scope.

It is important to distinguish language *disorders* from language *differences*. Many students come to school speaking a language other than English as their first language or a dialect that differs from standard English. These children must not be labeled "language disordered" merely because they talk differently from their teachers or from some societal standard. However, some children may talk differently and have a language disorder. Later in this book, we will see how experts have devised ways to differentiate children with language differences from those with language disorders.

Language disorders can vary from mild (e.g., problems in using word endings but easily understood by others) to severe (e.g., extreme difficulty in understanding what others say or being understood by others). At times, terms such as *delay* and *deviance* may also be used in relation to language disorders; however, both of these terms are problematic. Most clinicians and researchers prefer not to use the term "deviance" because of the very negative connotations of the term. While children with language disorders may "deviate" from the typical course of development, there is nothing inherently "deviant" about them. The term "delay" suggests that there is nothing seriously "wrong" with the child. Given time, they will catch up. But is this always true? Is there a point where a delay becomes a disorder? If a child is a year behind? Two years? Ten years? In many cases, what looks like a delay at one point in time may be recognized as a plateauing of development later. That is, the child has stopped developing and is now recognized as having a language disorder. Therefore, most practitioners prefer to use the term "language disorders" to describe impairments in language development.

Often children with language and communication disorders experience related problems that may be the result of their language difficulties. They may have difficulty interacting with their peers. They may be shy and reluctant to approach others. Other children may ignore them or, even worse, reject their attempts at friendship. Some children with language and communication disorders have difficulty with cognitive functioning. They may have problems organizing information for recall, may be less attentive than their peers, and may be generally slower to respond. Sometimes children with language and communication difficulties exhibit behavior problems. These problems may be the result of their own frustration with communication, or they may result from the response of others to their difficulties. Some children with language and communication disorders have physical disabilities that either cause or exacerbate their difficulty. For example, children with cleft palate often have difficulty with articulation, and children with mild, fluctuating hearing loss are at risk for a variety of language and communication disorders.

Language disorders are often associated with disabilities such as autism and **intellectual disability**. Children with language disorders may be called "dysphasic," "dyslexic," "dysnomic," "communication handicapped," "language learning disabled," and so on. However, language disorders are not limited to children with classifications such as mental retardation and intellectual disability. Many students with mild language difficulties are never classified or are grouped under the general term *learning disabled*. In this book, I have chosen to organize the sections on specific language disorders by category of disability. This was no easy choice, and I recognize its potential for confusion. It might seem that the book is saying that all children with a particular disability (e.g., intellectual disability) have language disorders when, in fact, this may not be the case. Alternatively, it might seem that a child has to be classified with a disability label to have a language disorder. This also is not true. However, special education tends to be organized on the basis of diagnostic categories, and much of the research on language disorders is related to diagnostic categories. So, although these categories may sometimes be misleading, they provide an organizing framework for understanding language disorders.

The key criterion in determining whether a language difficulty is serious enough to require intervention is the impact the problem has on the child and on others. Does the child appear to be concerned about the problem? Is the language difficulty interfering with the child's ability to learn and/or socialize? Do other children tease or reject the child because of difficulties the child may be experiencing with speech, language, or communication? If the answer to one or more of these questions is yes, the child may require some sort of intervention.

Because children with language and communication disorders are at risk for academic and social failure, it is important that their difficulties be identified as early as possible. In many cases, it may be possible to correct or at least enhance their performance. Children with language and communication disorders may exhibit a wide variety of characteristics. Some of the more frequently occurring characteristics are listed in Figure 1.3. Students who are experiencing one or more of these characteristics for an extended period of time

FIGURE 1.3

Characteristics of Children with Language and Communication Disorders

Academic Performance

> Reluctance to contribute to discussions
> Difficulty organizing ideas
> Difficulty recognizing phonemes
> Difficulty producing sounds
> Failure to follow directions
> Difficulty finding the right word for things

Social Interaction

> Reluctance to interact with other children
> Exclusion or rejection by other children
> Difficulty carrying on a conversation
> Problems negotiating rules for games

Cognitive Functioning

> Difficulty organizing information for recall
> Slow responding
> Inattentiveness

Behavior

> High level of frustration
> Frequent arguments
> Fighting with peers
> Withdrawing from interaction

may have underlying difficulties with language and communication. A comprehensive evaluation should include language and communication skills to determine whether they may be contributing to the child's learning and/or behavior difficulties.

Recognizing the problem and determining the need for intervention is a necessary first step in helping children with language and communication difficulties. But it is only a first step. Knowing *what* the child should be able to do and how to help the child get to that point is the goal of the rest of this book.

Check Your Understanding 1.2

Click here to gauge your understanding of the concepts in this section.

Summary

In the beginning of this chapter, the definitions of speech, language, and communication were presented and the characteristics of each term and the differences between them were described. Communication is the broadest of these concepts, encompassing both verbal and nonverbal interaction. Speech refers to the neuromuscular act of sound production. Language is a complex phenomenon that involves the use of symbols that conform to rules that are used to express meaning. In addition, language disorders were defined as deviations (or differences) from typical development and/or appropriate use of language. It is important to identify language disorders as early as possible because such disorders can cause serious problems in learning and socialization. Moreover, with early identification, it may be possible to help children make significant improvement in their language skills.

Understanding the Elements of Language

Language has been described as consisting of several elements. In this chapter we will look in depth at the elements of language. We will see how linguists have described each element and the rules that govern its use. Knowing these elements forms the framework for understanding language disorders and for differentiating language disorders from language differences. We will also examine ways to support the development and use of the elements of language by children.

Learning Outcomes

After reading this chapter, you should be able to:

1. Explain what a *phoneme* is and how to recognize it.

2. Define the term *morpheme* and understand how to count morphemes in words.

3. Explain the rules that underlie syntax and recognize their application to sentence building.

4. Describe the challenges in developing rules for semantics.

5. Explain the concept of *pragmatics* and its application in communication.

Human language is extremely complex. In order to simplify and better understand language, linguists have developed various systems for dividing language into its components (or elements). Most linguists identify five major elements: phonology, morphology, syntax, semantics, and pragmatics. Alternatively, Bloom and Lahey (1978) describe language as consisting of three components: form, content, and use. This model recognizes the interrelatedness of language elements. Within the component they call "form," Bloom and Lahey include the elements of phonology, morphology, and syntax (see Figure 2.1). It is often difficult to separate morphology from phonology (for example, when children are learning that the plural form of *cats* makes an "s" sound but the plural of *dogs* has a "z" sound). Similarly, morphology and syntax are closely related in the emergence of language

Figure 2.1

Model of Language Components and Elements

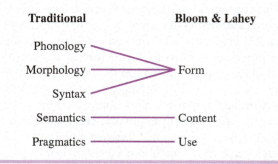

in young children. Nevertheless, in this chapter, we will use the model that includes five language elements because it describes language in its most elemental form. However, as you read the chapter, you should keep in mind the interrelated nature of these elements.

Phonology

As an exercise to illustrate the interrelatedness of language elements, imagine that your task is to program a computer to understand and use spoken language—in this case, English. This is a formidable task but one that has been pursued for some time and has begun to yield very promising results. What would you include in your program? What would the computer need to know in order to process language?

Since computers work best with the most elemental sort of information, the first step might be to input the sounds of the English language. This would not be a terribly difficult task. Linguists have identified approximately 43 (there are variations due to dialect and regional differences) distinctive sounds in English. These elemental units of language are called *phonemes*. A **phoneme** is the smallest linguistic unit of sound that can signal a difference in meaning. That is, native speakers recognize that because of the change of one sound, the meaning of the word changes.

A complete list of phonemes in both American and British English can be found at the Antimoon website (click on "How to learn English," then "Pronunciation," and then click "The sounds of English and their IPA symbols").

Linguists can determine whether a sound is a phoneme in a particular language by asking native speakers of that language whether the sound, when added to a root word, makes a new word that they recognize. For example, let's say that we have already established that *bill* is a word in English. Now, if we substitute a *p* sound for the initial *b* sound, will speakers of the language recognize this as a new word? Yes, they recognize the new word as *pill*. Therefore, it appears that *p* is a phoneme in English. Linguists call the two words *pill* and *bill* a **minimal pair** because the two words differ only with respect to one sound. Now, let's say that we have determined that the word *row* is a word in English. If we substitute a rolled *r* for the flat *r* in *row*, have we made a new word that speakers of English recognize as having a different meaning? No. Although the rolled *r* is a phoneme in Spanish, it is not a phoneme in English.

We can describe all of the sounds in English in terms of the way that those sounds are produced. Vowels are classified in terms of the height and position of the tongue and the shape of the mouth. Consonants are classified in terms of the **place of articulation** (the location of lips and tongue), **manner of articulation** (how the sound is produced), and whether the sound is **voiced** or **unvoiced** (whether the vocal folds vibrate during production of the sound). Now let's go back to our minimal pair: *pill* and *bill*. How do the two sounds "puh" and "buh" differ? Both sounds are considered **bilabial**, because they are made by putting the lips together. Both sounds are also classified as **stops** because the stream of air is stopped by the lips. But "buh" is voiced—that is, the vocal folds vibrate—whereas "puh" is **voiceless**—it is produced with a puff of air. Try saying both sounds. Can you feel the difference?

Watch this video for a demonstration of the way sounds are produced. What is the difference in the way that consonants and vowels are produced?
https://www.youtube.com/watch?v=dfoRdKuPF9I

As you have probably realized, the number of letters in English (26) does not match the number of phonemes (43, give or take a few). This creates a number of problems. Take the letter "a." How do you pronounce this letter? Is it pronounced like the "a" sound in the word "may" or like the "a" in the word "can." Clearly, there are several ways to pronounce the letter that we call "a" in English, depending on the other letters that precede or follow it.

This mismatch between the number of letters in the English alphabet and the number of sounds in the language contributes to the difficulty that some children have in acquiring reading and writing skills. We will have more to say about this dilemma in Chapter 6.

Having programmed our computer with the 40 or so sounds of English, we are ready to go. The first word our computer produces is *tphj*. Oh no! Something seems to be missing. In fact, what is missing are the rules that govern phonology. Remember, our definition of language said that it was a *rule-governed* system. In phonology there are constraints on which sounds can (and cannot) occur together. These are called **phonotactic constraints**. They determine that we can have a word like "team" but are unlikely to ever have a word like "lteam." There are also rules (or constraints) that tell when and how vowels must be used and how sound combinations are pronounced. Phonotactic constraints can sometimes make it difficult to learn another language, since the sound combinations in those languages may differ from ours.

While many linguists use the word "rules" to describe how language is structured, some are using the word "constraints" (as we did above in discussing which sounds can co-occur in English). The idea of "constraints" comes from **optimality theory**. This model of linguistics emphasizes the role of higher-order cognitive (thinking) processes in governing speech production and recognizes the flexibility in language (Stemberger & Bernhardt, 1999).

Phonology, the first of the form elements of language, is the study of the sound system of language. Linguists who are interested in phonology attempt to identify the phonemes of a language and the rules (or constraints) that govern the combination and pronunciation of these phonemes. Knowledge of these rules enables linguists to understand how native speakers of a language know which sound combinations are possible in their language.

Check Your Understanding 2.1
Click here to gauge your understanding of the concepts in this section.

Morphology

So it looks as though we are ready to proceed with our task of developing a computer program to process language. With the rules governing sound, our computer is now producing combinations that look a lot more like English. Some of them may not be words that we recognize (e.g., *blif* and *ulop*), but they are at least *possible* English words. Soon we notice that we are getting some larger words, such as *unpossible* and *deerses,* and we realize that something else is missing. Although these combinations of sounds conform to the rules of phonology, speakers of the language reject these combinations.

The problem is that there must be another set of rules—a set of rules that govern how words are made. In fact, there is such a group of rules. They are called *morphological rules*. **Morphology** is the study of words and how they are formed. Morphological rules determine how sounds can be put together to make words; they govern the structure of words.

Consider the word *base*. Any speaker of English would acknowledge this as a word in English. What about *baseball*? Of course this is a word, too, but it is different. It consists of two words—*base* and *ball*. Moreover, each of these words has a meaning that is related to the compound word. That is, both *bases* and *balls* are used in the game of baseball.

Based on this type of evidence, linguists have concluded that there are elemental building blocks of language called *morphemes*. A **morpheme** is the smallest unit of meaning in a language. To better understand morphemes, let's go back to the previous example. The word *base* is a morpheme. It cannot be broken into smaller pieces while retaining its original meaning. So what about *baseball*? As discussed previously, this *can* be divided into two parts that retain the meaning of the whole—*base* and *ball*. Therefore each of these words is a morpheme.

Actually, linguists say that there are two basic kinds of morphemes. To illustrate, let's return again to the example. We have already said that *baseball* consists of two morphemes. Each of these is called a *free* morpheme. In other words, each morpheme can stand on its own as a word with meaning. Now let's add a plural *s* to create the word *baseballs*. How many morphemes do we have now? There must be three, since we have already established that *baseball* alone has two morphemes. But what is this new morpheme? What does *s* mean? In this context the *s*, since it is used as a plural, means "more than one." Therefore, there are three morphemes in the word *baseballs: base, ball,* and *s* (plural). However, the plural *s* is a special kind of morpheme. It cannot stand alone but has meaning only when it is attached to other morphemes. It is called a *bound* morpheme. Prefixes (such as *un* and *pre*) and suffixes (such as *ing* and *able*) are examples of bound morphemes.

This video will help you better understand the concept of morphemes. How is the difference between free and bound morphemes explained?
https://www.youtube.com/watch?v=rfivuTgOxTl&list=PLiZlu2g-nRsfH9UjSCEFCnfsiBmRj8dZh&index=5

If all of this seems a bit complicated, just consider the kind of problems that linguists have with words such as *cranberry*. For years linguists thought that this was one morpheme, since there is no such thing as a *cran*. Then along came *cranapple* juice. This demonstrated that *cran* can be separated from *berry* and still retain its meaning. Therefore, maybe *cranberry* was really two morphemes all along. This is the sort of debate that linguists love to pursue.

For our purposes, the point of this discussion is that there are rules that determine what a word is and how words can be formed. Thus, native speakers of English recognize that the word *unlikely* is fine but *inlikely* does not mean anything, and that even though *boy* is pluralized as *boys*, more than one man is not *mans* but *men*. But how do we account for the fact that sometimes the plural "s" is pronounced like /s/ (as in cats) and sometimes like /z/ (as in dogs)? These variations in pronunciation are called **allomorphs** and can be explained by understanding how phonological and morphological rules work together. When "s" follows an unvoiced stop sound ("t"), it is pronounced as /s/, but when it follows a vowel or most voiced stops (like "g"), it is sounded as /z/.

Apply Your Knowledge 2.1: Morphology Exercise

To better understand the nature of morphological rules, complete this morphology exercise.

Morphology, then, as the study of words and how they are formed, includes the identification of morphemes (the basic *meaningful* units of language) and the rules for constructing words. With our computer programmed to identify and use morphemes, we can eliminate many of the strange letter sound combinations we were getting previously. Unfortunately, now we are getting sentences such as the following: *car the man hit the* and *the sweet is very child*. Clearly, there is still something wrong with our computer program. We need another set of rules. This additional group of rules is called *syntax*.

Check Your Understanding 2.2
Click here to gauge your understanding of the concepts in this section.

Syntax

Look at the following first stanza from Lewis Carroll's "Jabberwocky":

> 'Twas brillig, and _____ slithy toves
> Did _____ and gimble in the _____:
> All mimsy were the borogoves,
> And the mome raths outgrabe.

Can you guess what goes in each blank? You may not always get the exact word (*the*; *gyre*; *wabe*), but, even though this is a lot of nonsense, you probably guessed accurately about the *type* of word that must go in the blank. You undoubtedly knew that the first word was an article. You probably guessed that the second word was a verb and the third word was a noun. How did you do this? The answer is that you have rules of grammar (syntax) that help you accomplish tasks like this. You may or may not be able to formally state the rules. You may not even be aware that you possess these rules (until you are forced to use them in some ridiculous exercise), but they are there. These are *syntactic* rules. **Syntax** is the study of the rules that govern how words are put together to make phrases and sentences. What do these rules look like?

How would you describe the structure of the following sentences?

1. The dog is running.

2. The girl is reading a book.

For the first sentence, you might say that there is an article (*the*) and a noun (*dog*), an auxiliary verb (*is*), and a main verb (*running*). These are elements of the syntactic rules that linguists call **phrase structure rules**. These rules describe the structure of sentences.

Linguists have devised a shorthand code to describe these rules. For the first sentence, the code would look like the following:

S = NP + VP

NP = Art + N

VP = Aux + V

This notation says that the sentence consists of two elements—a noun phrase and a verb phrase. The noun phrase, in turn, consists of two elements—an article and a noun. The verb phrase also consists of two other elements—an auxiliary verb and a main verb.

If this were all that we knew about the English language, we could say that these were the rules of English syntax. But then we might find a sentence like the second example. Since this sentence is not completely explained by our original set of phrase structure rules, we must modify the rules somewhat. The second sentence example could be rewritten as:

S = NP + VP

NP = Art + N

VP = Aux + V + NP

NP = Art + N

This sentence introduces a new element into our phrase structure rules—a noun phrase that *follows* a verb phrase. If we were to continue examining sentences and refining our rules, we would end up with the finite (and surprisingly small) set of rules for the English language. Although small in number, these rules can be used to generate an infinite number of sentences, because of the *recursive* feature of phrase structure rules. This feature permits phrases to be joined together without limit. For example, in conjoined sentences (sentences that include a conjunction such as *and* or *but*), two or more noun phrases may be joined, as in the following example: *The boy and the girl sat outside the school.* Other nouns (e.g., *teacher, man, friend*) could be added to our sentence without limit. Similarly, more than one verb phrase may be embedded in a single sentence as in: *The girl who is here is my niece.*

For many years it was thought that phrase structure rules were all that were needed to describe a language. But there are certain kinds of sentences that are not easily explained by these rules. These include imperative sentences (*Go to bed!*) and questions (*Why are you crying?*). Such sentences bothered linguists for many years because they could not be adequately explained. Finally, Noam Chomsky (1957, 1965) developed a theory to account for these kinds of sentences. Called *transformational grammar*, his theory suggests that there are two levels in all languages—a surface structure and a deep structure. The surface structure is what we actually hear, but the deep structure is the underlying linguistic structure of the utterance. Between the deep structure and the surface structure, according to Chomsky, there is a set of rules (*transformational rules*) that can convert a deep-structure sentence to something else.

For example, take our question sentence, *Why are you crying?* The underlying (deep) structure of this sentence would be *You are crying* (deep-structure sentences are always simple, declarative sentences). In order to get the surface question, a question-transformation rule has to be applied, inverting the subject (*you*) and the auxiliary verb (*are*) and adding the appropriate *wh* word (*why*). This entire operation occurs subconsciously. In the case of the imperative, the deep-structure sentence is actually *You go to bed*. The imperative-transformation rule says that when the first noun is in the second person (*you*), it can be deleted, leaving the surface structure (*Go to bed*).

Apply Your Knowledge 2.2: Syntax Exercise

Complete this activity to understand how children develop their knowledge of complex sentences.

Transformational rules have served us well for many years; however, they have been found to have some limitations and Chomsky himself has rejected the notions of deep and surface structures. Some problematic sentences can be generated by the theory and its rules. For example, the ambiguity apparent in the sentence *The duck is ready to eat* (Is it the duck that is preparing to eat or is someone about to consume the duck?) cannot be resolved by reference to phrase structure and transformational rules. Additionally, the theory does not adequately explain the universality and learnability of languages (Leonard & Loeb, 1988).

More recent revisions of transformational grammar theory have attempted to describe these universal rules of language. For example, *government and binding theory* (Chomsky, 1981, 1982) attempted to account for the universality of language by describing the rules that relate the language we hear to the underlying mental representations we hold in our minds (Shapiro, 1997). X-bar theory (Pinker, 1994) can be used to explain how it is that in some languages (such as Japanese) the verb comes after the object (Akira sushi ate), whereas in others (such as English) the verb precedes the object (Mike ate chili). X-bar theory proposes "super-rules" to account for these differences; for example, "An X-bar is composed of a head (phrase) X and any number of role players, in either order" (Pinker, 1994, p. 111). In English, the X-bar is head first; that is, the verb precedes the object. Japanese is a "head-last" language. The point is that, according to Chomsky and his colleagues, the rules that underlie all languages can be described.

Watch this video about tree structures and X-bar theory. How is X-bar theory a more universal way to describe syntactic structure?
https://www.youtube.com/watch?v=jgRMBykXg4Q

So we can now program our computer with syntactic rules, including phrase structure and transformational rules. These will help us organize the words of English into coherent sentences that will easily be interpreted by native speakers of the language—sentences such as *Colorless green ideas sleep furiously*. Oh no! It looks like we have another problem.

The sentence *Colorless green ideas sleep furiously* was actually used by Chomsky (1957) to support his theory of the importance of structure in language. As he noted, there is nothing wrong with the syntax of this sentence. All of the words are in the right order. Still, the sentence does not mean anything (at least not in the literal sense). If we are to program our computer to understand and produce both grammatically correct and meaningful sentences, we will have to include yet another set of rules—semantic rules.

Check Your Understanding 2.3

Click here to gauge your understanding of the concepts in this section.

Semantics

Let's look at that sentence again—*Colorless green ideas sleep furiously*—to determine what, exactly, is wrong with this sentence. First of all, something cannot both have color (*green*) and be *colorless*. Additionally, ideas cannot have color, and they cannot sleep. Even if they could sleep, it is not actually possible to sleep furiously. That this sentence makes no sense suggests that there must be rules that govern which words can meaningfully go together. These rules are called *semantic rules*. **Semantics** is the study of how meaning is attached to the words and sentences of language.

The search for these rules has not been easy. There are several theories of semantics, none of which seems to fully describe how words are linked to ideas. For example, the *semantic feature theory* claims that there are certain fundamental features of all words. The word *husband* might consist of the features: + (is) male; + adult; + human; + (is) married. There are also **selection restrictions**. These rules govern which words can appear together. For example, someone would not be described as a *married bachelor* or *my sister the bachelor* or *my 2-year-old the bachelor* because of the component features of the word *bachelor*. You cannot be both married and a bachelor, nor can you be a female or a child and also be a bachelor. Of course, it *is* possible to talk about child bachelors and married bachelors in a nonliteral sense. Similarly, it is possible to interpret a phrase such as *colorless green ideas*. Surely many of us have had nights when we *slept furiously*. But we have to work to make sense of these expressions. They are not *literally* true; they have truth only in a metaphorical sense. It is this metaphorical feature of semantics that at times is what makes poetry interesting, and even beautiful.

Our fundamental-feature and selection-restriction rules could also be applied to the *colorless green ideas* sentence. Since one feature of green is that it is a color, it cannot be both a color and lack color. Since ideas are not animate, it is not possible for them to sleep. Fundamental-feature and selection-restriction rules help account for the contradiction that speakers find in a sentence, such as *My sister is married to a bachelor*, and for the ambiguity that we found previously in the sentence *The duck is ready to eat*.

The semantic-feature model is only one of many theories of semantics. It helps explain some of the ways in which adult speakers make distinctions between words, but it may not be a good explanation for how children learn word meanings. Additionally, it has limitations in explaining the acquisition of verbs, pronouns, and other word classes other than nouns. Contemporary theories of semantics emphasize the importance of social interaction and cognitive development in shaping word learning (e.g., Tomasello, 2003) and the development of semantic networks in which words are organized on the basis of the strength of the connections between words (Pence & Justice, 2012). We will have more to say about the acquisition of words in Chapter 5.

Now, after including some semantic rules in our computer program, we should be done. Although it may be difficult to describe all of the semantic rules, those that we have do a very good job of delivering meaningful sentences. Every once in a while, we might get a sentence that is difficult to interpret, but that happens in natural language as well.

Now, imagine trying to hold a two-way conversation with your computer. You type in statements or questions, and it types back responses. Suppose you type "Can you use a sentence with the word *dog*?" It types back "Yes." But that is not what you intended. You had wanted the computer to respond with a sentence using the word *dog*. Is there a problem? You bet there is. And you discover another problem. When you type a sentence such as "How are you today?" the computer might respond with almost anything—"The cat is on the mat," or "The car is at the shop." The response does not make any sense. What is wrong?

☑ **Check Your Understanding 2.4**
Click here to gauge your understanding of the concepts in this section.

Pragmatics

So far, our computer programming task has been relatively simple. We tried something. When it did not work, we changed the program and added another set of rules that got us closer to our goal of simulating human language. The rules could be discovered and were relatively few. Rules for semantics turned out to be a bit more difficult, but still it was possible to include these rules. But now we are faced with a major problem. Our computer seems insensitive to some of the subtle rules that govern conversation. It is misinterpreting the intent of some sentences and not responding to the content of other sentences. In short, we are having difficulty getting our computer to *use* language in conversation, suggesting that there must be yet another element of language. In fact, there is. This element is called **pragmatics**—the use of language for communication, or, as Gleason (2009) put it, "the use of language to express one's intentions and to get things done in the world" (p. 22).

Pragmatics includes the study of the rules that govern the use of language for social interaction. There are rules that govern the reasons for communicating, as well as rules that determine the choice of codes used in communication. Let's look more closely at one of these rules.

▶ Watch as Professor David Crystal explains the role of pragmatics in language. How does he define pragmatics?
https://www.youtube.com/watch?v=0xc0KUD1umw

I recall observing a student teacher in her placement in a classroom with 6- and 7-year-old children with language and communication disabilities. The student teacher was seated at a table at the front of the room, and the children were at their desks. Wanting the children to join her at the table, the student teacher asked, "Can you come to the table?" The children looked at the student teacher, then at each other, but they did not move. Naturally, this wanton disobedience angered the student teacher, so she raised her voice and quite sharply said, "Can you come to the table!" Once again, the only response was some puzzled looks and some foot shuffling. Finally, in exasperation, the student teacher said, "Please come to the table now." The children immediately got up and went to the table. What happened in this episode? Why were these children so reluctant to come forward?

The answer is that they were probably having difficulty interpreting the communicative intent of the student teacher. Like our computer, they may have interpreted the correct answer to the question, "Can you come to the table?" as "Yes." But, in fact, this was not meant to be a question at all, even though it had the form of a question. This is an example of an *indirect speech act*—an utterance for which the syntactic form does not match the communicative intention. In the context in which this sentence was uttered, the intent was clearly that of a command. Unfortunately, the intent may not have been so clear to the children, because indirect speech acts tend to be more difficult to interpret than direct speech acts. Direct speech acts are those in which the communicative intention is reflected in the syntactic form, such as *Can I have some cake?* (question) and *Stop that car!* (imperative). Every utterance, however, is a speech act, and linguists have identified speech acts and the rules that determine whether a conversation is intelligible.

Apply Your Knowledge 2.3: Pragmatic Language Exercise

To better understand the difference between direct and indirect speech acts, complete this pragmatic language exercise.

Pragmatics also includes the study of the rules of conversation. You may recall what happened when we tried to engage the computer in conversation. It did not respond appropriately to what we had typed. Our computer violated one of the principles (rules) of conversation identified by Grice (1975)—specifically, the *relation principle*. This principle says that a response must be relevant to the topic. Other principles involve the *quantity* of information provided by the speaker, the *quality* (or truthfulness) of that information, and the *manner* (directness) of the information. When these principles are violated, we know that something is wrong with the conversation. Similarly, there are rules of conversation that govern how one speaks to persons of different levels of social status, that determine how conversations are repaired, and how to maintain the topic of a conversation. But these "rules" can be difficult for children to understand because they are so dependent on the context of the conversation. For example, the conventions for politeness may differ in the home setting as compared to the school (Bryant, 2009).

It would be difficult, if not impossible, to program our computer with such pragmatic rules because these require not only a solid understanding of language but also an understanding of people and their social environment. How do we tell the computer to talk one way to someone wearing a black coat and white collar and another way to someone wearing jeans and a T-shirt? The wonder is that we are able to make these subtle distinctions ourselves and that children are able to develop these skills fairly quickly.

Check Your Understanding 2.5

Click here to gauge your understanding of the concepts in this section.

Summary

This chapter examined the elements of language in detail—considering how form (phonology, morphology, and syntax), content (semantics), and use (pragmatics) relate to language and noting the rules characterizing each in determining the structure and use of language. The rules, considered individually, seem manageable enough, but discussion of the interrelatedness of the elements in language reveals the complexity of the language system. For students who lag in the development in any or all of these language elements, there are methods that can be used to enhance their skills. These methods will be discussed in Chapter 13. The next several chapters will focus on how children acquire the language system and how the system develops as children mature.

Bases of Language Development

What is it about humans that enables us to learn language? What physical structures are necessary in order for language to be acquired? What role does cognitive development play in acquiring language? What about interaction with others? These are some of the questions that will be addressed in this chapter.

Learning Outcomes

After reading this chapter, you should be able to:

1. Describe the physical structures and processes that underlie speech.

2. Explain the relationship between *cognition* and *language*.

3. Describe the role that social interaction plays in language acquisition.

Physical Bases of Language Development

In Chapter 1, the work of Professors Beatrice and Allan Gardner with a chimp called Washoe was described. Although Washoe was able to learn a number of signs for words, the chimp was limited in her ability to develop new words (signs) and use the signs she had acquired in novel ways. Other researchers have tried without success to teach chimpanzees to talk. Why were these animals unable to develop true language skills? The answer lies primarily in the physiological structures that allow humans to learn and develop language. We will look at two types of structures that contribute to language development and use: those of speech production and the regions of the brain that control language.

Speech Production Structures

The speech production system is quite complex, and a thorough discussion of the physiology of speech would go beyond the scope of this book. There are several texts, however, that give a detailed description of the physiology of the speech production system (e.g., Anderson & Shames, 2011; Owens, Farinella, & Metz, 2015). Here, we will briefly look at the structures that contribute to the four processes of speech production—respiration, phonation, resonation, and articulation—and at how these processes and structures together produce speech sounds. Under the control of the brain, they function almost simultaneously in the speech production process (see Figure 3.1).

Respiration.   How is sound produced? First, we need air, for it is a stream of shaped and guided air that forms sounds. When we breathe normally, about half of the breathing cycle is spent on inhaling air and about half involves exhaling (Hulit, Fahey, & Howard, 2014). However, during speech, something very different happens. Muscles that control respiration—namely, the **diaphragm** (see Figure 3.2)—work to control the airstream so that the exhaling stage lasts close to 85 percent of the breathing cycle—15 seconds or more. Just imagine what speech would be like if we were limited to 2- or 3-second bursts.

Figure 3.1

The Processes of Speech

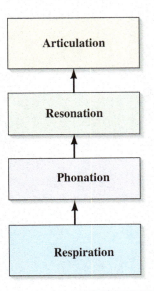

Figure 3.2

The Human Vocal Organs

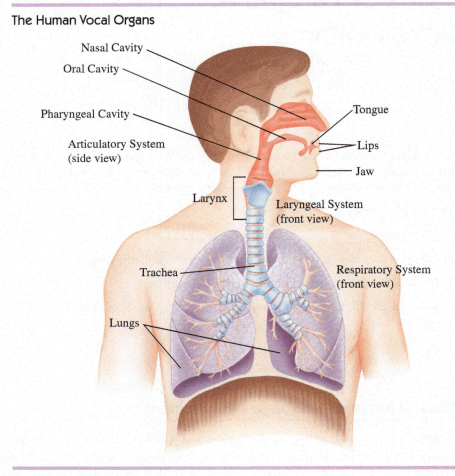

Nasal Cavity
Oral Cavity
Pharyngeal Cavity
Articulatory System (side view)
Tongue
Lips
Jaw
Larynx
Laryngeal System (front view)
Trachea
Respiratory System (front view)
Lungs

Phonation. In addition to maintaining a longer stream of air, the respiratory muscles allow air to be forced under pressure through structures in the **larynx**. The *vocal folds* contained in the larynx act as a valve that prevents foreign matter from entering the lungs. The vocal folds also obstruct the flow of air from the lungs, thus causing the vibrations necessary for speech. As the airstream is restricted and buffeted, it creates a buzzing sound.

Resonation. Moving upward from the larynx, the air resonates in the mouth, the nasal cavities, and/or the pharynx (see Figure 3.2). The tone of the resulting sound is affected by the size and shape of the resonating structures into which the air is expelled. In general, the larger the resonating cavity, the lower is the tone. Try making a vowel sound. This is the sound created by resonated air.

Articulation. **Articulation** of sound takes place when the airstream is further impeded by structures such as the lips, tongue, and/or teeth. The production of consonants requires the action of articulation. As we saw in Chapter 2, each phoneme has a unique combination of articulators and resonators that work together to form the sound. Vowel articulation can be described with respect to tongue and lip position. The tongue position varies along two dimensions: front–back and high–low (Kent & Vorperian, 2011). For example, the /ae/ sound (as in *hat*) is described as a low-front sound—that is, the tip of the tongue is placed in a low position at the front of the mouth when that sound is articulated. Try it. Now, say the word *heat*. What happens? You should feel your tongue move toward the roof of your mouth (the /i/ sound is high-front). Vowels are also described by lip position—rounded or unrounded. Similarly, each consonant sound can be described by a unique combination of three sets of characteristics: **place of articulation** (where sound is formed), **manner of articulation** (how a sound is formed), and **voicing** (whether the vocal cords are vibrated).

Watch this video about the mechanisms related to speech production. How do the various elements of the system work together to produce speech?
https://www.youtube.com/watch?v=-m-gudHhLxc

Apply Your Knowledge 3.1: Speech Production

Try this activity to better understand how speech sounds are articulated.

Central Nervous System

Control of speech production is governed by the central nervous system. The human nervous system can be divided into two major divisions: the peripheral nervous system and the central nervous system.

The **peripheral nervous system** is made up of the cranial and spinal nerves that carry sensory information to the brain while relaying motor information from the brain to the muscles of the body. The 12 cranial nerves directly connect from the brain to the ears, nose, and mouth, whereas the spinal nerves are connected to the spinal cord via long pathways.

The **central nervous system** includes the brain and spinal cord. In order to better understand this complex organ, scientists often describe the brain as being comprised of three major regions: the hindbrain, the midbrain, and the forebrain (see Figure 3.3). The **hindbrain** consists of structures of the brain stem, such as the medulla oblongata, the pons, and the cerebellum, which control functions such as respiration, digestion, and large motor movement. This part of the brain is sometimes called the most primitive, because these structures were the first to develop in animals and are the first to develop in the neonate. The **midbrain** consists of structures that assist in relaying information to and from the brain and the visual and auditory nerves.

The **forebrain** (cerebrum) is the largest part of the brain. The cerebrum is divided into two nearly equal hemispheres connected by a bundle of fibers called the **corpus callosum**. For purposes of study, each hemisphere of the cerebrum is divided into four regions: frontal lobe, parietal lobe, temporal lobe, and occipital lobe.

Each hemisphere of the cerebrum, and each region within the hemisphere, is believed to have a special function. In most people, language processing, both comprehension and production, takes place largely in the left hemisphere, although the right hemisphere *does* have a role to play in the processing of language. For example, research has shown that auditory syntactic information is processed primarily in the left temporal lobe and in part of the left frontal lobe, whereas the interpretation of paralinguistic cues such as stress and intonation takes place in the right hemisphere (Friederici, 2001). In addition, research on individuals with right hemisphere brain damage has suggested that they may have more difficulty participating in extended communicative exchanges (Obler & Gjerlow, 1999).

Two areas in the left hemisphere are thought to be especially important in language production and comprehension: Broca's area and Wernicke's area. **Broca's area** is located near the middle of the left cerebral hemisphere, where the frontal, parietal, and temporal lobes meet. This is the area where organization of the complex motor sequences necessary for speech production occurs. **Wernicke's area** lies closer to the rear of the left cerebral hemisphere in the temporal lobe and is the area involved in the comprehension of

Figure 3.3

View of the Brain Showing Major Regions

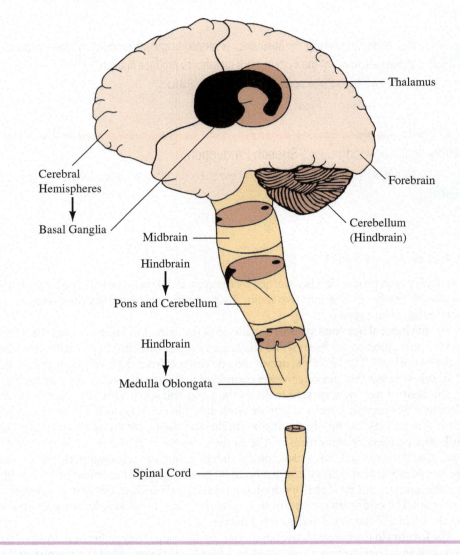

Source: Anderson, Noma B.; Shames, George H., *Human Communication Disorders: An Introduction*, 8th Ed., ©2011. Reprinted and Electronically reproduced by permission of Pearson Education, Inc., New York, NY.

language (see Figure 3.4). When these regions of the brain are damaged, the effect on language use can be devastating. The right hemisphere of the brain contains similar regions that may play a role in comprehension of speech (Hickok, 2001) (see Figure 3.5).

 Watch this video on the brain and language. How has evidence from studying individuals with aphasia helped us better understand what regions of the brain are involved in controlling language?
https://www.youtube.com/watch?v=5k8JwC1L9_k

Evidence from neuroimaging studies is revealing that although specific regions of the brain are, indeed, activated during language tasks, for many language functions, large regions of the brain are involved (Fedorenko & Kanwisher, 2009; Frackowiak et al., 2004). These results support connectionist (or neural network) models of human brain functioning, which emphasize the importance of interconnections between brain regions in cognitive processing. For example, neuroimaging studies have found that although the left hemisphere, specifically Wernicke's area, is critical for word recognition and retrieval, other parts of the left hemisphere are involved depending on the nature of the semantic task (Frederici, Opitz, & van Cramon, 2000). In fact, in some cases, the right hemisphere plays a role in the processing of semantic information such as figurative language and humor (Bookheimer, 2002).

The connectionist models of human brain functioning combined with neuroimaging studies are helping us to understand the complexities of the brain and language. Although specific regions of the brain are critical for language functioning, connections between regions are also necessary for optimal language processing. These results have implications for understanding the impact of brain damage (as in traumatic brain injury) and the more subtle impact of functional differences that may underlie language learning disabilities.

Why is the ability to understand and use language not fully developed at birth? The most likely explanation is that the brain is not fully developed. Synaptic connections are developing rapidly in the first year of life (Huttenlocher, 2002) as the result of new experiences, and the efficiency of communication between cells is improving as **myelination** (sheathing of nerves) continues. Over time, the combination of physiological maturation and experience causes the brain to develop both in capacity and in efficiency of processing. However, there appears to be a time limit within which this brain development must take place. Lenneberg (1967) proposed that there is a "critical period" for brain development, as it

Figure 3.4

Broca's and Wernicke's Areas

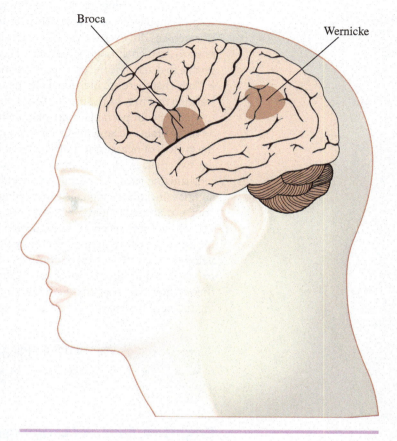

Figure 3.5

Comprehension and Production of Speech in the Brain

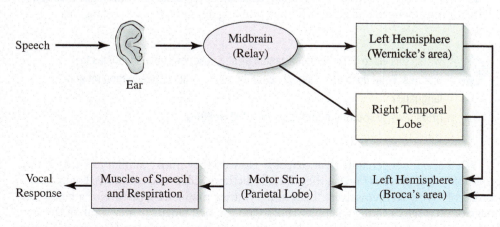

relates to language functioning. After this period (which Lenneberg claimed ends with the onset of puberty), acquisition of a first language is difficult, if not impossible. This theory is supported by research on individuals with brain damage that has found that adults recover language functioning much more slowly (if at all) than do children. In addition, learning a second language is much more difficult as an adult than as a child. On the other hand, recent research has discovered that some aspects of language (e.g., pragmatics and semantics) continue to develop through adolescence and beyond (Obler, 2012). In fact, researchers have been unable to determine the exact point at which language acquisition becomes more difficult. It is likely that there are individual differences in the extent of the "critical period" for language learning that may be the result of both physiological and experiential differences.

Another important feature of brain functioning is "plasticity." Plasticity refers to the ability of the brain to change in response to experience or to injury. Changes in the brain, including the growth of new connections between brain cells, occurs in children as the result of everyday experiences (Huttenlocher, 2002). But, remarkably, the brain can also adapt to injury by reorganizing itself. As a result, many individuals can recover some or all of their functional abilities (including language functioning) following brain injury (Kleim & Jones, 2008). Of course, this often requires intensive therapy, including speech and language therapy.

These findings about brain development and language have important implications for those interested in helping children with language learning difficulties. Since brain development continues throughout childhood, it may be possible, through appropriate experiences, to have some effect on development in those children. The critical period theory, however, suggests there is limited time to influence language acquisition, supporting the need for early intervention.

Check Your Understanding 3.1
Click here to gauge your understanding of the concepts in this section.

Cognitive Bases of Language Development

How are language and thinking (cognition) related? Is it possible to "think" without language? How is language development affected by the development of cognitive processes? These are incredibly difficult questions with very elusive answers.

Although a direct examination of how prelinguistic children think is not possible (since they cannot tell us), emerging assessment techniques in cognitive neuroscience have helped us learn a little more about the relationship between thought and language. Additionally, reports from people with disabilities can help us understand how thought and language are related. For example, Dr. Temple Grandin, a person with autism, says that she uses visual images to think. For her, language is not essential for thinking. Although it is hard for most of us to understand, for her, thinking does not depend on language.

Watch this video of Dr. Temple Grandin as she describes how she thinks in pictures. What does this suggest about the relationship between thought and language?
https://www.youtube.com/watch?v=rJ90_mX8qQk

What about congenitally **deaf** persons? How do they think? Similar to Dr. Grandin, profoundly deaf persons say that they think in pictures, video, and emotions. For example, instead of saying to themselves, "I am hungry," they might see a picture or a video-like image of themselves eating an apple. Those who use sign language may think of the sign for "apple." Many deaf persons have shared their insights into their thinking on the Quora website. Just submit the following question: Does someone who was born with a hearing loss "hear" an inner voice?

These reports from people with disabilities suggest that language and cognition are not necessarily related—that they can develop independently. This view of the relationship between language and cognition—that language and cognition develop *independently* as the result of physical maturation—is the position of the psycholinguist Steven Pinker. Pinker (1994) claims that all of the theories about cognition and language are wrong for one simple reason—language is not learned at all. He claims that language is an "instinct." By that, he means it is a skill that develops spontaneously, without conscious effort or formal instruction. Pinker further claims that what he calls the "language instinct" is a characteristic of the human species and is distinct from cognitive development. As the central nervous system matures, so too do language abilities. According to this model, disorders of language could be explained only by serious physiological disorders.

On the other hand, many theorists argue that *language is dependent on cognition*, a view whose theoretical basis was provided by the Swiss psychologist Jean Piaget and his followers (Piaget, 1954; Sinclair-DeZwart, 1973). According to this view, cognitive development precedes language development. Piaget claimed that "language is not enough to explain thought, because the structures that characterize thought have their roots in action and in sensorimotor mechanisms that are deeper than linguistics" (1954, p. 98).

Piaget believed that language was only one of several symbolic functions a child develops through growth and interaction with the environment. Language developed, Piaget claimed, only after prerequisite cognitive accomplishments had occurred. These accomplishments include development of such principles as distancing and object permanence. **Distancing** involves the gradual movement away from actual physical experiences to symbolic or representational behavior. **Object permanence** is the idea that objects exist even when they are not being touched, tasted, or seen. These and other developments of the sensorimotor period help move the child from being dependent on the physical world to relying more on the symbolic—a necessary prerequisite to language development, according to Piaget.

Apply Your Knowledge 3.2: Object Permanence

Watch as a mother plays a "hide-and-seek" game with her child, and then respond to the questions about object permanence.

Piaget's claim that cognitive development precedes language has been examined frequently by researchers with mixed results. On the one hand, there is evidence that some language milestones (such as the emergence of two-word combinations) often occur at about the same time as cognitive developments (sensorimotor development) (Bohannon & Bonvillian, 2009). On the other hand, there is little compelling evidence that these cognitive developments *cause* the resulting language outcomes. On the contrary, there is increasing evidence that children can understand and sometimes use language long before the time that would be expected within the Piagetian model. Although Piaget's model of language and cognition is still valuable in helping us think about the relationship between cognition and language, we should be cautious about claims that specific cognitive developments must precede language milestones.

A third model of language and cognition claims that *language and cognition are interdependent*. The Russian psychologist Lev Vygotsky most clearly stated this view (1962). According to Vygotsky, language and cognition develop as separate and independent systems. Initially language development occurs because of interaction with others, but, eventually, language becomes internalized. It is at this point that language and thought begin to merge, allowing the child to engage in abstract thought and symbolic reasoning. Without language, according to Vygotsky, thinking could not progress beyond the earliest stages of development. Recent work by cognitive neuroscientists has attempted to make sense of these competing theories about thought and language. They start with what we know—that the development of language and cognition depends on at least three (some say four) elements: social interaction, language input, and neurobiological development (MacWhinney, 1998). Each of these is conceptualized as a "neural network," developing separately at first but then connecting to extend development. So, when a young child is learning a new word (such as "dog"), the child has to link an auditory map (the sounds that make up the word) with a conceptual map (the features that characterize this "object"). In order for the child to say the word, an articulatory map must be accessed (MacWhinney, 1998).

This *emergentist* theory (also sometimes called the "connectionist" or "network" theory) of language and cognition has helped us get past the argument about which has to come first—language or cognition. The answer seems to be that both are needed in order for language to develop. As we have seen, however, language (at least spoken language) is not a prerequisite for cognitive development. Visual and spatial learning systems can work as well. But, when language and thought intersect, a highly efficient and effective system for learning is created. We will have more to say about neural networks and the "emergentist" theory of language acquisition in the next chapter.

So far, in examining the physiological and cognitive foundations for language acquisition, we have seen how cognitive and physical developments set the stage for language acquisition. We will now look at the role of social interaction.

Check Your Understanding 3.2

Click here to gauge your understanding of the concepts in this section.

Social Bases of Language Development

At the beginning of this chapter, you were asked to keep in mind this question: What is *necessary* for language to develop, and what is *sufficient* for development? So, what have we learned so far?

Physiological development appears to be absolutely *necessary* for the development of language. The role of cognitive development is less certain. But there is little doubt that without appropriate physical development, language is highly unlikely to develop. But is physical maturation sufficient to account for language development?

What would happen to a healthy baby who was somehow not exposed to language? Sadly, such cases have happened. Several decades ago, child welfare authorities discovered a 12-year-old girl who had been locked in a room by her parents with little or no opportunity for human interaction. When she was discovered, the girl (given the fictitious name of "Genie") seemed to be physiologically intact, but she was cognitively and socially delayed and had essentially no language development (Curtiss, 1977). After years of systematic work, speech-language specialists were able to help "Genie" develop a significant amount of language, but she never fully recovered. There has been a great deal of controversy about this case (see Rymer, 1993) and Genie has lived in a succession of group homes. This, and other purported cases of children raised without human interaction (such as Victor, the "wild boy of Aveyron") suggest that human interaction is essential for language to develop.

Watch this video that provides additional information about "Genie." How does Genie's history of isolation and her subsequent language and cognitive development help us understand the role of the environment in language learning?

https://www.youtube.com/watch?v=VjZoIHCrC8E

But what exactly do adults do to trigger language development in their children? Parents do not talk to their young children in the same way that they talk to older children and adults. They make a number of modifications in the way they talk, including reducing the length and complexity of their language, using a greater range of pitch in their voices, and using more limited vocabulary (Newman & Sachs, 2012; Trainor & Desjardins, 2002) (see Table 3.1). These alterations have been found in both males and females, in adults with little previous experience with infants, and in many different cultures and language groups (Trainor & Desjardins, 2002).

Table 3.1

Characteristics of Child-Directed Speech (Motherese)

Higher overall pitch; greater range of pitch

Exaggerated intonation and stress

Slower speech

More restricted vocabulary

More reference to here and now

Fewer broken or run-on sentences

Fewer complex sentences

More questions and imperatives

Shorter conversations

In addition to making alterations to the sound of their voices, parents alter their vocal interactions to their young children in other ways. For example, they tend to pronounce labels for objects more distinctly, using exaggerated stress and higher pitch; use a high number of questions and greetings; and tend to talk about things that are present in the immediate environment. The following sample is taken from an actual interaction between a mother and her 21-month-old daughter:

Mother: Hi baby. Want some lunch? (takes child from crib)

Child: Yunch! (arms outstretched to mother)

Mother: Would you like some turkey and cheese?

Child: Chee! Mmm! Cuppy? Cuppy?

Mother: Yes, honey, you can have your cuppy. Do you want juice or milk?

Child: Mook? Mook! (clapping and smiling)

Mother: Mommy loves you. You're such a happy baby!

Child: Happy. Monkey? Monkey? (looking around)

Mother: Where's monkey? Did you leave him upstairs?

Child: Up? Monkey?

What do you notice about this conversation? First, the mother is taking the lead in directing the conversation, asking questions to prompt her child to respond. But that is not always true. Note how the child requests her cup and how, toward the end of the interaction, the child changes the topic to request her monkey. Note, too, the length of the mother's utterances. They are short and simple, both in vocabulary and in sentence structure. This is clearly a rich interaction in which each partner takes an important role in the conversation.

As you watch this video of a mother and her young child, note how the mother engages her child and how the child responds. What are the implications for the role of parents in their young child's early language development?
https://www.youtube.com/watch?v=BABrm1ie5tg

Young children are highly responsive to talk directed to them. Studies have shown that babies prefer baby-talk patterns, even when they are only 2 days old (Cooper & Aslin, 1990). Research has also found that the exaggerated pitch contours that are characteristic of child-directed speech aid in the acquisition of vowels (Trainor & Desjardins, 2002). Other researchers have found that babies are responsive to the positive affect associated with child-directed speech (Singh, Morgan, & Best, 2002). In a study of mothers who were clinically depressed, the researchers found that the depressed mothers used less exaggerated speech to their children and that babies actually responded better to unfamiliar mothers who were not depressed (Kaplan, Bachorowski, Smoski, & Hudenko, 2002).

Further evidence for the critical role of socialization comes from more systematic studies such as that by Hart and Risley (1995). These researchers studied parent–child interactions in 42 families over an extended period of time. The families were carefully chosen to provide a cross-section of socioeconomic status levels and to include both white and African American families. Observers went into the home and attempted to record every interaction that took place during the observation period. The results were stunning and disturbing. Children from the higher socioeconomic groups developed a far larger vocabulary than did children in families that received welfare. Children from middle-class families were right in the middle of vocabulary development. Similar results were found for both white and African American families. The researchers also found that parents from higher socioeconomic families engaged in more language interaction with their children than did parents of children from welfare or from middle-class families and that the quality of their interaction differed in significant ways. For example, parents from lower socioeconomic status families tended to interact with their children primarily for the purpose of behavior management. Although there are many ways to look at the results of this study, it demonstrates very clearly that early experiences are important in shaping language development. In particular, the amount and quality of interactions shape language development.

Socialization provides the third piece in the puzzle of language development. Physiological development provides the "how," cognitive development the "what," and social development the "why" of language development. All of these may be *necessary* in order for language acquisition to take place, but none of them is sufficient to account for the emergence of language. In the next chapter, we will see how linguists have put this information into models that attempt to explain language development.

Apply Your Knowledge 3.3: Grandfather–Child Interaction

Watch the interaction between a grandfather and a young child, and then respond to the questions about caregiver–child interactions.

Check Your Understanding 3.3

Click here to gauge your understanding of the concepts in this section.

Summary

The physiological, cognitive, and social foundations of language acquisition were discussed in this chapter. Physiological development is a necessary prerequisite for language acquisition. However, physical development alone cannot explain the emergence of language. Children need something to talk about, and the exploration of their world that is part of cognitive development may provide that motivation. In addition, it is clear that parents and families actively provide socialization opportunities that encourage their children to interact in increasingly sophisticated ways. In trying to describe the complex relationship between physiology, cognition, socialization, and language, it is important to keep in mind that there are individual differences in development.

Language Acquisition Models

How do children acquire their first language? What motivates them to learn? These are questions that have challenged researchers in child language for many years.

This chapter presents theories of language acquisition, detailing how each theory explains the phenomenon of language acquisition and discussing both the contributions and limitations of each theory. Although no one model can fully explain the wonder of language acquisition, the effort to describe how children acquire language has helped us better understand the language-learning process and how we can help children with language and communication disorders.

Learning Outcomes

After reading this chapter, you should be able to:

1. Explain the principles of the behavioral model of language acquisition as well as its limitations.

2. Describe how the nativist model explains language acquisition.

3. Explain the role of semantic knowledge in language acquisition.

4. Describe the role of social interaction in language acquisition.

5. Describe the principles of contemporary models of language acquisition.

6. Explain the implications of language acquisition models for the teaching of language skills.

How do children acquire their first language? A satisfactory answer to this question has eluded linguists and psycholinguists (persons who study the relation of thought to language) for many years. The reason that this is such a difficult task lies with the phenomenon of language acquisition itself. Hirsh-Pasek and Golinkoff (1996) have suggested that any theory of first language acquisition must address the following questions:

1. What is present when grammatical learning begins?

2. What mechanisms are used in the course of acquisition?

3. What types of input drive the language-learning system forward?

Let's look at each of these questions in more detail.

First, in order to explain language acquisition, we have to understand what the child brings to the task. That is, what cognitive, social, and neurological developments are necessary for language learning to occur.

Second, by "mechanisms," Hirsh-Pasek and Golinkoff are referring to whether language acquisition emerges out of general development of cognitive skills such as problem solving or whether language develops separately, with mechanisms that are unique to language.

Finally, the third process that needs to be understood is the role that exposure to language and communicative interaction plays in language acquisition. How do children use the input they receive? What role does the environment play in helping children understand the rules of language?

We might add to this list of questions a fourth one: How is it that children from all social strata, from all types of environments (urban, rural, suburban) all over the world learn language at approximately the same rate? As Guasti (2002) noted, regardless of their specific language, all children go through similar stages of early language development (babble; first words; multiword utterances) at about the same age.

In developing their explanations (theories) of language acquisition, theorists have considered various factors that influence language acquisition and development:

- The linguistic environment
- Inherited abilities
- The individual's experiences
- The individual's opportunities for interaction
- The child's developing linguistic and cognitive abilities
- Brain development and organization
- Cognitive development and organization

Each of these factors has been emphasized in one of the major theories of language acquisition, and each contributes to the entire process of language acquisition. Additionally, theories of language acquisition have been influenced by the long-standing debate among developmental psychologists about the relative importance of the environment (nurture) compared to the child's intrinsic development (nature) in explaining how children learn. While the issue is really not one of either/or (few would claim that the environment has no effect or that intrinsic traits and abilities have no impact), the nature/nurture debate is evident in the language acquisition models we will discuss.

The Behavioral Model

Most people's response to the question of how children learn language is that they learn it through imitation. When pressed to describe how this might occur, people will say that the child hears what the adult says and tries to imitate it. Cattell (2000) provides the following vignette to illustrate how this might happen:

> Mother leans over the crib and says to the baby, "Say 'Mum-Mum.'"
> After a few gurgles and splutters, the baby says something that sounds a bit like "Mum-Mum."
> Mother smiles warmly and repeats the game until the child is clearly saying "Mum-Mum."

In a very simplified form, this commonsense explanation is similar to the actual process described in behavioral theories of language acquisition. This particular theory was set forth most completely by B. F. Skinner in his book *Verbal Behavior* (1957). As described by Skinner, the behavioral theory of language acquisition places a great deal of emphasis on the role of the environment in language acquisition. The child is seen as a relatively passive recipient of external influences—from parents, siblings, and others.

Language, according to behavioral theory, is learned like any other behavior. Children begin with no language. Gradually they begin to imitate (or model) sounds of those individuals to whom they are most frequently exposed. These individuals respond to the sound outputs (operants) by doing one of three things: reinforcing the verbal behavior (*Good!*), punishing the behavior (*Shut up!*), or ignoring the behavior. If reinforcement occurs, there is a good chance that the behavior in the child will occur again. If either of the other two responses happens, the likelihood of the verbal behavior recurring is reduced. Over time, as the child's verbal behavior is repeated, the parents (or others) become less responsive and force the child to produce a verbal output that is closer to the adult model (successive approximation). As Skinner put it, "Any response which vaguely resembles the standard behavior of the community is reinforced. When these begin to appear frequently, a closer approximation is insisted upon" (pp. 29–30). Eventually the child produces the adult word. Through the process of **chaining**, the child learns to string together several verbal behaviors to make an utterance. The actual process might go something like this:

Mother:	See Daddy. There goes Daddy.
Child:	*Da.*
Mother:	Yes, there's Daddy.
	(Later)
Mother:	Wave bye-bye to Daddy.
Child:	Da Da.
Mother:	Yes, that's right. There he goes.
	(Still later)
Mother:	Say good-bye to Daddy.
Child:	Bye-bye Da Da.
Mother:	Good girl.

Notice in this example how the initial simple response, "Da" becomes more fully formed ("Bye-bye Da Da") as "Mother" prompts a response. According to the behavioral theory, the mother is helping build a response chain in her child by reinforcing more complex language behaviors.

There is a good deal of support for the behavioral theory of language acquisition. This support comes both from structured research and from the less formal observations of parents and others. There *does* appear to be a process of imitation and reinforcement at work in the child's acquisition of language—at least for first words. Parents provide a model for these words and, when their child responds, they respond in turn with enthusiastic joy. Over time the child's verbal output does change in a way similar to that described by the theory—coming closer to the adult model. Moreover, there is some evidence that imitation is a critical component of language learning. For example, there is evidence that when mothers respond to their infants' vocalizations, the children appear to vocalize more (Velleman, Mangipudi, & Locke, 1989). Other support for the behavioral theory of language learning comes from work with people with disabilities that has found that children with significant language deficits can learn to acquire words through highly structured sequences based on a behavioral model such as discrete trial (e.g., Lovaas, 1987; McEachin, Smith, & Lovaas, 1993; Smith, Eikeseth, Klevstrand, & Lovaas, 1997).

 Watch this video about the behavioral model of language acquisition. What are the methods of instruction suggested by the model and the limitations of this approach?

There are, however, serious limitations to the behavioral explanation of language acquisition. First, the theory makes the wrong prediction about what children will learn—particularly the *order* of word acquisition. If imitation were the primary process involved in word acquisition, then one would expect that the child's first words would be those heard most frequently. In English, the words *a* and *the* are the most frequently heard words. But these words are rarely, if ever, found in the language of young children. A second problem for this theory of language acquisition is its difficulty in explaining the phenomenon of *novel productions*. Young children have been found to use constructions that they have *never* heard previously. Children may say things like *I wented* when they want to use the past tense of *go* and *womans* when they want to pluralize the word *woman*. Behavioral theory alone does not account for novel productions such as these.

A third problem with the behavioral theory of language acquisition is that systematic observations of parents indicate that parents actually tend to *ignore* grammatical errors and are more concerned about the truth value of what their children say. For example, if a child says, "I eated ice cream at grandma's," the parents are more likely to respond, "No you didn't—you ate Jello," than to say, "No, we don't say *eated*. Say *ate*" (Hirsh-Pasek, Treiman, & Schneiderman, 1984; Owens, 2016). Behavioral theory also cannot account for the observation that comprehension usually precedes production of language in children—that is, children can understand words and sentences before they can produce them. If language learning occurs by a process of reinforcement for language production, then how can it be that children can understand language before they can produce it? What about the "evidence" derived from children with disabilities to talk using behavioral techniques? Some researchers have questioned the methods and conclusions of Lovaas and his colleagues (e.g., Prizant & Rubin, 1999). We will have more say about these studies later in the book, but at this point, it is enough to say that even if children *can* be taught to imitate and acquire words through reinforcement, this does not mean that that is how they learn in natural environments.

Although behavioral theory is limited in its ability to explain all language acquisition, there is still some value to the theory. First, the theory highlights the essential role that parents and significant others play in the child's language learning. Second, the theory's description of the process of language learning, although flawed, has inspired others to develop alternative theories. Finally, the behavioral approach has been a successful tool in the development of intervention approaches to enhance the language skills of many persons with significant language disorders. For these reasons, it is important to know about the behavioral theory of language acquisition and to use the observations of behaviorists as one source of information for the language-intervention process.

Check Your Understanding 4.1
Click here to gauge your understanding of the concepts in this section.

The Nativist (Syntactic) Model

Noam Chomsky (1965, 1968) and others developed the nativist/syntactic theory of language acquisition partly in response to the behavioral theory of language acquisition. In developing this theory, Chomsky noted several interesting phenomena. First, it seemed highly unlikely to him that 4-year-old children could have learned all the language they know simply by being exposed to it and remembering what they heard. The memory load required for such a feat would seem to be well beyond that available to a child. Second, Chomsky noted the *universality* of language. That is, he pointed out that language is learned by people of all cultures, in all environments, and in very similar stages. Moreover, language appears to be *unique* to humans (as we discussed in Chapter 1). Third, it seemed clear to Chomsky that children were doing more than memorizing chunks of language—they were also learning language *rules*. This point is evident in the cute but revealing mistakes that children make as they are learning language.

Putting these pieces of information together, Chomsky concluded that language must be innate (hence the *nativist* label). Language, according to Chomsky, is inborn in the human species—hardwired at birth. Babies are born ready to learn language. As Steven Pinker (1994), one of Chomsky's followers, put it, "Language is not a cultural artifact that we learn the way we learn to tell time or how the federal government works. Instead, it is a distinct piece of the biological makeup of our brains" (p. 18).

Figure 4.1

Slobin's Operating Principles of Language

Principle A: Pay attention to the end of words.
Principle B: There are linguistic elements that encode relationships between words.
Principle C: Avoid exceptions.
Principle D: Underlying semantic relationships should be marked overtly and clearly.
Principle E: The use of grammatical markers should make semantic sense.

Source: Adapted from Slobin (1979).

> This video presents Professor Noam Chomsky discussing his theory of language acquisition. How does Professor Chomsky explain how language rules are learned across different languages?
> https://www.youtube.com/watch?v=xfiHd6DyuTU

Not only are children born ready to learn, but they also possess a mechanism that Chomsky called the **language acquisition device (LAD)**, which consists of basic grammatical categories and rules that are common to all languages. These basic rules might look something like the operating principles described by Slobin (1979) (see Figure 4.1). Alternatively, the LAD may consist of some inherent constraints and biases to respond to the language environment (Wexler, 1999).

In order for the LAD to operate, the child must merely be *exposed* to language. The quality of the adult language does not really matter nor do adults have to actively teach or reinforce language use. After a child's exposure to language input, according to the theory, the child's LAD will take over to help him or her discover the underlying rules of language. Once the rules are mastered (and a certain amount of vocabulary is acquired), the child will be able to understand and produce language. The exact nature of the LAD and its physical location continues to be debated (Ritchie & Bhatia, 1999), but the idea that there is a built-in human mechanism for language acquisition continues to be a powerful theory.

The nativist/syntactic theory addresses some of the unexplained phenomena associated with language acquisition. The nativist theory attempts to explain the universality of language as stemming from an inborn bias to learn language rules. The LAD model explains how children learn language rules merely by being exposed to language—that babies are programmed from birth to search out and discover the rules (**generalizations**) of language. The theory also accounts for the speed with which language is acquired, since it points out that children are able to process language rules right from birth.

Although the linguistic (nativist) model helps us understand many of the phenomena of language acquisition, there are some significant limitations to this theory. One of the most troublesome is the diminished role given to language input. In Wexler's (1999) view, language is not learned but develops due to the maturation of a genetic program for language learning. As we have noted earlier (Chapter 3), investigations of parent–child interactions have found that parents alter their language for their children in systematic ways—simplifying and clarifying. If mere exposure to language were all that was needed for language acquisition, why would parents continue to go to the trouble of altering their language for children? In addition, there is evidence that, although parents may not be explicitly teaching language rules, they do correct their child's language "errors" by modeling the correct structure (Bohannon, Padgett, Nelson, & Mark, 1996; Bohannon & Stanowicz, 1988; Saxton, Houston-Price, & Dawson, 2005). These results call into question the innateness of language and suggest a more important role for input than the nativist models generally recognize.

A second problem stems from the theoretical underpinnings of the model itself. Chomsky was interested in explaining the acquisition of *syntax* in children. He was much less interested in explaining the acquisition of the other elements of language. Although the theory adequately explains the acquisition of syntax, it does not account for the child's acquisition of semantic, morphophonological, or pragmatic rules.

Finally, the nativist theory appears to pose a dilemma to those who are interested in helping children with disabilities improve their language performance, as it seems to suggest that there is little hope for children who have sensory or neurological deficiencies. If language is innate, perhaps these children simply lack the ability to learn language. But, going beyond the biological issues, the model suggests that intensive and explicit instruction on language rules and on strategies to compensate for biological deficiencies may help children with significant language-learning difficulties.

 This video provides further explanation of the nativist model of language learning. What are the implications for intervention in children with language difficulties?

Chomsky's early theories on language acquisition marked a significant departure from the prevailing (behavioral) view that language input was the primary, even exclusive, influence on language development in children. Chomsky's revolutionary theories sparked a flood of research on language learning that continues to this day. Some of the subsequent research has supported Chomsky's claims, but some has supported competing theories of language acquisition. Although the nativist/syntactic model is a no more complete explanation of language acquisition than the behavioral theory, it too has made an important contribution by addressing some of the most challenging questions about language learning and by advancing our knowledge about language and language acquisition.

Apply Your Knowledge 4.1: Teaching Syntactic Rules

 Read this transcript of an interaction between an aunt and her 3-year-old niece to gain a better understanding of how the use of language rules develops, and then answer the question.

Check Your Understanding 4.2

 Click here to gauge your understanding of the concepts in this section.

The Semantic-Cognitive Model

"Mommy, sock." These two words helped lead Lois Bloom (1970) to contribute to a new interpretation of child language acquisition. Bloom had observed a child using this expression on two occasions. One time, the child used this expression to note that the sock belonged to her mother (possessive). The second time, she appeared to be making a request (e.g., "Put my sock on, Mommy."). Although we do not know precisely what the child meant to say, it is clear from this context that the same words were being used to express two different meanings. Observations such as these led Bloom to conclude that semantics precedes syntax in child language acquisition. In other words, children develop syntax because they already have something to talk about rather than because they have the grammar to express themselves. In this case, the child used one syntactic form ("Mommy, sock") to express two semantic functions (possessive and requesting).

The semantic model of language acquisition was developed from evidence such as the above, as well as from linguistic and cognitive theory. At about the same time Bloom was conducting her observations of children, Fillmore (1968) was publishing his ideas about the role of semantics in language structure. Fillmore noted that the selection of a word to be used in a sentence is determined more by the *meaning* of the sentence than by the syntactic structure of the sentence. Thus, in a sentence such as *The _____ hit the ball*, rules of syntax tell us that the word that goes in the blank must be a noun, but semantics tells us that only certain nouns will do. The word *boy* or *girl* would be fine but *clock* or *desk* would not do. Fillmore's theory—case grammar—forced linguists to rethink their assumptions about the relationship between syntax and semantics.

While Fillmore's and Bloom's work focused on the role of semantics in language acquisition, the Swiss cognitive psychologist Jean Piaget was interested in the relationship between cognition (thought) and language. Piaget did not propose a theory of language development as such, but his work was seen as implying that language development is secondary to cognitive development. According to Piaget (1954), language is but one of many symbol systems. Also, according to Piaget and his associates, cognitive developments such as object permanence must precede language development.

The combined influences of Fillmore's case grammar, Piaget's cognitive theories, and observations by researchers such as Bloom led to the development of the semantic-cognitive theory of language acquisition. This theory gives preeminence to the semantic aspect of language. The theory proposes that young children pay particular attention to the *meanings* of things. When they use language, they do so to talk *about* something they have already experienced. In other words, the experience comes first, then the language follows. According to this theory, syntax develops as the result of the need to talk about more and more things or experiences. In addition, certain cognitive accomplishments must take place before language can be acquired at all. As the child's understanding of and experience with the world grows, language develops as an outgrowth.

Like the other language acquisition theories we have reviewed, the semantic-cognitive theory has some strong support. It seems logical that children will talk when they have something to talk *about*. As they acquire more experiences, they need more sophisticated language to express their ideas. In addition, there is evidence that certain cognitive development steps usually do precede the emergence of language (Bohannon & Bonvillian, 2009). This theory helps explain why children tend to talk about the same kinds of things no matter what their socioeconomic background and environment.

The semantic-cognitive theory also has its shortcomings. While certain cognitive developments do appear at the same time as corresponding language milestones, that is not evidence that language relies on cognitive development. On the contrary, there is increasing evidence that cognitive and language development may go hand-in-hand. Sometimes known as "**bootstrapping**," this theory postulates that specific language skills (such as the understanding of "disappearance" words such as "all gone") correlate with the accomplishment of specific cognitive accomplishments (in this case, object permanence) (Gopnik & Meltzoff, 1987). Neither of these developments depends on the other. They emerge from the interaction between cognition and language (Pence & Justice, 2008).

Like the nativist theory, the semantic cognitive model gives little attention to the role of input language. These theoretical models would have us believe that adult input matters little, if at all. Like the other language acquisition models, the semantic-cognitive model has made important contributions to our understanding of language acquisition. It has forced theorists to look beyond syntax and to consider other aspects of language development. It has also had an impact on intervention practices, as we will see later. However, like the other models, although it has contributed pieces to the puzzle, it does not solve the entire enigma of language acquisition.

✔ Check Your Understanding 4.3
Click here to gauge your understanding of the concepts in this section.

The Social Interactionist Model

The social interactionist model of language acquisition is based on a very simple observation—people talk in order to communicate. Therefore, the model places greatest emphasis on the communicative function of language. According to this theory, language development takes place as children learn to choose the linguistic form that will best express their communicative intent (Ninnio & Snow, 1999; Tomasello, 2003).

This original impetus for the social interactionist model came from the study of pragmatics. At about the same time that linguists began to identify and classify the rules of pragmatics, psychologists and psycholinguists were observing and describing communication between parents and their children. As we have seen in Chapter 3, parents modify their speech to their young children. These modifications do not appear to be random but emphasize features of language that focus the child's attention on critical elements in the flow of language. But interaction is not a one-way street. As we will see in Chapter 5, young children play an important role in conversational interaction as well.

According to Bruner (1977), adjustments in adult language such as those described previously provide the framework, or *scaffolding*, for language development. By engaging in communication with their parents (and other significant adults), children learn that language can be used for communication, and they indirectly pick up structural aspects of language. Communication—especially repetitive, routine communication—makes it possible for children to hear and model the adult language forms.

Tomasello (2003) has a somewhat different view of the role of communicative interaction. His "usage-based" theory of language development suggests that language forms (phonology, morphology, syntax) emerge from the use of language. As children interact with others, they induce the correct language form from the result of the interaction.

Like the behavioral model, the social interactionist model of language acquisition puts a great deal of emphasis on events that take place in the environment around the child. Children learn language by being exposed to language during communicative interaction. Unlike the behavioral model, however, the social interactionist model does *not* claim that overt reinforcement is necessary in order for language to be acquired. Instead, it is similar to the nativist model in acknowledging the role of physiological maturation in determining the level of communicative interaction that can be handled by the child. The social interactionist model can be seen as an attempt to account for both the role of the environment (nurture) and the role of biological processes (nature) in language development.

The social interactionist model of language acquisition has much going for it. Any parent can attest to the fact that young children can communicate their needs long before they have the language to express themselves. This supports the claims of the social interactionist model that communication precedes language. Moreover, there is evidence that children who have limited opportunities for interaction with adults have more difficulty acquiring language (Christopoulos, Bonvillian, & Crittenden, 1988).

One of the limitations of the social interactionist model, though, is in how it accounts for the acquisition of specific syntactic structures. In other words, why do almost all children follow the same sequence of language development at about the same time? If children rely primarily on the adults in their environment for language input, then it would be logical to expect that both the quality and quantity of input (and thus the child's output) would vary widely. Yet, this is not the case. Clearly there must be other factors at work. There is also limited research on just how much interaction is needed to stimulate language development. Is there a minimum amount? Is there an optimal amount? Until these questions are answered, we cannot be sure about the role of communicative interaction in early language development.

The social interactionist model has had a significant influence on language-intervention techniques. Today, many clinicians are emphasizing the importance of engaging children in communication—especially in repetitive, routine interactions. Rather than breaking language down into small parts and teaching each part, some clinicians are using indirect methods of language stimulation, stressing the wholeness of language and the essential role of communication in the language-learning process.

Contemporary Models of Language Acquisition

The preceding models of language acquisition are rooted in research that was conducted primarily in the final decades of the 20th century. Although these models have helped us understand much about how children acquire language, they do not completely explain this phenomenon. Contemporary models of language acquisition have grown out of the development of machine information processing and from the rapidly expanding knowledge base on human neuropsychology.

Information-Processing Model

Information-processing models attempt to explain how learning takes place. These models originated as a way to develop machine-based learning (i.e., computers). Later, they were adapted to be applied to human learning.

Figure 4.2 illustrates a very simplified model of human **information processing**. As input enters the system, some initial processing takes place. Information previously stored in long-term memory is accessed in order to further process the information and to formulate a response. The entire system is managed by executive (decision-making) processes that can be influenced by factors such as attention and emotion.

An example might help in understanding how this system might work. Let's say you are walking down the street and you see something in the distance. You receive visual input and initially processing suggests that what you see is an animal. As you get closer, the image becomes clearer and (by accessing information in long-term memory) you recognize the animal as a cat. How are you going to respond? Your emotions tell you that cats are safe and that you like them. Your attention level is not too high. However, as you get closer and you can see the animal's coloring and distinctive white stripes, you realize that this is

Figure 4.2

A Schematic Model of Information Processing

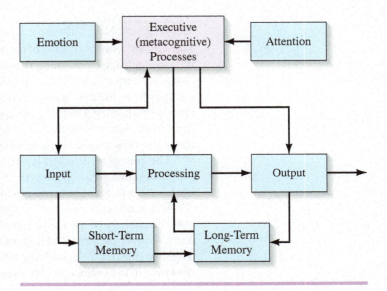

not a cat at all, but a skunk. Suddenly, your attention is at full alert. Your information processing quickens. You access information in long-term memory about skunks and realize they can be a real problem. You quickly formulate a response (stay calm, back up slowly) that will enable you to extricate yourself from the situation.

What we have described above is an example of **serial processing**, where each step in the sequence takes place one at a time. But much of human learning is not like this. Multiple steps happen simultaneously. This view of human information processing is called **parallel processing**.

 This video provides an illustration of the information-processing model. According to the model, what is the role of executive functioning?
https://www.youtube.com/watch?v=pMMRE4Q2FGk

The information-processing model of learning has been applied to language acquisition by psycholinguists such as Elizabeth Bates and Bryan MacWhinney in their *competition model* of language acquisition (Bates & MacWhinney, 1987). According to this model, language structures emerge from the communicative functions that drive language acquisition. There are multilayered connections between these functions and the linguistic forms that are used to express the function. The information-processing system, operating in a parallel-processing mode, makes matches between form and function. Over time, the matches that are most consistent with the language evidence the child is experiencing win out (thus, the "competition" model). These matches remain in the child's communication system.

The information-processing model has helped in understanding the complexity of the relationship between cognition and language. It recognizes that the processing of complex information is rarely done in a serial (step-by-step) manner. Instead, many levels of learning take place simultaneously. Thus, children are not only learning syntax but they are also learning meaning, and are doing so in the context of communication (pragmatics) at the same time. This model attempts to account for these many levels of learning.

Although the information-processing model has provided another view of language learning, research evidence for the operation of the model in children is limited. Most of the research thus far has been with adults or with theoretical language-processing models. In addition, the model does not appear to be able to account for the role of social interaction in language learning (Bohannon & Bonvillian, 2009).

Emergentist Model

The nativist/syntactic model of language acquisition attempts to explain the uniqueness of human language by claiming the existence of unique language structures—the so-called "language acquisition device." In contrast, the emergentist model suggests that language emerges from the interaction of social patterns and from the biology of the cognitive system (MacWhinney, 1998). According to this model, there is no need to have specific structures in the brain dedicated soley to language. Instead, language is acquired through the use of the same mechanisms by which all learning takes place.

The emergentist model is anchored to a great extent on the information-processing theory of human learning described previously. In brief, the theory claims that language is not innate in humans but emerges from the interaction of **neural networks**. MacWhinney (1998) describes the process of language acquisition as one of "interacting constraints." He uses the analogy of the formation of geographic features where forces such as ocean currents, weather patterns, and human construction interact to shape the shoreline. Similarly, language is learned through the interaction of cognitive development, changes in neural networks in the brain, and experience.

For example, consider how this model explains early word learning. As the child is exposed to new words, he or she uses **fast-mapping** to construct an initial tentative match between what the child hears (auditory map) and the concept (conceptual map). MacWhinney (1998) describes the process in this way:

> When the child hears a given auditory form and sees an object at the same time, the coactivation of the neurons that respond to the sound and the neurons that respond to the visual form produces an association across a third pattern of connections which maps auditory forms to conceptual forms. (p. 209)

As long as the child continues to hear examples that link the auditory input with the concept, the child will continue to maintain this word in his or her vocabulary. But, at the same time, the child's understanding of the world is changing. The child is constantly reworking his or her "conceptual map" of the world. Word acquisition *emerges* from the interaction of the experience of hearing words and the mapping of these words onto the ever-changing conceptual map.

The emergentist model of language acquisition is relatively new and still being developed. The model can help us understand how experience, biology, and social interaction can work together to shape language learning. In addition, the model seems to be supported by increasing neurological evidence that large regions of the human brain work together to accomplish complex tasks like language processing, reading, and writing. However, there is little direct evidence from research in language acquisition in support of the model.

Check Your Understanding 4.5
Click here to gauge your understanding of the concepts in this section.

Conclusion

Perhaps it is not possible to completely account for the phenomena of language development described at the beginning of this chapter. Although such a conclusion may seem discouraging, it may be that what is important is the search for answers itself. As a result of this search, our ideas about language have been clarified and the debate about language learning has been sharpened. Additionally, the search for answers has led to the development of language-intervention methods.

Implications for Language Intervention

Each of the language acquisition models has implications for language intervention. In subsequent chapters, we will describe a number of language-intervention methods that are grounded in one or more of the theoretical models of language acquisition.

The *behavioral theory* of language acquisition suggests that language is learned just like any other behavior; that is, the processes of imitation, modeling, and reinforcement are critical components in the child's acquisition of language. In the behavioral model, teachers choose specific, discrete language behaviors as the focus of instruction and, through assessment, determine that the child has acquired the prerequisite skills. The child is *prompted* to make a response (*Say, "I want a cookie"*) and is *reinforced* for making a correct response (*Good talking!*). Instruction continues until mastery of the skill is achieved.

Behavioral models of learning have been widely applied to teaching children with significant learning difficulties, including those with autism and intellectual disabilities. Under the general term, *applied behavior analysis*, those methods include discrete trial training, the mand-model and interrupted behavior chain methods, verbal behavior, and the Picture Exchange Communication System (PECS). These methods have generally been found to be effective in helping children with significant disabilities acquire some language skills, although there are concerns about the generalization of these skills to new environments.

The *nativist/syntactic theory* of language acquisition places most of its emphasis on biological development, on the idea that language emerges as the individual develops. Although there is little that teachers can do to directly influence biological maturation, they may still apply the nativist/syntactic model to language instruction. First, this theory suggests using *developmental guidelines* for instructional goals, and second, that instruction should focus on *rule learning.* According to the nativist/syntactic theory, the most important developments in early language learning involve the acquisition of the underlying rules of language. Instruction that helps children become aware of language rules, discover underlying rules, and apply these rules in new situations is most useful. In addition, methods, such as Fast ForWord, Earobics, and auditory training, that aim to change the way children process sound can address the neurobiological differences that make it difficult for some children to develop language.

Using the *semantic-cognitive model* of language learning as a guide to teaching language involves focusing on the acquisition of cognitive prerequisites to language and on the development of semantic concepts. As discussed earlier in this chapter, some theorists (e.g., Piaget) claim that certain cognitive prerequisites (e.g., object permanence) must precede the emergence of spoken language. If children lack these prerequisites, it may be necessary to help them acquire the necessary skills. Although there has been much debate as to whether it is possible to teach cognitive skills, many researchers believe it is possible to help children who are ready to take the next step do so just a bit more quickly. The formal name for this idea is the *zone of proximal development.* As proposed by Vygotsky (1962), the notion is that when children are just at the edge of developing a new skill, experiences and instruction can help them take this step. In addition to its helping children develop cognitive prerequisites, the semantic-cognitive model suggests that language learning can be facilitated by the development of new semantic concepts. When children have something to talk about, the theory suggests, they will find a way to express their new ideas.

The *social interactionist model* implies that the goal of language intervention should be to enhance communication. Children should be encouraged to interact with parents, peers, and teachers. Language facilitators should be responsive to the child, letting the child take the lead in language interaction by setting the conversational topic. The incidental teaching approach, with its emphasis on responding to the child's lead, is a method that is grounded in the social interactionist model.

The *information-processing model* and the *emergentist model* emphasize the importance of connections between different types of experience. Some children can absorb unrelated pieces of information but have difficulty processing this information to understand the world and to develop language. For example, children with learning disabilities have sometimes been reported to have difficulty with executive processes that help match experiences with long-term learning. The implications for language learning are clear. Some children may lack specific language skills, and some may have differences or delays in cognitive processing that may interfere with their understanding and/or use of language. Teaching methods that use strategy training, in which children are taught to use a multistep method for solving a problem, help children learn the skills that the information-processing and emergentist models identify as essential for learning.

Each of these models of language acquisition has contributed to the development of intervention methods. Yet none, by itself, appears to be an adequate model for intervention. In later sections of this book, we will see how these models have been applied to enhance the language performance of children with disabilities and to guide classroom practice.

 Check Your Understanding 4.6
Click here to gauge your understanding of the concepts in this section.

Model	Principles	Limitations
Behavioral	Language learned through imitation and reinforcement Language learned like other behaviors Parents reinforce meaning, not structure Comprehension precedes production	Makes wrong predictions about word acquisition How to explain novel utterances
Nativist/Syntactic	Inborn ability for language Language acquisition device (LAD)	What is role of input? What about parts of language other than syntax?
Semantic-Cognitive	Meaning precedes structure Same utterance can have multiple meanings (Bloom) Cognition precedes language (Piaget)	Relationship of cognition and language very complex
Social Interactionist	Need to communicate precedes language structures Parents alter language for their child	How to account for specific structures What about child's role?
Information Processing	Language structures emerge from communicative functions Competition eliminates unsuccessful forms	Limited research evidence
Emergentist	Language emerges from interaction between input and biology	Limited evidence

Table 4.1

Major Models of
Language Acquisition

Summary

Language acquisition is a complex, wondrous, and still somewhat mysterious phenomenon. Six theories of language acquisition—behavioral, linguistic (nativist), semantic-cognitive, social interactionist, emergentist, and information processing—were presented in this chapter (see Table 4.1). The support, both theoretical and observed, for each of these models was presented, as were shortcomings of the models. Each of these models has contributed something to our knowledge of language acquisition, yet none of them can completely account for the remarkable achievement that we call language.

Language Development: Birth Through the Preschool Years

Language development, from birth through the preschool years, is described in this chapter. Beginning with a description of the early communicative attempts of newborns and the role of parents and other caregivers, the chapter examines the emergence of language and development in the preschool years, describing the stages of syntactic, semantic, and pragmatic development. The relationship between early language development and the emergence of literacy skills is examined and discussed.

Learning Outcomes

After reading this chapter, you should be able to:

1. Describe the development of communicative skills during the prelinguistic stage of development and the role of parents and other caregivers in the development of early communicative interactions.

2. Describe the stages of language development in the preschool years.

3. Explain the relationship between language development and the emergence of literacy skills.

Having examined the physiological, cognitive, and social bases for language development, we are ready to turn our attention to describing the course of language development itself. For those interested in understanding and teaching children with language disorders, knowledge of patterns of language development is important. Imagine what it would be like if you had no idea about the progression of language development. Where would you begin teaching? What would you teach? What would you teach next? What examples would you use? How would you develop reasonable goals for instruction? Gaining knowledge of language development is the best way to answer these questions.

Before we begin to examine the course of language development in children, a note of caution is in order. There is wide variation in "typical" language development. Young children develop at different speeds and in different ways. When we refer to ages in this chapter (and others), we really mean the *average age* at which a structure or function develops. It is important to understand that there is a range of typical development around this average and that children sometimes follow individual patterns of development. Parents and teachers are often concerned if children do not adhere closely to the "norm." They are right to be concerned, but their concern should be tempered by an understanding of the variability of child development. However, when a child deviates significantly from the typical developmental sequence, it is important to intervene as early as possible. Therefore, a knowledge of language development is essential for understanding typical development and for recognizing deviations from the norm.

Prelinguistic Development

Birth to Age 6 Months

The traditional view of infant development is that babies come into the world as a "blank slate," ready to be filled with experiences that will guide their development through childhood to become fully functioning adults. However, research conducted during the past few decades has seriously challenged this traditional view of early childhood. We now understand that infants are born ready to learn in many ways. They are not merely passive recipients of information from their environment. They are active learners who influence and even shape their environment. Even during this prelinguistic stage, when babies do not exhibit what we would call language, they are developing the necessary prerequisites to the emergence of language.

Newborns have been found to have some surprising language (comprehension) abilities. For example, it appears that they can discriminate between languages. In one study, French babies who were played samples of French and Japanese speech sounds listened more attentively to the French, indicating that they recognized the language they were hearing in their environment (Nazzi, Bertoncini, & Mehler, 1998). Of course, if these babies had been exposed to Japanese, they would have showed a preference for that language. Using a technique called high-amplitude sucking, in which the frequency of sucking to stimuli is measured, researchers have found that infants as young as 1 month old can discriminate speech sound differences such as *pa* and *ba* (Eimas, Siqueland, Jusczyk, & Vigorito, 1971). Using cerebral blood flow as a measure, Saito et al. (2007) found that neonates attended more to child-directed speech from their mothers than when their mother spoke to another adult. Other research has found that babies as young as 7 months old can discriminate between familiar and unfamiliar words, although younger babies appear unable to do this (Jusczyk & Aslin, 1995).

Early Communicative Interaction.   From the moment of birth, and perhaps even before birth, babies communicate. Ask a pregnant woman. She is likely to tell you that her baby is telling her when he or she is awake or asleep, uncomfortable or agitated, from the movement and kicking the expectant mother experiences. This does not mean that the fetus *intends* to communicate these things, but the mere fact that mothers-to-be *interpret* the actions as communicative helps set the stage for the coming communicative interaction between mother (and father and others) and child.

How does this communicative interaction take place? Despite their limited repertoire of behavior, newborns engage their parents (and other family members) in a variety of ways. They move their head in response to the human voice. Their eyes widen and body tension increases in anticipation of attention from their caregiver. Through their wakefulness, fussiness, or other signs, infants let their parents know when they are tired or when they are ready for interaction. After a few weeks, *interactional sequences* begin to develop. The infant gazes at his or her caregiver's face and the caregiver responds with a smile and/or some comforting words (Owens, 2011). Feeding can be a wonderful interactional opportunity. The baby sucks and pauses, then gazes at her or his caregiver, who responds with a smile or a touch. The infant responds by resuming sucking. These sorts of interactions evolve into a give-and-take that begins to resemble conversational turn-taking with initiation and response (Newman & Sachs, 2013).

Vocalizations are also part of early communicative interaction. At first, most infants' sound productions are **reflexive** in nature—burps, gurgles, and other sounds that are responses to physical states. But parents respond to these vocal productions as if they were meaningful communication (Murray & Trevarthen, 1986). Look at this exchange between an English mother and her 3-month-old daughter (Ann) as described by Catherine Snow (1977):

> **Ann:**   (smiles)
> **Mother:**   Oh what a nice little smile.

> Yes, isn't that nice?
>
> There. That's a nice little smile.

Ann: (burps)

Mother: What a nice little wind as well!

Notice how the mother responds to her daughter's behaviors as if they were meaningful. She engages her daughter in conversational interaction (even if the conversation itself is one way). Parents typically claim that they can identify the meaning of their child's crying. They will say that their child is hungry, or wants to be changed, or is lonely. Parents may or may not be accurate in identifying the meaning of their child's crying. That seems to be less important than the fact that their child's vocalizations initiate a response by the parent. In their intensive study of language development, Hart and Risley (1999) reported that long before children began saying words, they had learned essential skills of interaction such as getting and holding their parents' attention, taking turns, and maintaining interaction.

As infants move through the first 6 months of life, their vocal repertoire increases from reflexive sounds to cooing and babbling. At first, these are mostly vowel-like sounds. Try opening your mouth and saying, "ah." The sound produced is similar to what infants of 2 to 4 months produce. Although this may not seem like a particularly significant event, it is important because the baby is gaining control over his or her sound-production apparatus. These early sounds are the result of control of the flow of air. In addition, as the baby progresses through this stage, these sounds are increasingly produced in response to the caregiver. This is the very beginning of vocal interaction.

Somewhere between 3 and 6 months of age, babies begin to babble. Consonant sounds begin to enter the baby's vocalizations. It is as if the baby is playing with sounds. There is a common belief that babies babble all of the sounds of every language, gradually filtering out those sounds that are not actually heard in their language. However, Stoel-Gammon and Menn (2013) point out that research has found that, rather than producing every sound, babies babble a limited set of sounds—especially those that appear earlier in speech development.

Parental Language Input.   Our focus so far has been on the infant's role in early interaction but, of course, parents play an essential role as well. Not only do parents respond in nonverbal ways to their child (by smiling, holding, stroking), but as we have seen in Chapter 3, they also talk to their baby differently from the way they talk to other people. This baby talk is much more than "goo-goo" and "gah-gah." It is a systematic alteration in the way that parents speak to their baby. It is natural, spontaneous, and appears across a variety of cultures (Fernald, 1992; Matsaka, 1992). Early communicative interaction provides the basis for pragmatic and semantic development and may even provide the examples and modeling that children need to develop syntax (Bohannon & Stanowicz, 1988).

Although the theoretical models of language acquisition differ in their emphasis on the role of parental input on language acquisition, there are some conclusions that we can draw. First, so-called baby talk is not harmful. Unfortunately, there are some parents who believe that if they talk to their babies in adult-like modes right from the beginning, their child will learn language faster and be "smarter." The research evidence suggests just the opposite. Young children benefit from engaging in early interaction with parents who speak to them in the characteristic patterns of baby talk. Second, parents should be encouraged to talk to their young children as often as possible. We may not know for sure how children benefit from hearing this language input, but the evidence strongly suggests that there is a benefit.

Age 6 Months to 12 Months: The Development of Communicative Intentions

From the moment of birth (and perhaps even before birth), parents and their baby are engaging in complex behaviors that set the stage for later language development. The parent picks up the baby, makes eye contact, and smiles. The baby relaxes into the parent's arms and perhaps gurgles or burps. The parent, in turn, reacts as if this were an attempt at communication and says, "Oh, you're hungry," or, "Yes, you are sleepy." Feeding rituals and games such as "Peek-a-Boo" provide opportunities for the development of early communication skills.

During the period from 6 to 12 months, there is a major change occurring in the way that young children communicate. Initially, babies are dependent on their caregivers to ascribe meaning to their behavior. That is, parents act as if their child is communicating, interpreting burps and giggles as attempts to interact. This early stage of communication has been called the **perlocutionary stage** (Bates, 1979; Bates, Camaioni, & Volterra, 1975). Consider the following interaction:

Baby cries. Mother enters the room and says, "Are you hungry? Do you want something to eat now?"

Baby quiets and turns toward mother. Mother says, "Yes, you are hungry, aren't you?"

Baby stretches, touching rattle lying in crib. "Do you want to play?"

Mother picks up rattle and shakes it. Baby gurgles. "Yes, that's what you wanted, isn't it?"

Note how much the mother is reading into this conversation. She is interpreting her child's behaviors as communicative attempts. The baby is really not capable of acting intentionally at this stage, but caregivers act as if their child did intend to communicate.

By age 7 months or so, there is a significant, but subtle, change in the infant's behavior. The baby follows the parent's movements with her or his eyes and head and becomes distressed if the parent leaves the room. Children of this age have been found to show interest in toys when their caregiver is present but to stop playing when the caregiver leaves (Owens, 2011). By 8 to 10 months of age, the infant begins to respond to social gestures such as hand waving to signal "bye-bye." The young child is beginning to enter what some linguists call the **illocutionary stage** of communication. At this stage, children begin to use intentional communication.

> ▶ Watch this video of a baby interacting with her caregiver. What does the baby do to get the attention of others and to indicate what she wants?

A significant development in this period is **joint attention**. During this period, the young child shows increasing interest in objects, such as a favorite cup, a toy animal, or a set of play keys. As babies begin to reach for preferred objects and play with them, they are beginning to show some intentionality in their play. They are making more than random movements, accidentally touching an object. Rather, they are intentionally reaching for and manipulating objects. When parents respond, joint attention takes place. Parents may join in the play, shaking their child's toy monkey to get the child's attention. They may label the item, saying something like, "See the monkey? Do you want the monkey?" Researchers have found that when mothers engage in joint attention and label the objects, their babies increase their vocabulary faster (Campbell & Namy, 2003). In addition, children whose parents respond to their initiation of interaction have been found to have greater language development later in life (Rollins, 2003).

Throughout the illocutionary stage, young children are learning to use gestures to get what they want. Bates (1979) identified two predominant types of communicative functions expressed by early gestures: protodeclaratives and protoimperatives. When young children use gestures such as pointing at an object not to request the object but just to participate in the conversation (as if to say, "Hey, look at that!"), this is what Bates calls a **protodeclarative**. It is a precursor to the development of declarative sentences. On the other hand, when the child gestures in an attempt to control or manipulate others (such as pointing to an object and vocalizing in order to get the adult to get the object), Bates calls this a **protoimperative**.

Somewhere between 10 and 15 months (remember, there is a broad range of typical development), children begin to make the transition to the **locutionary stage** of communicative development. Now, the developing child is beginning to combine vocalizations with gestures to request, demand, and comment. At first these vocalizations may just be sounds, but gradually they begin to take on the characteristics of adult speech and language.

It seems that children and adults are engaged in communicative interaction right from the beginning. Babies are active participants in communication, performing in ways that get the adults' attention and prompt a response. Adults are engaging their children in communication by altering their own language to fit the linguistic and cognitive abilities of their child. By the time babies are 9 months old (prior to the emergence of spoken language), they can express a wide range of communicative intentions, including requests, demands, and rejection.

At the same time that the young child is developing a greater repertoire of communicative functions, the child's vocalizations are becoming increasingly sophisticated. Although the child cannot yet produce adult-like language, his or her babbling gradually takes on many of the characteristics of adult language. At this stage, babbling is characterized by consonant–vowel clusters ("ba-ba") and sequences that are of a similar length as adult speech. At times, this **reduplicated babble** even sounds like adult sentences, with intonational contours that sound like questioning or demanding.

 Watch this video of a baby babbling. In what ways do the strings of sounds that the child makes sound like adult utterances?
https://www.youtube.com/watch?v=lyV2j4BsEM8

Remember, too, that babies are not just developing expressive language. At this stage, their receptive language is far ahead of their ability to express themselves. They are able to understand more and more words and respond to questions and commands. Parents often express amazement about the amount that their child can understand. Research has confirmed what parents have known to be true. In a series of studies that used a technique called a "preferential looking paradigm," Hirsh-Pasek and Golinkoff (1993) and Hirsh-Pasek (2000) found that children can understand a variety of language structures before they can use them.

Apply Your Knowledge 5.1: Receptive/Expressive Language

 Does receptive language really exceed expressive language in young children? Watch this video of a mother interacting with her young child, and then answer the questions.

By about 12 months of age, most children are on the verge of producing their first real words. But they have already learned a lot about language. They can understand much more than they can produce. They have learned to express a variety of intentional communicative functions and have learned how to participate in conversations. They have learned the sounds of their language and have practiced them incessantly through babbling. They are ready to take the next step in language development.

Emergence of Expressive Language

Most parents can remember the excitement of hearing their baby's first words. This remarkable achievement did not happen overnight, however. Indeed, most babies do not wake up one morning speaking in full sentences. In fact, the progression from the shrieking first heard in the hospital nursery to the controlled utterance of *da-da* or *ma-ma* is slow, systematic, and predictable for most children.

Stark (1979) developed a framework for describing prelinguistic development consisting of five stages. We will use Stark's model to guide us through these early stages of language development. Keep in mind that, although generalizations can be made about development, these generalizations are not true of *every* child. As we noted in the beginning of this chapter, there is wide variation in language development among children.

Stage I (0–8 Weeks).   At this stage, newborns are making reflexive cries and vegetative sounds. That is, they are opening their mouths and emitting whatever comes out. What comes out is generally a loud, piercing cry that does wonders for getting a parent's attention. It is difficult, even painful, to ignore this cry. The crying is typically in short, rapid bursts, although there are individual differences. Some babies are relatively quiet; others seem to cry all the time. Some have a loud, piercing cry; others whimper. In addition, babies produce sounds—such as burps, coughs, and sneezes—that parents may respond to as if they were attempts to initiate communication.

Stage II (8–20 Weeks).   This period is one in which the infant gains increasing control over her or his sound-producing apparatus. Crying becomes differentiated, and parents begin to identify different kinds of cries (hunger, discomfort, demands). The bursts of crying begin to smooth out in more sustained (but usually less frequent) occurrences. By the end of this period, most babies are making cooing sounds. These are vowel-like utterances that are often interpreted by parents as sounds of pleasure. Many babies also begin to laugh at this stage.

Stage III (16–30 Weeks).   Vocal play characterizes this stage. This is a period in which there is continued control over the vocal mechanism. Consonant sounds begin to enter the baby's vocalizations. These may be added to the cooing sounds heard previously. By the end of this stage, the baby is beginning to produce the sounds we call *babble*.

Stage IV (25–50 Weeks).   This is the true babbling stage. The baby is producing combinations of consonants and vowels such as *ba* and *na*. By the end of this period, these consonant–vowel (CV) combinations are being repeated in long strings (*ba ba ba ba*), often with changes in pitch and intonation.

Stage V (9–18 Months).   Now the child's babbling becomes increasingly complex. The range of consonant sounds increases. Jargon emerges in most children. This is a type of vocalization that produces sounds and intonation that are similar to adult language. In fact, when listening from another room, one might almost think that the baby is actually talking, since these strings of sounds take on the sound characteristics of sentences.

Stage V marks a transition to true language production. Parents detect first words being uttered, sometimes heard within the flow of jargon speech. At times, the words are articulated clearly, not to be heard again for days or weeks. Some children may use *protowords*, CV combinations that are used consistently to mean something. For example, a child might use the combination "an" to indicate that she or he *wants* something. What makes this a protoword and not just babble is that the sounds are used *consistently, in appropriate contexts* to signal their meaning. Owens (2011) has suggested that the following criteria should be used in deciding whether a vocal production is actually a word:

- The utterance must have a phonetic relationship to some adult word.
- The child must use the word consistently.
- The word must occur in the presence of a referent.

Our review of early vocalizations has taken us from the reflexive crying of the newborn to the emergence of true first words. We have noted the universality of this progression, while keeping in mind the individual variations that are found in developing

Table 5.1

Prelinguistic
Development

Stage	Form	Content	Use
I (0–8 wks)	Reflexive crying Vegetative sounds Sound discrimination	Biological and physical needs	Eye contact Body movement
II (8–20 wks)	Cooing and laughing Vowel-like sounds Cry more controlled	Differentiated crying (hunger, distress)	Games Routines
III (16–30 wks)	Increased control over speech Prolonged vocalizations Babble	Beginning of semantic functions	Intent to communicate
IV (25–50 wks)	Repeated syllable clusters Jargon speech Some words	Expansion of semantic functions	Illocutionary stage
V (9–18 mos)	Protowords Transition to language	Overextensions Underextensions	Locutionary stage

Source: Adapted from Stark (1979).

children. Table 5.1 summarizes the development of vocalizations (form) as well as communication (use) and content.

Check Your Understanding 5.1

Click here to gauge your understanding of the concepts in this section.

Language Development in the Preschool Years

In his pioneering book on language development, Harvard University psychologist Roger Brown described a longitudinal study of the language development of three children: Adam, Eve, and Sarah. Working with a group of remarkably talented assistants, Brown and his colleagues observed, recorded, and analyzed each step in the language growth of these children. Their observations were reported in the book *A First Language: The Early Stages* (Brown, 1973). This is still the most comprehensive description of language development available. One of Brown's key observations was that the *length* of a child's utterance is a better indicator of language development (especially syntactic development) than is the child's age. Brown developed a measure of syntactic development called **mean length of utterance (MLU)**. MLU is relatively simple to calculate (see Box 5.1) and has become a widely used measure of language development, even though it is only a rough measure of language complexity. MLU is calculated by counting the total number of morphemes in a sample of language and dividing by the number of utterances in the sample. For example, if there were 100 morphemes used in a sample of 50 utterances, the MLU would be 2.0 (100/50). Brown and his colleagues used MLU to describe the stages of language they observed in their subjects (see Table 5.2). Brown's stages are used in the following description of language development in the preschool years.

Stage I (MLU = 1.0–2.0; Age = 12–26 Months)

Stage I marks the emergence of true words. Researchers such as Nelson (1973) has found that nouns (animals, food, toys) predominate. Nelson found that approximately

---

Box 5.1 Measurement of Mean Length of Utterance

1. The language sample should be 50 to 100 utterances in length.

   Note: An utterance is a sentence or a shorter unit separated by a pause or signaled by a change in pitch (e.g., *Now?* with a rising pitch = an utterance).

2. Count the number of morphemes in each utterance.

   Note: Brown (1973) lists explicit rules for what to count. For example:

   a. Count as one morpheme: Compound words (e.g., *railroad*)

      Diminutives (e.g., *goggie*)

   b. Count as two morphemes: Possessive nouns (e.g., *mommy's*)

      Plural nouns (e.g., *kitties*)

      Present progressive verbs (e.g., *sleeping*)

   c. Do not count: Fillers (e.g., *um, ah*)

      Dysfluencies (e.g., *m-m-m mommy*) (only count full morpheme)

3. Divide the total number of morphemes by the total number of utterances to derive MLU:

$$MLU = \frac{\text{Total number of morphemes}}{\text{Total number of utterances}}$$

Example: 2-year-old child and grandmother

Child: Get donuts.

Grandmother: I know you want to get donuts. What kind of donuts do you want?

Child: I-I = icy.

Child's total number of morphemes = 4/2 (utterances) = 2.0 MLU

---

65 percent of first words were nouns. These are not just any nouns, however. They fall into what we might call the "midlevel" of nouns (e.g., *dog*)—not so specific that they name just one type (e.g., *collie*) but not so general as to cover an entire category (e.g., *animal*) (Anglin, 1995). The next most frequent words are action words (*hi, bye-bye*) and then modifiers (*hot, cold*).

What else do you notice about these first words? They are usually one or, at most, two syllables, and certain sounds tend to predominate (*b, p, m*). In addition, children often make systematic phonological errors at this stage. These include:

Reduction of consonant clusters (*green* becomes *geen*)

Deletion of unstressed syllables (*banana* becomes *nana*)

Devoicing of the final consonant (*bed* becomes *bet*)

Table 5.2

Brown's Stages of Language Development

Stage	MLU	Approximate Age (months)	Development
I	1.0–2.0	12–26	Use of semantic rules
II	2.0–2.5	27–30	Morphological development
III	2.5–3.0	31–34	Development of sentence forms
IV	3.0–3.75	35–40	Emergence of complex sentence forms
V	3.75–4.5	41–46	Elaboration and refinement of structures
VI	4.5+	47+	

Source: Based on Brown (1973).

Nelson found many similarities in the first words used by children, but she also discovered that there were clear individual differences among children. Some children tended to use language to describe and categorize, whereas others used language primarily for interpersonal interaction.

 Watch this video of a 19-month-old child interacting with a caregiver. What kinds of words does he use? Is this consistent with Nelson's observations of early utterances in children?

By the end of Stage I, children are beginning to use multiword utterances. Like first words, these utterances have a typical pattern, which has often been described as *telegraphic*. That is, they are characterized by the deletion of prepositions, conjunctions, articles, and pronouns. In their early two-word utterances, children typically talk about a limited set of items—objects, agents, and actions. They point to objects (demonstrative), and they talk about where the objects are (location). They talk about who owns the object (possessive) and about the appearance of the objects (attributive). These early semantic functions are characteristic of Brown's Stage I of language development.

Stage II (MLU = 2.0–2.5; Age = 27–30 Months)

As children's utterances grow longer, they also become more complex. One of the major developments identified by Brown and his colleagues in what they called Stage II of language development is the emergence of **grammatical morphemes** (prefixes, suffixes, prepositions). As we noted in Chapter 2, morphemes are linguistic elements that carry meaning. *Grammatical* morphemes are the type that add meaning only when attached to a root word. In Stage II, young children are learning to convey more subtle meanings by adding these grammatical morphemes to words they have already acquired.

Although the use of grammatical morphemes begins in Stage II, the development of the use of grammatical morphemes continues through Stage V. Brown found that there was a highly predictable sequence of acquisition of grammatical morphemes (see Figure 5.1). Prepositions (such as *in* and *on*) and the present progressive (*-ing*) are usually acquired first. Then comes the use of the plural *s* and so on. Of course, these constructions do not emerge fully formed or in the exact order that Brown and his colleagues claimed. As children learn to use these morphemes, they make a number of errors in usage, using the endings incorrectly (e.g., *deerses*) or failing to use them at times. As children continue to develop, however, they learn to use grammatical morphemes more consistently and accurately. Pronoun use also begins to develop in Stage II. The earliest pronouns used are *I* and *my*. Later (Stage III), *he, she,* and *you* emerge in usage. By Stage V (approximately 4 years old), most children are using even the most sophisticated pronouns.

Stage III (MLU = 2.5–3.0; Age = 31–34 Months)

The major developments of Stage III are the emergence of sentence types such as negation, the imperative, and questions, and the elaboration of the basic sentence elements (noun phrase and verb phrase). Each of the sentence types has a developmental progression.

We will examine negation as an example of the steps in sentence development. Any parent can tell you that long before 31 months of age, children can express negation. They do so by pushing the bottle away, by scrunching up their faces, and by using the word *no*. However, at Stage III, we begin to

Figure 5.1

Average Order of Acquisition of 14 Grammatical Morphemes by Three Children Studied by Brown

1. Present progressive
2/3. Prepositions (in and on)
4. Plural
5. Irregular past tense
6. Possessive
7. Copula, uncontractible
8. Articles
9. Regular past tense
10. Third-person present tense, regular
11. Third-person present tense, irregular
12. Auxiliary, uncontractible
13. Copula, contractible
14. Auxiliary, contractible

see the emergence of more adult-like ways of saying no. At first, the child simply adds the word *no* to the beginning of a sentence (*No the kitty eating*). Next, the child learns to place the negative marker inside the sentence, just before the verb (*The kitty no eating*). Still later, auxiliary verbs are used (*The kitty is not eating*).

> ▶ Watch this video of a 32-month-old child at play. What types of sentences does she use?

Development of the use of questions also follows a predictable order. Most children begin to ask questions by using a rising intonation (*Daddy?*), where a rise in intonation at the end of the word may mean, "Is that Daddy?" As their language develops, children begin to ask more sophisticated questions. Generally, children start by asking *wh* questions— who, what, when, where, and why. In order to ask such questions in English, the speaker must invert the subject and auxiliary verb and place the *wh* word at the beginning of the sentence (e.g., *Where is kitty?*). But, as they learn to use this type of construction, children typically drop the auxiliary verb, leaving something like, *Where kitty?* The next step in development is to add the auxiliary but not switch it with the subject (e.g., *Where she is going?*). Finally, children learn to use these constructions, as well as yes–no questions (e.g., *Is Daddy home?*), in the correct (adult-like) manner. The appearance of negation and questioning, like that of other sentence types, begins at Stage III and continues to develop through the preschool years (see Table 5.3).

As a variety of sentence types begin to emerge, the young child is adding elements to basic noun and verb phrases. Up to this point, noun phrases have generally consisted of a noun and, perhaps, a determiner (article). Now, the child begins to add adjectives, initiators (*all, both, only*), and postmodifiers (prepositional phrases and clauses) to the basic noun phrase. Similarly, verb use expands from simple verbs to inclusion of auxiliary verbs, the progressive (*-ing*), and modals (*can, will, may*).

Stage IV (MLU = 3.0–3.75; Age = 35–40 Months)

Stage IV marks the emergence of complex sentence types. Complex sentences are formed when two or more *clauses* (a group of words with a subject and predicate) are joined together. The first type of complex structure to emerge is that of *coordination*. Children begin by linking ideas with the word *and* (*I am going to the store and my dad is going to work*). Later, the child learns to use coordination of multiple ideas as a way to *shorten* sentences (*My mom and I are going to the bank*). Still later, children begin to use other conjunctions (*but, because, since*).

Negation	Questioning
■ "No" used alone	■ Yes/no questions
■ "No" added to other words (placed outside sentence) Examples: *No go. No sit down. No the girl run.*	Example: *Baby drink?* (rising intonation)
■ Negative moved within sentence Example: *The girl not running.*	■ "What" and "where" questions Example: *Where doggie?*
■ Use of auxiliary and contraction Example: *The girl is not (isn't) running.*	■ "What" and "where" + noun phrase + (going)/(doing) Examples: *Where daddy going? Why you crying?*
■ Elaboration of negative forms	■ Limited inversion and use of auxiliary Example: *What the boy is riding?*
	■ Inversion of auxiliary Example: *What is the boy riding?*

Table 5.3

Sequence of the Development of Negation and Questioning

Table 5.4

Use of Conjunction and Embedding

Conjunction: Joining of two *main* clauses
Embedding: Joining of a *main* clause with a *subordinate* clause

Development of Conjunction	Development of Embedding
1. Single words used together	1. Use of prepositions
2. Use of *and* to link sentences	2. Use of semi-auxiliary
3. Use of *and* to link clauses (with deletion)	3. Object noun phrase complements (*I think that I will go.*)
4. Use of *but* and *if* to link clauses	4. Infinitive (*I gotta go home.*)
	5. Relative clause (*I am going where it is nice.*)

At Stage IV, children also typically begin to use embedded sentences. These are sentences in which a subordinate clause (*who is my friend*) is embedded in an independent clause (*The boy is here*) to form a complex sentence (*The boy who is my friend is here*) (see Table 5.4).

 Watch as this 5-year-old boy tells a story. How does he use conjunctions?

Stage V (MLU = 3.75–4.5; Age = 41–46 Months)

There are no major new structures that emerge in Stage V. Instead, this stage is marked by elaboration and refinement of structures that emerged in earlier stages. The child continues adding grammatical morphemes; more frequently uses adjectives, adverbs, and embedded sentences; and more consistently uses inversion in questions (*Are you going to the store?*). In short, the child is learning to become a more effective (and more social) communicator.

This description of the syntactic development of children between 1 and 4 years of age is complete for the purpose intended here, although there has been no attempt to describe every feature that develops during this period. Instead, the goal has been to describe major accomplishments that illustrate the general course of development and provide background for an understanding of what happens when children fail to develop in the expected ways.

By the time most children enter kindergarten, they are able to understand and use quite complex and sophisticated language. They have mastered the use of pronouns and grammatical morphemes and can use all adult sentence forms, including compound and complex sentences. But they have not learned everything there is to know about language. There is still much to be learned after children enter formal schooling. Before examining syntactic development during the school years, however, we need to look at the development of two other aspects of language in the preschool years: semantics and pragmatics.

Apply Your Knowledge 5.2: Stage V+

 Watch the video of a 6-year-old boy having a conversation with an adult, and then answer the question.

Learning to Mean: The Development of Semantics

By the time they are 8 years old, most children have a receptive vocabulary of about 8,000 words and can use about 5,000 in their language (Menyuk, 1999). How did they acquire so many words, and how did they learn what each means?

Word learning starts very early in development. In one study (Tincoff & Jusczyk, 1999), 6-month-old infants watched videotapes of their parents while listening to an audiotape that said either "Mommy" or "Daddy." The experimenters found that the children looked longer at the picture when it was associated with the correct label, suggesting that the child understood the word. In another study, 10-month-old children were able to learn novel names for objects that differed in appearance (Pruden, Hirsh-Pasek, Michnick Golinkoff, & Hennon, 2006).

Did these very young children actually "learn" these words? It all depends on what we mean by "learn." What the infants may have been doing is what is called "fast-mapping," the development of an initial relationship between a word and its referent. As they learn more about the world, they develop a more sophisticated semantic map in which entries in their lexicon (vocabulary) are linked by experience (Turnbull & Justice, 2012). This process has sometimes been called "slow mapping" or "extended mapping." How does this process work?

At first, infants appear to focus primarily on the appearance of the object, as Pruden et al. (2006) discovered. In this study, the researchers found that the infants were more likely to learn the labels for objects that were "interesting" (objects that were brightly colored and made noise) than objects that were "boring." But within a few months, other factors appear to become important. Tomasello (2003) and others have claimed, for example, that social context is very important for early word learning. Social processes such as eye gaze and joint attention appear to help the child focus on the salient features of both words and objects and facilitate the word-learning process.

By about 24 months of age, children are becoming word-learning "experts." They can use social cues to attend to the important sounds in words and the essential perceptual information. They can "fast map" new words while sharpening their knowledge of existing words through building ever more sophisticated semantic maps. The "errors" they make can reveal a lot about how children are going about the word-learning process. For example, one day my wife and I were at a petting zoo watching some sheep. A young child next to us said, "Look mommy, doggie." This is an example of an *overextension*—the use of a word for a broad range of items. In this case, the child apparently had learned something like all animals are doggies. If the child's parents had said something like, "No, that's a sheep," then the child might have to reshape his semantic map to accommodate this new information. Now his lexicon might consist of two words—"dog" for all animals that live in houses and "sheep" for animals that live outside. Occasionally, children *underextend* meanings, by restricting a word to only one object (usually something they treasure, such as a cup or a pacifier). In this case, they will use the word only when that particular object is present.

But perceptual features are not the only clues that children use to learn words. Children also pay attention to the *action* related to objects. The *functional core* hypothesis claims that children learn about meaning by interacting with things, much as Piaget claimed that cognitive growth is spurred on by experience. If asked to differentiate between a red apple and a red ball, children might say that the ball is "something you play with," while the apple is "something you eat." The action helps define the object.

Although a complete understanding of semantic development remains elusive, research has given us some insights into the process children use to develop the semantic aspect of language. Children are *active* participants in the language-learning process, constantly adding new concepts and refining old ones. As their understanding of the world changes, they develop new words or adjust the meanings of existing words to match their new knowledge. This process is gradual at first, but builds in intensity as the child enters school.

At the same time, there is evidence that children use a variety of strategies to develop their semantic knowledge. What factors might explain how the child selects which strategy to use? First, there are individual differences in children. Some children may pay more attention to physical features of objects, whereas others are more action oriented. Second, at different stages of development, children may prefer one strategy over another. A third factor that may affect how children acquire meaning is the object itself. Some objects (e.g., pets and toys) are more likely to be discovered through action, whereas others (e.g., walls and clouds) are more likely to be viewed at some distance. So, in a sense, each of the models of semantic development may be right at a particular time, for specific children, for particular objects or items.

 In this video, a teacher is evaluating a child on her ability to identify types of animals. Can you identify the use of an overextension?
https://www.youtube.com/watch?v=CNAP3ahGQmE

Learning to Converse: The Development of Pragmatic Language

Earlier in this chapter, we discussed the development of conversational skills from infancy to the emergence of spoken language. We saw how, right from the start, infants appear to engage in exchanges that begin to take on the give-and-take characteristics of communicative interactions. Parents enhance their child's developing communication skills by responding as if they were intentionally communicating and by providing models for interaction.

With the development of spoken language comes a refinement in the use of the conversational skills, which linguists call *pragmatics*. As children develop, so too does the length of their conversational exchanges. Although the conversational interactions of 2 year olds tend to be limited to one or two turns, 3 and 4 year olds can maintain longer conversations, and the number of utterances in each turn increases (Logan, 2003). In addition, children learn to take turns in the conversation, with fewer interruptions and overlapping language (Elias & Broerse, 1996).

Besides engaging in longer conversations, preschool children develop a number of pragmatic functions that enable them to engage in more effective conversations. For example, they develop skills in using conversational repairs, such as asking for clarification (*What?*). They become more adept at staying on topic during a conversation and at setting the topic themselves. They also begin to understand and use politeness rules (such as saying *please* and *thank you*) and begin to understand indirect requests (such as, "Why don't you play outside?" which really means, "Go play outside").

Overall, as preschool children develop more sophisticated forms of language and a wider vocabulary, they are also learning to engage in longer, more complex conversational interactions. They are beginning to learn conversational skills that will enable them to fully participate in the challenging communicative environments found in school.

 Watch as this 5-year-old girl tries to tell an adult about her adventure with her class. What difficulties does she encounter when trying to tell her story?

 Check Your Understanding 5.2
Click here to gauge your understanding of the concepts in this section.

Language Development and Emergent Literacy

Our focus so far has been on understanding and describing the remarkable and still somewhat mysterious phenomenon known as language development in young children. But just as remarkable (and just as mysterious) is the development of literacy skills—reading and writing—in young children.

Research over the past two decades has led to the conclusion that reading and writing skills develop long before children begin to receive formal instruction in these skills in school (see Dickinson & Tabors, 2001; Teale & Sulzby, 1986). This model of reading and writing has come to be known as **emergent literacy**. It is based on research that has found that language and literacy develop concurrently and interdependently from an early age (Whitehurst & Lonigan, 1998). In other words, language and literacy develop at the same time, and the continuing development of one skill is dependent on the other. This is very different from the "reading readiness" model that suggests that reading and writing develop only after the child has acquired sufficient language (and other) skills.

Although the exact relationship between language development and reading and writing is still unclear, most researchers have concluded that early language experiences play a critical role in the development of literacy skills. The National Early Literacy Panel (2008) reviewed and synthesized a substantial amount of the research literature on early literacy development. The panel concluded that six early literacy factors were highly related to later reading and writing skills:

- Alphabet knowledge: knowledge of the names and sounds associated with printed letters
- Phonological awareness: the ability to detect, manipulate, or analyze the auditory aspects of spoken language
- Rapid automatic naming of letters or digits: the ability to rapidly name a sequence of random letters or digits
- Rapid automatic naming of objects or colors: the ability to rapidly name a sequence of repeating random sets of pictures of objects or colors
- Writing or writing name: the ability to write letters in isolation on request or to write one's own name
- Phonological memory: the ability to remember spoken information for a short period of time

In addition, the panel found five other factors to be moderately related to later reading and writing success:

- Concepts about print: knowledge of print conventions (e.g., left–right, front–back) and concepts (book cover, author, text)
- Print knowledge: a combination of elements of alphabet knowledge, concepts about print, and early decoding
- Reading readiness: a combination of alphabet knowledge, concepts of print, vocabulary, memory, and phonological awareness
- Oral language: the ability to produce or comprehend spoken language, including vocabulary and grammar
- Visual processing: the ability to match or discriminate visually presented symbols

The panel's report suggests that these skills are the most important ones for early literacy development. But the panel's conclusions and methodology have been questioned by several researchers, including Dickinson, Golinkoff, and Hirsh-Pasek (2010), who contend that the report does not place enough emphasis on the role of early language development in emergent literacy. Dickinson and colleagues argue that many of the effects of early language development are indirect and harder to measure than a discrete skill such as phonological awareness. Moreover, even the National Early Literacy Panel noted the importance of early language skills for later literacy development. Although early language skills may not be directly related to early word recognition skills, there is evidence that they are an important factor in the development of reading comprehension (Muter, Hulme, Snowling, & Stevenson, 2004).

Using data from a national study of child development, a group of investigators from the National Institute of Child Health and Human Development Early Child Care Research Network (NICHD-ECCRN, 2005) found significant relationships between language development at age 3 and both later language development (at 54 months) and reading. Specifically, oral language skills at age 3 were directly related to both vocabulary development and the development of phonological knowledge (awareness of phonemes). The researchers did not find a direct relationship between language skills at age 3 and word recognition, but they did find such a relationship with language at 54 months. Moreover, oral language competence at 54 months of age was found to be strongly related to both first-grade word recognition and to third-grade reading comprehension. These researchers concluded that early oral language skills are critical for success in later reading.

What is the role of parents and families in the development of their child's learning of language (and literacy)? This has been a key question for researchers. One factor that has been examined is home environment. We have already reviewed evidence (in Chapter 3) that some home environments are more conducive than others to the development of oral language skills. In the study by Hart and Risley (1995), children from lower socioeconomic families participated in fewer interactions and acquired a smaller vocabulary than children from families with middle or higher socioeconomic status. Interestingly, there is considerable evidence that children from lower socioeconomic families are also at risk for reading difficulties (Snow, Burns, & Griffin, 1998). A number of factors have been suggested as the cause of this phenomenon, including biological and health factors, discrimination, and home environment (Vernon-Feagans, 1996). Children from low-income families have been reported to visit libraries less often, have fewer print materials in the home, and are read to less by their parents. Although there are clearly cultural and economic forces at work here, most researchers have concluded that early literacy practices have a strong and enduring effect on children's language and literacy skills (Wasik & Hendrickson, 2004).

One of the most researched factors within the home environment is storybook reading. As Whitehurst and Lonigan (1998) pointed out, the image of a parent reading to his or her child is a cherished cultural icon. For most parents, reading stories to their child is an essential part of child rearing. We have the intuitive sense that it is an important part of the child's early literacy training. In fact, a highly influential book titled *Becoming a Nation of Readers* concluded that "the single most important activity for building the knowledge required for eventual success in reading is reading aloud to children" (Anderson, Hiebert, Scott, & Wilkinson, 1985, p. 23).

 Watch this video of an adult reading a book to a child. What does the adult do to engage the child in the story?

Research on shared book reading has generally found that it has a positive effect on the development of early reading skills in children, although questions have been raised about the strength of the effect (Senechal, LeFevre, Thomas, & Daley, 1998). What is less in doubt is that book reading has significant effects on language development. These effects are of two types. First, shared book reading creates an opportunity for language interaction. This is a chance for parents to converse with their children and for the child to practice his or her emerging language skills. Second, children are learning new vocabulary and are being exposed to new grammatical structures as part of the book-reading experience. So, although book reading itself may not be strongly linked to later reading success, there is evidence that children who are read to more often have enhanced language skills, which, in turn, leads to more success in reading.

What can we conclude about language and the emergence of literacy? It seems clear that there is a relationship. Language skills are an important factor in the early development of literacy. At the same time, literacy experiences positively influence language development. Although there is a need for more research on the most effective ways to enhance early literacy development, there is enough evidence to suggest that parents should be encouraged to read to their children and to discuss with them what they are reading.

Check Your Understanding 5.3

Click here to gauge your understanding of the concepts in this section.

Summary

This chapter presented the development of language from birth (or even before birth) through the preschool years. The role of both parents and children in the early development of language was reviewed. We examined the course of spoken language development, from the early vocalizations through the emergence of first words and sentences to the further refinements and elaborations that take place in early childhood. We examined evidence about the influence of early language development on the emergence of literacy skills and how language can be enhanced through engagement in literacy activities.

Language and Literacy in the School Years

Language development does not end when children enter school. In fact, growth in some areas of language actually accelerates during the school years. The demands of school also require that children use their knowledge of language to develop skills in reading, writing, and thinking. This chapter describes the course of language development during the school years and the important relationship between language and literacy.

Learning Outcomes

After reading this chapter, you should be able to:

1. Describe the major language developments accomplished during the school years and the implications of language development in the school years for classroom instruction.

2. Describe the relationship between language development and literacy development in the school years and the implications for literacy development.

Teacher Perspective: Alternative School Teacher for 9th and 10th Grades

I'm not sure how to handle my 12 teenagers. I don't think any of them come from a language-literate household. Often my students are speaking and writing in a "different language" using the English language! I'm not sure if it is street slang, or sayings they hear from the music they listen to, or what. I'm reading their papers and saying to myself, "What are they talking about?" They refer to an event as being "good lookin" or an act as being "handsome" and are always using words for different meanings. Sometimes I'll just sit and listen to the class interact with each other. They all understand each other and communicate using their "different language," but I'm the one that is now confused! I'll ask them to define the word they are using, and they do so with no problem but it's not the "English" definition. It's almost as if a culture is evolving with a new language. They think it's "corny" to use the old-fashioned meanings of words.

Language Development in the School Years

By the time most children enter school, they have acquired an enormous number of language skills. They can speak in complete sentences and use many different types of sentences, including complex sentences. They can talk about past, present, and future events, and they have a large and varied vocabulary. They are competent communicators, able to take their part in a conversation. One might ask, then, whether there is anything left to learn. The answer is yes—plenty.

The beginning of formal schooling marks a period in which there are new demands on language ability. Now, the child is expected not just to talk but to *understand* language itself. In school, children are asked to study language that for several years they have used without much thought and to become aware of the sounds and structures that underlie that language. Further, they must then apply their language skills to reading and writing. Schoolchildren are presented daily with new words to learn and relate to prior knowledge. At the same time, because of the social structure of school, students face new demands on their skills as communicators. Success in classroom discussions, playground negotiations, and lunchroom conversations all require maximum skills in communication. It should come as no surprise that children with minimal language skills begin to fall behind soon after beginning school.

As children move through the school years, new demands are made on their language and communication skills. Vocabulary becomes more complex and specialized. Writing demands the use of more complex syntactic and semantic features, including the use of figurative language. In addition to these academic demands, the growing importance of peers and peer groups demands sophisticated communication skills. The example at the beginning of this chapter from the 9th/10th-grade teacher shows how important language can be to teenagers and how frustrating teen language can be for adults!

Morphology and Syntax

During the school years, children complete their development of many of the morphological and syntactic forms that emerged earlier. You might recall from Chapter 5 that the development of morphological endings begins around age 2 in typically developing children, but, of course, development continues for some time. In fact, during the school years, children are still adding **inflectional prefixes** (such as *un-* and *dis-*) and **derivational suffixes** (word endings that change the type of word (e.g., *-ly* added to a verb to create an adverb) (Owens, 2015). Elaboration of noun and verb phrases continues during the school years. Children learn to use noun clause structures such as **reflexives** (*myself, himself*) and to identify the subject and object pronouns in a complex sentence such as *Tom's father had two tickets for the game. He hoped that Tom wanted to go with him.* School-age children use more modifiers in their language and learn to use them in new ways (e.g., as sentence starters, *Suddenly the sun came out*). They begin to understand and use gerunds—verbs that are turned into nouns by the addition of an *-ing* ending (*Swimming is lots of fun*). During the school years, children also learn to use subtle rules such as *adjective ordering* (e.g., *The big, fat cat* not *The fat, big cat*) (Owens, 2015).

The development of verb tenses, which began in Stage III, continues into the school years as children learn to use structures such as the perfect tense (have + be + verb; e.g., *has been eaten*), learn to use modal auxiliaries (*could, should*), and enhance their use of irregular verbs (Shipley, Maddox, & Driver, 1991).

In addition to developing greater elaboration of noun and verb phrases, school-age children continue their development of the use of various sentence types and begin to use new structures. For example, it is only after age 5 that children begin to use and understand passive sentences (*The ball was hit by the girl*). Most children have begun to use compound and embedded sentences before coming to school, but during the school years, they learn to use sophisticated variants of these basic sentence types, such as subordinating conjunctions (e.g., *when* and *although*) and coordinating conjunctions (*Henry likes chess and David likes checkers*) (Nippold, 1998). The use of embedded sentences (a sentence containing one independent clause and at least one dependent clause) increases during the school year, and children learn to understand and use more sophisticated forms, such as center embedding ("The cat *that ate the cheese* ran away").

As important as continued morphological and syntactic development are for school-aged children, an even more significant development is learning how to use existing structures with greater efficiency to enhance communication (Nippold, Hesketh, Duthie, & Mansfield, 2005). Although most children enter school able to use a wide variety of syntactic structures, they can rarely identify the rules that describe these structures. One of the outcomes of formal education is the development of **metasyntactic awareness**, the ability to identify and correct grammatical errors using syntactic rules.

As children move through the school years, they are also required to apply their increasingly sophisticated syntactic and morphological developments to tasks such as reading, writing, and the use of **expository discourse** (the use of language to convey information) (Nippold et al., 2005). For example, when a high school student has to explain the steps in a chemistry experiment, he or she is using expository discourse. Nippold et al. (2005) found that in tasks such as these syntactic complexity and sentence length increase with age. In addition, the complexity of expository discourse is greater than that found in typical conversations.

Similarly, Nippold, Ward-Lonergan, and Fanning (2005) studied the development of formal, persuasive writing in three groups of typically developing individuals: 11 year olds, 17 year olds, and 24 year olds. They found age-related changes in the writing of essays that included increases in essay length, mean length of utterance, and relative clause production. Combined with the evidence from the research on expository discourse, this study supports the contention that typically developing students are not only continuing to develop new and expanded morphological and syntactic forms, but they are also increasing their ability to apply their learning to more sophisticated language tasks.

Although typically developing children enter school as highly proficient users of spoken language, they continue to build on this foundation of syntactic and morphological knowledge during the school years. A summary of some of the major developments can be found in Table 6.1.

Semantics

Rapid expansion of vocabulary is one of the major developments during the school years. Children are reported to have a vocabulary of about 10,000 words by the end of first grade, increasing to about 40,000 words in grade 5 (Anglin, 1993). New vocabulary comes from exposure to a wide array of literature as well as to new concepts from the sciences and social studies. In addition to learning more words, school-age children deepen their understanding of words already in their vocabulary and are better able to define words. They can compare and contrast words, synthesize meanings, and begin to understand that some words have more than one meaning (e.g., *table*).

During the school years, a new development in the semantic domain is the ability to understand and use **figurative (nonliteral) language**. To use figurative language (metaphors, idioms, jokes, proverbs), one must have a firm grasp on the literal meanings of words, for only then can the beauty and humor of figurative language be properly used

Table 6.1

Development of Language Form in the School Years

Morphology	Syntax

Increased use of inflectional prefixes
Use of derivational suffixes
	Continued Expansion of Noun Phrase:
	  Reflexives
	  Modifiers
	  Gerunds
	  Adjective ordering

	Expansion of Verb Phrase:
	  Perfect tense
	  Modal auxiliaries (*could, should*)

	Understanding and use of passive voice Use of subordinating and coordinating conjunctions Use of center embedding

and appreciated. During the school years, children are asked to write poems and stories that go beyond the literal use of language to incorporate more and more figurative language. Social interaction also requires children to understand words used in nonliteral ways (*He is cool* does not mean that he is cold) and to understand increasingly sophisticated forms of humor.

This video is designed to help children learn more about figurative language. How could it be used with students who are having difficulty understanding figurative language?
https://www.youtube.com/watch?v=6qwUEztyKGE

Research has found that the ability to understand and use figurative language begins to develop around age 5 and continues through the school years (Nippold, 1998, 2000). For example, the comprehension of idioms (*He put his foot in his mouth*) has been found to develop slowly throughout childhood and even into the adult years (Nippold, 1985). Similarly, children often have a difficult time understanding proverbs (e.g., *One swallow does not a summer make*) and at first struggle to find literal explanations for them. They might say something like "It gets hot in the summer, so it is hard to swallow." Gradually, they are able to move away from the literal meaning of the words to the correct nonliteral interpretation (Nippold, Hegel, Uhden, & Bustamante, 1998). Similarly, the ability to understand irony (when the speaker says one thing but means another) has been found to emerge in typically developing children around age 5 but continues to develop through the school years (Dews et al., 1996).

Apply Your Knowledge 6.1: Figurative Language

In this exercise, you will review the responses that two children made to a figurative knowledge task and discuss the implications for understanding the development of figurative language.

The use of humor by children is a fascinating area of study (see Bernstein, 1986). If you have ever heard a 5 year old try to tell you a joke, you know the difficulty children have learning to use humor. There is actually a developmental sequence to the understanding and use of humor. For example, Fowles and Glanz (1977) found that children begin to use riddles between ages 6 and 9 years but often do not understand what they mean. Children may say things like:

Question: Why did the chicken cross the road?

Answer: Because it was there.

This is followed by a howl of laughter from the child and a puzzled look by the adult. The child is able to understand the *form* of a riddle but does not yet understand the point of the joke. Ely and McCabe (1994) identified four levels in the development of the understanding of riddles (see Figure 6.1). They found that most 6 year olds were at Level 1, whereas most 9 year olds performed at Level 3.

Between 9 and 12 years of age, children begin to use and understand humor that is based on the sound and meaning of words. For example, they are able to understand the humor in the old joke:

Question: What is black and white and red (read) all over?

Answer: A newspaper.

Figure 6.1

Stages in Solving Riddles

Target riddle: What dog keeps the best time? Answer: A watch dog.

Level 0

Absent or minimal response: "I don't know."

Level 1

Illogical or negative attempt at explication: "Because dogs don't really have watches."

Level 2

Explanation focuses on the situation to which the language referred, not the language itself: "Because a watch dog is a kind of dog and also it keeps time."

Level 3

Incongruity is clearly attributed to the language itself: "Because, well, watch dogs are really dogs to watch and see if anybody comes in but watch dogs. . . . It's a joke 'cause it's also another word for telling time."

Source: Based on Ely & McCabe (1994).

Although the ability to tell jokes and understand humor may seem a trivial matter, in fact it is an important component of social acceptance and an essential social skill. Children who lack the language skills to appreciate humor may be at risk for social rejection.

 Watch this video of children telling jokes. What do these attempts at humor indicate about the development of humor in children?
https://www.youtube.com/watch?v=aAbdQZ2L8u4

One of the characteristics of adolescence is the development of unique words or idiosyncratic meanings for common words. For example, do you know the meaning of the word "cray"? It is short for "crazy." How about "rachet"? In Internet slang, "rachet" means nasty. Other slang words and their meanings can be found on the Internet (search for the Internet slang website). But it is not just the meanings of words that differ. Intonational differences (such as the use of a rising intonation at the end of a sentence) can also be part of adolescent language (Eckert, 2004). The unique features of adolescent speech serve as a way to convey membership in a social group while excluding those (e.g., adults) who do not belong. However, because language is always evolving, it is not unusual for "slang" to become accepted usage. For example, "sexting" and "selfie" have become part of the mainstream culture and have been included in some dictionaries. Although adults may sometimes complain about the "misuse" of language by teenagers, in terms of language development, the use of unique words and meanings is a highly sophisticated use of language.

The development of semantics in the school years is also reflected in written language. Nippold, Ward-Lonergan, and Fanning (2005) examined the use of three kinds of semantic features associated with more sophisticated persuasive writing: adverbial conjuncts (words or phrases that introduce an independent clause and link it to a previous clause; e.g., *technically, personally*) abstract nouns (e.g., *decision, benefits, courage*), and "meta-verbs" (verbs that refer to acts of thinking or speaking; e.g., *discover, realize, reflect*). They found that the use of abstract nouns in written language increased rapidly throughout the school years but that the other two forms were used infrequently.

Pragmatics

Some of the most dramatic language development in the school years is in the area of pragmatics. Although most kindergarten-age children can express their wants and needs, they are not yet truly sophisticated communicators. They do not have command of some of the subtleties of communication. For example, a preschool child may launch into a conversation about Eduardo, forgetting to tell you that Eduardo is the name of her teddy bear. In any case, the child's entire conversation may be irrelevant to the topic being discussed.

During the school years, children continue to develop *conversational competence* as well as increasing sophistication in the use of **narratives**—that is, a storytelling monologue. In the domain of conversational skills, school-age children improve their ability to stay on topic, to have extended dialogues, to make relevant comments, to shift between topics, and to adjust their language to the context and to the speaker (Nippold, 1998). Pence and Justice (2012) have called the growing communicative skills of school-age children "functional flexibility." That is, children are developing the ability to communicate with a variety of people about many topics—to compare and contrast, hypothesize, classify, and perform many other sophisticated communicative acts. They are also learning how to adjust their communicative acts to the context—to different people, places, and subjects.

As you read the preceding paragraph, you may have wondered who these children are who possess such good conversational skills. You may have thought about children you know who butt in to conversations, who seem insensitive to the give-and-take of conversation, or who talk to teachers just as they talk to each other. But this is the point. We *expect* school-age children to be more competent and more sensitive conversational partners. When they let us down, we are justifiably disappointed. However, keep in mind that, as with other aspects of language, *competence* may exceed *performance*. In other words, although students may possess the language *ability*, they may fail to utilize their skill—for a variety of reasons.

As children become preadolescents and adolescents, important changes in communication continue to take place. Among these changes are a greater variety of conversational partners and the addition of new topics to their conversation (Nippold, 2000). It should not be surprising that researchers have found that adolescents spend an increasing amount of time talking to their peers (Raffaelli & Duckett, 1989). These researchers also found that conversations with family members do not decrease, even though peer interactions take on greater importance. Adolescents tended to talk about personal issues (such as dating) and affective topics (their feelings) much more with their friends than with their families. Researchers have also found differences in the quality of conversations with peers compared to adults. When talking to peers, adolescents tend to ask more questions, obtain more information, shift to new topics more often, and make more attempts to entertain their partners, especially with humor (Larson & McKinley, 1998).

In addition to their developing communicative competence, school-age children are developing other pragmatic skills. For example, their ability to understand and use **indirect requests** is increasing. This is a critical skill for school success. When a teacher says, "It's getting noisy in here," she is really saying, "Be quiet." The child who is not able to *understand* indirect requests may misunderstand the message and be punished for misbehavior. Indirect requests take place when the communicative intent differs from the linguistic form. In the preceding example, the linguistic form is that of a declarative sentence (*It's getting noisy in here*), but the communicative intent is a command (*Be quiet*). During the school years, children become more adept at using indirect requests, recognizing that they are more likely to get what they want by saying, "Gee, I'm hungry," than by saying, "Give me another cookie."

Another important pragmatic language development during the school years is increasing skill in storytelling (narratives). If you have been around preschool children, you know that this skill develops over time. Three year olds tend to tell incomplete stories. They may start in the middle, forget the ending, and throw in unknown characters with no explanation. However, by the time they enter school, most children have acquired the ability to tell a story from beginning to end. Stadler and Ward (2005) have identified five levels of narrative development in children: labeling, listing, connecting, sequencing, and narrating. They note that narrative skills have been found to be an important factor in emergent literacy.

 Watch these two videos of children telling a fictional story. The first features a 6-year-old child. The second features a 9-year-old child. What differences do you note in the narrative skills of the two students? What is similar? What is different?

Narrative skills are important for success in school. Children are often asked to report what they did over the weekend or on their summer vacation, or to write a story about an event that happened in the past. These activities require narrative skill. Although even young children can tell stories, as children mature, their stories take on more adult forms such as the use of beginning and end markers (e.g., *once upon a time* and *lived happily ever after*). Older children's narratives include the following elements:

- Fewer unresolved problems and unprepared resolutions
- Less extraneous detail
- More overt marking of changes in time and place
- More introduction, including setting and character information
- Greater concern for motivation and internal reactions
- More complex episode structure
- Closer adherence to the story grammar model (Johnston, 1982, as cited in Owens, 2015)

The last element in this list is *story grammar*. What is this? Stories tend to consist of several components with underlying rules that give the story structure. Stories have elements such as characters, setting, and plot. They have a beginning, middle, and end. Typically developing children become more aware of these structures and rules as they advance in school and increasingly use these structures in their own stories (Owens, 2015). Clearly, this is a development that sets the stage for the growth of literacy skills in the school years.

The school years are characterized by rapid expansion of vocabulary and increasingly sophisticated pragmatic language skills. These and other language developments both set the stage for literacy development and are influenced by encounters with text. A brief summary of the development of semantics and pragmatics in the school years appears in Table 6.2.

Table 6.2

Development of Semantics and Pragmatics in the School Years

Semantics	Pragmatics
Rapid expansion of vocabulary	Greater variety of conversational partners
Understand multiple meaning words	More variety in conversational topics
Increase understanding of figurative language, including:	Improved understanding of indirect requests
Metaphor	Development of narrative skills
Humor	
Proverbs	

Metalinguistic Ability

When we ask children to sound out words, to analyze sentences into their constituent parts, to complete a map of story elements, or to identify rules of language, we are asking them to use **metalinguistic abilities**. Metalinguistic ability allows the child to go beyond language use and to think *about* language.

By the time they enter school, children have a substantial amount of language ability, but they are generally not aware of what they know. Have you ever tried asking a first grader to differentiate grammatical from nongrammatical sentences? Many first graders can tell you which ones are the "bad" sentences, but when asked to explain their reasoning, they encounter difficulty. They may look at you with a blank stare or say something like, "It just doesn't sound right." They *know* the rules of grammar, but they cannot *say* them. By second or third grade, however, most children can state a rule to support their answer. They can tell you that nouns must come before verbs or that word endings must agree in number. This observation has been confirmed by research, such as that by Sutter and Johnson (1990).

One type of metalinguistic awareness is **phonemic awareness**. Phonemic awareness has been defined as "the ability to focus on and manipulate phonemes in spoken words" (Ehri et al., 2001, p. 253). Phonemic awareness is a key skill for learning to read and write English because a single letter may represent several different sounds. For example, the letter *c* may sound like *k* as in *cake* but sound like *s* in the word *celery*. Similarly, a single sound (such as *s*) may be represented by more than one letter. In order to figure out which sounds go with each letter, children must first learn to identify the sounds (phonemic awareness) within speech and then learn to match these sounds to letters (phonics).

In this video, a learning specialist explains phonological and phonemic awareness and how they are related to early reading. What kind of tasks does she suggest to enhance these skills?
https://www.youtube.com/watch?v=8JNVzioC7lc

By the time they enter school, most children can recognize all the phonemes of English. Once in school, they are required to become *aware* of these sounds and use them in reading. That is, they must bring to conscious awareness their underlying knowledge of the sound system of their language. This is what is meant by phonemic awareness. Children are asked to divide words into sounds, to become aware of rhyme, and to count the number of sounds in a word. In order to perform tasks such as these, children must have awareness of the phonological characteristics of their language. A great deal of research over the past 25 years has found that children who are more skilled in phonological awareness are usually better readers (Ehri et al., 2001), whereas children with reading disorders are often deficient in phonological skills (Vellutino, Fletcher, Snowling, & Scanlon, 2004).

The phonological theory of reading and reading disorders has become the dominant view among researchers interested in how children develop reading and writing skills. In fact, Stanovich (1991) went so far as to call this finding "one of the more notable scientific success stories of the last decade" (p. 78). The theory claims that children with poor phonological skills have difficulty identifying the sounds within words. As a result, these children have difficulty making the association between the sound of words and their print representations (letters). This leads to poor word recognition and, ultimately, to poor comprehension (since children cannot read the words on the page).

Phonemic skills have also been found to predict reading success. For example, Storch and Whitehurst (2002) examined reading development and language skills in 626 children who attended Head Start programs. They followed the progress of these children from age 4 through fourth grade. They found that phonological skills (along with print recognition) were the most important predictors of reading in the early grades but that other language skills became more important in grades three and four.

Metalinguistic skills are important for school success. School activities such as reading, spelling, and writing often require children to use their knowledge of language in new ways. Children are asked to break words down into sounds or other units, to identify word endings, and to learn to identify the parts of speech that they have been using naturally for years.

Implications for Instruction

Knowledge of language development during the school years can help teachers organize and plan for instruction. For example, the research on pragmatic language indicates that adolescents converse differently with their peers than with adults. They are more relaxed, more talkative, and more concerned that their conversation partners understand what they are saying. When older students are required to talk to adults or are asked to talk to the class, they may appear shy, be reluctant to talk, and use short responses. They probably are not interested in that type of conversational interaction. But it is important to remember that these characteristics may not represent the actual conversational competence of these students. Observing students in interaction with their peers, especially in informal settings, may give a more accurate picture of their conversational abilities. Likewise, for students with communication disorders, testing situations and structured intervention sessions with adults may be of limited value. Instead, observations of informal interaction and peer interaction are more likely to expose the student's conversational skills.

Children's literature often uses many forms of figurative language, including metaphor, simile, and proverbs. These can be cognitively and linguistically difficult to understand. Nippold (1998) developed an instructional approach for enhancing proverb understanding in adolescents. Working in small groups, students learn to use contextual cues to determine the meaning of difficult words contained in the proverb (e.g., *expectation, realization*), learn to ask and answer factual and inferential questions about the proverb, and think about how the proverb could be used in their own lives.

Knowing that school-age children are still developing their understanding and use of some language structures may help teachers in their interaction with students. For example, many children in the early elementary grades would have a difficult time understanding indirect requests. Likewise, young children may have a hard time understanding humor. Older children may have difficulty understanding and using more sophisticated linguistic forms such as gerunds and the passive voice. It is not uncommon for teachers to assume that students know all they need to know to be effective readers and productive writers by third or fourth grade. But the research on language development suggests that students are continuing to develop some language skills throughout the school years.

Conclusion

Language development in the school years evolves in two ways: elaboration of existing structures and acquisition of new structures. During the school years, children build on their earlier language development—refining previous structures and broadening their use of these structures—while, at the same time, they continue to develop new structures. They can understand and use increasingly complex sentences, passive sentences, figurative language, and subtle conversational rules for a summary. School-age children also develop metalinguistic ability—the ability to think about language and apply language to other purposes (e.g., reading and writing). It would be incorrect to think of language development as ending at age 5 or 6. In fact, language continues to change and develop throughout life.

Check Your Understanding 6.1

Click here to gauge your understanding of the concepts in this section.

Language Development and Literacy

Learning to read and write is key to success in school and in life after school. Children who read well are able to acquire more knowledge more quickly than other children. For example, researchers have reported that a middle school child who reads a lot could read as many as 10,000,000 words a year, compared to a poor reader who might read as few as 100,000 words (Nagy & Anderson, 1984). Avid readers are exposed to more new concepts and more words than unmotivated readers. As a result, the learning gap between good and poor readers widens over time.

Teachers and researchers have been searching for many years for ways to close the reading gap. The U.S. government has made the achievement of literacy skills one of the key objectives of the federal No Child Left Behind Act. The goal is for all children, including those from diverse socioeconomic groups and those with disabilities, to acquire the literacy skills that will enable them to achieve. Schools are told to adopt reading programs that have a record of success.

Despite lofty goals and the greater use of effective instructional practices, many students still struggle to acquire effective reading and writing skills. Most children with early reading problems continue to experience difficulty throughout their school careers. On the other hand, few children who start out as good readers end up having reading difficulties later in school (Scarborough, 1998). These findings have led researchers to focus on the skills that young children bring to school. One of these skills is language. What is the relationship between language acquisition and success in reading and writing?

There can be little doubt that language ability plays an essential role in the development of reading and writing. A great deal of research has been conducted in the past 30 years that has established the language basis for literacy (e.g., National Institute of Child Health and Human Development Study of Early Child Care Research Network, 2005).

A number of specific language skills have been identified as critical for reading success. These include syntax, semantics, vocabulary, phonological knowledge, and linguistic awareness (Whitehurst & Lonigan, 1998). Of these specific components of language, the one that has received the most attention from researchers is **phonological awareness**. As we noted earlier in this chapter, research has established that children's sensitivity to the sounds of their language and their ability to manipulate those sounds is related to the acquisition of reading skills (Bradley & Bryant, 1985; Wagner & Torgesen, 1987).

Phonemic Awareness and Reading

Phonological awareness is a term that is generally used to describe a range of skills that involve the understanding, use, and recall of sounds. Phonemic awareness is a type of phonological skill that involves language sounds (phonemes). Ehri and colleagues (2001) identified the following subskills related to phonemic awareness:

1. *Phoneme isolation*, which requires recognizing individual sounds in words; for example, "Tell me the first sound in paste." (/p/)

2. *Phoneme identity*, which requires recognizing the common sound in different words; for example, "Tell me the sound that is the same in bike, boy, and bell." (/b/)

3. *Phoneme categorization*, which requires recognizing the word with the odd sound in a sequence of three or four words; for example, "Which word does not belong: bus, bun, or rug?" (rug)

4. *Phoneme blending*, which requires listening to a sequence of separately spoken sounds and combining them to form a recognizable word; for example, "What word is /s/ /k/ /u/ /l/?" (school)

5. *Phoneme segmentation*, which requires breaking a word into its sounds by tapping out or counting the sounds or by pronouncing and positioning a marker for each sound; for example, "How many phonemes are in ship?" (three: /sh/ /i/ /p/)

6. *Phoneme deletion*, which requires recognizing what word remains when a specified phoneme is removed; for example, "What is smile without the /s/?" (mile)

There are both informal and formal methods that can be used to assess phonemic awareness in children. Informal assessment of phonemic awareness might include one or more of the following tasks (Al Otaiba, Kosanovich, & Torgesen, 2012):

- *Phoneme segmentation*: Counting, pronouncing, deleting, adding, or reversing phonemes in words (e.g., "How many sounds are in the word *cat*?")
- *Phoneme synthesis*: Blending sounds heard individually (e.g., /c/-/a/-/t/)
- *Sound comparison*: Identifying which sounds begin or end with the same sound as a target word

Another option is to use the Yopp-Singer Test of Phoneme Segmentation (Yopp, 1995). This 22-item test takes only about 5 minutes to give and gives a quick measure of the child's ability to divide words into their sound constituents.

 Watch as a teacher administers the Yopp-Singer Test to a 5-year-old child. What do the child's responses indicate about his development of phonemic awareness? https://www.youtube.com/watch?v=tJdw-kxnXM0

There are a number of formal tests of phonemic awareness such as the Preschool Individual Growth and Development Indicators (IGDIs) and the Phonological Awareness and Literacy Screening (PALS) for Preschool (PALS-PreK). The IGDIs assess language and literacy skills in children ages 3 to 5 (see the Infant and Toddler IGDIs website). The test includes subtests in picture naming, rhyming, and alliteration. The PALS-PreK measures children's phonological awareness skills with three subtests: beginning sound awareness (recognition of alliteration), rhyme awareness, and nursery rhyme awareness. You can find more information about the PALS tests at the University of Virginia website (search for "PALS University of Virginia"). Many formal tests of reading include subtests that assess phonemic awareness. A list of these tests can be found in Chapter 14.

Is phonological ability the only language-based skill that is essential for reading success? It is becoming clear that, although phonological skills are critical for early reading, other language skills may also be important. In fact, other language skills may be more important than phonological skills for older readers and for more difficult reading material. What is the evidence to support this conclusion?

The language and reading development of more than 1,000 children was studied by the National Institute of Health Early Child Care Research Network (2005). These children were followed from age 36 months through grade three. The researchers found that broad language skills, not just phonological skills, were related to first-grade word recognition and to third-grade reading comprehension. Other researchers (e.g., Catts, Fey, Zhang, & Tomblin, 1999; Tunmer, Herriman, & Nesdale, 1988) have also concluded that both phonological and other language abilities are important for early reading success. Scarborough (2005) has listed a number of arguments against the phonological model as the sole (or even most important) predictor of reading, including the following:

1. *Measures of phonological awareness are not the strongest predictors of the future reading levels of beginning students.* Phonological skills are a significant predictor, but letter-identification skills are more important, and other language skills (such as expressive vocabulary and sentence recall) are also significant factors.

2. *The risk of developing a reading disability is as great for preschoolers with nonphonological language impairments as for those with impairments in phonological skills.* Children with nonphonological language disabilities have been found to be at significant risk for reading difficulties.

3. *Severe deficits in decoding and word recognition skills can emerge after third grade in children who progressed satisfactorily in reading acquisition in the primary grades.* Some children can develop phonological disabilities at later ages. These children seemed to have intact phonological skills at an early age but developed word-level processing problems in later grades.

4. *Successful reading comprehension is often accomplished by students with severe word recognition and decoding deficiencies.* Although the phonological model suggests that students with poor phonological skills will have reading comprehension difficulties, some studies have not found this to be true.

What can we conclude about phonological abilities and reading? There can be little doubt that phonological ability—in particular, phonemic awareness—is strongly related to early reading success; this is especially true for word identification. Phonological ability may be an important factor in reading comprehension, but it appears that it is not the only factor. Some researchers have concluded that broad language ability, not just phonological skill, is most predictive of reading success, especially for reading comprehension (Storch & Whitehurst, 2002; Vellutino, Tunmer, Jaccard, & Chen, 2007). What are some of the specific language skills (in addition to phonological) that have been found to be related to reading?

Syntactic Skills and Reading

Earlier in this chapter, we cited research that had found that phonological knowledge, along with letter identification, was the best predictor of early reading success. However, when Scarborough (1998) reviewed a large number of research studies that examined kindergarten performance as a predictor of later reading scores, she found a number of other language measures (including general expressive and receptive language skills and sentence recall) to be as good or better predictors of reading success. Performance on these measures depends to a great degree on children's syntactic knowledge. Scarborough claims that syntactic knowledge (along with other language skills) is important for the development of reading comprehension. As children advance in reading, comprehension becomes more important, so syntactic knowledge becomes more critical. Other researchers (e.g., Tunmer, Herriman, & Nesdale, 1988) have found that successful reading may require both good phonological knowledge and good syntactic knowledge.

Semantic Skills and Reading

Semantic knowledge may also be a significant contributor to reading success. Research studies that have looked at factors that predict reading success have usually found that expressive and receptive vocabulary are important factors. Vocabulary knowledge becomes even more important as students begin to read in the content areas. Poor comprehenders have been found to use less effective strategies for storing semantic information (Nation & Snowling, 1999), which may affect their ability to understand what they read. The same researchers have reported that 8- and 9-year-old poor comprehenders were slower and less accurate at synonym judgments than age-matched control children (Nation, Clarke, Marshall, & Durand, 2004; Nation & Snowling, 1998). A study of the relationship between the oral vocabulary and literacy skills of 8- to 10-year-old children by Ricketts, Nation, and Bishop (2007) found that children with poor reading comprehension had weaker vocabulary skills but that vocabulary skills were not highly related to most word recognition skills. After reviewing the research on the relationship between vocabulary knowledge and comprehension, Elleman, Lindo, Morphy, and Compton (2009) concluded that, although the findings for competent readers were mixed, there was a much stronger link for students with reading difficulties. The results of research lend support to the conclusion that semantic skills are an important factor in the development of reading comprehension.

Narrative Skills

In addition to being able to understand and use language structure (syntax) and meaning (semantics), there is increasing evidence that good readers and writers also have good narrative (pragmatic) skills. Students with effective narrative skills are good at understanding and composing stories. They understand that most stories have a beginning, middle, and end and that it is important to make appropriate connections so that the listener (or reader) can understand what is going on. In typically developing children, narratives become longer and more complex with age. Children who have been exposed to extended discourse have been found to be better prepared for beginning reading (Tabors, Snow, & Dickinson, 2001). On the other hand, the narrative styles of some children have been found to be related to problems in reading (Vernon-Feagans, Hammer, Miccio, & Manlove, 2001).

Instructional Implications

Today there is little question among researchers and practitioners that language skills are an essential factor in reading success. But questions remain about which language abilities are most important. It seems clear that phonological abilities are important for success in word recognition. Children with good phonological skills tend to be better (initial) readers, whereas those with poor phonological skills often struggle. But reading is more than word recognition. As children progress beyond the initial stages of reading, comprehension becomes increasingly important.

The relationship between literacy and language is complex. There is consensus among researchers that language and literacy are related. Support for this conclusion comes from studies such as that by Hay, Elias, Fielding-Barnsley, Homel, and Freiberg (2007), which found that children with language difficulties who received classroom-based language intervention significantly outperformed similar children who did not receive this intervention on end-of-year measures of reading. But specifying just which language skills at which ages are related to specific aspects of reading has been challenging. As Dickinson, Golinkoff, and Hirsh-Pasek (2010) noted, because of its pervasive effects on development, the impact of language on reading can be difficult to measure.

What can we conclude about the relationship between language and literacy? First, it seems clear that one aspect of language, phonological skills, is clearly related to early reading success. This is likely due to the importance of phonemic awareness in word recognition. Second, it is becoming increasingly clear that other language skills, including semantic, syntactic, and pragmatic (narrative) skills, are related to reading comprehension skill.

The research on language and literacy has important implications for educational practice. First, it is important that all teachers understand the language basis of literacy. This was one of the conclusions reached by the authors of the National Academy of Education publication, *Knowledge to Support the Teaching of Reading* (Snow, Griffin, & Burns, 2005). Unfortunately, many teachers have little or no knowledge of language development and the relationship between knowledge and literacy.

Second, knowledge about the reading–language connection can help teachers and other education professionals identify children at risk for reading and writing difficulties. Observation and assessment of language skills, especially phonological knowledge in beginning readers, can help focus instruction on children who need it the most. Similarly, knowing the language skills that are related to successful reading comprehension can help identify children with potential comprehension difficulties.

Finally, knowledge about the relationship between language and literacy can help teachers improve reading and writing success. As we noted in the beginning of this section, despite a significant focus on reading, many children continue to struggle with literacy, falling further behind their peers. We now know a great deal about how to help children learn to read. Unfortunately, this knowledge has not always made its way into the classroom. It is essential that knowledgeable teachers, working in collaboration with other professionals (such as speech-language specialists and reading specialists), apply what research has documented as effective practices to the education of all students. In the next chapter, we will review several instructional programs that are designed to enhance phonemic awareness.

Check Your Understanding 6.2
Click here to gauge your understanding of the concepts in this section.

Summary

Language development does not end when children enter school. Indeed, elements of language continue to develop throughout the school years. Children learn to use more complex syntactic structures and combinations of structures in novel ways. Their vocabulary expands dramatically, and they become more sophisticated users of figurative language. Children become more sophisticated communicators as they expand their range of communicative partners and the topics of their interaction.

The development of reading and writing skills depends to a large extent on language. Students with better overall language skills have a greater chance for successful development of literacy skills. Phonological awareness is especially important for word recognition at the beginning stage of reading, but other language skills are important as well. It is important for teachers to understand language development and how it relates to academic success in order to identify children at risk for reading and writing difficulties and to be able to help all students succeed.

Language, Students with Learning Disabilities, and Students with Attention Deficit Hyperactivity Disorder

Students with learning disabilities comprise a large, if somewhat poorly defined, segment of the population of children with special needs. This chapter describes both the specific language characteristics of children with learning disabilities and the effects of these language difficulties on their academic and social performance. In addition, the language and communication difficulties of students with attention deficit hyperactivity disorder are reviewed. Although these are considered separate disorders, both children with learning disabilities and those with attention deficit disorders often have language difficulties that impact their school success. Some suggestions are provided for teaching children with language-learning disabilities.

Learning Outcomes

After reading this chapter, you should be able to:

1. Explain the difficulties in defining learning disabilities and attention deficit hyperactivity disorder.

2. Identify the major language difficulties experienced by many students with learning disabilities and those with attention deficit hyperactivity disorder and the impact of language difficulties on learning.

3. Identify appropriate instructional approaches for students with language-learning disabilities.

Keisha W.: A Case Study

Keisha W. is an 8-year-old African American student in a regular second-grade class. Her teacher is concerned about her lack of progress in reading and her poor socialization. The teacher also reports that Keisha is pleasant and cooperative but is very shy and reluctant to participate in groups. Keisha is reading at an early first-grade level, and her reading is slow and hesitant. Her first-grade teacher noticed similar problems with reading and socialization but hoped that the child would outgrow these problems.

Mrs. W. has struggled to provide for Keisha and her two brothers since her husband left her 3 years ago.

Mrs. W. has held a succession of low-paying jobs and has been unemployed several times. The family lives in public housing in a high-crime neighborhood. Mrs. W. has reported that Keisha's early development was normal, although she remembers that Keisha had frequent colds and earaches and was always a quiet child.

Keisha was observed in the classroom during a group reading lesson and during group work on a writing assignment that followed the reading lesson. When called on to read, she read very quietly. She hesitated frequently and misread a number of words. She needed a great deal of

(continued)

Keisha W.: A Case Study   Continued

assistance to complete a paragraph. However, when asked a question about the passage, she responded correctly. During the group activity, Keisha kept to herself; she joined in only when prompted to do so by her teacher.

Keisha was tested for possible classification for special educational services. Her Wechsler Intelligence Scale for Children–Fourth Edition (WISC-IV) scores in the major cognitive areas clustered within the average range. Within the verbal area, her results varied from the 6- to the 9-year levels. The Test of Language Development-3 (Primary) was administered and yielded a spoken language quotient (SLQ) of 84. This score placed Keisha in the below-average range. Her test profile indicated that her lowest scores were in word articulation and word discrimination—elements of phonology. Keisha scored highest in grammatical understanding and picture vocabulary.

What are we to make of a case like Keisha's? Here is a child who seems to be bright and does not have a behavior problem, yet she is struggling to succeed in school. What

is wrong? It is because of cases like Keisha's that the term *learning disability* was developed. Keisha must have a disability that diminishes her ability to learn, some would argue. As a result, she is not achieving to her potential. Yet, calling her "learning disabled" certainly does not solve Keisha's problems. We want to know more about her. What exactly is wrong? What can be done?

In this report, there are several hints that Keisha has some sort of language-based learning disability. For example, her difficulty reading words, her reluctance to talk, and results from the language testing could indicate a language-based disability. Yet, Keisha talks normally and can communicate when she is encouraged to do so. Her language disorder, if indeed there is one, is really quite subtle. In order to better understand Keisha and other children like her, we will examine the term *learning disabilities* and the relationship between language disorders and learning disabilities.

Defining Learning Disabilities and Attention Deficit Hyperactivity Disorder

What is a learning disability? How do we know that such a thing even exists? In 1960, there were no classes for children labeled *learning disabled*. In the 2011–2012 school year, there were over 2.3 million children classified as learning disabled in the public schools of the United States (4.7% of the entire school population). Although this is a very large number of children, the percentage of the school population identified as learning disabled has actually decreased from a high of 6.1 percent in the 2000–2001 school year to 4.7 percent in the 2011–2012 school year (U.S. Department of Education, 2015). Cortiella and Horowitz (2014) identified several factors that may explain the decrease in identification of students with learning disabilities, including expansion of early childhood education, improvements in reading intervention, and efforts such as the use of the response to intervention (RTI) approach (see the RTI Action Network website) to identify children with learning difficulties at an early age and provide intervention in the general education classroom without formal identification (Cortiella & Horowitz, 2014).

Where did all of these children with learning difficulties come from? The answer to this question lies partly in the history of the term *learning disability* and partly in its definition. Dr. Samuel Kirk proposed the term in 1963 to describe "a group of children who have disorders in development of language, speech, reading, and associated skills needed for social interaction" (Kirk, 1963, p. 2). Kirk's proposal resonated with professionals who worked with children who had been identified by a variety of labels, including perceptually impaired, brain damaged, borderline mentally retarded, dyslexic, childhood aphasic, and so on. Now there was one label that could be used to identify children with significant learning difficulties.

Although the term *learning disabilities* helped consolidate the young field of special education and channel research funding into better understanding of significant learning difficulties, it also set off a search for the "cause" of learning disabilities—a search that continues to this day.

Early theories of learning disabilities focused on perceptual deficiencies, especially auditory and visual perception, as the probable cause. It was hypothesized that students with learning disabilities had particular difficulty integrating perception with motor functions (perceptual–motor functioning).

Assessment batteries and intervention materials were developed and disseminated. Although some children may have been helped, the perceptual–motor theory of learning disabilities ultimately faltered on evidence that, in most cases, perceptual and perceptual–motor intervention simply did not work (Kavale & Mattson, 1983). Still, vestiges of the perceptual theory of learning disabilities linger to this day.

In the 1980s and 1990s, the information-processing theory of learning disabilities was predominant. This theory grew out of what was being learned about processing information in the rapidly developing computer field. Applied to humans, information-processing theory provided sophisticated models of learning that showed how information might flow and be altered during the learning process. It also helped researchers describe how learning might break down and cause the sort of learning problems seen in children identified as learning disabled. Intervention methods such as learning strategies were developed to help children overcome their information-processing deficiencies. Information-processing theory presented a more sophisticated explanation of what might be causing the academic and social difficulties characteristic of individuals with learning disabilities, but it has proved hard to implement in practice. In addition, many children with learning disabilities exhibit no clear pattern of information-processing difficulties.

One of the difficulties in defining learning disabilities is that we appear to be searching for a single underlying cause for a group of disabilities that is unlikely to have a single cause. Partly as a response to this dilemma, the **response to intervention (RTI)** model emerged as an alternative way to identify children with learning disabilities. Rather than searching for internal learning difficulties, the focus of the RTI model is on examining the outcomes of instruction. Students who fail to keep pace with their peers receive supplementary instruction designed to help them improve their learning and catch up with their classmates. In the past decade, the RTI model has become widely used in the United States, although, as Fuchs and Deshler (2007) note, a number of issues remain to be addressed, including the application of the model to older students and to content area reading and writing. The RTI Action Network has developed a checklist for identifying students with suspected learning disabilities on their website (search for RTI Action Network and click on "Checklists").

Another approach to understanding individuals with learning disabilities is to identify subgroups within the general population. The International Dyslexia Association (2012) estimates that approximately 85 percent of children with learning disabilities have difficulties primarily in reading and language. Although debate among researchers continues, there is a growing consensus that reading disorders are caused by difficulties with language. If true, this theory can help practitioners identify and intervene with children at risk for learning difficulties. Although there may be different causes of the learning difficulties experienced by other children labeled as learning disabled, the subgroup approach helps narrow the search for causative factors. Of course, in a sense, looking for subgroups marks a return to the days before the use of a single label, but that might be a necessary step in order to better identify and teach children with learning disabilities.

Another group of children that is sometimes included in discussions of learning disabilities is students with attention deficit hyperactivity disorders. Attention deficit hyperactivity disorder (ADHD) has been defined as "a persistent pattern of inattention and/or hyperactivity-impulsivity that interferes with functioning or development" (American Psychiatric Association, 2013). The symptoms of ADHD include inattention, hyperactivity, and impulsivity.

By definition, ADHD is not a type of learning disability. However, up to 45 percent of children with ADHD exhibit academic learning difficulties similar to those experienced by students with learning disabilities (Du Paul, Gormley, & Laracy, 2014).

Watch this video to learn more about ADHD. What are the types of ADHD discussed in this video?
https://www.youtube.com/watch?v=0Wz7LdLFJVM

Existing definitions have done little to resolve the dilemma of learning disabilities. The definitions tend to be broad and offer little help to practitioners seeking to identify children in need of intensive remediation. For example, the federal definition of learning disabilities, incorporated in the Individuals with Disabilities Education Act (IDEA, 2004), states:

> The term "specific learning disability" means a disorder in one or more of the basic psychological processes involved in understanding or in using language, spoken or written, which disorder may manifest itself in imperfect ability to listen, think, speak, read, write, spell, or to do mathematical calculations. Such disorders include such conditions as perceptual handicaps, brain injury, minimal brain dysfunction, dyslexia, and developmental aphasia. Such term does not include children who have learning problems which are primarily the result of visual, hearing, or motor handicaps, of mental retardation, of emotional disturbance, or of environmental, cultural, or economic disadvantage.

The definition was designed to be broad and inclusive, although its last section was meant to exclude other causes of learning problems from the category of learning disabilities. However, the definition has been difficult to apply in practice. Until recently, IDEA required local education agencies (school districts) to use discrepancy between achievement (usually defined as standardized test scores) and potential (IQ) to identify students with learning disabilities. The 2004 amendments to IDEA make the use of discrepancy optional and call for a process that determines if a child responds to "scientific, research-based intervention" (the RTI approach mentioned earlier in this chapter).

In this video by the National Center on Learning Disabilities, they call learning disabilities an "umbrella term." What does this mean for understanding the concept of learning disabilities?
https://www.youtube.com/watch?v=yG_xSBsFMPQ

The federal definition of learning disabilities identifies disorders of language (spoken or written) as the defining feature of the disorder. The definition recognizes that most children labeled as learning disabled have difficulty understanding and using language. However, IDEA also includes the disability category of "speech or language impairment," which is defined as "a communication disorder, such as stuttering, impaired articulation, a language impairment, or a voice impairment, that adversely affects a child's educational performance." As you might imagine, there can be a lot of confusion about the terms *learning disability* and *speech or language impairment*. After all, according to the definitions, many children with "learning disabilities" have a disorder of language. But many children with "speech or language impairment" have difficulties with educational performance. To make matters worse, many speech-language specialists use an entirely different term (*specific language impairment [SLI]*) to describe children who have "a language deficit, but without accompanying factors such as hearing loss, low intelligence scores, or neurological damage" (Kaderavek, 2014). Researchers have found that up to 50 percent of children with reading disorders (the most common type of learning disability) may also meet the criteria for SLI and that a similar percentage of children with SLI could be considered reading disabled (McArthur, Hogben, Edwards, Heath, & Mengler, 2000). See Table 7.1 for a summary of definitions of learning disabilities.

Although there is a lot of overlap between learning disabilities and specific language impairments, there may be differences as well. Children with specific speech and language impairments are typically identified prior to entering formal schooling. Their

Table 7.1

Definitions of Learning
Disabilities and Related
Disorders

Category Label	Definition	Characteristics
Learning Disabled	Disorder in one or more of the basic psychological processes involved in understanding or in using language, spoken or written.	Difficulties in thinking, listening, speaking, reading, spelling, or math.
Speech or Language Impairment	A communication disorder—such as stuttering, impaired articulation, a language impairment, or a voice impairment—that adversely affects a child's educational performance.	Speech and/or language difficulties, usually apparent early in development, that impact learning.
Specific Language Impairment	A language deficit, but without accompanying factors such as hearing loss, low intelligence scores, or neurological damage.	Significant language difficulties, usually first identified at an early age.

Sources: Based on IDEA (2004); Kaderavek (2014).

language delays and differences are so significant that they have caught the attention of their parents, preschool teachers, or family physicians. Their language disabilities are usually more significant and affect several areas of language (Bishop & Snowling, 2004). On the other hand, children with learning disabilities are not usually identified until they enter school. Their difficulties first show up in school-related tasks. Their language difficulties may be more subtle and less pervasive than those encountered by children with specific language impairments.

Most of the research on the relationship between language and learning disabilities has been conducted with students whose primary learning difficulty is in reading and writing. The *Diagnostic and Statistical Manual of Mental Disorders,* Fifth Edition (DSM-V) definition of learning disabilities (specific learning disorder) includes subcategories for impairments in reading, writing, and mathematics. Within the reading subcategory, children can be diagnosed with difficulties in word reading accuracy, reading rate or fluency, or reading comprehension. Reading disabilities have been estimated to occur in approximately 10 to 15 percent of the school-age population (Shaywitz et al., 1992). Over the years, a number of different theories about the causes of specific reading disabilities have been proposed (see Vellutino, Fletcher, Snowling, & Scanlon, 2004, for a review). Today, however, there is a broad consensus among researchers that specific reading disabilities are caused by language difficulties (Catts, Fey, Zhang, & Tomblin, 1999; Scarborough, 2005).

Whatever we call them—learning disabled, reading disordered, dyslexic, specific language impaired—it is clear that there are a number of children who, despite normal intelligence, fail to learn adequately in typical classrooms. Although this is clearly a heterogeneous population, many, if not most, children with learning disabilities have language difficulties. That does not mean that children with learning disabilities do not have other contributing learning difficulties such as attention deficits, memory difficulties, or organizational problems. But many of these learning problems may, in fact, be mediated by underlying language difficulties.

Check Your Understanding 7.1
Click here to gauge your understanding of the concepts in this section.

Language, Learning Disabilities, and Attention Deficit Hyperactivity Disorder

Historically, many different causes for learning disabilities have been proposed. Possible causal factors have included brain injury, perceptual disorders, and differences in neurological processing (Lerner & Johns, 2015). For most children with learning disabilities, however, there is no readily identifiable cause for their learning difficulties. But contemporary views of the causes of learning disabilities focus primarily on language difficulties.

The evidence for the relationship between learning disabilities and language comes from a variety of sources. First, children with language difficulties have been found to be at high risk for reading difficulties (Bishop & Adams, 1990; Catts, 1993; Snowling, Bishop, & Stothard, 2000). For example, in a study of approximately 200 kindergarten children with language impairments, researchers found that by fourth grade more than 50 percent of the children performed significantly below average on a test of reading comprehension—a rate more than five times greater than children with typical language development (Catts, Fey, Tomblin, & Zhang, 2002). In addition, the severity of the language impairment was found to be related to the reading deficit.

The second type of evidence for a relationship between language and learning disabilities comes from studies that have reported the existence of specific language deficiencies in children with learning disabilities. Most of these studies have been conducted with children whose primary learning difficulty was in reading. These studies have identified a variety of language-learning deficits related to poor reading performance (Vellutino, Fletcher, Snowling, & Scanlon, 2004). Although phonological processing difficulties have most often been found to be related to reading difficulties, researchers have more recently focused on children whose primary reading difficulties are in reading comprehension rather than in word attack. Children with reading comprehension difficulties have been found to have difficulty in many areas of language, including vocabulary knowledge and syntactic skills, but not phonological awareness (Nation, Cocksey, Taylor, & Bishop, 2010).

Although there is overwhelming evidence that reading disabilities are related to language disabilities, there continues to be debate about which aspects of language are most important. There is a growing consensus among researchers that there appear to be two types of reading disabilities. One type (often called "dyslexia") is caused primarily by deficits in phonological processing. The second type is caused by difficulties in various aspects of language (Catts, Adlof, Hogan, & Weismer, 2005). Moreover, Catts and others (e.g., Snowling & Hayiou-Thomas, 2006) have claimed that children with phonological disorders are more likely to have problems with word attack, whereas children with more general language difficulties have problems primarily in comprehension (Catts, Adlof, & Weismer, 2006). Let's examine in more detail the evidence for language-learning disabilities in students with reading and learning disabilities.

Phonology

Deficits in phonological awareness—especially phonemic awareness—have been found to be highly related to reading failure. Phonological awareness is an ability that develops over time in typically developing children. By 5 years of age, most children can divide words into syllables, but they are just beginning to be able to divide words into sound units (phonemes). There is a great deal of evidence that children's sensitivity to the sounds of their language and their ability to manipulate those sounds is related to the acquisition of reading skills (Bradley & Bryant, 1983; Wagner & Torgesen, 1987). In fact, phonological awareness and memory have been found to be highly predictive of reading success by both the National Early Literacy Panel (2008) and by the National Reading Panel (2000). As noted in Chapter 6, good readers tend to have good phonological skills, whereas poor readers lag behind in the development of phonological awareness.

> Watch this video of a therapist working with a young child on learning to associate sounds with letters. How does the therapist help the child make the association between letters and sounds?

Deficiencies in a number of phonological skills have been identified in children with reading disabilities, including difficulty dividing syllables into phonemes (Fox & Routh, 1980), identification of sounds, phoneme segmentation and detecting rhyme (Blachman, 2000; Bradley & Bryant, 1983; Brady, Shankweiler, & Mann, 1983; Snowling, 2000; Torgesen, Wagner, & Rashotte, 1994; Tunmer, 1989; Vellutino, Scanlon, & Spearing, 1995). Early difficulties with phonological processing have been found to be related to later reading and writing problems, especially when they co-occur with other language difficulties (Lewis, Freebairn, & Taylor, 2000).

In their review of the research, Vellutino and colleagues (2004) concluded that "there is now strong and highly convergent evidence in support of weak phonological coding as an underlying cause of the [specific reading disability] disorder" (p. 12). With so many studies reaching a similar conclusion, there can be little doubt that phonological awareness plays a very important role in reading disorders.

Morphology

There is increasing evidence that morphological skills also play an important role in the development of literacy skills and in explaining literacy disorders. Research has found that morphological knowledge is related to vocabulary development, word reading, spelling, and reading comprehension (Apel, Wilson-Fowler, Brimo, & Perrin, 2012; Nagy, Carlisle, & Goodwin, 2013; Tong, Deacon, Kirby, Cain, & Parrila, 2011). Morphological awareness is important because it helps children analyze and understand complex words. Poor morphological skills can contribute to learning disorders in reading. For example, Casalis, Cole, and Sopo (2004) studied morphological awareness in French children with reading disorders (dyslexia). They found that morphological awareness (as well as phonological awareness) was poorer for the children with reading disorders than for their peers without reading disorders. Siegel (2008) compared the morphological awareness skills of sixth graders with reading disorders (dyslexia) to a group of English language learners and children with English as their first language. She assessed each group on a variety of reading tasks that included both morphological and phonological skills. Although there was little difference between the English language learners and native English speakers, the children with reading disorders did much more poorly on the tasks that measured morphological awareness.

Syntax

Research on the syntactic skills of children with learning disabilities has been clouded by some of the issues in definition we discussed earlier in this chapter. In other words, the answer to whether children with reading and learning disabilities have deficits in syntax depends on how one identifies learning disabilities. That may explain why some researchers have reported that children with learning disabilities have deficiencies in syntactic skills, whereas others have not found such problems. For example, a number of studies that used standardized tests of language skills have found that children with learning disabilities, especially those with reading disorders, have poor syntactic skills when compared to their peers of the same age without reading disorders (e.g., Bishop & Snowling, 2004; Catts et al., 1999; Mokhtari & Thompson, 2006; Nation, Clarke, Marshall, & Durand, 2004). Students with learning disabilities have been reported to have difficulty understanding syntactic structures such as complex sentences (e.g., those that contain relative clauses and use the passive voice) (Vogel, 1974) and to use shorter and less complex sentences (Simms & Crump, 1983). Other studies have not found significant problems with syntax in children with reading and learning disabilities (Roth & Spekman, 1989; Shankweiler et al., 1995).

Why the differences in findings? Again, part of the answer lies in how one defines learning disabilities. Are we talking about students with reading disorders, language difficulties, math deficiencies, or all of the above? It would not be surprising to find different results depending on the nature of the learning problems of the children studied. In an attempt to get a more definitive picture of the syntactic skills of students with learning disabilities, Scott and Windsor (2000) carefully chose 20 children with language-learning disabilities. Each student had expressive language difficulties (measured by the Test of Language Development) and a specific reading impairment. These children were matched by the researchers with children of the same chronological age and to younger, typically developing children with a similar language age as the children with language-learning disabilities. All of the children watched videotapes and then were asked either to tell or to write a story about what they had seen. The researchers evaluated the children's responses on four major criteria: productivity, lexical diversity (vocabulary), grammatical complexity, and grammatical error. The results showed that children with learning disabilities produced shorter and less complex utterances than the group of the same chronological age but were similar to the younger children matched for language age. Similar results were found for grammatical complexity and for errors, although the group with language disabilities made more errors than either of the other groups. There were no differences found on lexical diversity (vocabulary), except in writing. The students with learning disabilities used less diverse vocabulary. The researchers concluded that children with the type of syntactic difficulties found in this study would have a very difficult time functioning in a regular education classroom. Their speaking and writing would be shorter, less grammatically complex, and filled with errors.

Although there has been conflicting evidence about the syntactic functioning of students with learning disabilities, there is sufficient evidence to suggest that syntax is an area of concern. The sort of problems experienced by children with learning disabilities may not always be obvious in spoken language, but these problems become more identifiable in reading and in written output.

Semantics

The acquisition and application of semantic knowledge are significant problems for many students with learning disabilities. In particular, research has discovered two main problem areas: **word finding** and the use of figurative language. Many studies have found that the expressive vocabulary skills of children with learning disabilities lag behind those of other children (e.g., Rudel, Denckla, & Broman, 1981). Children with a variety of learning disabilities, including reading disorders, take longer to retrieve words from memory than typically developing children (Bishop & Snowling, 2004; Catts et al., 1999). Some researchers believe that this word-finding problem is characteristic of children with reading disorders (Wolf, Bowers, & Biddle, 2000). In addition to their word-finding problems, students with learning disabilities have been reported to have difficulty with word meanings. Children with reading comprehension deficits have been found to have overall deficiencies in vocabulary (Catts et al., 2006).

Studies of children with learning disabilities have also reported specific problems with **figurative** (or nonliteral) **language**, such as understanding and using metaphors (Nippold & Fey, 1983), similes (Seidenberg & Bernstein, 1986), and idioms (Qualls, Lantza, Pietrzykb, Blood, & Hammera, 2004). Problems understanding and using nonliteral language may reflect the rigidity with which many students with learning disabilities seem to approach language. That is, it seems as though they become attached to the most concrete meaning of words, even when this clearly makes no sense in the context. Nonliteral language is often an important part of the curriculum; metaphors and similes are important language devices that are used in many stories. Students are asked to use such devices in their own writing (and are graded accordingly).

Pragmatics

Although most of the research on language and learning disabilities has focused on reading disorders, there are other ways that language may affect learning. For example, many children with learning disabilities experience significant difficulty with aspects of social skill development (Bryan, Burstein, & Ergul, 2004). Children with language-learning disabilities have been found to participate in fewer peer interactions and are less preferred communication partners (Weiner & Schneider, 2002). As a result, they often are less accepted by their peers and have difficulty establishing friendships. Since much of social interaction is language based, there is likely a relationship between social skills and the use of language for communication (pragmatics). Research has consistently found the area of pragmatics to be a major problem for children with learning disabilities (Boucher, 1986; Lapadat, 1991; Troia, 2011). Not only do these students have difficulties with language, but they often lack the ability (or the knowledge) to analyze social situations, to plan their responses, and to evaluate the consequences of their actions (Bryan, 1991; Vaughn, 1991).

 In this video, two boys are having a conversation. What does the video suggest as ways to improve social communication?
https://www.youtube.com/watch?v=3RjRZ9jMfs0

In addition to the research with children classified as learning disabled, a number of studies have found that children with specific language impairments are at risk for social difficulties (Brinton & Fujiki, 1993). Children with specific language impairments have been found to have difficulty with social tasks, such as cooperative learning (Brinton, Fujiki, & Higbee, 1998), and to experience social rejection (Paul, Looney, & Dahm, 1991). More recently, Hart, Fujiki, Brinton, and Hart (2004) found that social behavior problems were linked to the severity of language problems. Specifically, children with more severe language disorders were less prosocial (sympathetic, comforting, sharing) than their peers without language disorders. Although children with specific language impairments often have more significant language difficulties than children identified as language-learning disabled, there is considerable overlap between the two groups, adding further evidence that language difficulties may be a factor in the often reported social problems of children with learning disabilities.

Children with learning disabilities frequently have significant difficulties with pragmatics, especially with conversational skills. They have difficulty clearly expressing themselves to others, they frequently fail to adjust their language to the needs and/or level of their listener, and they are not sure what to do when they do not understand something being said to them. These difficulties have consequences for classroom interaction, social relationships, and the ability to understand and use written language.

Metalinguistic Skills

Metalinguistic skill refers to "the ability to reflect consciously on the nature and properties of language" (van Kleeck, 1994, p. 53). When children play word games, use rhyme, or recognize nongrammatical sentences, they are using metalinguistic skills. As van Kleeck points out, metalinguistic skills are not essential for the development of spoken language. We don't ask young children to tell us what parts of speech they just used (at least not before they enter school). However, many researchers believe that metalinguistic skills are essential for learning how to read and write.

We have already discussed one type of metalinguistic skill—phonological awareness. As children progress from the initial stages of reading to become more proficient readers, other types of metalinguistic skills become important. For example, children develop an awareness of the grammatical rules that underlie language and the pragmatic rules that govern conversation.

Children with learning disabilities have frequently been found to have difficulty developing metalinguistic skills, especially phonological awareness. But researchers have also found that children with learning disabilities have difficulty recognizing grammatical and morphological errors and making the appropriate corrections (Kamhi & Koenig, 1985). In a study of predictors of reading difficulty, Menyuk and colleagues (1991) found that measures of metalinguistic abilities (including word retrieval, phonological, and semantic) were the best predictors of later reading problems, but that different metalinguistic skills predicted the performance of different children. Tong and colleagues (2011) examined both the morphological and syntactic awareness skills of fourth-grade children with good reading comprehension skills compared to those with poor comprehension. They found that the students with poor comprehension had weaknesses in both morphological and syntactic awareness.

The research evidence suggests that children with learning disabilities, especially those with reading disorders, have a variety of language-learning deficits. Difficulty with phonological processing is the most often reported language difficulty, but a variety of other language problems are associated with reading and learning disabilities. The strongest source of evidence for a relationship between language and learning disabilities comes from intervention studies. Although children with language disorders may be more likely to have reading difficulties, and students with reading disorders may have language difficulties, neither of these findings is conclusive evidence that language and reading are causally related. In order to show cause, we need to see evidence that enhancing language skills improves reading outcomes. Fortunately, a number of studies have found just such a result. For example, Bradley and Bryant (1983) looked at the effects of sound-categorization training on the reading development of beginning readers. Children who were poor at sound categorization were taught to recognize and group words by their sounds. Children who were taught this skill did better on reading and spelling tests than other children who were taught to group by word meaning or who received no training. In a review of the research on the effects of phonemic awareness intervention, Ehri and colleagues (2001) found that phonemic awareness intervention was generally very effective. One of their analyses was on effect sizes on phonemic awareness training. Effect sizes measure the strength of an intervention. An effect size of 0.20 is considered weak, 0.5 is considered moderate, and anything above 0.8 is considered strong. Ehri and colleagues (2001) found the overall effect size for phonemic awareness interventions to be 0.86 for improving phonemic awareness itself. They also found that phonemic awareness training had a moderately positive effect on both reading (0.53) and spelling (0.59). The researchers found these effects to be true for typically developing children and for those who were identified as at risk for reading difficulties. The effects were less robust for children identified as having reading disorders.

Results such as these support the conclusion that phonological awareness difficulties are a cause of reading disabilities. The National Reading Panel (2000) concluded that "phonological awareness training improves reading performance in preschoolers and elementary students, and in normally progressing students, as well as in older disabled readers and younger children at risk for reading difficulties" (pp. 2–19).

Similarly, there is increasing evidence that instruction in morphological skills, including activities that focus on morphological word parts and patterns, can improve literacy outcomes for students with literacy difficulties (Goodwin & Ahn, 2010).

Although there is a lot of evidence that language skills are related to reading and that training in language can enhance reading, children with language-based reading disorders are often not identified as candidates for language intervention. Typically, their language-learning difficulties are more subtle than those of most children who are identified at an early age for speech and language intervention. It is interesting to note, however, that several researchers have found that the most effective interventions for reading difficulties combine instruction in phonological awareness with intensive language instruction (Hook, Macaruso, & Jones, 2001).

Language and Attention Deficit Hyperactivity Disorder

ADHD is one of the most common neurobehavioral disorders of childhood. The U.S. Centers for Disease Control and Prevention (2011) estimates that approximately 11 percent of children age 4 to 17 years (6.4 million) have been diagnosed with ADHD as of 2011. Although ADHD is not recognized as a category of disability under the Individuals with Disabilities Education Act, many children with ADHD receive special education and related services under the "Otherwise Health Impaired" category or other categories.

Although speech and language disorders are not a core characteristic of children with ADHD, research has found that a significant percentage of children with ADHD have speech and/or language difficulties. A review of studies that have examined the co-occurrence of ADHD and language impairments by Mueller and Tomblin (2012) found percentages of language impairments ranging from a low of 45 percent to a high of 90 percent. Despite the evidence that language disorders are frequently associated with ADHD, language is not usually part of the treatment plan for students with ADHD. Why is this so? Mueller and Tomblin (2012) have suggested a number of factors to explain the lack of focus on language issues, including an exclusive focus on social and behavioral issues, failure to assess language skills, and belief that literacy difficulties are the result of lack of motivation rather than language difficulties.

In this video, a girl with ADHD and a language disorder describes the impact of the language disorder on her life. What were some of the ways that her language difficulties affected her?

https://www.youtube.com/watch?v=RlRpgWl2bWs

A number of specific language disorders have been identified in the ADHD population. For example, Gremillion and Martel (2012) compared the semantic language skills of a large sample of children with ADHD (n = 266) between 6 and 12 years of age to those of a similar sample of children without ADHD. The children were tested on their word knowledge, working memory, and reading and mathematics achievement. The researchers found that the children with ADHD performed significantly lower than their peers on all of the measures. They concluded that semantic language difficulties combined with memory deficiencies could account for much of the reading and mathematics underachievement of the children with ADHD. Martinussen and Mackenzie (2015) reached a similar conclusion in their examination of the differences between children with ADHD with good reading comprehension as compared to those with poor comprehension. They found that the poor comprehenders in their sample of 45 adolescents with ADHD had significantly lower scores on a measure of expressive vocabulary than did their peers with good reading comprehension. Both of these studies suggest that semantic language difficulties, particularly vocabulary deficiencies, may be related to the academic underachievement that is characteristic of some children with ADHD.

Students with ADHD often have significant problems with social interaction and in developing peer relationships. A variety of factors may contribute to these difficulties, but problems with social communication (i.e., pragmatic language) have been found to be an important factor in social development deficiencies (Redmond, 2004). Children with ADHD have been reported to have significant difficulties in the domain of pragmatic language, especially in social communication (Bishop & Baird, 2001). Specifically, they have been found to have poor conversational initiation skills (Bishop & Baird, 2001), have difficulty in the role as speaker (Mikami, Huang-Pollock, Pfiffner, McBurnett, & Hangai, 2007) as well as listener (Nilsen, Mangal, & Macdonald, 2013), and have difficulty with discourse management and narrative discourse (Staikova, Gomes, Tartter, McCabe, & Halperin, 2013). For example, when Purvis and Tannock (1997) asked boys with ADHD age 7 to 11 years to retell a story, they found that, compared to non-ADHD peers, they made more errors in sequencing the story elements and made ambiguous references (using pronouns where the individual being referred to was

Teacher Perspective: Students with Reading Disabilities

In the resource room class that I taught in this year, many of the students were way below grade level in reading. They did not like to read during regular class time because they struggled. They would not raise their hand to answer any questions for fear they would answer wrong and get laughed at. I encouraged them to participate and helped them when I could. One young man never liked to do his bookmark after he read his book. He was always behind everyone else. He was also absent quite often. When I asked him to answer a question, he shut right down. Then he would make noises so he would get into trouble and be asked to leave the room. It took me a while to figure out what was happening. Once I figured out what was going on, I pulled him back to the table and worked with him one on one. He just struggled at reading. With a little more help, the behavior issues began to stop.

not clear), making it difficult for the listener to follow their retelling of the story. In the study by Staikova and colleagues (2013), the researchers concluded that the pragmatic deficits of children with ADHD appear to be highly related to their social skills difficulties.

The research on the language abilities of children with ADHD indicates that these children tend to have more language difficulties than might be expected. Their difficulties are primarily in the use of language for engaging in successful social communication. In addition, recent research suggests that language and cognitive difficulties may contribute to significant problems with written expression (Re, Pedron, & Cornoldi, 2007).

Impact of Language Impairments

Research has found that children with language disabilities are clearly at risk for academic failure, especially in reading. In fact, the incidence of reading disabilities in children with early language difficulties has been estimated to be between 4 and 75 percent (Bashir & Scavuzzo, 1992). There is some evidence that children with language-learning disabilities are also at risk for emotional problems (Baker & Cantwell, 1982). Therefore, it is essential that teachers and other professionals intervene as soon as possible to help these students.

For those who think that if we just wait long enough, children with language disabilities will get better, the news is not good. Although some studies have found that children with early language problems improve over time, most researchers have concluded that these children continue to be significantly impaired in their learning when compared to that of their peers (Rissman, Curtiss, & Tallal, 1990). In one study (Aram, Ekelman, & Nation, 1984), a group of children with early identified language disorders was examined 10 years later. Most adolescents (70%) continued to have difficulties with academic tasks and social acceptance. Although some children with early language problems do, indeed, grow out of them (30% of the children in the study just cited), it appears that most continue to experience significant problems. Therefore, it is important for teachers to recognize language disorders and use effective intervention approaches.

Check Your Understanding 7.2
Click here to gauge your understanding of the concepts in this section.

Instruction for Language-Learning Disabilities

What are some effective instructional approaches for enhancing the language skills of students with learning disabilities? This section will focus on instruction in two specific areas known to be problematic for students with learning disabilities: phonological processing and cognitive strategies. The methods discussed in this chapter were designed primarily to address the needs of students with learning disabilities, but they can be applied to other children experiencing similar problems. An overview of instructional approaches and methods for children with language and communication disorders is presented in Chapter 14 of this text, but specific methods developed primarily for specific populations of students with disabilities are presented within the chapter that addresses that disability.

Enhancing Phonological Awareness

Earlier in this chapter, we discussed the large research base that has implicated phonological awareness as a cause of the reading difficulties faced by most students with learning disabilities. As we noted, research studies have found that it is possible to teach phonological skills and have a positive effect on reading. Due to the strong and consistent findings linking phonological awareness to reading, a large number of phonological training programs have been developed during the past two decades (see Table 7.2 for examples). As a result, teachers and other educators are finding it increasingly difficult to decide which program to use. In their review of phonological training programs, Torgesen and Mathes (2000) suggested that any program should follow these principles:

1. *Instruction in phonological awareness should begin with easier tasks and move toward more difficult tasks.*

   Example: Instruction should begin with segmenting words, then sounds within words, then beginning and ending sounds.

2. *Instruction in phonological awareness should be a regular part of the curriculum.*

   Example: The authors suggest that phonological awareness activities should take place for 15 to 20 minutes a day in regular kindergarten classrooms.

Table 7.2

Phonemic Awareness Instructional Programs

Program	Developer/Date	Brief Description
Programs for Regular Classroom Instruction		
Ladders to Literacy: Preschool Kindergarten	Notari-Syverson, O'Connor, & Vadsey (2005) O'Connor, Notari-Syverson, & Vadsey (2005)	Activity books for phonological awareness and oral language skills for preschool and kindergarten ages.
Phonemic Awareness in Young Children	Adams, Foorman, Lundberg, & Beeler (1998)	Developmental sequence of activities in phonological awareness. Activities range from simple listening games to more advanced exercises in rhyming, alliteration, and segmentation.
Programs for Small Group or Individualized Training		
Launch into Reading Success: Book 2	Bennett & Ottley (2011)	In-depth, systematic phonological awareness training for young children.
Phonological Awareness Training for Reading (second edition)	Torgesen & Bryant (2013)	Small group activities for children with weaknesses in phonological awareness. Highly scripted lessons and activities.
Road to the Code	Blachman, Ball, Black, & Tangel (2000)	Small group instruction for children in kindergarten and first grade having difficulty learning to read.

3. *Teachers should expect that children will respond at widely varying rates to instruction in phonological awareness.*

   Example: Some may progress quickly while others will require more intensive and extensive instruction to acquire phonological awareness skills.

4. *Instruction in phonological awareness should involve both* analytic *and* synthetic *activities.*

   Example: Analytic activities require children to identify individual sounds within whole words (e.g., "What is the first sound in the word *dog*?). Synthetic activities involve blending together individual phonemes (e.g., "What word do these sounds make: /b/-/a/-/t/?").

5. *Because the first goal of instruction in phonological awareness is to help children notice the individual sounds in words, teachers should speak slowly and carefully, and should pronounce individual sounds correctly.*

   Example: Many teachers confuse the letter name with the sound made by the letter (e.g., the letter *p* makes the sound *puh*, not *pee*). Also, words with blends can be confusing (e.g., *church* has six letters but just three sounds (/ch/-/ur/-/ch/).

6. *It is not easy to pronounce individual phonemes correctly without some careful practice.*

   Example: Teachers need to be aware of issues such as regional and local accents and the distortion that takes place when sounds are used in context (e.g., /b/ sounds different in *beet* and *bought*).

7. *Methods to stimulate phonological awareness in students are limited only by the creativity of teachers.*

   Example: Good teachers embed phonological activities within many types of activities such as spelling and writing.

8. *Instruction in phonological awareness should be fun for teachers and students.*

   Example: Imagine the delight that a child in a kindergarten class for children with special needs experiences when he recognizes the letter *b* and identifies the sound it makes while participating in a story-reading activity.

Box 7.1 provides an example of a phonological training program first developed and tested by Blachman (1991) and now available for use in the classroom as "Road to the Code" (Blachman et al., 2000). This program uses a variety of classroom-based instructional activities that are both fun and effective. When Blachman taught teachers to use these techniques, their kindergarten students outperformed others on several measures of phonological awareness and letter names.

Now that it is well established that phonological training can improve the phonological processing and reading of some children with disabilities, the question becomes which instructional methods are most effective. Although research has not yet found a definitive answer to this question (and may never do so, given the heterogeneous nature of learning disabilities), the results do provide research evidence that will enable teachers and other professionals to select instructional methods for students with phonological-processing problems. These methods have been shown to be effective and to meet the mandate of legislation, such as the No Child Left Behind Act, that requires the use of evidence-based practices.

For example, Torgesen and colleagues (2001) assigned 60 students with reading disorders, ages 8 to 10 years old, to two groups. Each group received one-on-one instruction for two 50-minute sessions each day for 8 to 9 weeks for a total of 67.5 hours of instruction. This was followed by generalization training, during which the teacher supported the children in their regular classrooms. One group was taught with the Auditory Discrimination in Depth (ADD) program (now known as the Lindamood Phoneme Sequencing program [LiPS]) (Lindamood & Lindamood, 2011). This program provides intensive instruction in phonological and reading skills using a multisensory approach in which students learn to use sensory information from the ear, eye, and mouth to identify, label, and classify sounds. Children are taught to identify and label the place and manner of articulation of

Box 7.1 Example of a Phonological Training Program

1. *Say-It-and-Move-It Activity.* This is a phonological segmentation task in which children are taught to represent sounds by using manipulatives (such as disks, tiles, or buttons). The children are taught to represent, with a disk, each sound they hear. Each child is given a card that is divided in half. The top half is a disk storage area. On the bottom half of the card, there is an arrow pointing from left to right. If the teacher says, "Show me the *a,*" the children are to move a disk from the top half of the card to the left-hand end of the arrow and say the sound. After demonstrating mastery of this skill, the teacher progresses to two-phoneme words (*up, it, am*) and three-phoneme words (*sun, fat, zip*).

2. *Segmentation-Related Activity.* One of several segmentation activities is used in the second step of this lesson. For example, children might learn to group words based on rhyme, or they are taught to segment words using *Elkonin* cards. In this activity, the children are taught to identify the number of sounds in words using picture cards developed by the Russian psychologist Daniel Elkonin. The cards have a picture of a common word at the top (e.g., *sun*) and a series of boxes below the picture that represent the number of *phonemes* (not letters) in the word. Children are taught to move a disk along the boxes that correspond to each sound as they say the word.

3. *Letter Names/Letter Sounds.* Children are taught to use keywords and phrases to help them remember the sounds made by each letter. For example, they might see a card for the letter *t* that showed two teenagers talking on a telephone. Another activity described by Blachman is a post office game in which children select a picture that illustrates a word with a target letter (e.g., *pot* for *p*) and place it in the correct letter pouch. Later, as children learn the letter–sound relationships, letters are placed on the manipulatives used in the Say-It-and Move-It activity.

Source: Adapted from Blachman (1991).

---

phonemes using a special "language" (e.g., "lip popper" for the unvoiced, plosive sound /p/). The other group was taught using a program called Embedded Phonics, which was designed by Torgesen and colleagues (2001). Children in this program received intensive practice in word reading that was immediately applied to connected text. Instructional sessions included introduction of new words, spelling practice, word games, oral reading, and writing. The primary difference between the two approaches was in the amount of time spent on phonemic activities and on using phonemic skills in reading and writing. The ADD (LiPS) program emphasized learning phonemes out of context, whereas children in the Embedded Phonics program learned about sounds in the context of reading and writing activities.

The researchers found that children in both programs made substantial progress in both phonological processing and in reading. In fact, approximately half of the children in each group were reading at an average reading level 1 year after the intervention. Considering the severity of the reading deficiencies of the children in this study, this is an excellent result. Of course, that means that the other children were still behind their peers, even though their rate of reading progress did improve significantly. Surprisingly, there was no significant difference between the two approaches. The authors concluded that intensive remediation programs in phonological skills that are based on sound instructional practices, as were both of the programs in this study, can be effective for many children with significant reading difficulties.

The Institute for Education Sciences, a U.S. Department of Education program that reviews educational programs, reported that Ladders to Literacy was found to have potentially positive effects on alphabetics and fluency and mixed effects on comprehension (Institute for Education Sciences, 2010).

The Orton-Gillingham method is another intensive, individualized program for enhancing phonological processing. Based on the work of Samuel Orton in the early 20th century, the program uses a systematic, multisensory approach to teaching reading that emphasizes the development of phonological awareness, sound–symbol relationships, and the basic elements of language (syntax, semantics, etc.). Multisensory instruction, incorporating visual, auditory, and kinesthetic/tactile learning pathways, is an essential component of the program. Although the Orton-Gillingham method has been in existence for more than 50 years, there is surprisingly little research on its effectiveness. A review of research by Ritchey and Goeke (2006) found that reading programs based on Orton-Gillingham principles were moderately effective, particularly for word attack and nonword reading measures.

 Watch this video of an Orton-Gillingham reading lesson. What kinds of sensory inputs were used?
https://www.youtube.com/watch?v=zZgS8Ij1Ltg

A number of reading programs have been derived from the Orton-Gillingham model, including the Slingerland Approach (Slingerland & Aho, 1994–1996), Project Read (Enfield & Greene, 1997), and the Wilson Reading System (Wilson, 1996). The latter program has become widely used in the last decade, especially since the development of Fundations®, a program designed to be implemented in general education classes to prevent reading failure. There is limited research evidence to support the Wilson programs. An Institute for Education Sciences report (2007) found that the Wilson program had a "potentially positive" effect on learning alphabetics but no evidence for effectiveness in improving reading fluency or comprehension.

Many phonological training programs were initially designed for use with individuals or small groups. But a number of programs have now been developed to use in regular education classes with the entire class (see Table 7.2 for some examples). There is now some research that shows that the use of such programs with kindergarten and first-grade classes can help children develop phonological skills (Hatcher, Hulme, & Snowling, 2004) and may be particularly beneficial for children at risk for reading disorders.

Several phonological training programs use some form of technology in the delivery of instruction. Two that have received some attention by researchers are the Fast ForWord program (Scientific Learning Corporation) and Earobics (Cognitive Concepts). Fast ForWord is the general name for a series of programs that feature computer-based activities designed to build language and reading skills in individuals with language-learning difficulties, including, but not limited to, individuals with learning disabilities. The original program was designed for children between kindergarten age and 12 years old who have a wide range of language-learning difficulties. The program now has five levels that cover the age range from preschool through high school. Scientific Learning Corporation (the program's distributors) claims that students using the program "can achieve a one to two grade level reading gain in 8 to 12 weeks" (Scientific Learning Corporation, 2011).

 Watch this demonstration of some of the elements of the Fast ForWord language program. What cognitive and language skills does the program claim to improve?
https://www.youtube.com/watch?v=WuIFNyBnAAQ

Most of the research on Fast ForWord has focused on the language program, since this was the first program developed and has been in use for the longest time. Fast ForWord Language (FFW-L) consists of seven computer games designed to teach specific language skills. Children play five computer games a day for a total of 100 minutes. The computer constantly monitors their success, adjusting the difficulty level upward or downward as necessary. Children progress through five levels on each of the seven games. One of the unique (and controversial) aspects of Fast ForWord is that at the first level of each game, acoustic input is modified. That is, the sounds that the child hears are digitally manipulated to increase the duration and the intensity of the sound. It is hypothesized that children with language-learning difficulties cannot process incoming auditory input as quickly as other children. Therefore, slowing down this input should enhance their language-learning abilities. As the children progress through the levels, these sound enhancements are reduced until the child is hearing normal auditory input. Research on Fast ForWord has generally been mixed. Initial studies by Paula Tallal (the developer of the program) and her colleagues (1996) found that children with speech and language difficulties who played computer games that used modified auditory input outperformed similar children who played games without modifications. Later studies, however, generally failed to confirm the very dramatic results reported by the early studies. For example, in an intensive study of five children with significant language-learning difficulties, Friel-Patti, DesBarres, and Thibodeau (2001) reported significant gains in phonological processing for two of the participants but little improvement for the other three. In a study with a much larger number of children with language impairments, Cohen and colleagues (2005) compared the effectiveness of intervention using (1) Fast ForWord, (2) another series of computer-based language intervention activities, and (3) traditional speech and language therapy. Although children in all three groups benefited from instruction, those who received either of the computer-based intervention activities did no better than children who received traditional therapies. Similarly, Fey and colleagues (Fey, Finestack, Gajewski, Popescu, & Lewine, 2010) compared the effectiveness of the FFW-L program in combination with a more traditional narrative-based language intervention to determine if FFW-L could enhance the language training. In the narrative-based language intervention, children participated in several tasks designed to enhance grammar and storytelling skills. The authors found that children in the combined program (FFW-L + language intervention) did not outperform children who only received language intervention. Although research indicates that the FFW-L program can improve the phonological-processing ability of many (but not all) children with language-learning disabilities, it may be no more effective than other intensive language-intervention programs.

In addition to improvements in language skills, the developers of the Fast ForWord programs have claimed that children can improve their reading ability by participating in the program. Again, studies of these claims have yielded, at best, mixed results. For example, in a study comparing Fast ForWord with training based on the Orton-Gillingham program (a multisensory, structured language approach that emphasizes instruction in the alphabetic code), children with reading and language disorders made significant improvements in both language and reading with both approaches. Children trained using the Fast ForWord program did improve their reading skills, but not more than children using the other approach. Another study of children with learning disabilities found that Fast ForWord did not significantly improve either the language or the reading scores of most of the children. However, children with more severe learning problems did benefit from instruction using the program (Troia & Whitney, 2003). To test whether the acoustically modified speech used in FFW-L can improve reading, Loeb and colleagues (2009) compared the effects of FFW-L to those of a computer-based intervention for language that did not use acoustically modified speech and a traditional language intervention approach where a therapist worked with a child on a one-to-one basis on language tasks. The researchers found that all of the interventions improved blending skills, but none significantly improved reading. As is the case with language outcomes, there is little evidence FFW-L can improve reading skills as significantly as the program developers have claimed. However, new Fast ForWord products targeting reading have recently been developed that have not yet been tested in large-scale research studies.

Another computer-based program that has been used to teach language skills to children with language-learning disabilities is the Earobics Literacy Launch program (Cognitive Concepts). Earobics uses a series of computer-based activities to teach phonological awareness, auditory processing, and phonics skills. There are three versions of the program: one for children 4 to 7 years old, one for children ages 7 to 10, and a third program for adolescents and adults. In each program, the participant moves through a series of levels while playing interactive games. The computer automatically adjusts the difficulty level in response to the participant's answers. The authors claim, "Elementary school students across the country are making dramatic, statistically significant gains in essential literacy skills." The company's website (search for Earobics) presents reports from several school districts that have successfully used the Earobics Literacy Launch program. The Institute for Education Sciences (2009) found that the use of Earobics had positive effects on alphabetics and "potentially positive" effects on fluency.

> ▶ Watch this demonstration of some of the activities in the Earobics program. What are the skills being taught in this demonstration?
> https://www.youtube.com/watch?v=pEBOyJIT-fs

The effectiveness of Earobics Literacy Launch, Fast ForWord, and the LiPS programs was compared in a study of 60 children with reading and language deficits (Pokorni, Worthington, & Jamison, 2004). Children received 3 hours of instruction in one of the programs each day in a summer program. The authors found that the LiPS program was the most effective in improving phonological skills. The Earobics program was also effective, but the Fast ForWord program was not effective. None of the programs significantly improved reading skills.

In summary, there is now overwhelming evidence that phonological training programs can improve the phonological skills and perhaps the reading skills of many children with learning disabilities. There is, as yet, no clear evidence that technology-based programs such as Fast ForWord or Earobics Literacy Launch are superior to other programs. However, the research does suggest that intensive, long-lasting intervention can work. Phonological training has generally been used successfully with young children who are beginning readers to improve phonemic awareness and word identification skills. What about older children with language-learning problems? What can we do for them?

Mnemonic Strategies

One type of approach that has been frequently found to be useful in helping older students learn a variety of skills is mnemonic **strategy training**. With this approach, students are taught *how* to learn, not just *what* to learn. In other words, the children are taught a strategy to use as they are learning.

Many students with learning disabilities have difficulty learning new vocabulary words. Mastropieri (1988) described a strategy for vocabulary learning that she and her colleagues have applied successfully in a number of academic areas (Scruggs & Mastropieri, 1992). The keyword strategy includes the following steps:

1. *Recoding.* The new vocabulary word is recoded into a keyword that sounds similar to the target word, is familiar to the student, and can be easily pictured. For example, *forte* (meaning "loud") could be recoded as *fort.*

2. *Relating.* The student relates the keyword to the target word, using an illustration. A sentence that relates the word to the drawing is created. In our example, a picture of a fort during a battle might show guns firing. The sentence might read, *The guns at the fort are loud.*

3. *Retrieving.* The definition of the new vocabulary is recalled by thinking of the keyword, creating the drawing (either actual or imagined), thinking of the related sentence, and stating the definition—*forte* means "loud."

Although this technique may seem slow and cumbersome, it works. It has been applied successfully in a number of studies to improve the vocabulary learning of students with learning disabilities (e.g., Condus, Marshall, & Miller, 1986; Mastropieri, Scruggs, Levin, Gaffney, & McLoone, 1985). Use of the keyword mnemonic method does not have to be limited to students with disabilities. Uberti, Scruggs, and Mastropieri (2003) reported the results of a study in which the keyword approach was compared to more traditional vocabulary instruction—providing either a picture to illustrate a word or providing a definition only—in classrooms that included both disabled and typically developing 8- to 10-year-old students. The typically developing students learned approximately equally in all three conditions, but the students with learning disabilities did far better with the keyword approach—actually outperforming their peers.

The keyword method is just one example of a learning strategy that may be used to help older students with language-learning difficulties. The research on this and other instructional techniques suggests that it is possible to help these students overcome at least some of their learning difficulties.

Cognitive Learning Strategies

A number of studies have examined the use of cognitive learning strategies to enhance the language skills of students with learning disabilities, especially in the area of vocabulary learning. Cognitive strategy instruction provides students with a framework for understanding words and the relationships between words by helping students recognize the similarities and differences between words. For example, in a study by Bos, Anders, Filip, and Jaffe (1989), high school students with learning disabilities were taught to use a semantic feature strategy that used a relationship chart on which the most important ideas in a reading passage were listed across the top and related vocabulary terms were listed on the side. Students were guided to develop a definition of each word and then discuss how the word related to the ideas from the text. Students who used this method outperformed their peers who simply used a dictionary to look up definitions. After reviewing a number of studies that used some form of cognitive strategy instruction for word learning, Jitendra, Edwards, Sacks, and Jacobson (2004) concluded that this was a highly effective approach to teaching vocabulary to students with learning disabilities.

Another type of learning strategy is morphological analysis. This method involves teaching students to use word parts such as prefixes, suffixes, and root words to derive the meaning of a word. Harris, Schumaker, and Deshler (2011) compared a morphological analysis strategy to an alternative strategy approach for enhancing the vocabulary skills of high school students with learning disabilities. The researchers found that both students with disabilities and those without disabilities in both treatment groups made statistically significant gains in their ability to define the target vocabulary words. However, students in the morphological strategy group outperformed their peers who used the alternative vocabulary strategy as well as those in the control group on a test of morphological analysis skills.

Technological Applications

Emerging technologies show promise in helping children with learning disabilities overcome their learning difficulties. Two studies by Kennedy and his colleagues (Kennedy, Deshler, & Lloyd, 2015; Kennedy, Thomas, Meyer, Alves, & Lloyd, 2014) examined the use of podcasts to deliver vocabulary instruction in social studies content areas to high school students with disabilities. The content acquisition podcasts developed for these studies used a multimedia format based on universal design of learning principles. The podcasts present illustrations of the word to be learned with text and a voice-over that explains the word and its definition. The researchers found that when the students with disabilities were taught using the content acquisition podcasts, they had significantly higher scores on vocabulary probes and learned the words faster than when they were taught using the standard approach.

Speech recognition holds a lot of promise for students with reading and writing difficulties. Speech recognition programs translate the spoken word into text on the computer screen. Early systems were expensive and difficult to use, but current programs, such as Dragon Naturally Speaking (Nuance Communications) and IBM's Via Voice are making speech recognition more practical and accessible than ever. Speech recognition software (along with voice output programs that translate words on the computer into speech) will make computers more functional for children with a wide range of learning disorders.

Since word recognition software is relatively new, research on its use in classroom situations with children with disabilities is limited. However, the research in existence points out both the potential benefits as well as the limitations of this emerging technology. Higgins and colleagues (Higgins & Raskind, 2000, 2004; Raskind & Higgins, 1999) have conducted the most extensive research on the use of speech recognition programs with students with learning disabilities. They have found that students who use this technology can improve their word recognition, spelling, reading comprehension, and phonological processing.

Despite the positive results reported in these studies, speech recognition technology is not without difficulties. Many of the students reported experiencing frustration with the time it took to "train" the program to recognize their voice and with the errors the software produced. Additionally, most speech recognition programs are not as accurate in recognizing children's voices, especially when the children have language and/or reading difficulties, as is the case with most students with learning disabilities.

Read the following case study about James, and then respond to questions about the case in your Pearson eText.

James: A Case Study

EDUCATIONAL HISTORY, CURRENT PLACEMENT, AND PROGRESS

James is a 9-year, 6-month-old student who has been classified as special education under the "Specific Learning Disability" classification. James received basic skills instruction in reading in first grade. Due to a concern by his parents and teachers concerning his gains in reading, he was referred to the district's child study team at the beginning of his second-grade year. He was classified that same school year and began receiving services in an inclusion classroom and a pullout resource classroom (for reading and writing only). Throughout third grade, James continued to receive instruction in both an inclusion general classroom and a pullout resource setting (for reading and writing).

James is currently a fourth-grade student in an inclusion classroom. James has participated in the general classroom setting within the inclusion classroom for science, social studies, math, spelling, and grammar for the entire school year. From September through December, he received instruction in reading and writing in a pullout resource room setting. At that point, his parents requested that he be placed back into the general classroom. They believed his progress was stagnating in the resource room and that he felt isolated from his peers, and they wanted him to have the opportunity to rise to the occasion. Beginning in January, James began to receive all his academic instruction in the general classroom.

Academically, James has shown an aptitude for mathematics and has steadily earned grades of A and A– throughout the school year. James is also highly curious in science and social studies, and has earned high Bs and As in those subjects throughout the year. James has experienced ebbs and flows in rule-based subjects such as grammar and spelling. His performance generally falls within the high B to A range, with occasional dips in which he earns Cs. Reading is the area in which James has the most difficulty. He has deficits in expressive and receptive vocabulary, verbal memory, and attention in regard to reading. These deficits have made it difficult for James to comprehend reading materials and to demonstrate (in written and verbal means) his understanding. Despite his difficulties, James has worked extraordinarily hard since joining the general classroom environment and, through his efforts and the supports provided to him, has maintained a B average. In writing, James has difficulty structuring his work and completing his thoughts. This is largely due to his expressive vocabulary and verbal memory deficits (he can easily forget the direction of his writing as he writes). However, with the use of graphic organizers and teacher support, James is able to complete writing assignments at approximate grade level proficiency.

(continued)

James: A Case Study   Continued

In addition to the instruction James receives in the inclusion classroom, he also sees a speech-language pathologist three times per week for a total of 1 hour each week. They have focused on strategies to help James expand his receptive vocabulary such as breaking words into prefixes, roots, and suffixes (morphology) and defining new words through context clues and using word keyword strategies. Their sessions have also focused on expanding James's expressive vocabulary through strategies such as having James view a picture and then create a word web to describe the whole picture or parts of the picture using as many words as he can that are applicable.

James also receives services from an occupational therapist. He does not have regular sessions with this professional; instead, she observes James once a month in the classroom setting and makes recommendations for accommodations that may aid in James's classroom development. The occupational therapist and the teacher also meet briefly once a week to discuss James's progress, and the therapist sees James outside of the classroom as needed.

PHYSICAL/HEALTH DEVELOPMENT

Before describing James's language development, it is important to detail his physical and health development. James's mother gave birth to him after a 39-week pregnancy (which is about typical). He was reported to hit all physical and cognitive milestones within the range of typically developing children. James is an outstanding athlete, particularly excelling in swimming. Although his gross motor skills are above average, observations of James, tests, and collaborative discussions with the occupational therapist reveal a weakness in terms of fine motor skills. He struggles with tasks such as finger-thumb succession. According to the occupational therapist, this is a developmental issue that is linked to his sensory processing of touch sensation. This is the reason he receives occupational therapy services.

Just before the age of 2, James had his first ear infection. These ear infections would prove to be chronic. James has had numerous ear infections throughout his life and six separate surgeries to insert tubes in his ears to reduce the instances of infection. Ear infections still continue currently, with his mother reporting winter to be the worst season for infections. In 2012, his hearing was assessed at the Children's Hospital of Philadelphia under normal circumstances (without an ear infection). James was found to have normal hearing acuity bilaterally; however, he was found to need a higher signal-to-noise ratio. This indicates that James has trouble distinguishing between the primary auditory input and background noise.

Language Development

James's parents have self-reported to have interacted with James as much as his siblings and to have made literacy activities (such as reading to and with James) a key focus of his early childhood. Still, James's parents reported language deficits from an early age in terms of vocabulary and reading comprehension (both materials that James has read and stories that have been read/told to him). This may certainly, as has been suggested by professionals who have worked with and assessed James, be attributable (to at least some degree) to his history of chronic middle ear infections.

When James was first formally tested as a second-grade student, it was found that he had deficits in language in general. As a young student, James had struggles with elements of phonology, morphology, syntax, and semantics. Pragmatics was not an area of concern. He interacted properly with adults and peers. Throughout his school experience, James made significant gains in phonology and moderate gains in syntax. With the intensive strategies used by teachers and particularly the speech-language pathologist, James has made gains this school year in morphology through word attack strategies such as identifying prefixes, suffixes, and roots. Reading comprehension continues to be an area of weaknesses (and the target of many goals) as James continues to learn and implement semantic skills to improve expressive and receptive vocabulary strategies as well as strategies to improve verbal memory and aid James in organizing his thoughts.

EVALUATION OF LANGUAGE AND COMMUNICATION SKILLS

This section is broken up into two sections: informal and formal assessments. Although James has participated in comprehensive testing in speech, language, and communication skills in the past, the testing that is to be reported upon is limited in scope to skills related to expressive and receptive vocabulary. This decision was made based on the goals that have been prioritized for James by both the parents and the school for this school year. James's parents have made it clear to the school that it is their wish to have vocabulary acquisition skills and vocabulary usage strategies as the top priority in terms of the intervention services he receives in school as well as strategies that are expressly taught in the general classroom. School personnel (teacher, special education teacher, speech-language pathologist, and case manager) agree that, although there are other factors that contribute to James's school performance, expressive and receptive vocabulary skills are a significant deficit

(continued)

James: A Case Study   Continued

for James and that interventions to aid James in these areas would be greatly beneficial. It is for these reasons that expressive and receptive vocabulary skills were the focus of testing for this report.

Informal Assessment

James has been the focus of consistent informal assessments of vocabulary skills throughout the school year. This is partially due to general classroom practices by his teachers this year (both the general and special education teacher), but also due in part to his parents' wishes related to vocabulary skills. Informal assessments based on observations have been focused on independent reading (fiction and nonfiction), class work, and tests.

James has been periodically assessed on independent reading tasks by both the teacher and the special education teacher in the classroom who have collaborated to share results and findings. Independent reading task assessments have occurred during James's reading of textbooks, news articles, novels, and short stories (both fictional and nonfictional). He has been found to be below his peers in terms of defining grade level words. He has also been found to have poor skills in terms of monitoring his own understanding of words, such as stopping himself when he comes across words he does not know or recognize. As a result, he rarely uses word vocabulary strategies to learn new words and aid in his comprehension of his reading task independently. When prompted to use such strategies (identifying prefixes, suffixes, and roots and using context clues to infer meaning and then checking against a glossary or dictionary), he has been able to attempt them with moderate success. When asked a question or to summarize what he has read, James often will hesitate and give an answer of "I know the answer, but I don't know how to say it" (or a similar answer). With assistance from a teacher or peer with whom James is able to talk out his answer or when James is given assistance finding the "right words," he is generally able to express his opinion, although overly simple words are often used.

When working on independent class work (questions from a textbook or a worksheet), James has been observed in terms of his strategies when he does not know a word in the question. James rarely seeks help when he does not understand a question. He will occasionally look at his neighbor's paper; at times, he copies his neighbor's answer, but more often, he looks at his neighbor's response to help him understand what is being asked. Most often, however, James will guess at the meaning of a question he does not understand and formulate his answer based on his guess. When he asks for assistance or when a teacher approaches James about a question that is not fully understood based on the words used, James is typically able to understand the question through talking with a teacher or having the teacher explain or reword the question. When James understands the question, his responses are typically understandable, although the vocabulary used in answers is typically below grade level expectations.

James takes his grades very seriously, and when he is taking a test, he will ask for assistance with vocabulary that he does not know within a question. On vocabulary tests, he generally does well when he has had time to practice words ahead of time (typically above the class average). He does poorly, however, on vocabulary tests on words for which he has not had time to prepare. These words, for example, test to see if James has retained knowledge of the word from reading assignments, is able to properly use skills to determine word meaning based on word parts (prefix, suffix, roots), or is able to infer word meaning based on context clues. In responding to short response or essay questions on tests, he is typically able to respond appropriately, although his word choice is simpler than his peers and he is often unable to use specific words that would be expected on tests in areas such as science and social studies.

For informal assessments, the accommodations that are ensured by his individualized educational plan as well as those deemed appropriate by the teacher, special education teacher, speech-language pathologist, and his parents are in place. Accommodations pertinent to these assessments include rewording and rephrasing of questions and directions, preferential seating, tasks broken into manageable portions, checklists and graphic organizers, additional time on tests and quizzes, and testing in a small group setting.

Formal Testing

The results of three formal tests have been included in this report. The first test included, the Woodcock Johnson-IV (WJ-IV), was conducted by an independent learning consultant. This is a comprehensive language and literacy test; however, James's vocabulary scores will be used because they fall within the scope of the assignment. The second test was the Expressive One-Word Picture Vocabulary Test (EOWPVT-4) administered by James's teacher in conjunction with the speech-language pathologist. The third test, the Rapid Automatic Naming (RAN) subtest of the Clinical Evaluation of Language Fundamentals 4 (CELF-4), was administered by the teacher.

(continued)

James: A Case Study   Continued

Although the WJ-IV was not administered by the teacher, it is included in this report to give a more complete picture of James and to help clarify the objectives and goals that have been implemented based on the testing. Furthermore, the results of the WJ-IV have been found to conflict with the results of subsequent tests. The discrepancies between the results of these tests are important in formu-lating the objectives and goals, and possible factors that led to the differing results will be discussed in the analysis section of this report. Finally, the discrepancies underline the possible limitations of standardized testing and the importance of proper balancing between formal and informal assessments while developing goals and objectives.

FORMAL TESTING RESULTS

Woodcock Johnson–IV.   This is a standardized test that is normalized to James's same-aged peers. James was 9 years, 5 months old when he was given this assessment.

Subtest	Standard Score	Percentile Rank	Description	Grade-Level Equivalent
Reading Vocabulary	74	4	Limited	1.4
Oral Expression	79	8	Limited	2.2
Picture Vocabulary	64	1	Limited	Not listed

Expressive One-Word Picture Vocabulary Test (EOWPVT-4).   This is a standardized test that is normalized to James's same-aged peers. James was 9 years, 6 months at the time the assessment was given.

Raw Score	Standard Score	Percentile Rank
111	107	68

Rapid Automatic Naming (RAN) subtest of the Clinical Evaluation of Language Fundamentals 4 (CELF-4).   This subtest of the CELF-4 is normalized to James's same-aged peers. James was 9 years, 6 months at the time the assessment was given.

Color-Shape Time	143 seconds
Color-Shape Time Criterion	Non-normal*

*Based on the performance of James's peers, the assessment considers 95 seconds or less to be "normal," 96 to 114 seconds to be "slower than normal," and 115 seconds or above to be "non-normal."

Color-Shape Errors	4
Color-Shape Errors Criterion	Normal*

*Based on the performance of James's peers, the assessment considers five or fewer errors to be "normal," six to seven errors to be "slower than normal," and eight or more errors to be "non-normal."

Neither accommodations nor modifications for James as he took part in these formal assessments were deemed necessary. Although he has proper classroom accommodations and modifications, he was able to participate in these assessments fully.

Apply Your Knowledge 7.1: Case Study: James

Click here to assess your understanding of James's case.

Check Your Understanding 7.3

Click here to gauge your understanding of the concepts in this section.

Summary

In this chapter, we have examined the language difficulties of children with learning disabilities and children with attention deficit hyperactivity disorders. Problems with defining *learning disabilities* present one of the biggest challenges to identifying students with learning needs. Despite the uncertainty created by problems with definition, overwhelming research shows that language difficulties are an important cause of learning disabilities and that they do not usually get better on their own. In addition, research on students with ADHD has found increasing evidence of language difficulties in this population. Instructional approaches, including phonological training methods to enhance word identification ability, mnemonic strategies, cognitive learning strategies, and technological applications, were presented. After reading this chapter, you should be better able to identify language disorders in the classroom, understand some of the consequences of language disabilities, and be better prepared to teach children with learning disabilities and those with ADHD.

Language and Students with Intellectual Disabilities

This chapter examines the language and communication problems associated with intellectual disabilities. Ideas about intellectual disabilities are changing, and teachers, as well as other education professionals, should be aware of these changes. Children with intellectual disabilities are a diverse group, ranging from those with relatively minor developmental delays to those with severe impairments. An examination of the range of language and communication problems experienced by students with intellectual disabilities and the factors that contribute to these impairments leads to some approaches to helping students improve their language and communication skills.

Learning Outcomes

By the end of this chapter, you should be able to:

1. Explain the definition and causes of intellectual disabilities.

2. Describe the specific language and communication characteristics of children with intellectual disabilities, factors related to language development, and the impact of language on the literacy skills of individuals with intellectual disabilities.

3. Discuss methods for enhancing the language and communication skills of individuals with intellectual disabilities.

Karen: A Case Study

Karen, a 10-year-old girl with a measured IQ of 65, presently attends a regular third-grade class in a public school. An aide in the classroom assists Karen and two other children with mild disabilities. Karen has difficulty understanding directions, reading, and completing work independently. She reads at a late first-grade level, and her math achievement is at the second-grade level. Her teacher reports that Karen has made progress while in this classroom. She noted that Karen is reluctant to contribute during cooperative learning groups but will participate with prompting.

Karen's mother has reported that Karen had no apparent physical problems during her early development, although her development was a little slower than that of other children. Karen was late in crawling and could neither stand nor walk at 18 months. When Karen was about 2 years old, her parents became concerned about her lack of speech; however, the family physician told them not to worry—that Karen would catch up. Karen had persistent

otitis media (middle-ear infections) as a young child and continues to experience occasional earaches.

Prior to this year, Karen was in a self-contained, special education classroom. She appeared to make considerable progress in that class. She began to read and opened up to other children in the class. Before being placed in the special education class, Karen had spent 2 years in a regular first-grade program. Her teachers there described Karen as quiet and a hard worker, but also as slow and immature. She had particular difficulty with beginning reading skills and with working independently. She appeared to have few friends.

Karen's parents asked that she be returned to the regular education classroom after her year in special education. Although the district was reluctant to return her to regular education (since she appeared to be progressing in the special education classroom), they agreed to do so. At this point, Karen appears to be making slow but steady progress. It is likely that she will remain in regular education in the future.

Danny: A Case Study

Danny is a 14-year-old boy with Down syndrome (trisomy 21). He presently attends a special education class for children with moderate intellectual disabilities. Danny has a history of significant cognitive and language delays. He did not speak until he was approximately 3 years old. Even then, his speech was difficult to understand. Significant problems with articulation persist.

Danny has a measured IQ in the 40 to 45 range. However, his language age of 4 years (as measured by the Peabody Picture Vocabulary Test) is below his mental age of 5.6. A language sample analysis completed by the speech-language pathologist indicated that Danny had an mean length of utterance (MLU) of approximately 3.5. He used mostly simple, declarative sentences, and he appeared to have a limited vocabulary, although his poor articulation made this difficult to determine.

Danny is a very talkative, outgoing young man. He loves to hug his teachers and to dance. His school program is focused on functional skills and community-based training. The class makes frequent trips to local malls and restaurants, where students get the opportunity to practice their math and travel skills. Danny's speech and language instruction is focused on improving his articulation and on helping him make appropriate requests. Danny's parents hope that he will be able to live in a group home or an apartment setting and perhaps work in a service-type job.

Definitions and Causes of Intellectual Disabilities

The stories of Karen and Danny illustrate the diversity of the population of children known to have intellectual disabilities. Despite the widespread popular belief that individuals with intellectual disabilities are more alike than different, they actually exhibit a diverse pattern of abilities and deficits. Today, most live at home, but some reside in state or private institutions. An increasing number are educated in regular education classrooms, but many more continue to receive their education in separate classrooms or in special schools. Some work in the community after school, and a small but increasing number go on to higher education. Although all children with intellectual disabilities have deficits in cognition, each child has an individual pattern of strengths and weaknesses. In addition to cognitive deficits, most children with intellectual disabilities have problems with language and communication (Long, 2005).

Our understanding of intellectual disabilities and our expectations for persons with intellectual disabilities are undergoing rapid change. Examples of this change in attitudes and beliefs abound. In the last two decades, there has been a movement away from institutions as the primary sites for treatment and residence for persons with intellectual disabilities toward smaller, community-based, and even family-centered, residences. At the same time, there has been growing pressure on schools to educate children with intellectual disabilities in regular education classrooms. The 2004 Individuals with Disabilities Education Improvement Act and the No Child Left Behind (now, Every Student Succeeds) Act raised the standards and expectations for all children with disabilities, including those with intellectual disabilities. Now more than ever, students with intellectual disabilities are studying the same curriculum as other students, with modifications and supports that enhances their chances for success.

Changes in societal expectations for individuals with intellectual disabilities, especially inclusion in regular education classrooms, have significant implications for language skills. Clearly, there are higher expectations for students with intellectual disabilities to have language and literacy skills that will enable them to fully participate in the classroom. Therefore, we will look at what is known about the language of persons with intellectual disabilities and what can be done to enhance their language skills.

As we examine the research on the speech and language difficulties of children with intellectual disabilities, it is important to keep in mind the diverse nature of this population. In fact, as scientists learn more about the causes of intellectual disabilities, research has become more focused on specific disorders (such as **fragile X syndrome** and **Williams syndrome**), rather than looking at the population of persons with intellectual disabilities as a whole. This may help in understanding some of the variability that has characterized the research on persons with intellectual disabilities. It is important also to consider against whom children with intellectual disabilities are being compared. Some studies compare children with intellectual disabilities to typically developing children of the same chronological age; other studies match children with intellectual disabilities to children having the same mental age but who are chronologically younger; and still other studies use some measure of language age as the means of comparison. Each of these methods has drawbacks, and each can give quite different results.

On October 5, 2010, President Barack Obama signed into law an act entitled, "Rosa's Law." Modeled after a similar law that was enacted in Maryland, Rosa's Law honors Rosa Marcellino, a girl with Down syndrome. The law is more than symbolic. It removes the terms "mental retardation" and "mentally retarded" from federal health, education, and labor policy and replaces them with people-first language such as "individual with an intellectual disability" and "intellectual disability." The term "mental retardation" has many negative connotations and is often associated with unpleasant and inaccurate stereotypes. As a result, there is a growing consensus among experts and advocates to eliminate general use of the term *mental retardation* and substitute *intellectual disabilities* in its place.

According to the American Association on Intellectual and Developmental Disabilities (AAIDD), intellectual disability can be defined as "a disability characterized by significant limitations both in intellectual functioning and in adaptive behavior, which covers many everyday social and practical skills. This disability originates before the age of 18" (AAIDD, 2010). Intellectual function can be measured using a standardized test of intelligence. Individuals who score below an IQ of 75 can be considered intellectually disabled. In addition, they must score below the norm on an assessment of adaptive behavior that includes measures of:

- Conceptual skills—including language and literacy; math concepts such as money and time; and self-direction.

- Social skills—including interpersonal skills, social problem solving, and the ability to follow rules and obey laws.

- Practical skills—Including activities of daily living such as personal care, occupational skills, the use of transportation, and the use of the telephone.

Until the signing of Rosa's Law, the Individuals with Disabilities Education Act (IDEA) used the term "mental retardation." However, now IDEA also uses the term "intellectual disability" and defines it as follows:

> Significantly subaverage general intellectual functioning, existing concurrently with deficits in adaptive behavior and manifested during the developmental period, that adversely affects a child's educational performance. [34 CFR §300.8(c)(6)]

 This video explains the definition of intellectual disability in more detail and provides information on how to identify individuals with intellectual disabilities. According to the video, what factors are included in adaptive behavior?
https://www.youtube.com/watch?v=V_mTP9WLdcl

One of the most significant developments in our understanding of intellectual disabilities has been increased research on and understanding of the various conditions that cause intellectual disabilities. There are, in fact, a number of conditions that cause intellectual disabilities, including:

1. *Genetic conditions.* Disorders such as phenylketonuria (a genetic disorder that causes a buildup of an enzyme called phenylalanine, causing intellectual disability, **Down**

Table 8.1

Genetic Syndromes Related to Intellectual Disabilities

	Cause	Incidence	Major Characteristics
Down Syndrome (Trisomy 21)	Most children with Down syndrome have an extra 21 copy of chromosome. Instead of the normal number of 46 chromosomes in each cell, the individual with Down syndrome has 47 chromosomes.	1 in 800 to 1 in 1,100 live births	Usually smaller. Slower physical and mental development. Physical features include flattening of back of head, slanting of eyelids, slightly smaller ears, small mouth with narrow palate. Majority function in mild to moderate range of intellectual disability but wide variation in mental abilities.
Fragile X Syndrome	Mutation in the *FMR-1* gene on the X chromosome		Males generally more often affected than females. Physical features in males include large ears, loose joints and muscles, elongated face, and enlarged testicles. Mild to severe intellectual disability. Hyperarousal. Significant problems with social skills and attention.
Williams Syndrome	Random genetic mutation (deletion of a small piece of chromosome 7) most often causes the disorder	1 in 20,000 live births	Mild to moderate intellectual disability, a distinctive facial appearance, and a unique personality that combines overfriendliness and high levels of empathy with anxiety.

Sources: www.thearc.org (The ARC); www.ninds.nih.gov/disorders/williams/williams.htm (National Institute of Neurological Disorders and Stroke).

syndrome, or trisomy 21, a chromosomal anomaly in which there is an extra chromosome present on the 21st chromosome pair; see the National Down Syndrome Society website for resources about Down syndrome), fragile X syndrome (caused by a mutation in one of the genes on the X chromosome), and Williams syndrome (caused by the deletion of genetic material from a specific region of chromosome 7; see Table 8.1).

In this video, parents and doctors describe the symptoms of fragile X syndrome. What do they describe as the major physical characteristics?
https://www.youtube.com/watch?v=TEce4nhWFaw

Williams syndrome is described as a unique disorder in this video. What are some of the strengths and challenges of individuals with Williams syndrome?
https://www.youtube.com/watch?v=M6n4z0XjPh4

2. *Problems during pregnancy.* The use of alcohol (fetal alcohol syndrome) and maternal drug use during pregnancy.

3. *Problems at birth.* Low birth weight and difficulties during labor and delivery that cut off oxygen to the brain.

4. *Problems after birth.* Caused by childhood diseases, such as measles and chickenpox, that may lead to serious complications such as meningitis and encephalitis or by injuries or lead or mercury poisoning.

5. *Poverty and malnutrition.* Higher risk for malnutrition, poor medical care, and exposure to environmental hazards that may cause intellectual disabilities.

The resulting syndrome of characteristics (called **behavioral phenotypes**) caused by one or more of these conditions can differ in many ways. As Table 8.1 shows, individuals with intellectual disabilities can differ in physical appearance, level of intellectual impairment, social skills, behavior, and so on. As we learn more about the genetic syndromes that cause intellectual disabilities, we are discovering patterns of characteristics that are related to the underlying genetic disorder. In other words, we might think of the term "intellectual disabilities" as a generic term (much like "learning disabilities") that describes a group of disorders each of which has a distinct set of characteristics.

Until recently, most of the research in the field of "mental retardation" did not differentiate between subgroups of persons with this disability. It is only in the last decade that researchers have begun to examine the patterns of disabilities associated with specific syndromes. As we review the research on the language and cognitive functioning of individuals with intellectual disabilities, you will note that some of the research studies identify specific subpopulations (such as Down syndrome or fragile X), whereas others do not differentiate.

Check Your Understanding 8.1

Click here to gauge your understanding of the concepts in this section.

Language and Communication Characteristics

Although there is general agreement that language and communication disorders are an important characteristic of intellectual disabilities, there is less agreement about the causes of language deficits in this population and about the specific language difficulties that can be identified as characteristic of persons with intellectual disabilities.

One of the ongoing issues has been the question of whether the language and communication of individuals with intellectual disabilities are delayed or different. Is their language similar to that of typically developing individuals of a younger age, or does it develop differently? Another issue is whether the language deficits of this population are a direct result of the cognitive delays that are characteristic of intellectual disabilities or whether they are a separate problem. The prevailing view has been that language disorders in this population were the direct result of the cognitive deficiencies characteristic of persons with intellectual disabilities. Those individuals with more significant cognitive deficits were thought to have more significant language and communication difficulties. But there have always been puzzling reports of individuals with more severe cognitive deficits performing better in some domains of language than others with less severe disabilities. An emerging point of view is that the language and communication difficulties of individuals with intellectual disabilities may be more closely related to the specific genetic (or other) cause of their disability, rather than the severity of their cognitive deficits (Abbeduto, Evans, & Dolan, 2001; Rondal, 2001). In other words, language and communication difficulties are one of several problems associated with a specific disorder. Individuals with this disorder may have cognitive deficits, socialization difficulties, and specific language differences that are caused by the disorder itself.

Early Language Development

Most research on the early language development of children with intellectual disabilities has been conducted on children with Down syndrome. Young children with Down syndrome have been reported to use the same sort of nonverbal communication as other infants (e.g., smiling, laughing, reaching) but use vocalizations less often with these gestures (Chapman, 1997). In fact, the use of gestures may be a strength in babies with Down syndrome (Roberts, Price, & Malkin, 2007). When babbling emerges, it follows a pattern similar to that of typically developing young children, with early babbling that leads to more adult-like utterances over time (Stoel-Gammon, 1997). Some researchers have reported delays of up to 2 months in the onset of babble; others have reported no delays. Most children with Down syndrome continue to use babble longer than their typically developing peers, often continuing to babble into their second year of life. They tend to be less responsive to parental input and engage in less turn-taking and requesting than typically developing babies (Chapman & Hesketh, 2000; Rondal, 2001).

The acquisition of first words is significantly delayed in most children with Down syndrome. Children with this condition have generally been found to start using first words at a later age and acquire words more slowly than typically developing children of the same age (Stoel-Gammon, 1997). However, there is a great deal of variability among these children. For example, in a study of 336 Swedish children with Down syndrome, the investigators found that 10 percent of the children began to use recognizable words by age 1 and 80 percent were using words by age 2. However, between 10 and 20 percent of the children had fewer than 10 words by age 3, and some children had not started to talk at all by age 5 (Berglund, Eriksson, & Johansson, 2001).

In general, it appears that young children with Down syndrome are significantly delayed in early language development. These delays continue as the child develops, so that the gap between them and typically developing peers widens. For example, many children with Down syndrome do not begin to speak until age 2 or 3 or use multiword utterances until at least age 4 (Rondal, 2001).

Research on the early language development of children with Williams syndrome has found that language acquisition is usually delayed (Mervis & Becerra, 2007). Compared to children with Down syndrome, children with Williams syndrome have larger expressive vocabularies, although their receptive vocabularies do not appear to be significantly greater (Mervis & Klein-Tasman, 2000). However, children with Williams syndrome do experience delays in vocabulary acquisition compared to typically developing children. One reason for this finding may be their curious pattern of development in referential communication. Most babies point before they use words to describe objects. Pointing is a way to get the attention of adults and begin to engage in communication. But children with Williams syndrome have been found to use words to refer to objects before they point (Mervis & Klein-Tasman, 2000). This unusual pattern may be related to the problems in visuospatial processing (visual perception and discrimination) and to the preference of individuals with Williams syndrome for people rather than for objects.

Limited research on children with fragile X syndrome indicates that they also experience significant delays in early language development (Abbeduto, Brady, & Kover, 2007). Kover, McCary, Ingram, Hatton, and Roberts (2015) examined the early language skills of a sample of 13 children with fragile X syndrome at four points in development: 9, 12, 18, and 24 months of age. They found significant delays in language development by 12 months of age. However, the children did show evidence of growth in language skills over time, indicating that their sample of children with fragile X syndrome were developing language in a delayed manner and that the gap between them and typically developing children increases over time.

In general, delays in early language development, including the emergence of first words, appear to be characteristic of all children with intellectual disabilities. However, there are specific differences in the types of delays that are related to genetic phenotypes.

Speech Production and Phonology

Difficulties with speech production are more common among children with intellectual disabilities than among typically developing children (Griffer, 2012), but there is a good deal of variation both within and between different phenotypes (e.g., Down syndrome, fragile X syndrome, Williams syndrome). Estimates of the incidence of speech production deficits have been reported to be as low as 5 percent and as high as 94 percent (Shriberg & Widder, 1990).

Most of the research on speech sound disorders among individuals with intellectual disabilities has been conducted with persons with Down syndrome. Difficulties in speech intelligibility are characteristic of individuals with Down syndrome. They tend to be difficult to understand, and this problem continues through childhood and into the adult years (Barnes et al., 2009; Martin, Klusek, Estigarribia, & Roberts, 2009). In a comprehensive review of the research on speech sound disorders in this population, Kent and Vorperian (2013) reported that the research indicates that speech sound disorders, including difficulties in the domains of voice, speech sound production, fluency and prosody, and intelligibility, are frequently found. These difficulties may be caused by a variety of factors, including anatomical differences in the vocal tract, tongue, and facial musculature; impaired hearing; impaired motor functioning; or central processing disorders that affect language and cognitive functioning (Martin et al., 2009).

Delays and differences in phonological development are also frequently found in children with intellectual disabilities. For example, individuals with Down syndrome have been reported to have significant delays in the development of phonology that are characteristic of younger children (Roberts, Price, & Malkin, 2007). The most common phonological errors are reduction of consonant clusters (saying *bake* for *break*) and final consonant deletion (saying *cah* for *cat*) (Klink, Gerstman, Raphael, Schlanger, & Newsome, 1986; Sommers, Patterson, & Wildgen, 1988). As they grow older, the lag in phonological development increases, and the error patterns persist, even when compared to typically developing younger children matched for mental age (Roberts et al., 2005).

Compared to individuals with Down syndrome, those with fragile X syndrome have fewer phonological difficulties. Yet, persons with fragile X syndrome are usually delayed in the acquisition of phonology and can be difficult to understand (Roberts et al., 2005). These delays may become greater after age 10 and can affect their reading performance (Adolf, Klusek, Shinkareva, Robinson, & Roberts, 2015). In contrast, the limited research on the phonological skills of individuals with Williams syndrome suggests that their phonological abilities are similar to those of typically developing children. However, unlike their typically developing peers, their phonological skills seem to develop independently from other language skills (Stojanovik, Setter, & van Ewijk, 2007).

The research on the phonological development and speech production abilities of children with intellectual disabilities, especially those with Down syndrome, suggests that education professionals should be prepared to help these children enhance their phonological and speech production skills. Many children with intellectual disabilities have articulation difficulties that interfere with their ability to be successful in school and in social interactions. Intervention that includes both individual therapy and classroom-based applications may be useful in helping children with intellectual disabilities become more successful learners. In addition, for some, augmentative or alternative communication techniques may be needed.

Morphology and Syntax

As was true with phonology, research on the morphological and syntactic development in children with intellectual disabilities has generally focused on individuals with Down syndrome. In general, researchers have found that although there are significant delays in the development of morphology and syntax, the pattern of development is similar to that found in nondisabled children.

Although children with Down syndrome have generally been reported to develop grammatical morphemes in the same order as typically developing children, they lag significantly behind same-age peers (Roberts, Price, & Malkin, 2007) even when matched for mental age (Finestack, Sterling, & Abbeduto, 2013). This suggests that morphological development may be especially difficult for children with Down syndrome. Children with fragile X syndrome have also been found to lag behind in morphological development, but the gap between these children and their typically developing peers narrows as they get older (Finstack, Richmond, & Abbeduto, 2009).

Delays and some differences in the development of syntactic skills are commonly found in children with Down syndrome and fragile X syndrome. The syntactic delays of children with Down syndrome begin as soon as they make the transition from single to multiword utterances. As they age, their mean length of utterances (MLU) continues to lag behind that of typically developing peers, even when compared to younger children with the same mental age (Roberts, Price, & Malkin, 2007). They use shorter, less complex sentences. Researchers who have studied the receptive syntactic skills of children with Down syndrome have also reported significant delays in development (Price, Roberts, Vandergrift, & Martin, 2007). For example, like typically developing children, the MLU of individuals with Down syndrome generally increases with chronological age up to adolescence but at a much slower rate than that found in typically developing children (Rondal, 2001). While some researchers have claimed that individuals with intellectual disabilities reach a ceiling in their morphosyntactic development, others have found no evidence for such a ceiling (Chapman, Hesketh, & Kistler, 2002).

Price and colleagues (2007) found that boys with fragile X syndrome had delays in syntactic development compared to younger, typically developing boys, but that these delays were not as great as those of boys with Down syndrome. However, there is a lot of variability in this population, especially in regard to morphological and syntactic development. For example, Abbeduto and colleagues (2007) report some findings that the language of individuals with fragile X syndrome may be more complex than predicted by MLU. Males with fragile X syndrome have been reported to have receptive syntactic skills at about the level that would be expected for their mental age but also to have expressive syntax significantly below expectations (Abbeduto & Hagerman, 1997). Finestack, Sterling, and Abbeduto (2013) found a similar result and suggested that difficulties with expressive syntax may be due to social anxiety. Oakes, Kover, and Abbeduto (2013) examined the receptive syntactic skills of adolescents with fragile X syndrome compared to typically developing peers matched for nonverbal mental age and adolescents with Down syndrome. They found that the adolescents with fragile X syndrome achieved lower overall scores on receptive syntax than the typically developing group but higher scores than the subjects with Down syndrome. As is often true with fragile X syndrome, females outperformed males. So, although there is evidence for delays in syntactic and morphological development in this population, it may not be surprising to find that some children with fragile X syndrome may show unusual patterns of development that could be due, at least in part, to their difficulty expressing themselves in conversational situations.

In contrast to the patterns of delay found in most children with intellectual disabilities, the syntactic skills of individuals with Williams syndrome have often been reported to be at or even above what would be expected for their mental age. They can use a variety of grammatical forms, including complex constructions such as relative clauses and the passive voice (Bellugi, Lai, & Wang, 1997). However, according to Mervis (2009), recent research with children with Williams syndrome has found that their morphological and syntactic development is similar to or slightly behind that of typically developing peers.

The research on syntactic skills of children with intellectual disabilities suggests that there is more variation in the population than might be expected. Although most, if not all, can be expected to develop syntactic skills much more slowly than do typically developing children of the same age, for some (such as children with Williams syndrome), syntax is a relative strength. The research also suggests that most children with intellectual disabilities could benefit from continued instruction in syntactic skills throughout their school years.

As you watch this video of a 7-year-old girl with Down syndrome talking with her mother, note both her use of syntax and her articulation of words. In what ways is Ciarra's language development similar to and different from that of a typically developing child?

https://www.youtube.com/watch?v=RwlXyoHMfYA

Semantics

Earlier in this chapter, we noted that young children with intellectual disabilities, especially those with Down syndrome, are delayed in their development of first words. Parent reports indicate that only 12 percent of 12- to 23-month-olds, 80 percent of 24- to 35-month-olds, and 90 percent of 36- to 47-month-olds produced one word (Berglund et al., 2001). Compare that to typically developing children who generally produce their first word between 10 and 15 months of age. By age 4, only 50 percent of the children studied had at least 50 words in their spoken vocabulary. At age 5, the range of vocabulary acquisition was from no words to over 600 words.

In contrast to the above findings, some studies have found that the development of vocabulary is an area of strength for children with intellectual disabilities. For example, in a study of children and adolescents with Down syndrome, Chapman, Schwartz, and Kay-Raining Bird (1991) found that individuals with intellectual disabilities performed significantly better on the vocabulary-comprehension task than on tests of syntactic skills—in fact, they outscored a nonverbal mental age–matched control group on their vocabulary comprehension. Other studies have shown that examination of language produced in natural settings indicates that children with Down syndrome have a more diverse vocabulary than do nondisabled children matched for mental age (Miller, 1988). On the other hand, individuals with Down syndrome have been found to use both fewer words and a less diverse vocabulary than mental age–matched peers on narrative tasks (Chapman, 1997). To understand these conflicting results, one should consider two factors: the task and the age differences. First, the results of research suggest that individuals with intellectual disabilities may be able to perform better on structured tasks than when asked to produce open-ended narratives. Second, you should remember that students with intellectual disabilities matched for mental age will be older. As a result, they have had more exposure to diverse vocabulary. Despite this experience, their vocabulary skills are significantly below typically developing children of the same age, which can have an impact on their reading skills (Næss, Melby-Lervåg, Hulme, & Lyster, 2012).

Most studies of children with fragile X syndrome have found vocabulary development to be an area of relative strength. For example, Abbeduto and colleagues (2003) found receptive vocabulary to be similar to mental age in a sample of children with fragile X with a mean age of 16 years. On the other hand, in a study of boys age 3 to 15 years, Price, Roberts, Vandergrift, and Martin (2007) found that boys with fragile X syndrome had receptive vocabularies significantly below those of younger children with typical development, even when controlling for nonverbal cognition. The expressive vocabulary skills of individuals with fragile X syndrome have generally been found to be significantly reduced compared with developmentally matched peers (Finestack et al., 2009). Some of the variations in vocabulary in this population may be due to the different subtypes of fragile X syndrome. For example, there is a subtype that has autism as well as fragile X syndrome. This group generally is more significantly delayed in language development. In their comparison of children Down syndrome and children with fragile X syndrome, Finestack and colleagues (2013) found both expressive and receptive vocabulary of both groups to be similar to that of typically developing children matched for nonverbal mental age.

The semantic abilities of children with Williams syndrome are significantly different from others with intellectual disabilities. Children with Williams syndrome typically have an usually large and sophisticated vocabulary and may use words that not even typically developing children use. For example, one study reported that, when asked to name all the animals they could, adolescents with Williams syndrome gave responses including yak, ibex, and condor, whereas individuals with Down syndrome gave responses such as dog and cat (Bellugi et al., 1997). Other studies have found the semantic organization skills (Lee & Binder, 2014) and receptive vocabulary (Brock, Jarrold, Farran, Laws, & Riby, 2007) of children with Williams syndrome to be similar to those of typically developing children. However, children with Williams syndrome are likely to have more difficulty with spatial, temporal, and quantitative concepts (words such as "under" and "over" and "before" and "after") (Mervis & Becerra, 2007). This may be due to the often-reported difficulties of these children with visuospatial processing.

Clearly, there are significant differences in semantic abilities among persons with intellectual disabilities, but the primary pattern seems to be one in which production lags behind comprehension. Teachers and others who work with these children should help them use a more diverse vocabulary in their speaking and writing by using techniques such as word banks to enhance their semantic production.

Pragmatics

There has been good deal of research on the pragmatic abilities of individuals with intellectual disabilities. The research reveals a mixed pattern of strengths and weaknesses as well as some interesting differences between the different phenotypes of intellectual disabilities (e.g., Down syndrome, fragile X syndrome, Williams syndrome).

Conversational Competence.   To communicate effectively, it is necessary to develop pragmatic language skills such as turn-taking, topic management, and conversational repair. The conversational competence of persons with intellectual disabilities has been studied in each of these areas.

In typical conversations, participants take turns talking, occasionally speaking at the same time. Persons with intellectual disabilities have been found to have few problems with taking turns in conversations. Studies of young children with Down syndrome (Tannock, 1988), school-age children (Roberts, Martin, Moskowitz, Harris, Foreman, & Nelson, 2007) as well as adults (Abbeduto & Rosenberg, 1980), show that they take turns in conversations and make few errors, much as typically developing people do.

Although individuals with intellectual disabilities appear capable of taking turns in a conversation, what is even more important is what they do when it is their turn. Typically, people with intellectual disabilities do not make significant contributions to maintaining the conversation (Abbeduto & Hesketh, 1997). They might make comments such as *Okay* or *um-um* but do not *extend* the topic by adding new information. In their study involving school-age children with Down syndrome, Roberts and colleagues (2007) reported that, although the children initiated topics about as frequently as typically developing children matched for mental age, the quality of their conversational contributions differed. Specifically, although they responded to the speaker, their responses were limited and did little to encourage further interaction.

Research on the conversational skills of people with intellectual disabilities has also found that they have difficulty *repairing* conversations that break down. If you are talking with someone else and do not understand what is being said, you will usually do something to clarify the conversation. You might say, "What?" or "Excuse me?" as a signal to the speaker that you do not understand. People with intellectual disabilities are *capable* of using such conversational repairs but fail to use them when they are needed (Abbeduto, Davies, Solesby, & Furman, 1991; Robinson & Whittaker, 1986). Children with intellectual disabilities have also been found to be slow in responding to clarification requests made by others (Scherer & Owings, 1984). Moreover, researchers have found that the development of conversational repair skills appears to plateau during the school years and not improve with experience (Abbeduto, Short-Meyerson, Benson, & Dolish, 1997).

There is a small but growing body of research on the conversational skills of individuals with fragile X and Williams syndromes. Compared to children with Down syndrome, boys with fragile X syndrome use more "noncontingent" (off-topic) discourse and more perseveration (repeated words and phrases) in their conversation (Roberts et al., 2007). Adolescents with fragile X syndrome have also been found to produce more repetitive speech during conversation (e.g., *I—I—I left the house*) and more "tangential" language (utterances that are off topic) than other persons with intellectual disability or autism (Belser & Sudhalter, 2001; Sudhalter & Belser, 2001). Although individuals with fragile X syndrome may be better at using grammatical forms to express themselves, they are relatively poor communicators (Abbeduto, Brady, & Kover, 2007).

A significant percentage of individuals with fragile X syndrome also exhibit characteristics of autism. It has been estimated that between 60 and 75 percent of individuals with fragile X syndrome also meet the criteria for autism (Hall, Lightbody, & Reiss, 2008). Pragmatic language impairments are a defining feature of autism. Researchers who have compared the pragmatic language skills of children with fragile X syndrome who also exhibit symptoms of autism and those who do not have found similar impairments in pragmatics across both populations (Klusek, Martin, & Losh, 2014). Difficulties with pragmatic language were found to show up most clearly in conversational language samples, which suggests that individuals with fragile X syndrome as well as those with autism have difficulty communicating with others.

Individuals with Williams syndrome have frequently been described as being very sociable and friendly, to the point where they may, at times, put themselves in danger. For example, they may strike up conversations with complete strangers or express their "love" for someone they just met (Jones et al., 2000). After completing a series of studies examining several aspects of pragmatic language in children and adolescents with Williams syndrome, Jones and colleagues (2000) concluded that hypersociability (an unusually strong drive toward social interaction with others) is characteristic of individuals with Williams syndrome.

Despite their sociability, individuals with Williams syndrome have been found to have difficulty with aspects of pragmatic language, including turn-taking, topic maintenance, and a tendency to perseverate on topics that are of particular interest to them (Hoffman, Martens, Fox, Rabidoux, & Andridge, 2013; Rondal, 2001). In addition, individuals with Williams syndrome tend to provide too little information to their conversational partner and are more likely than typically developing children to misunderstand their conversational partner (Mervis & Becerra, 2007). For example, in a study of conversational skills of school-aged children (7–12 years old) with Williams syndrome, Stojanovik (2006) found that the Williams children used fewer "continuations" in their conversations (adding new information that tends to continue the conversation). Stojanovik found that, although the children with Williams syndrome had no obvious problems with topic maintenance, language structure, and turn-taking, their conversational behavior was typically characterized by very little exchange of information, speech that was heavily dependent on their conversational partner's lead, and general difficulties with interpreting meaning.

In considering all of the research on the communicative abilities of persons with intellectual disabilities, Abbeduto (1991) concluded that "deficits in verbal communication are a defining feature of intellectual disabilities and should figure prominently in assessments of adaptive behavior" (p. 108). Although problems with verbal communication do seem to be quite common among people with intellectual disabilities, there is considerable variability within the population.

Obviously, the ability to engage in effective communication with others is a critical skill for classroom success. Teachers and other education professionals should be alert to the problems that students with intellectual disabilities may have in expressing themselves and understanding others. Placing students in heterogeneous groups can be a good way to encourage communicative interaction if the groups are well managed and the group activities carefully chosen.

Speech Acts.   The concept of speech acts was described in Chapter 1. These acts occur whenever one has the intention to communicate. Requests, commands, and declarations are examples of speech acts. Children with intellectual disabilities have been described as being delayed in both their use and understanding of speech acts (Abbeduto & Hesketh, 1997). Although they have significant delays, their development of speech acts is similar to that of other children. That is, they can make requests, ask questions, and so on, like younger, typically developing children. In one study (Abbeduto, Furman, & Davies, 1988), children with and without intellectual disabilities were asked to interpret sentences requiring either a yes or no response or an action. For example, *Can you close the window?* could be either asking whether one is *able* to close the window or requesting that someone *actually close* the window. In their study, Abbeduto and colleagues found that in their ability to understand what the speaker actually wanted, adolescents with intellectual disabilities were similar to younger, nondisabled children matched for mental age. Although comprehension of speech acts is delayed, this has been found to be a relative strength, at least in children with Down syndrome. In fact, adults with Down syndrome may be quite good at understanding the messages that others are trying to convey.

One specific difference in speech-act usage by individuals with Down syndrome is the use of politeness. Children and adolescents with Down syndrome have been found to use less polite forms compared to typically developing children of the same mental age (Nuccio & Abbeduto, 1993). In other words, rather than saying, "May I please have the doll?" in requesting a toy, they were more likely to say, "You better gimme my doll." The study authors believe that this difference in the use of polite forms of request is not due to an inability to produce the polite form. In fact, the individuals with Down syndrome who were part of the study demonstrated the ability to use polite requests in certain contexts. Instead, the researchers concluded that individuals with Down syndrome fail to recognize the *need* to use a polite form. This finding suggests that teachers may need to monitor the conversation of students with Down syndrome and model a different form of requesting if this is a problem.

Referential Communication.   In **referential communication** tasks, children are evaluated on their ability to explain a task to another person. This procedure reveals their ability to take into account the information needed by someone else to complete the task. Individuals with intellectual disabilities have been reported to have problems with referential communication tasks. They have difficulty producing messages that make the task clear to others. They tend to pay less attention to the important features of the task or object that would help their listener complete the task. Although they are generally better at the listener role than the speaker role, they are still delayed relative to typically developing children of the same mental age.

One way to test referential communication is with a *barrier task*. For this procedure, children are seated across from each other with a barrier between them that prevents them from seeing each other. One child is the speaker; the other is the listener. Each has an array of blocks or other items. The speaker's blocks—the model—are arranged in a design. The speaker's task is to tell the listener how to arrange the blocks to match the model, using only verbal directions. Using just such a procedure to study the referential communication abilities of adolescents with intellectual disabilities, Longhurst (1974) found that when the individuals with intellectual disabilities were in the speaker's role, they were remarkably unsuccessful in directing the listeners to complete the task. However, when they were the listener, they were able to successfully perform the task when directions were given by nondisabled adults.

A second way to evaluate referential communication is by asking individuals to describe an activity (such as a game) to someone else. In one such study (Loveland, Tunali, McEvoy, & Kelly, 1989), adolescents and adults with Down syndrome were asked to explain a game to an experimenter. These individuals with intellectual disabilities performed quite well, giving the necessary information to the listener without a great deal of prompting. However, as Abbeduto (1991) points out, since we do not know how nondisabled persons would have handled this task, it is difficult to judge how good these results really are.

Most of the research on referential communication has been carried out with persons with Down syndrome. However, a recent study compared the referential communication of adolescents with intellectual disabilities caused by two different syndromes—Down syndrome and fragile X syndrome—to that of typically developing 5-year-old children matched for mental age (Abbeduto et al., 2006). The participants in the study were asked to play a game in which they had to describe a novel shape to a listener so that he or she could pick out the shape from among several choices. The researchers found that both the adolescents with Down syndrome and those with fragile X syndrome were less effective than the younger, typically developing children in helping their partner successfully complete the task. There were also some specific differences between the groups. Those with Down syndrome tended to give fewer descriptions to their partners, leaving it up to the partners to request more information. The individuals with fragile X syndrome used less consistent referents—sometimes inventing new descriptions for the same item, leaving their partners confused. These results suggest that, although referential communication can be difficult for all individuals with intellectual disabilities, the pattern of difficulties may vary due to the specific syndrome related to the disability.

It appears from the research on referential communication that persons with intellectual disabilities have some difficulty getting their messages across to others. This can cause significant difficulties in social interaction. Listeners may become confused and be less interested in carrying on a conversation. Classroom activities that require the use of referential communication skills can help children become better speakers and listeners. Guessing games, "20 Questions," and even "Show and Tell" provide opportunities for students to develop and use referential-communication skills.

Apply Your Knowledge 8.1: Communicative Interaction

Read this transcript of an 8-year-old student with Down syndrome as she talks with her teacher, and then respond to the questions.

Conclusion

Review of the research on the language and communication abilities of people with intellectual disabilities has revealed several things. First, in most cases, the language skills of this population can be described as delayed rather than different. That is, children with intellectual disabilities seem to develop through the same stages as nondisabled children, only much more slowly (see Table 8.2 for a summary). Second, there is a good deal of variation in the language and communication skills of persons with intellectual disabilities. These variations may be due to cognitive delays, physical characteristics, or the underlying cause of the individual's developmental disability. As research into the language and communication characteristics of specific syndromes continues, it is likely that we will better understand the variations in language performance among individuals with intellectual disabilities. In the section that follows, we will examine some of the factors that may contribute to the language and communication difficulties of individuals with intellectual disabilities.

Factors Related to Language and Communication Impairments

In most cases, it is not possible to say with certainty what causes the language and communication impairments of any individual (just as it is not possible to explain typical language development). It is true that in some individuals there are obvious physical characteristics (such as a cleft palate or protruding tongue) that can explain some of the communication difficulties of that person. But, in most cases, the best we can do is to talk about factors that may *contribute* to language and communication disorders. What are these contributing factors? We could have quite a long list, but we will limit our examination to three factors: cognitive functioning, specific language disorder, and input language.

Cognitive Functioning.   Deficits in cognitive functioning are *the* defining feature of intellectual disabilities. Cognitive abilities—as measured by intelligence tests—are the first criteria in determining whether an individual is intellectually disabled. There may be a temptation to assume a person having low measured intelligence is functioning at low levels across the board, but this is rarely the case. Each individual has a unique set of cognitive strengths and weaknesses. In addition, as we have seen with language and

Table 8.2

Language and Communication of Individuals with Intellectual Disabilities

Prelinguistic Development	Phonology and Morphology	Syntax	Semantics	Pragmatics
Nonverbal communication similar to other infants but uses vocalizations less often with gestures	Difficulties with speech production	Sentence length similar to mental age–matched controls	Problems understanding idiomatic expressions	Delays in understanding and use of speech acts
Use of gestures may be area of strength for babies with Down syndrome	Development similar to typical but delayed	Mean length of utterance of Down syndrome increases with chronological age, but more slowly	Delays in semantic development	Down syndrome: uses less polite forms
Babbling follows pattern similar to that of typically developing young children	Reduction of consonant clusters and final consonant deletion	Order of development of rules similar to typical	Vocabulary a relative strength for children with fragile X syndrome	Difficulty with speaker role
Children with Down syndrome start using first words at later age and acquire words more slowly	Children with fragile X experience delays in phonological development	Children with fragile X syndrome experience delays but not as great as those in Down syndrome	Williams syndrome: have relatively large vocabulary but specific deficits	Turn-taking intact
Young children with fragile X syndrome are delayed in early language development	Delays in morphophonological development	Syntax of those with Williams syndrome at or above expected for mental age		Less significant contributions to conversation
	May be some specific deficits in morphology			Difficulties with conversational repairs
				Fragile X: uses more tangential language and more repetition

Sources: Abbeduto et al. (1991); Abbeduto et al. (2003); Abbeduto et al. (2007); Abbeduto & Hesketh (1997); Bellugi et al. (1997); Chapman (1997); Chapman & Hesketh (2000); Goetz et al. (2008); Klink et al. (1986); Longhurst (1974); Mervis (2009); Mervis & Becerra (2007); Mervis & Klein-Tasman (2000); Nuccio & Abbeduto (1993); Roberts et al. (2005); Roberts et al. (2007); Rondal (2001); Shriberg & Widder (1990); Sommers et al. (1988); Stoel-Gammon (1997); Sudhalter & Belser (2001); Tannock (1988).

communication, there may be differences in cognitive function that can be attributed to specific syndromes that can result in intellectual disabilities. What is the relationship between cognition and language development for persons with intellectual disabilities?

Memory difficulties have long been associated with intellectual disabilities. However, as we learn more about memory, we learn that people with intellectual disabilities have both strengths and weaknesses in this domain. For example, there is evidence that long-term memory is a relative strength in individuals with Down syndrome, but most have significant difficulties with short-term memory, especially verbal short-term memory (Chapman & Hesketh, 2000; Laws & Gunn, 2004; Næss et al., 2012). Similarly, individuals with fragile X syndrome have been found to have difficulty with auditory short-term memory (Abbeduto, Brady, & Korver, 2007). On the other hand, individuals with Williams syndrome generally have relatively intact verbal short-term memory. However, they have significant difficulties with tasks that require them to match pictures or objects (visuospatial tasks) (Mervis & Klein-Tasman, 2000). Both long-term and short-term memory are associated with language development. Initial language learning requires short-term memory skills to identify and store information. Long-term memory is needed to retrieve previously stored linguistic information. So deficits in either of these skills could affect language development.

Attention is another cognitive function that is necessary for successful language learning. While the ability to attend to tasks is generally intact in individuals with Down syndrome, that is not the case for children with fragile X syndrome. In fact, difficulty in paying attention and sustaining attention has been found to be characteristic of children with this disorder (Cornish, Sudhalter, & Turk, 2004). Children with fragile X syndrome, especially boys, tend to be restless, impulsive, and easily distracted. These characteristics can interfere with learning in many domains, including language.

If nothing else, the research on cognition and language in persons with intellectual disabilities shows that knowing a child's IQ is not enough. One must consider the pattern of individual strengths and weaknesses. Often that pattern is determined by the behavioral phenotype associated with syndromes that cause intellectual disabilities.

Specific Language Disorders.   There is no doubt that most people with intellectual disabilities have impairments of cognitive functioning. They also have problems in several areas of language development. Might we conclude, then, that the cognitive impairments cause the language disabilities? Might it be just as true to assert that the language impairments cause delays in cognitive development?

These are not easy questions to answer because language and cognition are interrelated in very complex ways. To try to answer these questions, researchers have compared the language of children with intellectual disabilities to that of nondisabled children who are matched for nonverbal mental age. If their language performance is similar, this suggests that language development is dependent on cognitive development. If, on the other hand, the language development of the subjects with intellectual disabilities is less advanced than that of the nondisabled subjects, one could conclude persons with intellectual disabilities have a specific language disorder that cannot be explained by cognitive delays alone.

Research on the relationship between cognition and language in persons with intellectual disability has yielded inconsistent results. Our review of the research has revealed that delays in most aspects of language development are characteristic of children with intellectual disabilities. For the most part, their language development is like that of younger children matched for mental age and similar to children with specific language impairments (Eadie, Fey, Douglas, & Parsons, 2002). This suggest that children with Down syndrome may, in fact, have a specific disorder in language that goes beyond their cognitive differences. However, there are exceptions to this finding, for example, in pragmatics. In their review of the research on the language development of persons with Down syndrome, Roberts, Price and Malkin (2007) point out that the language disorders associated with this disorder occur early in development, occur in many domains of language, persist through life, and are generally greater than would be expected for mental age. They also point out, however, that this is not true of all individuals with Down syndrome or for all areas of language development.

Perhaps the answer is not to worry unduly about whether children with intellectual disabilities have an underlying language-processing disorder. Rather, teachers and clinicians should strive to identify the specific pattern of language and communication difficulties in each child and provide appropriate intervention and supports.

Parent–Child Interaction.   In the search for causes of language and communication difficulties in children with intellectual disabilities, another aspect is input language. We know from research on typical language development that children learn language by participating in communicative interactions with parents and other caregivers. We also know that parents alter their language to make it more compatible with their child's ability to comprehend.

Despite the fact that infants and young children with intellectual disabilities are delayed in development, recent research has found that parents of children with intellectual disabilities provide an adequate language environment for their child. They talk to their children as often as do parents of typically developing children and use similar speech acts. They respond to the communicative attempts of their children just like parents of typically developing children of the same language age. In fact, there is evidence that they respond to a broader range of behaviors in their children, including body movements, facial expressions, and made-up signs (Stephenson & Dowrick, 2005). Mothers of children with intellectual disabilities alter their linguistic input appropriately for the language-development level of their children (Rondal, 1978). Although they tend to use more directives in their communication with their children, they become less directive as their children become more linguistically advanced (Abbeduto & Hesketh, 1997).

It seems clear that parents of children with intellectual disabilities generally provide an appropriate language environment for their developing children. In most cases, differences in communicative interaction are an appropriate response by parents to their children's slower language development. On the other hand, these parents must be careful not to overcompensate for their children's language impairments. They must work hard at giving their daughters and sons the opportunity to initiate interaction and should be responsive to their children, even if they feel that the children may be acting inappropriately. Children with intellectual disabilities whose parents respond optimally to their child, for example, by putting nonverbal communication acts into words, being responsive to their child's requests, and imitating their child's vocalizations, either exactly or with slight modifications, have been found to have more advanced language and communication development (Yoder & Warren, 2004).

In the beginning of this section, we noted the difficulty in finding a specific cause for the language impairments experienced by most persons with intellectual disabilities. Indeed, our search for a cause has yielded some clues but no firm answers. Cognitive disabilities clearly play a role but do not account for all the language difficulties of people with intellectual disabilities. Parents and other caregivers may talk differently to children with intellectual disabilities, but it is likely that these differences are as much the *result* of language differences as the cause. Lack of motivation, adaptive behavior deficits, physical disabilities, and specific language impairments have been proposed as the cause of the language deficiencies of individuals with intellectual disabilities. Evidence increasingly supports the notion that genetic disorders such as Down syndrome, fragile X syndrome, and Williams syndrome may include specific language deficits as a characteristic of the syndrome. As research on these syndromes continues, we may be better able to understand the specific patterns of language strengths and deficits within subgroups of individuals with intellectual disabilities.

Literacy and Students with Intellectual Disabilities

Along with changing expectations for community living and inclusion in school, there have been changes in expectations for the academic achievement of individuals with intellectual disabilities, including those with moderate to severe disabilities. As Knight, Browder, Agnello, and Lee (2010) pointed out, under the Individuals with Disabilities Education Act (IDEA), students with disabilities must (a) *have access to* the general curriculum, (b) *be involved in* the general curriculum, and (c) *progress in* the general curriculum (IDEA, 2004). Recent research has provided evidence that when given the opportunity to learn academic content, students with moderate and severe developmental disabilities can do so (see Knight et al., 2010).

Teacher Perspective

One of my seventh graders has an IQ of 60. He received early intervention, but he did not learn to read until he was in fourth grade. He was taught to read by his speech teacher. He was developmentally ready at that time (not before). If he had been deemed hopeless as far as literacy was concerned, he probably would never have learned. His mother told me at the last teacher–parent conference that he reads all of the time now. I have given my students a 25-book goal for the year, and he is trying to reach it. (The books have to be at least 90 pages.) Now that we are getting more into nonfiction, I am going to have them obtain more information from resources and will also teach them life skills that use their literacy skills.

One of the most critical academic skill are for any student is literacy development. Developing skills in reading and writing is both an end in itself and a means to learning across the curriculum. However, until recently, it was generally assumed that most students with intellectual disabilities were incapable of developing significant literacy skills. As Browder, Wakeman, Spooner, Ahlgrim-Delzell, and Algozzine (2006) noted, historically, literacy development for persons with intellectually disabilities has received little attention. Whereas students with mild levels of intellectual disabilities might be expected to develop reading skills as high as the second- or third-grade level, individuals with lower measured intelligence were not expected to develop reading skills at all. However, there is now a good deal of evidence that, given appropriate instruction, students with intellectual disabilities can learn to read and write (Katims, 2000; Kliewer, 2008). The impetus to more fully include individuals with intellectual disabilities in the community, including in school, makes it even more important for educators to understand the literacy skills of individuals with intellectual disabilities and the most effective ways to enhance those skills.

Because the longstanding assumption has been that students with intellectual disabilities cannot learn to read and write, the prevailing approach to instruction has been "functional" in nature. Functional reading instruction typically involves teaching "survival" words through a sight-word approach. Students are taught to "read" specific words that are thought to be essential for survival in the world. For example, they might be taught to recognize the word *exit* on a sign or to read words on food labels. Research on the use of this approach has found that students with intellectual disabilities can learn to recognize a number of words using this method, but their ability to use this skill in real situations may be limited (Browder & Xin, 1998). In addition, for many students with intellectual disabilities, sight-word instruction is the only literacy training they receive in school. Some students learn (and relearn) the same words year after year, with little, if any, exposure to books or writing activities.

Currently, researchers are trying to discover more about the problems that underlie the reading and writing deficiencies of most students with intellectual disabilities. Undoubtedly, the language difficulties described in previous sections of this chapter are a factor. One of the specific skills that has been studied is phonological processing. Compared to students with learning disabilities, relatively little research has examined the phonological skills of individuals with intellectual disabilities. However, the limited research has confirmed that significant difficulties in phonological processing exist in this population and that reading instruction that incorporates phonological instruction can be effective (Allor, Mathes, Roberts, Cheatham, & Champlin, 2010; Channel, Lovell, & Conners, 2013; Conners, 1992; Joseph & Seery, 2004; Saunders, 2007).

One example of this research comes from a study by Conners, Rosenquist, Sligh, Atwell, and Kiser (2006). They taught 20 children with intellectual disabilities (mean IQ = 54), ages 7 to 12 years old, using a phonological training program of their own design. Students completed three units consisting of six to nine lessons per unit: oral practice in sound blending, letter–sound association, and sounding out. When compared to a matched group of students who did not receive this instruction, the phonological training group significantly outperformed their peers on measures of sounding out. However, there was significant variability in the results. About half of the children who received the instruction correctly sounded out 80 percent or more of the words on the posttest, whereas six students (30%) identified fewer than 20 percent of the words. The authors of the study found that previous instruction in phonological analysis and entering reading levels were important factors in success on the sounding-out task. Similarly, Goetz and colleagues (2008) found that intensive phonics instruction that included segmentation tasks and blending skills in the context of learning letter sounds and working with words in books significantly enhanced the reading skills of children with Down syndrome who were age 8 to 11.

Although phonological skills are an important factor in literacy development, other aspects of literacy have also been included in instructional programs for students with intellectual disabilities. For example, van Wingerden, Segers, van Balkom, and Verhoeven

(2013) examined the reading comprehension skills of children age 9 to 13 with intellectual disabilities in comparison to those of younger, typically developing first graders. They found that the children with intellectual disabilities were similar to the younger, typically developing students in their ability to perform low-level comprehension tasks (such as answer a factual multiple choice question). However, they had significant difficulty with higher level reading comprehension tasks, such as inferencing and choosing a title for the reading passage. Allor and colleagues (2010) have been examining the effects over time of a comprehensive reading program on the reading skills of children with intellectual disabilities whose IQs range from 40 to 69. They found that the children were able to make considerable progress in phonemic decoding, word attack skills, and comprehension.

The research on the literacy development of children with intellectual disabilities suggests that instruction in phonological skills should be part of a comprehensive reading program for students with intellectual disabilities. Moreover, a rich literacy environment in which children have an opportunity to listen to stories read to them, to talk about what they hear, and to write at the level of their ability should be part of a comprehensive literacy program for students with intellectual disabilities. The message from research and experience is that these children can develop literacy skills. They do so more slowly than their peers of the same age and may never reach the literacy levels of those peers, but they can do more than memorize lists of sight words.

There are many apps that can be useful for teaching literacy skills. Watch this video of a child using the "First Words: Animals" (Learning Touch) app. What elements of the app would be useful for teaching beginning literacy skills to children with intellectual disabilities?
https://www.youtube.com/watch?v=3VaZKErG5So

Check Your Understanding 8.2
Click here to gauge your understanding of the concepts in this section.

Language Instruction for Individuals with Intellectual Disabilities

Finding the cause of the language and communication disabilities of children with intellectual disabilities is not always possible. Fortunately, it is not essential to know the cause of the problem in order to do something about it. This section presents some general principles for intervention with students with intellectual disabilities, discussing two specific intervention approaches for language and communication impairments.

Instructional Principles

Roberts and colleagues (2007) suggested that the following language intervention guidelines could be effective for students with Down syndrome as well as those with other intellectual disabilities:

- **Initiate language intervention early in development:** There is evidence that interventions in the first 3 years of life foster prelinguistic skills and lead to enhanced development of language skills.

- **Provide intervention to increase speech intelligibility:** Speech intervention in individuals with Down syndrome and other intellectual disabilities should be individualized to target specific phonological processes and speech errors that persist.

- **Assess language in a variety of communication contexts to determine language goals for intervention:** Language should be assessed using standardized tests as well as language samples and a variety of elicitation methods. Language assessments should occur in a variety of contexts such as in the classroom, with peers, at home, and in the community.

- **Consider augmentative or alternative communication:** Use unaided systems such as pointing, body language, facial expressions, or manual sign language, or use aided methods such as voice output communication aids (VOCAS).

- **Manage otitis media and associated hearing loss:** Otitis media (middle-ear infections) can cause fluctuating hearing loss that can affect language development. It is important to test for otitis media and evaluate hearing on a regular basis.

Exciting research is being done incorporating early intervention with the use of technology to enhance the language skills of very young children with significant disabilities. Janice Light and Katherine Drager (2010) have reported that young children (under 1 year old) with Down syndrome and other developmental disabilities made significant increases in word usage, turn-taking, and other language skills after participating in individualized, home-based, instructional sessions that used computers to augment spoken language skills. You can find out more about this project by visiting their website, Early Intervention for Young Children with Autism, Cerebral Palsy, Down Syndrome, and Other Disabilities.

Specific Instructional Approaches

There are few instructional methods that have been developed to teach language and communication skills exclusively to students with intellectual disabilities. In general, instructional methods for enhancing language and communication in this population lie along a continuum from highly structured, didactic teaching to more naturalistic, child-oriented approaches (Yoder, Kaiser, & Alpert, 1991).

Among the more highly structured procedures are those that use applied behavior analysis methods such as imitation, modeling, and/or reinforcement. These approaches take the child through a highly structured sequence of steps toward a goal that is set prior to instruction. Instructional approaches based on applied behavior analysis (ABA) principles have been quite successful in enhancing the language and literacy of children with significant disabilities, including intellectual disabilities and autism.

Hicks, Rivera, and Wood (2015) used an ABA technique (direct instruction) to teach prepositions to three elementary-aged students with intellectual disability. The instructor followed a script to present the student with positive examples and nonexamples of the target preposition. For a positive example, the instructor picked a pencil out of a box and held it above the box while saying, "This is above." For a nonexample, the instructor picked a pencil out of a box and held it next to the box while saying, "This is not above." Using this approach, the experimenters were able to successfully teach each of the children the meaning of three prepositions.

One widely used ABA approach is discrete trial training. Discrete trial training involves teaching a specific task (e.g., naming an object) through individualized, intensive practice. Although discrete trial training has been used primarily with individuals with autism, Downs, Downs, Johansen, and Fossum (2007) evaluated its effectiveness in teaching receptive and expressive language skills, such as identification of objects, behaviors, emotions, colors, and shapes, and conversational skills to 4- and 5-year-old children with significant disabilities, including intellectual disabilities. The children received 10 to 15 minutes of discrete trial instruction each day for 27 weeks. The researchers found that the children who received the discrete trial training were able to master a large number of new words, although there was wide variation in the results.

Another ABA-based approach is constant time delay. When using this method, the instructor initially presents a stimulus item (e.g., a picture of a cup) and immediately provides a word prompt (e.g., "This is a cup") and asks the child to say the word. After establishing that the child can say the word, for the next trial, the instructor waits a prescribed time (3–5 seconds) for a response before prompting the child to respond. Hua, Woods-Groves, Kaldenberg, and Scheidecker (2013) used a constant time delay procedure to teach vocabulary to four young adults with intellectual disability. The instructor wrote the target word on a flashcard, modeled the pronunciation, and asked the participant to read it. Then the instructor showed the definition printed on the back of the flashcard, read the definition, and asked the participant to read it. Then the instructor asked the student to read the word and give a definition without referring back to the flashcard. If the student was unable to read the word or give the definition within 3 seconds, the instructor read the word and the definition. The participants in this study learned more words and retained those words over time when taught with the constant time delay method compared to a control condition where the participants simply read a passage and answered questions.

One of the concerns about ABA methods such as discrete trial training is that the behaviors that are taught may not generalize to new settings. Several instructional methods have been developed that apply ABA principles to more naturalistic settings. For example, incidental (or milieu) teaching uses a structured approach to instruction (arranging the environment to teach specific skills, use of prompts and reinforcement, and collecting data on outcomes) to teach specific skills. Ganz, Cook, and Earles-Vollrath (2007) described the steps in using an incidental teaching procedure as follows:

1. Choose a learning objective.

2. Arrange the environment to prompt an initiation from the student.

3. Wait for the student to initiate.

4. Prompt the student to elaborate.

5. If correct, give specific praise and access to the materials

> For more information about incidental teaching and an example of its use, watch the video. What are the key steps in incidental teaching described in this video?
> https://www.youtube.com/watch?v=VwoAYir7Vsk

Another naturalistic approach based on ABA principles is the **mand-model procedure**. In this approach, the adult initiates the interaction using activities and objects that the student is using at the moment; the adult prompts a response by using a "mand" (a demand or request). Like incidental teaching, this technique uses natural activities in the child's environment as the basis of instruction. However, modeling, rather than operant conditioning, is used to teach the language skill. Warren (1991) gives the following example:

Context: (The child is scooping rice with a spoon and pouring it into a bowl.)

Adult: Tell me what you are doing.

Child: Beans.

Adult: Well then, say, "Pour beans."

Child: Pour beans.

Adult: That's right, you're pouring beans into the pot.

In this example, the adult saying "Tell me what you are doing" elicited a response. If the child had not responded, the adult could have told the child to say the name of the object. Since the child did respond, the adult modeled for the child a more adult form of responding. This technique helped children with significant language impairments increase their communication (Rogers-Warren & Warren, 1980). In a study with four elementary-level students with moderate intellectual disabilities, Hemmeter, Ault, Collins, and Meyer (1996) found that using **incidental teaching** and mand-model techniques significantly increased the language interaction of the children in their study.

Still another hybrid approach to teaching language skills is the **interrupted-behavior-chain strategy**. In this approach, a targeted language skill is inserted in the middle of an already established sequence of behaviors. Caro and Snell (1989) give an example of the application of this strategy in grocery shopping. Having taught an individual to read a grocery list, locate items on the shelf, and pay the cashier, the teacher could interrupt the behavior sequence to ask the student to say which items had already been placed in the grocery cart, and then praise a correct response. If the student produced an incorrect response, the instructor would model the correct response and prompt the student to produce it. This is an example of the combination of a natural environment (grocery shopping) with a structured instructional technique (prompting, modeling, reinforcement).

Hunt, Goetz, Alwell, and Sailor (1986) describe the use of the interrupted-behavior-chain strategy with a student named Everett, a 7-year-old boy with severe intellectual disabilities. The first step in this intervention was to identify sequences of behaviors that Everett could presently perform or was currently being taught. In Everett's case, he was able to independently get a drink from the water fountain and get food from the refrigerator. He was being taught to start and listen to a record player and to play an arcade game. Then interruptions were inserted into these behavior sequences at particular points. For example, as he leaned down to take a drink, Everett would be asked *What do you want?* and then prompted to choose by pointing to the picture of the water fountain from among a group of four pictures. Using this approach, Everett increased his ability to identify the correct picture and learned to point to a picture to request water. The researchers suggested that interrupting a previously established chain of behavior may motivate students to learn the communication skill so they can continue with the activity. A review of research on the interrupted-behavior-chain strategy found that it can be an effective way of teaching language skills to students with varying degrees of intellectual disability (Carter & Grunsell, 2001).

Both traditional ABA approaches and milieu methods use instructional methods that might be useful in planning instruction for students with intellectual disabilities, including the following:

- Focus on a specific skill or skills that is/are needed in the child's environment.
- Use appropriate and desired reinforcers.
- Provide instruction in the most naturalistic setting possible.
- Consider the need to generalize a learned skill to new environments.

Enhancing Generalization

One of the most significant problems faced by teachers of students with intellectual disabilities is helping them generalize new learning. A number of research studies have found that difficulties with generalization can be reduced if children are taught in the settings in which they will need the skill they are learning (e.g., Caro & Snell, 1989; Stowitschek, McConaughy, Peatross, Salzberg, & Lignngaris/Kraft, 1988). If, for example, children learn to approach others by practicing this skill in the cafeteria, then it should be easier for them to ask someone in the cafeteria to share a table if they need to do so. Generalization of language skills can be enhanced by using a variety of communicative partners, teaching skills that are actually in demand in the natural environment, and practicing skills in situations that are as close as possible to real environments.

Check Your Understanding 8.3
Click here to gauge your understanding of the concepts in this section.

Summary

In this chapter, we have seen how changes in our understanding of intellectual disabilities have placed new demands on language instruction for persons with intellectual disabilities. We have reviewed recent trends in literacy and in educational services. Then, in describing the specific language and communication characteristics of persons with intellectual disabilities, we noted that although delays in language development are often found in people with intellectual disabilities, there appear to be some specific differences in their language abilities. We have examined possible causes of these language and communication impairments, including discussions of cognitive delay, specific language disorder, and deficiencies of input language. A discussion of intervention techniques included both structured and naturalistic instructional methods that have been used to help individuals with intellectual disabilities enhance their language and communication skills.

Language and Students with Autism Spectrum Disorders

Individuals with autism spectrum disorders have significant difficulties in both cognitive and language development. In this chapter, we will examine the characteristics, definition, and impairments of cognition and language that are usually associated with autism spectrum disorders, also reviewing explanations of the cause of the disabilities associated with autism spectrum disorders. We will examine some intervention approaches found to be effective in individuals with autism spectrum disorders, as well as look at some new, controversial techniques.

Learning Outcomes

After completing this chapter, you should be able to:

1. Define autism and explain the major characteristics associated with autism spectrum disorders.

2. Describe the language and literacy characteristics of children with autism spectrum disorders.

3. Describe intervention approaches that have been developed to help children with autism spectrum disorders develop their language and communication skills.

Aaron: A Case Study

Aaron is a 13-year-old boy who has been identified as autistic. He has hearing loss in one of his ears and has occasional facial tics. He is currently in seventh grade. He is doing well in both science and social studies but struggles in the math classroom. Aaron reads on level and enjoys reading higher level material, especially about topics that interest him, such as trains. Aaron is a polite young man who appears to enjoy being in the classroom. Aaron receives speech and language services in school. He has difficulty with pragmatic language skills, including conversational and communicative skills, as well as peer interactions. He also has difficulties in the area of morphology.

Aaron's parents are actively involved in his education. They work to ensure that he is prepared on a daily basis, completes all homework assignments, and is provided with any help or assistance he may need. Aaron receives counseling outside the school in addition to the services he receives at school.

Aaron's teacher believes that that even though Aaron produces sounds correctly, his speech is still sometimes difficult to understand. Aaron has been observed to use a variety of "voices" throughout the school day. His voice can sound robotic, nasally, high-pitched, or very quiet. Aaron's teacher has observed that a variety of things may affect the selection of voice, including the level of stimuli in the environment, his interest in what is going on, and the familiarity of the people who are around. For example, Aaron is fascinated by trains. When speaking about trains, he uses his robot voice. Aaron's teacher has also noticed that he may stop mid-conversation. Sometimes, when he stops, he begins to make humming noises. Aaron also makes these sounds while walking in the hallway between switching classes.

Aiden: A Case Study

Aiden is a 5-year-old male student who is in his second year of preschool. He has been identified as autistic. He is currently in a self-contained classroom for most of the educational day and receives speech therapy, occupational therapy, and applied behavior analysis (discrete trial) training. Aiden is also included in a general education classroom 3 days a week for large group and story time. Aiden receives additional speech therapy 1 day per week outside of school.

Aiden lives with his mother and grandmother. His mother also has a boyfriend who has been in Aiden's life since he was 10 months old. He calls him "daddy." His family is very supportive and tries to expose him to different activities and social settings. They are interested in Aiden's educational success and work collaboratively with his teachers and other team members.

According to his individualized education plan, Aiden's speech and language skills are significantly delayed. Receptively, Aiden is able to follow simple one-step commands. Expressively, he is able to label and use two- to three-word utterances such as, "It's a bird." However, at times, his utterances are unintelligible. Aiden also has difficulty with eye contact. He is able to make eye contact when prompted but cannot maintain it. An oral motor evaluation showed that he lacks mobility in his lingual and labial muscles.

Aiden's teacher uses the verbal behavior approach to help Aiden develop his spoken language skills. He is currently working on "manding" (requesting). His current goal is to mand for different items in the classroom without prompting.

These cases demonstrate the range of language, social, and behavioral characteristics of children on the autism spectrum. This disorder seems to fascinate both researchers and the general public. Researchers are intrigued by this mysterious disorder that defies their best efforts to find a cause and a treatment. The general public's interest in autism has been raised by numerous depictions of those with the condition in films, on television, and in media articles. What is it about autism and related disorders that make them so elusive and fascinating?

Understanding Autism Spectrum Disorders

Definition

Autism is a complex developmental disability that is characterized by significant problems with social interaction and communication and by restricted, repetitive patterns of behavior, interests, or activities (American Psychiatric Association, 2013). The 2013 revision of the *Diagnostic and Statistical Manual of Mental Disorders* (DSM-V) was very controversial in that it eliminated several previous types of autism as separate disorders, including **Asperger syndrome**, and combined them into one category with three levels of severity:

1. Requiring very substantial support: Characterized by severe deficits in verbal and nonverbal social communication.

2. Requiring substantial support: Characterized by marked deficits in verbal and nonverbal social communication.

3. Requiring support: Characterized by impairments in social communication when supports are not in place.

In addition, the definition requires that identification include whether or not the individual has intellectual impairment, an accompanying language impairment, and/or an associated medical or genetic condition (American Psychiatric Association, 2013).

In addition to eliminating some of the types of autism, the DSM-V revision added a new category called "social (pragmatic) communication disorder." This condition is characterized by deficits in social communication, difficulties matching communication to different contexts and persons and following conversational rules, and impairments in using nonliteral language (e.g., humor, metaphors) and drawing inferences. The definition of this category explicitly states that individuals with this condition are not autistic. Yet, it seems possible that there could be significant confusion about this disorder. Clearly, many individuals with autism exhibit the symptoms of social-pragmatic disorder. In addition, other children with disabilities such as learning and intellectual disabilities may have significant social communication difficulties. In practice, it may be more important to identify children with social-pragmatic communication difficulties and provide them with appropriate interventions and supports than to be overly concerned about which diagnostic category they best fit.

The Individuals with Disabilities Education Act (IDEA) recognizes autism as a disorder and defines it as follows:

> Autism means a developmental disability significantly affecting verbal and nonverbal communication and social interaction, generally evident before age three, that adversely affects educational performance. Characteristics of autism include irregularities and impairments in communication, engagement in repetitive activities and stereotyped movements, resistance to environmental change or change in daily routines, and unusual responses to sensory experiences. (IDEA, 2004)

The definitions contained in both the DSM-V and the IDEA contain what appear to be specific and easily recognizable symptoms. However, in practice, even highly skilled professionals have difficulty diagnosing autism. Frequently, children with autistic characteristics act like children with other disabilities, such as children with intellectual disabilities, pervasive language disorders, hearing impairments, or psychiatric disorders. Although children with autism share some characteristics with children with other disabilities, there are some distinct differences. For example, children with autism have more severe cognitive and behavioral impairments than those found among children with pervasive language disorders. Unlike children with other disabilities, children with autism do not respond to communicative attempts by others, and unlike children with severe hearing impairments, the sensory impairments of children with autism fluctuate from one extreme to the other.

Characteristics of Autism Spectrum Disorders

The DMS-V definition of autism identifies two major characteristics: impairments in social communication and social interaction and restricted, repetitive, and stereotyped patterns of behavior, interests, and activities. Let's look at each of these in more detail.

Impairments in Social Communication and Social Interaction.   Significant impairments in social interaction are the defining feature of autism (Rogers, 2000). Young children with **autism spectrum disorders** often are not responsive to parents and other caregivers. They do not respond to the subtle social stimuli of facial expressions and body movements that form the foundation of human social interaction (Dawson et al., 2004). In addition, children with autism have been found to engage in joint attention with their parents and others much less than typically developing children (Osterling, Dawson, & Munson, 2002). These early deficits in social interaction do not go away. They persist through the school years and into adulthood.

Children with autism spectrum disorders also have impairments in language, especially in using language for communication. A significant number of children with autism (up to half, in some estimates) never develop speech (Tager-Flusberg, Paul, & Lord, 2005). Language and communication difficulties are evident in most young children with autism spectrum disorders and persist through adulthood, even in adults with reasonably good language development (Howlin, 2003).

 Watch this series of video vignettes on social interaction and social communication of young children with autism. In what ways did the children with autism differ from the typically developing children?
https://www.youtube.com/watch?v=YtvP5A5OHpU

Restricted Repertoire of Activities and Interests. The "restricted repertoire" of activities and interests category includes the following characteristics according to DSM-V:

1. Stereotyped or repetitive motor movements in the way that objects are used (e.g., lining up objects) or in speech (repetition of phrases spoken by others)

2. Insistence on sameness, routines, or patterns of behavior (e.g., wearing the same clothes every day; becoming extremely upset by any change in schedule)

3. Highly restricted interests that are unusually intense or focused (e.g., preoccupation with particular objects, time periods, ideas)

4. Hyper- or hyporeactivity to sensory input (e.g., apparent indifference to pain/temperature, fascination with movement or water, inconsistent responses to sound)

Many children with autism spectrum engage in stereotypical behaviors, such as spinning objects, twirling their fingers in front of their face, slapping their heads, flapping their hands, and the like. These behaviors may increase or decrease in intensity based on the child's age and social situations (Boutot & Myles, 2011). Children with autism spectrum disorders are not the only individuals with disabilities who engage in such behaviors, but the behaviors seem to be particularly characteristic of autism spectrum disorders. In addition, individuals with autism spectrum disorders often have a compelling desire for sameness and routine. They may become upset if something in their room is out of place or if their usual schedule is changed in any way. This can cause many problems in schools, where classroom schedules can change for many reasons. In addition, many individuals with autism have an excessive interest in or focus on objects that it makes it difficult for them to communicate with others or participate in classroom interactions. No matter the topic of the conversation, they somehow bring the conversation around to talking about battles of World War II, or the history of the lightbulb, or whatever their particular interest happens to be.

Causes of Autism

So much has been written about the causes of autism that it is difficult to condense the research into a few paragraphs—or even a few pages. Any discussion of the causes of this disorder must attempt to explain the myriad symptoms associated with the syndrome. This is no easy matter. Even if we cannot say for certain what causes autism, understanding what does *not* cause the disorder is important.

Early theories of autism focused on the family and family interaction as the likely cause of the syndrome. Kanner (1943), and later Bettelheim (1967), suggested that autism was caused by parents who were unusually rigid and emotionally cold. Kanner talked about the "refrigerator" parents who interacted with their children in a cold, aloof manner. This behavior by parents was thought to cause emotional deprivation in the child, which, in turn, caused the child to withdraw from human interaction.

Although this psychoanalytic view of the cause of autism was widely accepted for many years, it is now rejected by most professionals. The reason is that controlled studies failed to find differences in either the personality traits of parents of children with autism or in the way they relate to their children (Prior & Werry, 1986). Although some differences have been found in interactions between parents and their autistic children, these can be attributed to the behavior of the autistic child rather than to psychopathology of the parent.

If parents do not cause autism, what does? More and more evidence points to a biological disorder underlying autism. However, the specific biological problem has been difficult to pinpoint. A recent review of research on the causes of autism (Hughes, 2008) identified a number of suspected causes, including:

- Genetic or chromosomal disorder: There is intriguing evidence for a genetic and/or chromosomal basis for autism. Studies of the incidence of autism within families have found that siblings, especially identical twins, are at much higher risk for autism (Folstein & Rutter, 1988). While a number of chromosomes and genetic structures have been implicated as possible causes of autism, no single chromosome or gene has yet been definitely linked with the disorder. Hughes (2008) suggests that this may be because autism has a complex genetic architecture and may be caused by a combination of genes and/or chromosomes.

- Central nervous system disorder: Many regions of the brain (including the frontal lobes, amygdala, hippocampus, and brainstem) have been identified as being either structurally or functionally different in autism. In addition, various neurochemicals (such as serotonin) have been implicated in the disorder. However, as with genetic and chromosomal disorders, no region of the brain or functional difference has been conclusively linked with autism.

- Vaccinations: There has been a lot of controversy about the possible link between vaccinations and autism. Specifically, it has been claimed by some that thimerosal, a substance that was added to some vaccines prior to 2001, may be linked to autism. However, a comprehensive review conducted by the Centers for Disease Control and Prevention (Price et al., 2010) has failed to find any evidence for such a link.

What can we conclude about the etiology of autism? Unfortunately, not much. Although there is significant evidence that autism is a neurobiological disorder that may have a genetic basis, scientists have not yet identified a single cause or a group of causes of autism. It is possible that what we call "autism" is really a group of disorders with various characteristics (e.g., severe social dysfunction, specific language disorders) that may manifest themselves in different ways with different individuals. As we learn more about the neurobiological basis of autism, we may find that specific symptoms can be explained by biological factors, even if the nature of the overall disorder remains a puzzle.

In this video about the causes of autism, several evidence-based risk factors for autism are discussed. What are these risk factors?
https://www.youtube.com/watch?v=AatBPbgNFak

Check Your Understanding 9.1
Click here to gauge your understanding of the concepts in this section.

Language and Literacy of Students with Autism Spectrum Disorders

Deficiencies in language and communication are an important factor in autism spectrum disorders—some would say the most important factor. Language and communication skills have been found to be an excellent predictor of future development (McEachin, Smith, & Lovaas, 1993). Children with better communication skills are more likely to be successfully included in school and the community and have better overall outcomes. As noted earlier in this chapter, many children with autism do not develop spoken language at all. For those who do develop spoken language, there are significant delays in development and a pattern of relatively preserved abilities and significant deficits.

Early Language and Communication Development

Since many children with autism are not identified until age 2 or later, it has been difficult for researchers to examine the very early language development of children with autism. Asking parents to recall the early development of their children who later were found to be autistic is not a very reliable method of determining early language and communication development. However, recent research has used new techniques to better identify the early development of children with autism.

For example, in two innovative studies studying the home videos of babies who were later identified as autistic, Osterling and her colleagues (Osterling & Dawson, 1994; Osterling, Dawson, & Munson, 2002) found that the 1 year olds with autism were less likely to look at people, look at objects held by people, orient to their name, and use gestures than typically developing 1 year olds. These results suggest that, right from the start, communicative development is a problem for children with autism.

Other studies have examined the language and communication development of young children at high risk for autism (because they had a close family member with autism) compared to that of same-age peers who were considered low risk for autism. In one study (Hudry et al., 2014), high- and low-risk children were tested four times between 7 and 38 months of age. The children at high risk for autism were significantly behind their low-risk peers in the development of receptive language. However, the high-risk children who subsequently did not develop autism improved significantly on measures of receptive language after 2 years of age. On the other hand, the high- and low-risk groups did not differ on other measures of language development or on parent reports on communicative development. Lazenby and colleagues (2016) studied the language and communication development of a large number of young children (12 to 36 months old), some of whom were considered to be at high risk for autism because they had a sibling who had been previously diagnosed as autistic. They found that the high-risk group had significant lower scores on both receptive and expressive language than the group of children who were considered at low risk for autism. The authors concluded that language deficits may occur early in development for children with autism.

You may recall from Chapter 5 of this text that one of the earliest communicative developments takes place when infants and their parents receive attention from each other. This interaction sets the foundation for the development of communication and eventually language. However, children with autism have been found to have significant deficits in joint attention (Kasari, Freeman, & Paparella, 2001). That is, they are less likely than typically developing children to share their attention with a caregiver over an object or activity. Young children with autism initiate and respond to joint interactions less frequently even when compared to other children with developmental disabilities (Chiang, Soong, Lin, & Rogers, 2008). It appears that these difficulties with joint attention do not improve over time. When Dawson and colleagues (2004) compared the joint attention skills of children with autism who were approximately 4 years of age to those of similar-age children with pervasive developmental disorder and to younger, typically developing children, they found that the autistic children made fewer attempts to initiate joint attention and were less likely to respond to the examiner's attempts to engage them in joint attention.

In addition to difficulties with joint attention, young children with autism use fewer vocalizations and fewer nonverbal gestures than children with language disorders and intellectual disabilities or typically developing children (Wetherby, Prizant, & Schuler, 2000). Clearly, both of these deficits place children with autism at significant risk for deficits in language and communication. Even when children with autism develop spoken language, they do so at a later age and develop more slowly than other children—even those with language disorders.

There is increasing evidence that many children with autism actually regress in language development during the early childhood years. For example, Landa and Garrett-Mayer (2006) found that children with autism between 6 and 24 months experienced a progressive slowing in rate of receptive and expressive language development. For the children in their study who were initially identified as autistic at 14 months of age, there were no significant gains in communication between 14 and 24 months. For those identified after 14 months, there was a pattern of declining communication skills over time.

Children with "high-functioning" (type 3) autism and Asperger syndrome (usually defined as those with IQ scores higher than 80) follow a pattern of early developmental difficulties that is largely similar to that of other children with autism. However, they do start to talk, on average, at about age 3 (Howlin, 2003). By age 5, they are beginning to use multiword phrases. Although this is certainly delayed compared to typically developing children, it is much better than most children with autism, many of whom develop no spoken language by age 5. In contrast, young children with Asperger syndrome do not have significant delays in their development of spoken language. The same study found that parents of children later identified as having Asperger syndrome reported first words emerging in their children, on average, at 14 months and phrases at 26 months—much like typically developing children.

Development in Specific Language Domains

As we noted earlier in this chapter, language disorders are one of the defining features of autism. However, that does not mean that all individuals with autism have the same language difficulties or the same level of severity. In fact, the language difficulties of children with autism can range from mild to severe and may be limited primarily to one domain (such as pragmatic language) or be found across all aspects of language. Although it has been estimated that up to 25 percent of children with autism are nonspeaking (Tager-Flusberg, Paul, & Lord, 2005), most develop at least some spoken language. In the following sections, we will examine the specific characteristics of the spoken language of children with autism.

Phonology. Studies of the speech production of children with autism have found that the development of phonological rules follows the same course found in typically developing children but with delays. The speech of most verbal children with autism spectrum disorders is intelligible and may even be more advanced than that of typically developing peers (Kjelgaard & Tager-Flusberg, 2001). In their study of high-functioning autistic and Asperger syndrome adolescents and adults, Shriberg and colleagues (2001) found that up to one-third of those in the study continued to have some speech errors (compared to 1 percent in the general population).

Many observers have reported that individuals with autism have considerable trouble with **suprasegmental features** of sound production (stress and intonation). Children with autism have been described as speaking in a singsong pattern, having fluctuations in vocal intensity (too loud or too soft), and using intonations that are not appropriate to the meaning of the sentence (using a rising intonation for sentences that are not questions). Individuals with autism often lack expression in their voices and may speak in a monotone. The study by Shriberg and colleagues (2001) confirmed these findings among high-functioning autistic and Asperger syndrome groups. These researchers found that a significant number of their study participants (30 to 40 percent) had difficulty with features such as phrasing, stress, and vocal modulation. Specifically, they often repeated sounds, syllables, and/or words, making their speech harder to follow. They placed stress at the wrong place in sentences, and their voices were often too loud and too high. Although some of these differences were subtle, they were significant enough to make it more difficult for a listener to understand.

Morphology and Syntax. As with phonological development, studies of the acquisition of morphological rules by children with autism have found some similarities to typically developing children and some differences. However, there are a few significant problems that may differentiate children with autism from typically developing children. One of those is the use of pronouns. Many children with autism (though not all) tend to mix up pronouns. They might say "you" when referring to themselves or "me" when referring to another person. For example, when asking for a drink of water, they might say, "You want a drink of water?" Pronoun reversal is not unique to children with autism. Other children with disabilities, especially children who are blind, may confuse the speaker and listener and use the wrong pronoun. However, pronoun reversal does seem to be more common in autistic children (Lee, Hobson, & Chiat, 1994).

 This video shows an interaction between a parent and a young child with autism. What pronoun does the child use to refer to himself?
https://www.youtube.com/watch?v=l0j9t89L3ck

Several explanations for the pronoun confusion and reversals of individuals with autism have been suggested, including:

1. *Echolalia.* Referring to our earlier example, the child saying, "You want a drink of water?" may have been using delayed echolalia (repeating a phrase she or he heard previously) or using immediate echolalia in response to the request, "Do you want water?"

2. *Cognitive development.* Words such as *I* and *you* are *deictic* forms—that is, words that change their referent in relation to the context. A *ball* is always a *ball,* but sometimes *I* is *I* and sometimes *I* is *you,* depending on the context. Cognitively, this is a more complex notion and one that may be more difficult for children with cognitive difficulties (Tager-Flusberg, 1981).

3. *Lack of attention.* Oshima-Takane and Benaroya (1989) have claimed that children with autism have trouble with pronouns because the children fail to attend to pronoun usage by others. They found, however, that when autistic children were guided to attend to an adult model, they *could* learn to use pronouns correctly.

It is possible that each of these factors plays a role for specific children with autism and perhaps at different stages of development. Some researchers have suggested that the phenomenon of pronoun reversal may be the result of a combination of difficulties that individuals with autism have with the concept of "self" combined with difficulty understanding the shifting roles of speakers and listeners in conversational exchanges (Tager-Flusberg, Paul, & Lord, 2005). The implication for teachers is to *recognize* pronoun reversal when it occurs, *respond* to the child's attempt to communicate, and *model* the appropriate form. In practice, the sequence might go something like this:

Student: You want water.

Teacher: Oh. You want water. I want water, too.

Studies of the syntactic development of children with autism spectrum disorders, especially those with autism, have generally found that, although there are significant delays, development follows a normal path (Tager-Flusberg, Paul, & Lord, 2005). For example, Tager-Flusberg and colleagues (1990) compared the language development of a group of children with autism to that of children with Down syndrome. They found that for most of the children with autism, mean length of utterance (MLU) increased over time and was a good indicator of level of language development. However, this was not true for one of the children. In addition, Tager-Flusberg and colleagues reported that the syntactic development of the children with autism followed a developmental course similar to that of both the typically developing children and the children with Down syndrome, although in children with autism, there appeared to be a leveling out of their development at higher stages of MLU. However, once again, there were exceptions; one child actually declined in syntactic development during the study. Difficulty in understanding and using past tense may be a particular problem for children with autism (Rice, Oetting, Marquis, Bode, & Pae, 1994; Tager-Flusberg, 1989).

Landa and Goldberg (2005) compared the morphological and syntactic development of high-functioning autistic children, ages 7 to 17, with a group of typically developing children matched for age and IQ score. The language skills of the children were similar on a number of measures, but the children with autism performed more poorly on a test of expressive grammar and on understanding figures of speech. The authors suggest that even though high-functioning individuals with autism may seem to have good expressive language, a careful analysis of their skills may indicate specific difficulties with some aspects of syntax.

In contrast to most of the research on the morphological and syntactic development of children with autism, Eigisti, Bennetto, and Dadlani (2007) found that 5-year-old children with autism (not Asperger syndrome) had significant syntactic deficits compared with typically developing children and children with other developmental disabilities. The children with autism produced less language, had lower MLUs, and were not showing the typical pattern of moving from less to more complex structures. On the other hand, the children with autism had relative strengths in lexical development, using more words than mental age–matched peers. The syntactic difficulties of children with autism appear to persist over time. A study by Eigisti and Bennetto (2009) found that, compared to typically developing individuals matched on age, IQ, and receptive vocabulary, individuals with autism ages 9 to 16 had significant difficulty judging the grammaticality of sentences.

Most of the research on the morphological and syntactic development of children with autism concludes that these domains of development are delayed. We should keep in mind that there is a great deal of variability in this population and that some children may deviate from this pattern of delayed development. In addition, several studies have reported significant problems experienced by children with autism in *applying* linguistic rules in social situations.

Semantics.   As is true with most aspects of language, individuals with autism spectrum disorders have a mixed pattern of strengths and weaknesses in semantics. Studies of the semantic skills of individuals with autism have not always found deficits. For example, when Tager-Flusberg (1985) directly examined the ability of children with autism to group information by conceptual categories, she found that the children with autism were no different from the nondisabled children in their categorization abilities. She concluded that the view of the world held by the children with autism that she tested was quite similar to that of the other children in the study. Similarly, Eskes, Bryson, and McCormick (1990) found that children with autism could comprehend both concrete and abstract words (such as *life* and *time*), much like children in a typically developing control group matched for reading ability. Research with high-functioning children with autism has shown that they score well on standardized tests of vocabulary, suggesting that this is a relative strength for many children with autism (Kjelgaard & Tager-Flusberg, 2001).

At the same time, a common finding of research studies is that children with autism use more idiosyncratic language and neologisms in their language. Volden and Lord (1991) defined **idiosyncratic language** as "the use of conventional words or phrases in unusual ways to convey specific meanings" (p. 111). For example, a child with autism in their study said, "It makes me want to go as deep as economical with it," which was interpreted to mean *withdraw as much as possible*. **Neologisms** are nonstandard (or invented) words. Subjects with autism in the Volden and Lord study said *bloosers* for *bruises* and *bells* for *rings*. Volden and Lord compared the frequency of idiosyncratic language and neologisms in language samples from two groups of children with autism (IQ > 80 and IQ < 80) to the language of children with intellectual disabilities and typically developing children matched for chronological age. They found that the children with autism made more semantic errors and produced far more neologisms than either of the comparison groups. Almost all of the children with autism produced unusual words or phrases, whereas few of the other participants did so. This study suggests that individuals with autism may have difficulty using words correctly.

One explanation for the inconsistent results on the semantic abilities of children with autism may have to do with their overall language abilities. McGregor and colleagues (2012) compared children with autism who had significant syntactic language difficulties to others with intact syntactic abilities. They found that children with impairments in syntax had more difficulty with semantic tasks.

Although the research on the semantic skills of individuals with autism may seem to be confusing and inconsistent, one thing stands out. Individuals with autism have difficulty using semantic concepts in natural situations. As educators, we can help children with autism by modeling correct usage, by pointing out when a word is misused or when there is an opportunity to apply a semantic concept, and by teaching students to use semantic strategies for thinking and problem solving.

Pragmatics.   One of the defining features of autism is withdrawal from social interaction. Thus, it should not be surprising to find that children with autism have significant impairments in the pragmatic aspects of language. A good deal of research evidence supports the claim that individuals with autism have significant problems with pragmatics. We have previously reviewed several research studies that have reported that young children with autism were very unresponsive to attempts by their parents to initiate communication. These studies have also found that children with autism rarely initiate communication spontaneously and produce fewer communicative acts than do mental age–matched children with language delays or typically developing children.

Researchers have found deficiencies in almost every aspect of pragmatic language that has been investigated, including speech acts, listening, using "polite" conversation, making irrelevant statements, staying on topic, and making bizarre and inappropriate comments (Eigisti, de Marchena, Schuh, & Kelley, 2011; Tager-Flusberg, Paul, & Lord, 2005). In studies that used either analysis of conversational samples or structured experimental tasks, specific pragmatic difficulties have included identifying the topic initiated by a speaker and making a relevant comment, knowing how much information is relevant to include in an utterance, and maintaining the topic of conversation (Volden, Coolican, Garon, White, & Bryson, 2009).

Although children with high-functioning autism (including those with Asperger syndrome) usually have relatively intact language and communication skills, the exception to this is in the area of pragmatics. Specific difficulties have been found in communicative abilities such as taking the lead in conversations, terminating conversations appropriately, and responding to others (Chuba, Paul, Miles, Klin, & Volkmar, 2003). In a study comparing the conversational skills of adolescents with Asperger syndrome to those of individuals with conduct disorder (matched for age and IQ), Adams, Green, Gilchrist, and Cox (2002) discovered that the Asperger group had many more problems successfully participating in conversations. They more frequently failed to mesh their response to their conversational partners even though they tended to talk a lot. Excessive talking by persons with Asperger syndrome has been reported by several researchers and by practitioners. Although the study by Adams and colleagues (2002) did not find that most of the adolescents with Asperger syndrome inappropriately dominated the conversation, a subgroup did fit that pattern.

Volden and her colleagues (Volden, Magill-Evans, Goulden, & Clarke, 2007; Volden & Sorenson, 2009) have examined the ability of children and adolescents with high-functioning autism (IQ > 80) and Asperger syndrome to adjust their language in different situations and with a variety of partners. In one study (Volden et al., 2007), the subjects were asked to explain how to act in a restaurant to listeners who differed in age and ability to understand (e.g., a nonnative speaker). They found that the children and adolescents with Asperger syndrome were able to adjust their language, but not as effectively as other children. In the other study (Volden & Sorenson, 2009), the children and adolescents with Asperger syndrome were able to successfully adjust their language to give "nice" or "bossy" commands to puppets. These results suggest that children and adolescents with high-functioning autism may have subtle pragmatic difficulties in some, but not all, aspects of communicative interaction.

Landa (2000) summarized the language and communication difficulties associated with Asperger syndrome as follows:

- Failure to adjust their language production in response to the context (e.g., using a formal greeting with someone who is already familiar)

- Tendency to initiate conversation without regard to the listener's interest in the topic

- Use of socially inappropriate topics (e.g., asking someone about his or her weight/age)

- Difficulty understanding nonliteral language

- Shifting conversational topics abruptly

These difficulties in language often have a negative impact on the ability of individuals with high-functioning autism to develop social relationships and to be accepted in the community. The pragmatic problems associated with autism, such as the use of overly formal language and failing to respond to a question, appear to persist through adolescence, even in individuals with higher IQs (Eales, 1993; Volden et al., 2009).

The research on pragmatic development in children with autism suggests that teachers and other education professionals can help these children with autism enhance their communication skills by interacting with them frequently, by being responsive to both verbal and nonverbal attempts to communicate, and by communicating with the children in comfortable, familiar contexts whenever possible. Children with Asperger syndrome are likely to have more subtle conversational difficulties, but these can lead to social rejection if not addressed.

Echolalia.   **Echolalia** is the literal repetition of speech produced by others (Prizant & Duchan, 1981). Echolalia that occurs immediately (or very shortly) after another person speaks is called **immediate echolalia**. **Delayed echolalia** involves the repetition of words or phrases that may have been heard days, weeks, or even years ago. Sometimes echolalic individuals repeat exactly what they hear, but often they change the structure of the original utterance. This is called **mitigated echolalia** (see Figure 9.1 for examples). Although echolalia is found among many individuals with disabilities (and even at certain stages of

Figure 9.1

Examples of Echolalia

Immediate Echolalia	Teacher says: "Gloria, what did you do last night?" Student responds: "What did you do last night?"
Delayed Echolalia	While working quietly at a desk, the child suddenly shouts: "What's the matter with you? You can't do that."
Mitigated Echolalia	Teacher says: "So, what did you do last night?" Student responds: "Night."

Category	Description
Interactive	
Turn-taking	Utterances used as turn fillers in an alternating verbal exchange
Declarative	Utterances labeling objects, actions, or location (accompanied by demonstrative gestures)
Yes answer	Utterances used to indicate affirmation of prior utterance
Request	Utterances used to request objects or others' actions; usually involves mitigated echolalia
Noninteractive	
Nonfocused	Utterances produced with no apparent intent and often in states of high arousal (e.g., fear, pain)
Rehearsal	Utterances used as a processing aid, followed by utterance or action indicating comprehension of echoed utterance
Self-regulatory	Utterances that serve to regulate subject's own actions; produced in synchrony with motor activity

Table 9.1

Seven Communicative Functions of Immediate Echolalia

Source: Adapted from Prizant & Duchan (1981).

normal language development), it occurs more frequently among individuals with autism and persists for far longer than in typically developing children (Howlin, 1982). However, as Tager-Flusberg and colleagues (2005) point out, echolalia is not unique to autism. Children with other disabilities, including children who are blind and children with intellectual disabilities, echo. Furthermore, studies have found that, although a significant number of children with autism use echolalia, many never echo.

The traditional view of echolalia has been that it indicates a lack of comprehension ability and is noncommunicative (Schreibman & Carr, 1978). Many language training programs have actively discouraged—and even punished—the use of echolalia by children with autism. However, views about echolalia have changed. Today, many believe that echolalia actually serves an important communicative role for individuals with autism. Barry Prizant (1983), for example, holds the position that people with autism may use echolalia in an intentional way to maintain social interaction. Prizant and Duchan (1981) went so far as to delineate seven communicative functions that echolalia may serve (see Table 9.1). Their research, as well as that by others, should remind us that we must look at the total context—not just at the spoken language produced—to fully understand what may be going on in an interaction.

Summary

Language and communication deficits are an important feature of autism spectrum disorders. With the exception of individuals identified with Asperger syndrome, most young children with autism have difficulties with language development prior to age 2. Some never develop spoken language. For those who do, some aspects of language, such as phonology and syntax, are relatively intact. There are delays, but for the most part, development progresses through the usual stages. Deficits in semantics and pragmatics are more significant and can affect academic and social success (see Table 9.2 for a summary).

Factors Related to Language and Communication in Autism

Recent research has focused on four factors that appear to be closely related to language development in children with autism:

- Parental responsiveness to communication attempts
- Cognitive factors (including theory of mind)

Table 9.2

Language Development of Individuals with Autism

Early Development	Morphology/ Phonology	Syntax	Semantics	Pragmatics
Less responsive to name	Typical but delayed development	Delays in nonverbal and written as well as spoken language	Categorization may be intact	Rigid, socially inappropriate
Does not look at others as much	Impairments in suprasegmental features (stress and intonation)	Less complex language than those with intellectual disabilities	Higher IQ and good vocabulary	Unresponsive
Difficulty with joint attention	Fluctuations in vocal intensity	Difficulty with some morphological rules (e.g., past tense)	Difficulty with pronouns	Problems persist
Fewer vocalizations and nonverbal gestures	Inappropriate intonation	More difficulties in unstructured conversations	Use more idiosyncratic language	Speech-act development intact
				Individuals with Asperger syndrome have difficulty with leading and terminating conversations and responding appropriately

- Socialization (joint attention; imitation; play)
- Neurological factors

We will examine each of these in greater detail in the following sections.

Parental Responsiveness to Communication.   As we know, one of the earliest theories on the cause of autism identified parents as the problem. Although research evidence has not generally supported this causal hypothesis, it is possible that deficiencies in parent–child interaction might have a negative effect on language development. In a series of studies, Siller and Sigman (2002, 2008) have examined the role of parents in fostering the language development of their children with autism. These studies have shown that parents of young children with autism who were more responsive to their children's focus of attention and ongoing activity during early play interactions had children who developed superior language during early and middle childhood than did children of parents who were less responsive initially. McDuffie and Yoder (2010) examined the associations between several types of parent verbal responsiveness and later spoken vocabulary for a group of young children with autism. They found that parent "follow-in commenting" (where the parent provided verbal comments that related to the child's current focus of attention and described what the child was looking at or playing with) was related to the child's development of spoken vocabulary. This study also found that vocabulary growth was affected by parents who more frequently repeated back what their child said and tried to expand their child's utterances to a more adult form. These studies suggest that how parents respond to the communicative attempts of their child with autism can make a difference in language development. That does not mean that parents "cause" autism. However, they do play an important role in helping their child develop.

Teachers and other education professionals may help parents of children with autism enhance the quality of interaction with their children by suggesting ways parents might engage their child's attention, comment on what their child is doing, and learn how to expand their child's communicative attempts.

Cognition.   Estimates of intelligence in autism have varied widely over time. A number of factors may have contributed to this variability, including the heterogeneous nature of autism and the difficulty of testing many children with autism. An epidemiological study by Charman and colleagues (2011) found that 55 percent of their sample of children with autism were intellectually disabled, but only 16 percent were in the severe disability range. Twenty-eight percent of their sample scored in the average range, with 3 percent in the above average range.

As we have noted earlier in this book, in typically developing children, there is a close relationship between cognitive and language development. A number of research studies have found that this relationship is true for children with autism as well. For example, Sigman and colleagues (1999) found that general cognitive ability at age 4 was related to receptive language level at age 4. However, cognitive ability did not differentiate those who gained receptive language by age 12 from those who did not. Similarly, Thurm, Lord, Lee, and Newschaffer (2007) found that nonverbal cognitive ability was a significant predictor of language development at age 5 for children with autism.

These studies suggest that the level of measured cognitive development is related to language acquisition and development in children with autism. But the relationship may be more complex than at first glance. In addition to level of cognition, it has been suggested that children with autism may think "differently." For example, it has been suggested by some that individuals with autism lack a **theory of mind** (Baron-Cohen, Leslie, & Frith, 1985). The theory of mind hypothesis states that typically developing children possess an understanding of mental states in others. If this ability is impaired, children have difficulty understanding the behavior (including the communicative behavior) of other people. For example, in order to communicate effectively, one must be able to understand the point of view of another person. What does that person know? What does that person need to know? For example, some individuals with autism provide their names and addresses to everyone they meet—even relatives who know all this information. Others may talk about their trip to the mall with Billy—never explaining who Billy is.

> ▶ This video shows children of different ages taking a series of tests on theory of mind. How do the responses of the children differ?

A number of research studies have found that individuals with autism have difficulty with theory of mind concepts (Baron-Cohen, 1995). Difficulty understanding another's viewpoint could certainly cause significant problems with communication. But it is not clear that, even if individuals with autism have difficulty with theory of mind concepts, this is the cause of the communication difficulties in this population.

Clearly, teachers and others need to consider the possible effects that cognitive abilities could have on the language development of children with autism. These students may benefit from participation in a variety of classroom and community experiences. But even more important is that teachers understand *how* children with autism have perceived these experiences, to know that their view may be quite different from what we *thought* they would experience. It may help for the teacher to recount what the group or individual did, to model analysis of new information, and to demonstrate how this information can be integrated with prior learning.

The theory of mind hypothesis has many implications for helping us to understand the language and communication difficulties of students with autism. For example, Tager-Flusberg (2000) claims that pragmatics deficits, such as difficulties with speaker–listener relationships and with storytelling (discourse), can be explained by the difficulty individuals with autism have in understanding the perspective of others. Tager-Flusberg (2000) also presents evidence that theory of mind differences in autism may also explain some difficulties with the acquisition of semantic concepts such as "think," "know," and "guess" and even some syntactic acquisition difficulties.

Socialization.   Earlier in this chapter, we reviewed evidence on the development of joint attention in children with autism. We noted that many researchers have found that the ability to participate in joint interactions with caregivers is often impaired in this population. Joint attention, the ability to imitate, and play behavior are three types of social skills that have been repeatedly found to be related to the language development of children with autism (Toth, Munson, Meltzoff, & Dawson, 2006). For example, in a study of vocabulary development (Smith, Mirenda, & Zaidman-Zait, 2007), although the researchers found wide variations in development among children with autism, the presence of verbal imitation skill, the use of objects to pretend, and the number of gestures to initiate joint attention were all found to be associated with greater vocabulary growth over time. Interestingly, cognitive development was not found to be a significant factor. Thurm and colleagues (2007) found a similar result with older (age 3) but not younger children with autism. They suggested that the greater importance of socialization factors in older children may be due to the greater demands for social skills as they enter school or other community-based settings.

Neurological Factors.   There is little doubt that autism spectrum disorders are neurodevelopmental disorders; that is, they are caused by some difference or dysfunction in the brain and/or central nervous system. But identifying the exact cause (or, more likely, causes) of this disorder has been extremely difficult. Numerous theories have been proposed, including biochemical agents, anatomical structures, and functional differences. However, at this point, there is no prevailing single cause or even group of causes.

However, advances in neuroimaging techniques have brought us closer to understanding the ways in which brain anomalies may contribute to the language difficulties experienced by individuals with autism. For example, in most typically developing, right-handed persons, the left hemisphere of the brain is slightly larger than the right—particularly in a region known as the planum temporale. It is thought that this hemispheric asymmetry is related to language functioning in the left hemisphere. But there is increasing evidence that many individuals with autism do not have the left hemisphere asymmetries found in most typically developing individuals (Muller et al., 1999). Functional magnetic resonance imaging (fMRI) can examine activity in the brain during real-time activities. Using this technique, researchers have found that individuals with high-functioning autism show lower activation in regions of the brain usually associated with the processing of grammar during a sentence-comprehension task (Just, Cherkassky, Keller, & Minshew, 2004).

Although still in their early stages, investigations of the brain structure and functioning of individuals with autism may allow us to better understand the underlying problems that contribute to the language and literacy difficulties associated with autism. Ultimately, this may help us focus intervention where it may do the most good.

Although the search for causes of the significant language and communication difficulties associated with autism continues, the picture is becoming somewhat clearer. Cognitive development plays a role, especially in early language development. But so do social skills such as imitation and joint attention. Parents can help their child develop language and communication skills by responding in ways that enhance interaction. As we learn more about the genetic and neurological bases of autism, we may be able to identify children at risk for language disorders earlier and better target interventions to their needs.

Literacy and Autism Spectrum Disorders

Students with autism spectrum disorders have a range of abilities that have a significant impact on their acquisition of literacy. As we have seen, some children with autism have significant deficits in cognitive and language development that are likely to cause significant difficulties in learning to read and write. However, higher-functioning children with autism may be able to acquire literacy skills in ways that are similar to typically developing students, and some may actually be more advanced than their typically developing peers in at least some aspects of reading and writing.

Students with autism who have significantly delayed language and cognitive development have faced many of the same literacy challenges as students with severe cognitive disabilities (see Chapter 8). As Mirenda (2003) points out, many students with autism were denied access to literacy because of the dominance of the reading "readiness" model. Until students achieved theoretical "prerequisite" skills (which most never did), they were not given the opportunity to participate in reading and writing activities, even if they were included in regular education classes. At best, they might be pulled aside to work on memorization of individual sight words. The problem with sight-word approaches, according to Kliewer and Biklin (2001), is that they severely limit the opportunity for further literacy development.

What is the alternative? In the past few years, approaches that combine new conceptualizations of literacy development that are based on emergent literacy (rather than "readiness" models of reading) coupled with intensive use of technology have enabled many students with autism to more fully participate in literacy activities. For example, Koppenhaver and Erickson (2003) described how they increased the literacy opportunities for three young children with autism who attended a preschool program for children with special needs. Prior to the intervention, the children had little exposure to literacy. No reading or writing materials were available to the children during free playtime. In fact, these materials were kept out of the reach of the children. Although the children occasionally listened to stories read to them, they took no active part in reading or writing activities. Interviews with the classroom teacher indicated that she felt that the children had little interest in reading and writing.

Koppenhaver and Erickson (2003) introduced a number of activities into the classroom to increase literacy opportunities. For example, they created an electronic writing center with a computer and word-processing software that was appropriate for young children. They supplemented the activities that were available during free play with a variety of toys and activities that encouraged literacy (e.g., erasable pads, letter stamps, and ink pads). They increased the variety of reading materials that were available in the classroom and helped the teacher integrate reading into regular class activities. The result of increasing literacy opportunities was that the children showed more interest in books and other literacy activities and began to show improvement in their literacy skills, such as writing.

Several research studies have focused on improving the writing skills of children with autism. Bedrosian, Lasker, Speidel, and Politsch (2003) used augmentative communication systems, story grammar maps, and peer support to enhance the written narratives of an adolescent student with autism. Blischak and Schlosser (2003) reviewed research that has found that students with autism can make progress in spelling through the use of speech-generating devices and talking word-processing software.

Light and McNaughton (2010) have reported preliminary results of a project designed to enhance the literacy skills of children with autism who also have limited speech abilities. They designed their intervention around five principles:

- Provide sufficient time for instruction: They suggest starting literacy instruction as early as possible and providing instruction on a daily basis, preferably for 2 hours or more a day.

- Use appropriate instructional content: They suggest following the National Reading Panel guidelines for literacy development.

- Use appropriate instructional procedures: They recommend providing frequent opportunities to apply skills in meaningful literacy activities.

- Use adaptations to allow active participation of individuals with autism spectrum disorders who have limited speech: These might including using **augmentative communication** or alternative communication modes and using pictures to replace words.

■ Establish positive rapport and motivating instruction: They suggest building on student strengths, providing students with choices, and starting with familiar tasks.

Using these principles, Light and McNaughton reported that all three of the children with autism they worked with were able to develop conventional literacy skills.

Although students with autism clearly face significant challenges to the acquisition of literacy, these and other studies strongly suggest that they can develop literacy skills when given the opportunity. Kluth and Darmody-Latham (2003) suggest that teachers can increase literacy opportunities for students with autism (and other severe disabilities) by taking the following steps:

■ *Recognize all literacies.* Recognize and build on the skills that students demonstrate. For example, students may not be able to write letters but they can use "pretend" (or emergent) writing to draw squiggles that represent letters for them.

■ *Capitalize on students' interests.* Students with autism sometimes have interests that occupy much of their time. Use these interests as the core for literacy activities in the classroom.

■ *Use a range of visual supports.* In addition to verbal input, students with autism may benefit from visual inputs such as graphic or visual organizers, flowcharts, and concept maps.

■ *Read aloud.* Give students many opportunities to listen to stories. Connect the listening to follow-up activities that actively involve students in thinking about what they have heard. For example, one teacher followed a story about leaves with a walk through the woods to gather leaves and then mounted and labeled the leaves in personal leaf books.

■ *Use and encourage different types of expression.* Provide students with a range of options for participation. For example, using the story about leaves, students might draw pictures, use emergent writing, or dictate words that are used in the book.

Higher-functioning students with autism present different types of literacy challenges. Typically they are able to read words at or above the level that would be expected for their age. However, their comprehension of text usually lags behind their word-reading ability (Loveland & Tunali-Kotoski, 1997). Some individuals with Asperger syndrome or high-functioning autism have been called **hyperlexic**; that is, they can read words at very high levels of proficiency. This can appear to be very impressive and lead parents and teachers to ignore the reading comprehension and other learning problems that may exist in these children.

Research has found that many students with Asperger syndrome have difficulty with reading comprehension (El Zein, Solis, Vaughn, & McCully, 2014). In an attempt to enhance reading comprehension among students with Asperger syndrome, O'Connor and Klein (2004) compared the effectiveness of three instructional methods: answering pre-reading questions, completing cloze sentences (where students attempt to fill in the blanks in sentences), and anaphoric cuing (where students are taught that some words can have more than one referent; for example, the word "he" can stand for various male individuals). The researchers found that anaphoric cuing was the most effective method. They also suggested that the use of graphic advance organizers might help improve reading comprehension for these students. Other methods, such as the use of graphic organizers and recognizing text structures such as cause and effect, have also been found to help students with autism better understand what they are reading.

Although there is still limited research on the reading comprehension difficulties of students with Asperger syndrome or high-functioning autism, it seems clear that these students will need intensive instruction in comprehension, including technology supports.

Check Your Understanding 9.2
Click here to gauge your understanding of the concepts in this section.

Intervention for Language and Communication Impairments

Because the language impairments of children with autism spectrum disorders are so pervasive and have such long-lasting effects, many intervention approaches have been developed. Parents, teachers, and clinicians have a bewildering number of choices of language-intervention programs that claim success with children with autism spectrum disorders. The challenge is to identify those programs that have proven to be most effective. However, keep in mind that there is no one program that is effective for all children. As Goldstein (2002) put it, there is no silver bullet when it comes to programs for enhancing the language and communication of individuals with autism spectrum disorders. We will look at several approaches that have a record of success in improving language and communication with children with autism, examining their strengths and limitations. This is a mere sample of the myriad of programs that are available (visit the Boston University website for information about exciting new research on interventions for language disorders in autism).

Applied Behavior Analysis Approaches

As noted in Chapter 8, applied behavior analysis approaches have been quite successful in enhancing the language and communication of children with significant language disabilities. These methods are based on the principles of operant conditioning, including the identification of discrete intervention targets based on a task analysis of the child's current behavior and target behavior and the use of principles such as positive reinforcement for correct responses and the chaining of behaviors to create longer responses.

One type of behaviorally based intervention program that has been used extensively with individuals with autism spectrum disorders is known as **discrete trial training** (Lovaas et al., 1980). Intervention targets are addressed through massed trials of antecedent–behavior–consequence chains, initiated by the adult, using adult-selected materials and tasks. In this approach, a "trial" is a single teaching unit that begins with a stimulus (the teacher's instruction), the child's response, the consequence, and a pause before the presentation of the next stimulus. Correct responses are reinforced, whereas incorrect responses are followed by verbal feedback (e.g., "no" or "wrong") followed by a correction.

This video provides additional information about discrete trial training and examples of its implementation. What are the three major components of a discrete trial?

https://www.youtube.com/watch?v=7pN6ydLE4EQ

In numerous studies, researchers have documented success using this type of approach with children with autism. For example, Lovaas (1987) reported that children with autism who received early, intensive, behavioral intervention (including language) scored higher on tests of intelligence and were more successful in school than similar children who received less intensive intervention. A follow-up study several years later found that these differences continued to exist (McEachin, Smith, & Lovaas, 1993). Smith, Eikeseth, Klevstrand, and Lovaas (1997) reported that preschoolers with severe intellectual disabilities and autistic features who received intensive behavioral treatment obtained a higher IQ score and had more expressive speech than similar children who received minimal treatment.

Despite the documented success of behavioral-intervention approaches such as discrete trial, some significant questions have been raised. Heflin and Simpson (1998) note four major issues that have been raised:

1. *Outcome claims.* Lovaas has sometimes claimed that intensive use of discrete trial training actually leads to autism "recovery" in up to one-half of the individuals with whom it is used. However, researchers such as Gresham and MacMillan (1997) have expressed a number of concerns about the design of the research that has led to the claims of success for discrete trial training and concluded that the Lovaas approach is "at best experimental, is far from producing a cure for autism, and awaits replication before school districts are required to provide it on a wholesale basis" (p. 196).

2. *Exclusivity.* Advocates of the use of intensive behavioral-intervention approaches argue that their method should be the only one used in treating a child with autism. Heflin and Simpson (1998) note that this argument ignores the evidence that other intervention techniques have been found to be as effective or more effective than discrete trial in addressing social skills, pragmatic language deficiencies, and other problems typically experienced by individuals with autism spectrum disorders.

3. *Extensive use.* Advocates for discrete trial training claim that, to be effective, the program must be implemented for 40 hours a week over several years. Yet, there is no empirical evidence that this level of intervention is required for all children. In fact, this requirement ignores the strengths and weaknesses of individual children that may have an impact on the effectiveness of the intervention.

4. *Personnel.* The appropriate preparation for discrete trial trainers is in dispute. Advocates for the program argue that there is no need for trainers to be certified teachers. Others argue that uncertified trainers may lack the skills to determine the appropriate intervention program for an individual child and to recommend alternative programs for children who either do not respond well to discrete trial training or who could benefit from another approach.

In addition, significant concerns revolve around the generalization of verbal behavior to natural, social situations (Prizant & Rubin, 1999) and about intensity of instruction. It remains unclear what the optimal amount of training time should be. Many educators and clinicians have raised concerns about the practicality of instruction that has to be delivered on such an intensive schedule. After reviewing a number of studies on the use of discrete trial training, Goldstein (2002) noted that, while early applications of the discrete trial training technique tended to focus on the acquisition of single words out of context, there has been increasing attention to teaching somewhat more sophisticated language and more of a focus on generalization of these skills to natural environments. Contemporary applied behavior analysis approaches modify the traditional discrete trial training paradigm by using the child's interests and activities that are readily available in the child's environment to identify therapeutic goals and activities. These methods focus greater attention on increasing the role of the child as a communicative partner in natural settings.

Picture Exchange Communication System

The Picture Exchange Communication System (PECS) (Bondy & Frost, 1994) uses pictures as the means of fostering meaningful communicative exchanges. Originally developed for individuals with autism, the program has been used successfully with students with a variety of significant disabilities. The PECS program uses a combination of behavioral methodology and incidental teaching techniques to enhance social communication. Students progress through six phases in which they are taught to communicate with a variety of people using increasingly complex language. A typical PECS Phase I training session might go as follows:

1. The trainer places an object in front of the child that the trainer has previously observed that the child wants.

2. When the child reaches for the item, the trainer places a picture into the child's hand.

3. The trainer then guides the child to hand the picture to the trainer.

4. When the child exchanges the picture, the trainer makes a verbal response and offers a reinforcer.

In later phases of the program, the child is helped to develop more spontaneous interactions, the ability to discriminate between pictured items, the use of sentence strings, and a broader repertoire of communicative functions and language concepts.

This video shows the elements of a PECS Phase I training session. What are the roles of the two trainers?
https://www.youtube.com/watch?v=mECl6PKVFiA

Bondy and Frost (1994) reported that of 66 children without functional speech who were taught to use PECS, 76 percent either developed speech as their means of communication or used a combination of speech and the picture system. In addition, the same authors reported significant improvements in behavior for children using the PECS program. Ganz and Simpson (2004) examined the use of the PECS program with three young children with developmental disabilities who were suspected to have autism. They found that the children progressed rapidly, acquiring new words and communication skills that generalized across environments. Yoder and Stone (2006) compared the PECS program to a naturalistic, milieu-based approach called Responsive Education and Prelinguistic Milieu Teaching (RPMT; Yoder & Warren, 2002). The RPMT system is composed of two components: one for parents (responsive education) and one for children (Prelinguistic Milieu Teaching [PMT]). The PMT component is a child-led, play-based incidental teaching method designed to teach gestures, nonword vocals, gaze use, and, later, word use as forms of clear intentional communication for turn-taking, requesting, and commenting pragmatic functions. Thirty-six young children with autism (with a mean age of 33 months) were taught with one or the other program. Although children in both programs made significant progress in the acquisition of words and the use of communication in a variety of contexts, the children who were taught with the PECS program made somewhat more progress than the other group.

Research on the use of PECS has increased rapidly. A review by Sulzer-Azaroff, Hoffman, Horton, Bondy, and Frost (2009) found 34 peer-reviewed studies. The authors (who included the developers of the PECS technique) concluded that PECS has been found to be an effective means of training functional communication for individuals with impaired or no speech. They noted that research had reported significant improvements in communication skills with a variety of partners and that, when compared to other methods for enhancing communication skills, PECS has been found to be equal or superior to those methods. They also concluded that PECS can enhance the development of spoken language skills. However, there is disagreement about this latter conclusion. In a more qualitative review of the research on PECS, Flippen, Reszka, and Watson (2010) concluded that, although there is evidence that PECS can improve communication, there is little evidence that it leads to increased speech.

There is an increasing amount of research support for the use of PECS to help children with autism initiate communication. Although PECS has limitations (for example, a limited repertoire of communicative functions and limited portability of the pictures), it can be an effective method for many children.

Pivotal-Response Model

Like PECS, the pivotal-response intervention model is a contemporary applied behavior analysis approach that is based on principles of applied behavior analysis but differs from the traditional discrete trial method in several ways, including the following:

- *Intervention settings.* Intervention is provided in the most inclusive settings possible, preferably in a context that includes typically developing children.

- *Amount of intervention.* The goal is to provide the most effective intervention within a relatively small number of hours. Children are not removed from their natural environment for intervention training.

- *Intervention agents.* Intervention is provided by a number of individuals, including family members.

- *Target behaviors.* These are individualized for each child and change over time (Koegel, Koegel, Harrower, & Carter, 1999).

One of the basic concepts of the pivotal-response intervention model is that instruction should focus on so-called pivotal areas. These include responsivity to multiple cues, motivation to initiate and respond appropriately, and self-regulation of behavior. Koegel et al. (1999) suggest that the following techniques can be used to enhance the language interaction of individuals with autism spectrum disorders:

- *Child choice.* Materials that the child prefers should be used during instruction.

- *Interspersing previously learned tasks with new tasks.* This leads to a higher degree of success and increases the child's motivation to respond.

- *Reinforcing the child's attempts.* A loose criterion for correct responding is preferable to a more narrowly defined goal.

- *Natural reinforcers.* A natural reinforcer is one that is directly related to the task. For example, in teaching a child to open the lid of a container, the natural reinforcer could be a sticker inside the container.

A typical teaching session using the pivotal-response model might begin with the presentation of a preferred object in an opaque bag. The trainer would attempt to prompt the child to initiate an interaction by saying to the child, "Say, 'What's that?'" If the child repeats the question, the adult responds by opening the bag and showing the child what is inside. Gradually, the prompt is faded until the child spontaneously asks the question. Later, the child is taught to ask other questions and to make other verbal initiations. In preliminary research with four children with autism, Koegel, Koegel, Shoshan, and McNerney (1999) found that pivotal-response training conducted for more than 2 years significantly increased the number of initiations as well as the overall pragmatic language of these children. Although still relatively untested, the pivotal-response intervention model appears to be a promising technique for enhancing the functioning of children with autism spectrum disorders. Two studies that compared pivotal-response training to other methods for improving language and communication skills, including a structured applied behavior analysis approach (Mohammadzaheri et al., 2014) and a parent education program (Hardan et al., 2015), found that pivotal-response training was superior to the other methods.

> You can watch Dr. Lynn Koegel, one of the developers of pivotal-response training, as she explains the basic principles and methods of this program. What are the "pivotal areas" according to this model?
> https://www.youtube.com/watch?v=5n9vlBtbji8

Auditory Training

Auditory problems are commonly found among children with autism and may, in part, account for some of the language problems associated with autism. Guy Berard, a French physician, developed a technique known as *auditory integration training* (AIT), which he claims can make a significant improvement in the language and communication of individuals with autism. The auditory training program entails 10 hours of listening to electronically modulated music over a 10-day period, using a variety of music (rock, pop, reggae), with high- and low-sound frequencies dampened on a near-random basis.

Research on auditory integration has found mixed results. Rimland and Edelson (1992) found that auditory integration training improved the behavior and reduced the auditory problems of eight children with autism compared with nine autistic children who did not receive the training. However, other researchers (e.g., Bettison, 1996; Mudford et al., 2000; Zollweg, Palm, & Vance, 1997) failed to find any effect for auditory integration training in children with autism or Asperger syndrome.

Early reports on auditory integration training appeared to be promising, but later research has failed to substantiate the effectiveness of this technique. Although auditory integration training may turn out to be effective for some individuals with autism spectrum disorders, the technique continues to be highly experimental and should be used with caution, if at all.

Facilitated Communication

Facilitated communication (FC) is another controversial intervention approach for children with autism. It is a technique for enhancing communication in persons who have difficulty communicating in the usual ways, such as those with autism, intellectual disabilities, or physical disabilities. The method is simple. A facilitator, using a special grip, holds the hand of the individual being facilitated. The facilitator is taught to provide resistance to the movement of the individual with whom he or she is working. The facilitator may place a hand over that of the other person or simply provide a light touch at the elbow or shoulder. It is hypothesized that this touch steadies the person with autism and allows the person to better focus his or her motor movements.

From the beginning, the technique has engendered both great excitement and profound skepticism. Many spectacular and controversial early claims were made about FC. For example, in one study (Biklen & Schubert, 1991), it was reported that after the implementation of FC, 20 of 21 people were able to type words. A number of research studies published since 1992 have raised significant concerns about the effectiveness of facilitated communication. Most of the studies have found that under clinical conditions, when the facilitator was "blind" to the stimulus item, the individual was unable to produce independent communication (e.g., Eberlin, McConnachie, Ibel, & Volpe, 1993; Regal, Rooney, & Wandas, 1994; Wheeler, Jacobson, Paglieri, & Schwartz, 1993). Instead, the communication appeared to be influenced, even guided, by the facilitator. This influence, although apparently unintended, nevertheless was real and pervasive. Study after study has found that when the facilitator did not know the content of the information to which the person had been exposed, the person was unable to identify the information being facilitated.

Because of concerns about claims regarding FC, the American Speech-Language-Hearing Association (ASHA) (1994) issued a position statement on FC that cautioned against using this technique. Although FC may help some students focus their attention and reduce off-task behaviors, it should not generally be part of clinical practice.

Making Instructional Decisions

With so many programs available to enhance the language and communication of children with autism spectrum disorders, it can be difficult for educators, clinicians, and parents to choose the right program. Prizant and Wetherby (2005) suggest that factors related to the individual child should be used in deciding which approach to use. These factors include:

- The child's current communication ability
- Development in other areas
- History of success with previous instruction
- Parental preferences

One of the most significant debates surrounding language and communication intervention for children with autism has been whether highly structured programs, such as

Teacher Perspective on Teaching a Child with Autism

I work within a self-contained pre-K autism classroom. There was a student who came in halfway through the school year from a school in a large urban area. We were informed that this child had little to no communication skills. In the beginning, we used a computer system called TEACH ME TO TALK. This system allowed for the student to touch pictures on the screen while the computer told him what the object was in a fun way. The pictures were in several different categories, ranging from food to toys to "m" words. We quickly learned that food was a huge motivation for this student. As we continued to teach him how to learn the program, we would choose the food category for the student to look at. As we sat at the computer, we would have his snack with us. If he had popcorn and chips for a snack, he had to point to the picture in order to get some of the food. When he was completely comfortable with the computer system, we began PECS with the student. As we ate the snack, he gave us the picture that corresponded with what he wanted. Gradually, we would have him give us the picture, along with trying to say the word. Eventually the student was saying the word without any pictures needed. Today, he is able to communicate far better than we ever expected.

discrete trial training, are superior to more naturalistic methods, such as the pivotal-response or incidental teaching methods. Paul, Campbell, Gilbert, and Tsiouri (2013) compared the effectiveness of discrete trial training to a naturalistic approach that included incidental teaching methods to teach spoken language skills to 22 preschool children with severe autism who had significant language impairments. The children were assigned to either a discrete trial or a naturalistic training group. Each group received 36 sessions of training that lasted for 45 minutes over 12 weeks. The researchers found that both groups of children made progress on language development as measured by factors such as the number of words used in conversations. However, they also noted that children with better receptive language skills made more progress with the naturalistic approach, whereas those with less developed receptive language did better with the discrete trial intervention. They also found that children with better joint attention skills performed better with either method. These results, if supported by future research, suggest that teachers and clinicians should evaluate factors such as the joint attention and receptive language skills of children with autism in order to select the most effective program to help those children develop their spoken language skills.

In the end, what matters most is outcomes. Is the child developing better language and communication skills? Can the child use these skills spontaneously and in a variety of communicative contexts? Is the child more successful in school and other community settings? Above is one teacher's approach to teaching a child with autism.

Case Study: CA—Autism Intervention Case

Read the following case study, and then respond to the related questions in your Pearson eText.

BACKGROUND INFORMATION

CA is a 12-year-old student with a premorbid medical history of fragile X syndrome, seizure disorder, and autism. CA has limited expressive communication skills; however, he is able to request most of his daily needs. Medications previously included Depakote, Trileptal, lithium, Tenex, melatonin, and clobazam. CA's mother recently stopped all medications, excluding those relating to seizures.

CA is currently in a self-contained classroom with a focus on functional skills. He is mainstreamed into a regular education setting for lunch and special events. CA receives related services of occupational therapy, physical therapy, and speech therapy.

(continued)

Case Study: CA—Autism Intervention Case   Continued

DESCRIPTION OF LANGUAGE AND/OR COMMUNICATION USED IN INTERACTIONS

Three observations were conducted in three different environments each with its own unique structure. Observation 1 occurred during a structured, well-regimented part of the student's day (arrival and morning routine). Arrival and morning routine is broken down into six activities:

1. Place book bag and coat on the table.
2. Get lion pictures and going to his desk.
3. Stand up and say the Pledge of Allegiance.
4. Unpack and hang up his book bag and coat.
5. Use the bathroom.
6. Sit down at the TV and watch *The Lion King*.

Observation 2 took place during a chance encounter (completely unstructured) in the hallway with another student from another class; CA had previous (positive) experiences with this other student. The third observation occurred in a mixed environment that contains both structured and unstructured portions (lunch). The structured parts include waiting in line and requesting what the student would like to eat; the unstructured parts are the actual eating of the meal and waiting at the table until lunch is over.

1. Initiation of communication.
   Arrival and morning routine: During the 30-minute period allocated for the arrival and morning routine, the student initiated interactions five times. Of the five initiations, four were verbal and one was nonverbal. The communicative initiations were centered on the last items of the student's activity schedule and those things that are highly desired for the student (lion pictures and *The Lion King*). Typically, his initiations to others are met with either immediate reinforcement in the form of what was requested or attention and guidance that after he completes the required task he will receive what he has asked for.
   Hallway transition: During this brief (5-minute) transition, the student did not initiate any interaction with individuals (peers, aide, or other staff members) in the hallway.
   Lunch: The only independent initiation occurred in a nonverbal form when the student poked his sandwich as a means to request help opening it. The aide interpreted this action and requested that CA use appropriate vocal language to request help.

2. Response to communicative attempts of others.
   Arrival and morning routine: In this structured environment, the communicative attempts by others were to redirect the students back to the activity schedule or vocal requests to complete tasks on the schedule. The communicative attempts by others resulted in the student completing the requested task. In this structured environment, CA responded positively to initiations by others and completed what was requested of him. He responded well to the one-on-one initiations by staff and seemed to enjoy the attention provided during these interactions.
   Hallway transition: When another student initiated communication with CA, he did not respond and continued down the hallway. When redirected and prompted by his support staff, CA responded by repeating what the aide directed him to say. Independent communication was nonexistent in this situation and was direct word-to-word prompting. The other student went on to ask CA about his holiday, which resulted in another lack of response that was followed by the aide structuring CA's response. When the student said "Bye" to end the conversation, CA did not respond.
   Lunch: Two communicative exchanges were attempted by staff members when they initiated interaction with CA. The first staff member (a lunch lady) said, "Hi," and was met with a response of "peanut butter," or what CA would like for lunch. After being prompted, the student responded with an appropriate "Hi" response. The second staff member said "Thank you" in response to receiving CA's tray and received no response until CA was prompted to provide a response.

3. Current language skills. Informal independent assessment was conducted to assess areas of phonology, morphology, syntax, semantics, and pragmatics.
   Phonology: Expressive phonological errors were substantial, including areas covered in the class text. Intelligibility of speech and accuracy of sound production were substantially low. Reduction of consonant clusters was seen in a few instances with the usage of the word "cose" to express close. Deletion of unstressed syllables was seen when the student was asked to say telephone and replied "Telphone." Receptive skills were limited.
   Morphology: CA's morpheme development/understanding, both expressive and receptive, is at best in its infancy, if existent at all.

(continued)

Case Study: CA—Autism Intervention Case   Continued

Syntax: CA is limited to the usage of crude simple sentences. Typically, sentences are limited to noun and verb usage with rare adjectives. One such example is when we talked about what he wanted to do at gym and he said, "Play big ball." Another example is his request for water: "Want water."

Semantics: Expressive and receptive vocabulary is severely limited. Use of figurative language and comprehension of humor are nonexistent.

Pragmatics: Expressive speech acts are a strength for CA; he is able to request, protest, greet, and answer. The depth of these acts is somewhat limited, but all are present in CA's repertoire. No understanding of conversational rules or receptive pragmatics was demonstrated.

Apply Your Knowledge 9.1: Case Study: CA

Click here to assess your understanding of CA's case.

Check Your Understanding 9.3

Click here to gauge your understanding of the concepts in this section.

Summary

In this chapter, we have seen that autism spectrum disorders are complex and still somewhat mysterious disorders. A variety of characteristics are associated with autism spectrum disorders, but severe impairments in socialization and in language appear to be most important. Many individuals with autism develop little or no spoken language. When language does develop, there are significant differences, especially in semantics and pragmatics. Most students with autism spectrum disorders have difficulty with the development of literacy skills, although the specific problems they encounter differ depending on their specific disability. A number of intervention programs to improve the language and literacy skills of individuals with autism spectrum disorders have been developed. Although success can be slow and frustrating, advances in research and practice are helping us to better understand and teach children with autism spectrum disorders.

Language and Students with Emotional and Behavioral Disorders

Individuals with emotional and behavioral disorders often have unexpected difficulties with language and communication. In this chapter, we will examine the evidence for the existence of language and communication problems in students with emotional and behavioral disorders. We will consider the implications for assessment and intervention and discuss some specific intervention approaches that may be effective with students with emotional and behavioral difficulties.

Learning Outcomes

After completing this chapter, you should be able to:

1. Describe the characteristics associated with students with emotional and behavioral disorders.

2. Explain the relationship between emotional and behavioral disorders, language impairments, and literacy.

3. Identify literacy difficulties related to emotional and behavioral disorders.

4. Describe evidence-based practices for assessing and enhancing the language and communication of students with emotional and behavioral disorders.

Najeem: A Case Study

Najeem is a fourth-grade male student, age 11 years, 11 months, who attends a day treatment program for at-risk adjudicated youth. Najeem was placed in the program for physically assaulting a teacher in his previous school. Najeem attended second grade for 2 years and then attended third grade for 1 year, and he is now in his third year as a fourth-grader. The initial testing he was given revealed that he reads at a middle first-grade level and has an instructional level of early third grade in mathematics. Najeem struggles with phonics skills, word decoding, spelling, and comprehension; therefore, reading materials, writing assignments, and mathematic word problems present a challenge for him. Additionally, Najeem has difficulty with expressive and receptive language skills. He frequently does not comprehend verbal prompts or directions, has difficulty explaining his thoughts, and does not understand humor or sarcasm.

Najeem is frequently uncooperative in the classroom. He often refuses to work, becomes angry, and has occasionally walked out of the room. His teachers report that he has limited interactions with his peers except for arguing and occasional fights. The goal is for Najeem to return to a regular education setting when he is able to control his behavior and improve his academic performance.

Defining the Population

One of the greatest challenges for researchers and practitioners is defining, identifying, and classifying students with emotional and behavioral disorders. Identification of this population can be very challenging because behavior can vary over time and by context and many assessment techniques have technical limitations. However, definition is important in order to identify children with difficulties that are so severe as to require specialized intervention procedures and/or special educational services.

A variety of terms have been used to describe this population of students, including *emotionally disturbed, behaviorally disordered, socially maladjusted,* and *psychiatrically disordered.* The Individuals with Disabilities Education Act (IDEA) uses the term *emotionally disturbed,* defined as:

(i) The term means a condition exhibiting one or more of the following characteristics over a long period of time and to a marked extent, which adversely affects educational performance:
   (A) An inability to learn which cannot be explained by intellectual, sensory, or health factors;
   (B) An inability to build or maintain satisfactory relationships with peers and teachers;
   (C) Inappropriate types of behavior or feelings under normal circumstances;
   (D) A general pervasive mood of unhappiness or depression; or
   (E) A tendency to develop physical symptoms or fears associated with personal or school problems.
(ii) The term includes children who are schizophrenic. The term does not include children who are socially maladjusted unless it is determined that they are emotionally disturbed. (IDEA, 2004)

The federal definition indicates that the problems experienced by children identified as "emotionally disturbed" must be *long-lasting* and *significant* and include both learning and social impairments. At the same time, the definition raises many questions. For example, what about students with attention deficits? Should they be included in this category? What about students with learning disabilities? If one follows the definition literally, then many students with learning disabilities could also be classified as emotionally disturbed. And what about students who are socially maladjusted? As Gresham (2005) points out, the definition indicates that "socially maladjusted" students must not be included in this population despite the fact that an "inability to build or maintain satisfactory relationships with peers and teachers," one of the core features of the IDEA definition of emotionally disturbed, is a defining feature of social maladjustment.

For the purposes of this chapter, we will use the term *emotionally and behaviorally disordered* (E/BD) because this is the term preferred by the Council for Children with Behavior Disorders of the Council for Exceptional Children (CEC). Within this category, we will include students with behavior problems that are so pervasive and persistent that they interfere with their academic and social development (the Center for Parent Information and Resources website includes a fact sheet on emotional disturbance in children; click on the "Resources" link, and then click on "NICHCY legacy resources"). Although many students with other disabilities (for example, those with attention deficits or autism) have behavior problems, these are not considered their primary problem but, rather, secondary difficulties that occur as part of a broader syndrome.

 In this video, a clinical psychologist provides a brief overview of emotional and behavioral disorders. What does she identify as possible causes?
https://www.youtube.com/watch?v=MbuqHvbSnCQ

Many professionals believe that students with serious emotional and behavior disorders have been underidentified and underserved for many years. For example, Kauffman, Mock, and Simpson (2007) point out that estimates suggest that about 5 percent of the school population may have significant behavior problems, but only about 1 percent are identified as E/BD. Kauffman and his colleagues (2007) suggest that there are several reasons for the underidentification of students as being emotionally disturbed, including:

- The stigma attached to the label "emotionally disturbed"
- The exclusion of students who are considered "socially maladjusted" from the federal definition
- Negative attitudes toward special education in general
- Problems in the identification of students with emotional and behavioral disorders

Students with E/BD tend to have an impact on schools far beyond the students' actual numbers. They are often the most difficult to include fully in regular education classrooms. When they are included, they may disrupt or distract other students. Long-term outcomes for students with E/BD are not good. One study (Greenbaum et al., 1999) reported that approximately two-thirds of adults who had been classified as E/BD in school had at least one contact with police in which they were believed to be the perpetrators of a crime and 43 percent had been arrested. Educational outcomes are also disturbing, as more than 75 percent of the adults in this study had low reading levels and 97 percent had low math levels.

Clearly, students with emotional and behavioral disorders present a significant challenge for schools. Despite a great deal of progress in the development of intervention techniques, the problems exhibited by students with E/BD remain resistant to change. Although there are, no doubt, many reasons why this is true, including family and community factors and continuing difficulties with assessment and identification, one factor that has been largely overlooked until recently is the language and communication difficulties of this population.

Why language and communication? As we will see, there is increasing evidence that children with E/BD often have significant deficiencies in spoken language. This could affect both their academic achievement and their social interaction. Moreover, these difficulties are often ignored by education professionals who are more focused on developing intervention methods for the most troubling surface problems (e.g., aggressive behavior, disruption, social withdrawal). As a result, language and communication difficulties are often unidentified or, if identified, are not included in the intervention plan for the child. In the remainder of this chapter, we will examine the evidence for language and communication deficiencies in students with E/BD and consider what can be done to address these problems.

Check Your Understanding 10.1
Click here to gauge your understanding of the concepts in this section.

Evidence for Language and Communication Difficulties

Until recently, the research basis for language and communication deficits associated with emotional and behavioral disorders was limited. Although many practitioners believed that students with emotional and behavioral problems had difficulty with aspects of language, there was limited systematic research to support their observations. However, there has been a dramatic increase in research on the relationship between language and communication difficulties and emotional and behavioral disorders. Researchers have found that children with speech and language disorders have a greater incidence of emotional and behavioral disorders than do other children. Similarly, children with emotional and behavioral disorders have high levels of language impairments.

Emotional and Behavioral Problems in Children with Speech and Language Disorders

A series of studies conducted by Lorian Baker and Dennis Cantwell and their colleagues at the University of California, Los Angeles (UCLA) Neuropsychiatric Clinic has reported a high incidence of emotional and behavior problems among children with speech and language disorders (Baker & Cantwell, 1987a, 1987b, 1987c; Cantwell & Baker, 1977, 1987). In one study, Cantwell and Baker (1987) examined 600 children with speech and language problems for evidence of emotional and behavioral disorders. Following an initial evaluation for speech and language problems, the children were divided into three groups: children with "pure" speech disorder; children with "speech and language disorders"; and children with "pure" language disorders. Psychiatric diagnoses were made after an interview with each child's parents and completion of four behavior-rating scales (two each by the child's parents and by a teacher). The results were that 31 percent of the children with "pure" speech disorders showed evidence of psychiatric disorder as compared to 58 percent of the children with both speech and language disorders and 73 percent of the children with "pure" language disorders. Both attention deficit disorders and **affective disorders** (e.g., separation anxiety, overanxious disorder) were commonly found, with the rates rising across the three groups of children.

A follow-up study done on the same population of children 5 years later (Baker & Cantwell, 1987c) showed that the prevalence of speech (but not language) disorders had decreased, but the prevalence of psychiatric problems had actually increased (from 44 percent initially to 60 percent). Attention deficit disorders were the most commonly reported problem.

Whereas Baker and Cantwell examined children who were receiving services from a university speech and language clinic, others studied children in regular school environments. For example, Beitchman, Nair, Clegg, Ferguson, and Patel (1986) investigated the prevalence of speech and language disorders and emotional and behavioral problems in 4,965 kindergarten children. They found that approximately 3 percent (142) of the children had significant speech and/or language disorders. These children, as well as a comparison group of children without speech and language disorders, were rated for emotional and behavior difficulties. The children with speech and language disorders were much more likely to have emotional and behavioral difficulties. Beitchman and colleagues (2001) have continued to follow this sample of children into adulthood. They have found significantly higher rates of psychiatric disorders in individuals with a history of early language impairments—especially social phobias and anxiety.

Another way to examine the relationship between speech and language impairments and emotional disorders is to follow a group of children with speech and language impairments over time to determine the prevalence of emotional and behavioral difficulties later in life. This approach was taken by Lindsay and Dockrell (2012). They identified a group of 65 children with speech and language impairments when they were 8 years old. They continued to follow this cohort of children as they went through school and completed a final evaluation of them at age 16 that included assessments of their verbal and nonverbal abilities, literacy skills, behavior, and self-perception of competence. They found that approximately 40 percent of their cohort had behavioral difficulties at age 16—approximately double the norm.

This and other studies indicate that children with speech and language disorders (especially those with language disorders) are at significant risk for having emotional and behavioral disorders. This may seem to be a surprising finding at first, since there seems to be no good reason why children with speech and language difficulties should have a higher incidence of emotional and behavior disorders. However, the evidence is overwhelming that this relationship does, in fact, exist. What is not clear is which problem is the cause and which is the result. In other words, do speech and language problems cause emotional and behavior problems or are language problems the result of an emotional or behavior disorder? Before attempting to answer this question, we need to look at the evidence for the existence of speech and language deficiencies in children with emotional and behavioral disorders.

Language and Communication Difficulties in Children with Emotional and Behavioral Disorders

An increasing number of studies have found that a majority of children with emotional and behavioral disorders have speech and language problems. A comprehensive review of the research on children with emotional and behavioral disorders in a variety of placements found that approximately 71 percent of children identified as E/BD had language and communication impairments (Benner, Nelson, & Epstein, 2002). A more recent review by Hollo, Wehby, and Oliver (2014) estimated the prevalence of language deficits in children identified as E/BD at 81 percent.

Much of the early research was conducted in children with significant emotional and behavioral disorders who were receiving services in psychiatric clinics or residential settings (Cohen, Davine, & Meloche-Kelly, 1989; Gualtieri, Koriath, Bourgondien, & Saleeby, 1983; Mack & Warr-Leeper, 1992). However, similar results have been found for children with less severe disabilities and those placed in regular education settings (Camarata, Hughes, & Ruhl, 1988; Nelson, Benner, & Cheney, 2005; Nelson, Benner, & Rogers-Adkinson, 2003).

Although there has been wide variation in the results for the incidence of language impairments in children with emotional and behavioral disorders, research has continued to find high rates of significant language difficulties in this population. For example, Nelson and colleagues (2005) reported that 68 percent of their sample of 166 E/BD students in public school special education placements had language deficits as determined by standardized tests. They also found that girls and boys had similar rates of language deficits and that the language impairments did not improve over time.

There is now strong and consistent research evidence that many (if not most) children with emotional and behavioral disorders also have significant language and communication impairments (see Table 10.1), but in most cases, the language difficulties go unrecognized because the focus of assessment and intervention is on the children's behavior. This is true in children served both in clinical settings (Cohen et al., 1989) and in school settings (Warr-Leeper, Wright, & Mack, 1994). These findings strongly suggest that it is important to identify and treat language and communication disorders both to improve language functioning and to prevent or diminish behavior problems.

Types of Language Difficulties. Although there is a great deal of evidence that children with emotional and behavioral disorders have language and communication difficulties at unexpectedly high rates, a number of questions remain about the nature of these problems. For example, researchers want to know whether certain kinds of language and communication problems are more prevalent than others.

As we know, language can be divided into two broad categories: expressive and receptive. Is either type of language disorder more common in children with emotional and/or behavioral disorders? Several studies have examined this question, with differing results. For example, the study by Hooper, Roberts, Zeisel, and Poe (2003) found that receptive language was the best predictor of behavior problems in grades one to three. Several other studies have reported similar results in regard to receptive language problems (Cantwell & Baker, 1987; Cohen et al., 1989). Other studies (e.g., Benner et al., 2002; Nelson et al., 2003) have reported that expressive language problems are more prevalent. There are several factors that might account for these different findings. We know that this population can be difficult to identify and define. Differences in the samples of children identified as E/BD may account for some of the variations in results.

Table 10.1

Research Evidence for Language Deficiencies in Students with Emotional and Behavioral Disorders

Study	Findings
Emotional/Behavioral Problems in Children with Speech-Language Disorders	
Baker & Cantwell (1987a)	Evaluated psychiatric status of 600 children with suspected speech-language disorders. Children with behavior disorders had significantly more language difficulties.
Baker & Cantwell (1987b)	Study of factors that might explain high incidence of psychiatric problems in children with speech-language disorders found most significant differences in language functioning.
Baker & Cantwell (1987c)	Follow-up study of 300 children with speech-language disorders found significant increase in psychiatric illness.
Beitchman et al. (1986)	Five-year-old children with speech-language disorders were more likely than a control group to have behavior disorders.
Beitchman et al. (2001)	Adults who were identified as having speech-language disorders as children had a high rate of psychiatric disorders.
Cantwell & Baker (1977)	Review of case study reports indicated that children with speech and language disorders have numerous psychiatric disorders.
Cantwell & Baker (1987)	Children with language disorders had higher rates of psychiatric problems than those with speech disorders.
Language Difficulties in Children with Emotional and Behavioral Disorders	
Camarata, Hughes, & Ruhl (1988)	Examined language skills of 38 children with mild to moderate behavior disorders in regular school; 71% fell two or more standard deviations on Test of Language Development–Intermediate.
Cohen, Davine, & Meloche-Kelly (1989)	Of 5- to 12-year-old children referred to a psychiatric clinic, 28% had a moderate to severe language disorder.
Cohen et al. (1998)	Of 380 children, age 7 to 14 years, referred to child psychiatric services, 40% had a language impairment that had never been suspected.
Mack & Warr-Leeper (1992)	Of 10- to 14-year-old boys from a psychiatric institute, 16 of 20 performed significantly more poorly than a control group on language measures.
Nelson et al. (2003)	Of students with an emotional disorder, 45% had a language deficit; learning difficulties were associated with language deficits.
Nelson et al. (2005)	Of 166 students with emotional and behavioral disorders in public school special education placements, 68% had language deficits; language impairments were stable over time.
Ruhl, Hughes, & Camarata (1992)	Thirty students with mild/moderate behavior disorders in public school setting scored more than one standard deviation below the mean on most language measures.
Trautman, Giddan, & Jurs (1990)	Of 6- to 13-year-old children attending a day program for severe behavioral difficulties, 54% demonstrated speech and/or language difficulties.

Another possibility is that there may be different types of language disorders associated with subgroups within the general population of students with emotional and behavior disorders. We will have more to say about this later in the chapter. A third possible explanation for the mixed findings about the type of language disorder is suggested by the results of a study by Benner, Mattison, Nelson, and Ralston (2009). When they tested 152 public school students classified as emotionally disturbed, they found that combined expressive-receptive language disorder was the most prevalent type of language difficulty (35.5 percent of the population), followed by receptive-only disorders; expressive-only disorders occured in just 6 percent of the subjects. What may be an even more important finding for teachers and clinicians was that the presence of language disorders, especially the combined receptive-expressive type, was highly related to learning difficulties. In other words, E/BD students who also had language disorders were at significant risk for learning disorders.

Specific Language Disorders. Most studies have found deficits in nearly every aspect of language in E/BD students. For example, Ruhl, Hughes, and Camarata (1992) gave a large battery of language tests to a group of 30 children who had previously been identified as emotionally disturbed and who were attending regular education classes. The researchers found that the students had deficiencies in language functioning in all areas that were measured, with particular problems in grammatical functioning and fewer problems in semantics. Specifically, the students with E/BD tended to use simple sentences that contained only one or two main ideas. Rinaldi (2003) studied what would appear to be a similar population—fourth- and fifth-grade students classified as E/BD who were placed in public school settings—but found somewhat different results. Although the majority of her sample of students scored significantly below the mean in all areas of language (as measured by the Test of Language Development), semantic functioning was the biggest problem area, followed by syntax and then pragmatics. However, Rinaldi concluded that the semantic and syntactic language difficulties contributed to the pragmatic language difficulties of students with emotional and behavioral disorders.

Since pragmatic language is closely intertwined with social interaction and many students with E/BD have significant problems in this area, it makes sense to explore pragmatic language in this population. In fact, several studies have found that students with E/BD have significant difficulty with pragmatic language. Specific problems include poor topic maintenance and inappropriate responses (McDonough, 1989) and failure to adequately consider the needs of the listener (Rosenthal & Simeonsson, 1991).

A review of research on language deficits in children with emotional and behavioral disorders by Hollo, Wehby, and Oliver (2014) found that deficiencies in expressive language skills were greater than deficiencies in receptive language skills. Similarly, participants in the studies that were included in the review scored lower on syntactic skills than they did on semantic skills. However, a limited number of studies included data on specific language skills, and most studies did not measure pragmatic language.

Language and Types of E/BD. Another question that has challenged researchers is whether differences in language and communication may be related to the type of emotional or behavioral problem of an individual. To explore this question, researchers have examined the language functioning of individuals with specific types of E/BD. Although there is a great deal of debate between experts as to how to classify children with emotional and behavioral disorders, two broad categories that are often used are "internalized" behavior disorders (such as withdrawal and depression) and "externalized" problems (such as aggression and hyperactivity). Are there differences in the language and communication of children with these differing types of problems, and if so, what are the implications for intervention?

Children with **internalized behavior disorders** often have limited social interactions. Because social interaction is an important contributor to language development, such children may be at risk for language difficulties. Research has found that children with language impairments are often more socially withdrawn. In particular, they tend to shy away from social interaction (Fujiki, Brinton, Morgan, & Hart, 1999). Additionally, depressed children have been found to have language difficulties, especially in aspects of pragmatics (Baltaxe & Simmons, 1988). Similarly, children with internalized behavior disorders have been reported to have significant language and communication difficulties—especially in pragmatic language (Hartas, 1995). As an example of this research, Evans (1987) examined the language and communication of what she called **reticent children**—children who spoke infrequently in the classroom. She found that, when compared their peers, these children talked about fewer topics, spoke in shorter utterances, and initiated interaction less often.

What about children with **externalized behavior disorders**? One of the first studies on the language and communication of children with conduct disorders was carried out by Mack and Warr-Leeper (1992). They administered a broad range of language tests to

20 residents of a psychiatric institute who had been referred for chronic behavior problems. The researchers reported that 13 of the participants showed evidence of significant language impairments, three had both language and speech impairments, and one had a specific speech impairment. Language difficulties were present in every area of language tested, so no specific area of language appeared to be more impacted than another. Increasing evidence shows that students with conduct disorders are more likely to have significant difficulty with expressive language. Specifically, they have more difficulty with the form and content of language (Nelson et al., 2005). This is not surprising, given the widespread observation by teachers that such students often seem to have difficulty expressing their feelings. (The American Academy of Child and Adolescent Psychiatry website includes information about types of emotional and behavioral disorders. Click on the "Resource Centers" link.)

Conclusion

Although many questions remain to be answered, there is more than enough evidence to indicate that language and communication difficulties are frequently associated with emotional and behavioral disorders. This is an important finding for three reasons. First, language and communication difficulties can have an impact on many of the areas of functioning that are problematic for children with emotional and behavioral disorders. In particular, problems with pragmatic language can contribute to difficulties in social interaction, the development of peer relationships, and interaction with teachers and others in authority. Imagine the child who does not adjust his language for different social situations. It may be acceptable for him interact with his friends on the playground by slapping hands and yelling, "Hey, what's happening?" but less so when he meets the principal in the hallway or his teacher on the first day of school. Students with language difficulties may also have problems using language to mediate their behavior—for example, thinking through the consequences of their behavior—and organizing their thoughts in writing.

Second, it is important to know that children with emotional and behavioral disorders are likely to have language and communication difficulties because these problems have often not been considered as part of the profile of E/BD students. Since their behavior is what gets the attention of teachers and parents, there is a tendency not to look past the behavior to consider what factors may contribute to their problems. The danger is that, if children have significant language and communication problems, these may go undetected and untreated, with the result that interventions for behavior problems may be less effective.

This leads directly to the third factor—intervention. Knowing that a student with emotional and behavioral difficulties may also have language and communication difficulties can lead to instruction that directly addresses the language problems while also enhancing the efficacy of behavioral interventions. For example, a child who frequently calls out in class may be on a behavioral program that rewards him or her for responding when recognized. The effectiveness of this program could be enhanced through instruction that teaches the child how to initiate interaction and how to respond when called on. Likewise, the research suggests that educators may be able to reduce the incidence of behavior (and reading) disorders through early identification and intervention for language and communication difficulties.

Check Your Understanding 10.2

Click here to gauge your understanding of the concepts in this section.

Literacy and Students with Emotional and Behavioral Disorders

Students with emotional and behavioral disorders experience a wide range of difficulties in school. In addition to the behavior problems that usually attract the attention of teachers and other school personnel, students with emotional and behavioral disorders also experience difficulties with social relationships and with academic skills. Because it is well established that many children with emotional and behavioral disorders have difficulty with language, it is not surprising that reading and writing skills are often poor in this population (Benner, Nelson, & Epstein, 2002; Benner, Nelson, Ralston, & Mooney, 2010). One study of children and adolescents with E/BD found that nearly 50 percent of the children (under age 13) and 36 percent of the adolescents had reading and/or writing scores well below average (Nelson et al., 2003). Another study (Trout, Nordness, Pierce, & Epstein, 2003) reported that the prevalence of underachievement in reading for students with emotional disorders ranged from 31 to 81 percent. Low reading achievement has been found to be a significant risk factor in the long-term outcomes of students with emotional and behavioral disorders (Epstein, Kinder, & Bursuck, 1989). Additionally, students with reading disorders have been found to be at higher risk for psychiatric disorders (including attention deficit hyperactivity disorder) than good readers (Carroll, Maughan, Goodman, & Meltzer, 2005; Willcutt & Pennington, 2000). Individuals with emotional and behavioral disorders have also been found to have significant difficulties with writing (Gage, Wilson, & MacSuga-Gage, 2014). In their study, Gage and colleagues (2014) noted that although reading difficulties were a major contributor to writing deficits, other skills, such as the ability to self-monitor and self-regulate, may also contribute to the writing difficulties of students with emotional and behavioral disorders.

Clearly, there is a relationship between emotional and behavior disorders, language impairments, and reading difficulties, but it is unclear which is cause and which is effect. In other words, do children who experience significant academic problems become behavior problems, or do children with behavior problems have more difficulty acquiring academic skills? And what is the role of language in both disorders? These questions were investigated in a study by Tomblin, Zhang, Buckwalter, and Catts (2000). The researchers intensively examined a population of 581 children by giving them a battery of tests that measured language, reading, and behavior. Approximately half of the participants had been identified as having language impairments in a previous study of a larger sample of children. The researchers found that the children with language impairments were about six times more likely to have reading difficulties than those without language impairments. They also discovered that children with language impairments were at significantly higher risk for behavior disorders—especially externalizing behavior problems. Further analysis of the data indicated that children with language impairments who also had reading disabilities were most at risk for behavior disorders. The authors concluded that it was most likely that language impairments preceded behavior disorders. Students with both language impairments and behavior disorders were most at risk for behavior problems.

Literacy Instruction

It is not enough to know that students with emotional and behavioral disorders have significant difficulty with reading and writing. Teachers and clinicians want to know how to help these students develop their literacy skills. A review of research on literacy instruction concluded that students with emotional and behavioral disorders can be responsive to appropriate reading instruction (Benner et al., 2010). The review revealed that supplemental instruction that focused on phonological awareness was especially beneficial. This was especially true for younger students. The review also concluded that older students with E/BD were responsive to comprehensive literacy instruction such as that provided in the *Corrective Reading* program (McGraw-Hill Education). A review of research on reading improvement methods for adolescents with emotional and behavioral disorders found that, although a number of approaches were effective, story mapping was the most effective strategy for these students (Garwood, Brunsting, & Fox, 2014).

Three other types of approaches have been found to be effective for improving the literacy skills of students with emotional and behavioral disorders: self-regulated strategy development (SRSD) (Lane et al., 2008; Rogevich & Perin, 2008); peer-mediated instruction programs, such as the Peer-Assisted Learning Strategies (PALS) program (Lane, Little, Redding-Rhodes, Phillips, & Welsh, 2007); and Corrective Reading (Allen-DeBoer, Malmgren, & Glass, 2006; McDaniel, Houchins, & Terry, 2011; Strong, Wehby, Falk, & Lane, 2004).

With the SRSD program, the teacher infuses literacy instruction with the self-regulation techniques of goal-setting, self-monitoring, self-instruction, and self-reinforcement. The ultimate goal is for students to internalize the literacy and self-regulation strategies so that they can comprehend text and write independently. Using a reading strategy called TWA (THINK before reading, WHILE reading, and AFTER reading), in combination with the SRSD approach, Rogevich and Perin (2008) reported significant improvements in the comprehension of science texts for adolescents with significant emotional and behavioral disorders. Lane and colleagues (2008) also used the SRSD approach to successfully improve the writing of second-grade students at risk for emotional and behavioral disorders. A review of research on the use of the self-regulated strategy development method for students with emotional and behavioral disorders concluded that SRSD is an evidence-based practice for improving the writing skills of these students (Sreckovic, Common, Knowles, & Lane, 2014).

 Watch this video to learn more about the principles and practices associated with self-regulated strategy development. What are some of the self-regulating strategies that are used?
https://www.youtube.com/watch?v=SkdJYqezAOs

The PALS program is a peer-directed, structured, supplemental reading program used to teach decoding and reading fluency skills (go to the Institute of Education Sciences website, put PALS into the search box, and then click on the link to the PALS overview for a description of this program). Teachers pair strong readers with weak readers. The students take turns being the tutor and tutee. Lane and colleagues (2007) implemented the PALS program with seven children ages 6 and 7 who had been identified as at risk for emotional and behavioral disorders. They found that the children increased their reading fluency and improved in academic engagement, although some of the children reported that they did not like their partner.

The Corrective Reading program (Englemann et al., 1999) uses direct, explicit instruction and scripted lessons to teach decoding and reading comprehension skills. Allen-DeBoer and colleagues (2006) implemented Corrective Reading with adolescents in a juvenile correctional facility. Each of these individuals had been identified as having an emotional disorder. Following 10 weeks of instruction that took place for 30 minutes a day, the students made significant gains in their reading levels. Other studies have found that found that the Corrective Reading program can improve reading fluency (Strong et al., 2004) and can be used as a supplementary program to improve the reading skills (McDaniel et al., 2011) of students with emotional and behavioral disorders.

 Watch this video of a teacher conducting a Corrective Reading lesson. How does the teacher prompt students to respond?
https://www.youtube.com/watch?v=ILDUjrNsnGY

Although there is no single best way to enhance the reading and writing skills of students with emotional behavioral disorders, a rapidly growing body of research is finding that the students can make significant progress with direct, explicit instruction on literacy skills. This, in itself, is a significant finding since academic skills often receive less emphasis than social and behavioral development in programs for students with emotional and behavioral disorders.

Check Your Understanding 10.3
Click here to gauge your understanding of the concepts in this section.

Assessment and Instruction

Students with emotional and behavioral disorders present some formidable challenges for education professionals. Their behavior, whether internalized or externalized, can be disturbing to both teachers and their peers. This may make it more difficult to implement effective intervention that requires the cooperation of teachers and/or peers. Moreover, the behavior of students with emotional and behavioral disorders may vary considerably from day to day or within the day. Children may come to school already angry or withdrawn. On other days, they may arrive at school in an upbeat mood but leave depressed or angry. These variations of behavior make it more difficult to assess the child and to provide consistent and appropriate instruction. In addition, many students with E/BD have "unexpected" language and communication difficulties. These problems can make assessment more difficult (since many assessment procedures are language based) and make instruction less effective. What, then, can be done to enhance the effectiveness of assessment and instruction for students with emotional and behavioral disorders?

Assessment

Assessment of speech and language skills, especially communicative abilities, should be part of the evaluation of any students suspected of having emotional and behavioral disorders. By now, the reasons for this suggestion should be obvious. In many cases, these children will have previously undetected speech and/or language problems. In a few cases, it may be that what was identified as a behavioral or emotional problem could, in fact, be primarily a language or communication difficulty. Therefore, it is essential that appropriate language and communication assessment be included as part of the assessment protocol. In many cases, however, persuading team members to include language and communication assessment in the evaluation of students with suspected emotional and behavioral difficulties may be a very difficult step. Many professionals are not aware of the impact of language and communication difficulties on behavior. As a result, they might be reluctant to include assessment of language and communication in the assessment plan of a child suspected of emotional and/or behavioral problems.

Audet and Hummel (1990) suggest that appropriate language assessment for students with suspected emotional and behavioral disorders should include a review of the child's history to identify possible psychological stressors and developmental history, a comprehension formal speech and language assessment including providing visual supports if needed, and informal assessment of the child's communicative skills. Many students with E/BD have difficulty applying their language skills to the task of communication. For them, testing may indicate that development of speech and language skills are at normal (or near-normal) levels, but their use of these skills in conversational contexts may be lacking.

Unfortunately, communication is not easy to assess. There are no formal, standardized tests of communicative competence (although there are tests of pragmatic language—a related skill). Instead, communication is best assessed in natural settings that are, by their very nature, difficult to control. A comprehensive assessment of communicative competence should include observation in several settings at different times during the school day. For example, observations could be done both in the classroom and in the cafeteria. Classroom observation should be done during more than one activity, since students may behave differently in response to various classroom activities. The observer must be trained in both what to observe and how to observe. Observers who get too close to students, for example, may interfere with natural interactions. In addition to observations in natural settings, it may be possible to structure situations in which children interact with a peer or in a group. Although these interactions may be less spontaneous, they have the advantage of being more easily controlled and observed. For example, teachers could assign two students to work together to write a story or could assign a group to collaborate on a science project. These activities provide opportunities for interaction that can be observed by the teacher or speech-language specialist.

Of course, the behaviors associated with children with emotional and behavioral difficulties make the assessment task more of a challenge. Their behavior may vary widely over the course of the school day. They may respond differently to various individuals and in different settings. Children who are withdrawn or depressed might be reluctant to participate at all. Students with attention deficits or conduct disorders may have a difficult time focusing on the assessment tasks. Therefore, it is important that the individual conducting the assessment understand the need to adapt the testing conditions to the child being evaluated. Assessment may have to be speeded up or slowed down. Children might need frequent breaks or no breaks at all. Some children may need a great deal of encouragement and reinforcement for responding; others will resent such feedback. The key is for the evaluator to be alert to each child's needs and respond appropriately. If this is done, a more complete and more accurate picture of the child may be achieved.

Instruction

As with assessment, the place to begin with intervention for students with emotional and behavioral difficulties is to be sure that language and communication are included in the instructional plan for the student. Unfortunately, this is rarely the case. Despite the overwhelming evidence for the presence of language and communication disorders, most children with emotional and behavioral disabilities do not receive speech and language instruction (Hyter, Rogers-Adkinson, Self, Simmins, & Jantz, 2001). Intervention plans usually focus primarily on the overt behavior exhibited by the student. For a student with a conduct disorder problem, this might be a plan to reward the student for reducing calling out during class. For a socially withdrawn student, the plan might address increased opportunities for peer interaction.

Although it is certainly important for intervention plans to address the specific problems that students are experiencing, for students with language and communication difficulties, such plans may not go far enough. In both of the cases just described, the inclusion of language and communication goals could enhance the effectiveness of the behavioral intervention. For example, rewarding a student for reducing the incidence of calling out in class may reduce disruption in the classroom, but it does not provide the student with appropriate classroom interaction skills. For this, direct instruction in pragmatic language skills—such as how to enter an ongoing conversation, how to stay on topic, and how to keep responses brief and focused—may be necessary.

There is evidence that language intervention can make a difference for students with emotional and behavioral disorders. For example, working collaboratively, special education teachers and speech-language pathologists taught six boys between the ages of 8 years 6 months and 12 years 11 months who attended a specialized educational facility for children with E/BD to improve their skills in describing objects, giving directions (step by step),

Problem	Intervention
Student engages in inappropriate interaction in class (e.g., calls out answers, strays off topic).	1. Teach student appropriate ways of attention and participating in classroom discussions. 2. Assign students to peers to ask and/or answer questions. 3. Ask students to self-monitor their interaction in the classroom.
Student interacts infrequently in class.	1. Provide opportunities to respond to a peer and/or small group. 2. Use class-wide voting as a strategy to involve all students.
Student dominates interaction when working in groups.	1. Assign a group member to keep track of who has already talked and act as the "referee"—reminding students to wait their turn. 2. Give each group member tokens that must be "spent" in order to participate.
Student interacts infrequently in groups.	1. Establish ground rules that require all group members to participate, and ask group to self-evaluate its achievement of this goal. 2. Provide training to the student outside group time on pragmatic language skills needed to participate in groups.

Table 10.2

Intervention Suggestions for Students with Emotional and Behavioral Disorders

stating personal opinions about inappropriate behavior (judgments), and negotiating for desired outcomes (Hyter et al., 2001).

Instructional Goals.   Although specific instructional goals should always be developed for each individual child, there are some general recommendations that can apply to many students with emotional and behavioral disorders (see Table 10.2). Giddan (1991) has suggested that one important instructional goal is to *help students learn vocabulary words that they can use to identify and describe their emotional states.* She suggests that helping students understand the subtle meaning differences between words such as *scared, worried,* and *embarrassed* may help them better express their feelings to others. To help them learn this new vocabulary, students can keep a notebook or journal in which they write down what they are feeling. Giddan suggests that the child can take this book to class, to counseling sessions, and home, where the words and the feelings they describe can be discussed.

Another important goal is to become a *more effective classroom communicator.* Students with emotional and behavioral disorders need to learn skills such as how to get the teacher's attention (without disrupting the class) and how to appropriately ask for repetition or clarification when they do not understand. In addition, they need to develop listening skills that will enable them to attend to important information in class and store it effectively. Instruction in classroom communication can take place in many ways. Teachers can use opportunities in the classroom to teach children appropriate ways of asking questions and responding. In addition to the traditional approach of asking children to raise their hands, teachers can use techniques such as picking names from a hat to ensure that all students are given an opportunity to participate, sharing an answer with a peer partner, or participating in class-wide "voting" on answers. These latter suggestions can be especially useful for children who may find talking in front of the class particularly stressful.

Interaction with peers is a significant problem for many students with emotional and behavioral disorders. Therefore, a third language and communication goal for these students is *enhancing peer interaction.* Many classrooms, especially at the secondary level, provide limited opportunities for peer interaction. In fact, students are often discouraged from or punished for interacting with their peers. Of course, there is an appropriate time and place for peer interaction, but that is the point. Teachers should provide that time and place where peer interaction *can* occur. However, for many students with emotional and behavioral difficulties, simply providing opportunities for interaction with peers is not enough. They need to be helped to develop skills such as how to initiate conversation, take turns (and wait their turn), and stay on topic. Teachers can help by assigning students particular roles in a group, giving students tokens to spend in order to participate in a group, and including assessment of interaction as part of an overall assessment of the group's performance. Gallagher (1999) suggests the following activities to enhance interaction:

- Teach communicative alternatives to socially penalizing behaviors.
- Build event-based/script knowledge for socially or emotionally difficult situations.
- Manipulate antecedent events to increase opportunities to display and practice positive communicative behaviors.
- Manipulate consequent events to increase frequency and salience of outcomes of socially positive communicative behaviors.
- Develop broader and more varied emotional vocabularies.

Even when additional communicative opportunities are created, many students with emotional and behavioral disorders are unable to take advantage of those opportunities because they lack skills in pragmatic language. Hyter and colleagues (2001) reported on the results of a classroom-based program to enhance the pragmatic language skills of six students, ages 8 to 12, with emotional and behavioral disorders. The students participated in 16 lessons, each lasting 30 minutes, that focused on four skill areas:

1. Describing objects
2. Giving step-by-step directions
3. Stating personal opinions about inappropriate behavior
4. Negotiating for desired outcomes

Each lesson included role-playing of the target skill. Following the instruction, all of the students increased their scores on the Test of Pragmatic Language. They also improved their skills in describing objects and giving directions. However, the students did not show significant improvement in the other areas. These results suggest that pragmatic language skills can be taught but that students need help (such as guided practice) in order to generalize these skills to real classroom situations.

Delivery of Instruction.   Service delivery issues are often a concern with students with disabilities. Questions about who should provide the service and where the service should be provided often impede the effective delivery of services. In the case of students with E/BD who may also have language and communication difficulties, the issues may be particularly complex. In addition to a regular education classroom teacher, there may be a special education teacher, a therapist, a speech-language specialist, and others involved with the child.

Although educators often recognize the importance a team approach when dealing with students with learning or intellectual disabilities, they may not recognize the need for an interdisciplinary team when working with children with emotional and behavioral disorders. As Brinton and Fujiki (1993) point out, most speech-language specialists have had little, if any, training in working with such students and have not usually thought of these students as within their area of expertise. Yet, the research clearly shows that language and communication impairments are an important factor in emotional and behavioral disabilities. Similarly, classroom teachers may be so focused on behavior that they lose sight of the important contribution of language skills. This is all the more reason why an interdisciplinary team can be an essential part of the intervention program for students with emotional and behavioral disorders.

The key to effective service delivery for this (or any) group of students is collaboration. Whenever possible, professionals should share their goals and methods of intervention with each other. For example, the teacher who is trying to get a withdrawn student to participate more frequently in the classroom could be assisted by a special education teacher who could prompt the student to respond. Similarly, a speech-language specialist could help by modeling a classroom interaction scenario with the child. Unfortunately, collaboration is often an elusive goal. In practice, teachers often feel that they are too busy to share their instructional goals with others. Specialists may feel that only they understand the complexities of their area of expertise and that teachers and parents would have little to contribute. Hopefully, education professionals and parents will overcome the impediments to collaboration and work together to provide an effective intervention plan for students with emotional and behavioral difficulties.

Even when instruction for students with E/BD is carefully planned and effectively delivered, there can be challenges due to the nature of the child's difficulties. Coleman and Vaughn (2000) interviewed eight teachers who work with students with emotional and behavioral disorders regarding the challenges they faced in teaching such students. Some of the themes that emerged included the following:

- *Emotional variability of students.* Progress can occur at unexpected rates due to the emotional state of the student. Long periods without progress can be followed by a sudden leap in performance followed by regression.

- *Fear of failure and trust issues.* Students will often refuse to attempt a task because fear of failure is so deeply ingrained. Because trust is often an issue, the teachers suggested establishing consistent routines in the classroom.

- *Keeping students engaged.* Many of the teachers indicated that they used games to keep their students engaged and motivated. Noncompetitive games were preferred.

Najeem: A Case Study

Read the following case study, and then respond to the questions in your Pearson eText.

Najeem, the fourth-grade student who attends a day treatment program for at-risk children who we discussed at the beginning of this chapter, is being evaluated for speech and language services. Available past educational and developmental records about Najeem are minimal because he has never been evaluated for special education services. It is known that Najeem attended second grade for 2 years and third grade for 1 year and that he is now in his third year as a fourth grader. His initial testing given at his current school revealed that he reads at a middle first-grade level and has an instructional level of early third grade in mathematics. Najeem often does not comprehend verbal prompts or directions, has difficulty explaining his thoughts, and does not understand humor or sarcasm.

ASSESSMENT INSTRUMENTS

The Test for Auditory Comprehension of Language (TACL-3) was given to Najeem as a formal assessment of his receptive language skills. The test was administered one on one in an office separate from the classroom, and it was given over three sessions on consecutive days. In addition, two informal assessments of receptive language were given one on one to Najeem, and a speech-language checklist was completed based on observations of him in the classroom.

ASSESSMENT RESULTS

TACL-3 Results

Subtest	Raw Score	Language Age Equivalent	Percentile
Vocabulary (V)	40/45	8 years, 6 months	37th
Grammatical Morphemes (GM)	36/46	7 years, 3 months	16th
Elaborated Phrases and Sentences (EPS)	39/48	8 years, 6 months	37th

(continued)

Najeem: A Case Study   Continued

Receptive Language Informal Assessments

Two similar informal assessments for receptive language were given to Najeem, each consisting of 10 questions. One asked questions about the days of the week, such as, "What day comes after tomorrow?" The other asked questions about numbers, such as, "What are the two numbers before 3?" These assessments were given orally in an office outside the classroom with only Najeem. He asked for questions to be repeated to him about 50 percent of the time. Najeem scored 7/10 on the days of the week and 8/10 on the numbers.

Speech-Language Assessment

A speech-language checklist that was filled out by Najeem's teacher based on classroom observations showed deficits in the following areas.

Expressive Language

√ Incorrect use of grammar

√ Tendency to ask questions that are too general

√ Difficulty expressing thoughts

√ Talkative but talk contains little real substance

> *Comments: Najeem uses incorrect grammar when speaking and writing. When he has a difficult time with classwork, he struggles to explain what it is he needs help doing.

Receptive Language

√ Seems unable to follow verbal instructions

√ Problems explaining the whys and wherefores of things; can't put grammar together

√ Difficulty requesting further information to aid understanding

√ Doesn't follow jokes, puns, sarcasm, or metaphors

√ Difficulties organizing information

> *Comments: Najeem is sometimes unresponsive when spoken to, as if he does not understand what is being asked of him or is not paying attention at all.

Pragmatic Language

√ Failure to understand or pay attention to rules of conversation, e.g., turn-taking

> *Comments: Najeem speaks loudly and tends to interrupt others in conversation.

Literacy

√ Word-letter reversal

√ Cannot segment syllables or words

√ Unable to blend or manipulate sounds

√ Confuses similar-sounding words

√ Difficulty discriminating vowel sounds

√ Poor word recognition

√ Difficulty reading orally

√ Avoids written work

√ Not using spelling/reading rules for decoding or encoding unfamiliar words

> *Comments: Najeem struggles with reading and writing; however, he does put forth effort. He has a difficult time decoding words and discriminating sounds in words. He sometimes confuses letters in writing and has to be reminded of what sound they produce.

Apply Your Knowledge 10.1: Case Study: Najeem

Click here to assess your understanding of Najeem's case.

Check Your Understanding 10.4

Click here to gauge your understanding of the concepts in this section.

Summary

Students with emotional and behavioral disorders exhibit a wide arrange of behaviors—from severely withdrawn to highly disruptive. Although their behavioral difficulties are the defining feature of this population, there is a substantial amount of research evidence that indicates that many students with E/BD often have unsuspected language and communication problems. Language and communication difficulties can interfere with classroom participation, peer interaction, and academic performance. It is important to include assessment of speech, language, and communication in the assessment plan for students with E/BD. In addition, instruction that includes language and communication goals may enhance the effectiveness of interventions with students with emotional and behavioral disorders.

Language and Students with Sensory Disabilities

Children with sensory disabilities, including hearing impairments and visual impairments, present significant challenges for education professionals. Sensory disabilities can have an impact on a number of areas of functioning, including language and communication. For children with **hearing impairments**, the problems are apparent. However, individuals with vision disabilities frequently have difficulties with language and communication that may limit their ability to fully participate in school and society. This chapter examines the impact of sensory impairments on language and cognitive development and on academic and social performance. The chapter also includes instructional methods that have been used effectively with children with sensory and motor impairments.

Learning Outcomes

After completing this chapter, you should be able to:

1. Describe how sensory impairments have been defined and classified and changes in the identification and treatment of children with hearing impairments.

2. Explain the impact of hearing impairments on the development of language and factors that influence the development of language in children with hearing loss.

3. Describe the educational performance of students with hearing impairments and compare the advantages and disadvantages of various intervention techniques for children with hearing impairments.

4. Describe the language characteristics associated with visual impairments and the implications for teaching students with vision loss.

Marisol: A Case Study

Marisol is a 6-year-old girl who is a student in Mrs. Wright's first-grade classroom. Marisol was born 2 months premature and developed retinopathy of immaturity, which left her with little residual vision. Marisol can see shadows but cannot see images.

Marisol has received intervention almost since the day she left the hospital. As a preschooler, Marisol attended a program that emphasized interaction with peers, hands-on learning, and play activities to promote language acquisition.

Marisol attended a regular kindergarten program in her community. She received support in the classroom from a full-time instructional aide. Marisol made very good progress in kindergarten both academically and socially. In addition to participating in class-wide activities such as circle time and listening to stories, Marisol began to learn to read braille with the assistance of a part-time instructor provided by the State Commission on the Blind. Although Marisol is still reluctant to initiate interactions

(continued)

Marisol: A Case Study   Continued

with her peers, she is included in social activities both within and outside the classroom.

Now that she is in first grade, Marisol continues to receive braille instruction from a part-time teacher. Unfortunately, there have been some problems with coordinating the braille lessons with classroom instruction provided by the regular first-grade teacher. The two teachers have found it difficult to find time to plan together so that Marisol receives a consistent program. Because there are no braille versions available for the math book used in class, Marisol's aide has been tape-recording those lessons. She is finding it difficult to keep the recordings up to date.

Marisol tends to be reluctant to initiate interactions with peers. She does have one friend in the classroom who she also sees out of school. However, most of the rest of the children in the classroom rarely interact with her.

Marisol's language skills seem to be close to those that would be expected for a child of her age. She is able to understand almost everything said to her. She can ask questions and initiate interactions, although she is often reluctant to do so. She has been receiving speech therapy for some lingering speech production problems but not for language skills. Marisol's teacher, Mrs. Wright, has reported that Marisol has some difficulty learning new words but can do so if given enough time.

Marisol is continuing to make good progress in the regular education classroom. Her aide assists her with mobility and with lessons that require reading. Her braille teacher reports that Marisol is making excellent progress in acquiring braille. Marisol's overall language skills are good. Her most significant challenge is in socialization. She is reluctant to initiate interactions and has few friends in the classroom. This will need to be a focus for intervention in the future.

Defining Hearing Impairment

Children with hearing impairments range from those with mild impairments to the profoundly deaf. They may have a disability that fluctuates, is stable, gets progressively worse, or is either hard to identify in the classroom or easily recognizable. With this much variation in the population with hearing impairments, it is essential that education professionals have a clear definition of hearing impairment.

The Individuals with Disabilities Education Act (IDEA, 2004) defines two categories of students with hearing impairments as follows:

Deafness: means a hearing impairment so severe that a child is impaired in processing linguistic information through hearing, with or without amplification, that adversely affects a child's educational performance.

Hearing impairment: means an impairment in hearing, whether permanent or fluctuating, that adversely affects a child's educational performance but is not included under the definition of "deafness."

If you think these definitions are not very specific, you are correct. There is no "legal" definition of deafness (as there is for blindness). As Karchmer and Mitchell (2003) note, the definitions of *deafness* and *hearing impairment* are "amorphous and contested" (p. 22).

The Conference of Executives of American Schools for the Deaf (CEAD) adopted the following definitions to classify persons with hearing impairments:

Hearing impairment: This generic term indicates a hearing disability that can range from mild to profound. It includes the subsets of deaf and hard-of-hearing.

Deaf: A person who is deaf is one whose hearing disability precludes successful processing of linguistic information through audition, with or without a hearing aid.

Hard-of-hearing: A hard-of-hearing person has residual hearing sufficient for successful processing of linguistic information through audition, generally with the use of a hearing aid.

The most important distinction made by these definitions involves the ability to process language. Children who are deaf are *unable* to use hearing to process language.

Figure 11.1

The Peripheral Auditory System

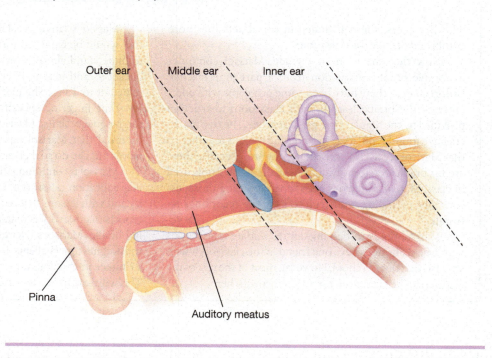

Source: From Owens, Robert E.; Farinella, Kimberly A.; Metz, Dale Evan, *Introduction to Communication Disorders: A Lifespan Evidence-Based Perspective, Enhanced Pearson eText—Access Card,* 5th Ed., ©2015. Reprinted by permission of Pearson Education, Inc., New York, New York.

Hard-of-hearing children can process spoken language, although they may experience delays and differences in development.

Another approach to the classification and definition of hearing impairments is by the type of hearing loss. There are three major types of hearing impairments. **Conductive hearing loss** is caused by a problem with transmission of sound from the outer to the middle ear (see Figure 11.1). This hearing loss is usually mild to moderate. The most common cause of conductive hearing loss is *otitis media* (middle-ear infection). Conductive hearing losses are usually treatable but, if left untreated, may cause significant problems. **Sensorineural hearing loss** results from damage to structures that transmit sound from the ear to the brain and often involves auditory nerve damage. This condition usually results in moderate to severe hearing losses and is usually not reversible. **Central hearing loss** is caused by damage to the brain resulting from many factors, including tumors, disease, or stroke. Central hearing losses are often difficult to identify because a child may seem to hear normally but may have problems in interpretation and integration of acoustic information.

 Watch this video for a demonstration of conductive hearing loss. What would be the impact of a mild hearing loss on a child's ability to participate in the classroom? http://www.youtube.com/watch?v=3yjc8NDtAZ4&feature=related

 Listen to Ashley as she describes what it is like to be a child with a hearing impairment. How does she feel about having hearing aids?

Figure 11.2

Two Audiograms

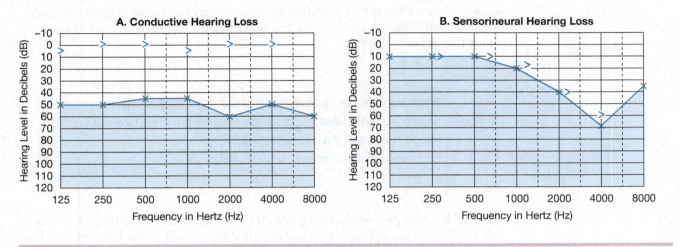

The most commonly used approach to the classification of hearing impairments is the *degree of hearing loss*. With this approach, hearing impairments are classified according to the results of audiometric testing. The speech-language clinician evaluates the child's hearing by determining how loud a sound or word must be in order for the child to recognize it. The results are recorded on an **audiogram** (see Figure 11.2). The audiogram shows the hearing threshold (the point at which the child can identify sounds) and the pitch frequencies of those sounds.

▶ For a better understanding of what an audiogram is and how to interpret it, watch this video. What are the two criteria measured by an audiogram?
https://www.youtube.com/watch?v=bP-nJp3yBK4

When the results for several different types of audiometric testing are averaged, that average indicates how seriously the child's hearing is impaired. Knowing the child's level of hearing impairment allows for predictions about that child's ability to learn and interact in the classroom. For example, children with **mild hearing loss** (15–30 dB) have minimal difficulty hearing, although they may have some problems hearing faint speech. However, these children may have some articulation difficulties, slight language delays, and some difficulty with reading and/or writing. It is important that teachers learn to recognize those with mild hearing disorders, since relatively simple interventions (such as preferential seating and the use of visual cues) may help these children.

Children with **moderate hearing loss** (31–60 dB) have more significant hearing and speech disorders. Many of these children experience significant delays in speech and language development, and they may have difficulty hearing in noisy environments or when speech is not directed at them. Children with moderate hearing losses may benefit from hearing aids and intensive speech and language instruction.

Children with **severe hearing loss** (61–90 dB) have considerable difficulty hearing normal speech and frequently have significant delays in speech and language development. Many have abnormal voice quality as well. Children with severe hearing losses will usually require some sort of amplification system or an alternative to spoken language. Therefore, early identification and intervention are important so these children can learn to use their residual hearing.

Watch this video that demonstrates the effect of a mild, moderate, and severe hearing loss. In the video, how does speech perception with a moderate hearing loss differ from that of a mild hearing loss?

http://www.youtube.com/watch?v=1EJ4g3J6cJM

Children with **profound hearing loss** (91+ dB) can hear little if anything. They learn to rely heavily on visual and tactile cues, and amplification is usually of little help to them. These children are most likely to benefit from training in the use of a manual communication system.

In addition to the degree of hearing loss, several other factors should be considered to understand the effects of a hearing impairment on a particular child. The *age of onset* of the disability is critical. Children who acquire hearing disabilities after the initial stages of language learning usually have less impairment than children whose disability is present at birth. *Age of identification of the hearing loss* is also very important. Children who are identified early and who receive appropriate intervention services are usually able to progress more quickly than children who are not identified early. *Stability of the hearing loss* should also be considered. Children with fluctuating or progressive hearing losses may require different types of instruction than children with stable hearing losses.

According to the U.S. Department of Education, 78,000 children ages 3 to 21 (about 0.2 percent of the school population) received services for deafness or hearing impairments in the 2011–2012 school year. However, this number may not represent the total number of children with hearing impairments. Some children may be identified as having another disorder (such as a communication impairment, learning disability, autism, or intellectual disability) as their primary disability yet may have a hearing impairment that contributes to their academic and social challenges.

Apply Your Knowledge 11.1: Simulation

It can be difficult for hearing individuals to understand how persons with hearing impairments experience the world. Try this simulation and respond to the questions.

There are profound changes taking place in our understanding and treatment of individuals with hearing impairments. These changes are due primarily to two factors: early newborn screening and cochlear implants. Universal screening of infants for potential hearing disorders is now the law in the United States and in many other countries around the world. The identification of children with hearing impairments holds promise for early intervention and, hopefully, a significant improvement in outcomes for children with significant hearing impairments.

Figure 11.3

Cochlear Implants

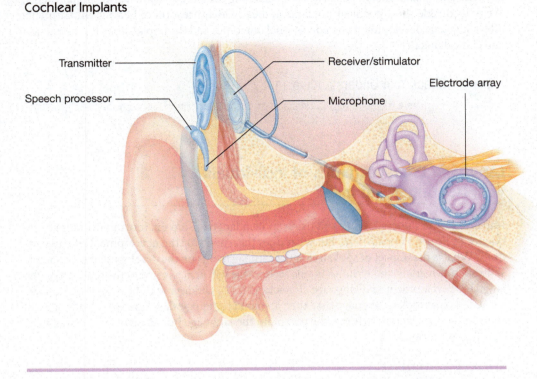

Transmitter

Speech processor

Receiver/stimulator

Electrode array

Microphone

Source: National Institutes of Health: Medical Arts, http://www.nidcd.nih.gov/health/hearing/coch.asp, U.S. Department of Health & Human Services.

Some of the children identified as hearing impaired may become candidates for **cochlear implants.** Cochlear implant work by directly stimulating the auditory nerve fibers, unlike conventional hearing aids that merely amplify sound. A microphone is contained within a wearable speech processor that filters out background noise while enhancing speech signals. These signals are transferred to a receiver implanted in the mastoid bone behind the ear and then to electrodes that have been implanted into the *cochlea* (inner ear), which, in turn, deliver the sound to the auditory nerve (see Figure 11.3).

> ▶ For more information about cochlear implants, watch this video. How does a cochlear implant enhance hearing?
> http://www.youtube.com/watch?v=SmNpP2fr57A

When cochlear implants were first developed, they were used primarily with adults. Now they are being used with children as young as 12 months old, or even younger. For many persons with hearing impairment, cochlear implants can improve speech perception and production as well as language development. However, there are cautions about cochlear implants as well. Some members of the deaf community have expressed concerns about the impact of cochlear implants on their community and on their language (sign language). Others have cautioned that cochlear implants are not a "cure" for hearing impairments.

Throughout this chapter, we will make reference to the emerging research on the impact of cochlear implants and universal hearing screening on children with hearing impairments. We will consider how cochlear implants and early identification of hearing impairments affect language development and educational outcomes and the implications for instruction and clinical practice.

 Check Your Understanding 11.1
Click here to gauge your understanding of the concepts in this section.

Language Characteristics of Individuals with Hearing Impairment

Impairments in understanding and using spoken language are the most important consequence of hearing impairment. But what does that mean for the development of language itself? What is the impact of spoken-language impairments on the development of academic skills such as reading and writing? In this section, we will review some of the research on the language development and language characteristics of children with hearing impairments. We will look at spoken language first, then at manual language development. Finally, we will examine several factors that may help explain the language impairments associated with significant hearing loss.

Spoken Language

Children with hearing impairments are at risk for delays in language development (Koehlinger, Van Horne, & Moeller, 2013). Those who are congenitally deaf have been found to have a language delay of at least 1 year by the time they enter school, and up to 50 percent have a severe language delay, even with hearing aids (Sarant, Holt, Dowell, Rickards, & Blamey, 2008). Even children with relatively mild hearing impairments often experience delays in some aspects of language development. Language impairments have been found to persist, at least into adolescence (Delage & Tuller, 2007).

Early Development of Language and Communication.   The early language and communication development of children with mild to moderate hearing impairments appears to follow a typical developmental sequence and pace (Yoshinaga-Itano & Seedy, 1999). Early communicative interaction with parents is intact, as is the early development of cooing and babbling (Oller, Eilers, Bull, & Carney, 1985). The intelligibility of early speech is also high for children with mild to moderate hearing impairments.

But what about children with severe and profound deafness? Experts know that early parent–child interaction sets the stage for language development. What is the impact of severe deafness on this interaction? Interestingly, research studies have found that hearing mothers produce comparable amounts of speech to their deaf and hearing children and modify their language in ways that are typical of parent–infant interaction (Gallaway & Woll, 1994; Lederberg & Everhart, 1998). However, babies who are deaf are limited in their ability to benefit from spoken-language input. They may benefit from the nonverbal communicative interaction sequences and from facial expressions, but they can learn little from the spoken language itself.

The early vocalizations of babies who are deaf have been found to be similar to those of hearing infants, but that changes when babbling begins. Babies who are deaf babble less frequently and use fewer different sounds in their babble, even when they have hearing aids and when parents emphasize spoken language (Oller & Eilers, 1988). Additionally, babies who are deaf have been reported to babble more disconnected consonants and vowels instead of consonant–vowel syllables (Stoel-Gammon, 1988). Vocalization differences increase as babies who are deaf approach the emergence of first words.

Phonology and Speech. Most of the research on the phonological abilities of children who are deaf has focused on their ability to *produce* language sounds. For the most part, researchers have found that speech production is delayed in these children and follows a developmental course that is similar to that of hearing infants. However, there may be some sounds that never fully develop (Blamey, 2003). Both the degree of hearing loss and the frequencies involved in the loss can affect speech intelligibility (Griffer, 2012).

Studies of older children have also found delays in the development of speech production. Children who are deaf or hard-of-hearing have been found to make more phonological errors and substitutions than do hearing children (Ratner, 2005). However, researchers have also discovered that children who are deaf develop the same phonological rules as do hearing children. These rules may develop more slowly, but when they do emerge, they are similar to those used by hearing children (Oller, Jensen, & Lafayette, 1978).

It is important for hearing-impaired children to acquire phonological rules, but it is even more important that these children be understood. Most people find the speech of children with significant hearing impairments difficult to understand. Intelligibility seems to be related to the degree of hearing impairment; that is, children with more serious impairments generally are more difficult to understand. However, several factors may affect a child's ability to be understood, one of the most important being the experience of the listener. Several studies indicate that those listeners who are more experienced in interacting with persons who are deaf are better able to understand such speakers (McGarr, 1983; Monsen, 1983). Other factors that affect speech intelligibility are the context of the conversation and the ability of the listener to see the face of the speaker (Monsen, 1983).

Research on the speech capabilities of children who are deaf or hard-of-hearing suggests that these children will have significant delays in speech development. These delays often result in speech that is difficult to understand, thus creating significant problems in the classroom. But research also suggests that teachers and others who work with these children can help them be better understood by seating them so they can be seen and by having listeners use context clues as an aid to understanding.

Morphology and Syntax. Word parts such as prefixes and suffixes are a rather subtle aspect of language and are sometimes hard to acquire, even for children without disabilities. In English, word parts are often unstressed, a situation making it all the more difficult for children with hearing disabilities to acquire these structures. Children with hearing impairments, not surprisingly, have been found to be delayed in their acquisition of morphological rules. This is true of both children with profound hearing impairments (Russell, Power, & Quigley, 1976) as well as individuals with less serious difficulties (Koehlinger et al., 2013). Although researchers have generally found that children who are hearing impaired follow the same sequence of morphological development, some studies (e.g., McGuckian & Henry, 2007) have reported differences in the morphological developmental sequence of children with moderate hearing impairments, with the third singular s (*she talks*), past -ed (*they walked*), and possessive s (*Mary's ball*) lagging behind in development.

Most of the studies on the syntactic skills of persons who are hearing impaired have found that these children experience significant delays relative to hearing children and that the delays are generally related to the degree of hearing loss (Griffer, 2012). For example, Schirmer (1985) examined the spontaneous spoken language of 20 children between the ages of 3 and 5 with severe to profound hearing impairments. The children were videotaped during a 1-hour play session. Analysis of their spoken language production indicated that the children with hearing impairments were developing a syntactic-rule system similar to that of hearing children, but with significant delays. Koehlinger and colleagues (2013) found that the mean length of utterance of 3- and 6-year-old children with hearing impairments was significantly lower than that of peers with typical hearing.

Some researchers have concluded that these delays are so great that some syntactic structures fail to develop at all. In their summary of a series of studies of the syntactic development of persons who are deaf, Quigley, Power, and Steinkamp (1977) reported that many of the syntactic structures usually acquired by hearing children between the ages of 10 and 18 had not been acquired by most 18-year-old persons who are deaf. These include the passive and embedded clauses. Quigley and colleagues also noted that persons who are deaf produce unique syntactic structures that are rarely, if ever, produced by hearing persons. For example, individuals who are deaf place the negative marker (*no*) outside the sentence, as in *Beth made candy no*. These structures appear to be rule based, since they are used consistently.

Research with children with mild to moderate hearing impairments has found that they have relatively good comprehension of syntactic structures. In one study of 5 to 10 year olds with mild to moderate hearing impairments, the children were found to achieve similar scores to age-matched peers without hearing impairments on a test of grammatical understanding (Briscoe, Bishop, & Norbury, 2001). Similarly, Nittrouer and Burton (2001) found that hearing-impaired children who had received intensive oral training performed similarly to hearing peers on a test of complex syntax understanding.

So, are children with hearing impairments *delayed* in their development of syntax, or is their language *different* from the norm? The research suggests that teachers and other educators can expect that most children with serious hearing impairments will be delayed in their understanding and use of morphology and syntax. Some structures may not develop at all, whereas some structures may be unique to children with hearing impairments. Children with mild to moderate hearing impairments are likely to lag behind their hearing peers but can make improvements with intensive intervention.

Semantic Development

Studies examining the development of semantic skills in children with hearing impairment have generally found significant delays and difficulties with receptive vocabulary (Mayne, Yoshinaga-Itano, & Sedey, 2000) as well as with expressive vocabulary (Mayne, Yoshinaga-Itano, Sedey, & Carey, 2000). In the latter study, the median expressive vocabulary score for 32- to 37-month-old children with normal cognition who were identified with hearing loss by 6 months of age fell under the 25th percentile for children with normal hearing at 30 months. Blamey (2003) has estimated that children who are deaf learn vocabulary at about half the rate of hearing children. Even children who have received cochlear implants have been found to lag significantly behind their same-age peers with normal hearing (Nott, Cowan, Brown, & Wigglesworth, 2009). Two factors have been frequently found to be associated with poor vocabulary development in children with hearing impairments: level of cognitive development and age of identification of the hearing disorder. Children with greater cognitive development who are identified before 6 months of age generally have more advanced vocabulary development, although it may still lag behind their hearing peers (Mayne, Yoshinaga-Itano, & Sedey, 2000; Mayne, Yoshinaga-Itano, Sedey, & Carey, 2000). Interestingly, degree of hearing loss has not been found to be associated with vocabulary development.

In addition to examining vocabulary development, researchers have also studied other aspects of semantic development in children with hearing impairments, including the ability to learn novel (nonsense) words and the development of categorical knowledge. The ability to learn new words has been found to be highly related to phonological skills, with hearing-impaired children with relatively intact phonological skills performing similarly to hearing peers and children with phonological deficits learning much more slowly (Gilbertson & Kamhi, 1995). The ability to form semantic categories and use them to learn has generally been found to be intact in children with hearing impairments (Jerger et al., 2006).

The results of research on semantic development in hearing-impaired children indicate that vocabulary learning is a particular problem and should be a focus of instruction with this population. However, overall semantic skills, including the ability to learn new words and to use semantic knowledge for learning, may be relatively intact.

Pragmatic Language

Given the significant speech and language difficulties of most children with significant hearing impairments, it should not be surprising that they have trouble in engaging in successful communicative interactions. In fact, research has generally found that children who are deaf or have significant hearing impairments have difficulty with the development of some pragmatic language skills (Thagard, Hilsmier, & Easterbrooks, 2011).

Young children with hearing impairments have been found to be both similar to and different from hearing children. For example, in a longitudinal study of children with severe to profound hearing impairments from ages 2 months to 3 years, Lederberg and Everhart (2000) reported that the children communicated as frequently with their parents as did hearing children. They initiated topics and maintained those conversational topics similarly to the hearing children. However, the hearing-impaired children relied much more on nonlinguistic means of communication. Over time, the researchers found that the hearing-impaired children continued to increase their communication, but fell behind their hearing peers. In particular, they had difficulty maintaining a conversation and asking questions. Nicholas, Geers, and Kozak (1994) looked at the use of communicative functions by 2-year-old children with hearing impairments compared to two control groups—one matched for chronological age and the other matched for language ability. The researchers found that the children with hearing impairments lagged well behind their same-age hearing peers but were actually ahead of the language-age-matched group. In other words, although they were delayed in the development of communicative functions, children with hearing impairments were ahead of where they should be for their level of language development. The authors suggested that these results may have been due to the fact that the children with hearing impairments participated in an educational program that emphasized communicative interaction.

What about later pragmatic development? Most older children with severe to profound hearing impairments interact with their hearing peers at rates that are similar to those found in same-age hearing children, although the nature of those interactions is somewhat different. For example, when trying to enter into an activity, they may "wait and hover" or disrupt the activity in order to be included, rather than joining in with the ongoing play. In a study of 12 preschool children with severe to profound hearing impairments (six of whom had cochlear implants), DeLuzioa and Girolamettoa (2011) found no differences between the hearing-impaired children and their hearing peers in either initiation of interactions or in responses. However, the hearing children systematically excluded their hearing-impaired peers from participation. They frequently ignored the initiations of the hearing-impaired children and initiated interactions infrequently with them. These results suggest that peer training in how to interact with hearing-impaired peers may be necessary.

This brief review of the spoken-language development of persons who are deaf suggests that significant delays, as well as some language differences, can be expected. There may be several causes of these language impairments. Obviously, the major factor is the hearing impairment itself. With limited opportunity to participate in oral–verbal conversations, children who are deaf do not have the same chance to learn the rules of language. This just seems like common sense. However, the relation between hearing impairments and language development may not be so simple. Research has led to mixed findings regarding the relationship between degree of hearing loss and language development. In addition to degree of hearing impairment, factors such as parents' efforts, educational programming, and individual differences intrinsic to the child may have significant effects on the language and cognitive development of a child with hearing impairments.

Manual Language

So far we have focused on the development of spoken language in children who are deaf. But some would argue that this focus is entirely wrong and that manual communication (i.e., sign language), not spoken language, is the natural language of those who are deaf. To understand the language development of children who are deaf, the argument goes, look at their development of manual language.

Support for the claim that manual language is the natural language of those who are deaf comes from studies of early communication such as that of Goldin-Meadow and Feldman (1977), who videotaped interactions between hearing parents and their children with hearing impairment. The parents were selected for the study because they had decided that their children should not acquire a manual sign language; therefore, the children were attending an educational program that emphasized spoken language. Yet, when the children were observed interacting with their parents, the researchers found something quite amazing. These children had acquired a number of gestures that could be called signs. They used these gestures consistently and even combined them into multiword phrases. Even more surprising was the discovery that the parents themselves, who were opponents of manual language, were unknowingly communicating via sign language. Through careful analysis of their videotapes, Goldin-Meadow and Feldman concluded that the children had developed the signs on their own, while their parents had unconsciously acquired signing from their children. Follow-up studies on one of the original children has found that the child's gestures became more language-like as he grew older. He learned to refer to objects that were not in his immediate environment and to express both noun and verb structures. Overall, it appeared that, despite a lack of formal sign language instruction, the child developed a communication system similar to sign language (Goldin-Meadow, Butcher, Mylander, & Dodge, 1994; Goldin-Meadow & Mylander, 1990).

Researchers who have looked at manual-language development in children who are deaf have found the development following a course similar to that found in hearing children as they acquire a spoken language (Bonvillian, Nelson, & Charrow, 1976; Klima & Bellugi, 1979). For example, children who are deaf developing a sign language appear to progress through similar stages of "manual babbling" as hearing children learning to speak (Petitto & Marantette, 1991). When first words (signs) develop, they have errors similar to those made by young children learning a vocal language (Schick, 2003). In fact, some researchers have claimed that children who are deaf learning sign begin to use "words" from 3 to 4 months earlier than hearing children developing spoken language (e.g., Anderson & Reilly, 2002). The research on the early development of children who are deaf learning to sign suggests that language development itself is not impaired in children who are deaf, but rather, the development of *spoken* language is delayed.

Research on the language development of children who are deaf has led to several important findings. First, spoken-language delays and even some language differences are characteristic of most children who are deaf. However, these delays are *not* found when manual-language development is observed. Therefore, although hearing impairment is clearly an important contributing factor to impairments in spoken-language development, teachers must recognize that other contributing factors (such as parental input and educational programming) are important as well. Perhaps the most significant consideration is that language needs *stimulation*. When children are exposed to a rich language environment and given the opportunity to interact, they are more likely to develop language skills.

Manual Language Versus Spoken Language

There is an ongoing and highly emotional debate in the deaf community about whether children should learn a spoken language or a manual language as their first language. Part of the debate is based on issues of culture and power. The most significant issue is what is best for the ultimate language development of children who are deaf.

One important question is whether the acquisition of a manual language interferes with the acquisition of spoken language. Marschark, Lang, and Albertini (2002) note that, although there is evidence that the unique syntactic structure of American Sign Language can affect the speech and writing of deaf children, there is no research evidence that the acquisition of manual language interferes with spoken-language acquisition. On the contrary, it may enhance spoken-language acquisition. The best advice for parents of children who are deaf is to interact frequently with their children using every modality available—spoken language, gesture, and sign. Over time, children tend to prefer one mode of communication over another, but there appears to be no harm in exposing them to multiple forms of communicative interaction.

Cochlear Implants and Language Development

As noted earlier in this chapter, cochlear implants are having a significant impact on our understanding and treatment of serious hearing impairments. According to estimates, the number of children receiving cochlear implants before 2 years of age has increased 40-fold from 1991 to 2002 (Drinkwater, 2004). Currently, over 50 percent of the children receiving implants are under 5 years old.

Cochlear implants can improve auditory perception and spoken-language production, but there is still disagreement about the extent of improvements. For example, a study of 39 congenitally children with congenital deafness with cochlear implants, ages 5 to 14, found that, compared to hearing children, the children who are deaf with implants obtained significantly lower scores on several measures of structural language. Surprisingly, the one area where the children were similar was in articulation (Schorr, Roth, & Fox, 2008). On the other hand, a number of studies have found significant improvements in language skills, especially in younger children who received cochlear implants (Svirsky, Robbins, Kirk, Pisoni, & Miyamoto, 2000; Tomblin, Barker, Spencer, Zhang, & Gantz, 2005). Geers, Moog, Biedenstein, Brenner, and Hayes (2009) tested 163 children with cochlear implants and found age-appropriate scores for approximately half of the children in the areas of expressive and receptive language.

A number of factors may account for the differences in reported findings. Age of implantation, parental interaction, nonverbal intelligence, and language instruction can have an impact on the eventual language development of children who receive cochlear implants. For example, in the study by Geers and colleagues (2009), it was reported that children who received their implants at young ages had higher scores on all language tests than children who were older at implantation. As research on the effects of cochlear implants continues, it seems likely that we will find that this intervention has a significant impact on the language learning of children with significant hearing impairments. At the same time, there are likely to be children who will continue to lag behind their hearing peers in language development and will need support to enhance their language skills. See the box for one teacher's perspective on cochlear implants.

A Teacher's Perspective on Cochlear Implants

A boy in kindergarten at my school had cochlear implants placed, and that was the first time I ever heard of them. He has done exceptionally well, having been mainstreamed into a general education setting with an in-class support aide. So, it came as a surprise to me that there was debate over the use of implants in deaf children. I believe that the use of these implants provides great benefit to children who are born deaf or who have lost their hearing, and if I had a child with such hearing challenges, I would find out all I could about the implants and pursue that option if appropriate.

The teacher's role is vital when a classroom has a child with cochlear implants. First and foremost, the teacher has to assess the student's academic performance in an ongoing manner and be alert to specific services and support that the child may require, such as periodic auditory and speech services. Some guidelines that teachers should follow in teaching children with cochlear implants include the following: differentiate instruction to accommodate the child's individual needs; use sign language to parallel visual language development, which helps the child understand what he or she is hearing; and use assistive technology to assist the child in communicating and acoustical enhancements such as microphones to help the child hear.

Factors Related to Language Development

Cognitive Development.   Contemporary research on the cognitive development of individuals who are deaf has focused on the cognitive differences between this population and hearing persons and the factors that contribute to these differences. Rather than absolute differences in ability, researchers are finding that factors such as early home experiences, exposure to language, and educational experiences can have an impact on cognitive development (Marschark et al., 2002). In addition to looking at measured intelligence, research has also been interested in the ability of deaf persons to receive, store, and process information. As an example, researchers have been interested in whether visual-processing abilities are superior in deaf persons. For a long time, it has been assumed that deaf persons compensate for their lack of hearing through enhanced visual skills. However, research has generally not supported this assumption. In fact, there is some evidence that young deaf children have poorer visual attention (Spencer, 2000). On the other hand, some research has suggested that deaf persons who use sign language have superior visual skills to those who use spoken language (e.g., Emmorey & Kosslyn, 1996). Marschark and colleagues (2002) concluded that, depending on the nature of the visual task, deaf persons may perform better, worse, or the same as hearing individuals. Similarly, various results have been found regarding the memory abilities of deaf persons. Research has found some subtle differences in the ways in which deaf persons organize information, but memory appears to be generally intact.

Another focus of research on the cognitive abilities of deaf persons has been on theory of mind. As you may recall from Chapter 9, many children with autism have difficulty understanding the mental states of other persons. Some researchers have reported that children with hearing impairments have difficulty with this skill as well (Peterson & Siegal, 1999). Others have reported that deaf children can understand mental states (Marschark, Green, Hindmarsh, & Walker, 2000). Part of the explanation for the differences in findings comes from the different tasks that were used to measure theory of mind. Another factor in explaining the different findings may be the child's family background and early use of language. As an example, Woolfe, Want, and Siegal (2002) found that deaf signing children who were raised by deaf parents had stronger theory of mind understanding than did children who developed signing later. These results suggest that deficiencies in theory of mind that have sometimes been reported in deaf children may have more to do with early socialization and language use than with a cognitive difference in the population.

So, what can we conclude about the cognitive abilities of persons who are deaf? It is likely that their intellectual abilities are similar to those found in the hearing population; that is, some persons with hearing loss have higher than average intellectual skills, with most falling around the norm and a few ranging below normal (assuming no other disabilities are involved). There may be some delays in the development of higher-order thinking skills. These delays could result from a lack of spoken language or a lack of opportunity to engage in challenging problem-solving tasks.

Parents and Families.   We know that parents and families have an important influence on early language development in children. There is every reason to think that this effect is as important, or even more important, in children with significant hearing impairments. We have already reviewed some of this research earlier in this chapter. Additional support for this claim comes from research such as that on theory of mind (mentioned earlier) that has found that early socialization is a factor in the development of the understanding of mental states in deaf children. Research has found that deaf children raised by deaf parents have certain advantages in language learning. They are typically exposed to sign language right from the start and develop relatively good receptive and expressive (manual) language skills. On the other hand, children who are deaf who have hearing parents usually have better developed speech skills (Griffer, 2012).

Otitis Media.   Parents of young children sometimes experience being awakened in the middle of the night by howling children who are holding their ears. These children may have otitis media, one of the most common childhood illnesses. By 3 years of age, about two-thirds of all children have experienced at least one bout of otitis media. During the worst phase of the infection, most children experience pain, fever, and fluid in their ears (*effusion*) (Teele, Klein, & Rosner, 1980). However, some children do not exhibit these outward signs of otitis media at all.

During episodes of otitis media, there may be a slight loss in hearing ability. This is of no great concern except when the child experiences frequent and long-lasting bouts of otitis media or when the infection goes untreated. Then the child may be at risk for more serious impairments. Because these fluctuating hearing losses occur just at the time when children are beginning to acquire language, there is concern about the effect of chronic, persistent otitis media on language development.

 Watch this video about otitis media. What are some of the symptoms that parents and teachers can watch for?
https://www.youtube.com/watch?v=FdhWivS3E88

Research on the effects of otitis media on the developing child has been mixed. Some studies have reported that children with otitis media experience delays in the development of expressive language (e.g., Teele, Klein, Chase, Menyuk, & Rosner, 1990) and in phonological and reading development (Winskell, 2006). These delays, if they exist, may be caused by the hearing impairment that results from otitis media (Friel-Patti & Finitzo, 1990). Other studies have failed to find a relationship between otitis media and the development of language in the young child (e.g., Grievink, Peters, van Bron, & Schilder, 1993; Paul, Lynn, & Lohr-Flanders, 1993; Shriberg, Friel-Patti, Flipsen, & Brown, 2000).

The best advice for parents is to have their child examined by a physician if they suspect their child may be having ear infections. Otitis media can often be treated with drug therapies, but when this approach is not successful, surgery may be necessary. Teachers of younger children can help by looking for the symptoms of otitis media—frequent colds, fluid from the ears, unusual crankiness, and/or difficulty hearing. Teachers of older children should be aware that a history of chronic and persistent otitis media may be related to later problems with language-related activities such as reading and writing. These children may benefit from additional practice on phonological analysis.

Check Your Understanding 11.2
Click here to gauge your understanding of the concepts in this section.

Educational Performance and Methods

Because cognitive ability and language development (with the exception of spoken language) are intact in most children with hearing impairments, there is no reason to expect that the educational performance of the children should be below normal. Yet, study after study has found that the educational performance of students with moderate to severe hearing impairments is below that of hearing students, especially in reading and language arts (e.g., Davis, Shepard, Stelmachowicz, & Gorga, 1981; Davis, Elfenbein, Schum, & Bentler, 1986; Gentile, 1972; Phelps & Branyan, 1990). These results have been consistent for many years (LaSasso & Mobley, 1998).

What factors cause the educational deficiencies of students who are deaf or hard-of-hearing? More importantly, what can be done to improve academic achievement in this population?

Watch this video as Ashley and her mother describe what it is like to be a student with a hearing impairment. What did Ashley's mother do to help to get her daughter the services she needed to be successful?

Reading

The reading achievement of students who are deaf and hearing impaired is an area of particular concern. The average high school graduate who is deaf reads at a level equal to the average 8- to 9-year-old hearing student, and about 30 percent leave school functionally illiterate (Paul, 1998; Traxler, 2000). Data from nationwide testing indicate that students who are deaf or hearing impaired underachieve in reading comprehension compared to same-age hearing students and that the gap widens over time (Qi & Mitchell, 2012). That is, with each year of schooling, students who are deaf or hearing impaired appear to fall further behind their hearing peers. This does not mean that every person who is deaf has poor literacy skills, but a significant portion of the population has literacy deficiencies that can affect subsequent employment and quality of life.

What might account for the reading difficulties of students who are deaf? From their review of the literature, Luckner, Sebald, Cooney, Young III, and Muir (2005/2006) identified five factors:

1. *Obstructed access to the phonological code.* Children who are deaf have been found to develop phonological skills more slowly than hearing children and may be less able to use those skills in reading (Sterne & Goswami, 2000).

2. *Limited fluency at the onset of formal schooling.* Many students who are deaf have limited (or no) experience with the English language. Therefore, they are like second-language learners who are simultaneously learning a new language while learning to read the language.

3. *Inadequate literacy experiences in early childhood.* Many students who are deaf or hearing impaired come to school with inadequate experience with print and books. Their parents read to them less often than parents of hearing children (Paul, 1998). When parents of children who are deaf do read to their children, they tend to be more directive with their child, providing less opportunity for interaction with the text (Aram, Most, & Mayafit, 2006).

4. *Delayed acquisition of vocabulary.* Research has found that students who are deaf or hard-of-hearing experience delays in developing their vocabulary knowledge, have smaller lexicons, and acquire new words at slower rates (Lederberg & Spencer, 2001).

5. *Problems with lower-level skills.* Skills such as word recognition, syntax, and morphology are inadequate. These form building blocks for reading success.

Research on specific factors that may impede the reading progress of children with hearing impairments has generally found that phonological awareness is deficient (Briscoe, Bishop, & Norbury, 2001; Gibbs, 2004). The study by Briscoe and colleagues (2001) found that phonological skills were related to degree of hearing impairment, with children with more severe impairments having poorer phonological skills. Although their phonological processing abilities were similar to those of children with specific language impairments, their overall language development was better than the language-impaired children. In addition to deficiencies in phonological awareness, Gibbs (2004) reported that lags in vocabulary development were related to the reading difficulties of 7-year-old children with hearing impairments. Difficulties with phonological awareness are evident in young children with hearing impairments and, in fact, appear to be the greatest difference between them and their hearing peers on emergent literacy skills (Easterbrooks, Lederberg, Miller, & Bergeron, 2008). There is some evidence that children who receive cochlear implants at an early age have better outcomes in both the development of phonological awareness skills and in reading (Johnson & Goswami, 2010).

In addition to these, three other factors may contribute to the reading difficulties of individuals who are deaf or hearing impaired prior knowledge, affect, and cognition. In order to understand what one reads, it is necessary to refer to previous knowledge. Paul (2003) has suggested that difficulties with the use of prior knowledge may have an impact on reading comprehension. Although there is limited research on affective factors (such as motivation and interest) in readers who are deaf, it may be that problems in this domain contribute to the poor performance of individuals who are deaf as well. Marschark and his colleagues (2009) have reported that difficulties with metacognition, specifically a lack of awareness of their own comprehension and learning, may impede the development of reading skills in college-aged students with hearing impairments. Other cognitive factors, such as attention, memory, and executive functions have also been found to differentiate good from readers who are deaf or hearing impaired (Daza, Phillips-Silver, Ruiz-Cuadra, & Lopez-Lopez, 2014).

What can teachers do to help children who are deaf or hearing impaired develop their reading skills? Marschark and colleagues (2002) suggest the use of a balanced literacy approach that combines the teaching of skills emphasized in a basal reader approach with the authentic text reading associated with whole-word approaches to literacy. Unfortunately, there is little research to indicate that this and other approaches commonly used with children who are deaf or hearing impaired (e.g., the language experience approach, bilingual approaches, dialogue journals, predictable books, teaching sight words, teaching figurative language, the use of story retelling) are consistently effective (Luckner et al., 2005/2006).

Since phonological awareness and vocabulary development appear to be significant challenges for many children with hearing impairments, it may be appropriate to focus on instruction in these areas. In a review of phonological instruction programs for children with hearing impairments, Wang, Trezek, Luckner, and Paul (2008) suggested that programs that emphasize the use of the visual system, such as cued speech and Visual Phonics, hold considerable promise for this population. In addition, teachers should provide as many literacy experiences as possible in the classroom, including shared book reading and writing activities, while working on the improvement of English language skills.

One approach that has been documented to be effective in a few studies is the use of the Reading Recovery program. Reading Recovery is a one-to-one intervention individually designed to accelerate literacy learning of children identified as at risk for reading difficulties. In a study in which first-grade students with severe and profound hearing impairments were included in a Reading Recovery program, all of the students made significant improvements in reading, and nine of the children were on grade level by the end of the year (Charlesworth, Charlesworth, Raban, & Rickards, 2005). Although it is not known if these improvements will hold up over time, the Reading Recovery program may prove useful for some children with significant hearing impairments.

Writing

Writing is another area of concern for students who are hearing impaired and deaf. Difficulties in written language are well documented (see Albertini & Schley, 2011; Williams & Mayer, 2015). Typically, the writing of students who are deaf is shorter and less complex than that of hearing students (Marschark et al., 2002). In addition, these students make more errors in their writing, including using unnecessary words, omitting essential words, substituting the wrong word, and using incorrect word order (Quigley & Paul, 1990).

When Everhart and Marschark (1988) asked students who were deaf or hearing impaired, ages 8 to 15 years old, to write a story about what they would do if they were picked up by a UFO, they found that the children who were deaf produced stories that were shorter, used simpler sentences, and used fewer modifiers. It is especially interesting that the written output of the children who were deaf was more literal and less imaginative than when they were asked to tell the story through sign language. Clearly, the students who were deaf had thoughts that were more sophisticated than they were able to express through written language.

Research on the academic achievement of students who are deaf can be viewed in two ways. The pessimistic view is that despite years of effort, the academic achievement of these students has not significantly improved. Children who are deaf still struggle with reading and writing, and the gap between their performance and that of hearing children generally widens with time. The optimistic view is that the factors that appear to cause these academic deficiencies also appear to be subject to remediation. Early intervention, consistent language development, and appropriate educational programs can make a difference. In the next section, we will take a look at some of the educational programs that have been developed for children with hearing impairments.

Educational Methods

Although there is general agreement that appropriate educational intervention is essential for children who are deaf, there continues to be a lack of consensus as to what constitutes an appropriate education. For decades, there has been a raging debate over the best way to enhance language development. Now there is a new debate about where children who are deaf should be educated. In the following sections, we will examine three aspects of educational programming for these children: language instruction, educational placement, and technological innovations.

Language Instruction. Since the early 19th century, when Thomas Gallaudet brought sign language from France to the United States, there has been an ongoing debate about the best way to enhance the language skills of individuals with deafness and hearing impairments. Today, three approaches coexist in the education of children who are deaf— oral, manual, and total communication. The goal of oral approaches is to help students become integrated into hearing society through development of skills in understanding and using spoken language. **Oral approach** programs use methods such as speech reading (lipreading), auditory training, and speech and language training to reach these goals, with mixed results. Although some programs claim to have high rates of success, many graduates have a difficult time using spoken language. Methods such as speech reading take a long time to learn and are limited in their usefulness.

 Watch this video to experience some of the challenges in using lipreading. What are some of the issues in using lipreading that are identified in the video?
https://www.youtube.com/watch?v=n1jLkYyODsc

The goal of **manual language programs** is to enable children who are deaf to develop a first language as quickly as possible. Manual programs use either American Sign Language or a manual language based on English syntax such as Seeing Essential English (SEE I) or Signing Exact English (SEE II) (see Table 11.1). The idea with SEE I and SEE II is

Table 11.1

Types of Sign Language

Sign System	Description	Advantages/ Disadvantages
Seeing Essential English (SEE I)	Uses ASL signs and invented signs with English syntactic structure	Uses some ASL signs English syntax should make transition to English easier
Signing Exact English (SEE II)	Modification of SEE I Closer to ASL Uses English syntax	Easier for ASL users
Signed English	Uses ASL signs in English word order	Even closer to ASL Still based in English syntax
American Sign Language (ASL)	Unique syntax Uses both abstract and iconic signs	"Natural" language of persons who are deaf Syntax differs from English

that the children with hearing impairments will make more academic progress if they are exposed to a manual language system that is based on the same syntactic structure as English. Many advocates argue, however, that American Sign Language should be the mode of instruction, since it is the natural language of the deaf; English, if introduced at all, should be used as a second language.

 To learn more about American Sign Language (ASL), watch this video. How did the hearing parents in the video describe their experience with ASL?
https://www.youtube.com/watch?v=FV69iJuXwP4

Many education programs for persons who are deaf follow a **total communication** approach. Quigley and Paul (1990) defined *total communication* as "the philosophy or system which permits any and all methods of communication to be used with deaf children" (p. 25). In actuality, total communication programs usually combine spoken-language instruction with manual communication. Two examples of total communication methods are cued speech and the Rochester method. With *cued speech*, hand signals are used near the face to differentiate speech sounds that look alike in speech reading (for more information about cued speech, visit the website for the National Cued Speech Association).

The *Rochester method* combines finger spelling with speech. Total communication approaches can use any combination of spoken and signed language to enhance students' learning. The logic behind total communication seems appealing, but some have argued that total communication approaches can slow down the natural language development children who are deaf.

This video provides more information about cued speech. How does cued speech differ from American Sign Language?
https://www.youtube.com/watch?v=B9emmTMswkE

An emerging approach to education of the deaf is the *bilingual-bicultural (bi-bi)* method. Modeled after English as a Second Language (ESL) programs, bi-bi programs use American Sign Language (ASL) as the basis of instruction in order to assure that the child who is deaf has a firm language foundation. These programs also include experiences in deaf culture that emphasize the child's place in a wider community of people who are deaf. English language skills are taught after children become competent in ASL. Bilingual-bicultural programs are growing in popularity, with over 40 percent of residential and day-school programs reporting the use of such a program (LaSasso & Lollis, 2003).

The emergence of cochlear implants for many children with significant hearing impairments may make moot the long-standing debate about the best approach to teach language to children with hearing impairments. Because these children have enhanced hearing skills, it would seem to make sense to use methods that focus on the development of spoken-language skills. However, Moores (2009) cautions that abandoning manual approaches may limit the early language development of these children. The debate about the best approach to teaching children who are deaf is likely to go on for some time. At this point, there is no one approach that addresses all the problems faced by persons with hearing loss (see Table 11.2).

Educational Placement Issues.　*Where* should children with hearing impairments be educated? In separate schools, as has been the case for most children with hearing impairments for most of the history of education? In separate programs within public schools?

Table 11.2

Intervention Approaches for Persons Who Are Deaf

Program Type	Goals	Methods	Outcomes
Oral/aural	Development of spoken language Integration into hearing society	Amplification Speech reading Instruction in English Speech therapy	Generally poor intelligibility Reading may be better
Manual communication	Development of a first language Integration into deaf culture	ASL or other sign language system	Good manual language development Generally poor academic outcomes
Total communication	Develop social, language, and academic skills	Uses both sign and spoken-language development	Generally fair academic outcomes Some spoken-language development
Bilingual/bicultural	Develop English as a second language	Builds English language skills on ASL base Emphasizes deaf culture	May improve academic performance

Or should children with hearing impairments be included in regular education classes? Although the debate about inclusion for all children with disabilities has become increasingly strident, the issue is of more than theoretical importance when it comes to the population with hearing impairments. Indeed, the question of inclusion goes to the heart of the debate about the culture and education of persons who are deaf—a topic that has been an underlying theme for many years in the community of persons who are deaf.

The question is at once simple and quite complex. Should the goal of education for students with hearing impairments be to integrate them into hearing society to the maximum extent possible, or should the goal be to prepare children who are deaf to be contributing members of their own culture? Advocates of such a culture argue that most persons who are deaf can never be fully integrated and successful in a hearing society. Therefore, children who are deaf will do best when taught by teachers like themselves and using sign language in programs that respect the beauty of their particular culture.

On the other hand, advocates for inclusion argue that all children, including those with hearing impairments, have the right to be included in regular education programs. Improved amplification technologies, increased use of computers, and other educational innovations increase the likelihood of success for students who are deaf. By including these children in regular education classes, the argument goes, the stigma of disability will be reduced, educational expectations will increase, and children with hearing impairments will have increased opportunities for socialization (see Box 11.1). Citing recommendations from the Individuals with Disabilities Education Act, Fiedler (2001) suggests that the following questions be asked when considering the appropriate educational placement for students with hearing impairments:

1. Communication needs
   - What does the student need in order to communicate?
   - Does this student use residual hearing efficiently?
   - Does this student need training in a specific communication mode?
2. Language and communication mode
   - What is the student's proficiency in spoken English (other spoken language)?
   - What is the student's proficiency in written English (other written language)?
   - What is the student's proficiency in manual communication?

> ## Box 11.1 Desiree: Student who is deaf in the Regular Education Classroom
>
> Desiree has a 95 percent hearing loss in each ear and has been diagnosed as "profoundly deaf." Desiree has learned American Sign Language and has also had speech therapy that included lipreading.
>
> For first and second grade, Desiree attended a special program for children with hearing impairments in her county. Students from throughout the county went to a community school where they were included in regular education classrooms most of the day but received intensive speech and language instruction from a speech-language specialist.
>
> Now that she is in the third grade, Desiree is fully included in a regular class in her home school. She still receives daily speech and language instruction. However, her progress has been very slow. Her speech is largely unintelligible. The speech-language specialist has recommended the use of an augmentative communication system, but Desiree's parents have been reluctant to agree so far.
>
> Desiree is supported by a full-time instructional aide who knows some American Sign Language. Mr. Morales, Desiree's third-grade teacher, makes a special effort to face Desiree when he talks to the class. He also tries to include Desiree in the classroom by using more charts and pictures than he has been accustomed to using. He has found Desiree to be eager to learn, but he is frustrated by his difficulty communicating with her.

3. Academic level
   - What academic skills does this student have?
   - Does this student have the academic skills to compete with hearing peers?
4. Full range of needs
   - What other needs does this student have that will affect academics, socialization, and emotional development?
   - What are the social and emotional implications of an educational placement for this student?
   - What are the specific needs of this student based on age?
5. Opportunities for direct instruction in the child's language and communication mode
   - Can the student communicate effectively with the teacher?
   - Can the student communicate effectively with other staff in the school?

While the political and cultural debate over where and how to educate children who are deaf continues, there is clearly a trend to educate these children in more inclusive settings. Data from the 2011–2012 school year show that most students who were deaf or hearing impaired (87 percent) were educated in regular education settings and that more than half of all hearing-impaired students spent the majority of their time in school integrated with hearing students. This is a monumental change in the education of children who are deaf that has profound implications both for the deaf community and for regular and special educators. "Regular" educators can expect to encounter more children with significant hearing loss in their classrooms. Special educators are likely to be asked to support these children and their teachers in the classroom.

Specialized Instructional Techniques. As we have seen, the development of literacy skills, especially related to phonological awareness, is often a significant challenge for children with hearing impairments. The good news is that systematic instruction in phonological skills can lead to both enhanced acquisition of these skills and to better literacy outcomes (Sterne & Goswami, 2000; Wang et al., 2008).

One technique that has shown particular promise for hearing-impaired students is visual phonics. Visual Phonics (see the International Communication Learning Institute website) is a multisensory system of 46 hand cues and written symbols to represent aspects of the phonemes of a language and the grapheme–phoneme relationships. Students are taught a hand cue that is associated in some way with the production of the particular sound. The written symbol is a simplified picture of the hand cue. For example, here is the Visual Phonics representation of the word "cat":

c   a   t
ɔ   –   ⅄

Although research on Visual Phonics is limited, it does appear that this can be a useful technique to enhance the literacy skills of children with hearing impairments (Wang et al., 2008). For example, a study of 20 kindergarten and first-grade children with hearing impairments who used Visual Phonics in combination with a phonics-based reading program found that the children made significant improvements in reading skills (Trezek et al., 2010). Although more research is needed to establish the effectiveness of Visual Phonics, it appears to be a promising technique to enhance the reading of children with hearing impairments.

 To learn more about how to implement Visual Phonics with children with hearing impairments, watch this video of a teacher using Visual Phonics. How does she teach the sounds to children with hearing impairments?
https://www.youtube.com/watch?v=BFO6cWUMkl4

Technological Aids

Advances in technology hold promise for individuals with hearing impairments. In the past 20 years, there have been remarkable advances in hearing aid technology. New developments in digital technology may mean that researchers are on the threshold of even greater advances. It is important for teachers and other education professionals to understand how to make the best use of these technological advances.

Amplification Devices.   Many types of amplification devices (hearing aids) are in use today. No matter what their shape or where they are worn, all amplification devices work in essentially the same way. A microphone picks up sound and converts it to electrical energy. An amplifier boosts the electrical signal, which is transferred to a receiver that converts the electrical signal back into sound waves. A battery supplies the electrical energy needed to power the components.

Behind-the-ear hearing aids are the most common type for children. It is essential that the hearing aid, which is shaped to fit behind the ear, be fitted properly to avoid feedback of sound. Because of this, the aid must be resized as the child grows. *In-the-ear* and *in-the-canal* hearing aids are small and inconspicuous, but they are powerful devices that can provide good sound amplification. However, they may not always be a good choice for young children because they have to be repaired and resized frequently. **FM radio hearing aids** are group amplification devices that permit a teacher's voice to be amplified for a group of students with hearing impairments. With this system, the teacher wears a microphone that transmits on an FM radio frequency being received in an earphone worn by the child. The FM system allows the teacher to move freely around the room and reduces background interference.

All hearing aids work by amplifying the sound entering the ear. Until recently, all sounds—speech and nonspeech—were amplified to the same extent. But today, some hearing aids (such as analog programmable aids and digital signal–processing devices) can be matched precisely to the individual's hearing loss. However, these devices can be expensive and may not be available to all children. Although hearing aids are not a perfect solution for every child, they can be useful in helping children in social interactions as well as in the development of language (Marschark et al., 2002).

A problem specific to children is the need to refit the hearing aid as a child grows. In addition, when batteries grow weak and the devices need to be repaired, children may go for days or weeks hearing a weak or nonexistent signal. Some individuals, especially those with more serious hearing impairments, may have hearing that is little improved by amplification. Teachers who work with children who wear amplification devices should check to see that the device is being worn properly and that it is still operational.

Cochlear Implants.   Earlier in this chapter, we discussed the impact of cochlear implants on language development. Cochlear implants differ from hearing aids in that they are surgically implanted in the skull to provide a direct connection between incoming sound and the nerves that carry auditory input to the brain. The use of cochlear implants has increased rapidly. By the year 2002, more than 70,000 adults and children were using cochlear implants (Marschark & Spencer, 2003). As evidence grows regarding the positive effect of these implants on language development, children as young as 10 months old are receiving the implants. However, cochlear implants are not a magic solution. In most cases, even after the implant, children need to receive extensive speech and language training. Still, evidence is growing that hearing-impaired children who are implanted early in life can develop more advanced language and literacy skills when compared to hearing-impaired children who do not receive cochlear implants.

Although cochlear implants hold great promise in decreasing the effects of many types of deafness, there has been significant controversy within the deaf community about their use. Some advocates claim that the use of an invasive surgical procedure sends a message that deafness is "bad" and needs to be eradicated—with the implication that deaf people are bad. Others express concern that children who receive the operation may be caught between the deaf world and the hearing world—not fully comfortable in either one. Ultimately, parents will need to decide whether cochlear implants are the right choice for their child and their family. Teachers and other education professionals can help by providing research-based information to the family as well as support for whatever decision is made.

Check Your Understanding 11.3
Click here to gauge your understanding of the concepts in this section.

Visual Impairment and Language

You were probably not surprised to learn that hearing impairments can have a significant impact on language learning. After all, language is usually relayed by speech and therefore relies on hearing. But what about visual impairments? What effect, if any, do impairments of vision have on language development? Is it possible that language abilities are actually *enhanced* in those who have visual impairments? There is a widespread belief that individuals with visual impairments develop heightened sensory abilities that enable them to compensate for their vision disability (Erin, 1990). Conversely, is it possible that visual impairments *interfere* with language development—causing delays and even developmental differences?

Defining Visual Impairment

Before examining the evidence on the language abilities of individuals with visual impairments, we first need to define this population. This is not such an easy task. Dekker and Koole (1992) note that the population with visual impairments is often divided into low vision and blind, but there is a good deal of disagreement as to just how to measure vision. The researchers go on to report that there are as many as 65 definitions of **blindness** in the professional literature. Disagreement among professionals about the best way to define visual impairments is likely to continue, but the Individuals with Disabilities Education Act (IDEA, 2004) defines *visual impairment* as follows: "Visual impairment including blindness means an impairment in vision that, even with correction, adversely affects a child's educational performance. The term includes both partial sight and blindness." For educational purposes, however, a child who learns primarily through tactile or auditory input is considered blind. For legal purposes, a person considered to be blind must have visual acuity of 20/200 or less in the better eye, after correction. A child is generally considered to be **low vision** if the child can benefit from the use of optical aids and environmental and instructional modifications (e.g., preferential seating or enlarged print) in order to learn.

 To get some understanding of what it is like to have a visual impairment, watch this video demonstration. What are some of the challenges portrayed in this video? https://www.youtube.com/watch?v=v9CawJSUy2c

Early Development

Studies of the early development of children who are blind have generally found that the timing and sequence of their language development is very much like that of sighted children, but there are some qualitative developmental differences. For example, Bigelow (1987) studied the emergence of the first 50 words in children who were congenitally blind (ages 9 to 21 months). She found that the timing and growth of these first words was quite similar to that of sighted children. In addition, Bigelow found that children who are blind tend to talk about the same kinds of things as sighted children. They use nouns and verbs that reflect their personal experiences. However, the specific referents named by children who were blind often differed from those reported in studies of sighted children. Not surprisingly, children who were blind tended to use words that described objects that could be heard (*piano, drum, bird*) or actually experienced (*dirt, powder*).

Other studies have discovered additional differences in the early language acquisition of children who are deaf or hearing impaired. For example, young children who are blind have been found to be slightly delayed in learning sounds that are visually distinctive (e.g., sounds that can be "seen" on the lips) (Perez-Pereira & Conti-Ramsden, 1998). Andersen, Dunlea, and Kekelis (1984) found that the children with visual impairments they studied rarely used overextensions or idiosyncratic forms of language. As children learn new words, it is not uncommon for them to extend these words incorrectly to other similar items (*overextension*) or to make up words (*idiosyncratic*). Yet Andersen and colleagues (1984) did not find this same phenomenon in the children they observed. They suggested that children who are blind were learning words as a whole—via imitation—not experimenting with words, as do sighted children. The result, they claim, is that children who are blind "have less understanding of words as symbolic vehicles and are slower to form hypotheses about word meaning than sighted children" (p. 661).

The early experiences of children who are blind may influence the subtle inconsistencies in their language development. For example, although the motor development of children who are blind in the first few months of life is similar to that of sighted infants, later motor development of children who are blind tends to be delayed. Also, children who are blind are often slower to crawl and walk. There may be many reasons for these delays, including lack of visual stimulation and parental overprotectiveness, but whatever the reasons, less movement means less opportunity to explore and experience the world. Limited experience may, in turn, lead to delays in the development of some cognitive concepts.

Bigelow (1990) examined the development of cognition and language in three children with vision loss. Mothers kept a record of the first 50 words spoken by their children, and the children were tested on 10 tasks that measure aspects of the development of object permanence. Bigelow found that the beginning of word usage and the rate of word acquisition by the three children were quite similar to those of sighted children. However, there were some differences in the development of object permanence. One child, who was not totally blind, showed no differences from the development of sighted children, but two other children, both of whom were totally blind, were delayed in their object permanence development. Bigelow suggested that children who are blind may have more difficulty *decentering*—that is, taking the perspective of another person. Consequently, it takes them longer to develop *object permanence*—the understanding that things that are not present are not gone forever. Understanding delays in object-permanence development may help us understand why at least some children who are blind talk primarily about present objects and events rather than those in the past and future.

In addition to some motor and cognitive differences, some researchers have reported that interaction between children who are blind and their parents differs from that observed between parents and their sighted children (Kekelis & Andersen, 1984; Urwin, 1984). This should come as no surprise. After all, many of the early communicative exchanges between infants and their caregivers are visual—baby looks at mom, mom smiles, baby gurgles. The baby who is blind lacks an important means of initiating interaction, while the mother is deprived of the subtle cues provided by her baby's eye contact. Infants who are blind do attempt to communicate, but their cues are often hard to discern and parents must be on the lookout for subtle hints that the baby wants to communicate. It is interesting to note that research has found that children who are blind whose parents were more responsive to them had better pragmatic language skills (Dote-Kwan & Hughes, 1994).

In their study, Kekelis and Andersen (1984) reported specific differences in the way that parents talk to their young children who are blind. For example, they found that parents of children who were blind used more commands and more requests for action, whereas parents of sighted children used more requests for information. Also, parents of children who were blind tended to label the objects with which their children interacted (*That's your belly*), whereas parents of sighted children provided richer, more detailed information about the objects. These differences, although subtle, may help account for the differences in early language development often found in children who are blind.

Other studies of early language development and parent–child interaction among children who are blind and their parents have found few, if any, differences between them and sighted children (Perez-Pereira & Conti-Ranisden, 2001). These researchers reported that the children who are blind that they studied initiated conversations as frequently or more frequently than sighted children and did not have more breakdowns in their communicative interactions. Parents of the children who were blind interacted in ways that supported the communicative interaction of their children, although they did initiate conversations more frequently than did parents of sighted children.

There appear to be some subtle differences in the early language development of children who are blind. Although the timing and sequence of their development are similar to that of sighted children, there are some qualitative differences. For example, children with significant visual impairments are more likely to talk about things they have *heard and touched,* they tend to learn words as a whole, and they appear to have delays in the development of object permanence—this is especially true for children with more serious visual impairments. These differences in language development may be the result of more limited opportunities to experience the world and/or a result of deficient parent–child interaction. However, we need to be cautious about these conclusions, since they are based on small samples of children and a limited number of studies.

Watch as these parents describe the early development of their child with visual impairments. What were some of the symptoms that indicated to them that their child had a visual impairment?
https://www.youtube.com/watch?v=6rbHOAtBNew

Language Characteristics

Like other children with disabilities, children with visual impairments are a heterogeneous group. Many factors other than their disability affect their learning, including the cause of their visual impairment, home environment, educational history, and opportunities for learning. However, in general, children with visual impairments have been found to follow a typical pattern of language development with relatively minor delays (Brambring, 2007).

Phonology.   Although research on the acquisition of phonology children who are blind is limited, the evidence suggests that perception of sound is not significantly different from that of sighted children. Although there may be delays in the acquisition of some sounds, the ability to perceive speech may actually be more advanced. Similarly, the rate and pattern of sound production have generally been found to be similar to those of sighted children.

Syntax.   Generally, researchers have found few differences between blind and sighted persons in their development of syntax. Utterance length, a measure of syntactic development, has been found to be the same (Landau & Gleitman, 1985) or slightly shorter in children who are blind when compared to sighted children (Erin, 1990). However, children who are blind use fewer different sentence types and tend to use a few types repeatedly (Erin, 1990). In addition, several studies have found that children who are blind have more difficulty understanding and using spatial prepositions such as "in," "on," and "under" (Andersen et al., 1984; Brambring, 2007).

Semantics.   Earlier we reviewed research that found that the early semantic development of children who are blind differs in subtle ways from that of sighted children. Children who are blind talk about different things. They talk more about items that are immediately present in their environment and less about the past and the future. Erin (1990) reported that the children with visual loss in her study used imaginative play less frequently. One specific problem that has been frequently reported regards pronoun usage (Brambring, 2007; Fraiberg, 1977; Perez-Pereira & Conti-Ramsden, 1998). Children who are blind often confuse pronouns such as *I* and *you*. Several explanations have been put forward for this finding, but Brambring (2007) believes that this has to do with the inability of children who are blind to use information from facial expressions to understand differences in the roles of speakers and listeners in conversations.

Another factor that may contribute to difficulties in the acquisition of pronouns and other semantic skills is differences in the acquisition of theory of mind. Theory of mind involves the understanding of intentions, beliefs, and desires in oneself and in others. You may recall that we discussed the concept of theory of mind in Chapter 9 in relation to children with autism. Researchers have also reported delays in the acquisition of theory of mind in children with congenital visual impairments (Brambring & Asbrock, 2010). Delays in the development of theory of mind can have an impact on pronoun development since this requires a basic understanding of self and other. Research has also found a relationship between theory of mind and the acquisition of some types of idioms (e.g., "break the ice") (Caillies & Le Sourn-Bissaoui, 2008).

Pragmatics.   Given the obvious limitations on visual input and feedback, it should not be surprising to find that visually impaired children might have some difficulties with pragmatic language. However, the differences between them and sighted children have generally been found to be limited. For example, children with visual impairments have been reported to use idiosyncratic gestures (Fraiberg, 1977) and changes in body posture (Urwin, 1984) that may cause the listener to misinterpret what they are trying to communicate. Parke, Shallcross, and Anderson (1980) also found some subtle differences in nonverbal communication when they compared the videotaped interactions of 30 children who were blind and a similar number of sighted children. Specifically, they found that many of the children who were blind constantly (and inappropriately), nodded less frequently to signal understanding, and raised their eyebrows inappropriately. Any one of these behaviors might seem trivial in itself, but any taken together could cause some misunderstanding of communicative intent. Differences in vocal quality have been found as well. Children who are blind often speak in a loud, strident voice (perhaps because they are not sure of the distance between them and the speaker) and show less awareness of the need to adapt their speech to the needs of the listener (Erin, 1990; Freeman & Blockberger, 1987).

The effects of visual impairments on language, as we have seen, tend to be subtle but widespread. In particular, there are delays in the development of some semantic concepts (pronouns and words that require vision) and in several aspects of pragmatics. These language differences may have an impact on the academic and social development of children with visual impairment.

Literacy Development

Children with mild to moderate visual impairments face significant challenges in learning to read. As a result, they generally lag behind their sighted peers in the development of reading skills (Fellenius, 1999; Gompel, van Bon, Schreuder, & Adriaansen, 2002). Explanations for the reading difficulties associated with low vision include difficulty fixating on text and extracting information from the peripheral vision field (Bosman, Gompel, Vervloed, & van Bon, 2006). In two studies, Bosman and colleagues (2006) compared elementary-age students to normally sighted peers matched for age or for reading scores. They found that, like their sighted peers, the children with low vision used phonological cues to support their reading. However, the children with visual impairments read much more slowly than their sighted peers. The authors suggested that both factors related to vision differences and other factors, such as a lack of reading practice, may have contributed to the results. These results, as well as those from other studies, suggest that children with low vision can benefit from instruction on phonemic awareness and should be given many opportunities to read both in the classroom and at home.

For children with very significant visual impairments, the use of braille may be the best way to access written text. Braille is a written language system that uses a series of raised dots to represent words (visit the website for the American Foundation for the Blind for an example). Children learning to read braille may start out at a disadvantage, since they would generally not have had any experience reading braille prior to starting school. In their own studies of 7- to 12-year-old children who were blind learning to read braille, Dodd and Conn (2000) found an average delay of 9 months in reading compared to sighted children. However, they attributed most of this difference to the structure of braille itself, rather than to the effects of blindness.

To learn more about the history of braille and how it works, watch this video. How was braille an improvement over previous reading systems for people with vision impairments?
https://www.youtube.com/watch?v=9IQKqPaICKI

Since braille is based on the same alphabetic principle as printed letters, children with visual impairments who read with braille also need to have intact phonological skills. Children with visual impairments who lack adequate phonological awareness skills have been found to lag behind in the development of braille reading skills (Gillon & Young, 2002).

Children with significant visual impairments are at risk for difficulties with reading comprehension. As Steinman, LeJeune, and Kimbrough (2006) note, children who are blind typically lack the early experiences available to sighted children. So, when they read a story about a fire truck, for example, they have no direct experience with this concept. Teachers should be aware of this potential problem and take the time to explain crucial concepts in text.

The limited research on the effects of visual impairments on reading and writing skills suggests that children who are blind may experience some delays, especially in comprehension, but that, with appropriate instruction and accommodations, they can attain high levels of literacy.

Implications for Teaching

Because there is a good deal of variation in the language and communication skills of children with visual impairments, teachers and other education professionals should be careful to observe and assess individual children. Do they have delays in development? Are essential vocabulary words missing? Do they have difficulty conveying their messages and understanding what others say? At times, language differences may be caused by other disabilities the child may have, in addition to impairment of vision. When intervention is necessary, Freeman and Blockberger (1987) suggest that strategies should focus on:

- Helping the child compensate for lack of visual stimulation through use of other sources of information
- Helping parents learn how to interact with their children who is blind
- Altering those behaviors that interfere with successful communication

Our review of the language problems associated with visual impairments suggests that the following areas may be appropriate targets for intervention:

- Vocabulary development
- Use of nonverbal communication
- Voice modulation
- Varying language for different communication situations
- Pronoun usage

Box 11.2 gives an example of classroom-based activities to enhance the learning of a child with low vision.

If teachers and parents create a stimulating environment where there is plenty of opportunity for learning about the world and for communicative interaction, it is likely that most children with visual impairment will develop good language skills. They may

---

Box 11.2   Instructional Modifications for a Student with Low Vision

- Description of the Student

Shylee is a 2½-year-old little girl with low vision. At this time, it is not known exactly how much Shylee sees, but we do know that she has some vision. Shylee is somewhat verbal, although at this time, her language mainly consists of repeating what others say. Additionally, Shylee has auditory and tactile sensory issues. She gets very upset when she hears a loud sound or is made to touch unfamiliar textures.

- Description of the Modifications

This modification is for a lesson reviewing the letters of the alphabet. For the first part of the lesson, a group of five or six children are shown a flashcard of a random letter along with a picture of an item starting with that letter. The children are then asked which letter is shown or what the picture is, depending on their current cognitive level. To modify this part of the lesson for Shylee, letters are printed from the computer using an enlarged font. The letters are printed in black ink on white paper for maximum contrast, which will have the best chance to be seen by Shylee. Pictures are also enlarged and printed out. During the lesson, the teacher holds one set of letter/picture flashcards while the teacher assistant holds the other enlarged letters and pictures. Shylee is seated close to the teacher assistant. After this part of the lesson, the children work in small groups of two or three to put capital letter puzzle pieces with knobs into their correct location on a puzzle board. This part of the lesson is modified for Shylee by coloring the cut-outs on the puzzle board with a black marker to increase the contrast with the rest of the board. Additionally, when Shylee is placing pieces into the puzzle, all but the letter she is trying to place will be covered, so that she can distinguish where the piece should go.

continue to have specific problems with words that rely on visual input (e.g., colors) and with nonverbal communication, but these difficulties should be minimized by effective teaching.

Apply Your Knowledge 11.2: Case Study: Marisol

Review the case study of Marisol presented at the beginning of the chapter—the child with a severe visual impairment who is included in a regular education classroom—and respond to the questions.

Check Your Understanding 11.4

Click here to gauge your understanding of the concepts in this section.

Summary

In this chapter, we have examined the impact of sensory disabilities on language and communication development, including the development of literacy skills. Hearing impairments can have significant effects on spoken-language development. Even so, the ability to develop a language (including sign language) remains intact. Children with hearing impairments frequently have a difficult time acquiring written language skills. Cochlear implants are having a significant impact on our understanding and teaching of children with hearing impairments and may have positive effects on the development of both language and literacy skills. Although language impairments do not generally come to mind when we think about children with vision disabilities, difficulties with language are also frequently present.

Teachers and other education professionals need to understand the impact of sensory disabilities on language, especially because so many children with these disabilities are being integrated into regular education settings. Effective management of instruction for these children will be critical for their academic and social success.

Language and Students with Neuromotor Disabilities and Traumatic Brain Injury

Children with neuromotor disabilities and brain injury have disabilities that are the result of developmental neurological disorders or traumatic brain injury. In most cases, their physical disability is the primary difficulty they face. However, many individuals with neuromotor disorders and traumatic brain injury have speech and/or language difficulties as well. This chapter examines the impact of neuromotor impairments and traumatic brain injury on language and cognitive development and on academic and social performance. The chapter also includes instructional methods that have been used effectively with children with neuromotor impairments and traumatic brain injury.

Learning Outcomes

After completing this chapter, you should be able to:

1. Describe the impact of neuromotor disorders on language development and educational performance and remediation methods that can be used.

2. Explain the impact that traumatic brain injury can have on language and academic performance and what can be done to support students with brain injury.

Charisse: A Case Study

Charisse is a young woman living with cerebral palsy who has a compelling life story. She had anoxia at birth that caused brain damage, leading to cerebral palsy. She was delayed in most aspects of motor development but was able to start walking at the age of 6 with the aid of a walker and leg braces. Later, she was able to walk on her own. She has attended general education classes throughout school. At first, most of her classmates were accepting of her disabilities, but as she grew older, she encountered bullying from other students. However, she persisted and eventually graduated from high school and is planning to go to college with the goal of becoming a special education teacher.

 As you watch this video of Charisse, a person with cerebral palsy, note both her difficulties with speech and her ability to tell her compelling story clearly as she describes her development. How did she handle bullying in school?
https://www.youtube.com/watch?v=0nnuHj5M5FE

Scott: A Case Study

Scott, a seventh-grader who is 12 years and 9 months old, is a returning student to the district. He suffered a concussion during a car accident 2.5 years ago, which affected his speech and fine motor skills. Scott is receiving special education services under the category of "Other Health Impaired." He functions in a low to average range of intellectual ability, is frequently off topic, and needs refocusing. Scott receives 30 minutes of small-group speech therapy once per 6-day cycle. He is currently receiving educational instruction in a resource room setting for mathematics, science, and social studies. He receives language arts and social skills instruction in a multiple-disabilities self-contained classroom. Scott engages in physical education, health, and related arts instruction with the general education population.

Scott has low reading comprehension scores, which are affecting his progress in content and core curriculum. He comprehends better when reading orally than silently. He struggles with segmenting words and lacks the phonological skills to decipher new words. Moreover, he struggles with recall of information and understanding the main idea of text. Scott's language and communication difficulties affect his interactions with classmates. He has difficulty understanding personal space and using appropriate body language and volume and tone of voice. His strengths are that he is an active and reliable worker, has a friendly smile, and is good at math computations. His weaknesses include difficulties in organizing his thoughts, making eye contact, turn-taking, written communication, and pragmatic and social skills.

Children with motor impairments caused by brain dysfunction face a number of serious challenges. Their primary difficulties are in the areas of motor development and movement, but they may have a number of other disabilities, including speech and/or language difficulties, social and emotional problems, and impairments in the development of literacy skills. Until recently, these problems usually resulted in social isolation and significantly reduced opportunities for life experiences. However, with new technologies and new attitudes toward individuals with physical challenges, the emphasis today is on including these persons in society to the maximum extent possible. An increasing number of children with neuromotor impairments are likely to be found in both regular and special education classes. With higher expectations and greater inclusion comes the need for enhanced language and communication skills.

Neuromotor Disorders

Cerebral Palsy

Cerebral palsy is the name given to a variety of disorders that cause neuromotor disabilities early in life. These disorders cause difficulties with movement and posture, as well as a variety of other problems, including cognitive delays and speech and language disorders. This damage often takes place during the birth process, but it may also be caused by trauma during prenatal development or by brain injury during early childhood. Cerebral palsy is a nonprogressive disorder; that is, the damage to the brain does not get worse over time. However, the associated motor problems may worsen if they are left untreated.

Until recently, there has been no widely accepted medical definition of cerebral palsy. However, a multidisciplinary group has proposed the following definition:

> Cerebral palsy (CP) describes a group of disorders of the development of movement and posture, causing activity limitation, that are attributed to non-progressive disturbances that occurred in the developing fetal or infant brain. The motor disorders of cerebral palsy are often accompanied by disturbances of sensation, cognition, communication, perception, and/or behaviour, and/or by a seizure disorder. (Bax, Goldstein, Rosenbaum, & Paneth, 2005)

Approximately 10,000 babies are born with cerebral palsy in the United States each year, or about 3.6 per 1,000 children (Yeargin-Allsopp et al., 2008). The incidence of cerebral palsy has remained stable in the United States and western Europe for the past 30 years. Today, there are approximately 800,000 persons with cerebral palsy living in the United States (National Institute of Neurological Disorders and Stroke [NINDS], 2011).

The Individuals with Disabilities Education Act (IDEA) includes children with cerebral palsy in a larger category of disabilities called "orthopedic impairments." These disorders are defined as follows:

Orthopedic Impairment: … means a severe orthopedic impairment that adversely affects a child's educational performance. The term includes impairments caused by a congenital anomaly (e.g., clubfoot, absence of some member, etc.), impairments caused by disease (e.g., poliomyelitis, bone tuberculosis, etc.), and impairments from other causes (IDEA, 2004) (e.g., cerebral palsy, amputations, and fractures or burns that cause contractures).

Types of Cerebral Palsy.   Cerebral palsy can be divided into several subtypes according to four criteria: area of brain that is damaged, the extent of the disorder, type of movement disorder, and part of the body affected (Best & Bigge, 2010). Five types of movement disorders are commonly recognized. **Hypertonia** (*spasticity*) is characterized by significant limitations in the individual's range of motion. Muscle tone is increased, and the muscles contract. Movement may be slow and jerky. Significant problems with posture can develop in this type of cerebral palsy. In **athetoid** (*extrapyramidal*) **cerebral palsy**, the limbs have involuntary movements. Individuals with athetoid cerebral palsy seem to have little control over their movements. They may lack head control, flail out their arms or legs when they try to move, or have writhing (choreoathetoid) movements. Individuals with **ataxic cerebral palsy** have difficulty balancing. When reaching for an object, they may overshoot their target. **Rigidity** is an extreme form of spasticity in which there is a simultaneous contraction of all muscle groups. Movement is very limited. Ataxia and rigidity are relatively rare disorders. Often several types of movement disorders may be identified in a single individual. This is known as **mixed cerebral palsy** (see Table 12.1).

 In this video, a doctor explains the causes, symptoms, and treatment of cerebral palsy. What are some of the causes she identifies?
https://www.youtube.com/watch?v=p5VNdy7_nlM

Disabilities other than serious motor impairments may also be associated with cerebral palsy. Approximately 40 percent of individuals with cerebral palsy have intellectual disabilities, and 80 percent have speech disorders (Odding, Roebrouck, & Stam, 2006). However,

Table 12.1

Subtypes of Cerebral Palsy

Subtype	Characteristic
Hypertonia (spasticity)	Significant limitations to range of motion Muscles contracted Movements slow and jerky
Athetoid (extrapyramidal)	Involuntary movement of limbs Lack head control Flail arms and legs Writhing (choreoathetoid) movement
Ataxic	Difficulty with balance Overshoot when reaching for object
Rigidity	Simultaneous contraction of all muscle groups—extreme form of spasticity
Mixed	Combination of two or more types

because individuals with cerebral palsy can be very difficult to test, it is possible that intellectual disabilities are overestimated in this population. Between 20 and 40 percent of children with cerebral palsy have epilepsy. Other related disorders that may occur in some children with cerebral palsy include delayed growth and development, impaired vision, and hearing impairments.

Speech and Language Impairments.   Children with cerebral palsy are at significant risk for speech and language difficulties. Because speech production involves the precise control and coordination of a variety of muscle groups, it is not surprising that speech impairments are common among children with cerebral palsy. A large-scale study found that 58 percent of children with cerebral palsy had communication difficulties (Bax, Tydeman, & Flodmark, 2006). Studies of school-age children with cerebral palsy have reported that approximately 40 percent have difficulty being understood (Kennes et al., 2002). The speech difficulties of children with cerebral palsy are extremely heterogeneous and depend, to a great extent, on the specific nature of the physical disability. Individuals with cerebral palsy may have speech production difficulties in one or several areas, including respiration (e.g., rapid, shallow breathing), phonation (inadequate airflow), resonation (hypernasality), and articulation (Owens, Metz, & Farinella, 2011). Articulation is often affected because of difficulty controlling the tongue, lips, or mouth.

In addition to difficulties with speech production, differences in early development may have an impact on language. Studies of the interactions between children with cerebral palsy and their parents has shown a pattern of conversational dominance by parents and child passivity. Typically, parents have been reported to initiate most conversational exchanges, introduce topics, ask many closed questions, and issue many commands. Children tend to reply with limited information and fail to take a similar number of turns, to initiate an equal number of exchanges, or to use a full range of pragmatic functions (e.g., Hanzlik, 1990; Pennington & McConachie, 2001). Several factors may account for these findings, including the physical dependence of children with cerebral palsy, the cognitive limitations of some children, and the intelligibility of the child. Children with cerebral palsy who have better speech intelligibility have been found to initiate more conversations and to use their communication for a wider range of functions compared with nonspeaking children (Pennington & McConachie, 2001).

What is the impact of speech disorders and early experiences on speech comprehension and language development in persons with cerebral palsy? This question was posed by Bishop, Brown, and Robson (1990). In a series of studies, they examined the ability of 48 individuals with cerebral palsy to discriminate sounds and understand language. Half of their sample exhibited serious speech production difficulties. The other half had no serious speech problems. The researchers found that the group with speech impairments had considerable difficulty with a phoneme discrimination task that used nonwords but did much better when real words were used. The group with speech impairments did poorly on a test of receptive vocabulary. However, there was no difference between the two groups on their syntactic development. After further testing, the authors concluded that individuals with cerebral palsy and speech impairments have more difficulty retaining meaningless strings of sounds in memory. The authors suggest that this problem may be the result of lack of opportunity to use spoken speech sounds. This may not seem like a significant problem, but Bishop and colleagues point out that this is the process children use when they are learning new words. At first, these strings of sounds are meaningless. Only later do they become meaningful words. Difficulty retaining sounds in memory may slow down vocabulary acquisition.

On the other hand, the results of the research reported by Bishop and colleagues (1990) also indicate that despite limited opportunities to use language, individuals with cerebral palsy who also have significant speech impairments can develop structural aspects of language (e.g., syntax) much like other persons. This suggests that language may be intact for these individuals. Yet many, if not most, children with cerebral palsy appear to lag behind their nondisabled peers in language development. There are several reasons why this may occur. Most significantly, cerebral palsy is often associated with other disabilities. It is not unusual to find children with cerebral palsy who also have hearing or vision problems or who have intellectual impairments. We know that all of these conditions can adversely affect language.

Other studies of phonological development in children with cerebral palsy have found conflicting results. For example, when Card and Dodd (2006) compared the phonological awareness of children with cerebral palsy who could speak to a similar group of nonspeaking children and a younger, typically developing group, they found the phonological awareness of both groups of children with cerebral palsy to be largely intact. Other studies have found significant difficulties in acquiring phonological skills (e.g., Peeters, Verhoeven, van Balkom, & de Moor, 2008). As with the research on early communicative development, speech intelligibility and measured intelligence, as well as differences in the phonological awareness tasks, may account for some of the differences in these findings. It appears that children with cerebral palsy who can speak and have higher measured intelligence have intact phonological skills.

Redmond and Johnston (2001) examined the morphological skills of 11- to 15-year-old children with severe speech and physical impairments, three of whom had cerebral palsy. The participants in their study were asked to judge whether test sentences were correct. Although the children with speech impairments had some difficulty identifying past-tense errors, overall there was little difference between these children and typically developing peers. These findings support the view that receptive language is relatively intact in children with cerebral palsy.

In addition to their obvious difficulty in producing spoken language, students with cerebral palsy may sometimes appear to have more significant language difficulties because of the ways in which they are assessed. Many tests of language require children to perform a motor movement. For example, the Peabody Picture Vocabulary Test requires a pointing response to a verbal command. Other tests ask parents or caregivers to rate the observed performance of the child. Of course, these sorts of procedures may tell nothing about language comprehension. Cauley, Golinkoff, Hirsh-Pasek, and Gordon (1989) reported on a procedure they developed to more accurately assess the language skills of children with motor disorders. Children were shown two different pictures on screens simultaneously as a target word was spoken. An observer recorded which screen the child looked at in response to the word by noting the child's eye fixation. The results suggested that children with motor impairments seemed to be able to respond to this sort of testing. This kind of procedure may enable researchers to more accurately assess the language development of children with motor disorders.

Given the variability in physical and cognitive development in individuals with cerebral palsy and the difficulties in testing children with motor disorders, it is not surprising that there is disagreement about the language skills of this population. Although many persons with cerebral palsy experience significant delays in language, for some, language is intact. Both speech intelligibility and measured intelligence appear to be important factors with children with more intelligible speech and higher measured intelligence having fewer language difficulties (Pirila et al., 2007). Unless there is specific brain damage in regions of the brain that process language, there is reason to expect that most children with cerebral palsy will have the capacity to develop language, although some will require augmentative or alternative means of communication to express themselves.

Literacy Development in Individuals with Cerebral Palsy.   Students with cerebral palsy often experience significant difficulty developing literacy skills (Koppenhaver & Yoder, 1992). In fact, their literacy development has been found to lag behind both their language skills and their cognitive development. It has been suggested that factors such as early home literacy experiences, school curriculums that focus more on physical development than literacy, and physical limitations associated with the child's disability may contribute to the literacy difficulties of children with cerebral palsy (Smith, 2001). In addition to these factors, the phonological awareness difficulties of some children with cerebral palsy may also contribute to their knowledge of the sound system for reading and spelling tasks (Sandberg, 2001).

The impact of home literacy experiences on the development of literacy skills in children with cerebral palsy has been the subject of several research studies. In general, these studies have found these environments to be less supportive of literacy development than those of typically developing children. For example, parents have been reported to be less actively involved in storybook reading, and their children had less opportunity to use printed materials (Dahlgren Sandberg, 1998; Light & Kelford Smith, 1993). This is especially true for children with cerebral palsy who have no speech or very limited speech intelligibility. A longitudinal study that followed children with cerebral palsy from kindergarten through first grade found that three home literacy factors were especially important for the development of literacy skills: parent literacy mediation (defined as frequency of rhyming games, reading letters, and involving the child in the parents' own reading activities), child story orientation activities (such as asking questions about the story, retelling, and relating the story to daily life experiences), and child word-orientation activities (naming pictures, reading, and pointing at letters or words) (Peeters, Verhoeven, de Moor, van Balkom, & van Leeuwe, 2009). These results suggest that parents of children with cerebral palsy should be involved in their child's reading and writing activities, such as reading letters and words with their child, and playing rhyming games.

Students with cerebral palsy clearly face significant challenges to their development of literacy skills. Some of these challenges may be the result of lack of opportunity, and some may be the result of differences in language processing that could affect the development of reading and writing skills. Teachers and speech-language specialists can help develop literacy skills in this population by ensuring they have frequent opportunities to participate in literacy activities, including listening to text, and developing phonological awareness skills.

Other Neuromotor Disorders

Other neuromotor disorders, such as spina bifida and muscular dystrophy, can also affect language acquisition and development. **Spina bifida** refers to a group of conditions in which a portion of the spinal cord is not completely enclosed by the vertebrae in the spinal column. In some cases, part of the spinal cord protrudes. In the most serious form of the disorder, **myelomeningocele**, damage to the spinal cord can cause sensory and motor losses. In addition, in about 80 percent of the cases, fluid accumulates in the brain, causing the condition known as **hydrocephalus**. If not treated quickly, hydrocephalus can cause Intellectual disabilities. Surgery can often correct the spinal cord abnormality in spina bifida, but some sensory and motor disabilities can remain (Best, 2010).

> The causes and outcomes of spina bifida are explained in this video. What are some of the consequences of spina bifida?
> https://www.youtube.com/watch?v=6li_v3t9hpU

Impairments in language are characteristic of many children with spina bifida, especially those who also have hydrocephalus. Although children with spina bifida often have strengths involving vocabulary and grammar, difficulties with the use of language in context have frequently been reported. Sometimes called the "cocktail chatter" phenomenon (Tew, 1979), their communicative interactions have been described as "chatty" conversations that remain at a superficial level. In addition, although their speech may be fluent and well-articulated, it may include verbal perseveration, excessive use of stereotyped social utterances, and overfamiliarity (Barnes & Dennis, 1998).

Many children with spina bifida have difficulties with academic skills including math (Barnes et al., 2006) and reading comprehension (Barnes, Faulkner, Wilkinson, & Dennis, 2004). Although children with hydrocephalus (which is associated with a number of neurological disorders, not just spina bifida) typically have good vocabulary and word attack skills, they have difficulty making inferences, understanding literal story content, and producing their own stories (Barnes & Dennis, 1998; Barnes, Faulkner, & Dennis, 2001).

Muscular dystrophy is a progressive disorder that produces weakness in muscles. Over time, the muscles waste away, and children become unable to walk and talk. There are several forms of muscular dystrophy. The most common is the Duchenne type, which affects about one in 3,500 children, mostly males, and begins in early childhood. Children may have problems with balance and in climbing stairs and eventually lose the ability to walk and sit up as muscle weakness spreads and muscles deteriorate. Children with muscular dystrophy usually live only into adolescence or early adulthood (Best, 2010).

 The symptoms associated with muscular dystrophy are illustrated in this video. What are some of the symptoms of muscular dystrophy that are discussed? https://www.youtube.com/watch?v=6wLnR7GJakY

Language and cognitive abilities can also be affected by *Duchenne muscular dystrophy.* On average, the mean IQ in children with Duchenne muscular dystrophy is approximately one standard deviation below the population mean, with verbal IQ scores lower than performance IQ scores (Cyrulnik, Fee, De Vivo, Goldstein, & Hinton, 2007). Language delays are apparent even in young children with Duchenne muscular dystrophy, suggesting that the disorder may affect regions of the brain responsible for both cognitive and language development (Cyrulnik et al., 2007). In an intensive analysis of 15 children with Duchenne muscular dystrophy, Dorman, Hurley, and D'Avignon (1988) found that six of the 15 children had very low measured intelligence and significant problems in reading, writing, and spelling, functioning much like children with severe dyslexia. The other children had performance levels similar to those found in nondisabled children. The implication of this research is that Duchenne muscular dystrophy may manifest itself in different ways. In some cases, language-based abilities are significantly impacted, but in other cases, they remain intact. With time, however, most children with this disorder have increasing difficulty communicating because of the deterioration of muscles involved in speech production.

Children with Duchenne muscular dystrophy have also been found to have lower performance on academic tasks such as math, reading, and writing (Hinton, De Vivo, Fee, Goldstein, & Stern, 2004). Some researchers have found lower phonological processing scores (e.g., Dorman et al., 1988), whereas others have identified verbal memory as the primary cause of reading and writing difficulties in this population (Hinton et al., 2004). Although the cause of academic learning difficulties is still not clear, the research on children with Duchenne muscular dystrophy should alert us to the need to identify language and learning difficulties in this population in order to help them develop their learning potential.

Epilepsy is a brain disorder in which clusters of nerve cells, or neurons, in the brain sometimes signal abnormally. In epilepsy, the normal pattern of neuronal activity becomes disturbed, causing strange sensations, emotions, and behavior, or sometimes convulsions, muscle spasms, and loss of consciousness. This disorder has a number of causes, including illness, brain damage, or abnormal brain development. However, in most cases, no cause can be identified (NINDS, 2011). Seizure disorders are generally divided into two types: generalized and partial. Generalized seizures affect both hemispheres of the brain, whereas partial seizures are focused on one side.

In some cases, epilepsy can cause disturbances in thinking and in language. For example, Caplan and colleagues (2002) examined the social communication skills of children with complex partial seizures (CPS) (a type of seizure in which a person may not lose consciousness but cannot interact with others), children with generalized epilepsy, and non-epileptic children. They found that the children with CPS had significant deficits in social communication. Specifically, these children underused conjunctions to tie together thoughts and used fewer pronouns and definite articles to refer to people or objects in their conversation. Children with generalized epilepsy also had some difficulty with social communication, but it was not as serious.

To learn more about epilepsy, watch this video. According to the video, how is epilepsy defined?

https://www.youtube.com/watch?v=MNQIq004FkE

Although most children with mild epilepsy may not have language difficulties, some children—especially those with CPS—may have difficulty developing and using language for social communication. In addition, children with epilepsy have been found to be at higher risk for learning disabilities, especially writing difficulties (Fastenau, Shen, Dunn, & Austin, 2008). Teachers and other education professionals who work with children with epilepsy need to know about the type of epilepsy affecting these children and be aware of the possible impact on language, cognitive, and social development.

Implications for Intervention

Typically, intervention for individuals with motor disorders has focused on speech therapy. For children with cerebral palsy, speech therapy often focuses on developing the muscles used in eating and swallowing. Most children with neuromotor disorders at some point will need help with breathing, vocal production, and articulation. Although speech therapy is important and should not be ignored as part of an instructional program, it can often be very slow in producing results and frustrating for both the child and the therapist.

Watch as this child with cerebral palsy receives speech therapy. What kind of skills does the therapy focus on?

https://www.youtube.com/watch?v=LIEAnhxasFs

In addition to receiving speech therapy, children with motor impairments should be given numerous opportunities to engage in literacy-based activities and to communicate with a variety of people. Literacy-based activities may include listening to stories, watching movies or videotapes of stories, and using computer word-processing programs that permit the user to write with a minimum of motor movement. It is essential that children with neuromotor disorders be involved in as many communicative interactions as possible. Teachers can facilitate these interactions through appropriate positioning. It is essential that teachers encourage children with neuromotor disabilities to communicate with others and that the teachers themselves engage the children in communicative exchanges whenever possible. Some examples of classroom modifications for a student with spina bifida can be seen in Box 12.1.

For many children with neuromotor disorders, the use of augmentative communication devices will be an important option. When properly designed and used effectively, these devices can open up new worlds of communication to children who were previously unable to communicate. Chapter 15 provides more information about augmentative

Box 12.1   Classroom-Based Modifications for a Student with Spina Bifida

Overview of Student: Isaac

Age: 3   **Sex:** M   **Disability:** Spina Bifida

This student wears leg braces that begin at his hips and cover his legs, wrapping around his feet. He uses a walker for mobility. From his hips down, sensation has not yet been found. He also has two shunts on the back of his head that drain the fluid from his brain. Isaac is significantly younger (by at least 6 months) than his peers. These developmental differentiations create difficulties with Isaac effectively participating in group activities.

Material 1: Morning Meeting: Open-Ended Questions
Adaptations: During morning meeting, a message is read. This message contains new vocabulary and an open-ended question at the end. The students respond to this question using their previous knowledge from prior learning experiences during our unit.

Isaac is developmentally behind the class. These cognitive delays create difficulties in responding to "WH" questions. Isaac will be provided with picture cards. These cards will have pictures that do and do not answer the closing question. Isaac will be able to choose a card to respond to the question.

By providing Isaac with these cards, he is shown possible answers. The cards eliminate the time that it would take him to come up with the vocabulary word, but from a teaching standpoint, I will still be able to determine if his answer is on target. If the picture he holds up is a correct choice, then I know that he understands the question and

is unable to process quickly enough without the picture assistance. The use of these cards will help me to understand his developmental delays and allow me to accurately evaluate his knowledge.

Material 2: Story Time: Preteaching Using Sequencing Pictures
Adaptations: Isaac will be provided with a preteaching opportunity each day prior to the next story time. During this preteaching session, sequential pictures will be used to help reiterate events and meaning from the text.

Due to Isaac's developmental delays, he is unable to connect sequential events. By providing Isaac with a preteaching opportunity, using text pictures to sequence, Isaac will have a stronger understanding of the story before participating in story time the next day.

The pictures will be placed on a clothesline that he will be able to view without distractions. Each picture will be placed as read in the text. The pictures should help eliminate other distractions from the text so that he will be able to follow the basic storyline and attach meaning to the pictures.

Implementing a clothesline sequential story will allow Isaac to have a better understanding of what the story is about so that he will be able to effectively participate in story time activities with his peers. Once Isaac has begun to understand the clothesline process, he will then hang the pictures and retell the story. This will be an evaluation period where the teacher will be able to evaluate his progress in understanding print concepts.

---

communication devices, but most important to this discussion is that users be taught and encouraged to use these devices for communication. Too often the child with an augmentative communication device sits idly in a classroom until called on to respond. Children who use such devices must continually be encouraged to use the device to initiate interaction and to respond appropriately.

As we have noted previously in this chapter, many parents of children with neuromotor disabilities tend to be very controlling of the conversational interaction with their children. They initiate most interactions, set the topic of the conversation, and use many directives (e.g., "Be quiet"). Parents are not doing this intentionally to hurt the development of their children. On the contrary, in most cases, they are trying to connect with their child and protect them from harm. But the unintended consequence is to provide their children with fewer opportunities to develop their own communicative skills.

A number of intervention programs have been developed to help parents learn to adopt a more responsive approach to interaction, including milieu teaching (Yoder & Warren, 2002) and the *It Takes Two to Talk: The Hanen Program for Parents* (Girolametto, Greenberg, & Manolson, 1986). The latter program was implemented with parents of 11 young children with cerebral palsy (age 19 to 36 months). The parents participated in a number of activities that taught them how to interact with their child, including role-playing, discussions, and watching videotapes. Following eight sessions of 2.5 hours, the parents were videotaped interacting with their child. Analysis of the videotapes showed that the parents became more responsive and less directive with their child and that the children initiated more and exerted more control in interactions (Pennington, Thomson, James, Martin, & McNally, 2009). These results suggest that parent training should be a part of the intervention package for enhancing the language and communication of children with neuromotor disorders.

Check Your Understanding 12.1
Click here to gauge your understanding of the concepts in this section.

Traumatic Brain Injury and Language

Traumatic brain injury is a leading cause of death and disability in children and adolescents in the United States. According to the U.S. Centers for Disease Control and Prevention (CDC, 2016), the rates of emergency room visits for children age 0 to 4 for brain injury and concussion increased by more than 50 percent from 2007 to 2010. This group had an injury rate nearly twice as high as that for the next largest group (age 15 to 24). Although most of these injuries are minor and leave no lasting problems, some result in significant impairments in motor, cognitive, and language functioning.

IDEA includes traumatic brain injury as a separate category of disability. It is defined as follows:

> An acquired injury to the brain caused by an external physical force, resulting in total or partial functional disability or psychosocial impairment, or both, that adversely affect a child's educational performance. The term applies to open and closed head injuries resulting in impairments in one or more areas, such as: cognition; language; memory; attention; reasoning; abstract thinking; judgment; problem-solving; sensory, perceptual, and motor abilities; psychosocial behavior; physical functions; information processing; and speech. The term does not apply to brain injuries that are congenital or degenerative, or brain injuries induced by birth trauma. (IDEA, 2004)

As the IDEA definition indicates, there are two types of head injuries. **Open-head injury** (also known as *localized*) is characterized by a visible injury, often a gunshot wound. The brain damage is usually confined to one portion of the brain. **Closed-head injury** is caused by a rapid acceleration and deceleration of the head, during which the brain bounces around inside the skull. Closed-head brain damage is most often caused by automobile accidents but can also be caused by falls and sports injuries.

Learn more about the causes and types of traumatic brain injury by watching this video. What are some of the major causes of traumatic brain injury described in the video?
https://www.youtube.com/watch?v=OiLBPsTRLnQ

Head injuries can cause a variety of problems, depending on the location and severity of the injury and the age of the victim. Symptoms can include:

- *Physical impairments.* Speech, vision, hearing, and other sensory impairments; headaches; problems with coordination; spasticity and/or paralysis

- *Cognitive impairments.* Memory difficulties; slowness in thinking; problems concentrating; problems with perception and attention; problems planning and sequencing

- *Behavior and personality problems.* Fatigue; mood swings; anxiety; depression; difficulty with emotional control (NINDS, 2011; Telzrow, 1987)

In most cases, children with head injuries show improvement over time, but there may be lasting effects that can have an impact on classroom performance.

Outcomes of Traumatic Brain Injury

Traumatic brain injuries can have a significant impact on school performance and on life after school. Researchers have found that children with traumatic brain injury have difficulty in many functional areas, including cognitive performance and reading, social skills, and behavioral skills (Arroyos-Jurado et al., 2000). The result is that, in many cases, children with traumatic brain injury end up being referred to special education.

Researchers have been interested in discovering the factors that can predict the severity of disability following brain injury and the likelihood of recovery. A study by Arroyos-Jurado and colleagues (2000) examined the outcomes of traumatic brain injury on 43 children and adolescents. The children were tested shortly after their injury and 3, 12, and 24 months later. They found that the most important factor in explaining functioning after injury was the child's abilities prior to her or his injury. Although severity of injury was important, especially in behavioral functioning, it was the child's skills in reading and writing prior to injury that were most predictive of performance following the injury. That is, children with good skills in these domains tended to have better outcomes than children with poor skills prior to injury.

A review of research on the academic and language skills of children with traumatic brain injury found that children with mild brain injuries had no significant deficits. However, those with moderate brain injury experienced slight losses in academic skills, but those deficits persisted over time. Children who had experienced severe traumatic brain injuries had significant deficits in reading, spelling, and mathematics but also made the most rapid recovery. However, they, too, never completely recovered functioning (Vu, Babikian, & Asarnow, 2011).

Language Characteristics

Many children with traumatic brain injury experience losses in language skills. Children who lose language functioning as a result of brain injury are said to have *acquired aphasia*. In other words, they have lost some language functions that they had acquired earlier. Language difficulties resulting from traumatic brain injury can involve expressive language, receptive language, or both and can range from mild to severe (Catroppa & Anderson, 2004).

Two aspects of language have most frequently been reported to be affected by brain injuries: syntax and pragmatic skills. For example, Campbell and Dollaghan (1990) found that children with severe brain injuries age 6 to 16 years significantly underperformed age-matched peers on several measures of syntactic functioning, including mean length of utterance, total number of words used, and use of complex sentences. Morse and colleagues (1999) found that, compared to children with mild and moderate brain injury, the language of children with severe brain injuries was more likely to be unintelligible, incomplete, and less complex. Children with traumatic brain injuries have been found to have difficulty understanding and using communicative processes such as negotiating and hinting (Didus, Anderson, & Catroppa, 1999) and difficulty with the use of narratives (Chapman et al., 1992). Turkstra (2007) reported on research that found that individuals with traumatic brain injury had difficulty with several aspects of social cognition, such as recognizing emotions in others and making judgments about conversational partners.

The research review by Vu and colleagues (2011) also examined language outcomes for individuals with mild, moderate, and severe traumatic brain injury. They concluded that children who had experienced moderate brain injuries generally had deficits in receptive but not expressive language. Those with severe brain injuries had significant difficulties in both expressive and receptive language as well as in pragmatic language skills, although they recovered much of their language functioning within 2 years after their injury.

Although there is considerable evidence that brain injury can lead to diminished language skills, the good news is that many children with brain injuries do frequently show marked improvements in their language abilities (Hanten et al., 2009). Campbell and Dollaghan (1990) investigated the phenomenon of language recovery by evaluating the language abilities of nine brain-injured children during the 13 months following their injuries. When first tested, the brain-injured children scored far below a group of nondisabled children matched for age and gender on all measures of expressive language. However, by the end of the 13-month period, the groups differed on only one measure—total number of utterances. There were, however, big differences in the language recovery of each of the brain-injured children. Two of the children showed no significant expressive language problems, even at the first session. Two other children eventually caught up to the nondisabled children their own age. However, five of the brain-injured children never fully recovered their language skills, although they did show improvements. The results of this study show just how difficult it is to make generalizations about the recovery of children with brain injuries.

Although severity of injury has generally been found to be related to the extent of language loss, it is not always predictive of recovery. In fact, children with severe impairments may actually make more progress than those with mild or moderate injuries (Catroppa & Anderson, 2004). Other factors, such as age at injury (younger children have worse outcomes), family socioeconomic status (higher socioeconomic status is associated with better outcomes), and preinjury communication and language skills, have been found to be related to recovery from brain injury (Catroppa & Anderson, 2004; Hanten et al., 2009).

In addition to impacting language and communication development, brain injuries can also have an impact on literacy skills. Children with traumatic brain injuries have been found to score significantly lower than age-, gender-, and race-matched uninjured children on achievement tests of reading, language, and mathematics (Ewing-Cobbs et al., 2006).

Teachers can expect children with brain injuries to have a variety of language impairments. Some may have no obvious problems; others might have subtle language impairments that may only show up in conversation or in reading and writing; and still others might have significant difficulties with word retrieval, speech fluency, and syntactic skills affected.

> To better understand the impact of traumatic brain injury on children and their families, watch this video. What were some of the challenges that the children faced in their recovery from their injury?
> https://www.youtube.com/watch?v=I5YBR1zQpQg

Intervention

The best intervention for head injury is prevention. Most head trauma is preventable. Use of seat belts, bicycle helmets, and appropriate sports equipment can reduce the incidence of head injury, as can efforts to reduce drunk driving and child abuse. Despite efforts aimed at prevention and education about brain injuries, they continue to occur at high rates.

With the high frequency of brain trauma and the trend toward inclusion of children with disabilities in regular education settings, most teachers are likely to have a child with traumatic brain injury in their classroom at some time. A child's return to school following a head injury can be very difficult for the child as well as the teacher. As

Harrington (1990) put it, "The dilemma of returning to school after a traumatic brain injury is that life is just not the same" (p. 479). There can be changes in thinking, in behavior, in language, and in academic skills such as reading and writing. The child may also have physical problems such as headaches and difficulty staying alert.

Telzrow (1987) has suggested 10 elements that should be part of an educational program for children with traumatic brain injury. These include the following:

1. *Maximally controlled environment.* The child may need a highly structured environment where distraction is reduced.

2. *Low pupil–teacher ratio.* It may be necessary to provide a classroom aide or other assistant to work with the child.

3. *Intensive and repetitive instruction.* The brain-injured child often needs more time to learn. Reducing nonacademic activities and lengthening the school year can provide more learning time.

4. *Emphasis on process.* The child may need to be helped in learning how to learn. Instruction should include help in sustaining attention and on memory.

5. *Behavioral programming.* Instructional strategies that use task analysis and careful measurement of progress have been found to be successful.

6. *Integrated instructional therapies.* Integrate allied therapies such as speech and physical therapy into the student's primary instructional setting to facilitate generalization and transfer of skills.

7. *Simulation experiences.* Use simulations to enable the child to transfer skills to a new setting.

8. *Cuing, fading, and shadowing.* Students may require cues to respond, which should be faded as soon as possible. When shadowing, the teacher closely monitors the child attempting a new task or moving to a new environment.

9. *Readjustment counseling.* This may help the child adjust to his or her new environment and abilities.

10. *Home-school liaison.* It is essential to build and maintain a strong link between parents and the school.

Some students with traumatic brain injury may need modifications to regular classroom instruction in order to become successful learners again. These may include relatively simple accommodations such as sitting near the teacher or a peer helper and frequent breaks for students who get tired easily. Bowen (2005) suggested that technological aids, such as an FM wireless communication system to help students with attention difficulties, electronic organizers, or word-processing software, can be useful to support the learning of individuals with brain injury.

For those with language impairments, a range of services and methods may be necessary. Some will need speech and language therapy; others may need more help than most children do when learning (or relearning) to read and write; and still others will need augmentative communication devices to enable them to communicate effectively. Teachers can help by responding to the child and being alert to her or his language abilities. In some cases, teachers may need to adjust their language so the child can better understand directions and assignments. In addition, it may help to put the child in many situations where there are opportunities to interact with other children.

Teachers and other education professionals who work with children with traumatic brain injury must be prepared for just about anything. These children may have few problems or many disabilities. They may readily adjust to their disabilities or be emotionally upset. Parents may be overly protective of their child or deny that there are any problems. If teachers are aware of the range of needs and abilities that brain-injured children might bring to the classroom, they can better help these children reach their learning potential.

To learn more about classroom accommodations for children with traumatic brain injury, watch this video. What are some of the suggestions for educating students with traumatic brain injury?
https://www.youtube.com/watch?v=dVRc0hVcGg0

Check Your Understanding 12.2
Click here to gauge your understanding of the concepts in this section.

Summary

This chapter examined the impact of neuromotor disabilities and brain injury on language and communication development. Children with neuromotor disabilities such as cerebral palsy face a number of challenges. Often, their speech, language, and communication difficulties do not receive much attention. In some cases, this is because these problems are treated as secondary to the motor disabilities that are the primary focus for intervention. Language and communication deficits, however, play a significant role in the development of socialization and literacy skills that are critical for success in school and in the community.

Teachers and other education professionals need to understand the impact of neuromotor disabilities and brain injury on language, especially since so many children with these disabilities are being integrated into regular education settings. Impairments of mobility are certainly important and have an impact on instruction, but recognition of their associated speech and language impairments can also be critical to the academic and social success of children with neuromotor disabilities.

Language Assessment and Instruction in the Classroom

Changing models of service delivery are impacting the way that children are identified for educational services. There is greater emphasis on classroom-based methods of identifying children with language and communication disabilities. In this chapter, we will examine classroom-based approaches to the identification of language and communication difficulties and instruction that addresses those difficulties. The goal is to enable teachers and speech-language professionals to be able to collaborate in the identification and remediation of language and communication difficulties in children.

Learning Outcomes

After completing this chapter, you should be able to:

1. Describe methods for identifying language and communication difficulties.

2. Identify classroom-based methods that can be used to enhance language skills in children across different ages and ability levels.

Teacher Perspective

I taught an eighth-grade student last year who was classified as communication impaired. Although he had been maintaining "D" averages for most of his schooling, no teachers had referred him until the eighth grade because he was never "a behavioral problem." He would simply sit in class and look at the teacher, and the teacher would assume he was paying attention and learning. On his tests, he would frequently mix up words from the questions and turn them into a sentence, and he had difficulty recalling information from novels. As I started working with him more, I noticed he had few friends, rarely spoke in conversations, and was picked on for his shy behaviors. In conversations, he would usually repeat what I had just said instead of responding to me, and he had trouble following directions. Once I referred him and he was eligible for services, he finally received the language therapy he needed

for his expressive/receptive skills and more support in the classroom. I learned that although he struggled with language, he excelled greatly at anything and everything visual—I taught him the lattice method of multiplication, and he could duplicate what I had done after only seeing it done once! As he received more support, he became much more confident, and his other teachers told me he started talking to them more. He participated in sports during recess, and he stood up for himself when his "friends" would try to make fun of him. At the end of the year, his father asked me what magic I was using on his son! It was so nice to see the academic improvements but also, more importantly, the social changes in my student as a result of giving him what he needed.

(Eighth grade, co-teacher)

Parent Perspective

My daughter has childhood apraxia of speech, and when she was about 18 months old, I started to get concerned that something might not be right. Most people assured me that she would grow out of it and that I should not be concerned. Instead I followed my gut and called early intervention for her. She qualified for services and started speech therapy within the next 4 to 6 weeks. She continued to receive these services until she turned 3, at which point she entered the local school district and received services there.

Even with services, she still had difficulties acquiring verbal communication. She started with American Sign Language and acquired approximately 8 to 10 new signs in about 2 months, but no new words. I realized that she was a child with a capacity for communication and could express her needs and wants, but for some reason, verbal language eluded her. That is when she was seen by a neurologist who gave her a diagnosis of apraxia. My point is,

we cannot assume that children will "outgrow" speech and language difficulties. If I had not contacted early intervention and started her in speech therapy, I can't imagine the kind of deficit she would have now going into kindergarten 2 to 3 years behind her peers with no support.

In my case, I compared her with her peers. When I saw her interact with other children her own age, I saw that she would want to play and interact with other children, but never spoke, even when they encouraged her to do so by asking questions or otherwise requesting her attention. I realized that if she wasn't able to interact with them in the same way that they were able to interact with her, then she was probably exhibiting a significant delay. It was then that I requested a referral to New Jersey Early Intervention, which I had to fight for. Her doctor did not seem concerned since she didn't show any signs of autism, so the doctor assumed that she was fine, which is yet another example of someone assuming that she would "outgrow" it.

Language Assessment in the Classroom

Changes in education service deliver models, including the Response to Intervention (RTI) model, and the inclusion of children with exceptional learning needs in general education classrooms place a greater responsibility on the classroom teacher to identify and teach children with all kinds of disabilities, including those with language difficulties. After all, in most cases, it is the classroom teacher who sees the child most often, in many different settings, interacting with a variety of communicative partners. Teachers can help identify children at risk for language-learning disabilities and help focus assessment on specific areas of concern. In addition, classroom teachers can observe children's use of language in the classroom. Ideally, classroom teachers should be collaborating with speech-language specialists to identify language and communication difficulties and plan appropriate instruction, but school schedules and caseloads often make comprehensive planning difficult.

In Chapter 7, we mentioned the changes that the RTI model has brought to the identification and treatment of students with learning disabilities. This model uses universal screening of students to identify those who are falling behind their peers as well as a tiered system of intervention that starts with the use of evidence-based instruction in the general education classroom and proceeds to more individualized, intensive intervention for those children who do not respond adequately to less intensive instruction (Ehren & Nelson, 2005; Fuchs & Fuchs, 2005). The Response to Intervention Action Network website provides more information and lots of resources that can be used to implement RTI in the classroom.

In this chapter, as well as the next chapter, we will use the RTI model as the framework for discussing the identification of students with language difficulties as well as instructional methods that can be used to enhance language skills. Even if your school has not adopted the RTI model, elements of the model, such as early identification of learning difficulties and levels of intervention, can be useful for any classroom.

In this chapter, the focus will be on classroom-based methods that can be used to identify and provide tier 1 (whole class) and tier 2 (targeted) interventions for children with language difficulties. In Chapter 14, we will discuss more intensive and specialized methods of assessment and intervention that can be used with students who do not show adequate improvement from tier 1 or tier 2 instruction or whose language impairments are so significant that they required specialized instruction.

Classroom-Based Observation

The formal assessment of language and communication is primarily the responsibility of speech-language specialists. They play an important role in determining whether or not the child meets the criteria for receiving services and for identifying best practices for delivering those services. But classroom teachers play an important role in identifying children at risk for language impairments and in planning and implementing instruction that will help students improve their language and communication skills. Classrooms provide a rich environment for the use of language. Children have to understand and follow directions, ask questions, participate in discussions, interact with their peers, and use language skills for reading and writing. All of these functions present opportunities for assessment of language skills. Nelson (1989) suggests that teachers observe the child's ability to use the various language rule systems (phonological, morphological, and so on) in all modalities demanded by the curriculum (listening, speaking, reading, writing, and thinking).

In addition to simply observing children in their classrooms, teachers can gather informal, classroom-based information about language use in many other ways—for instance, by participating with the child in answering questions at the end of a chapter. In this way, teachers can evaluate the ability of the child to understand text, to paraphrase, and to formulate a response. Other possibilities are to ask the student to retell a story or explain the steps in solving a math problem. Each of these activities can yield important information about the child's ability to understand and use language in the classroom.

Of course, teachers and other education professionals have limited time and opportunities to observe children and assess their performance. The use of checklists can be helpful to provide a framework for the observation. Catts (1997) developed a checklist to help teachers identify children at risk for reading disorders based on their language skills. Another example of a checklist is the one developed by Olswang, Coggins, and Svensson (2007), which was designed to assess the social communication of school-age children. An excellent resource that contains checklists for a number of language skills was developed by the Tennessee Department of Education. You can find this guide by going to the department's website. Type "special education evaluation and eligibility" into the search bar, click on the first result "Special Education Evaluation & Eligibility," click on "Resource Packets–Questions & Answers–Instructional Guidance," and then click on the "Speech and Language Impairments: (Languages) Resources Packet" link.

Classroom-based assessment can be useful both for determining the child's current status as well as looking at performance over time. As such, it is consistent with the RTI model of continuous assessment for identification of learning problems.

Language Elicitation Tasks

Sometimes observation of the child in the classroom is not sufficient for assessing language skills. Opportunities for observation may be too limited, or the use of some language structures may be too infrequent to be useful. As an alternative, it may be useful to structure a language elicitation activity in a way that will prompt a certain kind of response. Let's say, for example, that you have noticed that a child seemed to have difficulty understanding and/or using the past tense (-ed) ending. There may not be a lot of opportunities to observe the child's use of this structure in the classroom. So you might want to use a task that prompts the use of -ed endings—for example, by showing a brief video of a cartoon character fishing and then asking questions about what the child saw. The responses should be mostly in the past tense.

One widely used method to elicit specific language responses is imitation. Using this technique, the examiner says a sentence and asks the child to repeat it. To prompt the use of the present progressive ending, the examiner might say *The girl is riding a bike.* The idea behind the use of imitation tasks is that children will be able to repeat only those language structures that they have already mastered. Imitation can be a useful way to quickly assess the child's knowledge of a particular language structure, although the usefulness of this technique has been found to vary from child to child (Fujiki & Brinton, 1987). Imitation tasks can be useful but they should be used in combination with other measures of language use, such as those that follow.

Other language elicitation tasks use a variety of activities that can be fun for the child while yielding valuable information about language skills. Here are some examples.

Morphology.   Berko (1958) developed a classic task that requires children to complete a sentence that describes a picture. For this task, the examiner prompts a response by saying *This is a wug. Now there are two of them. There are two _____*. The child has to fill in the blank. By using nonsense words, this task is able to assess the child's knowledge of morphological rules.

Kirby and colleagues (2012) developed an informal assessment of morphological awareness. The children were asked to complete the ending when given a series of words such as run/ran and walk/walk _____. The tester said, "I am going to ask you to figure out some missing words. If I say 'push' and then I say 'pushed'; then I say 'jump,' so then you should say _____?" If the child did not respond correctly (jumped), the experimenter explained how push and pushed were alike, and then how jump and jumped were alike the same way. There were 5 practice items and 20 test items.

Syntax.   Owens (2010) gives two suggestions for eliciting negatives. He calls the first "The Emperor's New Clothes." The examiner makes an untrue statement (*Oh Shirley, what beautiful yellow boots*), which should prompt the child to respond with a negative (*I'm not wearing boots*). Owens calls the second technique "Screw-Up." The examiner makes a statement that does not match the action (*Here's your snack*—said as the examiner hands the subject a pencil). The subject should respond by saying *That's not a snack*. These examples show the creativity that teachers and others can apply to elicit specific syntactic structures. For example, to elicit the use of possessives, one could say *Who does that book belong to?* as a way to prompt the response, *It's Jack's book*.

Semantics.   Howell, Fox, and Morehead (1993, p. 281) present several ways to elicit vocabulary knowledge. One suggestion goes as follows:

Target word: *drill*

Directions: "Select the words which make sentence 2 most like sentence 1."

Sentence 1: We need drill on our skills.

Sentence 2: If we want to get better at our skills we should
  . . . study them.
  . . . put a hole in them.
  . . . do them a lot.

Apply Your Knowledge 13.1: Elicitation Tasks

In this activity, you will develop your own informal language elicitation tasks.

Ecological Assessment

Ecological assessment examines the child's behavior in the context of environmental demands and expectations (McCormick, 2003) rather than comparing children to population norms. Ecological assessment is often used to evaluate students with severe disabilities because normed tests may not be useful with this population and functional goals may be of great importance.

The basic idea behind ecological assessment is to intensively evaluate the functioning of the individual in the real environments in which he or she must function. The results of this evaluation become the basis for functional intervention goals for the child and guide needed adaptations in the environment. McCormick (2003) has identified 10 steps in the ecological assessment process:

1. Get to know the student.
   - Identify the resources and supports available at home and in school.
   - Identify the student's strengths.
   - Develop goals for (and with) the student.

2. List activities/routines in a typical school day.
   - Observations and/or interviews can be conducted.

3. Prioritize activities/routines and develop a broad goal statement.

4. Observe and record the behavior of a nondisabled peer and/or conduct interviews to determine the key behavioral expectations for each activity/routine.
   - Nondisabled peers are observed in order to understand what skills the student with disabilities needs to perform the target task.

5. Observe and record the behavior of the student from initiation to completion of each activity/routine.

6. Compare the behavior of the student with expectations for each activity/routine.
   - Note when the student does not meet expectations to determine skills to be learned.

7. Highlight language and communication skills.

8. Try to ascertain why key language/communication behaviors are not demonstrated.
   - The student may not recognize what he or she is supposed to do or say (strategy deficiency).
   - The student may be unable to perform the skill.
   - The student may be unmotivated to perform the skill.
   - The student has never learned how to perform the skill.
   - The physical environment makes it difficult for the student to perform the skill.

9. State the language/communication objectives for each activity.

10. Develop an individualized instructional plan for each objective.

Ecological assessment can be a complex and difficult approach to assessment, but it can yield very useful results, especially for students for whom test norms may not be relevant. There is an inseparable relationship between assessment and instruction in the ecological approach (see Box 13.1).

Universal Screening

Earlier in this chapter, we mentioned the use of universal screening as an element of the response to intervention (RTI) model. In practice, this means that teachers use a formal assessment instrument with the entire class to identify their current level of performance and periodically repeat the assessment to monitor student progress. Those students who fall behind the rate of progress of their peers become candidates for tier 2 (targeted intervention) or tier 3 (intensive intervention).

Two measures that can be used to identify elements of language are the Preschool Individual Growth and Development Indicators (IGDIs) and the Phonological Awareness and Literacy Screening for Preschool (PALS-PreK). The IGDI (see the My IGDIs website) assesses language and literacy skills in children ages 3 to 5. The test includes three subtests that specifically address language issues: Picture Naming (Oral Language); Rhyming (Phonological

---

Box 13.1   Example of an Ecological Assessment

Tricia is an 8-year-old student with cerebral palsy and mild cognitive disability who is placed in a regular education classroom. She is supported by a classroom aide.

Following a meeting with Tricia's classroom teacher, her aide, her parents, and Mrs. Kline, a special education teacher assigned to consult with the regular classroom teacher, it was determined that one of the priority goals for Tricia would be requesting food in the cafeteria. (Steps 1, 2, and 3)

Step 4
Observations of Tricia's peers indicate that, in most cases, they are asked by a cafeteria aide to make a verbal response to indicate their choice.

Steps 5 and 6
Observation of Tricia by Mrs. Kline indicates that Tricia responds to the verbal prompt from the cafeteria aide by pointing. If the aide is not sure what Tricia wants, she points to various choices until Tricia nods her head.

Step 7
The language/communication goal for Tricia is for her to make a verbal request in response to the cafeteria aide's verbal prompt.

Step 8
Mrs. Kline has determined that several of the common choices that Tricia needs to make are not currently available on her augmentative communication device.

Steps 9 and 10
Requesting food choices is established as an instructional goal for Tricia. Common menu choices are added as options on her communication device and practiced with the classroom aide. Tricia is given several opportunities to practice this skill in the cafeteria with the cafeteria aide when her peers are not in the cafeteria. Her classroom aide observes and collects data on Tricia's performance of this goal.

Awareness), and Alliteration (Phonological Awareness). The PALS-PreK (see the PALS-PreK website) measures children's phonological awareness skills with three subtests: Beginning Sound Awareness (recognition of alliteration), Rhyme Awareness, and Blending.

This video about the IGDI instrument provides a description of its elements and some examples of children completing the assessment. What are some of the skills assessed with this instrument?
https://www.youtube.com/watch?v=RzsAwt2UrzM

Another popular screening measure is the Dynamic Indicators of Basic Early Literacy Skills (DIBELS). DIBELS is a set of procedures and measures for assessing the acquisition of early literacy skills from kindergarten through sixth grade. The measures are designed to be short (1-minute) fluency measures used to regularly monitor the development of early literacy and early reading skills. DIBELS (sixth edition) consists of seven measures (or indicators), three of which can be useful for identifying language skills: Initial Sound Fluency, Phoneme Segmentation Fluency, and Word Use Fluency (which includes assessment of vocabulary and oral language). The first two indicators specifically relate to phonemic awareness.

Watch this introductory video about DIBELS to better understand how the assessment works. What skills does the DIBELS oral reading fluency subtest evaluate?
https://www.youtube.com/watch?v=e2GywoKm2pI

Screening instruments are one example of formal assessments. We will examine some additional formal assessments of language in the next chapter.

Summary

Identifying children who are experiencing difficulties with language is an important first step in helping children succeed academically and socially. We discussed four methods that teachers can use to identify language difficulties: observation, language elicitation, ecological assessment, and universal screening. Having identified children with language difficulties, the next step is to provide instruction that will help them enhance their language skills.

Check Your Understanding 13.1

Click here to gauge your understanding of the concepts in this section.

Language Instruction in the Classroom

We know from numerous research studies that young children with language disorders are much more likely to have academic, social, and language difficulties later in life than are children with typically developing language (Clegg, Hollis, Mawhood, & Rutter, 2005; Law, Rush, Schoon, & Parsons, 2009). If these children do not receive language intervention, their language disorders are likely to persist (Johnson et al., 1999; Law, Garrett, & Nye, 2004).

Fortunately, there is increasing evidence that early instruction that focuses on improving communication skills can significantly enhance both language skills (e.g., Gallagher & Chiatt, 2009; Law et al., 2004) and the academic success of children, especially in reading (Moats, 2001). For this reason alone, it would be important to provide instruction in support of enhanced language and communication skills. But there are other reasons to intervene as well. Language is a critical skill for classroom interaction. If students are to fully participate, they must have the language and communication skills to understand classroom instruction and to ask and answer questions. Moreover, social skills are as important as (some would say more important than) academic skills in success during and after the school years.

Although there are a number of good reasons to provide language instruction, many children still do not receive the instruction they need. One explanation is that some educators still rely primarily on intervention provided by specialists as the major source of language and communication instruction for children. The term **intervention** suggests that this service takes place after a period of time in which the individual has been exposed to research-based instruction. But some children have limited (or no) exposure to such instruction. Moats and Lyon (1996) note that many teachers lack the depth of understanding of language and language instructional approaches that is necessary in order to deliver effective instruction. These teachers may not recognize the language and communication needs of their students. Even if they do recognize the need, they may not be able to provide effective instruction. Another reason is that instruction, when it occurs, may focus on the wrong skills. Despite a trend in the field of speech and language away from a primary focus on speech sound disorders to a broader view of the role of speech and language for communication and literacy development, school speech services are still often focused largely on helping young children improve their speech. Even when instruction is well planned and delivered effectively, it may not be sufficient for some children. They may need more focused and intensive instruction that can best be provided through intervention. Since intervention is a costly and limited commodity, it is important that it be delivered only when necessary and to those who need it most. The classroom is the primary locus of instruction in language and communication for most students. In this section, we will identify techniques that can be used by teachers to enhance the language and communication of their students in the regular or special education classroom.

Enhancing Classroom Interaction

One of the most important things teachers can do is to teach in ways that will enhance the language and communication of children in their classroom. Increased opportunities for the use of language in the classroom will give children practice in the use of language skills. Unfortunately, sociolinguists who have carefully observed classroom interactions have found that teachers usually dominate the conversation, ask a lot of questions that require minimal responses (one-word answers), and initiate most of the interactions (Cazden, 1986). As a result, in the typical classroom, children are rather passive recipients of communication rather than active partners in such interaction. Even worse, many teachers actively discourage interaction between students and even between the student and the teacher. Of course, there is a limit to how much interaction can be tolerated, but if language learning is an important goal, some interaction should not only be tolerated but also encouraged. Without the chance to interact, children with language-learning difficulties will have little opportunity to develop crucial language skills.

Fortunately, it is possible to enhance classroom communication. After examining research on classroom language intervention, Dudley-Marling and Searle (1988) developed four recommendations that teachers can use to enhance the language-learning environment: (1) the physical setting must promote talk; (2) the teacher must provide opportunities for children to interact and use language as they learn; (3) the teacher needs to provide opportunities for children to use language for a variety of purposes and for a variety of audiences; and (4) the teacher needs to respond to student talk in ways that encourage continued talk. Let's look at each of these suggestions in more detail.

- *The physical setting must promote talk.* Dudley-Marling and Searle (1988) note that many classrooms are organized to discourage interaction. Individual workstations, carrels, and widely spaced rows are all designed to help students concentrate, but they also have the effect of reducing interaction. Certainly, there is a need for concentration, but many students also need opportunities to interact with their peers. Providing large tables where groups can work, learning centers, and interactive classroom displays can give students opportunities to interact in the classroom.

- *The teacher must provide opportunities for children to interact and use language as they learn.* Teachers can structure classroom conversation around academic tasks. For example, children reading a story about fishing can be encouraged to share their previous fishing experiences with the group. Teachers are sometimes reluctant to let students engage in these kinds of conversations because students may stray from the topic. If this happens, students can be redirected back to the topic. Remember, communication is a goal for many students, and conversation is not an off-task behavior. Other examples of using instructional activities for language interaction are encouraging the students to say aloud their strategies for solving a math problem or having them read a story to the class.

- *The teacher needs to provide opportunities for children to use language for a variety of purposes and for a variety of audiences.* Teachers can encourage class decision making and problem solving and provide opportunities for discussion and sharing. Teachers can provide opportunities for students to talk to each other, to younger children (through cross-age tutoring), and to adults (parents and visitors).

- *The teacher needs to respond to student talk in ways that encourage continued talk.* Teachers often ask questions in ways that give students little opportunity to respond. When students do reply, the teacher may not respond in ways that encourage further interaction. Dudley-Marling and Searle (1988) give an example of a teacher discouraging interaction:

    S: Boy, you should have seen the neat stuff at the circus.
    T: Really, James, you shouldn't say "neat stuff."

The authors suggest that this interaction could have been turned into a longer communicative interaction if the teacher had said something like, *Oh, you had a good time at the circus?* Teachers should be careful not to dominate the conversation, and they should follow the child's lead in setting the conversational topic. One simple but effective strategy for increasing interaction is to pause several seconds for a response to a question. Teachers generally wait less than 1 second for a response. Longer wait time increases the likelihood that students will respond (Rowe, 1986).

The techniques considered so far for enhancing language and communication skills are useful in nearly any classroom. But there are some strategies that are more effective in particular classroom environments or with children at certain ages or developmental levels.

Preschool Classrooms

Language and communication development should be a major goal in preschool classrooms. Teachers of preschool children usually include many activities to involve their students in such interaction. For example, Watson, Layton, Pierce, and Abraham (1994) describe a preschool program for children with language disorders that incorporates instruction in emerging literacy skills into activities that most teachers of preschool children will recognize. These activities include:

1. *Circle time.* When the bell rings, children get their mats and bring them to the circle. Children must recognize their names in order to get their mats. After an opening song, children discuss the job chart that has jobs listed in print, supplemented by pictures. When there is a song, the words are written out on a poster board and the teacher points to the words as they are sung.

2. *Story time.* Books that follow a classroom theme (animals, communities, etc.) are selected. As the teacher reads the story, each child is asked for some kind of response. In addition, there are opportunities for choral responding. Because repeated readings help children improve their comprehension skills, the story is reread at least three times in a week.

3. *Story-related group activity.* The teacher uses follow-up activities to reinforce concepts from the story. Children may role-play parts from the story or make puppets to represent characters from the story.

4. *Literacy-rich centers.* Watson and colleagues (1994) describe three literacy centers that are used in their classroom. At the *art and writing center,* children draw pictures related to the "story of the week" and tell about their picture. The *role-playing center* contains dress-up clothes, dolls, and toys that the children can use to act out action from the story or from their own scripts. During free time, the children can go to the *book and library center* to look at books and listen to tapes.

5. *Snack time.* Often snack time is integrated with the weekly theme. Snack packaging may be used as reading material for the child.

6. *Gross motor play/outdoor activities.* Even during gross motor activities, there are opportunities to practice literacy skills. When teaching exercises, the teacher also introduces the written word (e.g., *arm, body*).

7. *Closing circle.* This provides a final opportunity during the day for children to recall and talk about their experiences. When children are given printed materials to take home, the child is told about the purpose of the message, reinforcing the idea that print has a purpose.

Although the preschool classroom provides many opportunities for language interaction and instruction, it is important that teachers and other professionals know how to maximize these opportunities to enhance language skills. Ostrosky and Kaiser (1991) suggest seven strategies that they believe will increase the likelihood that children will show an interest in their environment and make communicative attempts, and that will increase the likelihood that the adult will prompt the use of language.

1. *Use interesting materials.* Provide materials and activities that children enjoy. Children's preferences can be identified through observation during free playtimes and from parents' reports. Rotating materials from time to time will keep the children interested.

2. *Place items out of reach.* Place some desired items in view but out of reach in order to prompt requests by the children. During snack time, for example, the teacher can place a cookie on the table out of reach from the child. If the child reaches for the cookie, the teacher can prompt the child to make a request or, if the child is nonspeaking, ask the child to point or use his or her communicative device to request.

3. *Provide inadequate portions.* Provide children with small or inadequate portions of a material, such as blocks. When the children need more, they are likely to make a request.

4. *Give children opportunities for choice making.* Children can be prompted to make a choice by being presented with two objects and asked to make a choice. For example, during snack time, the child may be asked to choose between a cookie and fruit. For children who are nonspeaking, pointing may be accepted. For other children, a verbalization may be required.

5. *Provide assistance.* Creating a situation in which the children will need assistance provides communicative opportunities. A windup toy or an unopened bottle of bubbles may provide opportunities for children to request adult assistance.

6. *Use sabotage.* A "sabotage" is created when children are not provided with all the materials they need to complete a task. For example, students may be asked to cut out pictures and paste them on a chart but are given no paste. Alternatively, in a group setting, each child may get some, but not all, of the needed materials. In order to complete the project, they will have to request materials from their peers.

7. *Use "silly" situations.* Children may be prompted to communicate by creating silly or absurd situations. For example, during circle time, the teacher may hold a picture upside down or place a weather symbol on the calendar instead of the date.

Each of these techniques is designed to increase communicative interaction. However, in many cases, the goal is to move beyond interaction to more adult forms of communication. When materials and activities are carefully selected and adults are aware of and use effective techniques for enhancing communicative interaction, the preschool classroom can be a rich environment for language learning.

Elementary Classrooms

Language development does not stop when children enter school. Earlier in this book, we reviewed research that described continuing growth in language development during the school years (Chapter 6). This growth occurs in nearly all aspects of language. At the same time, students are continuing to develop their reading and writing skills. What can teachers and other education professionals in elementary classrooms do to support and extend language learning—oral and written?

As we have noted earlier in this book, there is considerable evidence that phonological-processing abilities are related to initial success in reading. Many reading programs include activities to develop phonological skills, but many students need more practice on these skills than is generally provided by most basal reader series. Teachers can provide assistance by helping students identify words that begin with the same sound (not necessarily the same letter), pay attention to rhyme, and practice dividing words into parts and putting the parts back together to make words.

A number of approaches for improving phonological awareness were discussed in Chapter 7. In general, these techniques have helped children improve both their phonological skills and their reading success. In addition, some structured programs for improving phonological skills such as the *Ladders to Literacy* program (Notari-Syverson, O'Connor, & Vadasy, 2007; O'Connor, Notari-Syverson, & Vadasy, 2005) have been used successfully to teach phonological skills in the elementary and preschool classroom (Institute for Education Sciences, 2007).

Reading success requires more than just phonological awareness. As children progress in reading, other language-based skills, such as vocabulary and grammatical knowledge, play an important role. Narrative (storytelling) skills (an aspect of pragmatic language) are important for both reading and writing.

How teachers present information in the classroom can have a significant impact on student learning. This is the conclusion of a study by Lapadat (2002). Second-grade students were asked to listen to taped lectures that varied in the pace of the delivery (slow to fast) and the amount of redundancy in the lecture (high or low). Lapadat found that students with greater language ability learned more, no matter how the lecture was delivered. Presentation style, however, did matter. Overall, slow-paced instructional language was positively related to learning, but students attended less to it than to fast-paced talk. For most students, slow-paced, nonredundant instruction seemed to work best. However, students with special needs learned best when instruction was faster paced. Perhaps the lesson for teachers from this research is to understand that the pace of a lesson matters considerably. Although the optimal pace may vary for different learners, teachers need to be aware of the effect of their instructional delivery on their students' learning.

Secondary Classrooms

During the secondary-school years, language continues to grow and develop. Development in advanced syntactic skills, in vocabulary, and in subtle communicative skills is characteristic of the secondary years. Children with speech and language difficulties do not necessarily outgrow their problems. Instead, as they respond to the demands of the secondary setting, their problems may surface in new ways. Lecturing, note taking, and independent research projects pose difficult challenges to the student with language difficulties. Despite their need for continuing support, many secondary-age students with language and communication impairments fail to receive the supportive instruction that they need to be successful (Starling, Munro, Togher, & Arciuli, 2011).

An instructional approach that has been used with success with secondary-age students is **learning strategies**. Many students lack an efficient strategy to use when they encounter unknown words. The learning strategies approach helps students recognize and use a strategy. For example, the DISSECT strategy was developed by Lenz and Hughes (1990) to help secondary students decode words. Students are taught to follow seven steps that require them to use context clues, break words into their constituents, and use additional resources when needed. The seven steps of the strategy are as follows:

D: *Discover* the context. Students are reminded to use the context as an aid to identifying the target word.

I: *Isolate* the prefix. Students are instructed to find and separate the prefix and then try to say the word.

S: *Separate* the suffix. Students are instructed to find and separate the suffix and then try to say the word.

S: *Say* the stem. Once the prefix and suffix have been removed, what remains is the word stem. Students are now told to try to identify the stem.

E: *Examine* the stem. Students are taught to use the "rule of twos and threes" to identify the stem. That is, if the stem begins with a vowel, students pronounce units of two letters. If the stem begins with a consonant, students separate and pronounce units of three letters.

C: *Check* with someone. If students have followed the first five steps and still do not recognize the word, they can check with a peer, teacher, or someone else.

T: *Try* the dictionary. Another (perhaps preferable) alternative is to check the dictionary.

In one study, DISSECT was found to significantly reduce the oral reading errors of eighth-grade students with learning disabilities after only 6 weeks of use (Lenz & Hughes, 1990). In addition to improving word identification skills, strategy instruction has been used successfully to enhance the development of a variety of language-related skills, including metalinguistic skills (Starling et al., 2011), written expression (Ellis & Lenz, 1987), and reading comprehension (Fuchs, Fuchs, & Kazdan, 1999).

The continued development of semantic skills, especially vocabulary, is also essential for academic success at the secondary level. Vocabulary skills have been found to be related to reading comprehension (Elleman, Lindo, Morphy, & Compton, 2009) as well as to overall reading level (Scammacca et al., 2007). Research on vocabulary instruction for secondary-age students has found that systematic instruction on vocabulary can improve vocabulary learning (Kuder, 2016). The most effective instructional methods include mnemonic instruction, morphemic analysis, direct instruction, and multimedia instruction. In several studies, Michael Kennedy and his colleagues (Kennedy, Deshler, & Lloyd, 2015; Kennedy, Thomas, Meyer, Alves, & Lloyd, 2014) found that when secondary-age students with disabilities used podcasts that included multimedia resources, the students learned new vocabulary faster than when the standard drill and practice methods were used.

In addition to its role in academic success, language is an essential part of social competence as well. There is considerable research and clinical evidence that language skills play an important role in successful social interaction (Brinton & Fujiki, 1993). This is true for children at all ages, but, since social skills and social acceptance are such a crucial part of adolescence, the use of appropriate social language may be of even greater importance for secondary-age students. The social skills that adolescents develop and practice are essential for success in school as well as in life outside of school.

Teachers can support the development of social interaction skills by providing opportunities for interacting with a variety of communicative partners during many different activities. Formal reports and presentations are one type of activity. These provide opportunities for teachers to give feedback on pragmatic skills such as introducing a topic, taking the audience's perspective, elaborating on a theme, and providing an appropriate conclusion.

Although these are important skills for students to acquire, even more critical may be the opportunities for peer interaction. Group activities provide teachers with opportunities to observe their students in interaction with peers, model appropriate interaction, and assure that all students are given the opportunity to participate. Taking the time to set ground rules for interaction and discussing what the teacher has observed during group time can be as important as the content that the groups are assigned to complete. A review of research found that peer tutoring had a moderately large effect on improving the social and behavioral skills of both elementary and secondary-age students (Bowman-Perrott, Burke, Zhang, & Zaini, 2014).

Language skills continue to play an important role in learning at the secondary level. Unfortunately, in many cases, students with language and communication difficulties fail to receive the instruction they need at the secondary level. The result is that some students continue to fall behind their peers and do not reach their potential. It is important for teachers and other education professionals to recognize the importance of language skills for the academic and social growth of secondary-age students and to attempt to enhance these skills in their students.

Instruction for Students with Significant Disabilities

Academic expectations for students with moderate to severe disabilities are higher than ever. Changes in federal and state policies as well as research into instructional methods for these students have significantly raised the bar for this population (Knight, Browder, Agnello, &

Lee, 2010). Increasingly, students with significant disabilities are receiving some or all of their academic instruction in general education classrooms. Because language and communication skills play such an important role in reading, writing, and speaking, it is important to consider how to enhance the language and communication of children with significant disabilities in the classroom, whether it is a general or special education classroom.

Classroom-based language instruction for students with significant disabilities is similar to instruction for other students in many ways. For example, using naturally occurring opportunities throughout the school day to model and teach language skills, using peers to prompt language from students with significant disabilities, systematic instruction in specific language structures, and instruction in phonological awareness should all be part of instruction for this population. In other ways, language instruction may be quite different. For example, many of these students will be using an augmentative or alternative communication system (such as a voice output communication device or sign language). These require that teachers and peers learn how to communicate effectively with the student. Most students with significant disabilities will need more intensive instruction in order to achieve skill objectives. That means instruction that is delivered more frequently, with more examples and more opportunities for practice.

Recently, the author was asked by a local school to work with the staff to identify principles for teaching language and communication skills to students with significant disabilities. This is the list that we developed:

- **Use typical development as a framework for instruction:** Although children with significant disabilities do not always follow the typical developmental sequence, typical development can still be a good guide for planning an instructional sequence.

- **Teach functional skills:** It is possible and preferable to teach developmental skills in functional ways. Suppose, for example, you want the student to learn to identify nouns. Using items that the child needs for classroom success (e.g., pencil, paper) would be a functional application of this skill.

- **Develop clear and measurable objectives:** This principle should apply to all students, but it is critically important for students with significant disabilities. Progress is often slow and in small increments for this population. If objectives are carefully written, it is possible to measure success and know when it is time to move ahead.

- **Consider the student's sensory strengths and weaknesses:** Some students with significant disabilities have sensory disabilities that make it difficult for them to learn through listening or seeing. These need to be considered in planning instruction.

- **Use age-appropriate methods and materials:** Although it is not always easy to find appropriate materials for students with significant disabilities, it is important to try to find or create such materials. For example, using a television schedule may be a great way to teach sequencing skills.

Until recently, it was often assumed that individuals with moderate to severe disabilities were unable to acquire useful literacy skills. At best, perhaps they could learn a few "survival" words that would help them in an emergency. But that view has changed rapidly. Today there are greater literacy expectations for this population and better outcomes for many. In addition, there is now a growing body of research that indicates that these goals are achievable (Allor, Champlin, Gifford, & Mathes, 2010; Cooper-Duffy, Szedia, & Hyer, 2010; Erickson, Hatch, & Clendon, 2010).

Koppenhaver and Erickson (2003) described an approach to enhancing the language and literacy skills of students with severe disabilities in a preschool classroom. None of the children used speech. The authors worked with the teachers to use natural opportunities in the classroom to foster language and literacy skills. For example, they created an electronic writing center in the classroom that used a (previously unused) computer and a basic children's writing program. To enhance reading skills, they added a variety of reading materials to the classroom, including books with sound effects, wordless picture books, books on tape, and touch-and-feel books. Reading was also integrated into regular classroom activities. For example, at the beginning of each day, the students took attendance by identifying pictures of their classmates. Nametags were added to the pictures so children would become familiar with the written form of their names. The children were also given increased opportunities for language interaction. As an example, during drawing activities, the teachers were encouraged to describe what the children were drawing. The authors reported that, as a result of these and other activities, the students showed much greater interest in reading and writing.

As technology advances, new techniques and devices have emerged. Blischak and Schlosser (2003) reported on research studies that have found that speech-generating devices and talking word-processing programs can be useful for enhancing the spelling skills of nonspeaking students. Lee and Vail (2005) developed a program to teach sight words to 6- and 7-year-old students with moderate to severe disabilities. The program combined a multimedia presentation with a constant-time-delay procedure. When a task direction (i.e., "Click the word _____") was presented in the intervention program, a participant was given 5 seconds to initiate a response. Using this procedure, the children in the study were able to successfully learn the target words.

One of the key ingredients to improving literacy skills for students with significant disabilities is to increase the intensity of instruction. Increasing the intensity of instruction has been found to lead to significant improvements in literacy skills for students with significant disabilities. In one study, Allor and colleagues (2010) taught teachers to use the following strategies:

- **Present fast-paced lessons:** Activities focusing on letter sounds and words were very short, ranging from 1 to 5 minutes.
- **Move quickly from one activity to the next.**
- **Use appropriate pacing:** Pacing within activities was as quick as possible, while allowing students adequate processing time.
- **Promote automaticity:** Teachers gradually reduced processing time until student responses became quick and automatic.
- **Use behavior management techniques to decrease time off task:** Teachers developed routine prompts to quickly remind students to stay on task, and they reinforced on-task behavior.
- **Spend less time on clearly mastered skills:** Allow more practice time for skills not mastered.

There are undoubtedly significant challenges to teaching students with significant disabilities. But higher expectations for these students means that more of them will be expected to achieve language and literacy skills that will enable them to be successful in school and in life after school. Intensive instructional methods, clear and measurable outcomes, and technology are helping practitioners meet the needs of this challenging population.

Teaching Specific Language Skills

Although increasing communicative interaction in the classroom is important, many students can benefit from instruction in specific language skills. Most children acquire the essential elements of their first language without direct instruction. They simply learn to understand and use the elements through a process of trial and error (or, more formally, "hypothesis testing"). But, when children come to school, they are expected to identify the elements of language in order to develop literacy (reading and writing skills). Additionally, some children come to school with more limited acquisition of the basic language rules. For both of these reasons (learning to identify language elements and further developing language skills) teachers and other school professionals may want to help children develop their knowledge of the elements of language. That instruction can be delivered in whole-class lessons to all students (tier 1) or to individuals or small groups who have been identified as needing targeted instruction (tier 2).

A variety of professionals may be called on to deliver tier 2 services, including the classroom teacher, a special education teacher, an instructional assistant, and/or a speech-language specialist. Tier 2 instruction is designed to replicate instruction delivered in tier I; therefore, special strategies are usually not used. Instead, the goal is to deliver more focused instruction in small groups. Let's look at some examples of instructional methods that can be used to teach specific language skills.

Phonology. Gillon (2000) studied the effect of phonological awareness training on 91 children aged 5 to 7 years old. The subject sample included 61 children who had been previously identified as having delays in the development of phonological awareness. The remainder of the children had no identified language disorders. The children were divided into one of three groups: a phonological awareness intervention group, a "traditional" language-intervention (articulation therapy) group, and a minimal intervention (control) group that received a monthly consultation from a speech-language pathologist. After several months of instruction, the children in the intensive phonological awareness instruction group had made significant gains in phonological awareness and actually reached the level of their typically developing peers. This, and other studies (e.g., Blischak, Shah, Lombardino, & Chiarella, 2004; Seger & Voerhoeven, 2005) indicate that phonological awareness training can enhance the phonological skills of children with delays in the development of those skills.

The Florida Center for Reading Research is an especially rich source for activities for teaching phonological (and other) language skills. Classroom-based lessons by grade level are available for skills such as phoneme segmentation, phoneme blending, syllables, and many other areas. Another source for phonics and rhyming activities is the Kids Learning Station website. The Florida Assessments for Instruction in Reading (FAIR) website includes lots of activities for teaching language and literacy skills. Go to the FAIR search tool to access the activities.

There are numerous apps available that are designed to help children develop their phonological and phonemic skills. Here are a few examples:

ArtikPix	Flashcards and matching activities for phonological development
Articulate It	Picture cards with audio model of every phoneme in English
Speech Trainer 3D	Provides demonstration of speech sounds with illustration of position of mouth, lips, and tongue
Say It Again	Uses a "Bingo" game format to hear and practice sounds
Speech Stickers	The child chooses one of the five character stickers, and the teacher/therapist places it on the screen and repeats the sound the character makes
ABC Phonics Rhyming	Both versions use a matching game format to help children identify words that rhyme

▶ Watch this demonstration of the features of ArtikPix. What kind of methods does this app use to teach articulation skills?
https://www.youtube.com/watch?v=dO1ZVwsnM8E

Morphology. Connell and Stone (1992) studied the use of a computer-based program to teach 3- to 5-year old children with language impairments to recognize morphological rules under two instructional conditions: modeling (listening to a morpheme being used) and imitation (in which the participant both heard and was prompted to repeat the morpheme). Results indicated that the children with language learning disabilities did much better when taught in the imitation condition than in the modeling condition while the typically developing children did well under both conditions. This study suggests that children with language-learning difficulties can learn better when they are actively involved in instruction.

Based on their review of evidence-based practices to teach morphology, Kirby and Bowers (2012) suggested several instructional practices for teaching morphology, including:

- **Word detective:** Encourage students to search for examples of word patterns (such as addition of the "ing" ending) in class texts.

- **Word sums and word matrices:** Present words that might be related by a base (e.g., interrupt, corrupt, eruption). Have students identify a common base and test their hypotheses using word sums (e.g., inter + rupt, cor + rupt, e + rupt). Then construct a word matrix around this base.

- **Data banks of morphemes:** Create a sticky note morpheme chart in the class, adding affixes and bases as you encounter them.

- **Color-coded morpheme cards:** Students can use one color for prefixes, another for suffixes. As new base words are introduced, have students create corresponding white cards to use in conjunction with their affix cards.

Here is another idea to teach morphology. It is called "Flip-A-Chip" (Mountain, 2002). For this activity, the teacher (or a student) writes syllables or other word parts on each side of four poker (or other plastic) chips. For example, the chips might read, "pro," "re," "duce," and "voke." When the student flips the chips, he or she reads the word parts and says the complete word ("revoke" or "reduce"). The author followed up this activity by having the students fill in the blanks in a paragraph with the words they had created with the chips. The author reported that the students loved playing this "game" and improved their vocabulary skills as well.

Roots to Words (see the Tap to Learn website) is an app that helps children identify word roots and their meaning. The words are organized in categories (e.g., numbers, people, shapes). When the user taps on a category, the meaning of the root (morpheme) appears at the top of the screen (e.g., *tri* = *three*). This is followed by sample words that include the root (e.g., _____angle) and the definition.

Syntax. Eisenberg (2013) identified several evidence-based practices for teaching syntactic skills based on previous research. These included the following:

- **Explicit instruction:** Drill and practice on specific skills.

- **Imitation:** Presenting the child with sentences in the correct form and asking the child to repeat the sentence.

- **Partial imitation:** Presenting a model from one source (such as a picture) and then asking the child to describe a similar picture.

- **Modeling:** The child listens to a set of models while looking at the pictures before being asked to talk about the same set of pictures.

- **Corrected practice:** Prompting the child with a stimulus such as a picture or a sentence fragment; for example (showing a picture of a horse and rider), "Look at the girl. What do you think she is going to do?" If the child makes a grammatical error, the instructor models the correct form and asks the child to repeat it.

Here are some additional suggestions to directly teach syntactic skills:

- **Play the "WH" Twenty Questions game:** The teacher shows the group a bag containing an object. The students must guess what the question is by using "wh" questions (e.g., what, where, who, why).

- **Use a "Mad Libs"–type activity:** Have students dictate (or write, depending on the developmental level of the class) a story. Then the teacher (or a student) can blank out a class of words (for example, all of the nouns). Meanwhile, the students are generating a list of nouns that can be placed in the blanks in the order in which they were listed.

Some additional, web-based games for building sentence skills can be found at the Cookie.com website.

Watch this video of a speech-language specialist working with a child on identifying and using adjectives. How does the specialist help the student apply her knowledge of parts of speech?

Many apps have been developed to teach grammar/syntax skills. Here are two examples:

Sentence Builder | Enables users to drag and drop words from a given sentence into their correct order, building grammar and comprehension skills.
Preposition Builder | Helps elementary-aged children learn the correct use of prepositions and learn how prepositions can change the meaning of a sentence.

Semantics. Several methods for improving the vocabulary knowledge of students with vocabulary-learning difficulties have been developed, including mnemonic strategy instruction (such as the keyword method; Terrill, Scruggs, & Mastropieri, 2004) and semantic mapping (Harris, Schumaker, & Deshler, 2011).

The keyword method uses a three-step process to aid the learner in vocabulary:

Step 1: The target word (e.g., *forte*) is recoded into a word that the student already knows that is acoustically similar word to the target (e.g., keyword = *fort*).

Step 2: An interactive picture is created that contains an action related to the keyword to illustrate the meaning of the target word (e.g., there could be a picture of a fort with guns firing with the sentence, *The guns of the fort were loud.*).

Step 3: The student is prompted to state the meaning of the target word (*forte* means *loud*) using the keyword (*fort*), the action depicted, and the description.

The word mapping strategy used by Harris and colleagues (2011) includes four steps:

Step 1: Break words into their morphemic parts (prefix, suffix, root).
Step 2: Attach meaning to each word part.
Step 3: Make a prediction about the meaning of the unknown word based on the meaning of the parts.
Step 4: Check the dictionary for the definition.

There are also many apps that are available to teach vocabulary and categorization skills to students across different age ranges. Here are two examples:

Category TherAppy | Teaches categorization skills using words and/or pictures
Shape Puzzle | Jigsaw puzzle word-learning game for children

Pragmatics. All students need to have effective communication skills in order to interact with their peers, work in groups, participate in classroom interaction, and negotiate and resolve conflicts with peers. Teachers and other educators can help children develop better skills in communicative interaction, but research has found that they rarely intervene, and when they do, their responses may reduce rather than increase interaction. For example, teachers were reported to primarily use directives (e.g., "You and Michael play together") rather than using less directive statements that would help the children learn on their own ("Teresa can help you tie your shoe") (Kempel, David, & Hysmith, 1997).

Goldstein, Schneider, and Thiemann (2007) identified three methods for teaching pragmatic language skills that have been demonstrated to be effective for both students with and without disabilities. The three methods were as follows:

1. **Peer-mediated methods:** This approach uses peers to engage children who are having difficulty with social communication in communicative interactions. An essential aspect of peer-mediated methods involves teaching the peer how to effectively engage

their partner in conversation. One version of a peer-mediated method is called "Stay-Play-Talk" (Goldstein, English, Shafer, & Kaczmarek, 1997). Students were encouraged to *stay* with their partners during classroom activities such as snack time, *play* with them as appropriate, and *talk* with them during play.

2. **Sociodramatic script method:** Often called "social scripts," in this approach, students are pretaught language for specific situations. This can involve conversation starters, responses, and ideas to connect conversations or change the topic. For example, for a trip to a fast-food restaurant, children might be provided with a script that includes how to request food items. The script might be accompanied by pictures that illustrate some of the items.

3. **Text and graphic cueing:** The best-known application of this method is social stories. Originally developed by Carol Gray, social stories provide a narrative description of a situation that includes four types of sentences:

   - Descriptive: Tells where situations occur, who is involved, what they are doing, and why. Example: "At recess, there are many children playing with the ball."

   - Perspective: Describes the reactions and feelings of the student and of other people. Example: "When I take the ball without asking, it makes the other children angry."

   - Directive: Tells student what to do. Example: "When I want to play with the ball, I will ask the other children first."

   - Control: After the social story is read, the student writes sentences to help him or her remember the information from the social story (often considered optional). Example: The student may respond, "It can make other children angry if I take the ball without asking."

In addition, there are many apps that have been developed for teaching social-communicative skills. Between the Lines (Hamaguchi Apps) is designed for older elementary school students and up, who would benefit from practice interpreting vocal intonation, facial expressions, perspective-taking, body language, and idiomatic or slang expressions. Conversation Builder (Mobile Education Store) was designed to help elementary-age children learn how to have multiexchange conversations with their peers in a variety of social settings.

 This video provides an introduction to the Conversation Builder app. How can the teacher customize conversations with this app?
https://www.youtube.com/watch?v=gJw03l_mXec

Check Your Understanding 13.2
Click here to gauge your understanding of the concepts in this section.

Summary

In this chapter, we described techniques that can be used by teachers to enhance the language and communication of their students in the regular or special education classroom. We began with methods that could be applied in any classroom for all students (tier 1). Then, we focused on methods that could be most useful in specific types of classrooms. Finally, we explored methods that could be used to teach specific language skills either to a whole class or to specific students who need targeted instruction (tier 2).

Intensive Language and Communication Assessment and Instruction

As we know from the preceding chapters, there are children who, despite exposure to language, fail to develop language skills at the same rate or to the same extent as other children. For some of these children, effective instruction in the general education classroom or targeted intervention can be sufficient to enable them to improve their language and communication skills. But some students require more intensive instruction. In this chapter, we will examine effective practices in intensive language instruction.

Learning Outcomes

After completing this chapter, you should be able to:

1. Interpret the results of intensive language assessments.

2. Identify evidence-based methods of intensive instruction in language and communication and the rationale for selecting appropriate methods.

Sarah: A Case Study

Sarah is a seventh-grade student who is in a general education inclusion setting. She is 12 years, 7 months old. Sarah has cerebral palsy and has been classified as otherwise health impaired on her individualized education plan. Sarah has hypertonia, or spastic movements. She experiences significant limitations to her range of motion, and her movements are slow and jerky. Additionally, she experiences involuntary movements of her arms. Sarah is eligible for special education and related services. Sarah has received speech therapy from kindergarten to the present. She has worked on areas such as articulation, oral motor coordination, and most recently, vocal loudness.

During her sixth-grade year, Sarah received speech therapy on a consultative basis to monitor her vocal loudness. Sarah consistently exhibited appropriate speaking volume during the first half of the school year. However, beginning in the third marking period, Sarah became very depressed and withdrawn and refused to speak in class most of the time. Sarah preferred to communicate

by writing things down. To address this issue, positive behavior supports were implemented by her teachers. She exhibited significant inconsistencies using a loud, intelligible voice in the classroom until the end of the school year. In an effort to remedy this, she began to receive pull-out speech therapy sessions to review loud voice speaking strategies, such as sitting up straight and using diaphragmatic breathing. In therapy, during spontaneous speech with the therapist, she used appropriate loudness, but this did not transfer to her speech in the classroom.

In seventh grade, Sarah has made great strides in her classroom speech. She is not demonstrating a depressed demeanor, and she is speaking more in class. Sarah is using a better volume level that can be heard; however, she still has moments where she seems reluctant to speak in class when called upon. In the small-group setting or in partnerships, she will speak to her peers, but she rarely offers her opinion first. Additionally, at times, she has been observed working independently in a group

(continued)

setting. Sarah must be totally comfortable with her partner or group mates in order to fully communicate with them. Although Sarah does not vocalize frequently in class, she is excelling academically. For example, she is an excellent writer, enjoys social studies and science, and has frequently scored at the top of her section in math. Nonetheless, her classroom participation is low. When called on, she will answer with a voice that can be heard; however, she rarely volunteers to answer questions or give opinions to the entire class.

Intensive Assessment

Identification of language difficulties can enable teachers to intervene quickly to address problems that may be preventing children from succeeding academically and/or socially. But some children may not respond or may have disorders that are more significant. For these children, referral for a more detailed, comprehensive assessment might be required. Such assessment would typically be conducted by a speech-language specialist. However, it is the responsibility of the classroom teacher, whether general or special education, in collaboration with the speech-language specialist, to provide appropriate instruction that addresses the issues identified by the assessment. Therefore, it is important that teachers understand the methods and materials used in comprehensive language assessments and be able to interpret the results so that they can deliver instruction effectively.

Development of a comprehensive plan of language assessment should include the following elements:

- Testing of hearing
- Examination of the child's mouth, teeth, and tongue to determine whether malformations may be affecting language production
- Assessment of cognitive functioning
- Observation of language use in school
- A language sample (or other functional assessment of language)
- Formal tests of language

What to Assess

What should be included in a comprehensive assessment of language? Although the answer to this question is affected by factors such as the characteristics of the child and the purposes for testing, there are some broad areas that should be included in most assessments of language. At the core of any assessment of language are the five basic elements of language discussed previously: phonology, morphology, syntax, semantics, and pragmatics. Both the child's understanding and production of each of these elements should be considered. Specific elements of language that might be included in a comprehensive assessment are described in Table 14.1.

A comprehensive assessment of language might also include the evaluation of social, cognitive, and physiological bases of language. We know, for example, that typically developing children engage in a number of prelinguistic communicative routines with their parents. These include turn-taking exchanges, gaze behavior, and the like. Observation of these routines could be included in the assessment of a nonspeaking child. An evaluation of the child's level of cognitive development may provide helpful information on whether the child engages in symbolic play or whether the concept of object permanence seems to be established. Certainly, one would need to know whether the child's speech-processing abilities are

Table 14.1

Language Elements Used in Assessment

Element	Expressive	Receptive
Phonology	Articulation of speech sounds Phonological errors: reduction deletion devoicing substitution	Phonological awareness: rhyme division of words into sounds adding/deleting beginning and ending sounds
Morphology	Use of grammatical morphemes in real and nonsense words	Identification of grammatical morphemes
Syntax	Use of basic sentence elements (e.g., noun, verb) Use of sentence types (simple, complex) Use of transformational rules (question, passive)	Understanding and interpretation of sentence types and transformational rules
Semantics	Vocabulary use: amount types Speed of word retrieval Use of figurative language	Identification of words Comprehension of humor/proverbs
Pragmatics	Use of speech acts: requesting greeting answering Use of conversational rules: turn-taking repairs topic setting	Understanding of direct and indirect speech acts

intact. An examination of the child's mouth and teeth to determine whether they are healthy and intact may be necessary. In addition, a neurological evaluation may be necessary to determine whether the child is physically capable of using and understanding language.

Apply Your Knowledge 14.1: Planning Language Assessment, Case Study: Sarah

Review the case study of Sarah, who was introduced at the beginning of this chapter. Considering her age, history, and current functioning, what language assessments would be recommended for her?

Methods of Language Assessment

There are two basic types of assessment procedures: formal and informal. Formal procedures include tests, checklists, and observation systems. One type of formal assessment—screening tests—was discussed in Chapter 13. In that chapter, we also reviewed several types of informal methods include language sampling, language elicitation techniques, and a variety of classroom-based methods for assessing language skills. In this chapter, we will examine other examples of formal tests of language and discuss one type of informal language assessment procedure—language samples.

Formal Procedures.   **Formal assessment** procedures consist primarily of standardized tests—that is, tests that have a standard set of directions and format. Most standardized tests are also **norm referenced**, which means that the tests compare an individual's

Test Name	Author(s) and Date of Publication	Publisher
Fluharty Preschool Speech and Language Screening Test–Second Edition (FLUHARTY–2)	Fluharty (2000)	Pearson
Preschool Language Scale–5	Zimmerman, Steiner, & Pond (2011)	Pearson
Preschool Language Assessment Instrument–Second Edition (PLAI-2)	Blank, Rose, & Berlin (2003)	Pro-Ed
Receptive-Expressive-Emergent Language Test–Third Edition (REEL-3)	Bzoch, League, & Brown (2003)	Pro-Ed

Table 14.2

Examples of Language Screening Tests

performance to that of a comparison population. Unfortunately, norms do not always include children from a variety of cultural and socioeconomic groups and often do not include children with disabilities.

Despite concerns about norms and test **validity**, use of formal, standardized tests of language continues. Therefore, it is important for practitioners to be aware of the great variety of language tests available, to keep in mind the limitations of these tests, and to learn about alternative assessment procedures—such as those discussed later in this chapter.

Formal tests of language can be divided into three types: screening tests, comprehensive measures, and tests of specific language skills. **Screening** involves the testing of a large number of children in order to identify current levels of functioning and those children who might benefit from more intensive assessment and intervention. The instruments that are used must be relatively brief and easy to administer and interpret. As a result, screening measures may overidentify or underidentify children. In addition, screening tests may fail to identify subtle language difficulties (Reed, 2012). A few examples of screening tests for language skills can be found in Table 14.2.

> Watch the first few minutes of this video as a child is given part of the Preschool Language Scale. How does the tester establish rapport with this child?
> https://www.youtube.com/watch?v=oA5bkoY2H7o

Comprehensive tests of language are designed to test a broad range of language skills across a wide range of ages. For example, the Test of Language Development–Primary (fourth edition) (Newcomer & Hammill, 2008) is designed to assess both expressive and receptive language in children from ages 4 to 9 and comprises nine subtests that cover the areas of phonology, syntax, and semantics. Using scores for each subtest, practitioners can derive an overall language age, as well as gain composite scores for phonology, syntax, semantics, speaking, and listening. The test is relatively easy to administer and interpret. It requires no special training, other than requiring a very careful reading of the manual.

Comprehensive tests of language skills have several advantages, the most important being that they give a reasonably complete picture of the child's language functioning. They provide information about the child's skills in syntax and semantics, and some (but not all) evaluate skills in phonology (e.g., the Test of Language Development–Primary) and pragmatics (see Table 14.3 for some examples). Most of these tests evaluate both receptive and expressive language skills. Because these tests evaluate a wide range of skills, the results reflect the child's skills in various domains of language.

Table 14.3

Examples of Comprehensive Language Tests

Test Name and Author(s)	Age Range (year, month)	Areas Assessed Receptive	Expressive
Clinical Evaluation of Language Fundamentals–5 (Semel, Wiig, & Secord, 2013)	6–0 to 21–0	syn, sem	syn, sem, pho, prag
Comprehensive Assessment of Spoken Language (CASL) (Carrow-Woolfolk, 1999)	3–0 to 21–0	sem, syn, prag	sem, syn, prag
Test of Language Development–Primary (4th edition) (Newcomer & Hammill, 2008)	4–0 to 8–11	pho, syn, sem	pho, syn, sem
Test of Language Development–Intermediate (4th edition) (Hammill & Newcomer, 2008)	8–0 to 12–11	syn, sem	syn, sem
Test of Adolescent and Adult Language (4th edition) (Hammill, Brown, Larsen, & Wiederholt, 2007)	12–0 to 24–11	syn, sem	syn, sem

Sarah (the student presented at the beginning of this chapter) was given the Comprehensive Assessment of Spoken Language (CASL) test. Here were her scores:

Subtest	Raw Score	Standard Score	Test-Age Equivalent (year, month)
Antonyms	24	62	8–8
Synonyms	19	64	8–10
Sentence Completion	30	64	9–6
Syntax Construction	33	64	9–0
Grammatical Morphemes	10	48	6–10
Grammaticality Judgment	27	41	5–4
Nonliteral Language	18	59	10–4
Meaning from Context	5	65	10–2
Pragmatic Judgment	53	75	10–10
Core Composite Score	304	59	N/A

The CASL assessment shows that Sarah is below age expectations in all areas of language. Based on the results of the subtests, Sarah is having particular difficulty with expressive syntax (Grammaticality Judgment and Grammatical Morphemes subtests).

Although comprehensive tests of language can give us valuable information to use in making classification decisions, by their very nature, they are limited in depth. Because they are designed to test a wide range of skills, they do not have a sufficient number of items for in-depth exploration of a specific language domain. Often such in-depth analysis is important for making instructional decisions because teachers need to know whether *specific* language structures are present or absent. Tests of specific domains of language can provide more detailed information about a single area of language. These tests evaluate phonological, syntactic, semantic, or pragmatic skills in greater depth than most general tests of language can (see Table 14.4 for some examples).

Table 14.4

Examples of Tests of Specific Language Skills

Test Name and Author(s)	Age Range (years, month)
Phonology	
Bankson-Bernthal Test of Phonology (Bankson & Bernthal, 1999)	3–0 to 9–0
Test of Phonological Awareness–Second Edition (Torgesen & Bryant, 2004)	5–0 to 8-0
Goldman-Fristoe Test of Articulation–Third Edition (Goldman & Fristoe, 2015)	2–21
Syntax	
Structured Photographic Expressive Language Test–Third Edition (SPELT-3) (Dawson, Stout, & Eyer, 2005)	4 to 9–11
Test of Auditory Comprehension of Language–Fourth Edition (Carrow-Woolfolk, 2004)	3 to 9–11
Semantics	
Boehm Test of Basic Concepts–3 (Boehm, 2000)	K to grade 2
Comprehensive Receptive and Expressive Vocabulary Test–Third Edition (Wallace & Hammill, 2013)	5–0 to 17–11
Peabody Picture Vocabulary Test–4 (Dunn & Dunn, 2007)	2–6 to 90+
Pragmatics	
Test of Pragmatic Language–2 (Phelps-Teraski & Phelps-Gunn, 2007)	6–0 to 18–11

▶ Watch as the Goldman-Fristoe Test of Articulation is administered in this video. What happens when the child fails to identify an item correctly?
https://www.youtube.com/watch?v=kd55ZWoTDc8

Formal, standardized tests can provide important information for making classification and instructional decisions. However, there are significant limitations to the use of standardized tests. Salvia and Ysseldyke (2010) note three particularly troubling issues regarding language assessment. First, standardized tests may not accurately reflect the child's spontaneous language abilities. Because standardized tests must be administered in a very particular way, they do not allow for spontaneous language expression. The child may talk incessantly before and after the testing session, but this cannot be counted as part of the test. A good tester, however, will be sure to note everything about the testing session. A second issue raised by Salvia and Ysseldyke (2010) involves problems associated with the use of test results to plan intervention. They note that many language tests do not easily translate into therapeutic goals. They also caution, as an aside here, that clinicians may be tempted to teach in ways that will improve test scores rather than focus on the skills the child needs for success in the classroom and the community. Third, there is a danger that tests may not adequately assess children from diverse social and cultural backgrounds. This is an especially important concern with language testing, since language is so closely intertwined with social and cultural norms.

Informal Procedures: Language Sampling

One useful way to obtain information about a child's language abilities is by collecting and analyzing a sample of his or her language (Costanza-Smith, 2010). Language samples can be a rich source of information, but they can be difficult to collect and analyze. Most speech-language specialists are trained in methods for eliciting and analyzing language samples in detail. But it is possible to collect brief samples of language in the school setting that can reveal important information about a child's language skills.

The best context in which to obtain a language sample is a realistic setting. In other words, the child's classroom, home, and lunchroom are ideal places to record the sample. If possible, the child should be engaged in real activities, such as working together on a group project or playing a game. Of course observing language in real settings has its drawbacks. Usually there is background noise, and there may be a variety of other distractions in the classroom and the lunchroom. Therefore, the ideal of assessment in a natural setting must be balanced by the realities of the limitations. Sometimes it may be necessary to adapt the setting to make it more possible to get a language sample, for example, by bringing mom into a clinic room that is furnished in a homelike way or by sectioning off a portion of the classroom for language sampling. A representative language sample length of 50 to 100 utterances is optimal (Owens, 2010).

After the language sample has been collected, it must be analyzed. A typical language sample analysis would include some or all of the following elements:

- A measure of syntactic development such as *mean length of utterance* (MLU) for younger children or *t-unit analysis* for older children and adolescents. A t-unit consists of one main clause plus any attached or embedded subordinate clause. This measure has been found to be a rough measure of syntactic complexity in older children (Nippold, 2000).

- A measure of semantic development such as *type-token ratio* (TTR). TTR is calculated by counting the number of *different* words used in a language sample and dividing by the total number of words in the sample.

- Analysis of pragmatic language elements such as initiating or concluding a conversation, topic maintenance, and adjusting language to different speakers.

Language samples are a good way to find out more about the language of a particular child. They can give a more realistic picture of the child's use of language in realistic conversational contexts. Careful analysis of the samples can yield information that can be used for instructional planning.

> ☑ **Check Your Understanding 14.1**
> Click here to gauge your understanding of the concepts in this section.

Intensive Language Instruction

When students continue to lag behind their peers, despite good classroom instruction and appropriate supplementary support, they may be assigned to receive more intensive, individualized instruction. This type of instruction should be targeted at specific language skills, be supported by evidence from research and practice, and be sufficiently intensive to cause an improvement in these skills. Intensive instruction is an expensive and, therefore, a limited commodity, so it is important to be able to identify children who need and may benefit from intervention and to select intervention methods that have the greatest likelihood of success.

There are many types of intensive language instruction (also known as intervention) methods. Some were developed to meet the needs of specific groups of individuals with language and communication disorders. Others are designed to remediate particular aspects of language. Several examples of intensive language-intervention methods have been discussed in earlier chapters of this book (see Table 14.5 for a complete list). Many of these methods were developed for a specific population (such as the Picture Exchange Communication System [PECS] for individuals with autism). Others (such as milieu instruction) have been applied to individuals with many types of disabilities. But even those methods that were originally developed for a specific population could be useful for

Table 14.5

Intervention Methods from Previous Chapters

any child who is having significant difficulty acquiring the types of skills taught by that method. For example, there is no reason that PECS could not be applied to any child with limited spoken language skills.

Every teacher or therapist faces the difficult task of choosing the best method for their students or clients. To determine what kind of intensive instructional method to use, practitioners should consider:

- The abilities and challenges of the individual student
- The child's developmental and instructional history
- The goals (short and long term) for the individual
- Who will deliver the instruction
- Where and how instruction will be delivered
- The evidence that supports the use of this method

The choice of which approach to use can be a daunting one for education professionals. Intervention methods range from highly structured methods (such as discrete trial training) to less structured approaches, like milieu or naturalistic instruction. Some rely on typical development to guide the selection of intervention goals, whereas others emphasize a more functional approach. In practice, many intervention programs combine elements of several of these dimensions (see Figure 14.1).

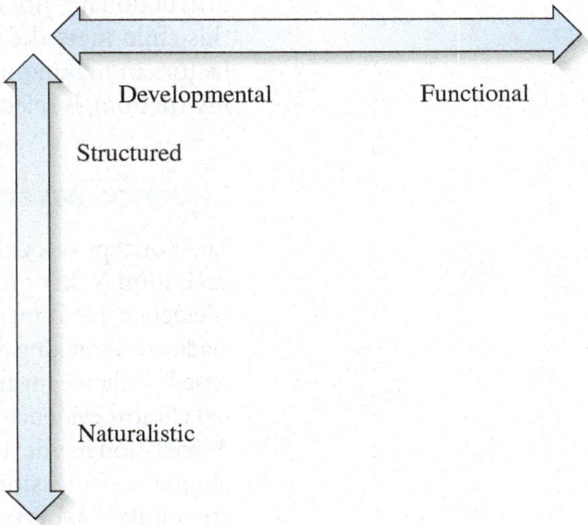

In schools where a more traditional model of problem identification and intervention is in place, children in need of more intensive instruction in language and communication skills may be referred by a parent and/or a classroom teacher for an evaluation of their current level of performance and identification of any related disabilities. When deciding whether a child might benefit for intervention, teachers and parents might want to ask the following questions:

1. *Is the child having difficulty with academic tasks?* For example, does the child have difficulty with reading, spelling, or writing?

2. *Does the child have difficulty participating in classroom interactions?* Does the child have problems understanding directions, following discussions, or contributing to classroom interactions?

Figure 14.1

Dimensions of Language-Intervention Approaches

Developmental — Functional

Structured

Naturalistic

3. *Does the child have difficulty getting along with others?* Are language difficulties causing the child to be teased by others, be misunderstood, or be left out of social activities?

4. *Is the language problem getting worse, getting better, or staying about the same?* If the child is making steady progress, intervention may not be needed. Instead, the child may need to be carefully monitored for a while.

If the answer to at least one of the first three questions is yes, and the problem appears to be getting worse or not improving, the child should be considered for intervention for the speech or language difficulty. This intervention might take place in a clinical setting, such as a speech-language therapy room or a special education resource center, but, increasingly, language intervention is being delivered in the classroom (Reed, 2012).

In a response to intervention service delivery model, intensive instruction is known as tier 3. Children who are continuing to fall behind their peers on measures of academic performance despite supplementary instruction may be candidates for tier 3 intervention. Additionally, children who are experiencing very severe or significant academic, behavioral, or social-emotional problems might be placed directly into tier 3 (Ervin, 2011). Tier 3 instruction is usually delivered by a specialist. In the case of language or literacy difficulties, this might be a special educator and/or a speech-language specialist. The intervention might be delivered in the classroom but is typically provided in a separate therapy or resource room. Intervention might consist of more intensive and more frequent instruction using materials used in tiers 1 and 2, but specialized intervention methods and materials are often used. In some cases, tier 3 might be the point where children are referred for special educational services.

Ervin (2011) suggests that the following considerations should guide the development of tier 3 intervention:

1. What the intervention will look like (i.e., its steps or procedures)

2. What materials and/or resources are needed and whether these are available within existing resources

3. Roles and responsibilities with respect to intervention implementation (i.e., who will be responsible for running the intervention, preparing materials, etc.)

4. The intervention schedule (i.e., how often, for how long, and at what times in the day?) and context (i.e., where, and with whom?)

5. How the intervention and its outcomes will be monitored (i.e., what measures, by whom, and on what schedule?) and analyzed (i.e., compared to what criterion?)

Of these considerations, perhaps the most critical one is what methods will be used. After all, this is a child who has already experienced significant difficulties. Previous instruction has not been successful. The question now becomes, what can we do to help this child meet the performance expectations of his or her age group? One of the key factors in making instructional decisions at any level, but certainly at tier 3 (intensive instruction), is selecting evidence-based practices.

Evidence-Based Practice

The concept of evidence-based practice comes from the medical field. An often-cited definition is that proposed by Sackett, Rosenberg, Gray, Haynes, and Richardson (1996): "Evidence based medicine is the conscientious, explicit, and judicious use of current best evidence in making decisions about the care of individual patients. The practice of evidence based medicine means integrating individual clinical expertise with the best available external clinical evidence from systematic research." The American Speech-Language-Hearing Association has developed a position statement on evidence-based practice for speech and language professionals that includes both the use of high-quality research evidence and clinical expertise in making intervention decisions (you can review the statement on their website).

This video explains the concept of evidence-based practice and how it can be used in decision making. What factors does the video suggest are needed to make evidence-based practice effective?
https://www.youtube.com/watch?v=Xiv75BLGtrs

Although the idea that teachers and other school professionals should use research to guide practice should hardly seem to be controversial, it is, in many cases, a departure from past practices. Slavin (2002) and others have noted that it is only very recently that educators have begun to rely more on scientific evidence than on past practice or opinion. Similarly, in the speech and language field, practitioners have traditionally been taught to consider their clients' wishes and their own experience in making clinical decisions rather than relying on research to guide practice (Gillam & Gillam, 2006).

The No Child Left Behind legislation called for educators to use "scientifically based" practices in delivering education. In response, the U.S. Department of Education has established the Institute of Education Sciences (visit the institute's website for more information) to disseminate information about effective practices, and many professional organizations (including the American Speech-Language-Hearing Association and Council for Exceptional Children) are at work to identify and inform their members about educational practices that are supported by research.

Implementing evidence-based practices in the classroom and in clinical practice is not always as easy as it may seem at first glance. As Ratner (2006) has pointed out, sometimes there is too little valid research available on a particular practice. Sometimes there is conflicting evidence. Ratner (2006) also reminds us that effective methods are only as good as the practitioners who implement them. Still, it is essential that teachers and other professionals attempt to use research-validated instructional practices and, when the research is not available, that they participate in studies of educational practices whenever feasible.

Gillam and Gillam (2006) proposed a seven-step process for using evidence-based practice for decision making as follows:

Step 1: This step involves creating the clinical question. The authors suggest that clinicians should specify the instructional target, the developmental level of the child, and the type of learning difficulty of the child.

Step 2: In the next step, the clinician (or teacher) should look for research evidence on interventions designed to address the type of problem identified in step 1. Resources such as research databases (e.g., the Education Resources Information Center [ERIC] or the What Works Clearinghouse; see the websites for these databases) can be the place to start the search.

Step 3: The practitioner evaluates the quality of the evidence. That can be difficult when there are many studies and contradictory findings. One approach is to consider the preponderance of the evidence. If 9 out of 10 studies have reached a similar conclusion, it is more likely that this approach is effective.

Step 4: Consider student and family factors, such as cultural values and beliefs, student interests, and family resources.

Step 5: Consider personal and agency factors. The practitioner may be better prepared to carry out one type of intervention over another. Similarly, school district or agency policies, practices, and finances may need to be factored into the decision-making process.

Step 6: Integrate the evidence to make a final decision. This can be simple when the research evidence, previous practice, the practitioner's preparation, and the school's ability to support the approach match. But in some cases, parents prefer one approach over another or the school may have invested in an approach that does not appear to meet the criteria for being evidence-based. Gillam and Gillam (2006) suggest that greater emphasis should be placed on the research evidence for making instructional decisions.

Step 7: Evaluate the outcomes of the selected procedure.

Developmental and Functional Approaches

One of the major questions in language instruction is how information about language development can and should be used in planning therapy for children with language disorders. Knowledge of the usual steps and timing of typical language development can provide a benchmark against which the language development of any individual child can be compared. Knowing what *should* come next can help in determining what should be taught next. However, at times, developmental evidence has been used to deny children access to instruction. For many children with significant learning difficulties, waiting for children to develop so-called "prerequisite" skills before engaging them in reading or writing or using augmentative communication methods may mean that they will never have these opportunities.

Because we know that children with disabilities often acquire language in the same sequence (although more slowly) as nondisabled children, it makes sense to follow developmental guidelines in planning language goals. This was the hypothesis tested by Dyer, Santarcangelo, and Luce (1987). In a series of studies, they taught phonetic sounds and syntactic structures to children with severe language disabilities. They found that earlier-emerging forms (e.g., /b/ sounds) were learned in fewer trials than were later-emerging forms (e.g., /z/ sounds). Moreover, later-emerging forms were never acquired unless the earlier forms had been learned. Here, using typical language development as a guideline turned out to be a useful way of planning instructional goals for these students with severe language disorders.

Although knowledge of typical language development can be helpful in planning language instruction, Owens (2010) suggests that we should be cautious in using development too strictly to guide intervention. He points out, for example, that it would be a mistake to teach children with language delays to go through all the steps that typically developing children use to get to the final form of a language structure. It is not necessary for a child to say *goded* before learning the correct irregular past-tense form, *went*. Owens suggests that developmental hierarchies can best be used as broad guidelines for instruction—for help in determining which structures are less complex—and should therefore be taught prior to more complex structures. Having knowledge of language development can also help the instructor avoid leaps that are too great for the child to master.

Largely as a result of concerns about the role of typical development in planning language instruction, some have suggested that instruction should focus on teaching specific skills that the children will need in their immediate environment. Sometimes called **functional approaches**, these instructional programs seek to identify skills that the children need in order to be successful in their present environment or in one that they will soon be entering. For example, if a child needs to request materials in the classroom, then practice on requesting might be an instructional goal. Although functional goals can be very useful to help a child master a short-term task, they may not lead to generalization of the skill to new environments.

It is possible to combine a developmental approach to language instruction with a functional approach. Language development should be seen as a framework within which there can be considerable variation. This is true for typically developing children and even more true for children with disabilities. Information about typical language development should be used as a way to identify children at risk for language disorders and as a way to develop an overall sequence of skills. The child's age and status should most importantly determine how developmental guidelines are used. In general, developmental hierarchies are less valid for older children and children with more severe disabilities. These children are more likely to benefit from programs that focus on skills needed in their current environment, skills of functional communication and general literacy. But instructional objectives can always be put in functional terms. In other words, typical development can be used as a guideline for the selection of instructional objectives. The objectives themselves can be put in functional terms that will enable the child to enhance their functionality in natural settings.

Remember Sarah, the 12-year-old student with intellectual disabilities. Sarah's teacher completed a speech and language checklist in which she identified a number of areas of difficulty, including poor or limited vocabulary, incorrect use of grammar, difficulty expressing thoughts, and difficulty with storytelling. Sarah's teacher decided that one skill that Sarah needed to work on was vocabulary development. Using Quizlet, a website that enables students to develop their own flashcards, Sarah's teacher gave her three vocabulary words to learn each week. The words were not taken from a standardized word list but rather from areas of high interest for Sarah, including sports and community activities. In this way, Sarah's teacher combined a developmental goal (expansion of vocabulary) with functional objectives (computer use and words that Sarah would need in the community).

Structured and Naturalistic Methods

Structured language instructional approaches are typically used with a standardized set of instructions and materials. They take the child through a sequence of steps toward a goal that is set by the teacher or therapist prior to instruction. Instruction is usually delivered for extensive periods of time over a long duration. Earlier in this book, some highly structured intervention methods, such as direct instruction (Chapter 8) and discrete trial training (Chapter 9), were discussed. Although highly structured programs can work, they have been criticized for being unnatural. That is, the instructional procedures are unlike what the child is likely to encounter in the real world, and as a result, children may master *splinter skills*—skills that are relatively useless. For example, a child might learn to identify a picture of a "spoon" by pointing to the picture of when it is presented along with two other pictures of utensils. However, the child may be unable to request a spoon when she needs one to eat her lunch.

Naturalistic approaches emphasize the delivery of language intervention in natural settings, using dispersed trials that follow the child's lead and using reinforcers indicated by the child's preferences (Warren & Kaiser, 1986). Although language-instruction goals may be set prior to instruction, the language facilitator is encouraged to be responsive to the child. The language facilitator may structure the environment in ways that will lead toward a language goal but should follow the child's lead and be responsive to the child rather than to a set of instructions. Therefore, if the child uses structures that were not anticipated or wants to talk about topics that were not part of the plan, the facilitator should follow the child's lead.

A number of different instructional approaches can be grouped under the general heading of naturalistic instruction, including:

1. *Modeling.* A verbal model is presented that is related to the student's interests. The student is reinforced if a response occurs. If there is no response, the model is repeated. For example, if a child were playing with a favorite toy, the teacher might say, "Barney." If the child responds with the word, the teacher could extend the conversation, such as, "I like Barney." If the child made no response, the teacher would repeat the sequence.

2. *Time delay.* When using this procedure, the language facilitator moves close to the child and looks at the child for 5 to 15 seconds while waiting for the child to talk. If the child does not initiate an interaction, the adult can provide a verbal prompt or model an initiation.

3. *Incidental teaching.* Warren and Kaiser (1986) describe incidental teaching as including the following elements:

   - Arranging the environment to increase the likelihood that the child will initiate to the adult
   - Selecting language targets appropriate for the child's skill level, interests, and environment
   - Responding to the child's initiations with requests for elaborated language
   - Reinforcing the child's communicative attempts with attention and access to the objects and activities with which the child has expressed interest

Research on Intervention Efficacy

In general, research has found that language intervention can be effective. A meta-analysis of a large number of studies found that language intervention was effective for children with phonological or vocabulary difficulties and somewhat effective for children with syntax difficulties. Intervention was not found to be effective for children with receptive language difficulties (Law, Garrett, & Nye, 2004). Cirrin and Gillam (2008) pointed out that although a number of intervention methods have shown promise, there is still a limited research base to support the effectiveness of language-intervention methods.

Some intervention methods have been found to work better with particular groups of children. For example, research by Connell (1987) and Connell and Stone (1992) found that modeling correct language was sufficient to improve the language skills of typically developing children but did not have the same effect on the language of children with specific language impairments. For those children, modeling combined with imitation was much more effective for improving the acquisition of grammatical morphemes.

One major question about the efficacy of language-intervention methods is whether highly structured methods (such as discrete trial training) are more effective than more naturalistic methods (such as milieu teaching). This question was directly studied by Yoder, Kaiser, and Alpert (1991). In their study, a less structured (milieu) approach was compared to a more structured (communication training program) language-instruction program. They found that the milieu approach worked best for the children with the most serious language impairments. The more structured program worked best for the higher-functioning children. The authors speculated that one reason for their findings may have been that the lower-functioning children benefited more from a program that emphasized the generalization of language skills (the milieu approach). A number of research studies have found that milieu teaching methods can be effective for enhancing the language skills of children with disabilities (Kaiser, Yoder, & Keetz, 1992). However, other studies have found that highly structured programs, such as discrete trial training, can also be effective (e.g., Downs, Downs, Johansen, & Fossum, 2007).

The results of research on language intervention suggest that factors such as the child's age and degree of disability, as well as the aspect of language being taught, should be considered when making decisions about the goals and methods of intervention. Developmental guidelines seem to be most appropriate for younger children. Goals developed from the demands of the environment (functional goals) are also useful, especially for older students and students with more severe disabilities. Structured-intervention procedures may work best for teaching discrete skills such as vocabulary. Instruction that takes place in natural settings can be effective if there are clear goals.

Generalization

The ultimate goal of language intervention should always be to make the child a more effective communicator. Therefore, no matter what intervention method teachers and speech-language specialists choose to use, they should always consider that the skills taught need to be generalized to new situations. Because many individuals with disabilities have difficulty generalizing learned skills, it is especially important to teach those skills in ways that will enhance generalization.

Some strategies to enhance the generalization of language skills include:

- Teaching in contexts that are as close to the natural environment as possible
- Using a variety of materials and examples to teach a new task
- Using a variety of communicative partners
- Teaching skills demanded by the environment
- Using reinforcers that are available in the natural environment (e.g., praise)

Let's try an example. We are trying to help Jason, a 10-year-old student with autism, to initiate conversations with his peers. Currently, he gets the attention of his peers by touching them. If they do not respond, he may escalate to hitting them. So, Jason's teacher decided to use modeling and coaching of communication skills to help Jason replace his current behavior with one that is more socially acceptable. His teacher modeled for Jason how to request something he needs, for example saying, "Please give me a marker." Then she had Jason practice this skill several times with her, receiving feedback from the teacher. But Jason's teacher did not stop there. She sometimes had the classroom assistant provide the modeling and feedback. She also used other objects and situations in the training. After Jason demonstrated that he had learned how to request different kinds of things in several situations, she asked one of his peers to provide the model. Finally, she created opportunities in the classroom for Jason to use his new requesting skills and was there to provide coaching to Jason as he performed his newly learned skill. Using multiple instructors, a variety of materials and situations, and practice in the actual settings where Jason would need to perform his newly learned skills, the teacher provided many opportunities for generalization of the skill.

This video shows methods that can be used to enhance the generalization of skills. What does the video suggest that teachers do to increase generalization of skills in their students?

https://www.youtube.com/watch?v=xU395HgXI2s

Apply Your Knowledge 14.2: Generalization of Instruction

Give two suggestions for how Sarah's teacher could enhance the generalization of the vocabulary words that Sarah is learning.

Collaboration

One of the keys to the success of any type of instruction is the collaboration among those who are responsible for the planning, implementation, and evaluation of the intervention. For students with language and communication disorders, a team approach that includes the child's parent, classroom teacher, and one or more specialists such as a speech-language pathologist and/or a special educator is required. Each of these partners brings essential knowledge and skills to bear on identifying the child's challenges and designing an effective program to address the issues. Parents can provide essential background information about the child as well as insights on how the child performs at home and in the community. The classroom teacher knows how the child interacts with peers and adults in the classroom and how the child is progressing in literacy skills and academic subjects. The specialist brings his or her knowledge of child development, language training, and instructional supports to the task.

Ideally, all of the team partners work together to help the child develop the skills he or she needs for success in school, at home, and in the community. Unfortunately, that ideal is not always achieved. That is why it is important for school professionals to understand the principles for successful collaboration and how to apply those principles to instructional planning and delivery.

Collaboration has been defined as "a style for direct interaction between at least two co-equal parties voluntarily engaged in shared decision making as they work toward a common goal" (Friend & Cook, 2007, p. 7). There are some key words in this definition. The first is the word "style." Friend and Cook (2007) claim that successful collaboration requires that partners engage with each other in a style that encourages free and open interaction. The participants must be willing to listen to the contributions of others and respond to their suggestions in ways that value what is said. A second key word is "equal." Ideally, all partners should feel that they have an equal role in the planning or implementation of instruction. In reality, sometimes there can be defensiveness and claims of ownership over some aspects of the discussion. Parents may not be included as full partners on the team or may insist on the use of a strategy that the rest of the team believes is not appropriate for the child. A third critical concept is "shared" decision making. Instructional planning and delivery work best when everyone shares responsibility for the success of the program and is willing to objectively examine the results of the intervention.

Friend (2014) identified five elements as essential for successful collaboration:

1. *Personal commitment:* There must be a commitment to collaboration as a worthwhile approach to intervention planning and delivery.

2. *Communication skills:* Participants must be able to engage in active listening, where each participant is encouraged to contribute to the discussion. Additionally, participants should strive to describe a behavior rather than make an evaluative comment that cuts off discussion. For example, instead of saying, "Jose is disrespectful of others," his teacher might say, "On two occasions last week, Jose tried to take a toy away from one of his classmates."

3. *Interaction processes:* The team should develop a process for problem solving that includes identification of the problem, generation of alternative methods for addressing the problem, a process for deciding which method to implement, and deciding the criteria for success and how that will be evaluated.

4. *Programs/services:* The team must decide which programs and services will be required and how they will be delivered.

5. *Context:* In order for collaborative planning and instruction to be successful, there needs to be a culture of collaboration. School leaders need to understand the value of collaboration and provide the time and resources that are required to make collaboration work.

 Watch this video of a collaborative planning discussion. What does the team leader do to engage each team member in the discussion?

Implementing a successful collaboration model can be challenging. At first, all of the pieces suggested by Friend (2014) may not be in place. The team may need to work hard to ensure that all members are heard and that a plan is developed that all support. However, when collaboration works, it can enhance the success of any intervention program.

 Check Your Understanding 14.2
Click here to gauge your understanding of the concepts in this section.

Apply Your Knowledge 14.3: **Sarah's Instructional Plan**
 Review Sarah's instructional plan and develop at least two additional suggestions for teaching one language or literacy skill.

Summary

In this chapter, we discussed methods that can be used when students require more intensive instruction. Assessment procedures and methods that could be used to identify more precisely the language and communication needs of students were presented. A discussion of methods for planning and delivering language intervention followed. The use of evidence-based practices, teaching for generalization, and the importance of collaboration were emphasized.

Augmentative and Alternative Communication

Some school-age children have significant disabilities that make it difficult for them to develop spoken language. Until recently, there was little that could be done for these children. They were often relegated to the back wards of institutions or employed in nonproductive sheltered workshop activities. Today new technologies offer hope for these individuals who previously lacked access to that most important human characteristic—communication. These new approaches are called augmentative and alternative communication (AAC).

This chapter examines the rapidly developing field of augmentative and alternative communication, describing a variety of approaches—from sign systems to sophisticated electronic devices. Most important, instructional methods that are designed to develop the functional use of AAC systems are discussed. The goal of this chapter is to help you become aware of the many options that are available for persons who do not speak and how to best use these procedures in classroom settings.

Learning Outcomes

After completing this chapter, you should be able to:

1. Describe the components of augmentative and alternative communication systems.

2. Describe effective methods and procedures for implementing augmentative and alternative communication and the outcomes associated with these methods.

Howard, a student with fragile X syndrome, has severe articulation problems that make his speech difficult to understand. He carries a communication wallet with pictures he shows others so they can understand what he is talking about. When he goes to McDonald's, he uses pictures from the wallet to help him order his meal.

Melissa, a 16-year-old girl with autism, rarely talks. She has learned to communicate with a Touch Talker. Now, she can respond to questions from her teacher by touching a symbol on her display, activating a voice output device that serves as her voice.

Tony, a 9-year-old student with cerebral palsy, attends a general education classroom. Because of his limited motor abilities, he uses a head pointer to touch an electronic keyboard to formulate written messages and produce a voice output.

Tanya, a student with Down syndrome, has learned a repertoire of eight signs that she uses to supplement her limited spoken output.

What all of these individuals have in common is that they are using some type of augmentative or alternative communication (AAC) procedure. For many, if not most, children with severe disorders of language and communication, AAC represents their best hope for the development of communication skills.

According to the American Speech-Language-Hearing Association (ASHA), more than two million people in the United States with significant language impairments use AAC devices. Although there are no nationwide data on the number of school-age children who use AAC devices, surveys within states have indicated that the percentage of preschool special education students who use AAC devices ranges from 12 percent in Pennsylvania (Binger & Light, 2006) to 30 percent in Connecticut (Worah, 2011). In the latter survey, it was found that 3 percent of students who were identified as in need of special education were receiving AAC services.

Federal law in the United States has recognized the growing importance of AAC systems by including provisions regarding the use of AAC in the Americans with Disabilities Act and the Individuals with Disabilities Education Act (IDEA). IDEA regulations now require that assistive technology be considered as part of the planning for children with disabilities. If it is determined that an assistive technology such as AAC is required, the school must purchase the device and train staff in its use.

Components of Augmentative and Alternative Communication

Augmentative and alternative communication (AAC) systems are designed to supplement or replace the natural language and communication of persons with disabilities. The International Society for Augmentative and Alternative Communication (ISAAC) has defined augmentative and alternative communication as "a set of tools and strategies that an individual uses to solve everyday communicative challenges." The ISAAC website includes information about and resources to increase understanding of AAC. AAC may include existing speech or vocalizations, gestures, manual signs, and aided communication (Sevcik & Romski, 2007).

 Watch this video about AAC. In what ways can AAC systems be used to support language and learning?
http://www.youtube.com/watch?v=r3m8_YmTDDM

AAC systems typically are thought of as consisting of four components: *communication aids* (or *devices*), *communication techniques*, *symbol systems*, and *communication strategies* (Sevcik & Romski, 2007). Each of these components must be considered when an AAC procedure is being developed. Sometimes most attention is lavished on the communication device, especially if it is a particularly high-tech system. Teachers and speech-language specialists must be careful not to become so caught up in the technical sophistication of the device that they ignore the other components of AAC systems. After all, the device is of little use if the user cannot understand it or does not use it.

Techniques

There are two basic kinds of AAC techniques, aided and unaided. **Unaided augmentative communication techniques** do not require external support devices or procedures in order to operate. They include techniques such as sign language and gestural cueing systems. Unaided techniques have the obvious advantages of portability and speed of message preparation (Wilkinson & Hennig, 2007). There are no concerns about electrical outlets or battery packs. Of course, when a sign language is used as the mode of communication (e.g., American Sign Language or Signed English), there will be a more limited number of potential communication partners.

Aided augmentative communication techniques use communication means that may be as simple as a communication board or as complex as a computer with a synthetic speech output device. Low (or light) technology-aided systems include symbol boards, communication books, or picture systems such as the Picture Exchange Communication System (PECS) (Bondy & Frost, 2001). Wilkinson and Hennig (2007) point out that since light-technology methods require the communication partner to speak the words that the child selects, the result can be a highly interactive communicative exchange. However, low-technology communication systems require that the communication partner be very familiar with the user's communication style and experiences.

High-technology systems use microcomputers or, increasingly, a handheld device and specialized software or applications to provide the user with a voice. As technology has changed, these devices have become more powerful and more portable. The use of high-technology systems such as speech-generating devices (SGDs) have been found to be very effective for increasing the communication of individuals with significant language and communication disorders (Rispoli, Franco, van der Meer, Lang, & Carmargo 2010; Schlosser, 2003). As powerful and useful as high-technology devices can be, they are not always the best choice for every individual. Concerns about cost, vulnerability to damage, voice quality, and speed of interaction continue to exist despite technological advances (Wilkinson & Hennig, 2007).

A relatively new development that has the potential to revolutionize the use of AAC is the development of communication apps for mobile devices. In Chapter 13, we reviewed a few of the apps that are available to teach language skills. Similarly, there has been a proliferation of apps to enhance communication. Perhaps the best known is Proloquo2Go (AssistiveWare). Although this and other communication apps may have limitations not found in the most advanced augmentative communication devices, they have the advantage of being relatively inexpensive and easy to use. However, at this time, there is no published research on their effectiveness.

 One of the developers of Proloquo2Go is interviewed in this video. What does he describe as the advantage of this app over other kinds of AAC methods?
https://www.youtube.com/watch?v=vomkNSluWW4

Four features are common to all communication aids, electronic or not: output, selection technique, vocabulary capability, and portability.

Output refers to the appearance of the display and how it enhances communication with a listener. Communication boards typically consist of a flat surface on which drawn or written symbols are displayed. They can be placed on a wheelchair lap tray, bound in a book, or folded into a wallet-sized container. The output is a visual display that the user accesses by pointing. Electronic devices may use a visual display, a printed output, or a voice output. Visual displays allow listeners to check their understanding of the message and to even offer corrections or suggestions for extension of the communication. SGDs, also known as **voice output communication aids (VOCAs),** have the advantage of being the closest approximation to natural speech and can be used at a distance.

There are two types of voice output devices currently in use: *synthesized speech* and *digitized speech.* Synthesized speech devices generate speech-like sounds by electronically combining speech sounds. They can be used in text-to-speech applications where typed text is converted to vocal output. Digitized voice output systems use real speech that is converted to a digital format that is then reconverted into speech output. Digitized speech output is superior to synthesized speech in producing the inflections of human speech and has been found to be more intelligible than synthesized speech in children as young as 3 to 5 years of age (Drager et al., 2006).

A second common feature of communication aids is the **selection technique** employed. Users of a communication aid must indicate to their communication partner which letter or symbol they wish to select. Individuals with intact motor skills may use *direct selection.* In this case, the "speaker" simply points to a selected item. For those who have little or no voluntary control of their arms, adaptations can be used to allow them to make direct selections. These might be a head pointer (a rod attached to a headband) or an eye gaze system that identifies the selected item when the user looks at it for a period of time.

Direct selection is usually the fastest type of selection technique; however, some individuals with significant motor impairments need another type of selection method. *Scanning* is an alternative. Scanning involves making a selection from the presented choices. Rather than directly selecting the desired word or symbol, with scanning, choices are displayed for the individual. Typically, scanning is associated with electronic displays that present a blinking light (cursor) that moves from item to item on the display panel. The user selects an item by merely pressing a button (or a switch or pad) or making some other motor movement that stops the scanning. The cursor may move across the display in a linear motion, in up-and-down columns, or in any other preprogrammed way. Scanning devices can be coupled with various types of switches so that the individual who has any voluntary muscle control at all can operate a communication device.

Vocabulary capability varies with the type of system and the type of displays. Static displays include a limited number of vocabulary items that are presented in a fixed format so that the user always sees the items in the same presentation order. In order to present new vocabulary, the page is changed. Dynamic displays use linked pages and a branching structure to display vocabulary. Touching one symbol may take the user to related pages with multiple words. Although static displays can present only a limited number of items at a time, they may be useful for individuals who are learning new words. Dynamic displays provide greater flexibility but are also more complex.

Communication boards use static displays with overlays that can be changed for various settings and activities. Most electronic devices can be reprogrammed and the overlay changed to meet changing communicative needs. The ease with which such changes can be made and the number and usefulness of the items on the display are factors that should be considered in the design or selection of a communication aid.

▶ This video explains how a communication board can be organized. How does the presenter suggest that the board be used to enhance communication?
https://www.youtube.com/watch?v=UwxoJQvZkZY

▶ Watch this video to understand more about augmentative communication devices. What is the advantage of dynamic displays?
https://www.youtube.com/watch?v=OU_fj310t80

Portability is the final feature of communication aids. Portability is an important concern in an era when emphasis is on the integration of persons with disabilities into their schools and communities. As technology advances, the devices are becoming smaller and more powerful. Clearly, a communication device is of little help if it cannot be used in the settings where it is really needed. Therefore, it is essential that portability be considered when decisions about communication devices are being made.

There are advantages and limitations to the use of either aided or unaided procedures (see Table 15.1). Ideally, unaided communication techniques would be the choice for everyone. But there are many individuals who are unable to develop spoken language or understand and use nonverbal communication or sign language. For these persons, aided communication methods are the best alternative. When appropriately designed or selected, aided communication devices permit people with severe impairments in motor and/or cognitive abilities to communicate with others.

	Advantages	Disadvantages
Unaided Systems	No external support devices needed Portable No cost (other than training)	Potential communication partners limited Relies on user's memory ability Signs may be difficult to learn
Aided Systems	Can produce message that is more complex than user's own language Can communicate at a distance (with VOCAs)	Electronic device may break or lose power Portability may be limited May be expensive

Symbol Systems

Unaided AAC systems use language—spoken or signed. Studies examining the acquisition of sign systems by individuals with disabilities have generally found that such persons can acquire at least a basic sign vocabulary (Tincani, 2004). Although a sign language system may be a useful form of communication for some students, for many students with disabilities, sign language is not an effective approach to the development of communication skills. With signing, there is the obvious problem of the limited number of potential communication partners available. If the goal for persons with disabilities is community inclusion, sign language may not be the most effective approach. Therefore, many of these students require some sort of alternative approach that might include an aided AAC system.

Any AAC device must have some sort of symbol system as the mode of communication. For individuals with severe motor disorders but good literacy skills, letters and words can be the symbolic mode. But many users of AAC systems either have not had the opportunity to acquire literacy skills or have cognitive disabilities that impair their acquisition of written language. A variety of symbol systems ranging from real objects to photographs to abstract-symbol systems have been developed to aid these persons in communicating with an AAC system.

Photographs have the advantage of clearly representing an item. Of course, the quality of the photograph will affect its usefulness. Photos that include a contextual background (a spoon that appears next to a plate) are more recognizable. Additionally, in general, color photographs are more easily recognized than black-and-white photos (Mirenda & Locke, 1989). An alternative to photos is line drawings. These usually are composed of black lines drawn on a white background.

A number of abstract-symbol systems are available, including *Picture Communication Symbols* (PCS) (Johnson, 1981), *Picsyms* (Carlson, 1984), *Sigsymbols* (Creagan, 1982), and *Blissymbols* (Bliss, 1965). All of these graphic symbol systems include pictorial representations of the items they name. In addition, Sigsymbols include ideographs (ideas represented through graphic symbols) and Blissymbols include both ideographs and arbitrary symbols (ideas assigned arbitrary configurations of lines). *Rebus* symbols are another form of line drawing used with AAC systems. Rebuses use pictures of objects to replace the word in a sentence. A number of rebus systems are commercially available (e.g., see the Widgit Software website).

Communication Skills

AAC procedures and devices present wonderful opportunities for nonspeaking persons to communicate with others. Yet, if the systems are not used or not used effectively, the intervention is of no use, no matter how high-tech the device.

Research on the use of AAC systems has found that users tend to be relatively passive communicative partners. They rely on their speaking listeners to direct the conversation, rarely initiate interaction themselves, and often fail to respond to attempted conversational initiations from their peers (Chung, Carter, & Sisco, 2012; Mirenda & Iacono, 1990). One factor in this breakdown of communication may be the nature of the communicative opportunities provided by partners. Communicative partners have often been observed to provide instructions or make comments that do not encourage continued interaction (Chung et al., 2012; Reichle, 1991).

In addition to their rarely initiating conversation, AAC users have been found to have difficulty terminating conversations (Reichle, 1991). Some simply do not know how to do this. Others want to extend the conversation as long as possible, even if the interaction is no longer meaningful. Some AAC users have even been reported to make untrue statements simply to keep a conversation going (Reichle, 1991).

Check Your Understanding 15.1

Click here to gauge your understanding of the concepts in this section.

Implementing AAC Systems

Prerequisite Skills

One of the major issues in AAC involves prerequisites to its use. For many years, it was claimed that in order to be successful, potential users of AAC systems had to have achieved certain cognitive and language prerequisites. Sometimes called the *candidacy* model, this approach suggested that the potential AAC user should be able to demonstrate development to at least stage V (means-end relations) on Piaget's description of cognitive development and show evidence of intentional communication before being introduced to an AAC system (Cress & Marvin, 2003). The idea that AAC users needed these cognitive and language prerequisites was based on data from spoken language acquisition in normally developing children. These data indicated that specific cognitive and communicative behaviors preceded the emergence of spoken language. However, as Romski and Sevcik (2005) have noted, the exact relationship between cognition and communication development and language acquisition has never been clearly defined. Moreover, research indicates that persons with disabilities can benefit from AAC systems even if they lack these cognitive and communicative prerequisites. For example, Reichle and Yoder (1985) were able to teach preschoolers who functioned at Stage IV on a Piagetian scale to label objects using graphic symbols. Although the preschoolers were unable to generalize this skill to functional communication, such as commenting and requesting, they were able to label. Romski, Sevcik, and Pate (1988) taught young adults with severe intellectual disability to request foods and objects by using graphic symbols on a computer display panel, despite the subjects' lack of spoken language comprehension skills.

Because of research such as that described earlier and the realization that research from normal language development is not always easily translated to individuals with disabilities, today most clinicians and researchers are suggesting a try-and-see, rather than a wait-and-see, model for potential AAC users (McGregor, Young, Gerak, Thomas, & Vogelsberg, 1992). As Cress and Marvin (2003) put it, the only prerequisites needed for use of an AAC system are, "natural actions and behaviors," that is, any behavior or actions that others interpret as communicative.

Preassessment

As with any kind of intervention, the development of an AAC system begins with assessment. The most useful kind of assessment is one that is ecological in nature, that is, one that surveys the communicative environments and communicative needs in which the individual will function. McCormick and Wegner (2003) described a comprehensive assessment system for potential AAC users that includes the following elements:

- *The student:* They suggest that the assessment team ask questions such as the following:

  How does the student communicate now and for what purposes?

  What are the student's communication needs and goals?

  Where and with whom does the student need to communicate?

  What are the student's language, cognitive, sensory, and motor skills and capabilities?

  What are the potential barriers to the student communicating in his or her natural environment?

- *Mobility assessment:* Including seating, positioning, and ambulation.

- *Motor assessment:* To what extent can the student use hands for signing, pointing, and typing? Can the student have control over head movement, eye gaze, or other motor movements to communicate?

- *Communication assessment:* Interviews with teachers and family members and direct observation can address questions such as the following:

  How does the student currently communicate in different contexts?

  What communicative modes and functions does the student use?

  How effective are the student's present communication modes?

  What does the student communicate about?

  What motivational factors may have the potential to affect the student's communication?

- *Cognitive/linguistic assessment:* Including receptive language and cognitive development to determine the following:

  How does the student currently understand the world?

  How can communication be best facilitated within this understanding?

  To what extent can the student meet the cognitive demands of various symbol sets and systems?

- *Sensory/perceptual assessment:* How does the student process incoming information? Which sensory systems are intact?

- *Literacy assessment:* Including print and phoneme recognition, word recognition, reading comprehension, and spelling.

- *The environment:* What curricular and social activities could the student access with the use of an AAC system? Assessment should include the following:

  Communicative preferences and skills of potential partners

  Potential barriers in the environment such as attitudes, skills, and knowledge of teachers, support staff, and peers

  Opportunities to use AAC systems in natural environments

 Watch this video to learn more about the implementation of AAC in schools. What procedures are used for conducting a preassessment?
https://www.youtube.com/watch?v=BWy0hPggcBc

Developing an AAC System

Using the results of assessment, the AAC development team needs to design a system that will help the user participate in academic, functional, and social activities in a variety of environments and improve the quality and quantity of the child's language and communication skills. Decisions need to be made about the *type* of system to be used (aided or unaided), the nature of the *symbol system* (e.g., gestural, pictorial, symbolic), and the communication instruction required.

Deciding the type of system to be used—aided or unaided—is the first decision needed in designing an AAC system. The provider must weigh the advantages and limitations of each type of system in combination with information about the learner and the communicative environment. Characteristics of the learner, such as sensory and motor skills, may determine what kind of system is possible. Similarly, environmental demands and opportunities will also have an impact on this decision. If potential communication partners are not familiar with American Sign Language, this might be a poor choice for an AAC system.

In many cases, the choice of a communication system is not as critical as it might seem. Frequently, a combination of communication systems, including both aided and unaided, are preferable. For example, *Aided Language Stimulation* is a term for an AAC intervention strategy in which the interventionist highlights a symbol on the child's communication board while providing verbal stimuli (Goossens, 1989). The selection of a graphic symbol by the interventionist is always paired with a verbal model to show children that the symbols in front of them could be combined in new ways to exchange information. Keogh and Reichle (1985) suggested that a mixed mode, in which some vocabulary items are taught via one mode and others are taught in another, might be beneficial for some learners. Another alternative is to teach students to use two modes of communication. Depending on the situation, the student can choose the method that works best. For example, signing may work well in school with a teacher who knows sign language, but a communication wallet might be necessary when ordering at McDonald's (Reichle, Mirenda, Locke, Piche, & Johnston, 1992; Romski, Sevcik, Robinson, & Bakeman, 1994).

Once a method of communication (or combination of methods) has been selected, the next decision involves selection of an appropriate symbol system. For an unaided communication procedure, the choice will be among the variety of gestural languages in existence. For aided systems, there are several factors that should be considered in selecting a symbol system, including guessability, learnability, and generalization. Symbols range in **guessability** from those that are *very transparent* (easily guessed) to those that are *translucent* (need additional information to decode) (Mustonen, Locke, Reichle, Solbrack, & Lindgren, 1991). The term *iconic* is also used to describe guessability. Iconic symbols are similar in appearance to the items that they represent. In general, Picsyms and Rebus symbols have been found to be easier to guess than the meanings of Blissymbols (Musselwhite & Ruscello, 1984). Research by Mirenda and Locke (1989) on subjects with mild to severe intellectual disability found the following order of guessability: real objects, color photographs, black-and-white photographs, miniature objects, black-and-white line symbols (Picsyms, Picture Communication Symbols) (Mayer-Johnson Co., 1986), Rebuses, Self-Talk symbols (Johnson, 1986), Blissymbols, and written words.

Learnability refers to the ease or difficulty of learning a particular symbol set. Generally, studies with nondisabled children have found that learnability is related to iconicity (guessability). Symbols that are more iconic (similar to the object being named) are more easily learned. Rebus symbols are easier to learn than Blissymbols, which are in turn easier to learn than Non-SLIP chips or words (Carrier & Peak, 1975; Clark, 1981). Research on persons with disabilities has found that, for them, matching photographs with objects is easier than matching line drawings with objects (Sevcik & Romski, 1986) and that Rebus symbols are also more easily learned than Blissymbols (Hurlbut, Iwata, & Green, 1982).

According to Mustonen and colleagues (1991), iconic symbols facilitate the acquisition, generalization, and maintenance of graphic communication systems. The researchers acknowledge, on the other hand, that for students who can acquire higher-order symbolic information, iconic symbols may not be necessary. Another consideration is determining the ease with which symbols can be combined to make sentences. Lexigrams and Blissymbols are readily combined into sentences.

When graphic symbols are selected for use with an AAC system, Reichle (1991) suggests that four questions should guide their selection:

- *What types of symbols should be used?* Choices include photographs, line drawings, abstract symbols, and the like. The selection should be made based on what works for a particular learner.

- *How large will the symbols be?* Learners with poor visual acuity will require larger displays.

- *How will the learner select the symbols?* Direct selection, scanning, or a combination of these could be used.

- *How will the symbols be displayed?* A board (electronic or nonelectronic), wallet, or book could be used to display the symbols.

In the end, symbol selection should be guided by the abilities and needs of the user and his or her potential communication partners.

Regardless of which communication system is selected, a decision must be made about which vocabulary items to include. Unfortunately, decisions about vocabulary are often based on what the teacher or clinician *thinks* the student needs to know rather than on what the environment demands (Reichle et al., 1992). In fact, when Reichle (1983) asked interventionists how they made decisions about vocabulary selection, he got the following responses (in order of frequency): (1) selected vocabulary that the interventionist thought would be important; (2) selected vocabulary from the first 50 word developmental data; (3) selected vocabulary from word lists obtained from surveying service providers; and (4) selected vocabulary from word lists derived from vocabulary used by learners with developmental disabilities. A better strategy would be to select vocabulary demanded by the learner's environment. This vocabulary could be derived from the results of the preassessment ecological inventory.

Enhancing Communication

As with most decisions involving AAC, the decision about which symbol system to use must include considerations of the abilities and needs of the individual student—the student's literacy skills, cognitive abilities, and potential communicative partners. However, the most important decisions may regard the instructional strategies for enhancing communicative competence rather than the mode of communication employed.

Earlier in this chapter, we reviewed some of the research on the communication difficulties encountered by users of AAC and found that AAC users often lack opportunities to communicate. When they do communicate, they have been reported to have difficulty communicating effectively with others and are, therefore, relatively passive communicators who rarely initiate interactions.

Natural environments have proven to be the best place to teach conversation skills (Carter, 2003). When instruction is designed so that students have opportunities to talk about real situations with conversational partners who actually exist in those settings, not only does interaction increase, but there is also a greater chance for generalization of the skill as well. In addition to being provided with opportunities for interaction in natural environments, AAC users should be taught to use their systems for functional purposes—that is, to accomplish some real task in the environment rather than one contrived for instructional purposes.

Spiegel, Benjamin, and Spiegel (1993) give an example of the integration of functional communication within natural environments. They taught a 19-year-old male with cerebral palsy and moderate intellectual disability to increase his use of an AAC device (Touch Talker) (Prentke-Romich). Although the student had learned to use the Touch Talker, he used it infrequently for interaction with others. He learned to respond to conversational prompts that used sentences he had previously learned. For example, the student learned to produce the sentence *I need to go to the bank*. After demonstrating that he could produce this sentence, he was given the following prompt: *You just received your S.S.I. check in the mail. You want to put it in your savings account, and Ruby can drive you to the bank. Now, here comes Ruby to talk to you.* The student was then expected to type his previously learned sentence. Using this procedure, the student not only learned to respond to the vignettes appropriately, but also increased his spontaneous use of his AAC device.

Merely teaching an individual to use an AAC device is not enough to ensure that the person will use it. The results of the study by Spiegel and colleagues (1993) suggest this. Johnston, Reichle, and Evans (2004) identified three major problems with the use of AAC systems:

- Students who do not use their systems

- Communication partners who do not participate fully with a person using an AAC system

- Students who use socially or contextually inappropriate strategies for communication

Not only the AAC user, but also the listener, requires training. Often, listeners have to be very patient as AAC users formulate their messages. But patience alone may not be enough. Researchers have found that instruction in understanding the speech produced by voice output communication devices can increase the responsiveness of listeners to AAC messages (Rounsefell, Zucker, & Roberts, 1993). Communication between AAC users and their conversational partners can also benefit from instruction given to the listener on how to elicit communication from others (Hunt, Alwell, & Goetz, 1991). For example, Chung and Carter (2013) trained paraprofessionals and peers to enhance the communicative interaction of two children with intellectual disabilities who used speech-generating devices for communication (target students). The paraprofessionals were taught to use seven strategies to enhance interaction:

- **Increasing proximity to peers:** Helping the target student orient toward peers; including the student in class activities.

- **Increasing access to the device:** Ensuring that the device was present and working properly and contained items that could be used in the classroom.

- **Creating opportunities for use of the device:** Encouraging students to work with each other; using questions to promote peer interaction.

- **Monitoring interaction:** Using continuous monitoring to determine if additional prompts and interventions were needed to increase interaction.

- **Encouraging students:** Providing feedback to students on their interaction attempts.

- **Reducing support:** Fading prompts and questions once interaction was established.

- **Scoring interactions:** Using observations to determine if interactions were increasing.

Training for peers included strategies for getting the attention of the target student (such as using their name); using a variety of methods to communicate, including gestures and signs as well as the AAC device; asking questions; waiting for a response; helping the target student find a response on his or her device, if necessary; and learning how to respond when they did not understand what the target student was trying to say. The results showed that the target students significantly increased their interactions with peers and that these interactions persisted over time. A review of research on the use of peers to increase the interactions of AAC users found that the use of such methods can significantly increase interaction (Therrien, Light, & Pope, 2016).

There is increasing evidence that users of AAC can be helped to be effective communicators. It seems clear, however, that general instruction in the use of an AAC system is not sufficient. Rather, AAC users and their communicative partners have to be taught specifically how to use the system in effective communication interactions.

To summarize, the process of planning an AAC instructional program consists of five steps:

1. **Preassessment**, including an ecological inventory and assessment of the learner
2. **Development of goals** that should enhance the child's ability to participate in all environments
3. **Selection of a mode of communication**, either aided, unaided, or a combination
4. **Selection of a symbol system**, gestural or graphic
5. **Selection of methods to enhance communication** for both the AAC user and communication partners

There is evidence from research that with careful planning and the use of effective instructional techniques, nonspeaking individuals can develop effective communication skills.

Integrating AAC Use into General Education Classrooms

As more and more students with significant disabilities, including students with severe communication disabilities, are included in general education settings, it becomes increasingly important for teachers—both general and special education—to be aware of methods that will help these students become more fully integrated. For students who use AAC systems, there are many challenges. Not only may teachers and students be unfamiliar with AAC devices, but also many AAC users require a significant amount of help with their own communication skills.

Although most students with disabilities who use AAC systems can benefit from being included in general education classrooms, they will not all be able to participate equally. Beukelman and Mirenda (2005) describe three levels of participation to show how AAC users can participate in the general education classroom:

Competitive Educational Participation: Students with disabilities participate in the same educational activities as their peers and are expected to meet the same academic standards, although they may not complete the same amount of work in the same amount of time (and with the same independence) as their peers. AAC users may require more time to complete assignments and tests.

Active Educational Participation: Students with disabilities participate in the same educational activities as their peers. However, the expected outcome is not the same as that of their peers. Their progress is evaluated according to individualized goals. Active students may receive supplementary instruction in specific skill areas. They usually benefit from adaptations or modifications to instruction.

Involved Educational Participation: Students with disabilities participate in the same educational activities as their peers, but they are expected to learn in cross-curricular areas such as communication, social, and motor skills. Their progress is evaluated according to individualized goals. Such students may require extensive adaptations in order to participate with their peers (see Box 15.1).

The goal is for all students with disabilities to participate to the maximum extent possible with typically developing peers in the general education curriculum. Unfortunately, the academic and social outcomes for students with disabilities, especially those with more significant disabilities, are not as positive as we would hope. That is what Kent-Walsh and Light (2003) found when they interviewed teachers of students with significant disabilities who were AAC users. While finding that teachers reported increased interaction between the AAC users and their peers and greater acceptance by their peers, the researchers also reported somewhat disappointing results for academic and social skill development in the AAC users. Based on input from the teachers themselves, Kent-Walsh

---

Box 15.1 Examples of Levels of Participation in the General Education Classroom

CORAN: A COMPETITIVE STUDENT

Coran is a student with cerebral palsy who uses a computer with a word prediction program to write. Coran is expected to meet the same educational goals as her peers. For example, on a social studies assignment, Coran is expected to read independently. She answers the assigned questions using her computer. When she takes a test, she receives additional time to complete the test.

TIM: AN ACTIVE STUDENT

Tim is a student with autism who uses a communication book based on the Picture Exchange Communication System (PECS) model. Tim participates in the same instructional activities as his classmates but with adaptations and modifications to instruction. For example, for a social studies reading assignment, Tim is assigned to read with a peer. The peer reads the selection aloud while Tim follows along with a partially completed outline. Tim and his classmate then complete the outline together. A classroom aide assesses Tim's knowledge of the reading by asking questions that Tim can answer by constructing picture "sentences."

HEATHER: AN INVOLVED STUDENT

Heather is a student with significant intellectual disabilities who communicates primarily through vocalizations and by use of a simple voice output device. During social studies class, Heather participates in many of the same activities as her peers, but her learning goals focus primarily on communication. For example, while the rest of the class is reading the assignment, Heather watches a brief video from an online social studies website, then answers "yes/no" questions posed by her instructional aide by using her communication device. Heather is evaluated on her level of participation in the activity and the number of times she correctly responds to the questions.

---

and Light (2003) made the following suggestions to facilitate the inclusion of AAC users in the general education classroom:

- Communicate capabilities and limitations with respect to the inclusion process honestly.
- Develop competencies with AAC system operation.
- Request additional planning time.
- Remember students' humanity at all times.
- Include students in all classroom activities.
- Carefully match assistive technology to individual activity demands.
- Provide classmates with information related to the inclusion of students using AAC.
- Maintain effective team collaboration.
- Provide adequate training for team members.
- Provide the general education teacher with supports from individual team members (e.g., speech-language pathologist, paraprofessional).
- Implement effective transition planning.
- Select an AAC system with functions appropriate for the individual student.

As team members responsible for working with students using AAC systems, special educators may be called on to perform a variety of functions. A survey conducted by Locke and Mirenda (1992) found that many of these functions are traditional teacher-related responsibilities: adapting the curriculum, preparing and maintaining documentation, and writing goals and objectives for AAC users. However, some of the responsibilities are less traditional: identifying vocabulary, determining students' motivation and attitudes toward AAC techniques, and determining the communication needs of students. Two of the major concerns expressed by the teachers in this survey were the need for more training in AAC and the need for more time to work as a team.

Beukelman and Mirenda (2005) reviewed research that has identified a number of factors that contribute to the successful inclusion of AAC users with disabilities. These factors include the following:

- Administrative support for and commitment to inclusion of all learners
- Availability of an AAC system with functions that are appropriate to meet individual student needs
- Attitudes among AAC team members that include creativity, flexibility, and open-mindedness
- Willingness of the general education teacher to develop skills in both the use of AAC systems and inclusion
- A team whose members have a working knowledge of the general education curriculum as well as strategies for adapting/modifying the curriculum
- A team with expertise in assistive technology and other learning technologies
- A team with expertise in how to use inclusive educational practices
- A clear understanding of the roles and responsibilities of each AAC team member
- Sufficient time for AAC team members to meet generally, in collaboration with parents

Watch as this student uses an iPad to participate in the classroom. How did the teachers in the video prompt the students to use their devices?
https://www.youtube.com/watch?v=U_cwZxC6bPc

Literacy and AAC

As we have noted throughout this book, one of the key issues for all students is the development of literacy skills. Appropriate use of AAC systems in the classroom (and in the home) can enhance literacy skills. Unfortunately, many AAC users have limited access to and instruction in literacy skills. A review of the research on the literacy skills of AAC users showed that between 50 and 90 percent cannot read at all or read below age expectations (Koppenhaver & Yoder, 1992).

In addition to physical limitations, children who use AAC systems typically have reduced literacy-learning opportunities (Beukelman, Mirenda, & Sturm, 2005). Parents of children with severe speech and language impairments read aloud less often to their child. When they do read, they ask their child for fewer labels and make fewer requests for their child to point to pictures. Many parents of children with disabilities place more value on physical needs and on basic communication, rather than on the development of literacy skills (Light & Kelford Smith, 1993). In school, AAC users have been found to have more limited literacy-learning opportunities than their peers (Beukelman et al., 2005).

What can be done to provide children who use AAC systems with more and better opportunities for the development of reading and writing skills? Students with significant disabilities have been found to benefit from literacy instruction that includes the following components:

- Creation of a well-stocked, accessible library that includes both familiar and predictable books (those that include repeated passages and/or themes)
- Daily storybook readings in which children choose the book to be read
- Opportunities for children to write about functional and meaningful events
- Provision of a wide variety of reading and writing tools as well as time to explore use of those tools
- Adult scaffolding during storybook reading that draws attention to the form, content, and use of written language

- Routine integration of text into classroom routines

- Individual and small-group activities that expose children to new reading and writing activities (Koppenhaver & Erickson, 2003)

The reading skills of AAC users can be enhanced by the use of communication tools that support their participation during reading. For example, communicative devices can be programmed to include symbols from a story. Students can comment on their reading by having access to multiple choice responses to questions (e.g., "I thought the book was:" funny/sad). Additionally, communication devices need to be designed to include letters and words that students are likely to encounter frequently. After reviewing research on reading and its application to students with disabilities, Wilkins and Ratajczak (2009) developed some specific suggestions for literacy activities for AAC users, including using theme pages on the device to sort vocabulary words into groups, using picture keys to help the student activate his or her knowledge before reading a passage, and using peers to help the AAC user construct syntactically correct sentences from words and phrases produced by the user.

In addition to reading, the writing skills of AAC users should also be a focus of instruction. Bedrosian, Lasker, Speidel, and Politsch (2003) described a program to enhance the writing of a 14-year-old student with autism who used an AAC device (Lightwriter/Zygo) to communicate. At the beginning of the study, the student had limited written language skills. The authors paired the student with autism with a typically developing peer. They used an additional AAC device (Alphatalker/Prentke-Romich) that was programmed with phrases designed to enhance communication between the students. In addition, they used a computer with story-writing software ("My Words"/Hartley-Jostens Learning) to facilitate written language production. The students were taught to use these devices as well as story grammar maps and storyboards to plan and execute their writing. Using these techniques, the AAC user significantly improved his writing. The student took an active, even dominant, role in planning the stories. He learned to use a story map effectively to plan and write his stories. The typically developing peer reported that he enjoyed writing the stories with his disabled peer and would do so again.

Using techniques such as those described above, students who use AAC systems can more fully develop their literacy skills. Blischak (1995) described the case of Thomas, a 9-year-old boy with cerebral palsy and vision impairments. Thomas received early intervention for speech and language disabilities that included the development of an AAC system. In school, Thomas used an AAC device called a "Talking Screen," which enabled him to use his limited movement and vision skills to scan an array and produce a voice output. This system enabled Thomas to more fully participate in literacy activities. Using this device, Thomas was able to initiate interactions, answer questions, spell words, and write stories. For example, after listening to a story, questions were recorded by the teacher. Thomas was required to listen to the passage and use his Talking Screen to select and print answers. A project at Pennsylvania State University directed by Dr. Janice Light is focused on enhancing the literacy skills of children with disabilities who use AAC. You can find out more about this project and watch some of their students in action at the project website (search for "AAC Literacy PSU").

Outcomes of AAC System Usage

How effective is AAC? Answering this question requires examining answers to three other questions. First, has the student increased his or her communication ability? Second, what, if any, effects are there on other areas of functioning? And third, how is the AAC user accepted by others? All of these questions could be used in determining the success or failure of an AAC system.

The first question is, without a doubt, the most important one. After all, the primary reason for using an AAC system is to improve the communication skills of the student. There is considerable evidence from both research and clinical practice that AAC, when properly instituted, can enhance the communication skills of nonspeaking individuals.

A review of research on the use of speech-generating devices with individuals with developmental disabilities (Rispoli et al., 2010) found that most of the studies (86%) reported positive outcomes for improving communication, although they expressed concern about the design of some of the studies. Similarly, a review of single-subject research on the effectiveness of AAC on individuals with autism (Ganz et al., 2012) found that both speech-generating devices and the Picture Exchange Communication System (PECS) were effective for enhancing communication skills. In addition, there was some evidence for reduction of challenging behaviors and improvements in social and academic skills.

There is also evidence that individuals who use AAC devices and systems can increase their production of spoken language. Many parents and professionals are concerned that using AAC systems with individuals who speak may reduce their spoken language, but a review of research on the speech production of AAC users found that, in nearly 90 percent of the studies, AAC users increased their speech production (Millar, Light, & Schlosser, 2006). Moreover, there were no decreases in speech in subjects in any of the studies. This is powerful evidence that not only does AAC use not decrease spoken language, but also in most cases, it actually increases speech production.

The third area of consideration in evaluating the AAC system is acceptance by peers. If students with disabilities are to be fully included in school settings, it is essential that they become accepted by their peers. If speaking peers have negative attitudes toward them, nonspeaking AAC users may shy away from interacting with peers. Although there is little research on this issue, there is evidence that improved ability to communicate is associated with improved peer acceptance (Guralnick, 1986). When Blockenberger, Armstrong, O'Connor, and Freeman (1993) compared the attitudes of fourth-grade children toward a child using an alphabet board, an electronic device, and signing, they found that there was little difference in the children's reactions. Their research suggests that children are not heavily influenced by the type of AAC system used by another child. Although there is clearly a need for more research in this area, teachers often report that children are more accepting of peers with disabilities than adults would expect.

Check Your Understanding 15.2
Click here to gauge your understanding of the concepts in this section.

Summary

Every child can communicate. Physical and cognitive limitations are no longer impenetrable roadblocks to the development of communication skills. The rapid development of AAC procedures means that there are now a variety of options available to help nonspeaking persons develop communication skills.

Despite the rapid proliferation of AAC techniques, there are still many nonspeaking persons who do not have access to communication aids. This may be due to factors such as lack of funding or lack of knowledge about AAC on the part of teachers and clinicians. Whatever the reasons, to deny an individual access to effective means of communication is to deny that person the right to be part of the community. Therefore, it is incumbent upon teachers and clinicians to educate themselves about AAC and to advocate for the right of their students/clients to have access to AAC systems.

For those who need help getting started with AAC, many states have an AAC resource center. If no center is listed for your state, you might try contacting a university medical center to see if they have someone with expertise in AAC systems.

Language, Culture, and English Language Learners

Emily E. Kuder, M.A.

In this chapter, we will examine the influence of culture on language and the special problems posed by children learning to speak English—English language learners. Although most of these children do not have language disorders, many require help in order to achieve in school. We will examine instructional approaches that can be used successfully with these children, and we will also consider the necessity of adjustments to assessment procedures in order to fairly and accurately assess this population.

Some English language learners or students with dialect differences also have language disabilities. These children pose unique problems for educators. In this chapter, the special needs of this group of children are considered and recommendations for effective instructional practices and assessment procedures are provided.

Learning Outcomes

After completing this chapter, you should be able to:

1. Explain the ways in which children differ from one another according to their culture and language in addition to possible learning or developmental disabilities.

2. Identify appropriate assessment procedures for students with language differences.

3. Describe effective instructional practices for students with dialect differences, English language learners, and English language learners with disabilities.

Gabriel: A Case Study

Gabriel is an 11-year-old boy in fourth grade. He was born in Puerto Rico and has lived in the United States since he was a few months old. He began schooling at an English-speaking preschool where he was labeled as limited English proficient (LEP). Gabriel's kindergarten and first-grade classrooms were bilingual and equipped with English as a Second Language (ESL) services, whereas his subsequent classrooms have been English speaking with ESL support. Gabriel was documented as having incomprehensible speech and articulation difficulties in both English and Spanish in kindergarten and began receiving speech services. His second-grade teacher was concerned about his limited progress in reading as well as attention difficulties. He was assessed in both languages for special education services and was classified as communication impaired. Currently, Gabriel receives pullout resource center services for language arts and math five times a week. He also receives 30 minutes twice a week of speech and language services provided by an English-speaking special education teacher and speech-language pathologist. ESL services involve 30 minutes of pullout instruction a day, five times a week, by an English-speaking ESL teacher. Gabriel has continued to struggle with reading, making minimal

(continued)

Gabriel: A Case Study   Continued

progress during the last 2 years. His attendance is good, but his behavior has hindered his learning, and it can be a struggle for him to remain focused. It has been reported that beginning last year he was medicated for attention deficit hyperactivity disorder, although this has not been documented formally in his individualized educational plan.

Gabriel's case clearly illustrates some of the challenges faced by children who speak a language other than English. There may be limited resources to assist them. They may fall behind their peers in academic achievement, to the point that they may be classified for special education services. Those who have both learning difficulties and language differences may not receive educational services that are appropriate for all of their learning needs. As a result, language-minority children face significant challenges both in school and in life after school (August & Shanahan, 2006). In the United States the percentage of English language learners in public schools has increased from 8.7 percent in 2002 to 9.2 percent in 2012, and the numbers are still rising, particularly in urban areas (Kena et al., 2015). Because the number of children with language differences is increasing in schools, the challenge of meeting the educational needs of these children is increasing as well.

Language and Cultural Diversity

It should come as no surprise to anyone that in the United States and, indeed, in many other parts of the world, there is increasing diversity in the population. Language is an important part of one's culture. It unites groups of people and helps them form a common identity. At the same time, culture influences language. Children who speak a dialect other than "standard" English, or English language learners, may also have cultural differences that can have an impact on their ability to be understood and accepted by the mainstream culture.

For example, some Chinese-American children become easily embarrassed when receiving praise (Fung & Roseberry-McKibben, 1999). Their reaction to praise may be confusing to teachers and therapists who are trying to use positive rewards. In the Hispanic culture, physical proximity and touching during conversations is not uncommon (Cole, 1989). Some African American children have been taught that making eye contact is disrespectful (Terrell & Terrell, 1993). Table 16.1 gives additional examples of cultural differences in communication style and nonverbal behavior.

Table 16.1

Some Cultural and Conversational Differences

Cultural Group	Cultural Norms	Conversational Characteristics
African Americans	Touching of someone's hair may be seen as offensive. Verbal abuse is not necessarily a precursor to violence. Asking personal questions of new acquaintances may be seen as improper.	Children may avoid eye contact with adults. Discourse may be loosely connected. Conversation may be emotionally intense.
Hispanics	Official or business conversations are preceded by lengthy greetings and pleasantries. Mexican-American children seldom ask for help. Students may deny responsibility for mistakes.	Respect is shown through use of formal language. Hissing to gain attention is proper. Avoidance of eye contact may be a sign of respect. Relative distance between speakers is close. Straightforward communication is impolite.
Asians	Touching or hand-holding between members of same sex is acceptable. A slap on the back is insulting.	Talk about sensitive or unacceptable topics is not proper.

Sources: Based on Grossman (1995); Cole (1989).

Making generalizations about any culture is risky. There are often differences within cultures that are caused by country of origin, exposure to different cultures, and other factors. The important point for teachers is to be aware of the cultural differences that may exist in students from their community.

For educators, gaining an awareness of cultural differences and respect for different cultural values can be an important first step in building a functional classroom environment. Students who are linguistically and culturally different from other students also are at risk for problems in socialization. There are many reasons why this may be so. For example, there are different cultural norms for social interaction. Children from diverse cultures can be expected to have different patterns of eye gaze, speaker distance, and use of facial expressions. Other factors, such as prejudice and language differences themselves, can also affect socialization (Damico & Damico, 1993).

> In this video, educator James Alvarado discusses the importance of awareness of cultural differences among students. What does he suggest that educators should do to better understand students from different cultures?

Many of the diverse peoples of the United States also speak a language other than the dominant language of the region in which their children attend school. In the United States, data from 2009 indicate that an estimated 21 percent of school-age children (approximately 15 million) spoke a language other than English at home. Although many of these children are competent English language users, approximately 16 percent (or about 2.5 million) have difficulty using English in school, and 32 percent are living in homes below the federally defined poverty level (Federal Interagency Forum on Child and Family Statistics, 2011). Hispanic students compose 75 percent of all students in English as a Second Language (ESL), bilingual, and other English-language support programs, whereas Asian students accounted for almost 10 percent of all English language learners (Echevarria, Short, & Powers, 2006).

Although changes in demographic patterns have an impact throughout society, they disproportionately affect schools. Younger people and people with families are more likely to immigrate to a new country, and higher birth rates for minority groups mean more children in the schools. The rise in the number of students with limited English proficiency (LEP) is related strongly to the increased immigrant population in the United States. The 2006 American Community Survey administered through the U.S. Census Bureau (Kominski & Shin, 2008) determined that 20.4 percent of school-aged children spoke a language other than English at home, and out of those students, 6.5 percent spoke English at a proficiency level below the "very well" rating. So, in many parts of the United States, the schools have become the microcosms of our new society.

As a nation of immigrants, the United States has been built on cultural diversity. Yet, there has always been tension between the newer arrivals and those who were already here. Throughout most of the 20th century, it was expected that immigrants would assimilate into the mainstream culture. In other words, they would give up their distinctive dress, food, and—most importantly—their language to become a part of the "American" society. As a result, the myth of the "melting pot" developed. However, more recently, scholars have rejected the idea of a homogeneous America and recognized that the United States is less a melting pot than a "tossed salad" of many different cultures living together (Emihovich, 1988). In fact, terms such as "cultural pluralism" have been coined to describe a society in which several subcultures coexist in a world of mutual respect and thrive off of their cultural differences (Bernstein, 2015). As Adler (1993) noted, there has been an ongoing debate between those who advocate assimilation of immigrant groups and those who urge the preservation of cultural diversity.

Whatever the outcome of the cultural diversity debate, educators have to deal with the reality of schoolchildren who hold varying cultural norms and speak many different languages. Although this diversity can enrich our schools as well as our communities, it can also bring new problems. For example, a school district in New Jersey has struggled for years with how to celebrate holidays. Should it permit decorations for Christmas and Hanukkah? If so, what should it do about the Muslim, Hindu, and Buddhist children who have their own holidays? In this particular community (a midsized suburb), it is estimated that over a hundred languages are spoken.

Language poses one of the biggest dilemmas for educators. We may acknowledge and accept the desire of persons from different cultural groups to maintain their cultural heritage. But what about their language? After all, the language of instruction in U.S. schools is English. If children are to be successful in school, as well as in the larger community, won't they need to have good English-language skills? But what, then, do we do about their native language? Should we allow, or even encourage, students to use their first language? And what about children who speak English but in a different way? Should they be taught the "right" way to talk?

This is no mere theoretical issue. Some have responded to the increasing cultural and linguistic diversity in our society by calling for a declaration that English should be the only language spoken in the United States. Over half of the states in the United States have adopted laws that specify English as the official language of the state; others are considering similar action. An organization called U.S. English has been lobbying Congress for an amendment to the Constitution to make English the official language of the United States. These developments indicate just how important language is to people and how strongly they feel about preserving their language.

These are a few of the problems posed by children from different cultural and language backgrounds. In addition, there is the issue of language disability. It is important to be able to distinguish children who talk differently from children with a language disorder. Yet, because of deficiencies in assessment materials and procedures, this is often difficult to do. As a result, some children are inappropriately referred to special education, whereas others who could use additional help do not receive appropriate services (Gage, Gersten, Sugai, & Newman-Gonchar, 2013).

Dialect Differences

Regional Dialects.   A dialect is a variant of a particular language. Wolfram and Schilling (2016) defined a dialect as "any variety of a language that is shared by a group of speakers." Dialects share most of the features of the main language but differ in pronunciation, vocabulary, and/or stylistic features. For example, in some parts of Boston, words that end with an "uh" sound, such as *pizza*, are pronounced "er" (as in *pizzer*). President Kennedy, a Boston native, was faced with the challenge of the missile crisis in "Cuber." In some parts of the United States, the words *Mary, merry,* and *marry* are each pronounced the same. In other regions, they are differentiated from each other. In England, one works in a la-bor-a-tree, whereas in most regions of the United States, this word is pronounced lab-ra-tory. If you order a large sandwich on a roll, you get a *hoagie* in Philadelphia, a *hero* or *torpedo* in different areas of New York, a *grinder* or *sub* in New England, and a *po' boy* in New Orleans. People from the east and west coasts of the United States often feel that people from the South speak very slowly.

 Listen as a New York native models the dialectal variation present across the five boroughs of New York City. What do the variations suggest about the role of location in dialect differences?
https://www.youtube.com/watch?v=1hrA9-6o4tl

All of these are examples of regional dialect variations. Often these variations are minor; they may create brief moments of embarrassment or humor. However, some regional dialect differences are so great that it may be difficult for speakers and listeners to communicate easily. Some speakers from the Appalachian Mountains and those from isolated communities around the Chesapeake Bay area may use dialects that are very difficult to follow.

What we must keep in mind is that there is nothing "wrong" with these regional dialect differences. There is no one "right" way to talk, because the "right" way is different in different regions of the country. On the other hand, there is a widely held belief that there is (or should be) a standard dialect. A *standard dialect* is the one spoken by highly educated people in formal situations. The American Speech-Language-Hearing Association (ASHA, 2003) holds the position that each dialect is adequate as a functional and effective variety of American English and that dialect differences are not a sign of a language disorder.

Social Dialects.   In addition to regional dialects, there are social dialects. Social dialects are ways of speaking that are associated with a particular social group. The haughty, sometimes mumbled speech of the "aristocrat" and the dropped endings (*I'm goin'*) often heard in the speech of working-class persons are both examples of social dialects. Some social dialects carry with them the stigma of discrimination and the widespread belief that some are inferior versions of English. Nowhere is this truer than in the case of African American English (AAE) (sometimes called "Ebonics" or "Black English").

The debate about social dialects, specifically AAE, heated up in 1996 when the Oakland, California, school board enacted a resolution directing teachers to recognize and appreciate the language used by their students (called "**Ebonics**") and to use this language to help students make the transition to standard American English (SAE) (Applebome, 1996). The board's actions set off a wave of debate about language, dialects, and the role of education. The board was widely criticized for claiming that Ebonics was not a dialect at all but a separate language that was genetically programmed in African Americans, claims the board later dropped. However, the reaction to the board's actions shows just how sensitive issues of language and culture can be.

African American English is a dialect of English that is used by some, but not all, African American speakers. In actuality, there is a great deal of variation in language use within the African American community (Craig, Thompson, Washington, & Potter, 2003). A number of different terms have been used to describe this dialect, including Ebonics, AAE, Black English, and Black English Vernacular (BEV). We will use the term *African American English* (AAE), because it is preferred by some scholars (e.g., Day-Vines et al., 2009), although it is important to note that not all African Americans use this dialect.

AAE is characterized by differences in phonology, syntax, and pragmatics, as well as in aspects of conversational discourse (Day-Vines et al., 2009). Some of the unique features of AAE include deletion or substitution of medial and final consonant sounds (*brother = brovah; walked = walk*), deletion of auxiliary verb (*The boy is running = The boy running*), deletion of the possessive suffix (*boy's = boy* as in *It is the boy ball*) (Craig et al., 2003; Day-Vines et al., 2009) (see Table 16.2 for additional examples).

Even those African Americans who use AAE do not do so at all times. They may use this type of language in some settings, with some people, but not in other situations. This

Grammatical Feature	Example
Deletion of past-tense ending	cashed = cash
Variation in past tense of irregular verbs	saw = seen did = done
Use of double negatives	He didn't do nothing.
Use of *be* as a main verb	I be here in the evening.
Deletion of final *s* in third-person singular present tense	He walk.

Table 16.2

Examples of Grammatical Features of Black English Vernacular

Sources: Based on Craig et al. (2003); Day-Vines et al. (2009).

phenomenon in which people switch from one language or one dialect to another is called **code switching**. It means that the individual is aware of environmental conditions that affect the choice of language.

Social dialects such as AAE are often considered inferior by speakers of a more standard form of a language. Not only do social dialects differ linguistically from the standard language, but also when used by people of color or by lower socioeconomic groups, they carry the additional stigma of racism and discrimination. The idea that social dialects are inferior forms of a standard language was reinforced by research on the language of lower socioeconomic groups that was conducted during the 1950s, 1960s, and 1970s. Today, most scholars agree that there is nothing inherently wrong with social dialects such as AAE.

 Watch this video about the school experience of former students who spoke an AAE dialect. How did their language skills influence how they were perceived by the school?
https://www.youtube.com/watch?v=WWIbIA9BItQ

Despite a near unanimous consensus among researchers and clinicians that social dialects such as AAE are not inferior, concerns about what to do about speakers of these dialects continue to exist. Grossman (1995) notes three reasons for many educators' continued concerns about children who use nonstandard English dialects:

1. Although nonstandard English dialects are not substandard, they interfere with students' academic progress.

2. Competency in oral standard English is necessary for students to learn to write standard English.

3. Standard English is necessary for vocational success and in other areas in which nonstandard dialect speakers are branded as uneducated and ill prepared.

Grossman's concerns have been reflected in recent studies on the achievement gap between students from nonstandard dialect backgrounds. For instance, Brown and colleagues (2015) found that children who use AAE at home are at greater risk for delays in literacy. Educators are left with questions about whether to encourage or discourage students from using their particular dialect, and these questions are haunted by issues of race and class. Later in this chapter, we will examine the different approaches to teaching students with dialect differences.

English Language Learners

Like children with cultural or dialectal differences, children who come to school speaking a language other than English as their first language can pose significant challenges to teachers and other professionals. These children may be misunderstood as much for their cultural differences as their language differences. Sometimes these children are mislabeled as having learning disabilities or emotional and/or behavioral disorders and are inappropriately placed in special education. Hispanic children, especially those who speak Spanish as their first language, lag behind their native English-speaking peers in all grades and content areas (Kieffer, Lesaux, Rivera, & Francis, 2009). Our challenge as educators is to provide a program that will enable a child who speaks a language other than English to fully develop, both academically and socially.

There is not a consensus on what to call children who speak a language other than English. The terms *limited-English-proficient (LEP)* or *non-English-proficient (NEP)* have sometimes been used to describe these children. Other terms like **English as a second language (ESL)** students or *language-minority* students have sometimes been used.

However, there seems to be a developing preference among researchers and practitioners alike to use the term *English language learners (ELLs)*. This term has been defined as, "Students who speak another language other than English, who are in the process of acquiring English as a second language or additional language, and who have not yet achieved full English proficiency" (Klingner, Artiles, & Barletta, 2006, p. 126, note 1).

Bilingualism refers to the ability to understand and use two languages. Bilingualism is not an all-or-nothing principle, but ranges from minimal ability to complete fluency in more than one language (Baca & Almanza, 1991). Montrul (2013) distinguishes between several kinds of bilingual speakers. Bilinguals who acquire two languages during the first 12 years of life are called "early bilinguals," whereas those who begin learning their second language during adolescence or later are called "late bilinguals." Within early bilinguals, Montrul further distinguishes between "simultaneous bilinguals" and "sequential bilinguals" or "subsequent bilinguals." Simultaneous bilinguals are individuals who begin learning two languages at the same time. This is typical of children raised in families with guardians who speak different languages. Sequential bilinguals or subsequent bilinguals learn one language at birth and then begin learning a second language early in life. This is typical of children who immigrate at a very young age to countries where a language other than their home language is spoken by the majority, for example.

For teachers and other education professionals, it is important to keep in mind that while generalizations can be made about ELLs, they are still a heterogeneous group. They come to school with a variety of language and cultural experiences. Some are very familiar with the mainstream culture, whereas others are largely unfamiliar with any culture other than their native one. Some have good English language skills, whereas others have limited or nonexistent English language skills.

ELLs and Literacy.

ELLs have been found to lag behind their peers in the development of academic skills, especially literacy skills (Echevarria et al., 2006; Lenski, Ehlers-Zavala, Daniel, & Sun-Irminger, 2006). For example, an analysis of data from the National Assessment of Education Progress (NAEP) indicated that reading and math scores for ELLs, regardless of race, were lower than those of their native English-speaking peers (Hemphill & Vanneman, 2011). Although the data show that reading scores for ELLs have improved, they still lag far behind their peers.

Why do ELLs have difficulty acquiring literacy skills? This is a more complex question than it might appear at first. Are we interested in literacy in English-based text or in their first language? Although it is true that many ELLs struggle with the acquisition of English reading and writing skills, there is no reason to believe that they are deficient in the acquisition of literacy in their first language. The ELL population itself is diverse. It includes children from a variety of cultures, languages, and socioeconomic levels. Factors such as parents' educational levels, length of time that the family has been in the United States, and opportunities for education can influence the acquisition of literacy skills. However, even after considering all of these factors, we are left with the problem of explaining the significant lag in development of literacy skills among ELLs.

Obviously, skill in the English language is one factor. As we have noted earlier in this text, there is a close relationship between spoken language skill and reading and writing. It should not be surprising to find that children with limited spoken English language skills may struggle with the development of reading and writing in English. Halle, Hair, Wandner, McNamara, and Chien (2012) found that age of oral proficiency in English was directly correlated with ELLs' development of reading skills. ELLs who were not proficient in spoken English by first grade lagged behind their peers in reading to a greater extent than those who were proficient in English by first grade. More specifically, knowledge of English vocabulary has been found to be a particularly important predictor of reading success (Pollard-Durodola, Mathes, Vaughn, Cardenas-Hagan, & Linan-Thompson, 2006). However, the population of ELLs is not homogeneous by any means, and there is considerable variability across individuals. Peregoy and Boyle (2000) note that even ELLs with good English skills have been found to read more slowly than native English speakers.

However, important as it is, English language skill does not fully explain the literacy deficiencies of English language learners. Cultural factors appear to play a role, as well. For example, the NAEP results also showed that Hispanic students lagged significantly behind white students in fourth- and eighth-grade reading but that Asian American students' scores were equivalent to those of white children. There is also evidence that quality of schooling may have a significant impact on the literacy development of ELLs. In one study, kindergarten reading and spelling performance differences between children learning English as a second language and native English-speaking children largely disappeared by second grade following implementation of an intensive phonological awareness training program (Lesaux & Siegel, 2003).

The development of literacy skills in the English language is a critical factor in the school success of ELLs. Unfortunately, many children with limited English proficiency lag behind in the development of reading and writing skills. Later in this chapter, we will examine instructional programs that have been developed to help ELLs improve their literacy skills.

ELLs and Special Education.   Some students with limited English proficiency also have significant problems in learning, socialization, and/or behavior and require special education services. These children have needs that go beyond those of other ELLs because in addition to their learning disabilities or emotional and/or behavioral disorders, they also have language and cultural differences that may be inhibiting their learning.

One of the biggest challenges facing educators is appropriate identification of these students. Ironically, these students tend to be both overidentified and underidentified. Many researchers have found that students with language differences are misidentified as having learning disabilities and overrepresented in special education classes (Artiles, Rueda, Salazar, & Higareda, 2005; Hoover, 2012; Zeitlin, Beltran, Salcido, Gonzalez, & Reyes, 2011). A study by Artiles and colleagues (2005) found that ELLs in 11 urban school districts in California were overrepresented in special education classes by grade 5 and continued that way through grade 12. The study also found that ELLs in immersion programs (those that use little of the students' native language) were more likely to be referred to special education. At the same time, general education teachers sometimes hesitate to refer ELLs to special education because they are not sure whether they have a learning problem or a language difference (Klingner et al., 2006). The study by Gage and colleagues (2013) found that the odds of being identified with an emotional and/or behavioral disorder were significantly less for ELLs than for their native English-speaking peers. The misidentification of language disabilities and disorders among ELLs in many cases is due to the use of identification practices that rely largely (or solely) on testing performed in English. Without a proper way of distinguishing a language difference from a disorder, children from language-minority groups may receive inappropriate services that do not target their needs.

There is no inherent reason why second language learners should receive special education services more or less often than their peers. Yet, in some schools, this is the case. Conversely, ELLs can be expected to have learning disabilities as well as emotional and/or behavioral disabilities just as often as other children. It is incumbent on teachers and other education professionals to try to determine the factors that may be limiting the learning of individual children.

Check Your Understanding 16.1

Click here to gauge your understanding of the concepts in this section.

Appropriate Assessment

One of the great challenges for education professionals is to assess children from culturally and linguistically diverse backgrounds in a fair, appropriate, and accurate manner. As Campbell, Dollaghan, Needleman, and Janosky (1997) noted, children from different ethnic, cultural, or economic backgrounds may perform poorly on tests because they lack experience with the test's format or stimuli. As a result, it becomes difficult to distinguish between children whose language differences reflect their differing experiences and backgrounds and children who have fundamental language disorders. In addition, norm-referenced tests have problems that affect the accuracy of their use with children from diverse language and cultural backgrounds. These problems include content bias (the assumption that all children have had similar life experiences), linguistic bias (differences between the child's language or dialect and the test), and disproportionate representation in normative samples of students with limited English proficiency (the fact that, until recently, most norm-referenced tests failed to include diverse samples in their norm sample) (Laing & Kamhi, 2003). These issues lead to the misclassification of ELL students.

The Individuals with Disabilities Education Act (IDEA, 2004) contains provisions that spell out the obligations of schools to conduct nonbiased assessments when evaluating children for special educational services. Among these provisions are the following:

■ Testing and evaluation materials and procedures used for the purposes of evaluation and placement of handicapped children must be selected and administered so as not to be racially or culturally discriminatory.

■ Testing and evaluation materials and procedures must be provided and administered in the language or other mode of communication in which the child is most proficient, unless it is clearly not feasible to do so.

■ Tests must be administered to a child with a motor, speech, hearing, visual, or other communication disability, or to a bilingual child, so as to reflect accurately the child's ability in the area tested rather than the child's impaired communication skill or limited English language skill unless those are the factors the test purports to measure.

To summarize, IDEA requires that when students who are culturally or linguistically diverse are assessed for special education, testing must be culturally fair, conducted in the child's own language, and designed so that it examines the area tested rather than the child's communication skills in English. These goals are supported by most educators who are interested in identifying those children from diverse backgrounds who need special education services. Unfortunately, there are many challenges in creating and implementing the test regulations that IDEA advocates (Guler, 2013). Among the reasons that testing regulations may not be followed are:

■ Disagreement about what constitutes cultural bias in testing

■ A shortage of appropriate assessment materials for students from diverse cultural and linguistic backgrounds

■ A shortage of personnel trained in the assessment of children from diverse cultural and linguistic backgrounds

Let's look at each of these problems in turn. First, although many educators are concerned about the possibility of bias in testing, the bias has often been difficult to prove. Court decisions have only added to the confusion. Throughout the 1970s, most court decisions supported the notion that there was bias inherent in standardized testing. But in *PASE v. Hannon* (1980), the court ruled that although black children were disproportionately represented in special education classes in the Chicago school system, there was little evidence that the tests used to determine placement were biased. The results of court decisions have caused continued disagreement about what constitutes fairness in testing. Even as the courts cannot agree on what constitutes bias in testing, many educators continue to have concerns about fairness in assessment procedures.

A second reason that the listed mandates of IDEA may not be carried out is that appropriate tests may not be available. For example, after an extensive review of the research literature, Figueroa (1989) concluded that psychological testing for children with varying levels of language proficiency and differing home backgrounds was inadequate. He criticized technical aspects of the tests, the knowledge base used for constructing psychological tests, and regulations regarding testing. These problems are still prevalent today. Guler (2013) discussed the changes facing test writers, namely test validity, or whether or not the test is actually evaluating the skill it is targeting. Limited language proficiency can sometimes come across to a test evaluator as limited knowledge of the content area. Baca and Almanza (1991) expressed similar concerns about educational testing. They noted that there is widespread concern about the content of test items, lack of cultural sensitivity by testers, and lack of test-taking strategies for students from diverse cultural and language backgrounds.

One solution to the problem of test fairness is to use a version of the test in the child's native language. Yet, even this is not always a totally satisfactory solution. Payan (1989) has pointed out that even if such tests are available, the test items may still be inappropriate for children from diverse cultural backgrounds. In addition, the tests are often translated into a standard dialect that may not be the one used by the child.

Cole and Taylor (1990) noted that researchers have often raised concerns about speech and language testing of African American children, claiming that few standardized tests of language contain items that are truly representative of the variety of dialects in use within the United States. When Cole and Taylor used three widely accepted tests of articulation in testing African American children, they found that the results varied considerably, depending on what norms were used. They suggest, then, that clinicians would get more reliable results by using language samples and other techniques that measure the *use* of language skills in communication rather than by using tests of specific language skills.

A third obstacle to the implementation of the IDEA testing requirements is a shortage of trained personnel. There are two problems related to personnel. One involves language abilities. It is often not possible to find a qualified test administrator who speaks a particular child's native language. Frequently, schools have to use a test administrator who is only familiar with standard English. The second problem involves possible bias. Testers may also hold inaccurate expectations for children from particular cultural and language backgrounds and may interpret the test results to confirm those expectations.

Recommendations for Assessment

Considering all of the potential problems in testing children from diverse cultural and language backgrounds, what can educators do to try to fairly and accurately assess these children? One option is to provide accommodations to support students during testing, especially on high-stakes tests such as state or national assessments. Kieffer and colleagues (2009) examined the effectiveness of six commonly used testing accommodations for ELLs:

- Bilingual dictionaries and glossaries
- Spanish versions of the assessment
- Extra time
- Simplified English
- English dictionaries and glossaries
- Dual language booklets and test items

They found that only simplified English and English dictionaries and glossaries were generally effective in improving the performance of ELL students. The authors suggest that the limited effectiveness of test accommodations for this population may be due to the close relationship between language skills and content knowledge.

Payan (1989) has suggested a seven-step process for the assessment of ELL students being evaluated for special educational services. Step 1 is the *referral*. Payan (1989) provides a rather lengthy form that includes information about who referred the student for assessment, a description of the student's present program, and the student's language and communication abilities. This information is useful for planning the assessment, as well as for discouraging inappropriate referrals.

Table 16.3

Some Standardized Tests of Language Proficiency for English Language Learners

Name (Creators and Year)	Ages or Grades	Language(s)	Language Skills Assessed
Bilingual Verbal Ability Tests (Riverside; 1998)	Pre-K to grade 12	17 languages	Overall verbal ability
Dos Amigos Verbal Language Scales (Academic Communication Associates; 1999)	Ages 5 to 13	Spanish, English	Expressive vocabulary
Language Assessment Scales (CTB/McGraw-Hill; 1991)	Grades 1 to 12	Spanish, English	Phonemic, lexical, syntactic, and pragmatic aspects of language
Woodcock-Munoz Language Survey–Revised (Riverside; 2004)	Ages 4 to 90	Spanish, English	Receptive and expressive semantics

Step 2 is the *parent interview.* This is an especially important step for children who speak a language other than English at home. In order to completely understand the child's language and cultural background, the interviewer must ascertain what languages are spoken at home, who speaks them, and any concerns the parents may have about their child's language development. A parent interview is also an opportunity to find out about the cultural norms and cultural background of the family.

Step 3 is an assessment of *language proficiency.* Several standardized tests have been developed for the purpose of assessing the language skills of children with limited English (see Table 16.3). However, most of these tests have been developed for use with Spanish-speaking persons.

Step 4 is determining the *language for assessment.* The examiner should consider information from the parent interview and from assessment of the child's language in deciding in which language the assessment should be conducted.

Step 5 is an in-depth analysis of the child's *native language abilities,* including assessment of receptive and expressive skills in all areas of language.

Step 6 is a similar assessment of *English language skills.*

Finally, Payan (1989) recommends that in Step 7, the clinician *summarizes the results and makes recommendations.*

Given the limitations of norm-referenced testing of ELLs and other children with cultural and/or linguistic differences, an alternative assessment model may be useful. One approach that has been used successfully with such children is called **dynamic assessment (DA)**.

DA evaluates how children learn during the assessment process. Instead of measuring static knowledge that a student has, DA measures how much a student can learn. Gutiérrez-Clellen and Peña (2001) described three steps in implementing the model:

- *Testing the limits:* The goal is to find out what children really know and can do. For example, children might be provided feedback during testing, including explanations of why they got items wrong. Children might also be asked to explain how they arrived at their answers. This can help children realize why they are making mistakes and help them to self-correct.

- *Graduated prompting:* Responses are elicited through the use of increasingly more specific prompts. For example, a response may be *modeled* ("This is a baby"), *modeled with an elicitation question* ("This is a baby. What is it?"), or *modeled with an object obstacle* (withholding the object until the child attempted to produce the word). The child's readiness to learn specific target items is determined by the level of prompting needed by the child.

- *Test-Teach-Retest:* Initial testing is used to determine what the child does (and does not) know. Then intervention focuses on unknown items. Finally, the child is retested to see whether the child has acquired the newly taught information.

Gutiérrez-Clellen and Peña (2001) demonstrated that effective use of these techniques could provide more accurate information about the vocabulary knowledge of bilingual (Spanish/English) children than the standard administration of a norm-referenced test. The effectiveness of DA methods has been verified, with more recent studies showing that it may help to minimize test biases (Kapantzoglou, Adelaida Restrepo, & Thompson, 2012).

Educators may also administer a wide range of different types of alternative or authentic assessments (AAs) in order to get a more complete picture of each student's abilities (Lenski et al., 2006). Assessments given incrementally throughout a school year are called *formative assessments*, whereas *summative assessments* are given at the end of the unit or school year and test the student's comprehensive knowledge of the course material. Tracking a child's progress through formative assessments can reveal their academic strengths and weaknesses. AAs can include anything from teacher observations of student work (in the form of checklists, records, or ratings), journals (personal reflections or dialogue journals), questionnaires, self-assessments, or writing portfolios. Criterion-referenced tests and informal procedures, such as language samples, are other alternative means for assessing language proficiency.

> Watch this video to learn more about how to appropriately assess ELL students' language abilities and disabilities. What can teachers do to ensure that all students are tested fairly?
>
> https://www.youtube.com/watch?v=ILTwEJ8V8d4

Fair and accurate testing of linguistically and culturally diverse students, including those learning English, is a continuing and growing challenge for schools. Teachers and other professionals need to use a variety of techniques to assess such children and be willing to modify testing procedures to give children the opportunity to demonstrate what they really know. Only then will we be able to determine whether such children truly have learning difficulties or if their performance is largely the result of language or cultural differences.

Apply Your Knowledge 16.1: ELL Assessment Plan: A Case Study

In this exercise, you will assess a student's need for special education services.

Check Your Understanding 16.2

Click here to gauge your understanding of the concepts in this section.

Instructional Programs

In the previous sections, we noted that children with cultural and language differences are a diverse group. They come to school with different degrees of skill in their first language and in English; they differ in their exposure to the mainstream culture; and they differ in their learning and social skills. Therefore, there is no one program that will suit everybody. The task for educators is to find the most effective program for each individual.

Although each individual's program of study may differ, certain broad goals are appropriate for all learners with language and/or dialect differences. One goal is to develop *competence* in English. But what is competence? Cummins (1980, 1984, 2000) describes two types of language skills: **basic interpersonal communicative skills (BICS)** and **cognitive/academic language proficiency (CALP)**. Cummins cautions that children may develop BICS fairly quickly (1–2 years) but that CALP takes much longer to develop (5–7 years). Thus, when we say that a child is competent in English, we should clarify whether we mean that the child is able to engage in interpersonal interaction or the more advanced skill of applying English language skills to academic tasks. There is a danger that some children will be transferred out of programs that help them develop their English skills because they are able to demonstrate basic communication skills. But many of these children will not be prepared to use their language for the complex learning tasks posed in the classroom. Handscombe (1994) has suggested that in addition to the development of skills in English, programs for children with language and/or cultural differences should also help students enhance their academic achievement and social integration.

Cummins (1994) reminds us that a number of factors are working against the development of effective programs for children who speak a language (or a dialect) other than standard English. These include government policies that ignore the research on second language learning, curriculum that is skewed toward white, middle-class values and experiences, and a shortage of professionals who share the language and/or cultural background of many of the students in today's schools. Despite these obstacles, effective programs have been developed. In subsequent sections of this chapter, we will examine instructional programs for students with dialect differences, ELLs, and students with both language differences and special needs.

Instruction for Students with Dialect Differences

The question of how and what to teach children with cultural and dialect differences continues to be a very sensitive one. The issue clearly involves more than what is best in terms of language development or educational practice. It is closely related to our society's struggles with the issues of race, poverty, and equity. For instance, in 1979, a U.S. district court judge ruled in favor of a group of African American children who had brought suit against the Ann Arbor, Michigan, school district. The suit claimed that these children were being denied an equal education because their school did not take into account their use of Black English. The judge noted that there was evidence that teachers had unconsciously indicated to the children that Black English is wrong. As a result, the judge argued, the children had been made to feel inferior and became disenchanted with school. The court ruled that teachers had to attend in-service education programs about nonstandard dialects and that a child's dialect had to be considered when the child was being taught to read and write (*Martin Luther King Junior Elementary School v. Ann Arbor School District Board*, 1979).

This case caused many educators to rethink their attitudes toward dialect differences. In addition, it prompted debate (that continues even today) about the relationship between dialect differences and the development of literacy skills. Grossman (1995) described the debate as between those who argue for **bidialectalism** and those who argue for the *appreciation* of dialect differences.

Those who argue for a bidialectal approach to instruction for children who speak nonstandard dialects of English (such as BEV) contend that although there is nothing wrong with such dialects, they interfere with the child's ability to achieve success in the mainstream society. As Sol Adler, one of the advocates for a bidialectal approach, put it, "So long as linguistic and cultural prejudices dominate the thinking of these establishment members of our society, nonstandard speakers will continue to need to learn the language of the mainstream culture if they wish to have an equal opportunity to enter into the mainstream" (1993, p. 21). Adler argues that bidialectal programs must be mandatory, not voluntary, since most children will not pick up standard English without formal instruction.

Proponents of bidialectal programs generally give three reasons for the need for such programs (Adler, 1993):

1. *Educational reasons:* They cite evidence that the reading skills of speakers of BEV lag behind those of other children, both white and black. Furthermore, because "standard" English is the language of instruction in classrooms, speakers of BEV and other nonstandard dialects are at a disadvantage.

2. *Employment reasons:* They cite evidence that use of standard English is an important factor in hiring decisions. They argue that it is unfair to speakers of nonstandard dialects not to teach them the language skills they will need for employment.

3. *Ethical and pragmatic reasons:* Ethically, it is wrong to deny children the use of their dialect. But, it is equally wrong to deny them the opportunity to learn standard English. The pragmatic argument is that, like it or not, standard English is required for success in the United States and children must be given the opportunity to acquire the standard dialect.

The objectives of a bidialectal program are to create in students an awareness of the need to adjust language for different purposes, to help them understand the importance of communication skills, and to provide them with opportunities to develop and practice standard English while continuing to use their dialect (Harris-Wright, 1987). Many bidialectal programs use an instructional technique called *contrastive analysis,* in which children are given examples of nonstandard and standard English forms for communicating and are taught to analyze and recognize the differences between the two dialects. In fact, Godley, Sweetland, Wheeler, Minnici, and Carpenter (2006) outline ways in which teachers can use the dialects that their students bring to the classroom as a tool when teaching standard English:

1. Teachers should use and build on the dialectal variants used in the classroom and avoid referring to these variants with diminutive terms such as "nonstandard," "ungrammatical," or "slang."

2. Teachers should explicitly teach students about dialect diversity so that they learn to recognize the different language forms they use and their relative appropriateness in different situations.

3. Teachers should try to understand the grammatical patterns of dialectal variant forms in order to be able to distinguish them from errors.

In contrast with the bidialectal approach, the appreciation approach to dialect differences urges respect for dialect differences and the development of language skills in whatever dialect the child speaks. Grossman (1995) has summarized the arguments in support of the appreciation position:

1. Efforts to teach students to speak standard English do not work.

2. Dialect speakers who are required to speak standard English become less fluent and have difficulty expressing themselves.

3. Teaching students standard English before they are completely fluent in their original dialects stunts their language development.

4. It is not possible to encourage students to learn a second dialect without also communicating that their way of speaking is less desirable.

5. Acceptance and appreciation of nonstandard dialects by schools and teachers improve students' self-esteem.

6. Teaching standard English to nonstandard-dialect speakers is a form of political and cultural subjugation.

While the research base in support of many of these arguments is limited, the arguments do represent points of view that should be considered. At one time in the late 1960s and 1970s, some linguists were urging the development of Black English texts so that children who used this dialect would be less disadvantaged as they began to read (e.g., Baratz, 1969). Today, however, most educators recognize the need for all children to develop reading and writing skills in standard English.

Clearly the debate about what to do about children who speak nonstandard dialects of English, especially BEV, is about more than education. Issues of race and class inject highly emotional feelings into the debate. While most can agree that nonstandard dialects are not inferior forms of English and that speakers of such dialects deserve respect, they differ on the extent to which standard English should be taught. In making decisions about what kind of program to adopt, educators should consider the research base on nonstandard dialects and literacy, as well as the desires of parents, students, and the community as a whole.

Instruction for English Language Learners

Students who come to school with competence in both their native language and English (bilingual) will usually not need any type of special program. But many children whose first language is not English have limited skills in English and do need some type of instruction that helps them acquire the English skills they need for success in school. Instructional programs for ELLs range from those that require children to use English right from the beginning to those that emphasize the use of the child's native language. Rossell (2005) has described six types of programs that have been used in the United States to educate students learning English as a second language (ESL):

- *Structured immersion—or sheltered English immersion:* provides instruction in all content areas almost entirely in English, but in a self-contained classroom consisting only of ELLs.

- *ESL pullout programs:* supplements regular, mainstream classroom instruction with instruction in a small-group setting outside the mainstream classroom aimed at developing English language skills.

- *The sink-or-swim approach:* provides mainstream classroom instruction with no special help or scaffolding.

- *Transitional bilingual education:* initially delivers instruction and develops students' literacy in the students' native language but puts a priority on developing students' English language skills.

- *Two-way bilingual education:* (also known as two-way immersion) is designed to develop fluency in both the students' first language and a second language; teachers deliver instruction in both languages to classes consisting of both native English speakers and speakers of another language (most commonly Spanish).

- *Bilingual maintenance programs:* generally consist of non-English speakers and, like two-way bilingual education programs, place equal emphasis on maintaining students' primary language and developing their English proficiency.

Which type of program is most successful? Unfortunately, there is no simple answer to this question. Research on the outcomes of bilingual education programs is limited by factors such as individual differences between students and variations in the ways that school districts choose to implement the basic models described above. Despite these limitations, some trends have emerged.

Sheltered English instruction (or sheltered immersion) programs have been found to be one the most successful programs for building both English language skills and content area knowledge in ELLs (Abadiano & Turner, 2002). Sheltered instruction programs are designed to help ELLs develop continued competence in English while learning in academic content areas, such as social studies, mathematics, and science (Hansen-Thomas, 2008). Instruction is delivered in English but usually at a slower pace and with more repetition than in typical content area classrooms. Teachers in these classrooms are typically skilled in ESL techniques and use effective teaching strategies, such as visuals and demonstrations, scaffolded instruction, targeted vocabulary development, connections to student experiences, student-to-student interaction, adaptation of materials, and use of supplementary materials.

Sheltered instruction is used in mainstream classrooms that include a combination of ELLs and native English speakers or in classrooms with ELLs only. Research on sheltered immersion programs has reported that students in such programs outperform their peers on expository writing assignments (Echevarria et al., 2006). Although further research is needed, the sheltered immersion model is a promising approach to enhancing the language and academic skills of ELLs.

Bilingual education programs—programs that combined instruction in a first language with instruction in a second language—have also been proven to be generally effective (Baca & Cervantes, 1989; Gersten & Woodward, 1994; Rossell, 2005). Learning to read in the home language can boost one's literacy in a second language and promote academic development. Indeed, most of the research confirms that students in bilingual education programs perform as well as or better than their monolingual peers in assessments of academic, cognitive, and social functioning. This research has been conducted throughout the world, with speakers of a wide variety of languages.

However, the debate goes on as to the relative effectiveness of immersion and bilingual programs. A multiyear study found that children in a structured English immersion program showed more significant gains than children in a transitional bilingual education program at first, but by grade four, the difference in reading and language outcomes between the two programs was not significant (Slavin, Madden, Calderón, Chamberlin, & Hennessy, 2011). The researchers concluded that the language of instruction is not an important factor in determining whether a program is effective or not and, therefore, our focus should be on quality of instruction. Unfortunately, despite strong evidence for the effectiveness of immersion and bilingual education programs, many school districts choose other kinds of programs for these children, and the reasons for such decisions often have more to do with politics than with educational outcomes. As Rossell (2005) notes, the "sink-or-swim" model is the most prevalent approach to educating ELLs despite little research to support its effectiveness. Teachers and speech-language specialists should advocate for decisions based on the individual child's needs and program effectiveness rather than on factors such as prejudice, fear, and cost.

Although research has not clearly determined which approach to teaching ELLs is most effective, it has helped us to identify effective instructional practices for these students. In their review, Coleman and Goldenberg (2009) identified the following methods as being effective ways of teaching ELLs:

1. **Use explicit, direct instruction and interactive approaches:** Students should be explicitly taught the elements of English (e.g., vocabulary, syntax, conventions) and social conventions (e.g., greetings, conversational conventions). Teachers should use elements of effective instruction such as having clear objectives, providing opportunities for adequate practice, using frequent assessment, and reteaching when necessary.

2. **Provide opportunities for authentic communication:** ELLs need to have numerous opportunities to use their English language skills in interactions. Activities such as cooperative learning groups provide students with opportunities for more communicative interaction with their native English-speaking peers.

3. **Provide daily oral English language instruction that targets language acquisition:** While the authors note that research has not firmly established the optimum amount of direct instruction in oral language that ELLs need, they recommend about 45 minutes per day.

4. **Students need to be taught *both* expressive and receptive language skills:** ELLs need to be able to speak and write effectively as well as understand the content of classroom instruction.

5. **Group by proficiency level:** The authors caution that ELLs should not be segregated by language proficiency but that grouping by proficiency may help during English language instruction.

6. **Emphasize the acquisition of academic language as well as conversational language:** ELLs need to learn the vocabulary and complex language forms that will enable them to understand the more abstract and challenging content in social studies, mathematics, and the sciences.

Literacy Instruction for English Language Learners

An important component of most instructional programs for ELLs is the development of literacy skills (reading, writing, and spoken language). As we noted earlier in this chapter, many ELLs lag behind their peers in the development of reading and writing skills. How can we help these students develop literacy skills?

One approach that has been successful is intensive instruction in phonological awareness skills. For example, Lesaux and Siegel (2003) studied the effects of combining an intensive phonological awareness training program with a balanced literacy instruction on ELLs at risk for reading difficulties. The "at-risk" students (both those who spoke a language other than English and English-language-proficient children) received intensive instruction in phonological awareness. By second grade, the ELLs had caught up to (and, in some cases, surpassed) the native English language speakers. Culatta, Reese, and Setzer (2006) reported the results of the use of the Systematic and Engaging Early Literacy (SEEL) instruction program with 11 ELLs from two kindergarten classrooms. The program uses meaning-based instruction to teach phonological skills in both English and Spanish, including:

■ *Rhyming:* Activities designed to teach rhyme made the common word ending noticeable by targeting one rhyme per activity, highlighting the rhyme ending using intonation and stress, providing multiple examples of target words, and explicitly labeling the same word endings as rhyme.

■ *Alliteration:* Instructors used the same techniques to highlight literacy targets as in the rhyming activities. When instructing in Spanish, they highlighted an initial syllable in an activity such as passing things that began with /pa/ (e.g., "Pasa la papa para papá con el papel o pala" ["Pass the potatoes to the father with a piece of paper or a shovel"]).

■ *Sound blending and letter–sound associations:* Opportunities to segment and blend sounds and to make letter–sound associations were incorporated into the rhyme and alliteration activities.

Students who participated in the program made significant improvements on all of the skills taught by the program. Although the researchers did not evaluate whether the instruction led to better reading outcomes, they reported that the students were very motivated to participate.

Another approach to enhancing the literacy skills of ELLs has been to provide explicit instruction in vocabulary. ELLs are at risk for vocabulary difficulties (Lugo-Neris, Jackson, & Goldstein, 2010), so instructional methods that can help them improve their vocabulary learning are important. One approach is to embed vocabulary instruction into reading.

This is the approach that was taken by Lugo-Neris and colleagues (2010). They studied the effect of English as compared to Spanish vocabulary expansions (where the teacher explained the meaning of a word that the child encountered in print) on the vocabulary learning of 4- to 6-year-old children who spoke Spanish as their first language. They found that the children who received instruction in Spanish outperformed the children who were taught in English. They concluded that shared reading and the use of the child's first language to bridge between their first language and reading in their second language were effective methods to enhance literacy skills in young ELLs.

Nelson, Vadasy, and Sanders (2011) developed a tier 2–type intervention to supplement the vocabulary learning of kindergarten-age children who spoke Spanish as their first language. Children in the experimental group received vocabulary instruction that used the following techniques:

1. **Word blending and spelling:** Students were taught to blend target words, using multiple opportunities to develop rapid reading of words and phonetically accurate spelling.

2. **Word meaning:** Children were presented with child-friendly definitions for target words. The meaning for each target word was depicted by a picture and used in a sentence. The teacher alternated between being the listener and being the questioner for students' explanations of the meaning for target words.

3. **Fast read passage:** Students were asked to read a fully decodable short passage that used the target word in a context that was decodable and meaningful to young children. Each passage was first read aloud together by the teacher and student. The teacher–student read-aloud was followed by a student read-aloud. Each read-aloud was repeated until students could read the passage fluently and show comprehension of the text.

4. **Sentence completion:** Students were required to "fill in the blanks" in a cloze procedure task. The cloze procedure required the student to use the sentence context to choose the appropriate word that goes in the blank.

5. **Word meaning match:** Students identified the picture for the target word from a pair of pictures illustrating an example and nonexample of the meaning for target words.

6. **Say a sentence:** Instructors prompted the children to use the target vocabulary words in oral language activities. For example, for the words *hot* and *damp*, the prompt might be "Tell me how *hot* is different from *damp*."

The researchers reported that the children who received explicit vocabulary instruction significantly outperformed a similar group of children who engaged in interactive book reading.

Linan-Thompson, Vaughn, Hickman-Davis, and Kouzekanani (2003) also provided supplemental reading instruction to second-grade ELLs for 30 minutes a day, five times a week, for 13 weeks. The instruction consisted of five components:

- *Fluent reading:* Repeated reading of familiar text designed to help students develop automatic recognition of words.

- *Phonological awareness:* Students were given the opportunity to blend, segment, delete, substitute, and manipulate phonemes in words. Teachers used picture cards to provide context for words.

- *Instructional-level reading:* Students read books at their instructional level. Teachers previewed vocabulary words and activated students' background knowledge.

- *Word study:* Students received specific instruction in word analysis strategies.

- *Writing:* Students wrote as many words as they could in 1 minute.

Most of the children who received this instruction made significant gains on measures of reading outcomes and continued those gains even after the supplemental instruction was discontinued. Similarly, Denton, Anthony, Parker, and Hasbrouck (2004) studied the effects of providing tutoring to second- through fifth-grade ELLs. The tutoring sessions took place three times a week, for 40 minutes a session, over 10 weeks. The researchers compared two instructional programs: *Read Well* (Sprick, Howard, & Fidanque, 1998), in which students receive explicit, systematic instruction in English decoding, and *Read Naturally* (Ihnot, 1992), which uses a repeated reading approach. Students who received direct instruction in decoding (the *Read Well* program) made significant gains in reading. Most students in the *Read Naturally* program did not show improvement. The authors speculated that students may have not done as well in the latter program because they lacked the necessary vocabulary to be successful readers.

Hudelson (1994) described additional strategies for literacy development for second-language learners (see Table 16.4). Hudelson's suggestions are based on a whole-language theory of instruction. While this approach can work for students with limited English proficiency (LEP) (Gersten & Woodward, 1994), Reyes (1992) cautions that this approach should be used with care. She suggests that literature-based programs must include literature from the cultural traditions of *all* of the students in the class. Furthermore, teachers should not be afraid to correct syntax and spelling when necessary. Reyes observed that modeling was not always adequate to teach English grammar rules to LEP students. In addition, Reyes suggests that second-language learners be given the opportunity to use their native language for both academic and nonacademic purposes.

Although research on effective literacy instruction for ELLs is still limited, it is becoming clear that early identification of children at risk for reading and writing difficulties, coupled with intensive instruction that focuses on skills such as phonological awareness, can improve the literacy skills of these students.

Table 16.4

Strategies for Literacy Development of Second-Language Learners

- **Create a literate classroom environment:** The classroom should be a language-rich environment. Charts for attendance, favorite songs, and academic tasks; a classroom library; a writing center; and displays of children's written work can be used to enhance the classroom environment.
- **Encourage collaborative learning:** A collaborative learning environment has been found to be an important factor in the success of classrooms for linguistically diverse learners (Reyes & Laliberty, 1992). Children should be encouraged to work together, to rely on each other, and to support each other.
- **Use oral and written personal narratives:** Although second-language learners may take longer to feel comfortable producing personal narratives, this can be an effective procedure. Reyes (1992) notes that many second-language learners will need help with some of the mechanics of writing in order to be successful.
- **Use dialogic writing:** Dialogue journals enable students and teachers to communicate with each other in a nonjudgmental way. Second-language learners get the opportunity to see examples of standard written English.
- **Use predictable books:** Such books reinforce the idea that reading is a process of prediction. Students can be asked to predict what is likely to happen and to fill in missing words.
- **Include opportunities for self-selected reading:** Students need opportunities to select and read books of their own choice.
- **Include literacy development as a part of content study:** Content area study provides many opportunities for reading, researching, and writing. When students with limited English proficiency are grouped in classrooms with native English speakers, heterogeneous grouping can be used to give the LEP students an opportunity to be successful.

Source: Adapted from Hudelson, S. (1994). Literacy development of second language children. In F. Genesee (Ed.), *Educating second language children* (pp. 129–158). New York: Cambridge University Press.

Watch this elementary school teacher use explicit instructional techniques with her ELLs. What methods did the teacher use to elicit responses from her students?

Apply Your Knowledge 16.2: English Immersion Instruction

Watch a video of Janie Ruiz's first-grade English immersion class at Sammons Elementary School and answer the questions.

Instruction for Students with Language Differences as Well as Language Disorders

An earlier discussion in this chapter described a group of ELLs who also have disabilities affecting learning ability and/or social development. These students are sometimes *culturally and linguistically different exceptional (CLDE) students* (Baca & Almanza, 1991). These students can be very difficult to identify. As noted earlier, sometimes ELLs are misidentified as having a disability when they do not. Therefore, teachers and language specialists may be reluctant to consider the possibility that these children may have a learning difficulty as well as a language difference. But, as Garcia and Tyler (2010) point out, these students will have difficulty in learning not only in English but in their first language as well. To help these students with both their language-learning needs and their learning challenges, Garcia and Tyler (2010) suggest that teachers:

- Use teaching methods that draw on students' preferred or stronger modalities (e.g., listening versus reading, oral versus written)
- Reduce information students must generate independently (e.g., providing checklists, reading and/or study guides, peer assistance with note taking)
- Teach study skills, self-monitoring skills, or other coping strategies to support areas affected by the disability
- Modify test formats to accommodate language and disability-related needs (e.g., reading questions to the student, allowing extra time, performance-based assessments)
- Teach students discipline-specific language and symbols, as well as strategies to comprehend technical language and increase engagement with texts
- Provide supplementary, intensive reading interventions by a reading specialist or a special education teacher who is familiar with ESL adaptations

Just as there is disagreement about what constitutes the best instructional program for ELLs, there is also great disagreement within the special education field about the most effective instructional practices. Often, this disagreement comes down to an argument between those who advocate a direct instruction approach versus those who favor instruction addressing cognitive-learning processes. This debate is especially relevant with regard to ELLs with disabilities. Many educators have expressed concerns about the use of direct instruction techniques with these students (Cummins, 1984; Yates & Ortiz, 1991). They are concerned that programs focusing on the acquisition of specific language skills (such as phonics and vocabulary acquisition) may actually interfere with the child's acquisition of English. Some educators have suggested that programs that emphasize more naturalistic approaches may be more effective. At the same time, we cannot ignore the fact that many ELLs with disabilities will need extra help in identifying and correcting errors in language usage.

Check Your Understanding 16.3

Click here to gauge your understanding of the concepts in this section.

Summary

In looking at the impact of language and cultural differences on schools and schooling, educators must have an awareness of the difference between a *language disability* and a *language difference.* Many children come to school speaking a dialect that differs from standard English or a language other than English. There is nothing "wrong" with most of these children, and most of them do not require special educational services. But many do need special programs that will allow them to retain their first language or dialect while learning standard English.

We have seen that most research favors a *holistic* approach that emphasizes the development of *literacy skills* through use of the child's *first language*—that students are then better able to make the transition to English. It is important that teachers show respect for the child's language and culture as they try to help the child make this transition.

Some children with language and cultural differences also have learning and/or behavior disabilities. These children not only need help in learning English but also need the intensive instructional support that can be provided through special education.

Teachers and other education professionals need to be aware of the special needs of children with language and cultural differences. They should also respect the contribution that cultural diversity makes to our society.

References

Chapter 1

American Speech-Language-Hearing Association, Ad Hoc Committee on Service Delivery in the Schools. (1993). *Definitions of communication disorders and variations.* Retrieved from http://www.asha.org/policy/RP1993-00208/

Backus, A. (1999). Mixed native language: A challenge to the monolithic view of language. *Topics in Language Disorders, 19*(4), 11–22.

Battison, R. (2000). American Sign Language linguistics 1970–1980: Memoir of a renaissance. In K. Emmorey & H. Lane (Eds.), *The Signs of Language Revisited.* Mahwah, NJ: Lawrence Erlbaum.

Bishop, D. V. M., & Bishop, S. J. (1998). "Twin language": A risk factor for language impairment? *Journal of Speech, Language, and Hearing Research, 41,* 150–161.

Gardner, R., & Gardner, B. (1969). Teaching sign language to a chimpanzee. *Science, 165,* 664–672.

Hauser, M. D., Chomsky, N., & Fitch, W. T. (2002). The faculty of language: What is it, who has it, and how did it evolve? *Science, 298*(5598), 1569–1579.

Hulit, L., Fahey, K., & Howard, M. (2014). *Born to talk* (6th ed.). Boston, MA: Pearson.

Lewis, M. P. (Ed.). (2009). *Ethnologue* (16th ed.). Dallas, TX: SIL International. Online version: www.ethnologue.com/

MacWhinney, B. (Ed.). (1999). *The emergence of language.* Mahwah, NJ: Lawrence Erlbaum.

National Institute on Deafness and Other Communication Disorders. (2015). *Statistics on voice speech and language.* Retrieved from http://www.nidcd.nih.gov/health/statistics/pages/vsl.aspx

Owens, R. (2015). *Language development: An introduction* (9th ed.). Boston, MA: Pearson.

Owens, R., Farinella, K., & Metz, D. (2015). *Introduction to communication disorders* (5th ed.). Boston, MA: Pearson Education.

Pinker, S. (1994). *The language instinct: How the mind creates language.* New York, NY: William Morrow.

Pinker, S., & Jackendoff, R. (2005). The faculty of language: What's special about it? *Cognition, 95,* 201–236.

Savage-Rumbaugh, E. S., Shanker, S. G., & Taylor, T. J. (1998). *Apes, language, and the human mind.* New York, NY: Oxford University Press.

Terrace, H. (1980). *Nim.* New York, NY: Knopf.

U.S. Department of Education, National Center for Education Statistics. (2015). *Digest of Education Statistics, 2013* (NCES 2015-011), Chapter 2.

Chapter 2

Bloom, L., & Lahey, M. (1978). *Language development and language disorders.* New York, NY: Wiley.

Bryant, J. (2009). Language in social contexts: Communicative competence in the preschool years. In J. B. Gleason (Ed.), *The development of language* (7th ed., pp. 192–226). Boston, MA: Pearson.

Chomsky, N. (1957). *Syntactic structures.* The Hague, Netherlands: Mouton.

Chomsky, N. (1965). *Aspects of the theory of syntax.* Cambridge, MA: MIT Press.

Chomsky, N. (1981). *Lectures on government and binding.* Dordrecht, Netherlands: Foris.

Chomsky, N. (1982). *Some concepts and consequences of the theory of government and binding.* Cambridge, MA: MIT Press.

Gleason, J. B. (2009). The development of language: An overview and a preview. In J. B. Gleason (Ed.), *The development of language* (7th ed., pp. 1–36). Boston, MA: Pearson.

Grice, H. (1975). Logic and conversation. In P. Cole & J. Morgan (Eds.), *Syntax and semantics, Volume 3: Speech acts.* New York, NY: Academic Press.

Leonard, L., & Loeb, D. (1988). Government binding theory and some of its applications: A tutorial. *Journal of Speech and Hearing Research, 31,* 515–524.

Pence, K., & Justice, L. (2012). *Language development: From theory to practice* (2nd ed.). Saddle Brook, NJ: Pearson.

Pinker, S. (1994). *The language instinct: How the mind creates language.* New York, NY: William Morrow.

Shapiro, L. P. (1997). Tutorial: An introduction to syntax. *Journal of Speech, Language, and Hearing Research, 40,* 254–273.

Stemberger, J., & Bernhardt, B. (1999). The emergence of faithfulness. In B. MacWhinney (Ed.), *The emergence of language.* Mahwah, NJ: Lawrence Erlbaum.

Tomasello, M. (2003). *Constructing a language.* Cambridge, MA: Harvard University Press.

Chapter 3

Anderson, N., & Shames, G. (2011). *Human communication disorders: An introduction* (8th ed.). Boston, MA: Allyn & Bacon.

Bohannon, J. N., & Bonvillian, J. D. (2009). Theortical approaches to language acquisition. In J. Berko-Gleason (Ed.), *The development of language* (7th ed., pp. 227–284). Boston, MA: Pearson Education

Bookheimer, S. (2002). Functional MRI of language: New approaches to understanding the cortical organization of semantic processing. *Annual Reviews of Neuroscience, 25,* 151–188.

Cooper, R. P., & Aslin, R. N. (1990). Preference for infant-directed speech in the first month after birth. *Child Development, 61,* 1584–1595.

Curtiss, S. (1977). *Genie: A psycholinguistic study of a modern-day "wild child."* New York, NY: Academic Press.

Fedorenko, E., & Kanwisher, N. (2009). Neuroimaging of language: Why hasn't a clearer picture emerged? *Language and Linguistics Compass, 3*(4), 839–865.

Frackowiak, R., Friston, K., Frith, C., Dolan, R., Price, C., Zeki, S., ... Price, C. J. (2004). *Human brain function* (2nd ed.). San Diego, CA: Academic Press.

Friederici, A. D. (2001). Syntactic, prosodic, and semantic processes in the brain: Evidence from event-related neuroimaging. *Journal of Psycholinguistic Research, 30,* 237–250.

Friederici, A., Opitz, B., & van Cramon, D. (2000). Segregating semantic and syntactic aspects of processing in the human brain: An fMRI investigation of different word types. *Cerebral Cortex, 10,* 698–705.

Hart, B., & Risley, T. R. (1995). *Meaningful differences in the everyday experience of young American children.* Baltimore, MD: Paul H. Brookes.

Hickok, G. (2001). Functional anatomy of speech perception and speech production: Psycholinguistic implications. *Journal of Psycholinguistic Research, 30,* 225–235.

Hulit, L., Fahey, K., & Howard, M. (2014). *Born to talk* (6th ed.). Upper Saddle River, NJ: Pearson.

Huttenlocher, P. R. (2002). *Neural plasticity: The effects of environment on the development of the cerebral cortex.* Cambridge, MA: Harvard University Press.

Kaplan, P. S., Bachorowski, J. A., Smoski, M. J., & Hudenko, W. J. (2002). Infants of depressed mothers, although competent learners, fail to learn in response to their own mothers' infant-directed speech. *Psychological Science, 13,* 268–271.

Kent, R. D., & Vorperian, H. K. (2011). The biology and physics of speech. In N. B. Anderson & G. H. Shames (Eds.), *Human communication disorders: An introduction* (8th ed., pp. 54–83). Boston, MA: Allyn & Bacon.

Kleim, J., & Jones, T. (2008). Principles of experience-dependent plasticity: Implications for rehabilitation after brain damage. *Journal of Speech, Language, and Hearing Research, 51,* 225–239.

Lenneberg, E. (1967). *Biological foundations of language.* New York, NY: Wiley.

MacWhinney, B. (1998). Models of the emergence of language. *Annual Review of Psychology, 49,* 199–277.

Newman, R., & Sachs, J. (2012). Communication development in infancy. In J. Gleason & N. Ratner (Eds.), *The development of language* (8th ed., pp. 30–51). Upper Saddle River, NJ: Pearson.

Obler, L. (2012). Developments in the adult years. In J. B. Gleason & N. Ratner (Eds.), *The development of language* (8th ed., pp. 366–392). Upper Saddle River, NJ: Pearson.

Obler, L. K., & Gjerlow, K. (1999). *Language and the brain.* New York, NY: Cambridge University Press.

Owens, R., Farinella, K., & Metz, D. E. (2015). *Introduction to communication disorders: A lifespan evidence-based perspective* (5th ed.). Upper Saddle River, NJ: Pearson.

Piaget, J. (1954). *The construction of reality in the child.* New York, NY: Basic Books.

Pinker, S. (1994). *The language instinct: How the mind creates language.* New York, NY: Morrow.

Rymer, R. (1993). *Genie: Escape from a silent childhood.* London, United Kingdom: Michael Joseph.

Sinclair-DeZwart, H. (1973). Language acquisition and cognitive development. In T. Moore (Ed.), *Cognitive development and the acquisition of language.* New York, NY: Academic Press.

Singh, L., Morgan, J. L., & Best, C. T. (2002). Infants' listening preferences: Baby talk or happy talk? *Infancy, 3,* 365–394.

Trainor, L., & Desjardins, R. (2002). Pitch characteristics of infant-directed speech affect infant's ability to discriminate vowels. *Psychonomic Bulletin & Review, 9*(2), 335–340.

Vygotsky, L. (1962). *Thought and language.* Cambridge, MA: MIT Press.

Chapter 4

Bates, E., & MacWhinney, B. (1987). Competition, variation, and language learning. In B. MacWhinney (Ed.), *Mechanisms of language acquisition* (pp. 157–194). Hillsdale, NJ: Erlbaum.

Bloom, L. (1970). *Language development: Form and function of emerging grammars.* Cambridge, MA: MIT Press.

Bohannon, J., & Bonvillian, J. (2009). Theoretical approaches to language acquisition. In J. B. Gleason & N. Ratner (Eds.), *The development of language* (7th ed., pp. 227–284). Boston, MA: Pearson.

Bohannon, J., Padgett, R., Nelson, K. E., & Mark, M. (1996). Useful evidence on negative evidence. *Developmental Psychology, 32,* 551–555.

Bohannon, J., & Stanowicz, L. (1988). Adult responses to children's language errors: The issue of negative evidence. *Developmental Psychology, 24,* 684–689.

Bruner, J. (1977). Early social interaction and language acquisition. In R. Schaffer (Ed.), *Studies in mother-infant interaction.* New York, NY: Academic Press.

Cattell, R. (2000). *Children's language: Consensus and controversy.* New York, NY: Cassell.

Chomsky, N. (1965). *Aspects of the theory of syntax.* Cambridge, MA: MIT Press.

Chomsky, N. (1968). *Language and mind.* New York, NY: Harcourt, Brace, & World.

Christopoulos, C., Bonvillian, J., & Crittenden, P. (1988). Maternal language input and child maltreatment. *Infant Mental Health Journal, 9,* 272–286.

Fillmore, C. (1968). The case for case. In E. Bach & R. Harmas (Eds.), *Universals in linguistic theory* (pp. 1–88). New York, NY: Holt, Rinehart and Winston.

Gopnik & A.N. Meltzoff (1987). Language and thought in the young child: Early semantic developments and their relationship to object permanence, means-ends understanding and categorization. In K. Nelson & A. Van Kleeck (Eds.), *Children's language* (Vol. 6). Hillsdale, NJ: Lawrence Erlbaum.

Guasti, M. T. (2002). *Language acquisition: The growth of grammar.* Cambridge, MA: MIT Press.

Hirsh-Pasek, K., & Golinkoff, R. (1996). *The origins of grammar: Evidence from early language comprehension.* Cambridge, MA: MIT Press.

Hirsh-Pasek, K., Treiman, R., & Schneiderman, M. (1984). Brown and Hanlon revisited: Mother's sensitivity to ungrammatical forms. *Journal of Child Language, 11,* 81–88.

Lovaas, O. I. (1987). Behavioral treatment and normal educational and intellectual functioning in young autistic children. *Journal of Consulting and Clinical Psychology, 55,* 3–9.

MacWhinney, B. (1998). Models of the emergence of language. *Annual Review of Psychology, 49,* 199–277.

McEachin, J., Smith, T., & Lovaas, O. (1993). Long-term outcome for children with autism who received early intensive behavioral treatment. *American Journal on Mental Retardation, 97,* 359–372.

Ninnio, A., & Snow, C. (1999). The development of pragmatics: Learning to use language appropriately. In W. Ritchie & T. Bhatia (Eds.), *Handbook of child language acquisition* (pp. 347–386). New York, NY: Academic Press.

Owens, R. (2016). *Language development: An introduction* (9th ed.). Boston, MA: Pearson.

Pence, K., & Justice, L. (2008). *Language development from theory to practice.* Upper Saddle River, NJ: Pearson.

Piaget. J. (1954). *The construction of reality in the child.* New York, NY: Basic Books.

Pinker, S. (1994). *The language instinct: How the mind creates language.* New York, NY: Morrow.

Prizant, B., & Rubin, E. (1999). Contemporary issues in interventions for autism spectrum disorders: A commentary. *Journal of the Association for Persons with Severe Handicaps, 24,* 199–208.

Ritchie, W., & Bhatia, T. (1999). Child language development: Introduction, foundations, and overview. In W. Ritchie & T. Bhatia (Eds.), *Handbook of child language acquisition.,* (pp. 1–33). New York, NY: Academic Press.

Saxton, M., Houston-Price, C., & Dawson, N. (2005). The prompts hypothesis: Clarification requests as corrective input for grammatical errors. *Applied Nativist Syntactics, 26,* 393–314.

Skinner, B. F. (1957). *Verbal behavior.* New York, NY: Appleton-Century-Crofts.

Slobin, D. (1979). *Nativist-syntactics* (2nd ed.). Glenview, IL: Scott, Foresman.

Smith, T., Eikeseth, S., Klevstrand, M., & Lovaas, O. (1997). Intensive behavioral treatment for preschoolers with severe mental retardation and pervasive developmental disorder. *American Journal on Mental Retardation, 102,* 238–249.

Tomasello, M. (2003). *Constructing a language.* Cambridge, MA: Harvard University Press.

Velleman, S., Mangipudi, L., & Locke, J. (1989). Prelinguistic phonetic contingency: Data from Down syndrome. *First Language, 9,* 169–173.

Vygotsky, L. (1962). *Thought and language.* Cambridge, MA: MIT Press.

Wexler, K. (1999). Maturation and growth of grammar. In W. Ritchie & T. Bhatia (Eds.), *Handbook of child language acquisition* (pp. 55–110). New York, NY: Academic Press.

Chapter 5

Anderson, R. C., Hiebert, E. H., Scott, J. A., & Wilkinson, I. A. G. (1985). *Becoming a nation of readers: The report of the Commission on Reading.* Washington, DC: National Academy of Education, Commission on Education and Public Policy.

Anglin, J. (1995). Classifying the world through language: Functional relevance, cultural significance, and category name learning. *International Journal of Intercultural Relations, 19,* 161–181.

Bates, E. (1979). *The emergence of symbols: Cognition and communication in infancy.* New York, NY: Academic Press.

Bates, E., Camaioni, L., & Volterra, V. (1975). The acquisition of performatives prior to speech. *Merrill-Palmer Quarterly, 21,* 205–216.

Bohannon, J., & Stanowicz, L. (1988). Adult responses to children's language errors: The issue of negative evidence. *Developmental Psychology, 24,* 684–689.

Brown, R. (1973). *A first language: The early stages.* Cambridge, MA: Harvard University Press.

Campbell, A. L., & Namy, L. L. (2003). The role of social referential context and verbal and nonverbal symbol learning. *Child Development, 74,* 549–563.

Dickinson, D., Golinkoff, R., & Hirsh-Pasek, K. (2010). Speaking out for language: Why language is central to reading development. *Educational Researcher, 39,* 305–310.

Dickinson, D. K., & Tabors, P. O. (2001). *Beginning literacy with language.* Baltimore, MD: Brookes.

Eimas, P., Siqueland, E., Jusczyk, P., & Vigorito, J. (1971). Speech perception in infants. *Science, 171,* 303–306.

Elias, G., & Broerse, J. (1996). Developmental changes in the incidence and likelihood of simultaneous talk during the first two years: A question of function. *Journal of Child Language, 23,* 201–217.

Fernald, A. (1992). Human maternal vocalizations to infants as biologically relevant signals: An evolutionary perspective. In J. H. Barlow, L. Cosmides, & J. Tooby (Eds.), *The adapted mind: Evolutionary psychology and the generation of culture* (pp. 391–428). New York, NY: Oxford University Press.

Hart, B., & Risley, T. R. (1995). *Meaningful differences in the everyday experience of young American children.* Baltimore, MD: Brookes.

Hart, B., & Risley, T. R. (1999). *The social world of children learning to talk.* Baltimore, MD: Paul H. Brookes.

Hirsh-Pasek, K. (2000). Beyond Shipley, Smith, and Gleitman: Young children's comprehension of bound morphemes. In B. Landau, J. Sabini, J. Jonides, & E. Newport (Eds.), *Perception, cognition, and language: Essays in honor of Henry and Lila Gleitman* (pp. 191–208). Cambridge, MA: MIT Press.

Hirsh-Pasek, K., & Golinkoff, R. M. (1993). Skeletal supports for grammatical learning: What the infant brings to the language learning task. In C. K. Rovee-Collier (Ed.), *Advances in infancy research* (Vol. 10). Norwood, NJ: Ablex.

Jusczyk, P., & Aslin, R. (1995). Infants' detection of the sound patterns of words in fluent speech. *Cognitive Psychology, 29,* 1–23.

Logan, K. J. (2003). Language and fluency characteristics of preschoolers' multiple-utterance conversational turns. *Journal of Speech, Language, and Hearing Research, 46,* 178–188.

Matsaka, N. (1992). Pitch characteristics of Japanese maternal speech to infants. *Journal of Child Language, 19,* 213–223.

Menyuk, P. (1999). *Reading and linguistic development.* Cambridge, MA: Brookline.

Murray, L., & Trevarthen, C. (1986). The infant's role in mother-infant communication. *Journal of Child Language, 13*, 15–31.

Muter, V., Hulme, C., Snowling, M. J., & Stevenson, J. (2004). Phonemes, rimes, vocabulary, and grammatical skills as foundations of early reading development: Evidence from a longitudinal study. *Developmental Psychology, 40*(5), 665–681.

National Early Literacy Panel. (2008). *Developing early literacy: Report of the National Early Literacy Panel.* Washington, DC: National Institute for Literacy. Retrieved from http://www.nifl.gov/earlychildhood/NELP/NELPreport.html

National Institute of Child Health and Human Development Study of Early Child Care Research Network. (2005). Pathways to reading: The role of oral language in the transition to reading. *Developmental Psychology, 41*, 428–442.

Nazzi, T., Bertoncini, J., & Mehler, J. (1998). Language discrimination by newborns: Toward an understanding of the role of rhythm. *Journal of Experimental Psychology: Human Perception and Performance, 24*, 756–766.

Nelson, K. (1973). Some evidence for the cognitive primacy of categorization and its functional basis. *Merrill-Palmer Quarterly, 19*, 21–39.

Newman, R., & Sachs, J. (2013). Communication development in infancy. In J. Gleason & N. Ratner (Eds.), *The development of language* (8th ed., pp. 30–51). Boston, MA: Allyn & Bacon.

Owens, R. (2011). *Language development: An introduction* (8th ed.). Upper Saddle River, NJ: Pearson.

Pruden, S., Hirsh-Pasek, K., Michnick Golinkoff, R., & Hennon, E. (2006). The birth of words: Ten-month-olds learn words through perceptual salience. *Child Development, 77*, 266–280.

Rollins, P. R. (2003). Caregivers' contingent comments to 9-month-old infants: Relationship with later language. *Applied Psycholinguistics, 24*, 221–234.

Saito, Y., Aoyama, S., Kondo, T., Fukumoto, R., Konishi, N., Nakamura, K., Kobayashi, M., & Toshima, T. (2007). Frontal cerebral blood flow change associated with infant-directed speech. *Archives of Disease Fetal and Neuronal Edition, 92*, 113–116.

Senechal, M., LeFevre, J., Thomas, E. M., & Daley, K. E. (1998). Differential effects of home literacy experiences on the development of oral and written language. *Reading Research Quarterly, 33*, 96–112.

Snow, C. (1977). Mothers' speech research: From input to interaction. In C. Snow & C. Ferguson (Eds.), *Talking to children: Language input and acquisition* (pp. 31–49). Cambridge, MA: Harvard University Press.

Snow, C., Burns, S., & Griffin, M. (1998). *Preventing reading difficulties in young children.* Washington, DC: National Academy Press.

Stark, R. (1979). Prespeech segmental feature development. In P. Fletcher & M. Garman (Eds.), *Language acquisition* (pp. 15–32). New York, NY: Cambridge University Press.

Stoel-Gammon, C., & Menn, L. (2013). Phonological development: Learning sounds and sound patterns. In J. Gleason & N. Ratner (Eds.), *The development of language* (8th ed., pp. 52–88). Upper Saddle River, NJ: Pearson.

Teale, W. H., & Sulzby, E. (Eds.). (1986). *Emergent literacy: Writing and reading.* Norwoord, NJ: Ablex.

Tincoff, R., & Jusczyk, P. (1999). Some beginnings of word comprehension in 6-month-olds. *Psychological Science, 10*, 172–175.

Tomasello, M. (2003). *Constructing a language: A usage-based theory of language acquisition.* Cambridge, MA: Harvard University Press.

Turnbull, K., & Justice, L. (2012). *Language development: From theory to practice* (2nd ed.). Upper Saddle River, NJ: Pearson.

Vernon-Feagans, L. (1996). *Children's talk in communities and classrooms.* Cambridge, MA: Blackwell.

Wasik, B. H., & Hendrickson, J. S. (2004). Family literacy practices. In C. Stone, E. Silliman, B. Ehren, & K. Apel (Eds.), *Handbook of language and literacy* (pp. 154–174). New York, NY: Guilford.

Whitehurst, G. J., & Lonigan, C. J. (1998). Child development and emergent literacy. *Child Development, 69*, 848–872.

Chapter 6

Al Otaiba, S., Kosanovich, M., & Torgesen, J. (2012). Assessment and instruction for phonemic awareness and word recognition skills. In A. Kamhi & H. Catts (Eds.), *Language and reading disabilities* (3rd ed., pp. 112–145). Boston, MA: Pearson.

Anglin, J. (1993). Vocabulary development: A morphological analysis. *Monographs of the Society for Research in Child Development, 58*(10), 1–86.

Bernstein, D. (1986). The development of humor: Implications for assessment and intervention. *Folia Phoniatrica, 39*, 130–144.

Bradley, L., & Bryant, P. (1985). *Rhyme and reason in reading and spelling.* Ann Arbor, MI: University of Michigan Press.

Catts, H. W., Fey, M. E., Zhang, X., & Tomblin, J. B. (1999). Language basis of reading and reading disabilities. *Scientific Studies of Reading, 3*, 331–361.

Dews, S., Winner, E., Kaplan, J., Rosenblatt, E., Hunt, M., Lim, K., McGovern, A., Qualter, A., & Smarsh, B. (1996). Children's understanding of the meaning and functions of verbal irony. *Child Development, 67*, 3071–3080.

Dickinson, D., Golinkoff, R., & Hirsh-Pasek, K. (2010). Speaking out for language: Why language is central to reading development. *Educational Researcher, 39*, 305–310.

Eckert, P. (2004). Adolescent language. In E. Finegan & J. Rickford (Eds.), *Language in the USA: Themes for the twenty-first century.* Cambridge, United Kingdom: Cambridge University Press.

Ehri, L. C., Nunes, S. R., Willows, D. M., Schuster, B. V., Yaghoub-Zadeh, Z., & Shanahan, T. (2001). Phonemic awareness instruction helps children learn to read: Evidence from the National Reading Panel's meta-analysis. *Reading Research Quarterly, 36*, 250–287.

Elleman, A., Lindo, E., Morphy, P., & Compton, D. (2009). The impact of vocabulary instruction on passage-level comprehension of school-age children: A meta-analysis. *Journal of Research on Educational Effectiveness, 2*(1), 1–44.

Ely, R., & McCabe, A. (1994). The language play of kindergarten children. *First Language, 14,* 19–35.

Fowles, B., & Glanz, M. (1977). Competence and a talent in verbal riddle comprehension. *Journal of Child Language, 4,* 433–452.

Hay, I., Elias, G., Fielding-Barnsley, R., Homel, R., & Freiberg, K. (2007). Language delays, reading delays, and learning difficulties: Interactive elements requiring multidimensional programming. *Journal of Learning Disabilities, 40,* 400–409.

Johnston, J. (1982). Narratives: A new look at communication problems in older language disordered children. *Language, Speech, and Hearing Services in the Schools, 13,* 144–145.

Larson, V. L., & McKinley, N. L. (1998). Characteristics of adolescents' conversations: A longitudinal study. *Clinical Linguistics and Phonetics, 12,* 183–203.

Nagy, W. E., & Anderson, R. C. (1984). How many words are there in printed school English? *Reading Research Quarterly, 19,* 304–330.

Nation, K., Clarke, P., Marshall, C. M., & Durand, M. (2004). Hidden language impairments in children: Parallels between poor reading comprehension and specific language impairment? *Journal of Speech, Language, and Hearing Research, 47,* 199–211.

Nation, K., & Snowling, M. J. (1998). Semantic processing and the development of word recognition skills: Evidence from children with reading comprehension difficulties. *Journal of Memory and Language, 39,* 85–101.

Nation, K., & Snowling, M. J. (1999). Developmental differences in sensitivity to semantic relations among good and poor comprehenders: Evidence from semantic priming. *Cognition, 70,* B1–B13.

National Institute of Child Health and Human Development Study of Early Child Care Research Network. (2005). Pathways to reading: The role of oral language in the transition to reading. *Developmental Psychology, 41,* 428–442.

Nippold, M. (1985). Comprehension of figurative language. *Topics in Language Disorders, 3,* 1–20.

Nippold, M. (1998). *Later language development* (2nd ed.). Austin, TX: Pro-Ed.

Nippold, M. (2000). Language development during the adolescent years: Aspects of pragmatics, syntax, and semantics. *Topics in Language Disorders, 20,* 15–28.

Nippold, M. A., Hegel, S. L., Uhden, L. D., & Bustamante, S. (1998). Development of proverb comprehension in adolescents: Implications for instruction. *Journal of Children's Communication Development, 19,* 49–55.

Nippold, M., Hesketh, L., Duthie, J., & Mansfield, T. (2005). Conversational versus expository discourse: A study of syntactic development in children, adolescents, and adults. *Journal of Speech, Language, and Hearing Research, 48,* 1048–1064.

Nippold, M., Ward-Lonergan, J., & Fanning, J. (2005). Persuasive writing in children, adolescents, and adults: A study of syntactic, semantic, and pragmatic development. *Language, Speech, and Hearing Services in Schools, 36,* 125–138.

Owens, R. (2015). *Language development: An introduction* (9th ed.). Boston, MA: Pearson.

Pence, K., & Justice, L. (2012). *Language development from theory to practice* (2nd ed.). Upper Saddle River, NJ: Pearson.

Raffaelli, M., & Duckett, E. (1989). "We were just talking . . .": Conversations in early adolescence. *Journal of Youth and Adolescence, 18,* 567–582.

Ricketts, J., Nation, K., & Bishop, D. (2007). Vocabulary is important for some, but not all reading skills. *Scientific Studies of Reading, 11,* 235–257.

Scarborough, H. S. (1998). Early identification of children at risk for reading disabilities: Phonological awareness and some other promising predictors. In B. K. Shapiro, P. J. Accardo, & A. J. Capute (Eds.), *Specific reading disability: A view of the spectrum* (pp. 75–119). Timonium, MD: York Press.

Scarborough, H. S. (2005). Developmental relationships between language and reading: Reconciling a beautiful hypothesis with some ugly facts. In H. Catts & A. Kamhi (Eds.), *The connections between language and reading disabilities.* Mahwah, NJ: Lawrence Erlbaum.

Shipley, K., Maddox, M., & Driver, J. (1991). Children's development of irregular past tense forms. *Language, Speech, and Hearing Services in Schools, 22,* 115–122.

Snow, C. E., Griffin, P., & Burns, M. S. (2005). *Knowledge to support the teaching of reading.* San Francisco, CA: Jossey-Bass.

Stadler, M., & Ward, G. (2005). Supporting the narrative development of young children. *Early Childhood Education Journal, 33,* 73–80.

Stanovich, K. E. (1991). Cognitive science meets beginning reading. *Psychological Science, 2,* 70–81.

Storch, S. A., & Whitehurst, G. J. (2002). Oral language and code-related precursors to reading: Evidence from a longitudinal structural model. *Developmental Psychology, 38,* 934–947.

Sutter, J., & Johnson, C. (1990). School-age children's metalinguistic awareness of grammaticality in verb form. *Journal of Speech and Hearing Research, 33,* 84–95.

Tabors, P. O., Snow, C. E., & Dickinson, D. K. (2001). Home and schools together: Supporting language and literacy development. In D. K. Dickinson & P. O. Tabors (Eds.), *Beginning literacy with language* (pp. 313–334). Baltimore, MD: Brookes.

Tunmer, W. E., Herriman, M. L., & Nesdale, A. R. (1988). Metalinguistic abilities and beginning reading. *Reading Research Quarterly, 23,* 134–158.

Vellutino, F. R., Fletcher, J. M., Snowling, M. J., & Scanlon, D. M. (2004). Specific reading disability (dyslexia): What have we learned in the past four decades? *Journal of Child Psychology and Psychiatry, 45,* 2–40.

Vellutino, F., Tunmer, W., Jaccard, J., & Chen, R. (2007). Components of reading ability: Multivariate evidence for a convergent skills model of reading development. *Scientific Studies of Reading, 11,* 3–32.

Vernon-Feagans, L., Hammer, C. S., Miccio, A., & Manlove, E. (2001). Early language and literacy skills in low-income African-American and Hispanic Children. In S. B. Neuman & D. K. Dickinson (Eds.), *Handbook of early literacy research* (pp. 192–210). New York, NY: Guilford.

Wagner, R. K., & Torgesen, J. K. (1987). The nature of phonological processing and its causal role in the acquisition of reading skills. *Psychological Bulletin, 101*, 192–212.

Whitehurst, G. J., & Lonigan, C. J. (1998). Child development and emergent literacy. *Child Development, 69*, 848–872.

Yopp, H. (1995). A test for assessing phonemic awareness in young children. *The Reading Teacher, 49*(1), 20–29.

Chapter 7

Adams, M., Foorman, B., Lundberg, I., & Beeler, C. (1998). *Phonemic awareness in young children: A classroom curriculum.* Baltimore, MD: Brookes.

American Psychiatric Association. (2013). *Diagnostic and statistical manual of mental disorders* (5th ed.). Washington, DC: Author.

Apel, K., Wilson-Fowler, E., Brimo, D., & Perrin, N. (2012). Metalinguistic contributions to reading and spelling in second and third grade students. *Reading and Writing, 25*, 1283–1305.

Aram, D., Ekelman, B., & Nation, J. (1984). Preschoolers with language disorders: 10 years later. *Journal of Speech and Hearing Research, 27*, 232–244.

Baker, L., & Cantwell, D. (1982). Psychiatric disorder in children with different types of communication disorders. *Journal of Communication Disorders, 15*, 113–126.

Bashir, A., & Scavuzzo, A. (1992). Children with language disorders: Natural history and academic success. *Journal of Learning Disabilities, 25*, 53–65.

Bennett, L., & Ottley, P. (2011). *Launch into reading success: Book 2.* Bloomington, IN: Trafford.

Bishop, D. V. M., & Adams, C. (1990). A prospective study of the relationship between specific language impairment, phonological disorders, and reading retardation. *Journal of Child Psychology and Psychiatry, 31*, 1027–1050.

Bishop, D. V. M., & Baird, G. (2001). Parent and teacher report of pragmatic aspects of communication: Use of the Children's Communication Scale in a clinical setting. *Developmental Medicine and Child Neurology, 43*, 809–818.

Bishop, D. V. M., & Snowling, M. J. (2004). Developmental dyslexia and specific language impairment: Same or different? *Psychological Bulletin, 130*, 858–886.

Blachman, B. (1991). Early intervention for children's reading problems: Clinical applications of the research in phonological awareness. *Topics in Language Disorders, 12*, 51–65.

Blachman, B. A. (2000). Phonological awareness. In M. Kamil, P. Mosenthal, P. Pearson, & R. Barr (Eds.), *Handbook of reading research* (Vol. III, pp. 483–502). Mahwah, NJ: Lawrence Erlbaum.

Blachman, B. A., Ball, E. W., Black, R. S., & Tangel, D. M. (2000). *Road to the code: A phonological awareness program for young children.* Baltimore, MD: Brookes.

Bos, C., Anders, P., Filip, D., & Jaffe, L. (1989). The effects of an interactive instructional strategy for enhancing reading comprehension and content area learning for students with learning disabilities. *Journal of Learning Disabilities, 22*(6), 384–390.

Boucher, C. (1986). Pragmatics: The meaning of verbal language in learning disabled and nondisabled boys. *Learning Disability Quarterly, 9*, 285–295.

Bradley, L., & Bryant, P. (1983). Categorizing sounds and learning to read: A causal connection. *Nature, 301*, 419–421.

Brady, S., Shankweiler, D., & Mann, V. (1983). Speech perception and memory coding in relation to reading ability. *Journal of Experimental Psychology, 35*, 345–367.

Brinton, B., & Fujiki, M. (1993). Language, social skills and socioemotional behavior. *Language, Speech, and Hearing Services in Schools, 24*, 194–198.

Brinton, B., Fujiki, M., & Higbee, L. M. (1998). Participation in cooperative learning activities by children with specific language impairment. *Journal of Speech, Language, and Hearing Research, 41*, 1193–1206.

Bryan, T. (1991). Social problems and learning disabilities. In B. Wong (Ed.), *Learning about learning disabilities* (pp. 195–231). San Diego, CA: Academic Press.

Bryan, T., Burstein, K., & Ergul, C. (2004). The social-emotional side of learning disabilities: A science-based presentation of the state of the art. *Learning Disability Quarterly, 27*, 45–51.

Casalis, S., Cole, P., & Sopo, D. (2004). Morphological awareness in developmental dyslexia. *Annals of Dyslexia, 54*, 114–138.

Catts, H. W. (1993). The relationship between speech-language impairments and reading disabilities. *Journal of Speech, Language, and Hearing Research, 36*, 948–958.

Catts, H. W., Adlof, S. M., Hogan, T. P., & Weismer, S. E. (2005). Are specific language impairment and dyslexia distinct disorders? *Journal of Speech, Language, and Hearing Research, 48*, 1378–1396.

Catts, H. W., Adlof, S. M., & Weismer, S. E. (2006). Language deficits in poor comprehenders: A case for the simple view of reading. *Journal of Speech, Language, and Hearing Research, 49*, 278–293.

Catts, H. W., Fey, M. E., Tomblin, J. B., & Zhang, X. (2002). A longitudinal investigation of reading outcomes in children with language impairments. *Journal of Speech, Language, and Hearing Research, 45*, 1142–1157.

Catts, H. W., Fey, M. E., Zhang, X., & Tomblin, J. B. (1999). Language basis of reading and reading disabilities: Evidence from a longitudinal investigation. *Scientific Studies of Reading, 3*, 331–361.

Centers for Disease Control and Prevention. (2015). *ADHD homepage.* Retrieved from http://www.cdc.gov/ncbddd/adhd/index.html

Cohen, W., Hodson, A., O'Hare, A., Boyle, J., Durrani, T., McCartney, E., Mattey, M., Naftalin, L., & Watson, J. (2005). Effects of computer-based intervention through acoustically modified speech (Fast ForWord) in severe mixed receptive-expressive language impairment: Outcomes from a randomized controlled trial. *Journal of Speech, Language, and Hearing Research, 48*, 715–729.

Condus, M. M., Marshall, K. J., & Miller, S. R. (1986). Effects of the keyword mnemonic strategy on vocabulary acquisition and maintenance by learning disabled children. *Journal of Learning Disabilities, 19*, 609–613.

Cortiella, C., & Horowitz, S. H. (2014). *The state of learning disabilities: Facts, trends and emerging issues.* New York, NY: National Center for Learning Disabilities.

Du Paul, G., Gormley, M., & Laracy, S. (2014). Comorbidity of LD and ADHD: implications of DSM-5 for assessment and treatment. *Journal of Learning Disabilities, 46*(1), 43–51.

Ehri, L. C., Nunes, S. R., Willows, D. M., Schuster, B. V., Yaghoub-Zadeh, Z., & Shanahan, T. (2001). Phonemic awareness instruction helps children learn to read: Evidence from the National Reading Panel's meta-analysis. *Reading Research Quarterly, 36,* 250–287.

Enfield, M. L., & Greene, V. (1997). *Project read.* Bloomington, MN: Language Circle Enterprise.

Fey, M., Finestack, L., Gajewski, B., Popescu, M., & Lewine, J. (2010). A preliminary evaluation of Fast ForWord Language as an adjuvant treatment in language intervention. *Journal of Speech, Language, and Hearing Research, 53,* 430–449.

Fox, B., & Routh, D. (1980). Phonemic analysis and severe reading disability. *Journal of Psycholinguistic Research, 9,* 115–119.

Friel-Patti, S., DesBarres, K., & Thibodeau, L. (2001). Case studies of children using Fast ForWord. *American Journal of Speech-Language Pathology, 10,* 203–215.

Fuchs, D., & Deshler, D. (2007). What we need to know about responsiveness to intervention (and shouldn't be afraid to ask). *Learning Disabilities Research and Practice, 22*(2), 129–136.

Goodwin, A., & Ahn, S. (2010). A meta-analysis of morphological interventions: Effects on literacy achievement of children with literacy difficulties. *Annals of Dyslexia, 60,* 183–208.

Gremillion, M., & Martel, M. (2012). Semantic language as a mechanism explaining the association between ADHD symptoms and reading and mathematics achievement. *Journal of Abnormal Child Psychology, 40,* 1339–1349.

Harris, M., Schumaker, J., & Deshler, D. (2011). The effects of morphological analysis instruction on the vocabulary performance of secondary students with and without disabilities. *Learning Disability Quarterly, 34*(1), 17–33.

Hart, K. I., Fujiki, M., Brinton, B., & Hart, C. H. (2004). The relationship between social behavior and severity of language impairment. *Journal of Speech, Language, and Hearing Research, 47,* 647–662.

Hatcher, P. J., Hulme, C., & Snowling, M. J. (2004). Explicit phoneme training combined with phonic reading instruction helps young children at risk of reading failure. *Journal of Child Psychology and Psychiatry, 45,* 338–358.

Higgins, E. L., & Raskind, M. H. (2000). Speaking to read: A comparison of continuous vs. discrete speech recognition in the remediation of learning disabilities. *Journal of Special Education Technology, 15,* 19–30.

Higgins, E. L., & Raskind, M. H. (2004). Speech recognition-based and automaticity programs to help students with severe reading and spelling problems. *Annals of Dyslexia, 54,* 365–392.

Hook, P. E., Macaruso, P., & Jones, S. (2001). Efficacy of Fast ForWord training on facilitating acquisition of reading skills by children with reading difficulties—A longitudinal study. *Annals of Dyslexia, 51,* 73–96.

Individuals with Disabilities Education Act. (2004). Washington, DC: U.S. Government Printing Office.

Institute for Education Sciences. (2007). *What works clearinghouse intervention report—Wilson Reading.* Washington, DC: Author.

Institute for Education Sciences (2009). *What works clearinghouse intervention report–Earobics.* Washington, DC: Author.

Institute for Education Sciences (2010). *What works clearinghouse intervention report–Ladders to Literacy.* Washington, DC: Author.

International Dyslexia Association (2012). *Dyslexia basics.* Baltimore, MD: International Dyslexia Association.

Jitendra, A., Edwards, L., Sacks, G., & Jacobson, L. (2004). What research says about vocabulary instruction for students with learning disabilities. *Exceptional Children, 70*(3), 299–322.

Kaderavek, J. (2014). *Language disorders in children* (2nd ed.). Upper Saddle River, NJ: Pearson

Kamhi, A., & Koenig, L. (1985). Metalinguistic awareness in normal and language-disordered children. *Language, Speech, and Hearing Services in Schools, 16,* 199–210.

Kavale, K. A., & Mattson, P. D. (1983). "One jumped off the balance beam": A meta-analysis of perceptual-motor training. *Journal of Learning Disabilities, 16,* 165–173.

Kennedy, M., Deshler, D., & Lloyd, J. (2015). Effects of multimedia vocabulary instruction on adolescents with learning disabilities. *Journal of Learning Disabilities, 48*(1), 22–38.

Kennedy, M., Thomas, C., Meyer, J. P., Alves, K., & Lloyd, J. (2014). Using evidence-based multimedia to improve vocabulary performance of adolescents with LD: A UDL approach. *Learning Disability Quarterly, 37*(2), 71–86.

Kirk, S. (1963). Behavioral diagnosis and remediation of learning disabilities. In *Proceedings of the Conference on the Exploration into the Problems of the Perceptually Handicapped Child.* Evanston, IL: Fund for the Perceptually Handicapped Child.

Lapadat, J. (1991). Pragmatic language skills of students with language and/or learning disabilities: A quantitative synthesis. *Journal of Learning Disabilities, 24,* 147–158.

Lerner, J., & Johns, B. (2015). *Learning disabilities and related disabilities* (13th ed.). Stamford, CT: Cengage.

Lewis, B., Freebairn, L., & Taylor, H. (2000). Follow-up of children with early expressive phonology disorders. *Journal of Learning Disabilities, 33,* 433–444.

Lindamood, P., & Lindamood, P. (2011). *LiPS: The Lindamood Phoneme Sequencing Program for Reading, Spelling, and Speech–4th ed.* Austin, TX: Pro-Ed.

Loeb, D. F., Gillam, R., Hoffman, L., Brandel, J., & Marquis, J. (2009). The effects of Fast ForWord Language on the phonemic awareness and reading skills of school-age children with language impairments and poor reading skills. *American Journal of Speech-Language Pathology, 18,* 376–387.

Martinussen, R., & Mackenzie, G. (2015). Reading comprehension in adolescents with ADHD: Exploring the poor comprehender profile and individual differences in vocabulary and executive functions. *Research in Developmental Disabilities, 38,* 329–337.

Mastropieri, M. (1988). Using the keyword method. *Teaching Exceptional Children, 20,* 4–8.

Mastropieri, M. A., Scruggs, T. E., Levin, J. R., Gaffney, J., & McLoone, B. (1985). Mnemonic vocabulary instruction for learning disabled students. *Learning Disability Quarterly, 8,* 57–63.

McArthur, G. M., Hogben, J. H., Edwards, V. T., Heath, S. M., & Mengler, E. D. (2000). On the "specifics" of specific reading disability and specific language impairment. *Journal of Child Psychology and Psychiatry, 41,* 869–874.

Menyuk, P., Chesnick, M., Liebergott, J., Korngold, B., D'Agostino, R., & Belanger, A. (1991). Predicting reading problems in at-risk children. *Journal of Speech and Hearing Research, 34,* 893–903.

Mikami, A. Y., Huang-Pollock, C. L., Pfiffner, L. J., McBurnett, K., & Hangai, D. (2007). Social skills differences among attention deficit/hyperactivity disorder types in a chat room assessment task. *Journal of Abnormal Child Psychology, 35,* 509–521.

Mokhtari, K., & Thompson, H. B. (2006). How problems of reading fluency and comprehension are related to difficulties in syntactic awareness skills among fifth graders. *Reading Research and Instruction, 46,* 73–94.

Mueller, K., & Tomblin, J. B. (2012). Examining the comorbidity of language impairment and attention-deficit/hyperactivity disorder. *Topics in Language Disorders, 32*(3), 228–246.

Nagy, W., Carlisle, J., & Goodwin, A. (2013). Morphological knowledge and literacy acquisition. *Journal of Learning Disabilities, 47*(1), 3–12.

Nation, K., Clarke, P., Marshall, C. M., & Durand, M. (2004). Hidden language impairments in children: Parallels between poor reading comprehension and specific language impairment? *Journal of Speech, Language, and Hearing Research, 47,* 199–211.

Nation, K., Cocksey, J., Taylor, J. S. H., & Bishop, D. (2010). A longitudinal investigation of early reading and language skills in children with poor reading comprehension. *Journal of Child Psychology and Psychiatry, 51,* 1031–1039.

National Early Literacy Panel. (2008). *Developing early literacy: Report of the National Early Literacy Panel.* Washington, DC: National Institute for Literacy. Retrieved from http://www.nifl.gov/earlychildhood/NELP/NELPreport.html

National Reading Panel. (2000). *Report of the National Reading Panel: Reports of the subgroups.* Washington, DC: National Institute of Child Health and Human Development Clearinghouse.

Nilsen, E., Mangal, L., & Macdonald, K. (2013). Referential communication in children with ADHD: Challenges in the role of a listener. *Journal of Speech, Language, and Hearing Research, 56*(2), 590–603.

Nippold, M., & Fey, S. (1983). Metaphor understanding in preadolescents having a history of language acquisition difficulty. *Language, Speech, and Hearing Services in Schools, 14,* 171–180.

Notari-Syverson, A., O'Connor, R. E., & Vadsey, P. F. (2005). *Ladders to literacy: A preschool activity book* (2nd ed.). Baltimore, MD: Brookes.

O'Connor, R. E., Notari-Syverson, A., & Vadsey, P. F. (2005). *Ladders to literacy: A kindergarten activity book* (2nd ed.). Baltimore, MD: Brookes.

Paul, R., Looney, S. S., & Dahm, P. S. (1991). Communication and socialization skills at ages 2 and 3 in "late-talking" young children. *Journal of Speech, Language, and Hearing Research, 34,* 858–865.

Pokorni, J. L., Worthington, C. K., & Jamison, P. J. (2004). Phonological awareness intervention comparison of Fast ForWord, Earobics, and LiPS. *Journal of Educational Research, 97,* 147–157.

Purvis, K. L., & Tannock, R. (1997). Language abilities in children with attention deficit hyperactivity disorder, reading disabilities, and normal controls. *Journal of Abnormal Child Psychology, 25,* 133–144.

Qualls, C. D., Lantza, J. M., Pietrzykb, R. M., Blood, G. W., & Hammera, C. S. (2004). Comprehension of idioms in adolescents with language-based learning disabilities compared to their typically developing peers. *Journal of Communication Disorders, 37,* 295–311.

Raskind, M. H., & Higgins, E. L. (1999). Speaking to read: The effects of speech recognition technology on the reading and spelling performance of children with learning disabilities. *Annals of Dyslexia, 49,* 251–282.

Re, A., Pedron, M., & Cornoldi, C. (2007). Expressive writing difficulties in children described as exhibiting ADHD symptoms. *Journal of Learning Disabilities, 40,* 244–255.

Redmond, S. M. (2004). Conversational profiles of children with ADHD, SLI and typical development. *Clinical Linguistics and Phonetics, 18,* 107–125.

Rissman, M., Curtiss, S., & Tallal, P. (1990). School placement outcomes of young language impaired children. *Journal of Speech Language Pathology and Audiology, 14,* 49–58.

Ritchey, K., & Goeke, J. (2006). Orton-Gillingham and Orton-Gillingham–based reading instruction: A review of the literature. *Journal of Special Education, 40,* 171–183.

Roth, F. P., & Spekman, N. J. (1989). The oral syntactic proficiency of learning disabled students: A spontaneous story sampling analysis. *Journal of Speech and Hearing Research, 32,* 67–77.

Rudel, R., Denckla, M., & Broman, M. (1981). The effect of varying stimulus context on word finding ability: Dyslexia further differentiated from other learning disabilities. *Brain and Language, 13,* 130–144.

Scarborough, H. S. (2005). Developmental relationships between language and reading: Reconciling a beautiful hypothesis with some ugly facts. In H. Catts & A. Kamhi (Eds.), *The connections between language and reading disabilities.* Mahwah, NJ: Lawrence Erlbaum.

Scientific Learning Corporation. (2011). *Fast ForWord.* Retrieved from http://www.scilearn.com/products/fastforword-reading-series/

Scott, C. M., & Windsor, J. (2000). General language performance measures in spoken and written narrative and expository discourse of school-age children with language-learning disabilities. *Journal of Speech and Hearing Research, 43,* 324–339.

Scruggs, T., & Mastropieri, M. (1992). Effective mainstreaming for mildly handicapped students. *Elementary School Journal, 92,* 389–409.

Seidenberg, P., & Bernstein, D. (1986). The comprehension of similes and metaphors by learning-disabled and nonlearning-disabled children. *Language, Speech, and Hearing Services in Schools, 17,* 219–229.

Shankweiler, D., Crain, S., Katz, L., Fowler, A. E., Liberman, A. M., Brady, S. A., . . . Shaywitz, B. A. (1995). Cognitive profiles of reading-disabled children: Comparison of language skills in phonology, morphology, and syntax. *Psychological Science, 6,* 149–155.

Shaywitz, S. E., Escobar, M. D., Shaywitz, B. A., Fletcher, J. M., & Makuch, R. W. (1992). Evidence that dyslexia may represent the lower tail of a normal distribution of reading ability. *New England Journal of Medicine, 326,* 145–150.

Siegel, L. (2008). Morphological awareness skills of English learners and children with dyslexia. *Topics in Language Disorders, 28*, 15–27.

Simms, R., & Crump, W. (1983). Syntactic development in the language of learning disabled and normal students at the intermediate and secondary level. *Learning Disability Quarterly, 6*, 155–165.

Slingerland, B., & Alho, M. (1994–1996). *Slingerland Reading Program.* Cambridge, MA: Educators Publishing Service.

Snowling, M. J. (2000). *Dyslexia.* Oxford, United Kingdom: Blackwell.

Snowling, M. J., Bishop, D. V. M., & Stothard, S. E. (2000). Is pre-school language impairment a risk factor for dyslexia in adolescence? *Journal of Child Psychology and Psychiatry, 41*, 587–600.

Snowling, M. J., & Hayiou-Thomas, M. E. (2006). The dyslexia spectrum: Continuities between reading, speech, and language impairments. *Topics in Language Disorders, 26*(2), 110–126.

Staikova, E., Gomes, H., Tartter, V., McCabe, A., & Halperin, J. (2013). Pragmatic deficits and social impairment in children with ADHD. *Journal of Child Psychology and Psychiatry, 54*(12), 1275–1283.

Tallal, P., Miller, S. L., Bedi, G., Byma, G., Wang, X., Nagarajan, S., ... Merzenich, M. M. (1996). Fast-element enhanced speech improves language comprehension in language-learning impaired children. *Science, 271*, 81–84.

Tong, X., Deacon, S. H., Kirby, J., Cain, K., & Parrila, R. (2011). Morphological awareness: A key to understanding poor reading comprehension in English. *Journal of Educational Psychology, 103*, 523–534.

Torgesen, J. K., Alexander, A. W., Wagner, R. K., Rashotte, C. A., Voeller, K. K. S., & Conway, T. (2001). Intensive remedial instruction for children with severe reading disabilities: Immediate and long-term outcomes from two instructional approaches. *Journal of Learning Disabilities, 34*, 33–58.

Torgesen, J. K., & Bryant, B. (2013). *Phonological awareness training for reading* (2nd ed.). Austin, TX: Pro-Ed.

Torgesen, J. K., & Mathes, P. G. (2000). *A basic guide to understanding, assessing, and teaching phonological awareness.* Austin, TX: Pro-Ed.

Torgesen, J. K., Wagner, R. K., & Rashotte, C. A. (1994). Longitudinal studies of phonological processing and reading. *Journal of Learning Disabilities, 27*, 276–286.

Troia, G. A. (2011). How might pragmatic language skills affect the written expression of students with language learning disabilities? *Topics in Language Disorders, 31*, 40–53.

Troia, G. A., & Whitney, S. D. (2003). A close look at the efficacy of Fast ForWord Language for children with academic weaknesses. *Contemporary Educational Psychology, 28*, 465–494.

Tunmer, W. E. (1989). The role of language-related factors in reading disability. In O. Shankweiler & I. Y. Liberman (Eds.), *Phonology and reading disability: Solving the reading puzzle.* Ann Arbor, MI: University of Michigan Press.

Uberti, H. Z., Scruggs, T. E., & Mastropieri, M. A. (2003). Keywords make the difference: Mnemonic instruction in inclusive classrooms. *Teaching Exceptional Children, 35*, 56–61.

U.S. Department of Education, National Center for Education Statistics. (2015). *Digest of Education Statistics, 2013* (NCES 2015-011), Table 204.30. Retrieved from https://nces.ed.gov/programs/digest/d13/tables/dt13_204.30.asp

Van Kleeck, A. (1994). Metalinguistic development. In G. Wallach & K. Butler (Eds.), *Language learning disabilities in school-age children and adolescents* (pp. 53–98). New York, NY: Merrill.

Vaughn, S. (1991). Social skills enhancement in students with learning disabilities. In B. Wong (Ed.), *Learning about learning disabilities* (pp. 408–440). San Diego, CA: Academic Press.

Vellutino, F. R., Fletcher, J. M., Snowling, M. J., & Scanlon, D. M. (2004). Specific reading disability (dyslexia): What have we learned in the past four decades. *Journal of Child Psychology and Psychiatry, 45*, 2–40.

Vellutino, F. R., Scanlon, D. M., & Spearing, D. (1995). Semantic and phonological coding in poor and normal readers. *Journal of Experimental Child Psychology, 59*, 76–123.

Visser, S., Danielson, M., Bitsko, R., Holbrook, J., Kogan, M., Reem, M.G., Perou, R., & Blumberg, S. (2011). Trends in the parent-report of healthcare provider diagnosed and medicated attention-deficit/hyperactivity disorder: United States, 2003–2011. *Journal of the American Academy of Child & Adolescent Psychiatry, 53*, 34–46.

Vogel, S. (1974). Syntactic abilities in normal and dyslexic children. *Journal of Learning Disabilities, 7*, 35–43.

Wagner, R., & Torgesen, J. (1987). The nature of phonological processing and its causal role in the acquisition of reading skills. *Psychological Bulletin, 101*, 192–212.

Weiner, J., & Schneider, B. (2002). A multisource exploration of friendship patterns of children with and without LD. *Journal of Abnormal Child Psychology, 30*, 127–141.

Wilson, B. A. (1996). *Wilson Reading System.* Millbury, MA: Wilson Language Training Corporation.

Wolf, M., Bowers, P. G., & Biddle, K. (2000). Naming-speed processes, timing, and reading: A conceptual review. *Journal of Learning Disabilities, 33*, 387–407.

Chapter 8

Abbeduto, L. (1991). Development of verbal communication in persons with moderate to mild intellectual disabilities. *International Review of Research in Mental Retardation, 17*, 91–115.

Abbeduto, L., Brady, N., & Kover, S. (2007). Language and development and fragile-X syndrome: Profiles, syndrome-specificity, and within-syndrome differences. *Mental Retardation and Developmental Disabilities, 13*, 36–46.

Abbeduto, L., Davies, B., Solesby, S., & Furman, L. (1991). Identifying the referents of spoken messages: Use of context and clarification requests by children with and without intellectual disabilities. *American Journal on Mental Retardation, 95*, 551–562.

Abbeduto, L., Evans, J., & Dolan, T. (2001). Theoretical perspectives on language and communication problems in mental retardation and developmental disabilities. *Mental Retardation and Developmental Disabilities Research Reviews, 7*, 45–55.

Abbeduto, L., Furman, L., & Davies, B. (1988). The development of speech act comprehension in mentally retarded individuals and nonretarded children. *Child Development, 59,* 1460–1472.

Abbeduto, L., & Hagerman, R. J. (1997). Language and communication in fragile X syndrome. *Mental Retardation and Developmental Disabilities Research Reviews, 3,* 313–322.

Abbeduto, L., & Hesketh, L. J. (1997). Pragmatic development in individuals with mental retardation: Learning to use language in social interactions. *Mental Retardation and Developmental Disabilities Research Reviews, 3,* 323–333.

Abbeduto L., Murphy, M., Cawthon, S., Richmond, E., Weissman, M., Karadottir, S., & O'Brien, A. (2003). Receptive language skills of adolescents and young adults with Down's syndrome or fragile X syndrome. *American Journal of Mental Retardation, 108,* 149–160.

Abbeduto, L., Murphy, M. M., Richmond, E. K., Amman, A., Beth, P., Weissman, M. D., . . . Karadottir, S. (2006). Collaboration in referential communication: Comparison of youth with Down syndrome or fragile X syndrome. *American Journal on Mental Retardation, 111,* 170–183.

Abbeduto, L., & Rosenberg, S. (1980). The communicative competence of mildly retarded adults. *Applied Psycholinguistics, 1,* 405–426.

Abbeduto, L., Short-Meyerson, K., Benson, G., & Dolish, J. (1997). Signaling of noncomprehension by children and adolescents with mental retardation: Effects of problem type and speaker identity. *Journal of Speech, Language, and Hearing Research, 40,* 20–32.

Adolf, S., Klusek, J., Shinkareva, S., Robinson, M., & Roberts, J. (2015). Phonological awareness and reading in boys with fragile X syndrome. *Journal of Child Psychology and Psychiatry, 56*(1), 30–39.

Allor, J., Mathes, P., Roberts, J. K., Cheatham, J., & Champlin, T. (2010). Comprehensive reading instruction for students with intellectual disabilities: Findings from the first three years of a longitudinal study. *Psychology in the Schools, 47*(5), 445–466.

American Association on Intellectual and Developmental Disabilities. (2010). *Intellectual disability: Definition, classification, and systems of supports* (11th ed.). Washington, DC: AAIDD.

Barnes, E., Roberts, J., Long, S, Martin, G., Berni, M., Mandulak, K., & Sideris, J. (2009). Phonological accuracy and intelligibility in connected speech of boys with fragile X syndrome or Down syndrome. *Journal of Speech, Language, and Hearing Research, 52,* 1048–1061.

Bellugi, U., Lai, Z., & Wang, P. (1997). Language, communication, and neural systems in Williams syndrome. *Mental Retardation and Developmental Disabilities Research Reviews, 3,* 334–342.

Belser, R. C., & Sudhalter, V. (2001). Conversational characteristics of children with fragile X syndrome: Repetitive speech. *American Journal on Mental Retardation, 106,* 28–38.

Berglund, E., Eriksson, M., & Johansson, I. (2001). Parental reports of spoken language skills in children with Down syndrome. *Journal of Speech and Hearing Research, 44,* 179–191.

Brock, J., Jarrold, C., Farran, E., Laws, G., & Riby, D. (2007). Do children with Williams syndrome really have good vocabulary knowledge? Methods for comparing cognitive and linguistic abilities in developmental disorders. *Clinical Linguistics and Phonetics, 21*(9), 673–688.

Browder, D., Wakeman, S., Spooner, F., Ahlgrim-Delzell, L., & Algozzine, B. (2006). Research on reading instruction for persons with significant cognitive disabilities. *Exceptional Children, 72,* 392–408.

Browder, D. M., & Xin, Y. P. (1998). A meta-analysis and review of sight word research and its implications for teaching functional reading to individuals with moderate and severe disabilities. *Journal of Special Education, 32,* 130–153.

Caro, P., & Snell, M. (1989). Characteristics of teaching communication to people with moderate and severe disabilities. *Education and Training in Mental Retardation, 24,* 63–77.

Carter, M., & Grunsell, J. (2001). The behavior chain interruption strategy: A review of research and discussion of future directions. *Journal of the Association for Persons with Severe Handicaps, 26,* 37–49.

Channel, M., Loveall, S., & Conners, F. (2013). Strengths and weaknesses in reading skills of youth with intellectual disabilities. *Research in Developmental Disabilities, 34,* 776–787.

Chapman, R. S. (1997). Language development in children and adolescents with Down syndrome. *Mental Retardation and Developmental Disabilities Reviews, 3,* 307–312.

Chapman, R. S., & Hesketh, L. J. (2000). Behavioral phenotype of individuals with Down syndrome. *Mental Retardation and Developmental Disabilities Reviews, 6,* 84–95.

Chapman, R. S., Hesketh, L. J., & Kistler, D. J. (2002). Predicting longitudinal change in language production and comprehension in individuals with Down syndrome: Hierarchical linear modeling. *Journal of Speech, Language, and Hearing Research, 45,* 902–915.

Chapman, R., Schwartz, S., & Kay-Raining Bird, E. (1991). Language skills of children and adolescents with Down syndrome: 1. Comprehension. *Journal of Speech and Hearing Research, 34,* 1106–1120.

Conners, F. A. (1992). Reading instruction for students with moderate mental retardation. Review and analysis of research. *American Journal on Mental Retardation, 96,* 577–597.

Conners, F. A., Rosenquist, C. J., Sligh, A. C., Atwell, J. A., & Kiser, T. (2006). Phonological reading skills acquisition by children with mental retardation. *Research in Developmental Disabilities, 27,* 121–137.

Cornish, K., Sudhalter, V., & Turk, J. (2004). Attention and language in fragile X. *Mental Retardation and Developmental Disabilities Reviews, 10,* 11–16.

Downs, A., Downs, R., Johansen, M., & Fossum, M. (2007). Using discrete trial teaching within a public preschool program to facilitate skill development in students with developmental disabilities. *Education and Treatment of Children, 30,* 1–27.

Eadie, P., Fey, M., Douglas, J., & Parsons, C. (2002). Profiles of grammatical morphology and sentence imitation in children with specific language impairment and Down syndrome. *Journal of Speech, Language, and Hearing Research, 45*(4), 720–732.

Finestack, L., Richmond, E., & Abbeduto, L. (2009). Language development in individuals with fragile X syndrome. *Topics in Language Disorders, 29,* 133–148.

Finestack, L., Sterling, A., & Abbeduto, L. (2013). Discriminating Down syndrome and fragile X syndrome based on language ability. *Journal of Child Language, 40,* 244–265.

Ganz, J., Cook, K., & Earles-Vollrath, T. (2007). A grab bag of strategies for children with mild communication deficits. *Intervention in School and Clinic, 42*(3), 179–187.

Goetz, K., Hulme, C., Brigstocke, S., Carroll, J., Nasir, L., & Snowling, M. (2008). Training reading and phoneme awareness skills in children with Down syndrome. *Reading and Writing, 21,* 395–412.

Griffer, M. (2012). Language and children with intellectual disabilities. In V. Reed (Ed.), *An introduction to children with language disorders* (4th ed., pp. 220–252). Boston, MA: Pearson.

Hall, S. S., Lightbody, A. A., & Reiss, A. L. (2008). Compulsive, self-injurious, and autistic behavior in children and adolescents with fragile X syndrome. *American Journal of Mental Retardation, 113,* 44–53.

Hemmeter, M., Ault, M., Collins, B., & Meyer, S. (1996). The effects of teacher-implemented language instruction within free-time activities. *Education and Training in Mental Retardation and Developmental Disabilities, 31,* 203–212.

Hicks, S. C., Rivera, C., & Wood, C. (2015). Using direct instruction: Teaching preposition use to students with intellectual disability. *Language, Speech, and Hearing Services in Schools, 46,* 194–206.

Hoffman, A., Martens, M., Fox, R., Rabidoux, P., & Andridge, R. (2013). Pragmatic language assessment in Williams syndrome: A comparison of the Test of Pragmatic Language-2 and the Children's Communication Checklist-2. *American Journal of Speech-Language Pathology, 22,* 198–204.

Hua, Y., Woods-Groves, S., Kaldenberg, E., & Scheidecker, B. (2013). Effects of vocabulary instruction using constant time delay on expository reading of young adults with intellectual disability. *Focus on Autism and Other Developmental Disabilities, 28*(2), 89–100.

Hunt, P., Goetz, L., Alwell, M., & Sailor, W. (1986). Using an interrupted behavior chain strategy to teach generalized communication responses. *Journal of the Association for Persons with Severe Handicaps, 11,* 196–204.

Individuals with Disabilities Education Act. (2004). Washington, DC: U.S. Government Printing Office.

Jones, W., Bellugi, U., Lai, Z., Chiles, M., Reilly, J., Lincoln, A., & Adolphs, R. (2000). II. Hypersociability in Williams syndrome. *Journal of Cognitive Neuroscience, 12*(suppl), 30–46.

Joseph, L. M., & Seery, M. E. (2004). Where is the phonics? A review of the literature on the use of phonetic analysis with students with mental retardation. *Remedial and Special Education, 25,* 88–94.

Katims, D. S. (2000). Literacy instruction for people with intellectual disabilities: Historical highlights and contemporary analysis. *Education and Training in Intellectual Disabilities and Developmental Disabilities, 35,* 3–15.

Kent, R., & Vorperian, H. (2013). Speech impairment in Down syndrome: A review. *Journal of Speech, Language, and Hearing Research, 56,* 178–210.

Kliewer, C. (2008). Joining the literacy flow: Fostering symbol and written language learning in young children with significant developmental disabilities through the four currents of literacy. *Research and Practice for Persons with Severe Disabilities, 33,* 103–121.

Klink, M., Gerstman, L., Raphael, L., Schlanger, B., & Newsome, L. (1986). Phonological process usage by young EMR children and nonretarded preschool children. *American Journal of Mental Deficiency, 91,* 190–195.

Klusek, J., Martin, G., & Losh, M. (2014). Comparison of pragmatic language in boys with autism and fragile X syndrome. *Journal of Speech, Language, and Hearing Research, 57,* 1692–1707.

Knight, V., Browder, D., Agnello, B., & Lee, A. (2010). Academic instruction for students with severe disabilities. *Focus on Exceptional Children, 42,* 1–14.

Kover, S., McCary, L., Ingram, A., Hatton, D., & Roberts, J. (2015). Language development in infants and toddlers with fragile X syndrome: Change over time and the role of attention. *American Journal on Intellectual and Developmental Disabilities, 120*(2), 125–144.

Laws, G., & Gunn, D. (2004). Phonological memory as a predictor of language comprehension in Down syndrome: A five-year follow-up study. *Journal of Child Psychology and Psychiatry, 45,* 326–337.

Lee, C., & Binder, K. (2014). An investigation into semantic and phonological processing in individuals with Williams syndrome. *Journal of Speech, Language, and Hearing Research, 57,* 227–235.

Light, J., & Drager, K. (2010). *Effects of early AAC intervention for children with Down syndrome.* Paper presented at the Annual Meeting of the American-Speech-Language-Hearing Association, Philadelphia, PA.

Long, S. (2005). Language and children with intellectual disabilities. In V. Reed (Ed.), *Children with language disorders* (3rd ed., pp. 220–252). Boston, MA: Allyn & Bacon.

Longhurst, T. (1974). Communication in retarded adolescents: Sex and intelligence level. *American Journal of Mental Deficiency, 78,* 607–618.

Loveland, K., Tunali, B., McEvoy, R., & Kelly, M. (1989). Referential communication and response adequacy in autism and Down's syndrome. *Applied Psycholinguistics, 10,* 301–313.

Martin, G., Klusek, J., Estigarribia, B., & Roberts, J. (2009). Language characteristics of individuals with Down syndrome. *Topics in Language Disorders, 29,* 112–132.

Mervis, C. (2009). Language and literacy development of children with Williams syndrome. *Topics in Language Disorders, 29,* 149–169.

Mervis, C., & Becerra, A. (2007). Language and communication development in Williams syndrome. *Mental Retardation and Developmental Disabilities, 13,* 3–15.

Mervis, C., & Klein-Tasman, B. (2000). Williams syndrome: Cognition, personality, and adaptive behavior. *Mental Retardation and Developmental Disabilities Research Reviews, 6,* 148–158.

Miller, J. (1988). The developmental asynchrony of language development in children with Down syndrome. In L. Nadel (Ed.), *The psychobiology of Down syndrome* (pp. 168–198). Cambridge, MA: MIT Press.

Næss, K.-A. B., Melby-Lervåg, M., Hulme, C., & Lyster, S. A. H. (2012). Reading skills in children with Down syndrome: A meta-analytic review. *Research in Developmental Disabilities, 33,* 737–747.

Nuccio, J., & Abbeduto, L. (1993). Dynamic contextual variables and the directives of persons with mental retardation. *American Journal of Mental Retardation, 97,* 547–558.

Oakes, A., Kover, S., & Abbeduto, L. (2013). Language comprehension profiles of young adolescents with fragile X syndrome. *American Journal of Speech-Language Pathology, 22*(4), 615–626.

Price, J., Roberts, J., Vandergrift, N., & Martin, G. (2007). Language comprehension in boys with fragile X syndrome and boys with Down syndrome. *Journal of Intellectual Disability Research, 51*(4), 318–326.

Roberts J., Long, S., Malkin, C., Barnes, E., Skinner, M., Hennon, E., & Anderson, K. (2005). A comparison of phonological skills of boys with fragile X syndrome and Down syndrome. *Journal of Speech. Language, and Hearing Research, 48,* 980–995.

Roberts, J. E., Martin, G. E., Moskowitz, L., Harris, A. A., Foreman, J., & Nelson, L. (2007). Discourse skills of boys with fragile X syndrome in comparison to boys with Down syndrome. *Journal of Speech, Language, and Hearing Research, 50,* 475–492.

Roberts, J., Price, J., & Malkin, C. (2007). Language and communication development in Down syndrome. *Mental Retardation and Developmental Disabilities, 13,* 26–35.

Robinson, E., & Whittaker, S. (1986). Learning about verbal referential communication in the early school years. In K. Durkin (Ed.), *Language development during the school years* (pp. 155–171). London, United Kingdom: Croom Helm.

Rogers-Warren, A., & Warren, S. (1980). Mands for verbalization: Facilitating the display of newly taught language. *Behavior Modification, 4,* 361–382.

Rondal, J. (1978). Maternal speech to normal and Downs syndrome children matched for mean length of utterance. In C. Meyers (Ed.), *Quality of life in severely and profoundly mentally retarded people.* Washington, DC: American Association on Mental Deficiency.

Rondal, J. (2001). Language in mental retardation: Individual and syndromic differences, and neurogenetic variation. *Swiss Journal of Psychology, 60,* 161–178.

Saunders, K. (2007). Word-attack skills in individuals with mental retardation. *Mental Retardation and Developmental Disabilities Research Reviews, 13,* 78–84.

Scherer, N., & Owings, N. (1984). Learning to be contingent: Retarded children's responses to their mother's requests. *Language and Speech, 27,* 255–267.

Shriberg, L., & Widder, C. (1990). Speech and prosody characteristics of adults with intellectual disabilities. *Journal of Speech and Hearing Research, 33,* 637–653.

Sommers, R., Patterson, J., & Wildgen, P. (1988). Phonology of Down syndrome speakers, ages 13–22. *Journal of Childhood Communication Disorders, 12,* 65–91.

Stephenson, J., & Dowrick, M. (2005). Parents' perspectives on the communication skills of their children with severe disabilities. *Journal of Intellectual & Developmental Disability, 30,* 75–85.

Stoel-Gammon, C. (1997). Phonological development in Down syndrome. *Mental Retardation and Developmental Disabilities Research Reviews, 3,* 300–306.

Stojanovik, V. (2006). Social interaction deficits and conversational inadequacy in Williams syndrome. *Journal of Neurolinguistics, 19,* 157–173.

Stojanovik, V., Setter, J., & van Ewijk, L. (2007). Intonation abilities of children with Williams syndrome: A preliminary investigation. *Journal of Speech, Language, and Hearing Research, 50,* 1606–1617.

Stowitschek, J., McConaughy, E., Peatross, D., Salzberg, C., & Lignngaris/Kraft, B. (1988). Effects of group incidental training on the use of social amenities by adults with intellectual disabilities in work settings. *Education and Training in Intellectual Disabilities, 23,* 202–212.

Sudhalter, V., & Belser, C. (2001). Conversational characteristics of children with fragile X syndrome: Tangential language. *American Journal on Intellectual Disabilities, 106,* 389–400.

Tannock, R. (1988). Mothers' directiveness in their interactions with their children with and without Down syndrome. *American Journal on Mental Retardation, 93,* 154–165.

van Wingerden, E., Segers, E., van Balkom, H., & Verhoeven, L. (2013). Cognitive and linguistic predictors of reading comprehension in children with intellectual disabilities. *Research in Developmental Disabilities, 35,* 3139–3147.

Warren, S. (1991). Enhancing communication and language development with milieu teaching procedures. In E. Cipani (Ed.), *A guide to developing language competence in preschool children with severe and moderate handicaps* (pp. 68–93). Springfield, IL: Charles Thomas.

Yoder, P., Kaiser, A., & Alpert, C. (1991). An exploratory study of the interaction between language teaching methods and child characteristics. *Journal of Speech and Hearing Research, 34,* 155–167.

Yoder, P., & Warren, S. (2004). Early predictors of language in children with and without Down syndrome. *American Journal on Mental Retardation, 109,* 285–300.

Chapter 9

Adams, C., Green, J., Gilchrist, A., & Cox, A. (2002). Conversational behaviour of children with Asperger syndrome and conduct disorder. *Journal of Child Psychology and Psychiatry, 43,* 679–690.

American Psychiatric Association. (2013). *Diagnostic and statistical manual of mental disorders (DSM-V).* Arlington, VA: American Psychiatric Association.

American Speech-Language-Hearing Association. (1994). *Position statement on facilitated communication.* Retrieved from http://www.asha.org/policy/PS1995-00089/

Baron-Cohen, S. (1995). *Mindblindness: An essay on autism and theory of mind.* Cambridge, MA: MIT Press.

Baron-Cohen, S., Leslie, A., & Frith, U. (1985). Does the autistic child have a "theory of mind"? *Cognition, 21,* 37–46.

Bedrosian, J., Lasker, J., Speidel, K., & Politsch, A. (2003). Enhancing the written narrative skills of an AAC student with autism: Evidence-based research issues. *Topics in Language Disorders, 23,* 305–324.

Bettelheim, B. (1967). *The empty fortress—Infantile autism and the birth of the self.* New York: Free Press.

Bettison, S. (1996). The long-term effects of auditory training on children with autism. *Journal of Autism and Developmental Disorders, 26,* 179–197.

Biklen, D., & Schubert, A. (1991). New words: The communication of students with autism. *Remedial and Special Education, 12,* 46–57.

Blischak, D. M., & Schlosser, R. W. (2003). Use of technology to support independent spelling by students with autism. *Topics in Language Disorders, 23,* 293–304.

Bondy, A. S., & Frost, L. A. (1994). The picture exchange communication system. *Focus on Autistic Behavior, 9,* 1–19.

Boutot, E., & Myles, B. (2011). *Autism spectrum disorders: Foundations, characteristics, and effective strategies.* Boston, MA: Pearson.

Charman, T., Pickles, A., Simonoff, E., Chandler, S., Loucas, T., & Baird, G. (2011). IQ in children with autism spectrum disorders: Data from the Special Needs Autism Project (SNAP). *Psychological Medicine, 41(3),* 619–627.

Chiang, C., Soong, W., Lin, T., & Rogers, S. (2008). Nonverbal communication skills in young children with autism. *Journal of Autism and Developmental Disabilities, 38,* 1898–1906.

Chuba, H., Paul, R., Miles, S., Klin, A., & Volkmar, F. (2003). *Assessing pragmatic skills in individuals with autism spectrum disorders.* Presentation at the National Convention of the American Speech-Language-Hearing Association, Chicago, IL.

Dawson, G., Toth, K., Abbott, R., Osterling, J., Munson, J., Estes, A., & Liaw, J. (2004). Early social attention impairments in autism: Social orienting, joint attention, and attention to distress. *Developmental Psychology, 40,* 271–283.

Eales, M. (1993). Pragmatic impairments in adults with childhood diagnoses of autism or developmental receptive language disorder. *Journal of Autism and Developmental Disorders, 23,* 593–617.

Eberlin, M., McConnachie, G., Ibel, S., & Volpe, L. (1993). Facilitated communication: A failure to replicate the phenomenon. *Journal of Autism and Developmental Disorders, 23,* 507–530.

Eigsti, I. M., & Bennetto, L. (2009). Grammaticality judgments in autism spectrum disorders: Deviance or delay. *Journal of Child Language, 19,* 1–23.

Eigisti, I., Bennetto, L., & Dadlani, M. (2007). Beyond pragmatics: Morphosyntactic development in autism. *Journal of Autism and Developmental Disorders, 37,* 1007–1023.

Eigisti, I., de Marchena, A., Schuh, J., & Kelley, E. (2011). Language acquisition in autism spectrum disorders: A developmental review. *Research in Autism Spectrum Disorders, 5,* 681–691.

El Zein, F., Solis, M., Vaughn , S., & McCulley, L. (2014). Reading comprehension for students with autism spectrum disorders: A synthesis of research. *Journal of Autism and Developmental Disorders, 44,* 1303–1322.

Eskes, G., Bryson, S., & McCormick, T. (1990). Comprehension of concrete and abstract words in autistic children. *Journal of Autism and Developmental Disorders, 20,* 61–73.

Flippen, M., Reszka, S., & Watson, L. (2010). Effectiveness of the Picture Exchange Communication System (PECS) on communication and speech for children with autism spectrum disorders: A meta-analysis. *American Journal of Speech-Language Pathology, 19,* 178–195.

Folstein, S., & Rutter, M. (1988). Autism: Familial aggregation and genetic implications. *Journal of Autism and Developmental Disorders, 18,* 3–30.

Ganz, J. B., & Simpson, R. L. (2004). Effects on communicative requesting and speech development of the Picture Exchange Communication System in children with characteristics of autism. *Journal of Autism and Developmental Disorders, 34,* 395–409.

Goldstein, H. (2002). Communication intervention for children with autism: A review of treatment efficacy. *Journal of Autism and Developmental Disorders, 32,* 373–396.

Gresham, F., & MacMillan, D. (1997). Autistic recovery? An analysis and critique of the empirical evidence on the Early Intervention Project. *Behavioral Disorders, 22,* 185–201.

Hardan, A., Gengoux, G., Berquist, K., Libove,, R. Ardel, C., Phillips, J., Frazier, T., & Minjarez, M. (2015). A randomized controlled trial of Pivotal Response Treatment group for parents of children with autism. *Journal of Child Psychology and Psychiatry, 56(8),* 884–892.

Heflin, L., & Simpson, R. (1998). Interventions for children and youth with autism: Prudent choices in a world of exaggerated claims and empty promises. Part I: Intervention and treatment option review. *Focus on Autism and Other Developmental Disabilities, 13,* 194–211.

Howlin, P. (1982). Echolalic and spontaneous phrase speech in autistic children. *Journal of Child Psychology and Psychiatry, 23,* 281–293.

Howlin, P. (2003). Outcome in high-functioning adults with autism with and without early language delays: Implications for the differentiation between autism and Asperger syndrome. *Journal of Autism and Developmental Disorders, 33,* 3–13.

Hudry, K., Chandler, S., Bedford, R., Pasco, G., Gliga, T., Elsabbagh, M., Johnson, M., & Charman, T. (2014). Early language profiles in infants at high-risk for autism spectrum disorders. *Journal of Autism and Developmental Disorders, 44(1),* 154–167.

Hughes, J. (2008). A review of recent reports on autism: 1000 studies published in 2007. *Epilepsy & Behavior, 13,* 425–437.

Individuals with Disabilities Education Act. (2004). Washington, DC: U.S. Government Printing Office.

Just, M. A., Cherkassky, V. L., Keller, T. A., & Minshew, N. J. (2004). Cortical activation and synchronization during sentence comprehension in high-functioning autism: Evidence of under-connectivity. *Brain, 127,* 1811–1821.

Kanner, L. (1943). Autistic disturbances of affective contact. *Nervous Child, 2,* 217–250.

Kasari, C., Freeman, S. F. N., & Paparella, T. (2001). Early intervention in autism: Joint attention and symbolic play. In L. M. Glidden (Ed.), *International review of research in mental retardation: Autism* (Vol. 23, pp. 207–232). San Diego, CA: Academic Press.

Kjelgaard, M., & Tager-Flusberg, H. (2001). An investigation of language impairment in autism: Implications for genetic subgroups. *Language and Cognitive Processes, 16,* 287–308.

Kliewer, C., & Biklin, D. (2001). School's not really a place for reading: A research synthesis of the literacy lives of students with severe disabilities. *Journal of the Association for Persons with Severe Handicaps, 26,* 1–12.

Kluth, P., & Darmody-Latham, J. (2003). Beyond sight words: Literacy opportunities for students with autism. *The Reading Teacher, 56,* 532–535.

Koegel, L., Koegel, R., Harrower, J., & Carter, C. (1999). Pivotal response intervention I: Overview of approach. *Journal of the Association of Persons with Severe Handicaps, 24,* 174–185.

Koegel, L., Koegel, R., Shoshan, Y., & McNerney, E. (1999). Pivotal response intervention II: Preliminary long-term outcome data. *Journal of the Association of Persons with Severe Handicaps, 24,* 174–185.

Koppenhaver, D. A., & Erickson, K. A. (2003). Natural emergent literacy supports for preschoolers with autism and severe communication impairments. *Topics in Language Disorders, 23,* 283–292.

Landa, R. (2000). Social language use in Asperger syndrome and high-functioning autism. In A. Klim, F. Volkmar, & S. Sparrow (Eds.), *Asperger syndrome* (pp. 125–155). New York, NY: Guilford Press.

Landa, R., & Garrett-Mayer, E. (2006). Development in infants with autism spectrum disorders: A prospective study. *Journal of Child Psychology and Psychiatry, 47,* 629–638.

Landa, R. J., & Goldberg, M. C. (2005). Language, social, and executive functions in high functioning autism: A continuum of performance. *Journal of Autism and Developmental Disorders, 35,* 557–573.

Lazenby, D., Sideridis, G., Huntington, N., Prante, M., Dale, P., Curtin, S., . . . Tager-Flusberg, H. (2016). Language differences at 12 months in infants who develop autism spectrum disorder. *Journal of Autism and Developmental Disorders, 46,* 899–909.

Lee, A., Hobson, R. P., & Chiat, S. (1994). I, you, me, and autism: An experimental study. *Journal of Autism and Developmental Disorders, 24,* 155–176.

Light, J., & McNaughton, D. (2010). *Evidence-based literacy intervention for individuals with autism who have limited speech.* Presentation at American Speech-Language-Hearing Association Conference, Philadelphia, PA.

Lovaas, O. (1987). Behavioral treatment and normal educational and intellectual functioning in young autistic children. *Journal of Consulting and Clinical Psychology, 55,* 3–9.

Lovaas, O., Ackerman, A., Alexander, D., Firestone, P., Perkins, J., & Young, D. (1980). *Teaching developmentally disabled children: The me book.* Austin, TX: Pro-Ed.

Loveland, K., & Tunali-Kotoski, B. (1997). The school-age child with autism. In D. Cohen & F. Volkmar (Eds.), *Handbook of autism and pervasive developmental disorders* (pp. 283–308). New York, NY: Wiley.

McDuffie, A., & Yoder, P. (2010). Types of parent verbal responsiveness that predict language in young children with autism spectrum disorder. *Journal of Speech, Language, and Hearing Research, 53,* 1026–1039.

McEachin, J., Smith, T., & Lovaas, O. (1993). Long-term outcome for children with autism who received early intensive behavioral treatment. *American Journal on Mental Retardation, 97,* 359–372.

McGregor, K. K., Berns, A. J., Owen, A. J., Michels, S. A., Duff, D., Bahnsen, A. J., & Lloyd, M. (2012). Associations between syntax and the lexicon among children with or without ASD and language impairment. *Journal of Autism and Developmental Disorders, 42,* 35–47.

Mirenda, P. (2003). He's not really a reader: Perspectives on supporting literacy development in individuals with autism. *Topics in Language Disorders, 23,* 271–282.

Mohammadzaheri, F., Koegel, L. K., Rezaee, M., & Rafiee, S. M. (2014). A randomized clinical trial comparison between Pivotal Response Treatment (PRT) and structured Applied Behavior Analysis (ABA) intervention for children with autism. *Journal of Autism and Developmental Disorders, 44,* 2769–2777.

Mudford, O. C., Cross, B. A., Breen, S., Cullen, C., Reeves, D., Gould, J., & Douglas, J. (2000). Auditory integration training for children with autism: No behavioral benefits detected. *American Journal on Mental Retardation, 105,* 118–129.

Muller, R. A., Behen, M. E., Rothermel, R. D., Chugani, D. C., Muzik O., Mangner, T. J., & Chugani, H. T. (1999). Brain mapping of language and auditory perception in high-functioning autistic adults: A PET study. *Journal of Autism and Developmental Disorders, 29,* 19–31.

O'Connor, I., & Klein, P. (2004). Exploration of strategies for facilitating the reading comprehension of high-functioning students with autism spectrum disorders. *Journal of Autism and Developmental Disorders, 34,* 115–127.

Oshima-Takane, Y., & Benaroya, S. (1989). An alternative view of pronomial errors in autistic children. *Journal of Autism and Developmental Disorders, 19,* 73–85.

Osterling, J., & Dawson, G. (1994). Early recognition of children with autism: A study of first birthday home videotapes. *Journal of Autism and Developmental Disorders, 24,* 247–258.

Osterling, J., Dawson, G., & Munson, J. (2002). Early recognition of one year old infants with autism spectrum disorder versus mental retardation: A study of first birthday party home videotapes. *Development and Psychopathology, 14,* 239–252.

Paul, R., Campbell, D., Gilbert, K., & Tsiouri, I. (2013). Comparing spoken language treatments for minimally verbal preschoolers with autism spectrum disorders. *Journal of Autism and Developmental Disorders, 43,* 418–431.

Price, C., Thompson, W., Goodson, B., Weintraub, E., Croen, L., Hinrichsen, V., . . . DeStefano, F. (2010). Prenatal and infant exposure to Thimerosal from vaccines and immunoglobulins and risk of autism. *Pediatrics, 126,* 656–664.

Prior, M., & Werry, J. (1986). Autism, schizophrenia, and allied disorders. In H. Quay & J. Werry (Eds.), *Psychopathological disorders of childhood* (pp. 156–210). New York, NY: Wiley.

Prizant, B. (1983). Language acquisition and communicative behavior in autism: Toward an understanding of the "whole" of it. *Journal of Speech and Hearing Disorders, 48,* 296–307.

Prizant, B., & Duchan, J. (1981). The functions of immediate echolalia in autistic children. *Journal of Speech and Hearing Disorders, 46,* 241–249.

Prizant, B., & Rubin, E. (1999). Contemporary issues in interventions for autism spectrum disorders: A commentary. *Journal of the Association for Persons with Severe Handicaps, 24,* 199–208.

Prizant, B. M., & Wetherby, A. M. (2005). Critical issues in enhancing communication abilities for persons with autism spectrum disorders. In F. R. Volkmar, R. Paul, A. Klin, & D. Cohen (Eds.), *Handbook of autism and pervasive developmental disorders* (pp. 925–945). Hoboken, NJ: Wiley.

Regal, R., Rooney, J., & Wandas, T. (1994). Facilitated communication: An experimental evaluation. *Journal of Autism and Developmental Disorders, 24,* 345–355.

Rice, M., Oetting, J., Marquis, J., Bode, J., & Pae, S. (1994). Frequency of input effects on word comprehension of children with specific language impairment. *Journal of Speech and Hearing Research, 37,* 106–122.

Rimland, B., & Edelson, S. (1992, June). *Auditory integration training in autism: A pilot study.* Autism Research Institute Publication, 112.

Rimland, B., & Edelson, S. (1994). The effects of auditory integration training on autism. *American Journal of Speech-Language Pathology, 3,* 16–24. doi 10.1044/1058-0360.0302.16.

Rogers, S. (2000). Interventions that facilitate socialization in children with autism. *Journal of Autism and Developmental Disorders, 30,* 399–409.

Schreibman, L., & Carr, E. (1978). Elimination of echolalic responding to questions through training of a generalized verbal response. *Journal of Applied Behavior Analysis, 11,* 453–464.

Shriberg, L. D., Paul, R., Jane, L., McSweeny, J. L., Klin, A., Cohen, D. J., & Volkmar, F. R. (2001). Speech and prosody characteristics of adolescents and adults with high-functioning autism and Asperger syndrome. *Journal of Speech, Language, and Hearing Research, 44,* 1097–1115.

Sigman, M., Ruskin, E., Arbeile, S., Corona, R, Dissanayake, C., Espinosa, M., Kim, N., Lopez, A., & Zierhut, C. (1999). Continuity and change in the social competence of children with autism, Down syndrome and developmental delays. *Monographs of the Society for Research in Child Development, 64,* 1–114.

Siller, M., & Sigman, M. (2002). The behaviors of parents of children with autism predict the subsequent development of their children's communication. *Journal of Autism and Developmental Disorders, 32,* 77–89.

Siller, M., & Sigman, M. (2008). Modeling longitudinal change in the language abilities of children with autism: Parent behaviors and child characteristics as predictors of change. *Developmental Psychology, 44,* 1691–1704.

Smith, T., Eikeseth, S., Klevstrand, M., & Lovaas, O. (1997). Intensive behavioral treatment for preschoolers with severe mental retardation and pervasive developmental disorder. *American Journal on Mental Retardation, 102,* 238–249.

Smith, V., Mirenda, P., & Zaidman-Zait, A. (2007). Predictors of expressive vocabulary growth in children with autism. *Journal of Speech, Language, and Hearing Research, 50,* 149–160.

Sulzer-Azaroff, B., Hoffman, A., Horton, C., Bondy, A., & Frost, L. (2009). The Picture Exchange Communication System (PECS): What do the data say? *Focus on Autism and Other Developmental Disabilities, 24,* 89–103.

Tager-Flusberg, H. (1981). On the nature of linguistic functioning in early infantile autism. *Journal of Autism and Developmental Disorders, 11,* 45–56.

Tager-Flusberg, H. (1985). Basic level and superordinate level categorization by autistic, mentally retarded, and normal children. *Journal of Experimental Child Psychology, 40,* 450–469.

Tager-Flusberg, H. (1989). A psycholinguistic perspective on language development in the autistic child. In G. Dawson (Ed.), *Autism: New directions in diagnosis, nature, and treatment* (pp. 92–115). New York, NY: Guilford Press.

Tager-Flusberg, H. (2000). Language and understanding minds: Connections in autism. In S. Baron-Cohen, H. Tager-Flusberg, & D. J. Cohen (Eds.), *Understanding other minds: Perspectives from autism and developmental cognitive neuroscience* (2nd ed., pp. 1–45). Oxford, United Kingdom: Oxford University Press.

Tager-Flusberg, H., Calkins, S., Nolin, T., Baumberger, T., Anderson, M., & Chadwick-Dias, A. (1990). A longitudinal study of language acquisition in autistic and Down syndrome children. *Journal of Autism and Developmental Disorders, 20,* 1–21.

Tager-Flusberg, H., Paul, R., & Lord, C. (2005). Language and communication in autism. In F. R. Volkmar, R. Paul, A. Klin, & D. Cohen (Eds.), *Handbook of autism and pervasive developmental disorders* (pp. 335–364). Hoboken, NJ: Wiley.

Thurm, A., Lord, C., Lee, L., & Newschaffer, C. (2007). Predictors of language acquisition in preschool children with autism spectrum disorders. *Journal of Autism and Developmental Disorders, 37,* 1721–1734.

Toth, K., Munson, J., Meltzoff, A., & Dawson, G. (2006). Early predictors of communication development in young children with autism spectrum disorder: Joint attention, imitation, and toy play. *Journal of Autism and Developmental Disorders, 36,* 993–1005.

Volden, J., Coolican, J., Garon, N., White, J., & Bryson, S. (2009). Brief report: Pragmatic language in autism spectrum disorder: Relationships to measures of ability and disability. *Journal of Autism and Developmental Disorders, 39,* 388–393.

Volden, J., & Lord, C. (1991). Neologisms and idiosyncratic language in autistic speakers. *Journal of Autism and Developmental Disorders, 21,* 109–130.

Volden, J., Magill-Evans, J., Goulden, K., & Clarke, M. (2007). Varying language register according to listener needs in speakers with autism spectrum disorder. *Journal of Autism and Developmental Disorders, 37,* 1139–1154.

Volden, J., & Sorenson, A. (2009). Bossy and nice requests: Varying language register in speakers with autism spectrum disorder (ASD). *Journal of Communication Disorders, 42,* 58–73.

Wetherby, A. M., Prizant, B. M., & Schuler, A. L. (2000). Understanding the nature of communication and language impairments. In A. M. Wetherby & B. M. Prizant (Eds.), *Autism spectrum disorders: A transactional developmental perspective* (pp. 10–142). Baltimore, MD: Brookes.

Wheeler, D., Jacobson, J., Paglieri, R., & Schwartz, A. (1993). An experimental assessment of facilitated communication. *Mental Retardation, 31,* 49–60.

Yoder, P. J., & Stone, W. L. (2006). A randomized comparison of the effect of two prelinguistic communication interventions on the acquisition of spoken communication in preschoolers with ASD. *Journal of Speech, Language, and Hearing Research, 49,* 698–711.

Yoder, P. J., & Warren, S. F. (2002). Effects of prelinguistic milieu teaching and parent responsivity education on dyads involving children with intellectual disabilities. *Journal of Speech, Language, and Hearing Research, 45,* 1158–1174.

Zollweg, W., Palm, D., & Vance, V. (1997). The efficacy of auditory integration training: A double blind study. *American Journal of Audiology, 6,* 39–47.

Chapter 10

Allen-DeBoer, R. A., Malmgren, K. W., & Glass, M. (2006). Reading instruction for youth with emotional and behavioral disorders in a juvenile correctional facility. *Behavioral Disorders, 32,* 18–28.

Audet, L. R., & Hummel, L. J. (1990). A framework for assessment and treatment of language-learning disabled children with psychiatric disorders. *Topics in Language Disorders, 10,* 57–74.

Baker, L., & Cantwell, D. P. (1987a). Comparison of well, emotionally disturbed, and behaviorally disordered children with linguistic problems. *Journal of the American Academy of Child and Adolescent Psychiatry, 26,* 193–196.

Baker, L., & Cantwell, D. P. (1987b). Factors associated with the development of psychiatric illness in children with early speech/language problems. *Journal of Autism and Developmental Disorders, 17,* 499–510.

Baker, L., & Cantwell, D. P. (1987c). A prospective psychiatric follow-up of children with speech/language disorders. *Journal of the American Academy of Child and Adolescent Psychiatry, 26,* 193–196.

Baltaxe, C., & Simmons, J. Q. (1988). Pragmatic deficits in emotionally disturbed children and adolescents. In R. Schiefelbusch & L. Lloyd (Eds.), *Language perspectives: Acquisition, retardation, intervention* (2nd ed.). Austin, TX: Pro-Ed.

Beitchman, J. H., Nair, R., Clegg, M. A., Ferguson, B., & Patel, P. G. (1986). Prevalence of psychiatric disorders in children with speech and language disorders. *Journal of the American Academy of Child Psychiatry, 25,* 528–536.

Beitchman, J. H., Wilson, B., Jophnson, C., Atkinson, L., Young, A., Adalf, E., Escobar, M., & Douglas, L. (2001). Fourteen-year follow-up of speech/language impaired and control children. *Journal of the American Academy of Child Psychiatry, 40,* 75–82.

Benner, G., Mattison, R., Nelson, J., & Ralston, N. (2009). Types of language disorders in students classified as ED: Prevalence and association with learning disabilities and psychopathology. *Education and Treatment of Children, 32,* 631–653.

Benner, G. J., Nelson, J. R., & Epstein, M. H. (2002). The language skills of children with emotional and behavioral disorders: A review of the literature. *Journal of Emotional and Behavioral Disorders, 10,* 43–59.

Benner, G., Nelson, J., Ralston, N., & Mooney, P. (2010). A meta-analysis of the effects of reading instruction on the reading skills of students with or at risk of behavioral disorders. *Behavioral Disorders, 35,* 86–102.

Brinton, B., & Fujiki, M. (1993). Language, social skills and socioemotional behavior. *Language, Speech, and Hearing Services in Schools, 24,* 194–198.

Camarata, S., Hughes, C., & Ruhl, K. (1988). Mild/moderate behaviorally disorders students: A population at risk for language disorders. *Language, Speech, and Hearing Services in Schools, 19,* 191–200.

Cantwell, D. P., & Baker, L. (1977). Psychiatric disorder in children with speech and language retardation: A critical review. *Archives of General Psychiatry, 34,* 583–591.

Cantwell, D. P., & Baker, L. (1987). Prevalence and type of psychiatric disorders in three speech and language groups. *Journal of Communication Disorders, 20,* 151–160.

Carroll, J. M., Maughan, B., Goodman, R., & Meltzer, H. (2005). Literacy difficulties and psychiatric disorders: Evidence for comorbidity. *Journal of Child Psychology and Psychiatry, 46,* 524–532.

Cohen, N. J., Davine, M., & Meloche-Kelly, M. (1989). Prevalence of unsuspected language disorders in a child psychiatric population. *Journal of the American Academy of Child and Adolescent Psychiatry, 28,* 107–111.

Cohen, N. J., Menna, R., Vallance, D. D., Barwick, M. A., Im, N., & Horoclezky, N. B. (1998). Language, social cognitive processing, and behavioral characteristics of psychiatrically disturbed children with previously identified and unsuspected language impairments. *Journal of Child Psychology and Psychiatry, 39,* 853–864.

Coleman, M., & Vaughn, S. (2000). Reading interventions for students with emotional/behavioral disorders. *Behavioral Disorders, 25,* 93–104.

Engelmann, S., Becker, W., Carnine, L., Eisele, J., Haddox, P., Hanner, S., et al. (1999). *Corrective reading.* Columbus, OH: SRA/McGraw-Hill.

Epstein, M. H., Kinder, D., & Bursuck, B. (1989). The academic status of adolescents with behavioral disorders. *Behavioral Disorders, 14,* 157–165.

Evans, M. A. (1987). Discourse characteristics of reticent children. *Applied Psycholinguistics, 8,* 171–184.

Fujiki, M., Brinton, B., Morgan, M., & Hart, C. H. (1999). Withdrawn and sociable behavior of children with language impairment. *Language, Speech, and Hearing Services in Schools, 11,* 183–195.

Gage, N., Wilson, J., & MacSuga-Gage, A. (2014). Writing performance of students with emotional and/or behavioral disorders. *Behavioral Disorders, 40*(1), 3–14.

Gallagher, T. M. (1999). Interrelationships among children's language, behavior, and emotional problems. *Topics in Language Disorders, 19,* 1–15.

Garwood, J., Brunsting, N., & Fox, L. (2014). Improving reading comprehension and fluency outcomes for adolescents with emotional-behavioral disorders: Recent research synthesized. *Remedial and Special Education, 35,* 181–194.

Giddan, J. L. (1991). School children with emotional problems and communication deficits: Implications for speech-language pathologists. *Language, Speech, and Hearing Services in Schools, 22,* 291–295.

Greenbaum, P. E., Dedrick, R. F., Friedman, R. M., Kutash, K., Brown, E. C., Lardieri, S. P., & Pugh, A. M. (1999). National adolescent and child treatment study (NACTS): Outcomes for children with serious emotional behavioral disturbance. In M. H. Epstein, K. Kutash, & A. Duchnowski (Eds.), *Outcomes for children and youth with emotional and behavioral disorders and their families: Programs and evaluation best practices* (pp. 21–54). Austin, TX: Pro-Ed.

Gresham, F. M. (2005). Response to intervention: An alternative means of identifying students as emotionally disturbed. *Education and Treatment of Children, 28,* 328–344.

Gualtieri, C. T., Koriath, U., Bourgondien, M., & Saleeby, N. (1983). Language disorders in children referred for psychiatric services. *Journal of the American Academy of Child Psychiatry, 22,* 165–171.

Hartas, D. (1995). Verbal interactions of children with internalizing behavior disorders. *B.C. Journal of Special Education, 19,* 11–19.

Hollo, A., Wehby, J., & Oliver, R. (2014). Unidentified language deficits in children with emotional and behavioral disorders: A meta-analysis. *Exceptional Children, 80*(2), 169–186.

Hooper, S. R., Roberts, J. F., Zeisel, S. A., & Poe, M. (2003). Core language predictors of behavioral functioning in early elementary school children: Concurrent and longitudinal findings. *Behavioral Disorders, 29,* 10–24.

Hyter, Y. D., Rogers-Adkinson, D. L., Self, T. L., Simmins, B. F., & Jantz, J. (2001). Pragmatic language intervention for children with language and emotional/behavioral disorders. *Communication Disorders Quarterly, 23,* 4–16.

Individuals with Disabilities Education Act. (2004). Washington, DC: U.S. Government Printing Office.

Kauffman, J., Mock, D., & Simpson, R. (2007). Problems related to underservice of students with emotional or behavioral disorders. *Behavioral Disorders, 33,* 43–57.

Lane, K., Harris, K., Graham, S., Weisenbach, J., Brindle, M., & Morphy, P. (2008). The effects of Self-Regulated Strategy Development on the writing performance of second grade students with behavioral and writing difficulties. *Journal of Special Education, 41,* 234–253.

Lane, K., Little, M., Redding-Rhodes, J., Phillips, A., & Welsh, M. (2007). Outcomes of a teacher-led reading intervention for elementary students at risk for behavioral disorders. *Exceptional Children, 74,* 47–70.

Lindsay, G., & Dockrell, J. (2012). Longitudinal patterns of behavioral, emotional, and social difficulties and self-concepts in adolescents with a history of specific language impairment. *Language, Speech, and Hearing Services in Schools, 43,* 445–460.

Mack, A., & Warr-Leeper, G. (1992). Language abilities in boys with chronic behavior disorders. *Language, Speech, and Hearing Services in Schools, 23,* 214–223.

McDaniel, S., Houchins, D., & Terry, N. (2011). Corrective reading as a supplementary curriculum for students with emotional and behavioral disorders. *Journal of Emotional and Behavioral Disorders, 21*(4) 240–249.

McDonough, J. M. (1989). Analysis of the expressive language characteristics of emotionally handicapped students in social interactions. *Behavioral Disorders, 14,* 127–149.

Nelson, J. R., Benner, J. R., & Cheney, D. (2005). An investigation of the language skills of students with emotional disturbance served in public school settings. *Journal of Special Education, 39,* 97–105.

Nelson, J. R., Benner, J. R., & Rogers-Adkinson, D. (2003). An investigation of the characteristics of K–12 students with comorbid emotional disturbance and significant language deficits served in public school settings. *Behavioral Disorders, 29,* 25–33.

Rinaldi, C. (2003). Language competence and social behavior of students with emotional or behavioral disorders. *Behavioral Disorders, 29,* 34–42.

Rogevich, M., & Perin, D. (2008). Effects on science summarization of a reading comprehension intervention for adolescents with behavior and attention disorders. *Exceptional Children, 74,* 135–154.

Rosenthal, S., & Simeonsson, R. (1991). Communication skills in emotionally disturbed and nondisturbed adolescents. *Behavioral Disorders, 16,* 192–199.

Ruhl, K. L., Hughes, C. A., & Camarata, S. T. (1992). Analysis of the expressive and receptive language characteristics of emotionally handicapped students served in public school settings. *Journal of Childhood Communication Disorders, 14,* 165–176.

Sreckovic, M., Common, E., Knowles, M., & Lane, K. (2014). A review of self-regulated strategy development for writing for students with EBD. *Behavioral Disorders, 39*(2), 56–77.

Strong, A. C., Wehby, J. H., Falk, K. B., & Lane, K. L. (2004). The impact of a structured reading curriculum and repeated reading on the performance of junior high students with emotional and behavioral disorders. *School Psychology Review, 33,* 561–581.

Tomblin, J. B., Zhang, X., Buckwalter, P., & Catts, H. (2000). The association of reading disability, behavioral disorders, and language impairment among second-grade children. *Journal of Child Psychology and Psychiatry, 41,* 473–482.

Trautman, R., Giddan, J., & Jurs, S. (1990). Language risk factors in emotionally disturbed children within a school and day treatment program. *Journal of Childhood Communication Disorders, 13,* 123–133.

Trout, A., Nordness, P., Pierce, C., & Epstein, M. (2003). Research on the academic status of children and youth with emotional and behavioral disorders: A review of the literature from 1961–2000. *Journal of Emotional and Behavioral Disorders, 11,* 198–210.

Warr-Leeper, G., Wright, N. A., & Mack, A. (1994). Language disabilities of antisocial boys in residential treatment. *Behavioral Disorders, 19,* 159–169.

Willcutt, E. G., & Pennington, B. F. (2000). Psychiatric comorbidity in children and adolescents with reading disability. *Journal of Child Psychology and Psychiatry, 41,* 1039–1048.

Chapter 11

Albertini, J. A., & Schley, S. (2011). Writing: Characteristics, instruction, and assessment. In M. Marschark & P. Spencer (Eds.), *Oxford handbook of deaf studies, language, and education* (2nd ed., pp. 130–143). New York, NY: Oxford University Press.

Andersen, E., Dunlea, A., & Kekelis, L. (1984). Blind children's language: Resolving some differences. *Journal of Child Language, 11,* 645–664.

Anderson, D., & Reilly, J. S. (2002). The MacArthur Communicative Development Inventory: Normative data for American Sign Language. *Journal of Deaf Studies and Deaf Education, 7,* 83–106.

Aram, D., Most, T., & Mayafit, H. (2006). Contributions of mother-child storybook telling and joint writing. *Language, Speech, and Hearing Services in Schools, 37,* 209–223.

Bigelow, A. (1987). Early words of blind children. *Journal of Child Language, 14,* 47–56.

Bigelow, A. (1990). Relationship between the development of language and thought in young blind children. *Journal of Visual Impairment & Blindness, 84,* 414–419.

Blamey, P. J. (2003). Development of spoken language by deaf children. In M. Marschark & P. Spencer (Eds.), *Deaf studies, language, and education* (pp. 232–246). New York, NY: Oxford University Press.

Bonvillian, J., Nelson, K., & Charrow, V. (1976). Language and language-related skills in deaf and hearing children. *Sign Language Studies, 12,* 211–250.

Bosman, A., Gompel, M., Vervloed, M., & van Bon, W. (2006). Low vision affects the reading process quantitatively but not qualitatively. *Journal of Special Education, 39*(4), 208–219.

Brambring, M. (2007). Divergent development of verbal skills in children who are blind or sighted. *Journal of Visual Impairment & Blindness, 101,* 749–762.

Brambring, M., & Asbrock, D. (2010). Validity of false belief tasks in blind children. *Journal of Autism and Developmental Disorders, 40*(12), 1471–1484.

Briscoe, J., Bishop, D., & Norbury, C. (2001). Phonological processing, language, and literacy: A comparison of children with mild-to-moderate sensorineural hearing loss and those with specific language impairment. *Journal of Child Psychology and Psychiatry, 42,* 329–340.

Caillies, S., & Le Sourn-Bissaoui, S. (2008). Children's understanding of idioms and theory of mind development. *Developmental Science, 11*(5), 703–711.

Charlesworth, A., Charlesworth, R., Raban, B., & Rickards, F. (2005). Reading recovery for children with hearing loss. *The Volta Review, 106,* 29–51.

Davis, J., Shepard, N., Stelmachowicz, P., & Gorga, M. (1981). Characteristics of hearing impaired children in the public schools: Part II—Psychoeducational data. *Journal of Speech and Hearing Disorders, 46,* 130–137.

Davis, J., Elfenbein, J., Schum, R., & Bentler, R. (1986). Effects of mild and moderate hearing impairments on language, educational, and psychosocial behavior of children. *Journal of Speech and Hearing Disorders, 51,* 53–62.

Daza, M., Phillips-Silver, J., Ruiz-Cuadra, M., & Lopez-Lopez, G. (2014). Language skills and nonverbal cognitive processes associated with reading comprehension in deaf children. *Research in Developmental Disabilities, 35*(12), 3526–3533.

Dekker, R., & Koole, E. (1992). Visually impaired children's visual characteristics and language. *Developmental Medicine and Child Neurology, 34,* 123–133.

Delage, H., & Tuller, L. (2007). Language development and mild-to-moderate hearing loss: Does language normalize with age? *Journal of Speech, Language, and Hearing Research, 50,* 1300–1313.

DeLuzioa, J., & Girolamettoa, L. (2011). Peer interactions of preschool children with and without hearing loss. *Journal of Speech, Language, and Hearing Research, 54,* 1197–1210.

Dodd, B., & Conn, L. (2000). The effect of braille orthography on blind children's phonological awareness. *Journal of Research in Reading, 23,* 1–11.

Dote-Kwan, J., & Hughes, M. (1994). The home environments of young blind children. *Journal of Visual Impairment & Blindness, 88,* 31–42.

Drinkwater, T. (2004). *The benefits of cochlear implantation in young children.* Sydney, Australia: Cochlear Ltd.

Easterbrooks, S., Lederberg, A., Miller, E., & Bergeron, J. (2008). Emergent literacy skills during early childhood in children with hearing loss. *The Volta Review, 108,* 91–114.

Emmorey, K., & Kosslyn, S. (1996). Enhanced image generation abilities in deaf signers: A right hemisphere effect. *Brain and Cognition, 32,* 28–44.

Erin, J. (1990). Language samples from visually impaired four- and five-year-olds. *Journal of Childhood Communication Disorders, 13,* 181–191.

Everhart, V., & Marschark, M. (1988). Linguistic flexibility in signed and written language productions of deaf children. *Journal of Experimental Child Psychology, 46,* 174–193.

Fellenius, K. (1999). Swedish 9-year-old readers with visual impairments: A heterogeneous group. *Journal of Visual Impairment & Blindness, 93,* 370–380.

Fiedler, B. (2001). Considering placement and educational approaches for students who are deaf and hard of hearing. *Teaching Exceptional Children, 34,* 54–59.

Fraiberg, S. (1977). *Insights from the blind.* London, United Kingdom: Souvenir Press.

Freeman, R., & Blockberger, S. (1987). Language development and sensory disorder: Visual and hearing impairments. In W. Yule & M. Rutter (Eds.), *Language development and disorders* (pp. 234–247). Philadelphia, PA: J. B. Lippincott.

Friel-Patti, S., & Finitzo, T. (1990). Language learning in a prospective study of otitis media with effusion in the first two years of life. *Journal of Speech and Hearing Research, 33,* 188–194.

Gallaway, C., & Woll, B. (1994). Interaction and childhood deafness. In C. Gallaway & B. Richards (Eds.), *Input and interaction in language acquisition* (pp. 197–218). Cambridge, United Kingdom: Cambridge University Press.

Geers, A., Moog, J., Biedenstein, J., Brenner, C., & Hayes, H. (2009). Spoken language scores of children using cochlear implants compared to hearing age-mates at school entry. *Journal of Deaf Studies and Deaf Education, 14,* 371–385.

Gentile, A. (1972). *Academic achievement test results of a national testing program for hearing impaired students: 1971.* Annual Survey of Hearing-Impaired Children and Youth, Gallaudet College Office of Demographic Studies, Ser. D, No. 9.

Gibbs, S. (2004). The skills in reading shown by young children with permanent and moderate hearing impairment. *Educational Research, 46,* 17–27.

Gilbertson, M., & Kamhi, A. G. (1995). Novel word learning in children with hearing impairment. *Journal of Speech and Hearing Research, 38,* 630–642.

Gillon, G., & Young, A. (2002). The phonological-awareness skills of children who are blind. *Journal of Visual Impairment & Blindness, 96,* 38–49.

Goldin-Meadow, S., Butcher, C., Mylander, C., & Dodge, M. (1994). Nouns and verbs in a self-styled gesture system: What's in a name? *Cognitive Psychology, 27,* 259–319.

Goldin-Meadow, S., & Feldman, H. (1977). The development of language-like communication without a language model. *Science, 197,* 401–403.

Goldin-Meadow, S., & Mylander, C. (1990). Beyond the input given: The child's role in the acquisition of language. *Language, 66,* 323–355.

Gompel, M., van Bon, W. H. J., Schreuder, R., & Adriaansen, J. J. M. (2002). Reading and spelling competence of Dutch children with low vision. *Journal of Visual Impairment and Blindness, 96,* 435–447.

Grievink, E., Peters, S., van Bron, W., & Schilder, A. (1993). The effects of early bilateral otitis media with effusion on language ability: A prospective cohort study. *Journal of Speech and Hearing Research, 36,* 1004–1012.

Griffer, M. (2012). Language and children with auditory impairments. In V. Reed (Ed.), *An introduction to children with language disorders* (pp. 303–351). Boston, MA: Pearson.

Individuals with Disabilities Education Act. (2004). Washington, DC: U.S. Government Printing Office.

Jerger, S., Damian, M. F., Tye-Murray, N., Dougherty, M., Mehta, J., & Spence, M. (2006). Effects of childhood hearing loss on organization of semantic memory: Typicality and relatedness. *Ear and Hearing, 27*(6), 686–702.

Johnson, C., & Goswami, U. (2010). Phonological awareness, vocabulary, and reading in deaf children with cochlear implants. *Journal of Speech, Language, and Hearing Research, 53,* 237–261.

Karchmer, M. A., & Mitchell, R. E. (2003). Demographic and achievement characteristics of deaf and hard-of-hearing students. In M. Marschark & P. Spencer (Eds.), *Deaf studies, language, and education* (pp. 21–37). New York, NY: Oxford University Press.

Kekelis, L., & Andersen, E. (1984). Family communication styles and language development. *Journal of Visual Impairment & Blindness, 78,* 54–65.

Klima, E., & Bellugi, U. (1979). *The signs of language.* Cambridge, MA: Harvard University Press.

Koehlinger, K., Van Horne, A., & Moeller, M. (2013). Grammatical outcomes of 3- and 6- year-old children who are hard of hearing. *Journal of Speech, Language, and Hearing Research, 56,* 1701–1714.

Landau, B., & Gleitman, L. (1985). *Language and experience: Evidence from the blind child.* Cambridge, MA: Harvard University Press.

LaSasso, C., & Lollis, J. (2003). Survey of residential and day schools for deaf students in the United States that identify themselves as bilingual-bicultural. *Journal of Deaf Studies and Deaf Education, 8,* 79–91.

LaSasso, C., & Mobley, R. (1998). National survey of reading instruction for deaf or hard-of-hearing students in the U.S. *The Volta Review, 99,* 31–58.

Lederberg, A., & Everhart, V. (1998). Communication between deaf children and their hearing mothers: The role of language, gesture, and vocalizations. *Journal of Speech, Language, and Hearing Research, 41,* 887–899.

Lederberg, A., & Everhart, V. (2000). Conversations between deaf children and their hearing mothers: Pragmatic and dialogic characteristics. *Journal of Deaf Studies and Deaf Education, 5,* 303–322.

Lederberg, A. R., & Spencer, P. E. (2001). Vocabulary development of deaf and hard of hearing children. In M. D. Clark, M. Marschark, & M. Karchmer (Eds.), *Context, cognition, and deafness* (pp. 88–112). Washington, DC: Gallaudet University Press.

Luckner, J. L., Sebald, A. M., Cooney, J., Young III, J., & Muir, S. G. (2005/2006). An examination of the evidence-based literacy research in deaf education. *American Annals of the Deaf, 150,* 443–456.

Marschark, M., Green, V., Hindmarsh, G., & Walker, S. (2000). Understanding theory of mind in children who are deaf. *Journal of Child Psychology and Psychiatry, 41,* 1067–1073.

Marschark, M., Lang, H. G., & Albertini, J. A. (2002). *Educating deaf students: From research to practice.* New York, NY: Oxford University Press.

Marschark, M., Sapere, P., Convertino, C., Mayer, C., Wauters, L., & Sarchet, T. (2009). Are deaf students' reading challenges really about reading? *American Annals of the Deaf, 154,* 357–370.

Marschark, M., & Spencer, P. (Eds.). (2003). *Deaf studies, language, and education.* New York, NY: Oxford University Press.

Mayne, A., Yoshinaga-Itano, C., & Sedey, A. (2000). Receptive vocabulary development of infants and toddlers who are deaf or hard of hearing. *The Volta Review, 100,* 29–52.

Mayne, A., Yoshinaga-Itano, C., Sedey, A., & Carey, A. (2000). Expressive vocabulary development of infants and toddlers who are deaf or hard of hearing. *The Volta Review, 100,* 1–28.

McGarr, N. (1983). The intelligibility of deaf speech to experienced and inexperienced listeners. *Journal of Speech and Hearing Research, 26,* 451–458.

McGuckian, M., & Henry, A. (2007). The grammatical morpheme deficit in moderate hearing impairment. *International Journal of Language and Communication Disorders, 42,* 17–36.

Monsen, R. (1983). The oral speech intelligibility of hearing-impaired talkers. *Journal of Speech and Hearing Disorders, 48,* 286–296.

Moores, D. (2009). Cochlear failures. *American Annals of the Deaf, 153,* 423–424.

Nicholas, J., Geers, A., & Kozak, V. (1994). Development of communicative function in young hearing-impaired and normally hearing children. *The Volta Review, 96,* 113–135.

Nittrouer, S., & Burton, L. (2001). The role of early language experience in the development of speech perception and language processing abilities in children with hearing loss. *The Volta Review, 103,* 5–37.

Nott, P., Cowan, R., Brown, P., & Wigglesworth, G. (2009). Early language development in children with profound hearing loss fitted with a device at a young age: Part I— The time period taken to acquire first words and first word combinations. *Ear and Hearing, 30*(5), 526–540.

Oller, D. K., & Eilers, R. E. (1988). The role of audition in infant babbling. *Child Development, 59,* 441–449.

Oller, D., Eilers, R., Bull, D., & Carney, A. (1985). Prespeech vocalizations of a deaf infant: A comparison with normal meta-phonological development. *Journal of Speech and Hearing Research, 28,* 47–63.

Oller, D., Jensen, H., & Lafayette, R. (1978). The relatedness of phonological processes of a hearing-impaired child. *Journal of Communication Disorders, 11,* 97–105.

Parke, K., Shallcross, R., & Anderson, R. (1980). Differences in coverbal behavior between blind and sighted persons during dyadic communication. *Journal of Visual Impairment & Blindness, 74,* 142–146.

Paul, P. V. (1998). *Literacy and deafness: The development of reading, writing, and literate thought.* Boston, MA: Allyn & Bacon.

Paul, P. V. (2003). Processes and components of reading. In M. Marschark & P. Spencer (Eds.), *Deaf studies, language, and education* (pp. 97–109). New York, NY: Oxford University Press.

Paul, R., Lynn, T., & Lohr-Flanders, M. (1993). History of middle ear involvement and speech/language development in late talkers. *Journal of Speech and Hearing Research, 36,* 1055–1062.

Perez-Pereria, M., & Conti-Ramsden, G. (1998). *Language development and social interaction in blind children.* Hove, United Kingdom: Psychology Press.

Perez-Pereria, M., & Conti-Ramsden, G. (2001). The use of directives in verbal interactions between blind children and their mothers. *Journal of Visual Impairment & Blindness, 95,* 133–149.

Peterson, C. C., & Siegal, M. (1999). Representing inner worlds: Theory of mind in autistic, deaf, and normal hearing children. *Psychological Science, 10,* 126–129.

Petitto, L. A., & Marantette, P. F. (1991). Babbling in the manual mode: Evidence for the ontogeny of language. *Science, 251,* 1493–1496.

Phelps, L., & Branyan, B. (1990). Academic achievement and nonverbal intelligence in public school hearing-impaired children. *Psychology in the Schools, 27,* 210–217.

Qi, S., & Mitchell, R. E. (2012). Large-scale academic achievement testing of deaf and hard-of-hearing students: Past, present, and future. *Journal of Deaf Studies and Deaf Education, 17*(1), 1–18.

Quigley, S., & Paul, P. (1990). *Language and deafness.* San Diego, CA: Singular Publishing.

Quigley, S., Power, D., & Steinkamp, M. (1977). The language structure of deaf children. *The Volta Review, 79,* 73–84.

Ratner, N. B. (2005). Atypical language development. In J. Gleason (Ed.), *The development of language* (3rd ed., pp. 324–394). Boston, MA: Allyn & Bacon.

Russell, W., Power, D., & Quigley, S. (1976). *Linguistics and deaf children.* Washington, DC: Alexander Graham Bell Association for the Deaf.

Sarant, J., Holt, C., Dowell, R., Rickards, F., & Blamey, P. (2009). Spoken language development in oral preschool children with permanent childhood deafness. *Journal of Deaf Studies and Deaf Education, 14,* 205–216.

Schick, B. (2003). The development of American Sign Language and manually coded English language systems. In M. Marschark & P. Spencer (Eds.), *Deaf studies, language, and education* (pp. 219–231). New York, NY: Oxford University Press.

Schirmer, B. (1985). An analysis of the language of young hearing-impaired children in terms of syntax, semantics, and use. *American Annals of the Deaf, 130,* 15–19.

Schorr, E., Roth, F., & Fox, N. (2008). A comparison of the speech and language skills of children with cochlear implants and children with normal hearing. *Communication Disorders Quarterly, 29,* 195–210.

Shriberg, L. D., Friel-Patti, S., Flipsen, P., & Brown, R. C. (2000). Otitis media, fluctuant hearing loss, and speech-language outcomes: A preliminary structural equation model. *Journal of Speech, Language, and Hearing Research, 43,* 100–120.

Spencer, P. E. (2000). Looking without listening: Is audition a prerequisite for normal development of visual attention during infancy? *Journal of Deaf Studies and Deaf Education, 5,* 291–302.

Steinman, B. A., LeJeune, B. J., & Kimbrough, B. T. (2006). Developmental stages of reading processes in children who are blind and sighted. *Journal of Visual Impairment & Blindness, 100,* 36–46.

Sterne, A., & Goswami, U. (2000). Phonological awareness of syllables, rhymes, and phonemes in deaf children. *Journal of Child Psychology and Psychiatry, 41,* 609–625.

Stoel-Gammon, C. (1988). Prelinguistic vocalizations of hearing-impaired and normally hearing subjects: A comparison of consonantal inventories. *Journal of Speech and Hearing Disorders, 53,* 302–315.

Svirsky, M. A., Robbins, A. M., Kirk, K. I., Pisoni, D. B., & Miyamoto, R. T. (2000). Language development in profoundly deaf children with cochlear implants. *Psychological Science, 11,* 153–158.

Teele, D., Klein, J., Chase, C., Menyuk, P., & Rosner, B. (1990). Otitis media in infancy and intellectual ability, school achievement, speech, and language at age 7 years. *The Journal of Infectious Diseases, 162,* 685–694.

Teele, D., Klein, J., & Rosner, B. (1980). Epidemiology of otitis media in children. *Annals of Otology, Rhinology, and Laryngology, 89,* 5–6.

Thagard, E., Hilsmier, A., & Easterbrooks, S. (2011). Pragmatic language in deaf and hard of hearing students: Correlation with success in general education. *American Annals of the Deaf, 155,* 526–534.

Tomblin, J. B., Barker, B. A., Spencer, L. I., Zhang, X., & Gantz, B. J. (2005). The effect of age at cochlear implant: Initial stimulation on expressive language growth in infants and toddlers. *Journal of Speech, Language, and Hearing Research, 48,* 853–867.

Traxler, C. B. (2000). The Stanford Achievement Test, 9th ed.: National norming and performance standards for deaf and hard-of-hearing students. *Journal of Deaf Studies and Deaf Education, 5*(4), 337–348.

Trezek, B., Wang, Y., Woods, D., Gamp, T., & Paul, P. (2010). Using visual phonics to supplement beginning reading instruction for students who are deaf or hard of hearing. *Journal of Deaf Studies and Deaf Education, 12,* 373–384.

Urwin, C. (1984). Language for absent things: Learning from visually handicapped children. *Topics in Language Disorders, 4,* 24–37.

U.S. Department of Education, National Center for Education Statistics. (2015). *Digest of Education Statistics, 2013* (NCES 2015-011), Chapter 2. Retrieved from https://nces .ed.gov/programs/digest/d13/ch_2.asp

Wang, Y., Trezek, B., Luckner, J., & Paul, P. (2008). The role of phonology and phonologically related skills in reading instruction for students who are deaf or hard of hearing. *American Annals of the Deaf, 153,* 396–407.

Williams, C., & Mayer, C. (2015). Writing in young deaf children. *Review of Educational Research, 85*(4), 630–666.

Winskell, H. (2006). The effects of an early history of otitis media on children's language and literacy skill development. *British Journal of Educational Psychology, 76,* 727–744.

Woolfe, T., Want, S., & Siegal, M. (2002). Signposts to development: Theory of mind in deaf children. *Child Development, 73,* 768–778.

Yoshinaga-Itano, C., & Sedey A. (1999). Early speech development in children who are deaf or hard of hearing: Interrelationships with language and hearing. *The Volta Review, 100,* 181–211.

Chapter 12

Arroyos-Jurado, E., Paulsen, J. S., Merrell, K. W., Lindgren, S. D., & Max, J. E. (2000). Traumatic brain injury in school-age children: Academic and social outcome. *Journal of School Psychology, 38,* 571–587.

Barnes, M., & Dennis, M. (1998). Discourse after early-onset hydrocephalus: Core deficits in children of average intelligence. *Brain and Language, 61,* 309–334.

Barnes, M., Faulkner, H., & Dennis, M. (2001). Poor reading comprehension despite fast word decoding in children with hydrocephalus. *Brain and Language, 76,* 35–44.

Barnes, M., Faulkner, H., Wilkinson, M., & Dennis, M. (2004). Meaning construction and integration in children with hydrocephalus. *Brain and Language, 89,* 47–56.

Barnes, M., Wilkinson, M., Khemani, E., Boudesquie, A., Dennis, M., & Fletcher, J. (2006). Arithmetic processing in children with spina biffida: Calculation accuracy, strategy use, and fact retrieval fluency. *Journal of Learning Disabilities, 39,* 174–187.

Bax, M., Goldstein, M., Rosenbaum, P., & Paneth, N. (2005). Proposed definition and classification of cerebral palsy. *Developmental Medicine and Child Neurology, 47,* 571–576.

Bax, M., Tydeman, C., & Flodmark, O. (2006). Clinical and MRI correlates of cerebral palsy. *Journal of the American Medical Association, 296,* 1602–1609.

Best, S. (2010). Physical disabilities. In S. J. Best, K. W. Heller, & J. L. Bigge (Eds.), *Teaching individuals with physical or multiple disabilities* (6th ed.). Upper Saddle River, NJ: Merrill/Pearson.

Best, S., & Bigge, J. (2010). Cerebral palsy. In S. J. Best, K. W. Heller, & J. L. Bigge (Eds.), *Teaching individuals with physical or multiple disabilities* (6th ed.). Upper Saddle River, NJ: Merrill/Pearson.

Bishop, D., Brown, B., & Robson, J. (1990). The relationship between phoneme discrimination, speech production, and language comprehension in cerebral-palsied individuals. *Journal of Speech and Hearing Research, 33,* 210–219.

Bowen, J. M. (2005). Classroom interventions for students with traumatic brain injuries. *Preventing School Failure, 49,* 34–41.

Campbell, T., & Dollaghan, C. (1990). Expressive language recovery in severely brain-injured children and adolescents. *Journal of Speech and Hearing Disorders, 55,* 567–581.

Caplan, R., Guthrie, D., Komo, S., Siddarth, P., Chayasirisobhon, S., Kornblum, H., Sankar, R., Hansen, R., Mitchell, W., & Shields, W. D. (2002). Social communication in children with epilepsy. *Journal of Child Psychology and Psychiatry, 43,* 245–253.

Card, R., & Dodd, B. (2006). The phonological awareness abilities of children with cerebral palsy who do not speak. *AAC: Augmentative and Alternative Communication, 22,* 149–159.

Catroppa, C., & Anderson, V. (2004). Recovery and predictors of language skills two years following pediatric traumatic brain injury. *Brain and Language, 88,* 68–78.

Cauley, K., Golinkoff, R., Hirsh-Pasek, K., & Gordon, L. (1989). Revealing hidden competencies: A new method for studying language comprehension in children with motor impairments. *American Journal of Mental Retardation, 94,* 55–63.

Centers for Disease Control and Prevention. (2016). Injury prevention and control: Traumatic brain injury and concussion. Retrieved from http://www.cdc.gov/traumatic-braininjury/data/rates_ed_byage.html

Chapman, S. B., Culhane, K. A., Levin, H. S., Howard, H., Mendelsohn, D., & Ewing Cobbs, L. (1992). Narrative discourse after closed head injury in children and adolescents. *Brain and Language, 43,* 42–65.

Cyrulnik, S., Fee, R., De Vivo, D., Goldstein, E., & Hinton, V. (2007). Delayed developmental language milestones in children with Duchenne's muscular dystrophy. *Journal of Pediatrics, 150,* 474–478.

Dahlgren Sandberg, A. (1998). Reading and spelling among nonvocal children with cerebral palsy: Influence of home and school literacy environment. *Reading and Writing, 10,* 23–50.

Didus, E., Anderson, V., & Catroppa, C. (1999). The development of pragmatic communication skills in head injured children. *Pediatric Rehabilitation, 3,* 177–186.

Dorman, C., Hurley, A., & D'Avignon, J. (1988). Language and learning disorders of older boys with Duchenne muscular dystrophy. *Developmental Medicine and Child Neurology, 30,* 316–327.

Ewing-Cobbs, L., Prasad, M., Kramer, L., Cox, C. S. J., Baumgartner, J., Fletcher, S., . . . Swank, P. (2006). Late intellectual and academic outcomes following traumatic brain injury sustained during early childhood. *Journal of Neurosurgery, 105,* 287–296.

Fastenau, P., Shen, J., Dunn, D., & Austin, J. (2008). Academic underachievement among children with epilepsy: Proportion exceeding psychometric criteria for learning disability and associated risk factors. *Journal of Learning Disabilities, 41,* 195–207.

Girolametto, L., Greenberg, J., & Manolson, H. A. (1986). Developing dialogue skills: The Hanen early language parent program. *Seminars in Speech and Language, 7,* 367–382.

Hanten, G., Li, X., Newsome, M., Swank, P., Chapman, S., Dennis, M., Barnes, M., Ewing-Cobbs, L., & Levin, H. (2009). Oral reading and expressive language after childhood traumatic brain injury. *Topics in Language Disorders, 29,* 236–248.

Hanzlik, J. R. (1990). Nonverbal interaction patterns of mothers and their infants with cerebral palsy. *Education and Training in Mental Retardation, 25,* 333–343.

Harrington, D. (1990). Educational strategies. In M. Rosenthal, E. Griffith M. Bond, & J. Miller (Eds.), *Rehabilitation of the adult and child with traumatic brain injury* (pp. 476–493). Philadelphia, PA: J. B. Lippincott.

Hinton, V., De Vivo, D., Fee, R., Goldstein, E., & Stern, Y. (2004). Investigation of poor academic achievement in children with Duchenne muscular dystrophy. *Learning Disabilities Research and Practice, 19,* 146–154.

Individuals with Disabilities Education Act. (2004). Washington, DC: U.S. Government Printing Office.

Kennes, J., Rosenbaum, P., Hanna, S., Walter, S., Russell, D., Raina, P., Bartlett, D., & Galuppi, B. (2002). Health status of school-aged children with cerebral palsy: Information from a population-based sample. *Developmental Medicine and Child Neurology, 44,* 240–247.

Koppenhaver, D. A., & Yoder, D. E. (1992). Literacy issues in persons with severe speech and physical impairments. *Issues and Research in Special Education, 2,* 156–201.

Light, J., & Kelford Smith, A. K. (1993). Home literacy experiences of preschoolers who use AAC systems and of their nondisabled peers. *AAC: Augmentative and Alternative Communication, 9,* 10–25.

Morse, S., Haritou, F., Ong, K., Anderson, V., Catroppa, C., & Rosenfeld, J. (1999). Early effect of traumatic brain injury on young children's language performance: A preliminary linguistic analysis. *Pediatric Rehabilitation, 3,* 139–148.

National Institute of Neurological Disorders and Stroke. (2011). NINDS Traumatic Brain Injury Information Page. Bethesda, MD: National Institutes of Health. Retrieved from http://www.ninds.nih.gov/disorders/tbi/tbi.htm

Odding, L., Roebrouck, M., & Stam, H. (2006). The epidemiology of cerebral palsy: Incidence, impairments and risk factors. *Disability and Rehabilitation, 28*(4), 183–191.

Owens, R., Metz, D. E., & Farinella, K. (2011). *Introduction to communication disorders* (4th ed.). Upper Saddle River, NJ: Pearson.

Peeters, M., Verhoeven, L., de Moor, J., van Balkom, H., & van Leeuwe, J. (2009). Home literacy predictors of early reading development in children with cerebral palsy. *Research in Developmental Disabilities, 30,* 445–461.

Peeters, M., Verhoeven, L., van Balkom, H., & de Moor, J. (2008). Foundations of phonological awareness in preschool children with cerebral palsy: The impact of intellectual disability. *Journal of Intellectual Disability Research, 52,* 68–78.

Pennington, L., & McConachie, H. (2001). Interaction between children with cerebral palsy and their mothers: The effects of speech intelligibility. *International Journal of Language and Communication Disorders, 36,* 371–393.

Pennington, L., Thomson, K., James, P., Martin, L., & McNally, R. (2009). Effects of it takes two to talk: The Hanen program for parents of preschool children with cerebral palsy: Findings from an exploratory study. *Journal of Speech, Language, and Hearing Research, 52,* 1121–1138.

Pirila, S., van der Meere, J., Pentikainen, T., Ruusu-Niemi, P., Korpela, R., Kilipinen, J., & Nieminen, P. (2007). Language and motor speech skills in children with cerebral palsy. *Journal of Communication Disorders, 40,* 116–128.

Redmond, S. M., & Johnston, S. S. (2001). Evaluating the morphological competence of children with severe speech and physical impairments. *Journal of Speech, Language, and Hearing Research, 44,* 1362–1375.

Sandberg, A. D. (2001). Reading and spelling, phonological awareness, and working memory in children with severe speech impairments: A longitudinal study. *AAC: Augmentative and Alternative Communication, 17,* 11–26.

Smith, M. (2001). Simply a speech impairment? Literacy challenges for individuals with severe congenital speech impairments. *International Journal of Disability, Development and Education, 48,* 331–353.

Telzrow, C. (1987). Management of academic and educational problems in head injury. *Journal of Learning Disabilities, 20,* 536–545.

Tew, B. (1979). The "cocktail party syndrome" in children with hydrocephalus and spina bifida. *British Journal of Disorders of Communication, 14,* 89–101.

Turkstra, L. (2007). Pragmatic communication disorders: New intervention approaches. *The ASHA Leader, 12*(12), 16–17.

Vu, J., Babikian, T., & Asarnow, R. (2011). Academic and language outcomes in children after traumatic brain injury: A meta-analysis. *Exceptional Children, 77*(3), 263–281.

Yeargin-Allsopp, M., Braun, K., Doernbery, N., Benedict, R., Kirby, R., & Durkin, M. (2008). Prevalence of cerebral palsy in 8-year-old children in three areas of the United States in 2002: A multisite collaboration. *Pediatrics, 121,* 547–554.

Yoder, P. J., & Warren, S. F. (2002). Effects of prelinguistic milieu teaching and parent responsivity education on dyads involving children with intellectual disabilities. *Journal of Speech, Language, and Hearing Research, 45,* 1297–1310.

Chapter 13

Allor, J., Champlin, T., Gifford, D., & Mathes, P. (2010). Methods for increasing the intensity of reading instruction for students with intellectual disabilities. *Education and Training in Autism and Developmental Disabilities, 45,* 500–511.

Berko, J. (1958). The child's learning of English morphology. *Word, 14,* 150–177.

Blischak, D. M., & Schlosser, R. W. (2003). Use of technology to support independent spelling by students with autism. *Topics in Language Disorders, 23,* 293–304.

Blischak, D., Shah, S., Lombardino, L., & Chiarella, K. (2004). Effects of phonemic awareness instruction on the encoding skills of children with severe speech impairment. *Disability and Rehabilitation, 26,* 1295–1304.

Bowman-Perrott, L., Burke, M., Zhang, N., & Zaini, S. (2014). Direct and collateral effects of peer tutoring on social and behavioral outcomes: A meta-analysis of single-case research. *School Psychology Review, 43*(3), 260–285.

Brinton, B., & Fujiki, M. (1993). Language, social skills, and socioemotional behavior. *Language, Speech, and Hearing Services in Schools, 24,* 194–198.

Catts, H. (1997). The early identification of language-based reading disabilities. *Language, Speech, and Hearing Services in Schools, 28,* 86–89.

Cazden, C. B. (1986). Classroom discourse. In M. C. Wittrock (Ed.), *Handbook of research on teaching* (pp. 432–464). New York, NY: Macmillan.

Clegg, J., Hollis, C., Mawhood, L., & Rutter, M. (2005). Developmental language disorders—A follow-up in later adult life. Cognitive, language and psychosocial outcomes. *Journal of Child Psychology and Psychiatry and Allied Disciplines, 46,* 128–149.

Connell, P. J., & Stone, C. (1992). Morpheme learning of children with specific language impairments under controlled conditions. *Journal of Speech and Hearing Research, 35,* 844–852.

Cooper-Duffy, K., Szedia, P., & Hyer, G. (2010). Teaching literacy to students with significant cognitive disabilities. *Teaching Exceptional Children, 42,* 30–39.

Dudley-Marling, C., & Searle, D. (1988). Enriching language learning environments for students with learning disabilities. *Journal of Learning Disabilities, 21,* 140–143.

Ehren, B., & Nelson, N. (2005). The responsiveness to intervention approach and language impairment. *Topics in Language Disorders, 25,* 120–131.

Eisenberg, S. (2013). Grammar intervention: Content and procedures for facilitating children's language development. *Topics in Language Disorders, 33,* 165–178.

Elleman, A., Lindo, E., Morphy, P., & Compton, D. (2009). The impact of vocabulary instruction on passage-level comprehension of school-age children: A meta-analysis. *Journal of Research on Educational Effectiveness, 2*(1), 1–44.

Ellis, E., & Lenz, K. (1987). A component analysis of effective learning strategies for LD students. *Learning Disabilities Focus, 2,* 94–107.

Erickson, K., Hatch, P., & Clendon, S. (2010). Literacy, assistive technology, and students with significant disabilities. *Focus on Exceptional Children, 42,* 1–16.

Fuchs, D., & Fuchs, L. (2005). Responsiveness to intervention: A blueprint for practitioners, policymakers, and parents. *Teaching Exceptional Children, 38,* 57–61.

Fuchs, L., Fuchs, D., & Kazdan, S. (1999). Effects of peer-assisted learning strategies on high school students with serious reading problems. *Remedial and Special Education, 20*(5), 309–318.

Fujiki, M., & Brinton, B. (1987). Elicited imitation revisited: A comparison with spontaneous language production. *Language, Speech, and Hearing Services in Schools, 18,* 301–311.

Gallagher, A., & Chiatt, S. (2009). Evaluation of speech and language therapy interventions for pre-school children with specific language impairment: A comparison of outcomes following specialist intensive, nursery-based and no intervention. *International Journal of Language and Communication Disorders, 44,* 616–638.

Gillon, G. (2000). The efficacy of phonological awareness intervention for children with spoken language impairment. *Language, Speech, and Hearing Services in Schools, 31,* 126–141.

Goldstein, H., English, K., Shafer, K., & Kaczmarek, L. (1997). Interaction among preschoolers with and without disabilities: Effects of across-the-day peer intervention. *Journal of Speech, Language, and Hearing Research, 40,* 33–48.

Goldstein, H., Schneider, N., & Thiemann, K. (2007). Peer-mediated social communication intervention. *Topics in Language Disorders, 27*(2), 182–199.

Gray, C. & Garand, J. (1993). Social Stories: Improving responses of students with autism with accurate social information. *Focus on Autistic Behavior, 8,* 1–10.

Harris, M., Schumaker, J., & Deshler, D. (2011). The effects of morphological analysis instruction on the vocabulary performance of secondary students with and without disabilities. *Learning Disability Quarterly, 34*(1), 17–33.

Howell, K., Fox, S., & Morehead, M. (1993). *Curriculum-based evaluation: Teaching and decision making* (2nd ed.). Pacific Grove, CA: Brooks/Cole.

Institute for Education Sciences. (2007). *WWC intervention report: Ladders to literacy for kindergarten students.* Washington, DC. Retrieved from http://ies.ed.gov

Johnson, C. J., Beitchman, J. H., Young, A., Escobar, M., Atkinson, L., Wilson, B., . . . Wang, M. (1999). Fourteen-year follow-up of children with and without speech/language impairments: Speech/language stability and outcomes. *Journal of Speech, Language, and Hearing Research, 42,* 744–761.

Kemple, K., David, G., & Hysmith, C. (1997). Teachers' interventions in preschool and kindergarten children's peer interactions. *Journal of Research in Childhood Education, 12,* 34–47.

Kennedy, M., Deshler, D., & Lloyd, J. (2015). Effects of multimedia vocabulary instruction on adolescents with learning disabilities. *Journal of Learning Disabilities, 48*(1), 22–38.

Kennedy, M., Thomas, C., Meyer, J. P., Alves, K., & Lloyd, J. (2014). Using evidence-based multimedia to improve vocabulary performance of adolescents with LD: A UDL approach. *Learning Disability Quarterly, 37*(2), 71–86.

Kirby, J. R., & Bowers, P. N. (2012). Morphology works. What works: Research into Practice, Research Monograph #41, Ontario Ministry of Education. Retrieved from http://www.edu.gov.on.ca/eng/literacynumeracy/inspire/research/whatWorks.html

Kirby, J., Deacon, S. H., Bowers, P., Izenberg, L., Wade-Woolley, L., & Parrila, R. (2012). Children's morphological awareness and reading ability. *Reading and Writing, 25*(2), 389–410.

Knight, V., Browder, D., Agnello, B., & Lee, A. (2010). Academic instruction for students with severe disabilities. *Focus on Exceptional Children, 42,* 1–14.

Koppenhaver, D. A., & Erickson, K. A. (2003). Natural emergent literacy supports for preschoolers with autism and severe communication impairments. *Topics in Language Disorders, 23,* 283–292.

Kuder, S. (2016). Vocabulary instruction for secondary students with reading disabilities: An updated research review. *Learning Disabilities Quarterly* (in press).

Lapadat, J. C. (2002). Relationships between instructional language and primary students' learning. *Journal of Educational Psychology, 94,* 278–290.

Law, J., Garrett, Z., & Nye, C. (2004). The efficacy of treatment for children with developmental speech and language delay/disorder: A meta-analysis. *Journal of Speech, Language, and Hearing Research, 47,* 924–943.

Law, J., Rush, R., Schoon, I., & Parsons, S. (2009). Modeling developmental language difficulties from school entry into adulthood: Literacy, mental health, and employment outcomes. *Journal of Speech, Language, and Hearing Research, 52,* 1401–1416.

Lee, Y., & Vail, C. O. (2005). Computer-based reading instruction for young children with disabilities. *Journal of Special Education Technology, 20,* 5–18.

Lenz, B. K., & Hughes, C. A. (1990). A word identification strategy for adolescents with learning disabilities. *Journal of Learning Disabilities, 23,* 149–158.

McCormick, L. (2003). Ecological assessment and planning. In L. McCormick, D. Loeb, & R. Schiefelbusch (Eds.), *Supporting children with communication difficulties in inclusive classrooms* (2nd ed.). Boston, MA: Allyn & Bacon.

Moats, L. (2001, Summer). Overcoming the language gap and invest generously in teacher professional development. *American Educator,* 5–7.

Moats, L., & Lyon, G. R. (1996). Wanted: Teachers with knowledge of language. *Topics in Language Disorders, 16,* 73–86.

Mountain, L. (2002). Flip-A-Chip to build vocabulary. *Journal of Adolescent and Adult Literacy, 46*(1), 62–68.

Nelson, N. W. (1989). Curriculum-based language assessment and intervention. *Language, Speech, and Hearing Services in Schools, 20,* 170–184.

Notari-Syverson, A., O'Connor, R. E., & Vadasy, P. F. (2007). *Ladders to literacy: A preschool activity book* (2nd ed.). Baltimore, MD: Brookes.

O'Connor, R. E., Notari-Syverson, A., & Vadasy, P. F. (2005). *Ladders to literacy: A kindergarten activity book* (2nd ed.). Baltimore, MD: Brookes.

Olswang, L., Coggins, T., & Svensson, L. (2007). Assessing social communication in the classroom: Observing manner and duration of performance. *Topics in Language Disorders, 27*(2), 111–127.

Ostrosky, M., & Kaiser, A. (1991). Preschool classroom environments that promote communication. *Teaching Exceptional Children, 23,* 6–10.

Owens, R. (2010). *Language disorders: A functional approach to assessment and intervention* (5th ed.). Boston, MA: Pearson/Allyn & Bacon.

Rowe, M. (1986). Wait time: Slowing down may be a way of speeding up! *Journal of Teacher Education, 37,* 43–50.

Scammacca, N., Robens, G., Vaughn, S., Edmonds, M., Wexler, J., Reutebuch, C. K., & Torgesen, J. K. (2007). *Interventions for adolescent struggling readers: A metaanalysts with implications for practice.* Portsmouth, NH: RMC Research Corporation, Center on Instruction.

Seger, E., & Voerhoeven, L. (2005). Computer supported phonological awareness intervention for kindergarten children with specific language impairment. *Language, Speech, and Hearing Services in Schools, 35,* 229–239.

Starling, J., Munro, N., Togher, L., & Arciuli, J. (2011). Supporting secondary school students with language impairment. *Acquiring Knowledge in Speech, Language and Hearing, 13,* 26–30.

Terrill, M., Scruggs, T., & Mastropieri, M. (2004). SAT vocabulary instruction for high school students with learning disabilities. *Intervention in School and Clinic, 39*(5), 288–294.

Watson, L. R., Layton, T. L., Pierce, P. L., & Abraham, L. M. (1994). Enhancing emerging literacy in a language preschool. *Language, Speech, and Hearing Services in Schools, 25,* 136–145.

Chapter 14

Bankson, N., & Bernthal, J. (1999). *Bankson-Bernthal test of phonology.* Austin, TX: Pro-Ed.

Blank, M., Rose, S. A., & Berlin, L. J. (2003). *Preschool Language Assessment Instrument* (2nd ed.). Austin, TX: Pro-Ed.

Boehm, A. (2000). *Boehm Test of Basic Concepts–Revised.* San Antonio, TX: Psychological Corporation.

Bzoch, K. R., League, R., & Brown, V. K. (2003). *Receptive-Expressive-Emergent Language Test* (3rd ed.). Austin, TX: Pro-Ed.

Carrow-Woolfolk, E. (1999). *Comprehensive Assessment of Language.* Circle Pines, MN: American Guidance Service.

Carrow-Woolfolk, E. (2004). *Test for auditory comprehension of language* (4th ed.). Austin, TX: Pro-Ed.

Cirrin, F., & Gillam, R. (2008). Language intervention practices for school-age children with spoken language disorders: A systematic review. *Language, Speech, and Hearing Services in Schools,* S110–S137.

Connell, P. J. (1987). A comparison of modeling and imitation teaching procedures on language-disordered children. *Journal of Speech and Hearing Research, 30,* 105–113.

Connell, P. J., & Stone, C. (1992). Morpheme learning of children with specific language impairments under controlled conditions. *Journal of Speech and Hearing Research, 35,* 844–852.

Costanza-Smith, A. (2010). The clinical utility of language samples. *Perspectives on Language Learning and Education, 17*(1), 9–15.

Dawson, J., Stout, C., & Eyer, J. (2005). *Structured Photographic Expressive Language Test–3rd ed.* (SPELT-3). Joliet, IL: Janelle.

Downs, A., Downs, R., Johansen, M., & Fossum, M. (2007). Using discrete trail teaching within a public school program to facilitate skill development in students with developmental disabilities. *Education and Treatment of Children, 30*(3), 1–28.

Dunn, L., & Dunn, L. (2007). *Peabody Picture Vocabulary Test* (3rd ed.). New York, NY: Pearson Assessments.

Dyer, K., Santarcangelo, S., & Luce, S. (1987). Developmental influences in teaching language forms to individuals with developmental disabilities. *Journal of Speech and Hearing Disorders, 52,* 335–347.

Ervin, R. (2011). Considering Tier 3 within a response-to-intervention model. Retrieved from http://www.rtinetwork.org/

Fluharty, N. B. (2000). *Fluharty Preschool Speech and Language Screening Test.* Austin, TX: Pro-Ed.

Friend, M. (2014). *Special education: Contemporary perspectives for school professionals* (4th ed.). Boston, MA: Pearson Education.

Friend, M., & Cook, L. (2007). *Interactions: Collaboration skills for school professionals* (5th ed.). Boston, MA: Pearson Education.

Gillam, S. L., & Gillam, R. B. (2006). Making evidence-based decisions about child language intervention in schools. *Language, Speech, and Hearing Services in Schools, 37,* 304–315.

Goldman, R., & Fristoe, M. (2015). *Goldman-Fristoe Test of Articulation–3rd ed.* New York, NY: Pearson Assessment.

Hammill, D., Brown, V., Larsen, S., & Wiederholt, J. (2007). *Test of Adolescent and Adult Language* (4th ed.). Austin, TX: Pro-Ed.

Hammill, D., & Newcomer, P. (2008). *Test of Language Development–Intermediate* (4th ed.). Austin, TX: Pro-Ed.

Kaiser, A., Yoder, P., & Keetz, A. (1992). Evaluating milieu teaching. In S. Warren & J. Reichle (Eds.), *Causes and effects in communication and language intervention* (Vol. 1, pp. 9–47). Baltimore, MD: Paul H. Brookes.

Law, J., Garrett, Z., & Nye, C. (2004). The efficacy of treatment for children with developmental speech and language delay/disorder: A meta-analysis. *Journal of Speech, Language, and Hearing Research, 47,* 924–943.

Newcomer, P., & Hammill, D. (2008). *Test of Language Development–Primary* (4th ed.). Austin, TX: Pro-Ed.

Nippold, M. (2000). Language development during the adolescent years: Aspects of pragmatics, syntax, and semantics. *Topics in Language Disorders, 20,* 15–28.

Owens, R. (2010). *Language disorders: A functional approach to assessment and intervention* (5th ed.). Boston, MA: Pearson/Allyn & Bacon.

Phelps-Teraski, D., & Phelps-Gunn, T. (2007). *Test of Pragmatic Language–2.* Austin, TX: Pro-Ed.

Ratner, N. (2006). Evidence-based practice: An examination of its ramifications for the practice of speech-language pathology. *Language, Speech, and Hearing Services in Schools, 37,* 257–267.

Reed, V. (2012). *An introduction to children with language disorders* (4th ed.). Boston, MA: Pearson.

Sackett, D., Rosenberg, W., Gray, J., Haynes, R., & Richardson, W. (1996). Evidence-based medicine: What it is and what it isn't. *British Medical Journal, 312,* 71–72.

Salvia, J., & Ysseldyke, J. (2010). *Assessment in special and inclusive education* (11th ed.). Belmont, CA: Wadsworth.

Semel, E., Wiig, E., & Secord, W. (2013). *Clinical evaluation of language fundamentals* (5th ed.). San Antonio, TX: Psychological Corporation.

Slavin, R. E. (2002). Evidence-based education policies: Transforming educational practice and research. *Educational Researcher, 31,* 15–21.

Torgesen, J. K., & Bryant, B. R. (2004). *Test of Phonological Awareness* (2nd ed.). Austin, TX: Pro-Ed.

Wallace, G., & Hammill, O. (2013). *Comprehensive Receptive and Expressive Vocabulary Test* (3rd ed.). Austin, TX: Pro-Ed.

Warren, S. E., & Kaiser, A. P. (1986). Incidental language teaching: A critical review. *Journal of Speech and Hearing Disorders, 51,* 291–299.

Yoder, P. J., Kaiser, A. P., & Alpert, C. L. (1991). An exploratory study of the interaction between language teaching methods and child characteristics. *Journal of Speech and Hearing Research, 34,* 155–167.

Zimmerman, I. L., Steiner, V. G., & Pond, R. E. (2011). *Preschool Language Scale* (5th ed.). San Antonio, TX: Harcourt.

Chapter 15

Bedrosian, J., Lasker, J., Speidel, K., & Politsch, A. (2003). Enhancing the written narrative skills of an AAC student with autism: Evidence-based research issues. *Topics in Language Disorders, 23,* 305–324.

Beukelman, D. R., & Mirenda, P. (2005). *Augmentative and alternative communication.* Baltimore, MD: Paul H. Brookes.

Beukelman, D. R., Mirenda, P., & Sturm, J. (2005). Literacy development of children who use AAC. In D. Beukelman & P. Mirenda (Eds.), *Augmentative and alternative communication* (pp. 351–390). Baltimore, MD: Paul H. Brookes.

Binger, C., & Light, J. (2006). Demographics of preschoolers who require AAC. *Language, Speech, and Hearing Services in Schools, 37,* 200–208.

Blischak, D. M. (1995). Thomas the writer: Case study of a child with severe physical, speech, and visual impairments. *Language, Speech, and Hearing Services in Schools, 26,* 11–20.

Bliss, C. (1965). *Semantography.* Sydney, Australia: Semantography Publications.

Blockenberger, S., Armstrong, R. W., O'Connor, A., & Freeman, R. (1993). Children's attitudes toward a nonspeaking child using various augmentative and alternative communication techniques. *AAC: Augmentative and Alternative Communication, 9,* 243–250.

Bondy, A., & Frost, L. (2001). The Picture Exchange Communication System. *Behavior Modification, 25,* 725–744.

Carlson, F. (1984). *Picsyms categorical dictionary.* Lawrence, KS: Baggeboda Press.

Carrier, J., & Peak, T. (1975). *Non-slip: Non-speech language initiation program.* Lawrence, KS: H & H Enterprises.

Carter, M. (2003). Communicative spontaneity of children with high support needs who use augmentative and alternative communication systems. II: Antecedents and effectiveness of communication. *AAC: Augmentative and Alternative Communication, 19,* 155–169.

Chung, Y.-C., & Carter, E. (2013). Promoting peer interactions in inclusive classrooms for students who use speech-generating devices. *Research and Practice for Persons with Severe Disabilities, 38,* 94–109.

Chung, Y., Carter, E. W., & Sisco, L. G. (2012). Social interaction of students with severe disabilities who use augmentative and alternative communication in inclusive classrooms. *American Journal on Intellectual and Developmental Disabilities, 117,* 349–367.

Clark, C. R. (1981). Learning words using traditional orthography and the symbols of Rebus, Bliss, and Carrier. *Journal of Speech and Hearing Disorders, 46,* 191–196.

Creagan, A. (1982). *Sigsymbol dictionary.* Hatfield, Hertsford, England: A. Creagan.

Cress, C., & Marvin, C. (2003). Common questions about AAC services in early intervention. *AAC: Augmentative and Alternative Communication, 19,* 254–272.

Drager, K., Postal, V., Carrolus, L., Castellano, M., Gagliano, C., & Glynn, J. (2006). The effect of aided language modeling on symbol comprehension and production in two preschoolers with autism. *American Journal of Speech-Language Pathology, 15,* 112–125.

Ganz, J. B., Earles-Vollrath, T. L., Heath, A. K., Parker, R. I., Rispoli , M. J.,& Duran, J. B. (2012). *Journal of Autism and Developmental Disorders, 42,* 60–74. doi:10.1007/s10803-011-1212-2

Goossens, C. (1989). Aided communication intervention before assessment: A case study of a child with cerebral palsy. *AAC: Augmentative and Alternative Communication, 5,* 14–26.

Guralnick, M. J. (1986). The peer relations of young handicapped and nonhandicapped children. In P. S. Strain, M. J. Guralnick, & H. M. Walker (Eds.), *Children's social behavior.* New York, NY: Academic Press.

Hunt, R., Alwell, M., & Goetz, L. (1991). Interacting with peers through conversation turntaking with a communication book adaptation. *AAC: Augmentative and Alternative Communication, 7,* 117–126.

Hurlbut, B. I., Iwata, B. A., & Green, J. D. (1982). Nonvocal language acquisition in adolescents with severe physical disabilities: Blissymbol versus iconic stimulus formats. *Journal of Applied Behavior Analysis, 15,* 241–258.

Johnson, J. (1986). *Self-talk: Communication boards for children and adults.* Tucson, AZ: Communication Skill Builders.

Johnson, R. (1981). *The picture communication symbols.* Salana Beach, CA: Mayer-Johnson.

Johnston, S. S., Reichle, J., & Evans, J. (2004). Supporting augmentative and alternative communication use by beginning communicators with severe disabilities. *American Journal of Speech-Language Pathology, 13,* 20–30.

Kent-Walsh, J., & Light, J. (2003). General education teachers' experiences with inclusion of students who use augmentative and alternative communication. *AAC: Augmentative and Alternative Communication, 19,* 104–124.

Keogh, W. J., & Reichle, J. (1985). Communication intervention for the "difficult-to-teach" severely handicapped. In S. R. Warren & A. K. Rogers-Warren (Eds.), *Teaching functional language* (pp. 157–196). Austin, TX: Pro-Ed.

Koppenhaver, D. A., & Erickson, K. A. (2003). Natural emergent literacy supports for preschoolers with autism and severe communication impairments. *Topics in Language Disorders, 23,* 283–292.

Koppenhaver, D., & Yoder, D. (1992). Literacy issues in persons with severe physical and speech impairments. In R. Gaylord-Ross (Ed.), *Issues and research in special education* (Vol. 2, pp. 156–201). New York, NY: Teachers College Press.

Light, J., & Kelford Smith, A. (1993). The home literacy experiences of preschoolers who use augmentative communication systems and their nondisabled peers. *AAC: Augmentative and Alternative Communication, 9,* 10–25.

Locke, R. A., & Mirenda, P. (1992). Roles and responsibilities of special education teachers serving on teams delivering AAC services. *AAC: Augmentative and Alternative Communication, 8,* 200–210.

Mayer-Johnson Co. (1986). *The picture communication symbols, books I and 2.* Solana Beach, CA: Mayer-Johnson.

McCormick, L., & Wegner, J. (2003). Supporting augmentative communication. In L. McCormick, D. Loeb, & R. Schiefelbusch (Eds.), *Supporting children with communication difficulties in inclusive settings* (2nd ed.). Boston, MA: Allyn & Bacon.

McGregor, G., Young, J., Gerak, J., Thomas, B., & Vogelsberg, R. T. (1992). Increasing functional use of an assistive communication device by a student with severe disabilities. *AAC: Augmentative and Alternative Communication, 8,* 243–250.

Millar, D. C., Light, J. C., & Schlosser, R. W. (2006). The impact of augmentative and alternative communication intervention on the speech production of individuals with developmental disabilities: A research review. *Journal of Speech, Language, and Hearing Research, 49,* 248–264.

Mirenda, P., & Iacono, T. (1990). Communication options for persons with severe and profound disabilities: State of the art and future directions. *Journal of the Association for the Severely Handicapped, 15,* 3–21.

Mirenda, P., & Locke, P. A. (1989). A comparison of symbol transparency in nonspeaking persons with intellectual disabilities. *Journal of Speech and Hearing Disorders, 54,* 121–140.

Musselwhite, C. R., & Ruscello, D. M. (1984). Transparency of three communication symbol systems. *Journal of Speech and Hearing Research, 27,* 436–443.

Mustonen, T., Locke, P., Reichle, J., Solbrack, M., & Lindgren, A. (1991). An overview of augmentative and alternative communication systems. In J. Reichle, J. York, & J. Sigafoos (Eds.), *Implementing augmentative and alternative communication: Strategies for learners with severe disabilities* (pp. 1–37). Baltimore, MD: Paul H. Brookes.

Reichle, J. (1983). *A survey of professional serving persons with severe handicaps.* Unpublished manuscript, University of Minnesota, Minneapolis, MN.

Reichle, J. (1991). Developing communicative exchanges. In J. Reichle, J. York, & J. Sigafoos (Eds.), *Implementing augmentative and alternative communication: Strategies for learners with severe disabilities* (pp. 123–156). Baltimore, MD: Paul H. Brookes.

Reichle, J., Mirenda, P., Locke, P., Piche, L., & Johnston, S. (1992). Beginning augmentative communication systems. In S. E. Warren & J. Reichle (Eds.), *Causes and effects in communication and language intervention* (pp. 121–156). Baltimore, MD: Paul H. Brookes.

Reichle, J., & Yoder, D. E. (1985). Communication board use in severely handicapped learners. *Language, Speech, and Hearing Services in Schools, 16,* 146–167.

Rispoli, M., Franco, J., van der Meer, L., Lang, R., & Carmargo, S. (2010). The use of speech-generating devices in communication interventions for individuals with developmental disabilities: A review of the literature. *Developmental Neurorehabilitation, 13,* 276–293.

Romski, M., & Sevcik, R. (2005). Augmentative communication and early intervention: Myths and realities. *Infants and Young Children, 18*(3), 174–185.

Romski, M. A., Sevcik, R. A., & Pate, J. L. (1988). Establishment of symbolic communication in persons with severe retardation. *Journal of Speech and Hearing Disorders, 53,* 94–107.

Romski, M. A., Sevcik, R. A., Robinson, B., & Bakeman, R. (1994). Adult-directed communications of youth with mental retardation using the system for augmenting language. *Journal of Speech and Hearing Research, 37,* 617–628.

Rounsefell, S., Zucker, S. H., & Roberts, I. G. (1993). Effects of listener training on intelligibility of augmentative and alternative speech in the secondary classroom. *Education and Training in Mental Retardation, 28,* 296–308.

Schlosser R. (2003). Roles of speech output in augmentative and alternative communication: Narrative review. *AAC: Augmentative and Alternative Communication, 19,* 5–27.

Sevcik, R. A., & Romski, M. A. (1986). Representational matching skills for persons with severe retardation. *AAC: Augmentative and Alternative Communication, 2,* 160–164.

Sevcik, R. A., & Romski, M. A. (2007). *AAC: More than three decades of growth and development.* Retrieved from http://www.asha.org/public/speech/disorders/Augmentative-and-Alternative.htm

Spiegel, B. B., Benjamin, B. J., & Spiegel, S. A. (1993). One method to increase spontaneous use of an assistive communication device: Case study. *AAC: Augmentative and Alternative Communication, 9*, 111–1118.

Therrien, M., Light, J., & Pope, L. (2016). Systematic review of the effects of interventions to promote peer interactions for children who use aided AAC. *AAC: Augmentative and Alternative Communication, 32*(2), 81–93.

Tincani, M. (2004). Comparing the Picture Exchange Communication System and sign language training for children with autism. *Focus on Autism and Other Developmental Disabilities, 19*, 152–163.

Wilkins, J., & Ratajczak, A. (2009). Developing students' literacy skills using high-tech speech-generating augmentative and alternative communication devices. *Intervention in School and Clinic, 44*, 167–172.

Wilkinson, K., & Hennig, S. (2007). The state of research and practice in augmentative and alternative communication for children with developmental/intellectual disabilities. *Mental Retardation and Developmental Disabilities Research Reviews, 13*, 58–69.

Worah, S. (2011). *A survey of augmentative and alternative communication services in Connecticut.* State Education Resource Center, Connecticut. Retrieved from http://www.ctserc.org/index.php/tie/item/72-a-survey-of-augmentative-and-alternative-communication-aac-services-in-connecticut

Chapter 16

Abadiano, H. R., & Turner, J. (2002). Sheltered instruction: An empowerment framework for English language learners. *NERA Journal, 38*, 50–55.

Adler, S. (1993). *Multicultural communication skills in the classroom.* Boston, MA: Allyn & Bacon.

American Speech-Language-Hearing Association. (2003). Technical report: American English dialects. *ASHA Supplement 23*, 45–46.

Applebome, P. (1996, December 20). School district elevates status of Black English. *New York Times*, p. 18.

Artiles, A. J., Rueda, R., Salazar, J. J., & Higareda, I. (2005). Within-group diversity in minority disproportionate representation: English language learners in urban school districts. *Exceptional Children, 71*, 283–300.

August, D., & Shanahan, T. (2006). *Developing literacy in second-language learners: Report of the National Literacy Panel on Language-Minority Children and Youth.* Mahwah, NJ: Lawrence Erlbaum.

Baca, L. M., & Almanza, E. (1991). *Language minority students with disabilities.* Reston, VA: The Council for Exceptional Children (ERIC Document Reproduction Services No. 339, 171).

Baca, L. M., & Cervantes, H. T. (1989). *The bilingual special education interface.* New York, NY: Merrill.

Baratz, J. C. (1969). Linguistic and cultural factors in teaching reading to ghetto children. *Elementary English, 46*, 199–203.

Bernstein, R. J. (2015). Cultural pluralism. *Philosophy and Social Criticism, 41*, 347–356.

Brown, M. C., Sibley, D. E., Washington, J. A., Rogers, T. T., Edwards, J. R., MacDonald, M. C., & Seidenberg, M. S.

(2015). Impact of dialect use on a basic component of learning to read. *Frontiers in Psychology, 6*, 196.

Campbell, T., Dollaghan, C., Needleman, H., & Janosky, J. (1997). Reducing bias in language assessment: Processing dependent measures. *Journal of Speech, Language, and Hearing Research, 40*, 519–525.

Cole, L. (1989). *E pluribus:* Multicultural imperatives for the 1990s and beyond. *ASHA, 31*, 65–70.

Cole, P. A., & Taylor, O. L. (1990). Performance of working class African-American children on three tests of articulation. *Language, Speech, and Hearing Services in Schools, 21*, 171–176.

Coleman, R., & Goldenberg, C. (2009). What does research say about effective practices for English learners: Introduction and part 1: Oral language proficiency. *Kappa Delta Pi Record, 46*, 10–16.

Craig, H., Thompson, C., Washington, J., & Potter, S. (2003). Phonological features of child African-American English. *Journal of Speech, Language, and Hearing Research, 46*, 623–635.

Culatta, B., Reese, M., & Setzer, L. A. (2006). Early literacy instruction in a dual-language (Spanish–English) kindergarten. *Communication Disorders Quarterly, 27*, 67–82.

Cummins, J. (1980). The cross-lingual dimensions of language proficiency: Implications for bilingual education and the optimal age issue. *TESOL Quarterly, 4*, 171–174.

Cummins, J. (1984). *Bilingualism and special education: Issues in assessment and pedagogy.* San Diego, CA: College-Hill Press.

Cummins, J. (1994). Knowledge, power, and identity in teaching English as a second language. In F. Genesee (Ed.), *Educating second language children* (pp. 33–58). New York, NY: Cambridge University Press.

Cummins, J. (2000). *Language, power, and pedagogy: Bilingual children in the crossfire.* Clevedon, England: Multicultural Matters.

Damico, J. S., & Damico, S. K. (1993). Language and social skills from a diversity perspective: Considerations for the speech-language pathologist. *Language, Speech, and Hearing Services in Schools, 24*, 236–243.

Day-Vines, N., Barto, H., Booker, B., Smith, K., Barna, J., Maiden, B., Zegley, L., & Felder, M. (2009). African American English: Implications for school counseling professionals. *Journal of Negro Education, 78*, 70–82.

Denton, C. A., Anthony, J. L., Parker, R., & Hasbrouck, J. E. (2004). Effects of two tutoring programs in the English reading development of Spanish-English bilingual students. *Elementary School Journal, 104*, 289–305.

Echevarria, J., Short, D., & Powers, K. (2006). School reform and standards-based education: A model for English language learners. *Journal of Educational Research, 99*, 195–210.

Emihovich, C. (1988). Toward cultural pluralism: Redefining integration in American society. *Urban Review, 20*, 3–7.

Federal Interagency Forum on Child and Family Statistics. (2011). *America's children: Key national indicators of well-being.* Retrieved from http://childstats.gov/americaschildren/index.asp

Figueroa, R. A. (1989). Psychological testing of linguistic-minority students: Knowledge gaps and regulations. *Exceptional Children, 56*, 135–153.

Fung, F., & Roseberry-McKibben, C. (1999). Service delivery considerations in working with clients from Cantonese-speaking backgrounds. *American Journal of Speech-Language Pathology, 8,* 309–318.

Gage, N., Gersten, R., Sugai, G., & Newman-Gonchar, R. (2013). Disproportionality of English learners with emotional and/or behavioral disorders: A comparative meta-analysis with English learners with learning disabilities. *Behavioral Disorders, 38,* 123–136.

Garcia, S., & Tyler, B. (2010). Meeting the needs of English language learners with learning disabilities in the general curriculum. *Theory into Practice, 49,* 113–120.

Gersten, R., & Woodward, J. (1994). The language-minority student and special education: Issues, trends, and paradoxes. *Exceptional Children, 60,* 310–322.

Godley, A. J., Sweetland, J., Wheeler, R. S., Minnici, A., & Carpenter, B. D. (2006). Preparing teachers for dialectally diverse classrooms. *Educational Researcher, 35,* 30–37.

Grossman, H. (1995). *Special education in a diverse society.* Boston, MA: Allyn & Bacon.

Guler, N. (2013). Assessing ELL students in mainstream classes: A new dilemma for the teachers. *English Journal, 102.3,* 126–129.

Gutiérrez-Clellen, V., & Peña, E. (2001). Dynamic assessment of diverse children: A tutorial. *Language, Speech, and Hearing Services in Schools, 32,* 212–224.

Halle, T., Hair, E., Wandner, L., McNamara, M., & Chien, N. (2012). Predictors and outcomes of early versus later English language proficiency among English language learners. *Early Childhood Research Quarterly, 27,* 1–20.

Handscombe, J. (1994). Putting it all together. In F. Genesee (Ed.), *Educating second language children.* New York, NY: Cambridge University Press.

Hansen-Thomas, H. (2008). Sheltered instruction: Best practices for ELLs in the mainstream. *Kappa Delta Pi Record, 44,* 165–169.

Harris-Wright, K. (1987). The challenge of educational coalescence: Teaching nonmainstream English-speaking students. *Journal of Childhood Communication Disorders, 11,* 209–215.

Hemphill, F. C., & Vanneman, A. (2011). *Achievement gaps: How Hispanic and white students in public schools perform in mathematics and reading on the national assessment of educational progress* (NCES 2011-459). Washington, DC: National Center for Education Statistics, Institute of Education Sciences, U.S. Department of Education.

Hoover, J. J. (2012). Reducing unnecessary referrals: Guideline for teachers of diverse learners. *Teaching Exceptional Children, 44,* 38–47.

Hudelson, S. (1994). Literacy development of second language children. In F. Genesee (Ed.), *Educating second language children* (pp. 129–158). New York, NY: Cambridge University Press.

Ihnot, C. (1992). *Read naturally.* St. Paul, MN: Read Naturally.

Individuals with Disabilities Education Act. (2004). Washington, DC: U.S. Government Printing Office.

Kapantzoglou, M., Adelaida Restrepo, M., & Thompson, M. S. (2012). Dynamic assessment of word learning skills: Identifying language impairment in bilingual children. *Language, Speech, and Hearing Services in Schools, 43,* 81–96.

Kena, G., Musu-Gillette, L., Robinson, J., Wang, X., Rathbun, A., Zhang, J., . . . Dunlop Velez, E. (2015). *The Condition of Education 2015* (NCES 2015-144). Washington, DC: National Center for Education Statistics, Institute of Education Sciences, U.S. Department of Education. Retrieved from http://nces.ed.gov/pubsearch

Kieffer, M., Lesaux, N., Rivera, M., & Francis, D. (2009). Accommodations for English language learners taking large-scale assessments: A meta-analysis on effectiveness and validity. *Review of Educational Research, 79,* 1168–1201.

Klingner, J. K., Artiles, A. J., & Barletta L. M. (2006). English language learners who struggle with reading: Language acquisition or LD? *Journal of Learning Disabilities, 39,* 108–128.

Kominski, R., & Shin, H. (2008). *Language needs of school-age children.* Washington, DC: U.S. Government Printing Office. Retrieved from http://www.census.gov/hhes/socdemo/language/data/acs/Language-Needs-of-School-Age-Children-PAA-2008.doc

Laing, S. P., & Kamhi, A. (2003). Alternative assessment of language and literacy in culturally and linguistically diverse populations. *Language, Speech, and Hearing Services in Schools, 34,* 44–55.

Lenski, S. D., Ehlers-Zavala, F., Daniel, M. C., & Sun-Irminger, X. (2006). Assessing English-language learning in mainstream classrooms. *The Reading Teacher, 60,* 24–34.

Lesaux, N. K., & Siegel, L. S. (2003). The development of reading in children who speak English as a second language. *Developmental Psychology, 39,* 1005–1019.

Linan-Thompson, S., Vaughn, S., Hickman-Davis, P., & Kouzekanani, K. (2003). Effectiveness of supplemental instruction for second-grade English language learners with reading difficulties. *Elementary School Journal, 103,* 221–238.

Lugo-Neris, M., Jackson, C., & Goldstein, H. (2010). Facilitating vocabulary acquisition of young English language learners. *Language, Speech, and Hearing Services in Schools, 41,* 314–327.

Martin Luther King Junior Elementary School Children v. Ann Arbor School District Board (1979). 473 R Suppl 1371.

Montrul, S. (2013). *El bilingüismo en el mundo hispanohablante.* Walden, MA: Wiley-Blackwell.

Nelson, J., Vadasy, P., & Sanders, E. (2011). Efficacy of a tier 2 supplemental root word vocabulary and decoding intervention with kindergarten Spanish-speaking English learners. *Journal of Literacy Research, 43,* 184–211.

PASE v. Hannon (1980). 3 EHLR 552:108. F. Suppl. 831, N.D. Illinois.

Payan, R. M. (1989). Language assessment for the bilingual exceptional child. In L. M. Baca & H. T. Cervantes (Eds.), *The bilingual special education interface.* New York, NY: Merrill.

Peregoy, S. F., & Boyle, O. F. (2000). English learners reading English: What we know, what we need to know. *Theory into Practice, 39,* 237–247.

Pollard-Durodola, S. D., Mathes, P. G., Vaughn, S., Cardenas-Hagan, E., & Linan-Thompson, S. (2006). The role of oracy in developing comprehension in Spanish-speaking English language learners. *Topics in Language Disorders, 26,* 365–384.

Reyes, M. de la Luz. (1992). Challenging venerable assumptions: Literacy instruction for linguistically different students. *Harvard Educational Review, 62,* 427–446.

Reyes, M. de la Luz, & Laliberty, E. (1992). A teacher's "Pied Piper" effect on young authors. *Education and Urban Society, 24,* 263–278.

Rossell, C. (2005). Teaching English through English. *Educational Leadership, 62,* 32–36.

Slavin, R. E., Madden, N., Calderón, M., Chamberlin, A., & Hennessy, M. (2011). Reading and language outcomes of a multiyear randomized evaluation of transitional bilingual education. *Educational Evaluation and Policy Analysis, 33,* 47–58.

Sprick, M. M., Howard, L. M., & Fidanque, A. (1998). *Read well: Critical foundations in elementary reading.* Longmont, CO: Sopris West.

Terrell, S. L., & Terrell, F. (1993). African-American cultures. In D. E. Battle (Ed.), *Communication disorders in multicultural populations* (pp. 3–37). Boston, MA: Andover Medical Publishers.

Wolfram, W., & Schilling, N. (2016). *American English: Dialects and variation* (3rd ed.). Malden, MA: Wiley-Blackwell.

Yates, J. R., & Ortiz, A. A. (1991). Professional development needs of teachers who serve exceptional language minorities in today's schools. *Teacher Education and Special Education, 13,* 11–18.

Zeitlin, A., Beltran, D., Salcido, P., Gonzalez, T., & Reyes, T. (2011). Building a pathway of optimal support for English language learners in special education. *Teacher Education and Special Education, 34,* 59–70.

Glossary

Affective disorders Behavioral disorders that affect mood and feelings.

Aided augmentative communication techniques Methods that utilize external support devices or procedures; for example, communication boards and voice output devices.

Allomorphs Morphemes that are pronounced differently in response to surrounding sounds and/or injury.

Articulation Shaping of the sound through impedance of airstream by the lips, tongue, and/or teeth.

Asperger syndrome Less severe form of autism, characterized by difficulties with social interaction.

Ataxic cerebral palsy Rare type of cerebral palsy that affects balance and depth perception.

Athetoid cerebral palsy A type of cerebral palsy in which the limbs have involuntary movements; individuals seem to have little control over their movement and have difficulty balancing.

Augmentative communication Methods and devices that supplement existing verbal communication skills.

Autism spectrum disorders A group of disorders that vary in severity but share the features of impairments in social interaction, communication, and behavior differences.

Basic interpersonal communicative skills (BICS) The ability to communicate with others using a second language.

Behavioral phenotypes Patterns of behavior associated with genetic syndromes.

Bidialectalism An instructional approach that seeks to provide opportunities for students to develop and practice standard English while continuing to use their dialect.

Bilabial Consonants that are produced by a flow of air that is stopped or restricted by the two lips.

Bilingualism The ability to understand and use two languages.

Bootstrapping A theory of language development according to which specific language skills are associated with corresponding cognitive accomplishments.

Broca's area Region of the cerebrum, located near the middle of the left cerebral hemisphere, where organization of the complex motor sequences necessary for speech production occur.

Central nervous system Major division of human nervous system that includes the brain and spinal cord.

Chaining According to behavioral theory, the process of learning to put together several verbal behaviors to create an utterance.

Closed-head injury A type of brain injury caused by a rapid acceleration and deceleration of the head, during which the brain bounces around inside the skull; most often caused by automobile accidents.

Code switching Changing from one language or dialect to another during conversation.

Cognitive/academic language proficiency (CALP) The ability to apply English language skills to academic tasks.

Communication The process participants use to exchange information and ideas, needs, and desires.

Corpus callosum Bundle of fibers that connect the left and right hemispheres of the human brain.

Deaf A hearing disability that precludes successful processing of linguistic information through audition, with or without a hearing aid.

Delayed echolalia The repetition of words or phrases that may have been heard days, weeks, or even years ago.

Derivational suffixes Word endings that change the type of word.

Dialect (a) A variation of a language that shares elements of structure and vocabulary with the base language but differs in significant ways; (b) systematic subvariants of a particular language that are spoken by a sizable group.

Diaphragm Muscle separating the thorax and abdomen used in inhalation.

Discrete trial training An instructional approach based on behavioral principles developed for persons with autism.

Distancing In cognitive theory, the principle that involves the gradual movement away from actual physical experiences to symbolic or representational behavior.

Down syndrome A genetic syndrome caused by an extra chromosome at pair 21.

Dynamic assessment Evaluates how children learn during the assessment process.

Ebonics Another name for Black English Vernacular, sometimes used to indicate a different language rather than a dialect difference.

Echolalia The literal repetition of speech produced by others.

Ecological assessment   Examines the child's behavior in the context of environmental demands and expectations.

Emergent literacy   A theory of reading and writing development that claims that literacy develops continuously from early childhood experiences.

English as a second language (ESL)   An instructional program in which students with limited English proficiency spend most of their day in a submersion classroom but receive some help with English.

Epilepsy   A condition that produces brief disturbances in the electrical functioning of the brain, causing seizures.

Expository discourse   Use of language to describe or explain a topic.

Externalized behavior problems   Behavior disorders such as aggression in which the individual acts on others.

Fast-mapping   A theory of semantics that describes the phenomenon of rapid word acquisition.

Figurative (nonliteral) language   (a) Nonliteral language such as metaphor and simile; (b) use of language that uses language in more creative, imaginative ways.

Forebrain (cerebrum)   Region of the human brain that controls cognitive functions and language.

Formal assessment   Published instruments that utilize a standard set of procedures to gather information to be used for assessment; can include tests, observation forms, rating scales, and so on.

Fragile X syndrome   A genetic disorder in which the X chromosome is deficient, causing intellectual disabilities.

Functional approaches   Intervention methods that identify skills that the children need in order to be successful in their present environment or in one that they will soon be entering.

Generalization   The ability to apply previous learning to novel situations and tasks.

Grammatical morphemes   Word affixes that signal a difference in grammatical usage.

Guessability   Refers to the degree of similarity in appearance between a symbol and the item it represents.

Hindbrain   Region of the human brain that controls basic life functions such as respiration.

Hydrocephalus   A condition caused by the accumulation of fluid on the brain that, if untreated, can cause brain damage.

Hyperlexia   A condition in which individuals can read individual words with great accuracy but lag in comprehension.

Hypertonia   A type of cerebral palsy characterized by significant limitations in the individual's range of motion; muscle tone is increased and the muscles contract; movement may be slow and jerky.

Idiosyncratic language   The use of conventional words or phrases in unusual ways to convey specific meanings.

Illocutionary stage   The stage of communication at which children begin to use intentional communication.

Immediate echolalia   Echolalia that occurs within a brief time period after the speaker talks.

Incidental teaching   Language instructional technique in which instruction is "incidental" to the communicative interaction between student and teacher.

Indirect requests   Communicative form in which the syntactic form of the request (e.g., *Can you close the door?*) is different from the intent of the message (e.g., *Close the door!*).

Inflectional prefixes   Prefixes that do not change the word class of the word (e.g., from verb to noun).

Information processing   Contemporary model of human cognition that emphasizes the interconnectedness of cognitive processes information.

Intellectual disability   Significant limitations both in intellectual functioning and in adaptive behavior.

Internalized behavior problems   Behavior disorders such as depression in which the individual turns his or her feelings inward.

Interrupted-behavior-chain strategy   Inserting a target skill in the middle of an established sequence of behaviors to teach the new skill.

Intervention   Intensive instruction usually delivered after a period of time in which the individual has been exposed to instruction.

Joint attention   Situation in which two individuals (e.g., parent and child) are paying attention to the same thing.

Language   A rule-governed symbol system for communicating meaning through a shared code of arbitrary symbols.

Language acquisition device (LAD)   Consists of basic grammatical categories and rules that are common to all languages.

Language disorder   Impaired comprehension and/or use of spoken, written, and/or other symbol systems.

Larynx   Structure in the neck that contains the vocal folds.

Learnability   Refers to the ease with which a symbol system can be acquired.

Learning strategies   Instructional approaches that teach students to use a strategy to solve problems and carry out tasks.

Locutionary stage   Use of words to express communicative intentions.

Mand-model procedure Instructional procedure in which the trainer attempts to prompt a response from the student by using a demand or request ("mand").

Manner of articulation How a speech sound is produced.

Mean length of utterance (MLU) A measure of syntactic development that is calculated by counting the total number of morphemes in a sample of language and dividing by the number of utterances in the sample.

Metalinguistic ability The ability to think about language itself.

Metalinguistic skill The ability to reflect consciously on the nature and properties of language.

Metasyntactic awareness The ability to identify and correct grammatical errors using syntactic rules.

Midbrain Region of the human brain that consists of structures that assist in relaying information to and from the brain and the visual and auditory nerves.

Minimal pair Two words that differ only by one sound.

Mitigated echolalia A type of echolalia in which the structure of the original utterance is changed.

Mixed cerebral palsy A type of cerebral palsy that is characterized by symptoms of two or more types of cerebral palsy.

Morpheme The smallest unit of meaning in a language.

Morphology The study of words and how they are formed.

Muscular dystrophy A progressive disorder that produces weakness in muscles and eventually is fatal.

Myelination Growth of sheathing around nerves that improves transmission of messages.

Myelomeningocele A form of spina bifida in which damage to the spinal cord causes significant sensory and motor losses.

Narrative A storytelling monologue.

Naturalistic approaches Instructional approaches that use the natural environment as the basis for language instruction.

Neologisms Nonstandard (or invented) words.

Neural networks Interconnected nodes of processing that run in parallel in human cognition.

Norm referenced Norm-referenced tests compare an individual's performance to that of a comparison population.

Object permanence The idea that objects exist even when they are not being touched, tasted, or seen.

Open-head injury A type of brain injury, usually confined to one portion of the brain, characterized by a visible injury, often a gunshot wound.

Optimality theory This model of linguistics emphasizes the role of higher-order cognitive (thinking) processes in governing speech production and recognizes the flexibility in language.

Output In AAC, the appearance of the display and how it enhances communication with a listener.

Parallel processing A theory of information processing that suggests that multiple levels of information can be processed simultaneously.

Peripheral nervous system Major division of the human nervous system that includes the nerves that carry messages to and from the extremities to the spinal cord and brain.

Phoneme The smallest linguistic unit of sound that can signal a difference in meaning.

Phonemic awareness The ability to focus on and manipulate phonemes in spoken words.

Phonological awareness The ability to understand, use, and recall the phonological segment used in an alphabetic orthography.

Phonology The study of the sound system of language.

Phonotactic constraints Limitations on sound combinations in a language.

Phrase structure rules The rules that describe the basic structure of sentences.

Place of articulation Where sound is formed in the mouth.

Pragmatics The rules that govern the social use of language.

Prelocutionary stage Nonintentional communication that relies on a partner for interpretation.

Protodeclarative Use of objects to get the attention of adults.

Protoimperative Use of an adult to get a desired object.

Reduplicated babble More sophisticated form of repeated babble that includes consonants.

Referential communication A measure of communicative ability in which individuals are evaluated on their ability to explain a task to each other.

Reflexive vocalizations Sounds produced by infants in response to physical needs.

Reflexives Pronouns that refer to another noun (e.g., *myself, himself*).

Response to intervention (RTI) (a) A multilevel system that utilizes students' response to instruction in the general education classroom as the basis for identification and treatment; (b) an emerging educational service-delivery model that emphasizes early identification of learning difficulties through classroom assessment and levels of instructional support.

Reticent children Children who are reluctant to speak in class.

Rigidity A type of cerebral palsy in which there is a simultaneous contraction of all muscle groups and movement is very limited.

Rule-based system A system that is built on underlying rules such as syntactic (grammar) rules.

Screening An assessment procedure that is brief and easy to administer to a large number of individuals.

Selection restrictions The rules that govern which words can appear together.

Selection technique In AAC, the method used by an individual to select symbols on his or her communication device.

Semantics The study of the rules that govern the assignment of meaning to words.

Serial processing Information-processing model where operations take place one at a time.

Shared code A symbolic system that is shared by its users. This could include spoken, written, or gestural language.

Sheltered English Instruction (Immersion) Type of program for English language learners that provides instruction almost entirely in English, but in a self-contained classroom consisting only of English language learners.

Speech The neuromuscular act of producing sounds that are used in language.

Spina bifida A group of conditions in which a portion of the spinal cord is not completely enclosed by the vertebrae in the spinal column.

Stops A consonant which is produced by blocking airflow by means of the lips, tongue, or glottis.

Strategy training An approach to instruction in which students are taught *how* to learn, not just *what* to learn.

Suprasegmental features The use of stress and intonation in speech.

Symbolic A system that uses symbols (something that represents something else) such as a word to represent an object.

Syntax The rules that govern how words are put together to make sentences.

Theory of mind A theory about the cognitive processing style of individuals with autism that asserts that there is a reduced ability to understand the state of mind of another.

Unaided augmentative communication techniques Methods that do not require external support devices or procedures in order to operate; for

example, speech, sign language, and facial expressions.

Unvoiced A sound produced without vibration of the vocal cords.

Validity The extent to which the instrument measures what it purports to measure.

Voice output communication aids (VOCAs) Communication devices that produce synthesized speech.

Voiceless Type of consonant produced by absence of vocal cord vibration.

Voicing Presence or absence of vocal cord vibration during sound production.

Voiced A sound that is produced with vibration of the vocal cords.

Wernicke's area Located close to the rear of the left cerebral hemisphere in the temporal lobe and is the area involved in the comprehension of language.

Williams syndrome A genetic disorder caused by a random genetic mutation that causes intellectual disabilities.

Word finding The ability to recall a word from memory.

Name Index

Subject Index